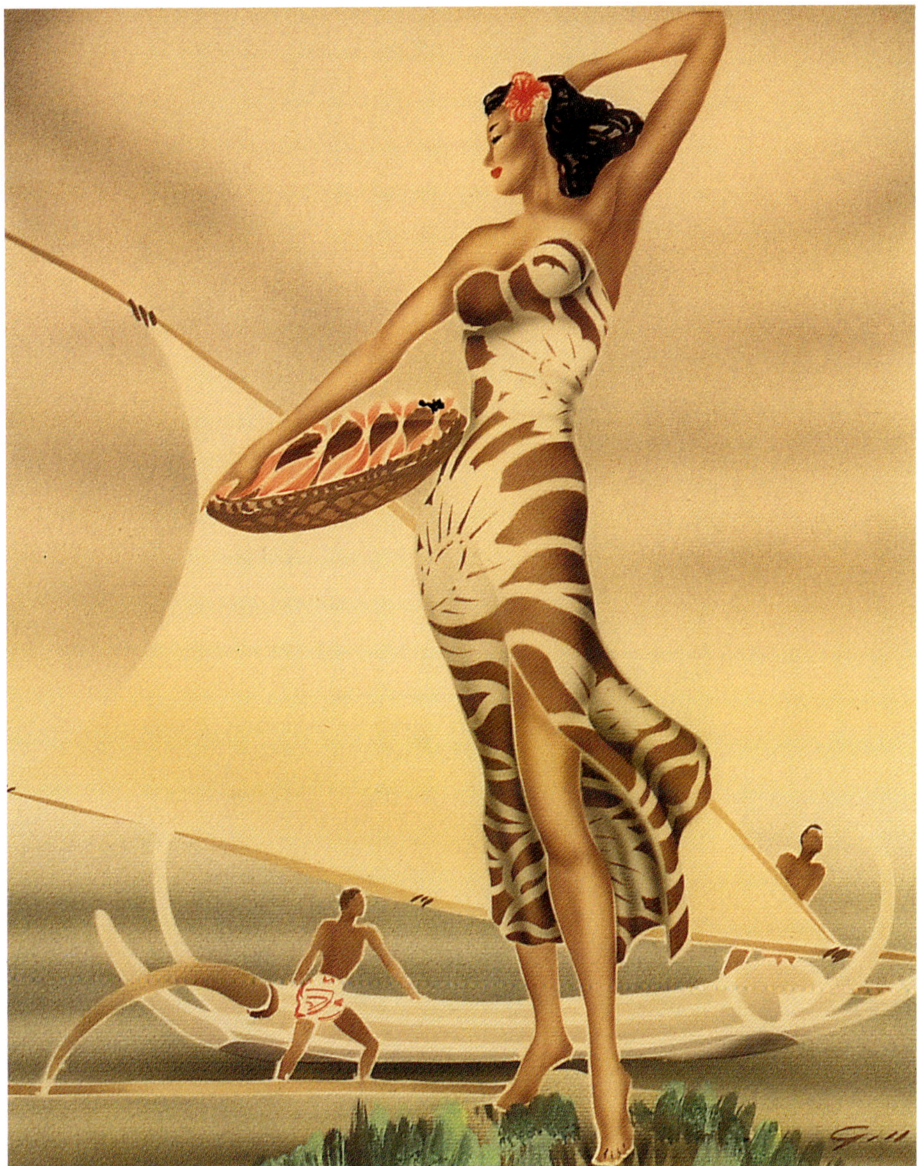

ALOHA SPIRIT

Hawaiian Art and Popular Design

Douglas Congdon-Martin

In Cooperation with the California Heritage Museum, Santa Monica, California

Schiffer Publishing Ltd

4880 Lower Valley Road, Atglen, PA 19310

In Memory of Harold E. Martin

Congdon-Martin, Douglas.
Aloha spirit / Douglas L. Congdon-Martin ; in cooperation with the California Heritage Museum, Santa Monica, California.
p. cm.
Catalog published in conjunction with an exhibition held at the California Heritage Museum, Apr. 16-July 27, 1997.
Includes bibliographical references.
ISBN: 0-7643-0489-5 (hardcover)
1. Hawaii--Collectibles--Exhibitions. I. California Heritage Museum. II. Title
NK6076.6.C66 1998
745'.09969'07479493--dc21 97-39000
CIP

Book design by Blair Loughrey

ISBN: 0-7643-0489-5
Printed in Hong Kong

Published by Schiffer Publishing Ltd.
4880 Lower Valley Road
Atglen, PA 19310
Phone: (610) 593-1777; Fax: (610) 593-2002
E-mail: Schifferbk@ aol.com
Please write for a free catalog.
This book may be purchased from the publisher.
Please include $3.95 for shipping.
Please try your bookstore first.

We are interested in hearing from authors
with book ideas on related subjects.

Contents

Acknowledgments

The author thanks the staff and volunteers of the California Heritage Museum for their willingness to undertake this project and their extraordinary efforts during the photo shoot and afterwards to produce the finest book possible. Tobi Smith did much of the preliminary work and twisted her schedule around to enable things to happen at what turned out to be a most inconvenient time. Michael Trotter literally disassembled the exhibit that he had worked so diligently to create in order to facilitate the photographic process. Linda Pearson helped identify items and gather valuable information. They and Steven Stanley spent much hard work on the exhibit, then after the photos were taken they and others spent many hours helping to identify objects and proofing the book.

In researching the exhibit and the book, three resources were used heavily, Mark Blackburn's *Hawaiiana: The Best of Hawaiian Design* (Schiffer Publishing Ltd., 1996); H. Thomas Steele's *The Hawaiian Shirt: Its Art and History* (Abbeville Publishers, 1984); and Nancy Schiffer's *Hawaiian Shirt Designs* (Schiffer Publishing, 1997). Their information was invaluable in identifying and labeling the exhibit.

The Lenders

Over forty lenders to the "Aloha Spirit" exhibition willingly parted with their most precious possessions for more than five months. Their support was greatly appreciated. They include the following people and organizations. We thank them for their generosity in making the Aloha Spirit Exhibit a success and this book a reality.

William S. Argonza
Stephen and Sandy Arterburn
Bishop Museum
California Heritage Museum Archives
California Surfing Museum
Julie Cline
Jim and Pam Cocores
Douglas A. Frazer Fine Art
Brian Goddard
Laurie Haslund
K.C. Heylin
Randy Hild
Sherry "Hula" Holt
Michele Leypoldt
Michele Leypoldt
Locals Only, Laguna Beach
Susan Mast Enterprises
M. Miller
Oceanic Arts
Gwen and Evan Olins, Hula Heaven
James O'Mahoney, S.B.S.M.
Dan Pincetich
Michael & Denise Queen
Dyana Sasse, Sante Fe, New Mexico
Sheila Silber and Chicken Little
Don Stewart
Jim and Susie Stiso
Gene Sweeney
Edward M. Smith
Tobi Smith
Tiki Trader
Tropical Sun Rattan, 20th Century Props
Michael Trotter
Cary B. Weiss
John Schell
Collection of Sue White
Donald F. Wilkes Collection
and others who desire to remain anonymous

The California Heritage Museum & the "Aloha Spirit" Exhibit

Built in 1894 by the nationally known architect Sumner P. Hunt for Roy Jones, the son of Santa Monica's founder, Senator John P. Jones, the California Heritage Museum has been open to the public since 1980. Rather than commemorate only the life of the Jones family, the Heritage Museum is committed to preserve the entire area's history. Thus the historic landmark building became a California history museum, not just a historic house. Community programming includes unique and innovative rotating exhibitions, lectures, workshops, and concerts.

The exhibition "Aloha Spirit - Hawaii's Influence on the California Lifestyle" was produced and designed by the staff at the California Heritage Museum, and was open from April 16 to July 27, 1997. The exhibition presented a look at the Golden Age of Hawaii and the objects manufactured for its tourist industry. It covered a period from the turn of the century to the post-war years, ending around 1960 when jet travel changed the Islands and their way of life forever.

If there is such a thing as "Aloha Spirit," it is the penchant that Islanders have for inviting the outdoors in and the indoors out. More than a specifically tropical ambience, it is this smooth, harmonious interplay between interior and exterior that is the signature of the Hawaiian style. Foliage, flowers, breezes, colors, light--in the island home they flow in and out unobtrusively, cheerfully blurring the boundaries between the two worlds.

The exhibition used the Heritage Museum's downstairs period rooms to present a 1940s-50s living room, dining room, kitchen, and pantry that were decorated with Hawaiian rattan and koa wood furniture, art work, tiki mugs, Vernon Ware, Tepco and Santa Anita china, Hawaiian quilts and tourist pillows, and colorful collectibles. The second floor formal galleries featured the best of Hawaiian design from 1890-1960, and included 1940s men's and women's vintage aloha clothing, paper Hawaiiana, musical instruments, a section on surfing, and a fine arts gallery. Several lectures were also presented in conjunction with the "Aloha Spirit" exhibition.

Tobi Smith, Executive Director
September, 1997

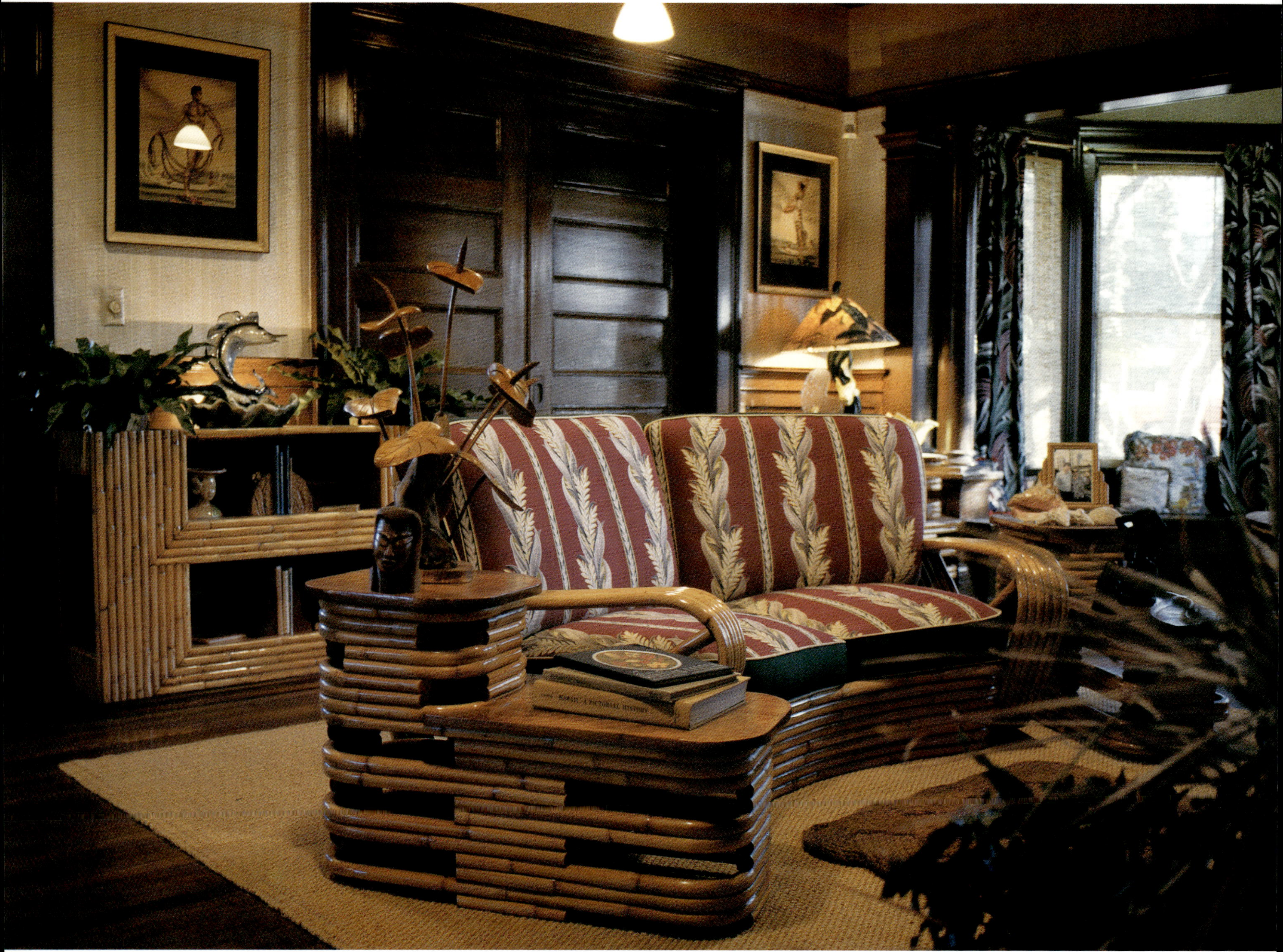

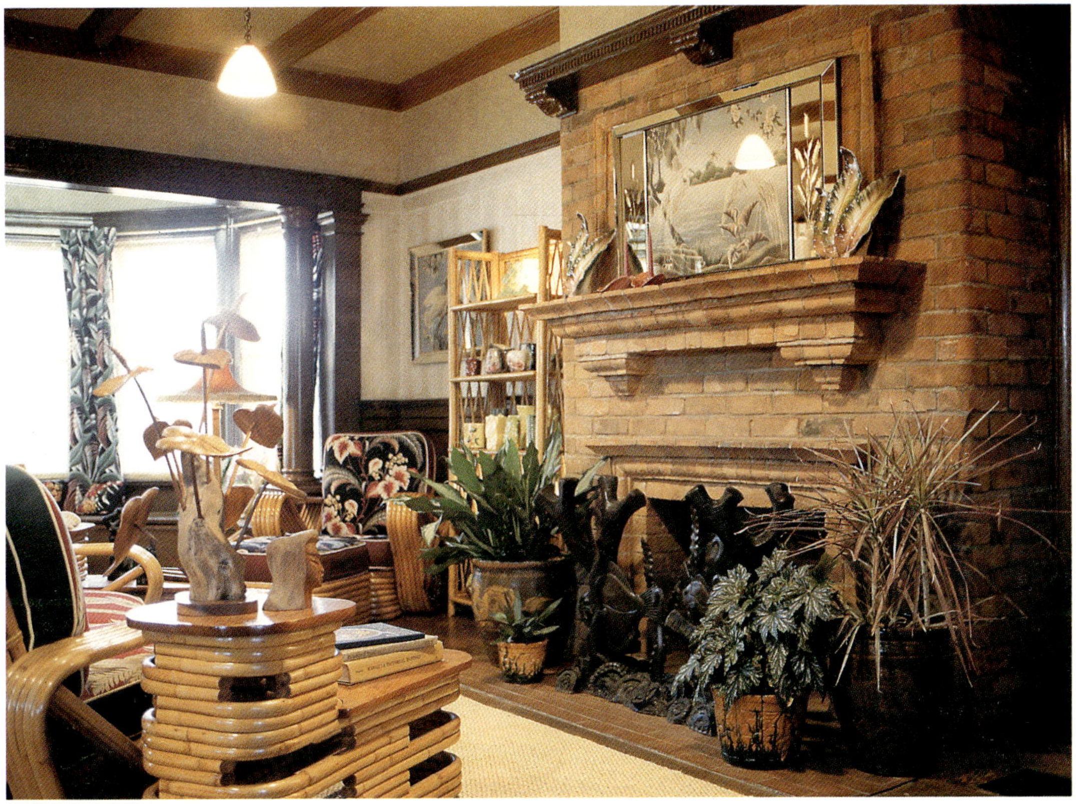

The fireplace has a mirrored flamingo print over it with a pair of ceramic lamps and a set of candlesticks. Beside it is an etagere filled with ceramic vases reflecting the Hawaiian style.

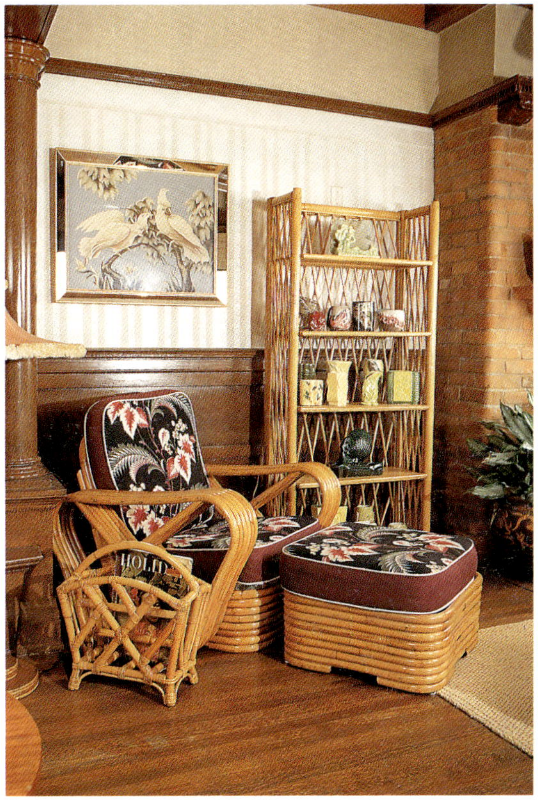

A reading corner next to the fireplace with chair, ottoman, magazine rack, lamp, and an etagere filled with pottery in the Aloha Spirit.

Opposite:
The enchantment of the aloha spirit begins as you enter the museum. The living room is decorated in rattan and rich fabrics. Everywhere you look the atmosphere of the Islands is captured. Tropical airbrush prints by Gill adorn the walls, bamboo shades and floral curtains are on the windows, and pottery in the tropical mode is everywhere.

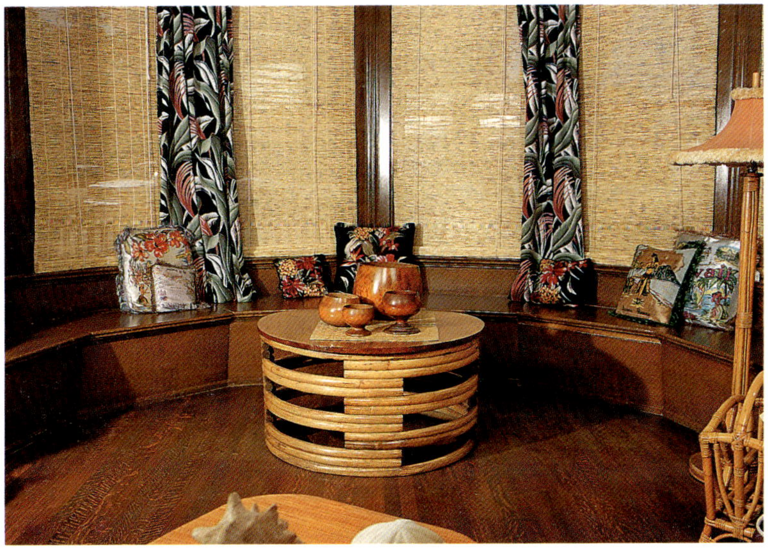

Tourist cushions soften the window seat.

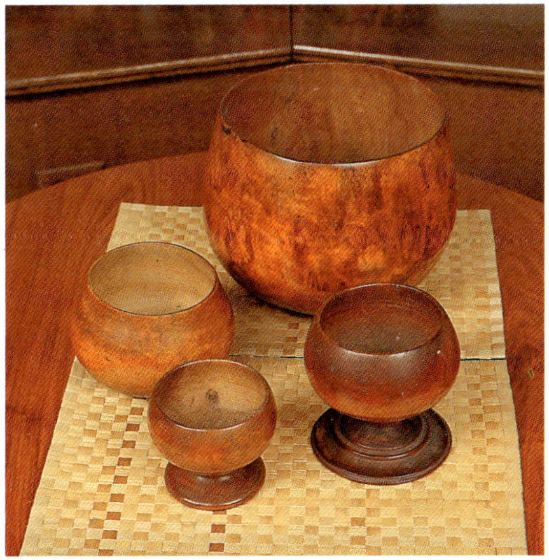

A round rattan coffee table holds calabash bowls and stem ware.

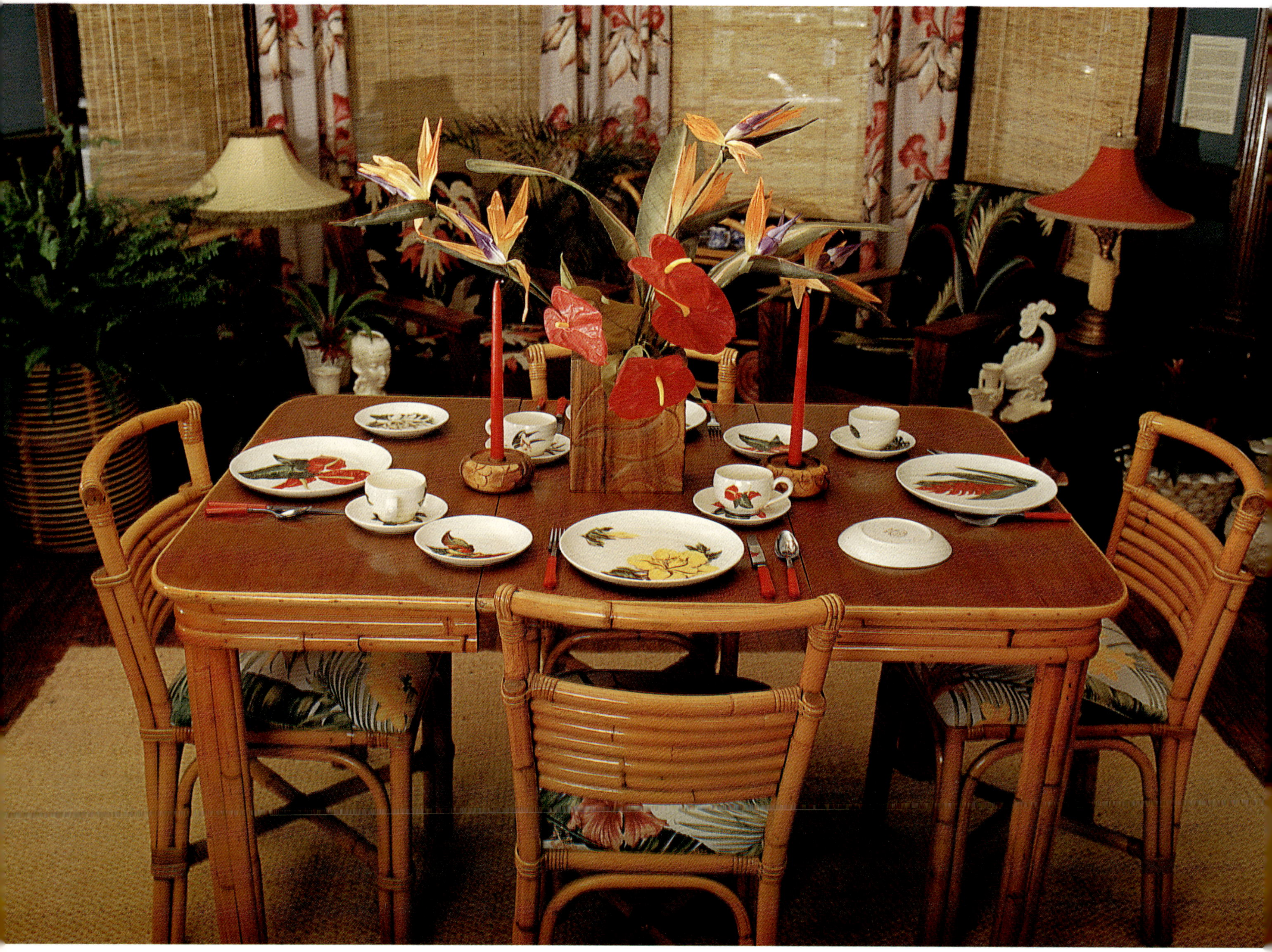

Moving to the right we come to the dining room. It too is packed with decorative items reflective of the Islands. In the center is the dining table with chairs in rattan.

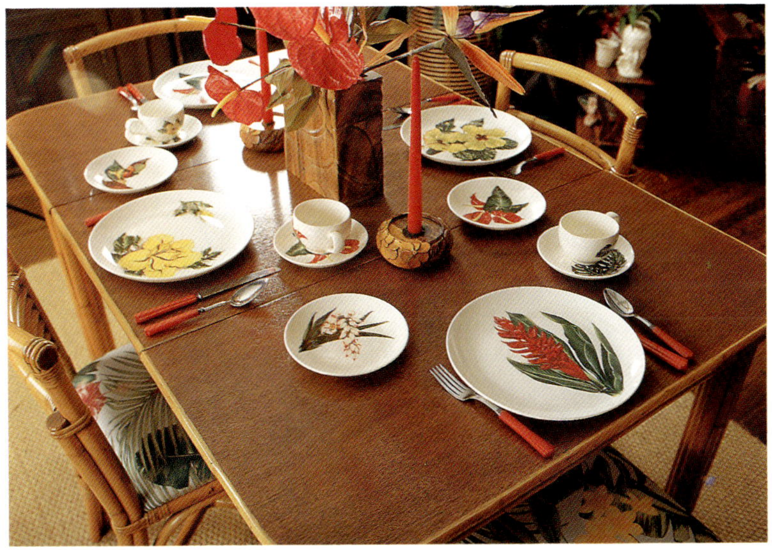

The table is beautifully set with Santa Anita Ware decorated with Hawaiian flora. In the center are carved koa wood candlesticks and a vase. The silverware has Bakelite handles.

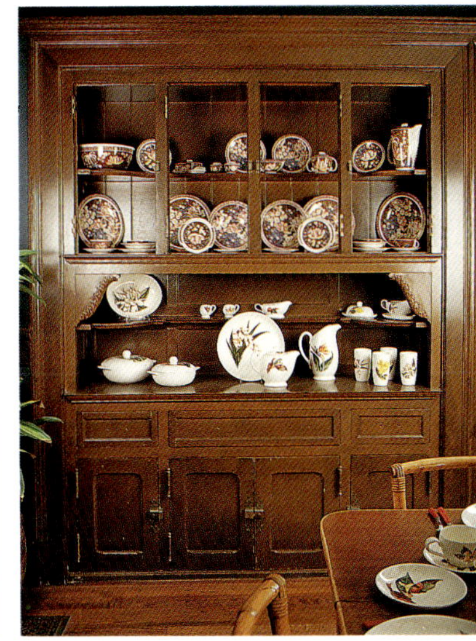

More Santa Anita Ware fills the built-in cabinets along with a set of Lei Lani ware from Vernon Kilns in the glass cabinets above.

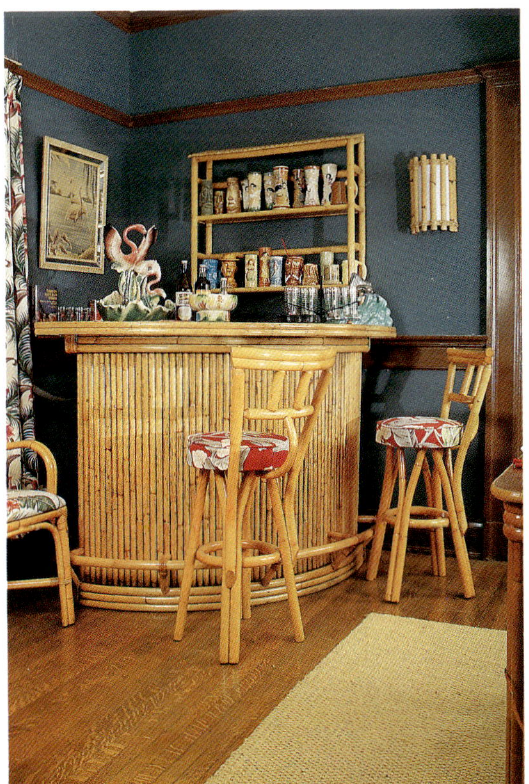

In a corner stands a rattan bar and stools. On the wall is a rattan hanging shelf filled with a wonderful collection of Tiki mugs. Beside it is a rattan sconce.

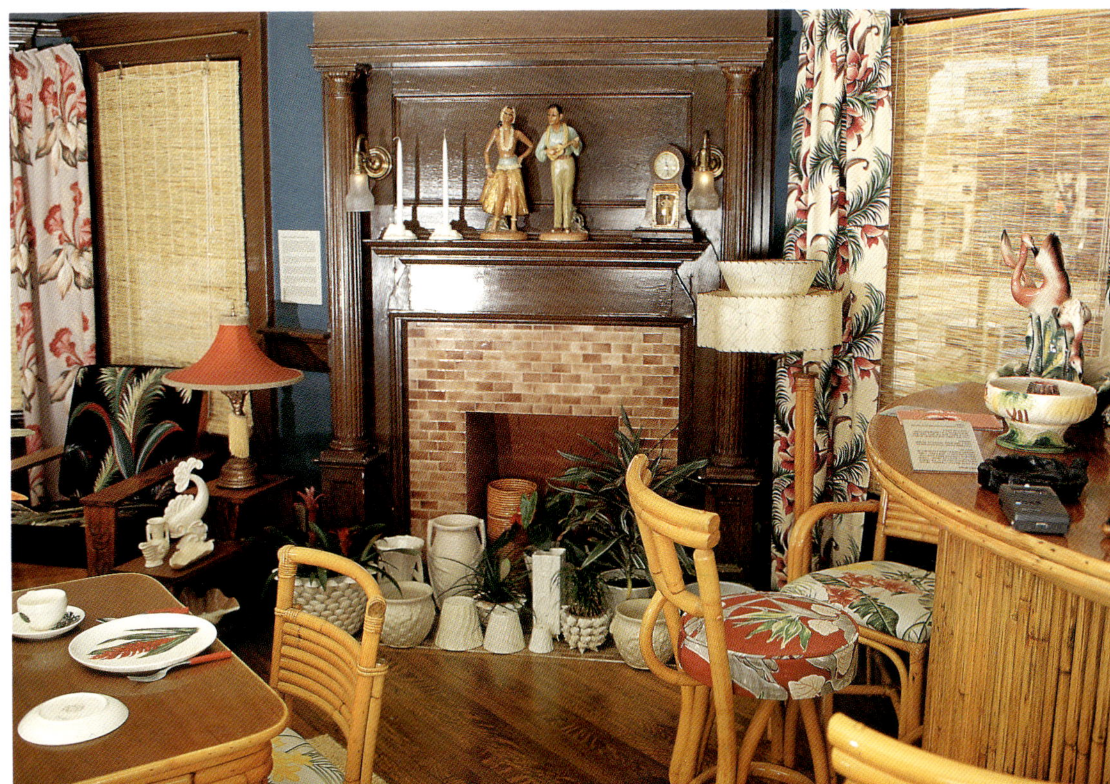

The dining room fireplace is also decked out in the Aloha Spirit, with white pottery on the floor and figural work on the mantel along with a hula clock.

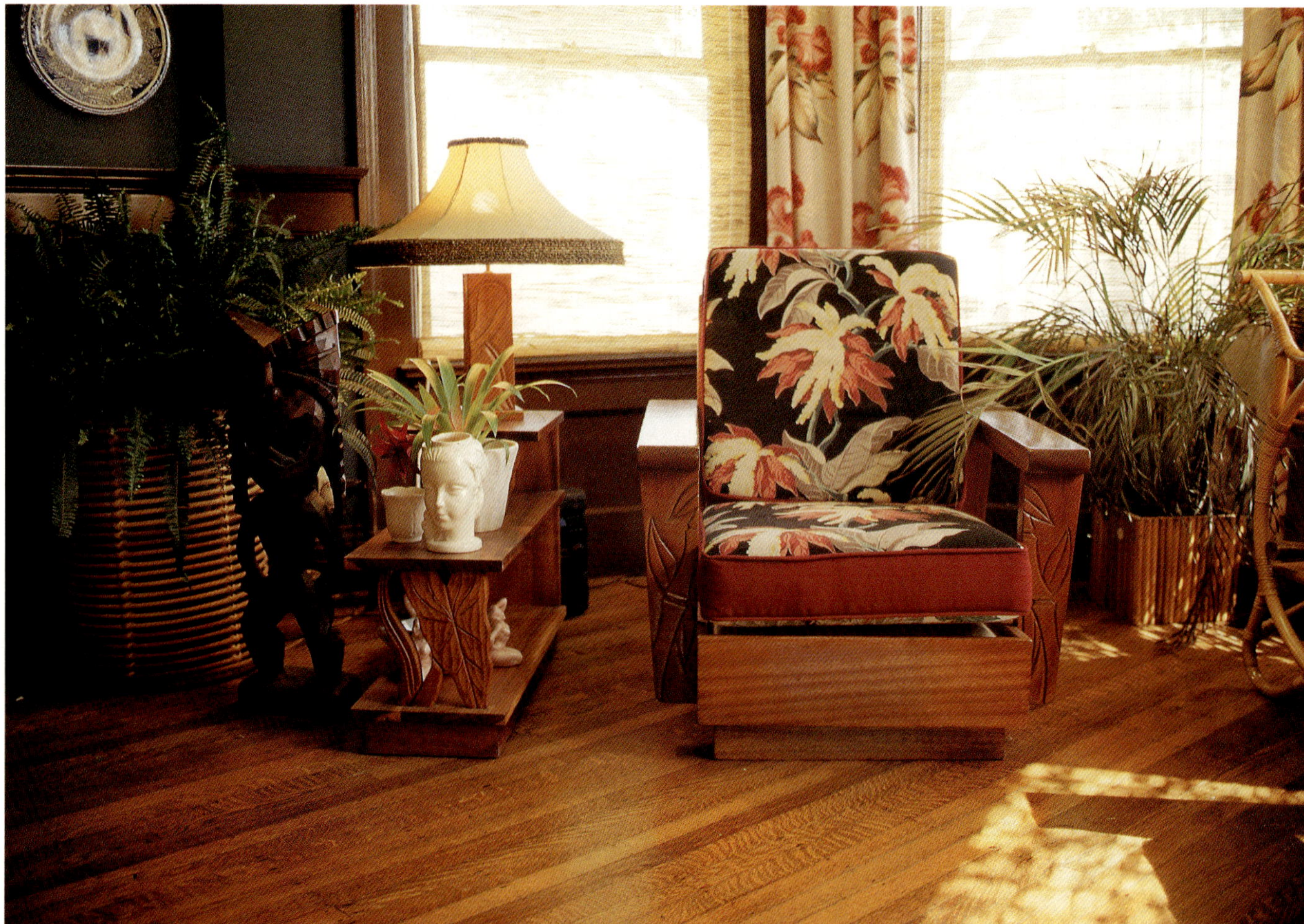

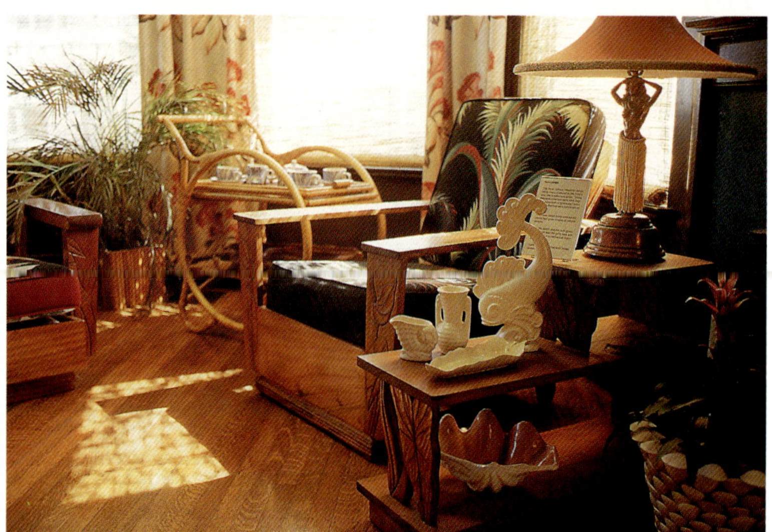

The dining room window bay is filled with koa furniture, a rattan serving cart, and other items shown in detail later.

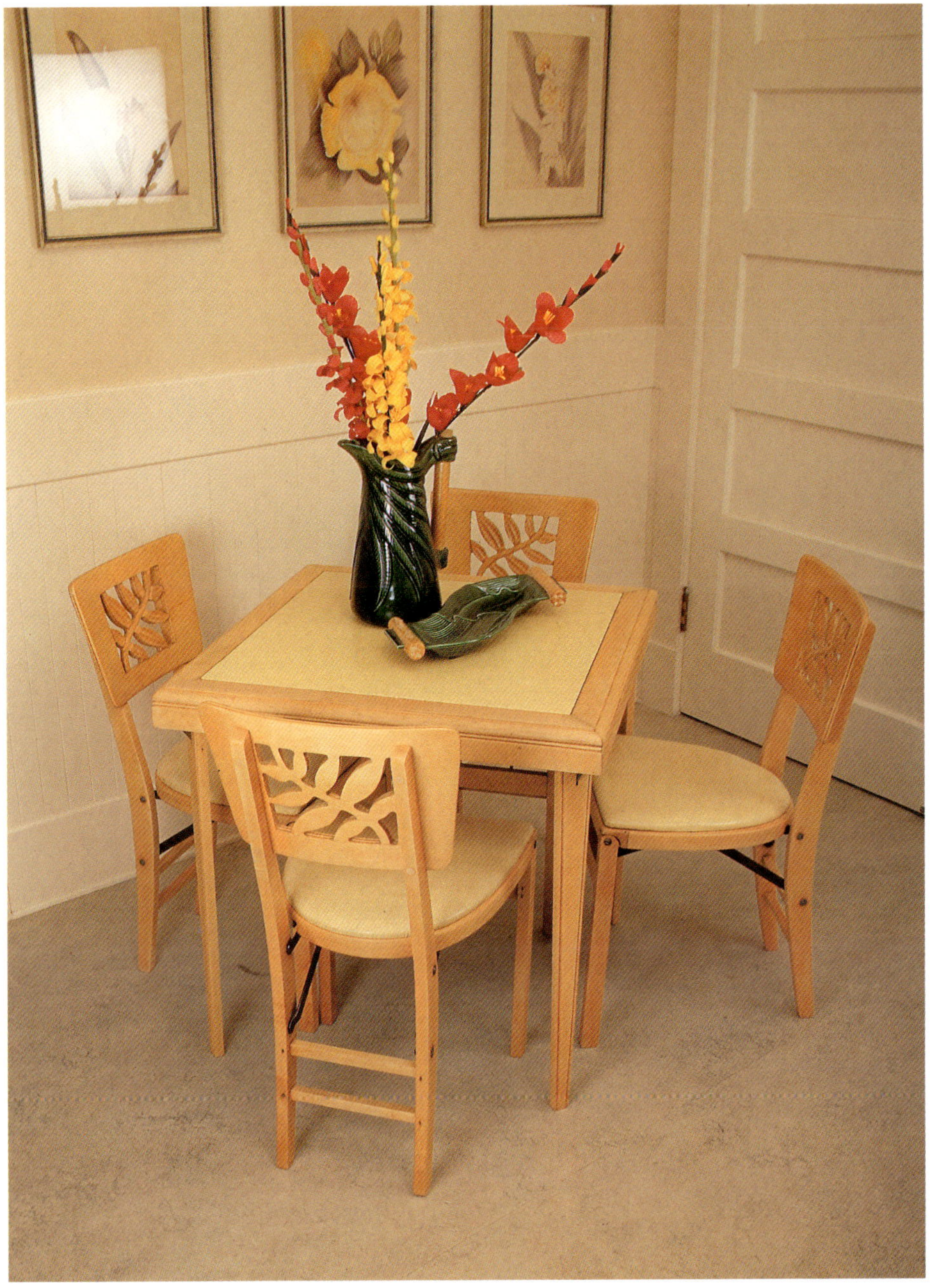

From the dining room the exhibit moves through the butler's pantry into the kitchen. Here we find a lovely folding card table and chairs decorated with some rich green pottery. *Courtesy: Michael & Denise Queen and the Collection of Brian Goddard & Gene Sweeney.*

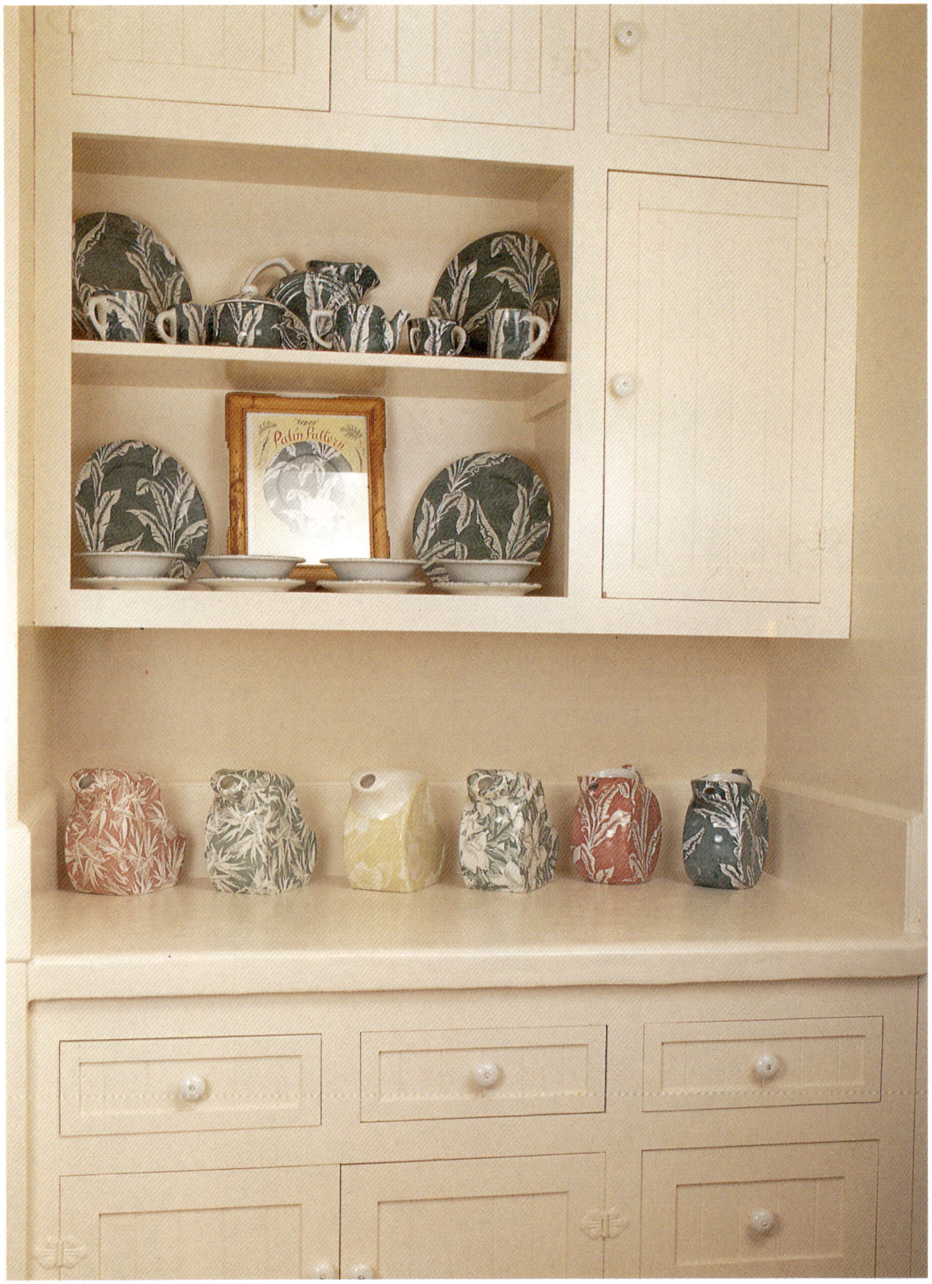

Palm Pattern ceramics fill the upper shells of the cabinets at one end of the kitchen, while various pitchers line the counter top.

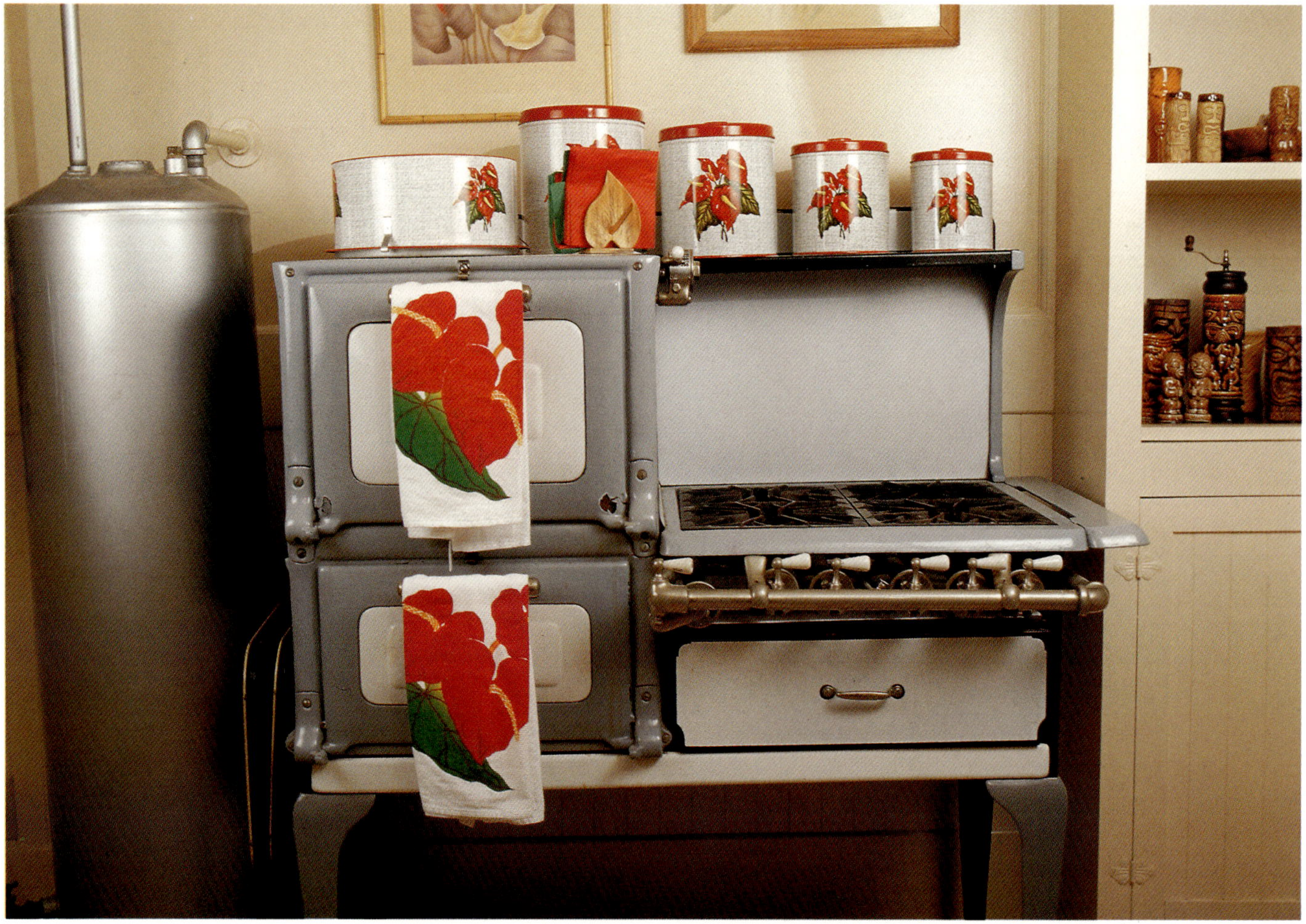

The old stove is decorated with Anthurium items, including towels, napkin holders, and tin canisters and cake pan.

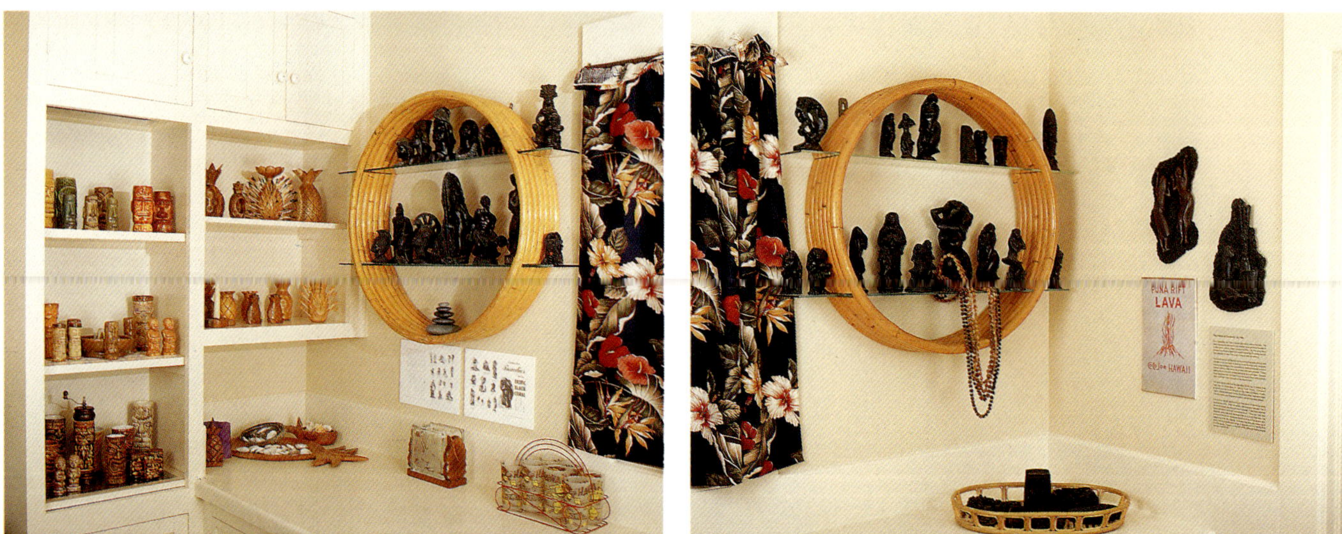

Around the sink are displayed various ceramic Tiki wear, as well as wooden pieces and lava souvenirs.

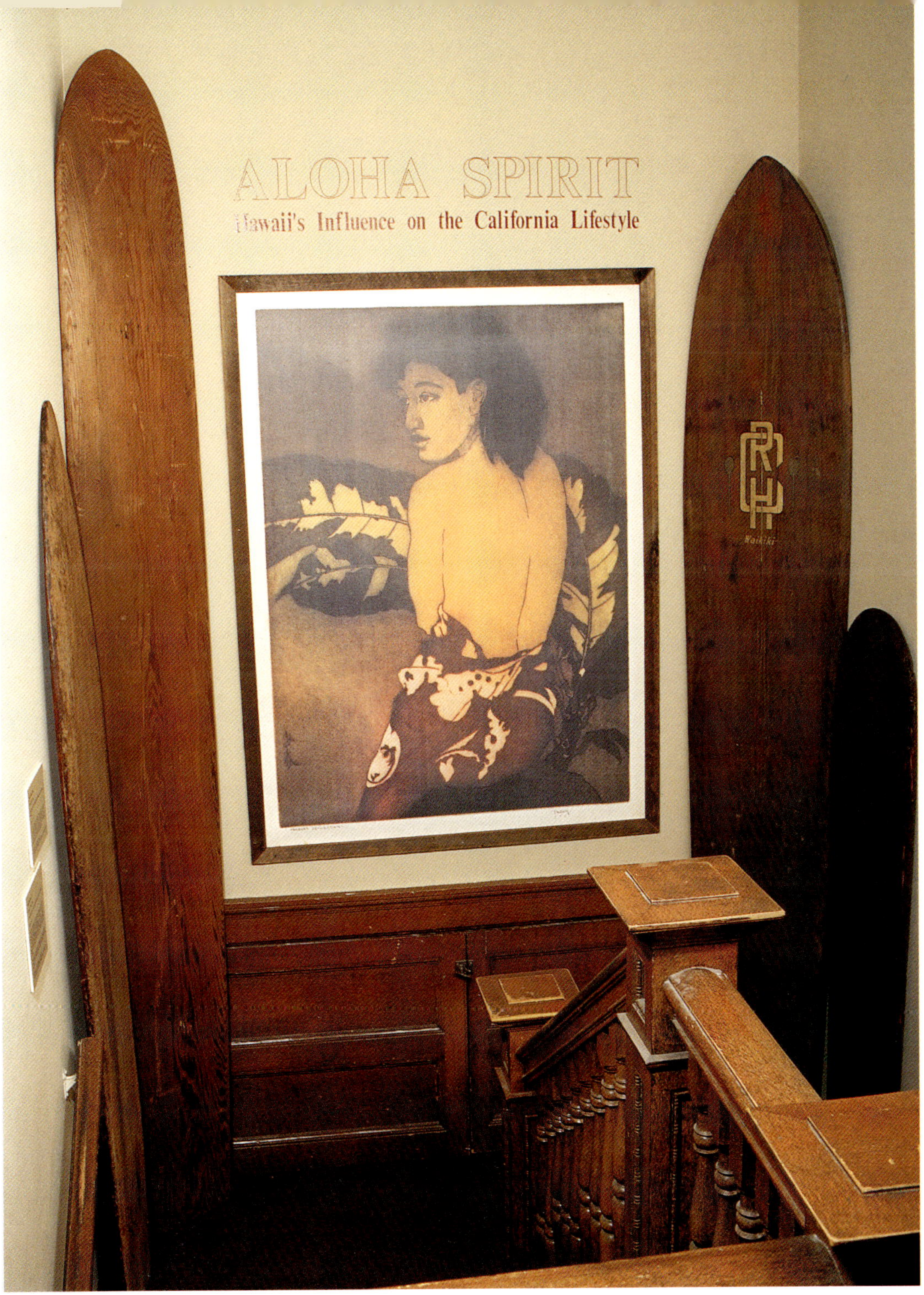

The exhibit then moves upstairs. At the landing are displayed four wonderful surfboards framing the centerpiece of the exhibit, the John Melville Kelly aquatint, "Hawaiian Decoration," 1937.

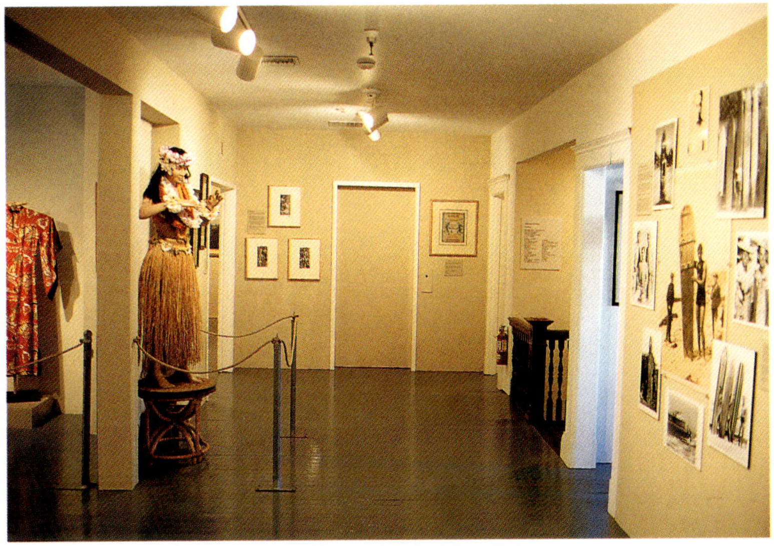

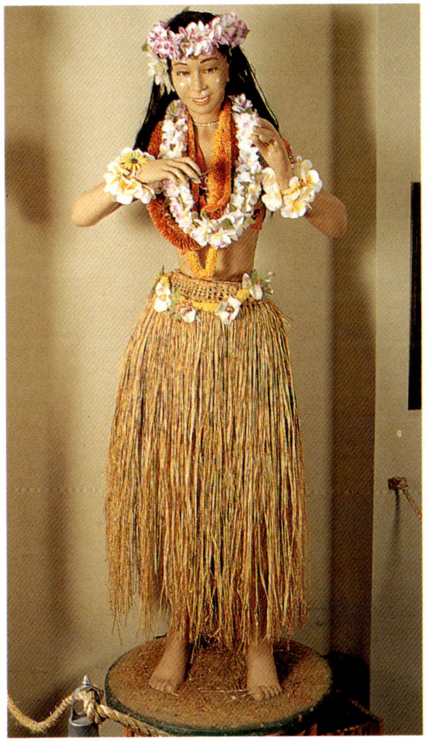

At the top of the stairs we enter the main hall. One end is dominated by a mechanical hula dancer, complete with leis and grass skirt. *Courtesy: the Donald F. Wilkes Collection.*

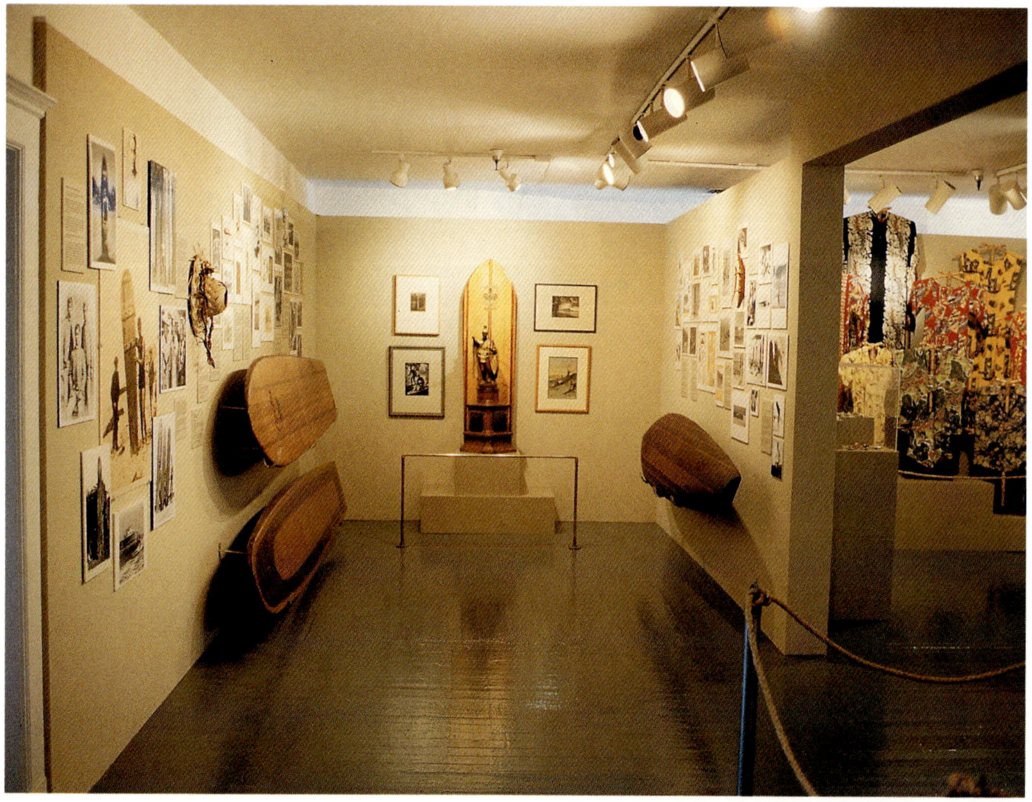

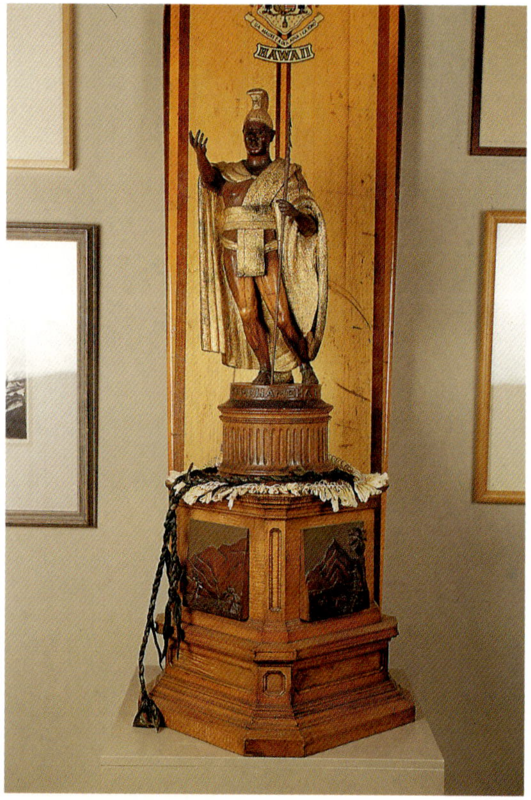

The other end is watched over by a wonderful carved and gilt statue of King Kamehameha. Its walls are lined with photographs and historical memorabilia documenting the spread of the sport of surfboarding from Hawaii to California.

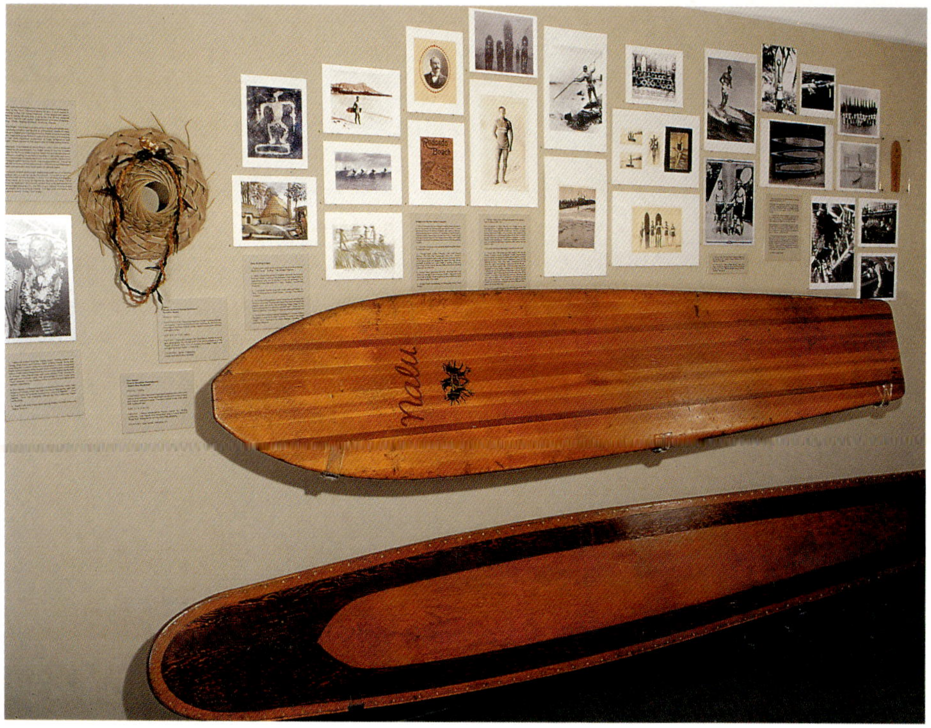

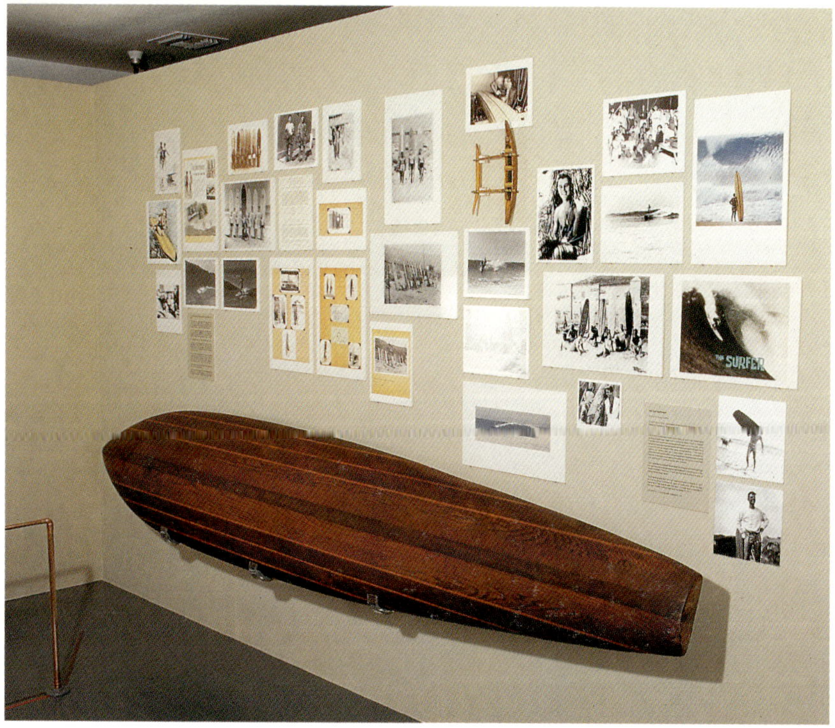

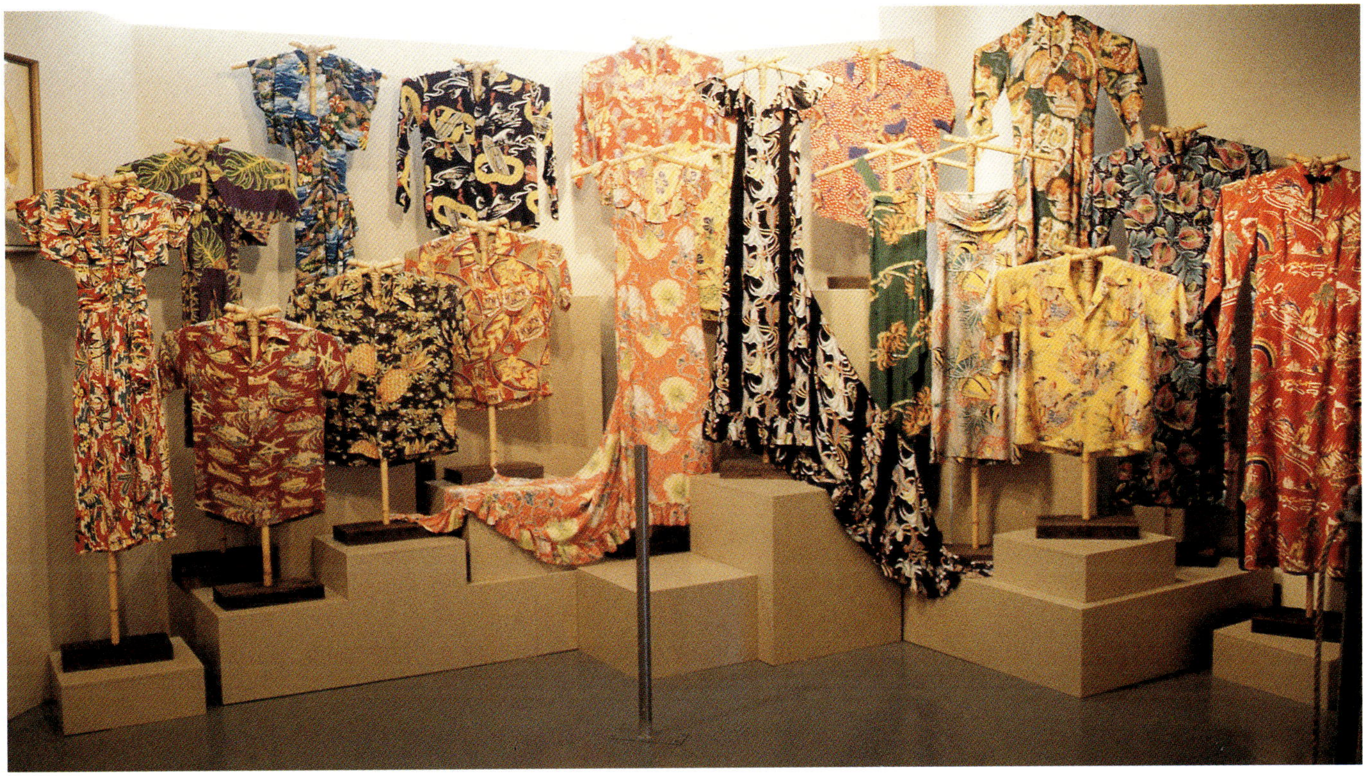

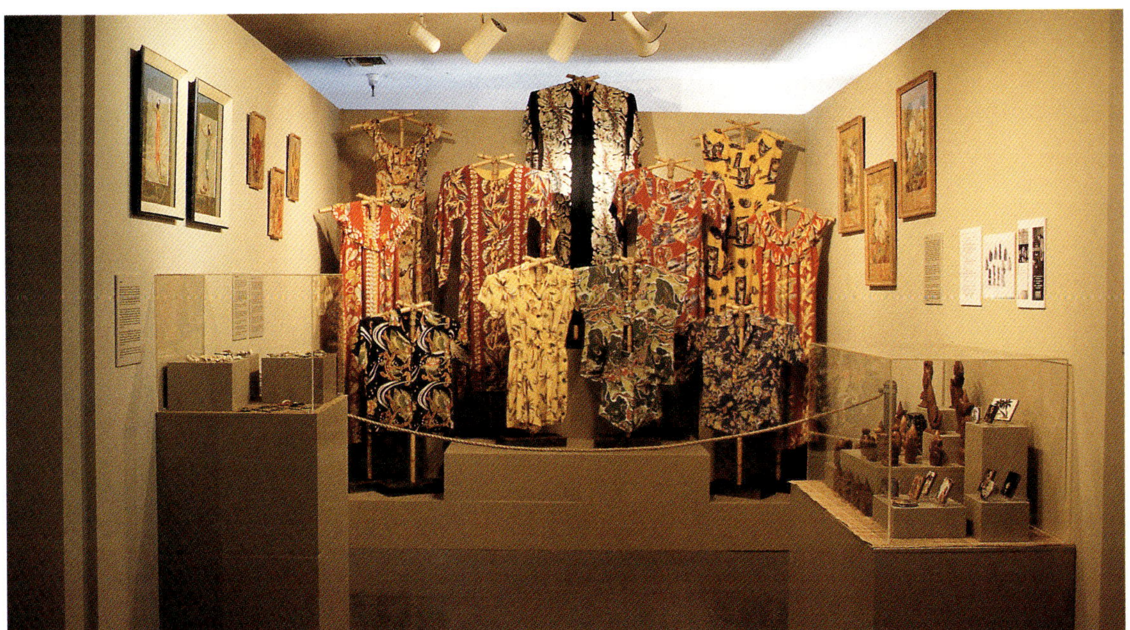

Three rooms run off of the main hall. In the first is a collection of clothing, jewelry, and other personal accessories that have caught the attention of tourists and others over the years.

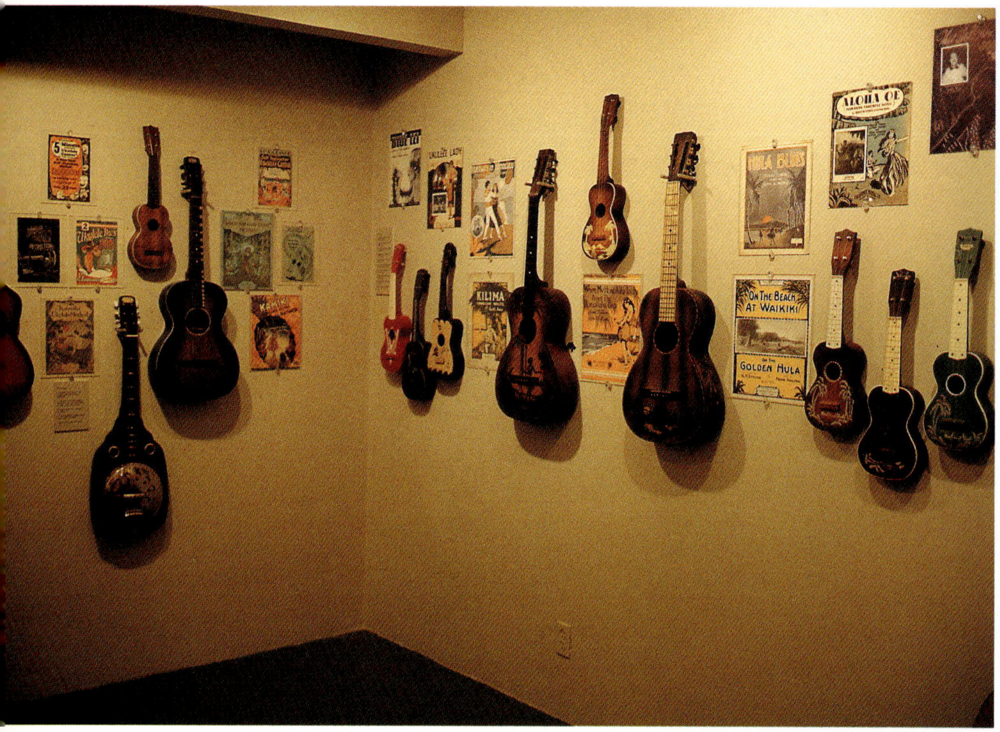

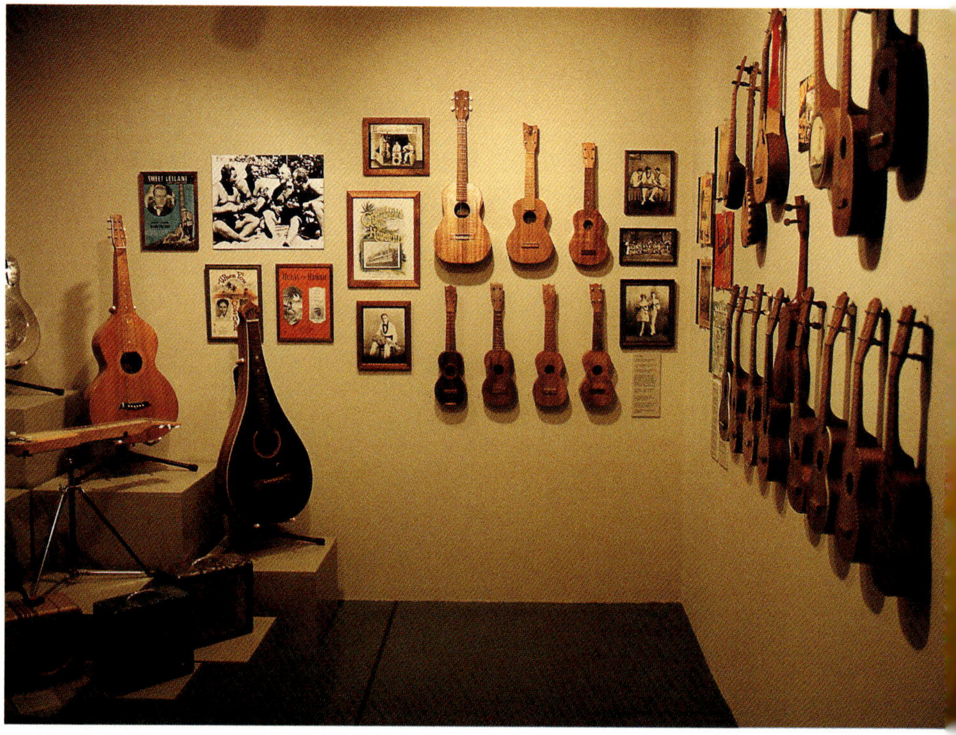

Another room off the main hall is the music room, its walls covered with ukuleles, Hawaiian guitars, sheet music, vintage photos, and record albums.

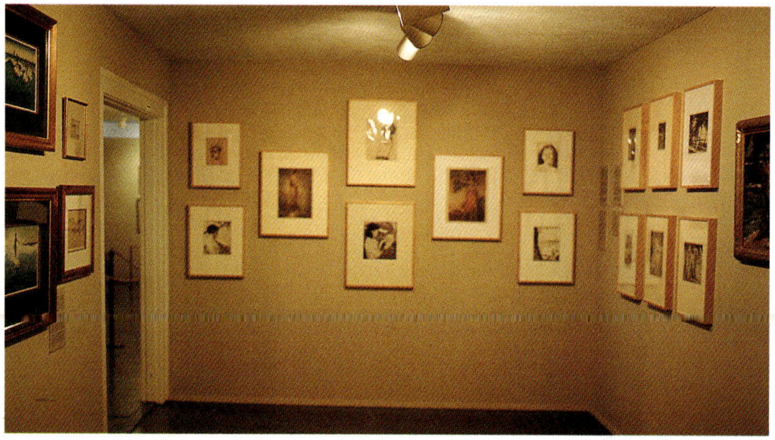

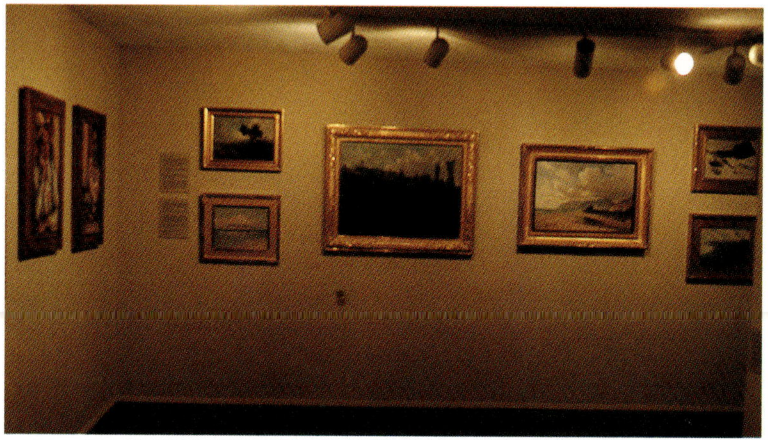

Finally there is a gallery of fine art representing some of the most prominent artists of Hawaii.

The Hawaiian Influence

As soon as I stepped out of the airport terminal at Hilo I could feel the Aloha Spirit. At once I relaxed. All the worries I had about the job that lay ahead vanished with the warm breezes. The dread of being a stranger in a strange land was dispelled with a smile and a fragrant, beautiful lei. The weariness of travel was soothed and I was refreshed.

Hawaii gives rise to the Aloha Spirit as naturally as plumeria release their heavenly scent. The love, friendship, good wishes, and welcome that Aloha means are engendered by the Hawaiian people and the Islands themselves. It is difficult to be otherwise here. Nature will not allow it. Everything that touches these shores is transformed, however subtly, by the magic.

This transforming spirit lies at the heart of the Hawaiian experience. Millions of years ago, when the tops of the volcanoes broke the water and established dry land in the middle of the Pacific Ocean, Hawaii was essentially a hard, barren place with only the most primitive of life forms. It was a new creation isolated by a vast, watery border. But even then the Aloha Spirit was at work, welcoming seeds carried to the Islands on the trade winds or on the wings of migrating birds, and providing rich volcanic soil in which they could root. Some of the birds made the new islands their homes, and other life came to there on ocean currents. So remote were the islands that for millions of years the only land mammal on them was the hoary bat.

Then as now the life that found its way to the Islands was transformed, though more biologically than psychologically. The isolation of the Islands resulted in unique evolutionary developments, giving them a flora and fauna all their own. And as each new life form arrived it was assimilated into the whole, both changing it and being changed by it at the same time.

One of the more recent species to inhabit the Island was homo-sapien...us. Polynesians, probably from Tonga and Somoa, developed the art and technology of navigation and seafaring and began moving out into the surrounding oceans. They explored the islands, establishing human communities in the Marquesas, Tahiti, Easter Island, New Zealand, and Hawaii. In the ancient legends of many of these islands these ancients appear as "Menehene" or a variation on the word. Scientists examining ancient sites have determined that the earliest human habitation on the Hawaii Islands dates to 500 to 750 A.D.

The human population of the Islands remained relatively undisturbed for hundreds of years. They lived in harmony with their surroundings. As explorers do, the Polynesians brought with them the things they needed for survival, introducing to the Islands the beauty of hibiscus and wild ginger, and the agricultural richness of yams, taro, gourds, ti, sugar cane, bananas, bamboo, mountain apple, coconut, turmeric, sweet potato, breadfruit, and paper mulberry. In addition they brought dogs, pigs, and chickens to the Islands, and, as unwelcome stowaways, rats and insects. The Islands gladly supported these new arrivals and they developed a rich culture of their own and had very few contacts with other cultures. Until the arrival of the English explorer Captain James Cook in 1778, only a few passing Spanish and Japanese ships had graced their shores.

Cook was on his third voyage of discovery when he came upon the Islands. His first two voyages had been in the South Pacific, but this time he was headed toward the northwest coast of the Americas, seeking a northwest passage back to Europe. On January 18, 1778, he landed on the Hawaiian Islands. A remarkable sight to the isolated Hawaiians, they mistook Cook and his men as gods arriving on great moving islands. Whatever awe they felt had disappeared by the following winter when Cook returned to the Islands from the northern waters to spend the winter. Over a misunderstanding, Cook, four of his men, and some Islanders were killed on February 14, 1779. His crew continued in vain to search for the northwest passage before returning to England in October, 1780.

Cook's first contact led to others between the Islands and the western world. These were of mixed blessing to the Hawaiian people. According to Eleanor Nordyke, in *The Peopling of Hawaii,* the Islands in the post-Cook era gained a written language, western education, metal, cloth, and manufactured goods, all generally thought of as positive influences. But they also gained disease, firearms, gun powder, and alcohol, interventions that would bring the Islands great pain. The years 1778 to 1853 saw political consolidation for the Islands and the rise of the monarchy. They brought changes in religion, land use, the economy, and health.

The Islands experienced a rapid depopulation after contact with the West. Nordyke attributes it to three general causes. First, as Cook foresaw from the first, the Islanders had no resistance to western disease, particularly venereal disease, and the epidemics that followed contact cost many lives. Second, there was a high infant mortality rate. Third, the contact opened new vistas on the world and many of Hawaii's people left to find new adventure or new homes. According to estimates there were 250,000 pure native Hawaiians in 1778. That number reduced to 1,000-10,000 by 1970.

As tragic as that is, it is not the whole of the story. Another of the reasons that the number of pure natives has declined so dramatically is the nature of the Aloha Spirit. It is a welcoming, transforming power. Newcomers to the Islands, whether from Europe, America, or Asia, are quickly integrated into the culture and its life. The barriers of race and ethnicity break down, and the love that is Aloha extends to all its many meanings. As John D. Spreckels wrote in *Overland* magazine in 1895, the stranger "will be welcomed by the people, if he shows himself to be the least bit friendly." The Aloha Spirit embraces all who wish to place themselves in its power.

Its power transforms not only those who stay, but those who visit for a time and return home. No one leaves the Island without taking a piece of it home. Perhaps it is something tangible...a shell, a lava rock, a koa wood souvenir, an Aloha Shirt. All around the world these grace knickknack shelves, table tops, or closets, invoking memories of warm days, pristine beaches, wonderful people. More important, though, are the intangible pieces of Hawaii that people take with them...the calm demeanor, the relaxed elegance, the accepting attitude.

The power and reach of the Aloha Spirit have led people in California and around the world to attempt to recreate it in their lives and homes. The warmth of rattan and koa wood furnishings grace distant living spaces. The color and exotic forms of tropical plants and flowers adorn fabrics, ceramics, clothing. Images of beautiful Hawaiian people adorn the walls. Soft fragrances of gardenia and plumeria are applied to the body. Hawaiian music stirs the heart. And the daring take to the sea on planks of wood or fiberglass to relive an ancient ritual with the surf. The Aloha Spirit—love, welcome, and friendship—is a contagious affliction, and one that is to be nurtured, celebrated, and cherished.

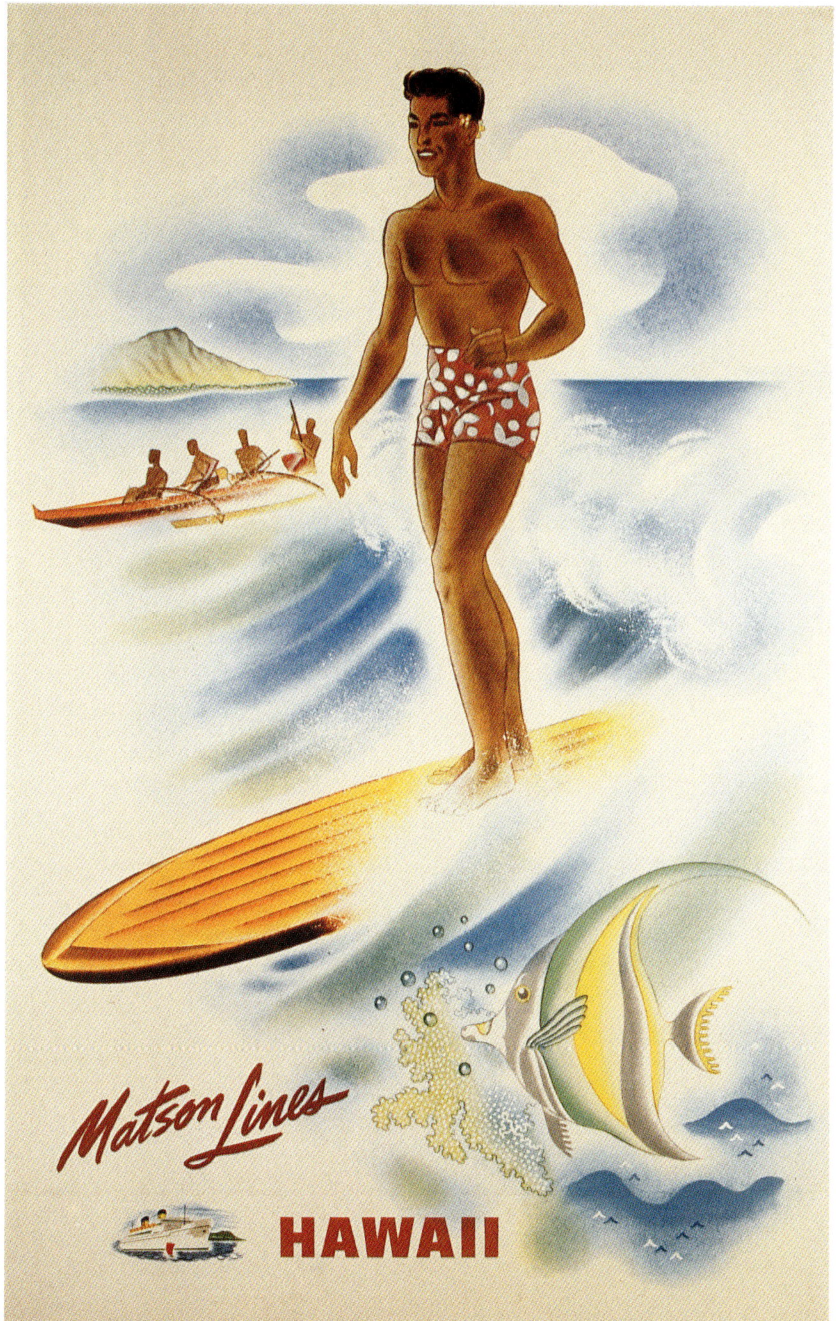

Travel poster by Frank MacIntosh, produced in the late 1930s or early 1940s for the Matson Line. *Courtesy: Randy Hild.*

Chapter 1

Tourism: The Spell of Aloha

The expansive reach of the Aloha Spirit can be laid largely at the feet of tourism. Today it is the largest element of the Hawaiian economy, bringing millions of people to the Islands every year. In earlier times, before jumbo jets winged their way across the Pacific, the numbers were a tiny fraction in comparison.

Among the early tourists were Mark Twain and Charles Warren Stoddard in the late 1800s. Twain wrote about his visit to Hawaii in his popular book *Roughing It*, and Stoddard did the same in his, *Cozy Letters from Low Latitudes*. The two books combined to spark an interest among Westerners in visiting this exotic site.

Getting there, however, was something of a problem. Prior to 1883, the only practical way to travel to Hawaii was on a Pacific Mail steamer, a cargo ship that stopped there on its way between San Francisco and Australia. In 1883 the Oceanic Steamship Company initiated the first round trip steamer service between Honolulu and San Francisco with two ten ton steamers, the *Mariposa* and the *Alameda*, providing semi-monthly service for 30-40 passengers on each. Two more ships, the *Zealandia* and the *Australia*, were added in 1886. From 1889 to 1890 Oceanic Steamship carried over 1,000 tourists to the Islands each month.

Writing in the June, 1895 issue of *Overland* magazine (an issue devoted entirely to Hawaii), John D. Spreckels, probably a relative of owners of the Steamship line, wrote, "There is but one Pacific Ocean, but one Hawaiian group—to sail for a week over the clear and calm waters of one and to luxuriate in the tropical beauty of the other are pleasures not to be duplicated the world over." He goes on to promote the warm climate amid abundant vegetation, the drama of the active and inactive volcanoes, and expansive coffee and sugar plantations.

Even at this date, the souvenir was important to the traveler. Spreckels assures them that there are many quarries available on the Islands for the avid memento hunter. "The lover of lonely prowls in unknown nooks may find corners...of aboriginal simplicity...where he may pick up for his studio or his cabinet curios that will make him the envy of all his acquaintances, idols and music instruments, kapa cloth, and the bones of ancient warriors that have lain in their rock sepulchers for generation protected by the dreaded taboo." That may be carrying souvenir hunting a bit over the edge!

Spreckels was optimistically prophetic about tourism on the Islands. "The best security for the growth of the tourist traffic of the Islands," he wrote, "are the facts that are more widely known than ever before and that the constantly increasing numbers of persons who have made the trip are everywhere and all the time doing missionary work in promoting their less fortunate fellows to follow their example."

Spreckels was not alone in his vision. In 1901 a group of Hawaiian businessmen sought ways to promote tourism. A report of their work (Feher, p. 418) stated "Recognizing the great commercial possibilities to be derived from visitors, sightseers, and health-and recreation-seekers, [they] took the first steps to organize and perpetuate a plan to attract visitors to the Islands. To insure a steady flow of tourists it was necessary to spread broadcast the witchery of Hawaii's native life, the spell of her natural wonders, and the charm of her scenery and climate—in other words, to advertise." To continue this work the Hawaii Promotion Committee was created in 1903.

One of the companies betting on the growth of tourism was the Matson Navigation Line. It was started by Captain William Matson with one ship in 1882, sailing between Hawaii and San Francisco. By 1909 it had four ships in service. At about that time it received the support of some of the most powerful businessmen in Hawaii, allowing it to go against the more dominant Oceanic Steamship line. Matson grew quickly, absorbing Oceanic in 1930 and expanding to 50 ships by 1935. It dominated Hawaiian tourism until the coming of age of air travel following World War II.

One of the charms of going to the Islands was getting there. A 1927 magazine advertisement by the Hawaii Tourist Bureau promotes a travel bargain: "...four thousand miles of sailing on the sunny Pacific, first class steamer fares both ways, two weeks at Hawaii's world-famed hotels, inter-island trips and sightseeing—and the cost need be no more than $400."

Change was in the air...literally. In 1935 Pan American Airways started exploratory flights to Hawaii from San Francisco. On October 22, 1936, the Hawaiian Clipper carried its first paying customers from San Francisco to Honolulu in a 20 hour flight. Suspending flights during the Second World War, Pan American resumed daily service on March 15, 1946. The flights took 12-1/2 hours and cost $195 (the price was $278 when service was suspended in 1941). By June, 1947 Pan American had 68 flights to the Islands per week.

Matson ships had been requisitioned for the military during the war. The line offered air passage in 1946 while their vessels were being refitted for civilian use.

Following the war the Honolulu Chamber of Commerce adopted a five year plan to promote tourism. It included building hotels, cleaning up towns and attractions, encouraging the start-up of stores, and the building of highways. In October, 1947 the first Aloha Week was held to promote the sale of Hawaiian products.

In the post war years tourism took a monumental leap, due principally to the increased ease of travel. In 1941 the number of visitors to Hawaii was about 25,000. In 1950 over 57,000 tourists visited the Islands. In 1960 the number topped 1,000,000 for the first time and by 1975 the number reached 3,000,000.

The Aloha Spirit lives and continues to attract millions of people to the Islands every year, and when they return home they take a little of that spirit with them.

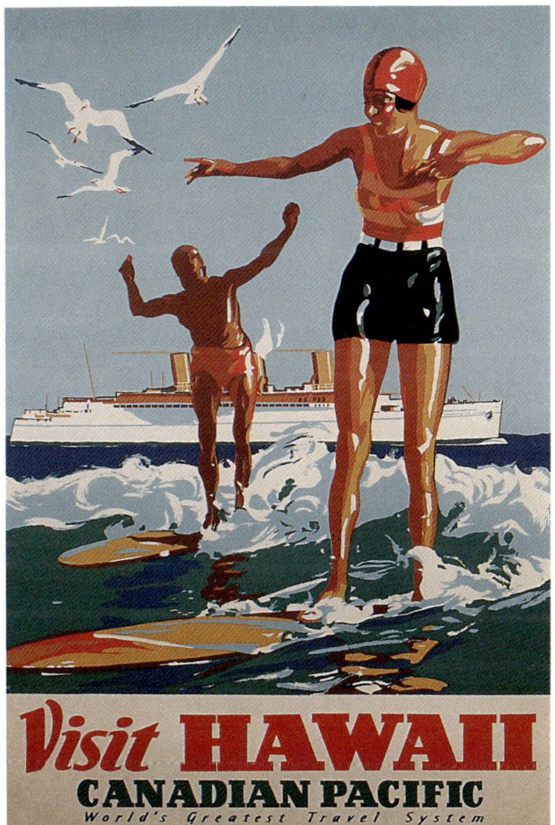

"Visit Hawaii," travel poster for Canadian Pacific. *Courtesy: Dan Pincetich*.

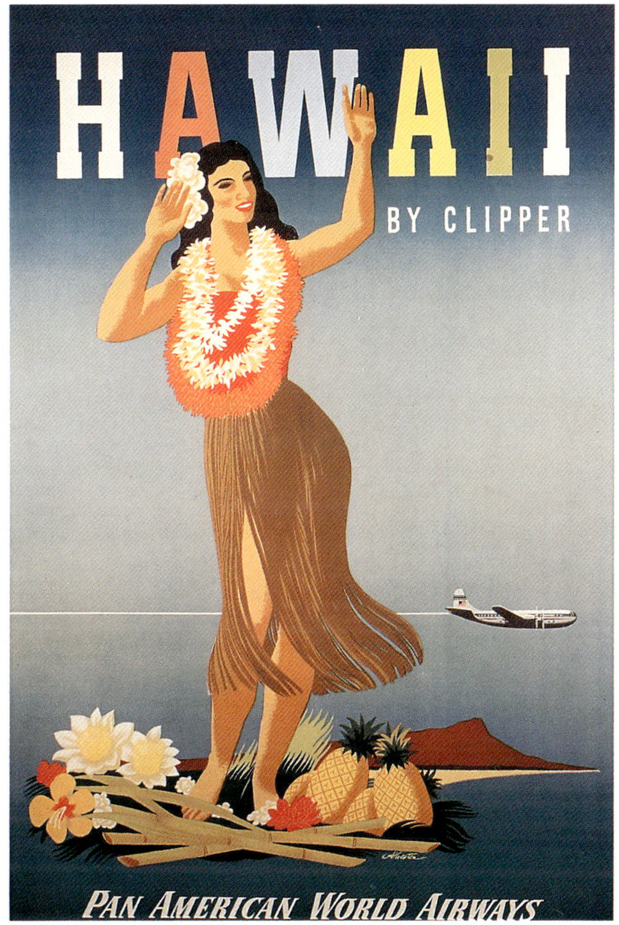

"Hawaii by Clipper," travel poster for Pan American World Airways with art by Atherton. *Courtesy: Randy Hild*.

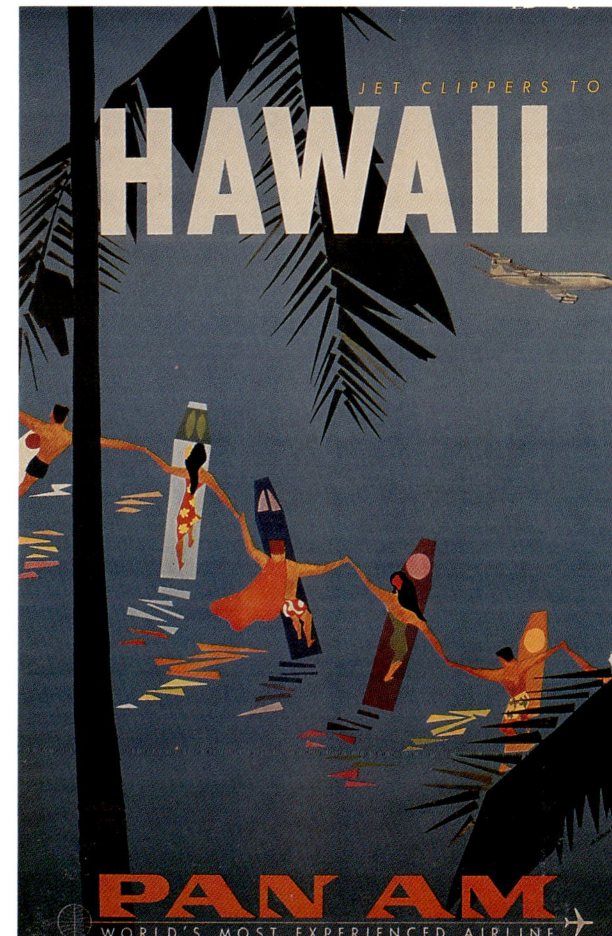

"Jet Clippers to Hawaii," travel Poster for Pan Am with art by Aaron Fino. *Courtesy: Randy Hild*.

Frank MacIntosh

Frank MacIntosh used vivid colors and bold graphic designs to capture the Aloha Spirit. His long association with Matson Lines produced travel posters and a remarkable series of menu covers. He also lent his hand to special Island events and created images for a Hawaiian promotion at Filene's department stores in Boston.

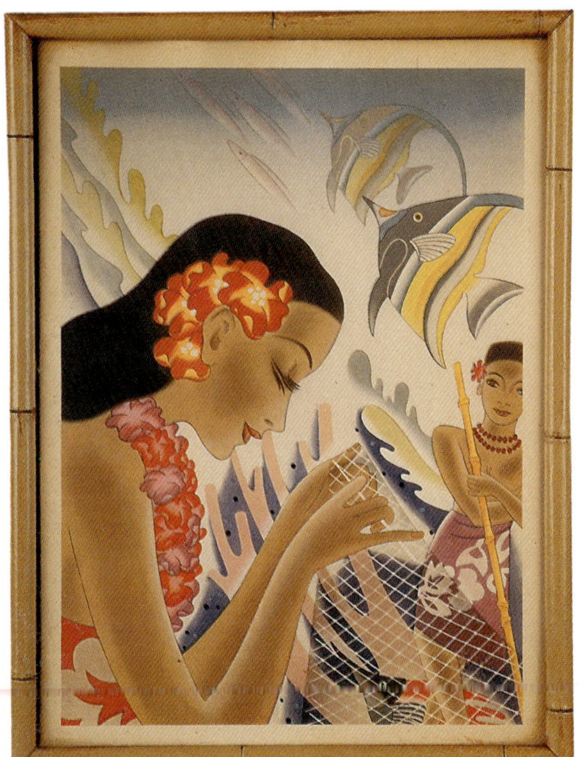

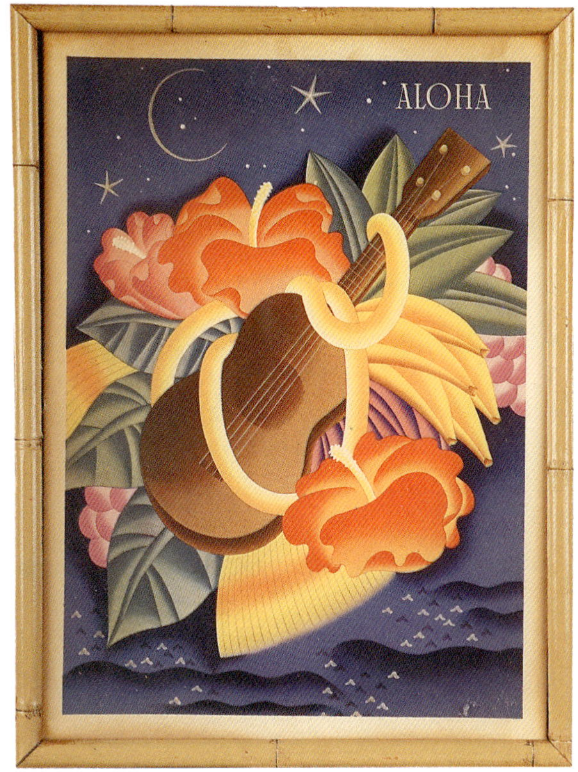

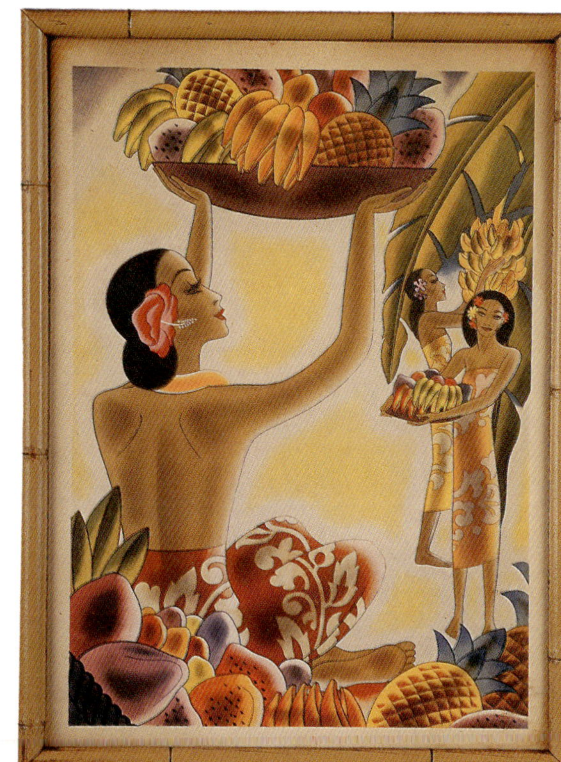

Menu covers designed for the Matson Lines in the 1930s. *Courtesy: Jim & Susie Stiso.*

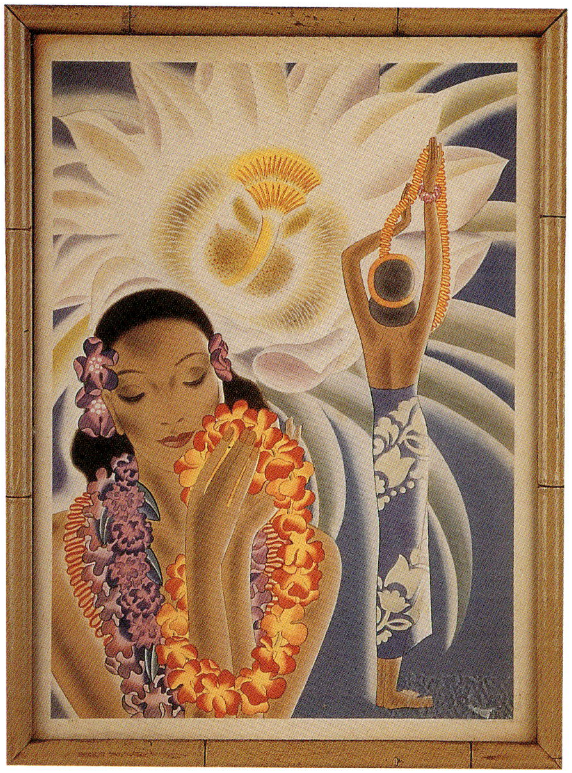

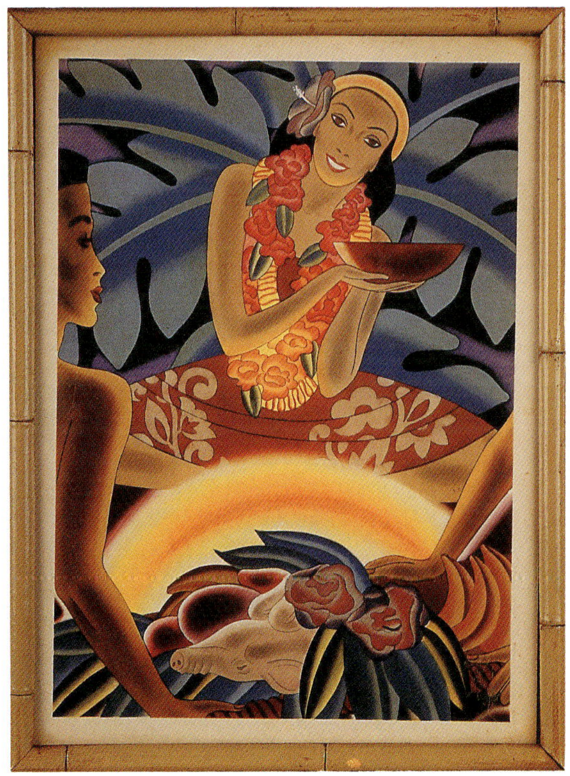

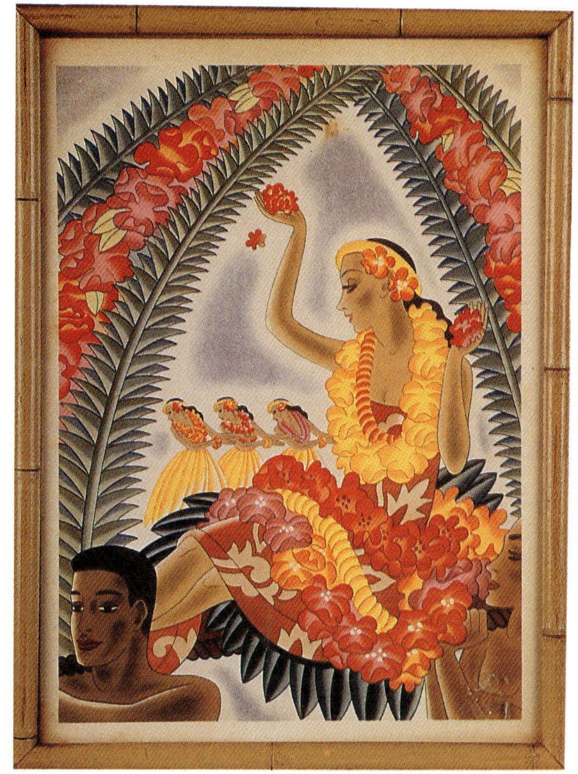

Eugene Savage

Eugene Savage (1883-1978) also produced menus for the Matson Lines. The *S.S. Lurline* was to be added to the passenger line in the early 1940s, but with the outbreak of World War II it was requisitioned for troop transport. The murals, four by eight feet, which Savage executed and which were meant to hang in the ship as well as serve as menu covers, were unceremoniously stowed away. When the *Lurline* was returned to private service in 1948, the menus were finally used. They received immediate acclaim from customers and critics alike. To meet the demand, Matson offered a set of prints for sale for a nominal amount. According to Blackburn in *Hawaiiana* over a quarter million sets were printed either as menus or prints.

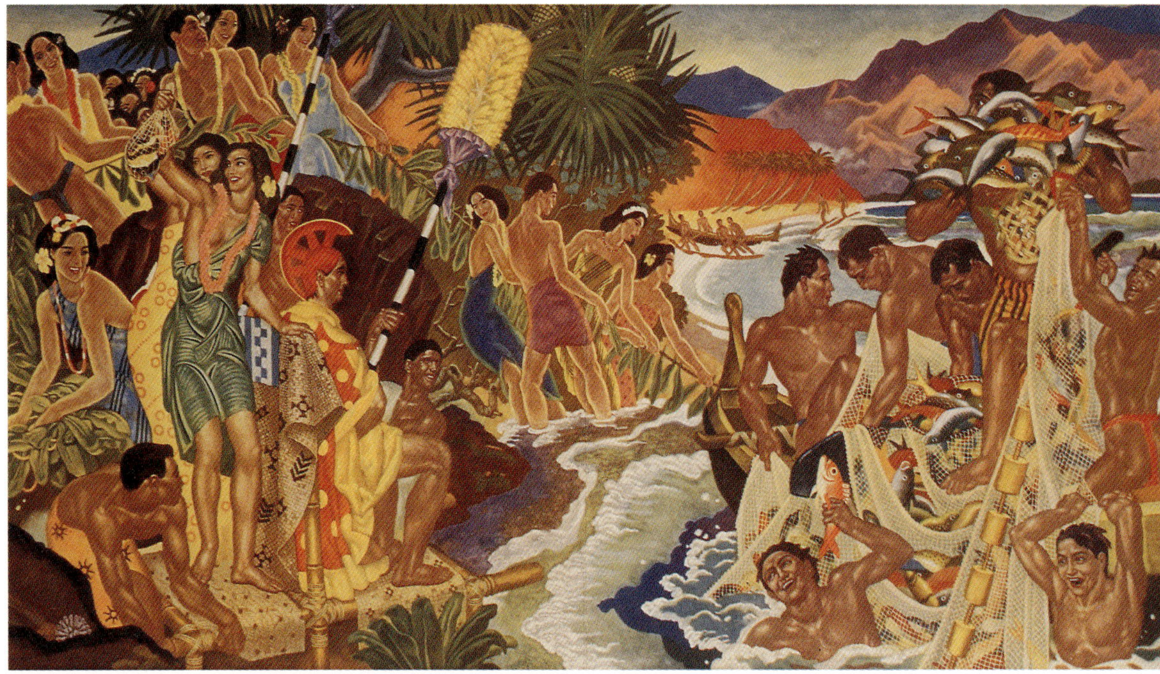

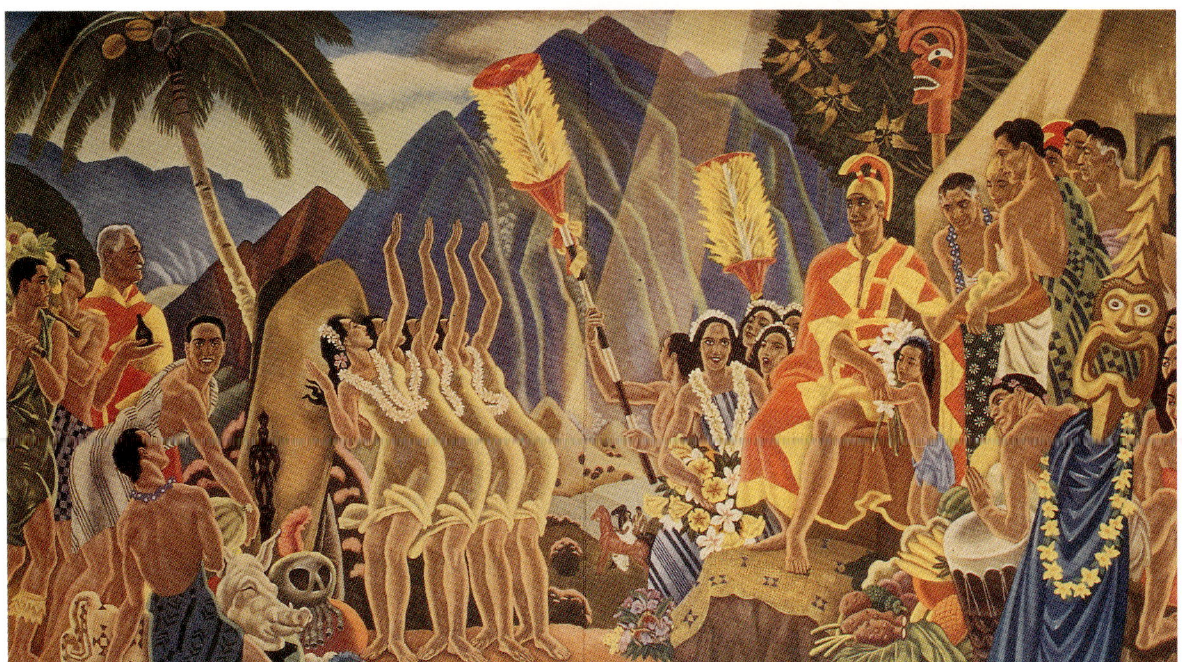

Above:
"Festival of the Sea," Eugene Savage menu. *Courtesy: Michael Trotter.*

Left:
"Pomp and Circumstance," Savage menu. *Courtesy: Michael Trotter.*

Chapter 2

The Aloha Home

Writing in the *New York Times Magazine* on July 3, 1960, the day before the ceremonies surrounding Hawaii's statehood, Cynthia Kellogg predicted that "Hawaii can be expected to contribute more decoration to the American scene than the fiftieth star that it adds to the flag...The new state has long been a symbol of the good life outdoors. Mainlanders have been charmed by its alfresco living to the point of 'importing' such samples of it as the *luau*...and, in housing, the *lanai*, a room open on one side or more to the outdoors, which is already popular with homeowners on the West Coast and Florida."

The outdoors is the essential element in Hawaiian decorative arts. Blessed as the Islands are with an ideal climate, there is, in reality, little need for shelter. So the line between outdoors and indoors tends to blur. Ingenuously simple solutions for comfort from the intense sun include high ceilings that allow space for warm air to rise, leaving the lower room cool, and broad, overhanging eaves that provide shade through the day. Beneath this sheltering roof, the homes tend to be open. They invite the fresh breezes to breathe through, carrying the fragrances of a host of flowers, which can be seen through wide expanses of window and screen.

So marvelous is the natural world of Hawaii that it becomes a central theme of Island decor. The furniture takes on the natural look of rattan or is carved with leaves and blossoms and is upholstered with multicolored bark cloth in patterns of tropical foliage. Pottery takes organic forms and dinnerware is decorated with a variety of Island flowers and plants. Even in the kitchen, the anthurium becomes a decorative motif.

It is little wonder that this oneness with nature was emulated in California and Florida, where the climate permits it, but as Kellogg predicted, it has spread beyond those warm places. As more and more tourists experienced the Islands, and their decor and ambience received more and more coverage in the popular press, their influence grew. Today, even in the most inhospitable of climates, great walls of glass look onto patios and gardens. Tropical gardens are brought indoors and in many homes the designs and furnishings of the Islands seek to recreate the magic of the Aloha Spirit.

Furniture and Accessories

The history of furniture making in Hawaii begins almost as early as the arrival of the first Western residents. Some who came to Hawaii virtually taught themselves to be skilled woodworkers, but as time passed professional craftspeople from America, Europe, and Asia established themselves in the Islands. They created a body of regional American furniture that is cherished and still popular in island homes.

The most important aspect of Hawaiian furniture was the use of certain native Hawaiian woods, koa wood being particularly beautiful. The possession of koa furniture became an expression of pride in Hawaii.

Koa trees grow in dense rain forests and develop straight trunks often reaching a height of forty feet. Growing in the mild climate of the Islands, koa trees have no discernable annual growth rings but are thought to have a maximum life span of around 400 years.

The designer who worked for the Honolulu branch of the San Francisco-based Gump's and Company created koa furniture and furnishings with relief carvings of flower and leaf patterns that were copied by cabinetmakers throughout the territory.

Koa wood was also used for most Hawaiian ukuleles, lamp bases, bookends, beautifully carved bowls, perfume bottles, serving trays, and a variety of souvenir items. The souvenir items were often found bearing the Hawaiian coat of arms and were carried by nearly every curio shop in the Islands between 1900 and 1930.

For those interested in recreating the Aloha Spirit back, rattan furnishings provided the perfect decorating touch. Long produced in Victorian forms and meant primarily for casual use, in the 1920s and '30s they were used to create marvelous Art Deco furniture. The individual pieces of wood combine to make eye-catching geometrical patterns as well as sensuous curves. When combined with a solid wood table top or tropical cushions, the relaxed ambience of the Islands is brought into the formal settings of distant living and dining rooms. Most of the finest rattan of the period was produced in California.

Rattan

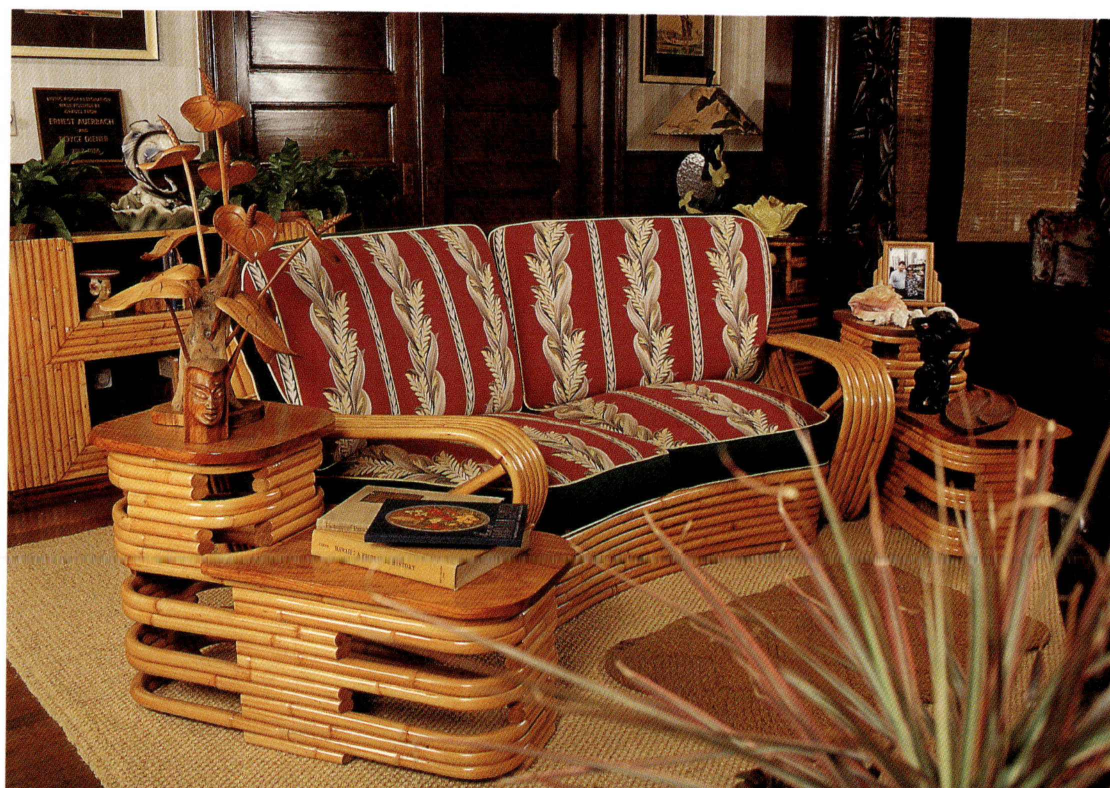

Stepped end-tables of rattan and wood with a curved rattan sofa, bedecked with cushions in a shell ginger pattern. *Courtesy: Michael & Denise Queen.*

Behind the sofa is this rattan bookcase. The pedestals at the ends have plant wells at the top and open display areas at the ends. This is the perfect place for displaying treasures as well as books. *Courtesy: Michael & Denise Queen.*

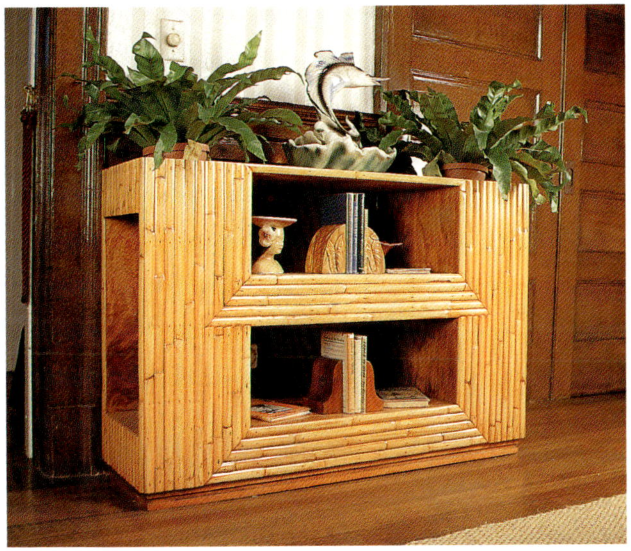

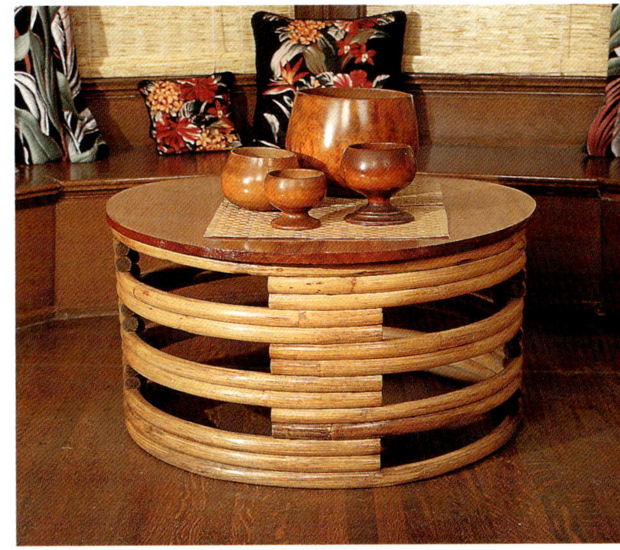

A round rattan and wood table. *Courtesy: Michael & Denise Queen.*

This comfortable reading nook contains a matching chair and ottoman with rich floral cushions, a five-shelf etagere, a magazine rack and a floor lamp.

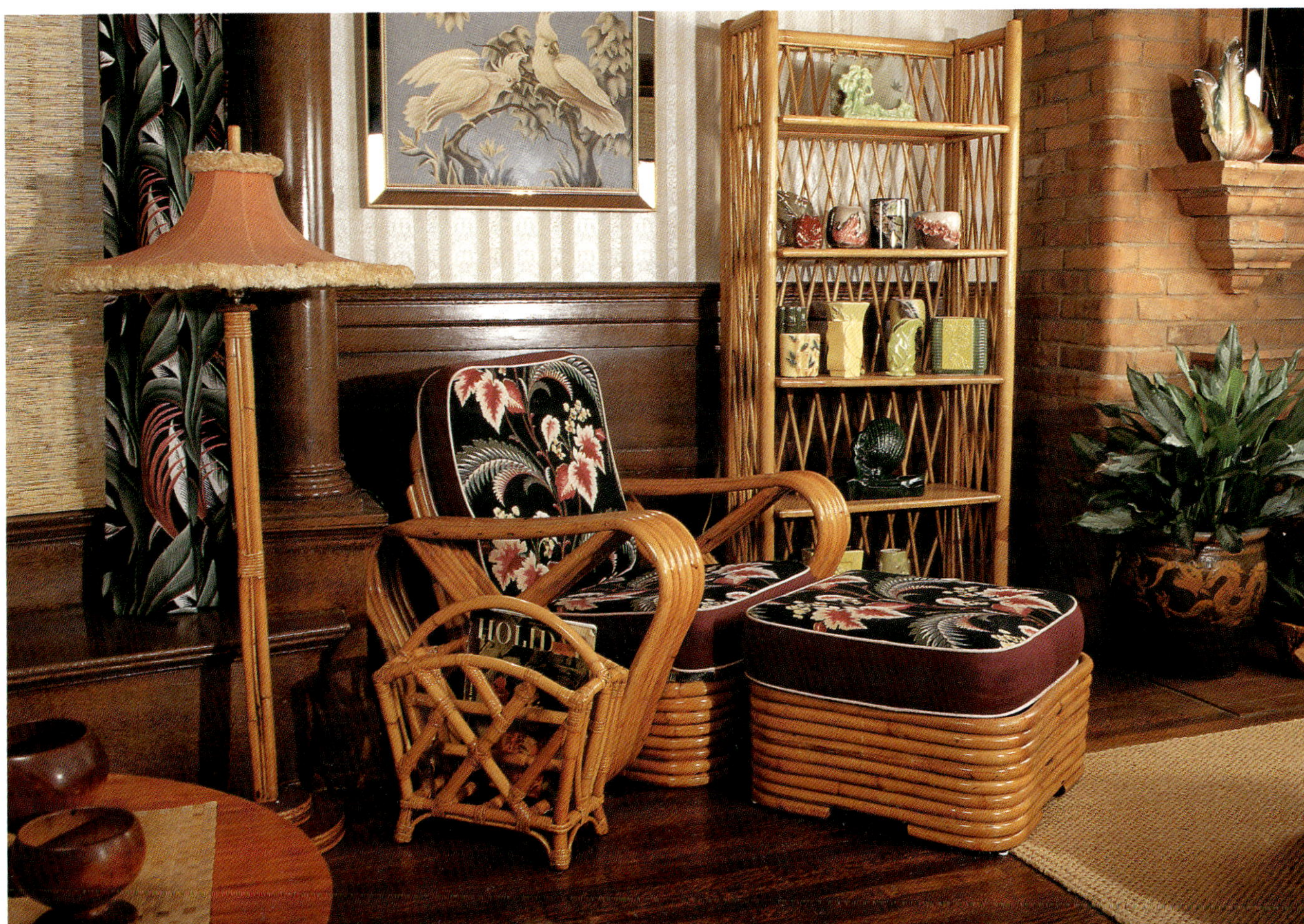

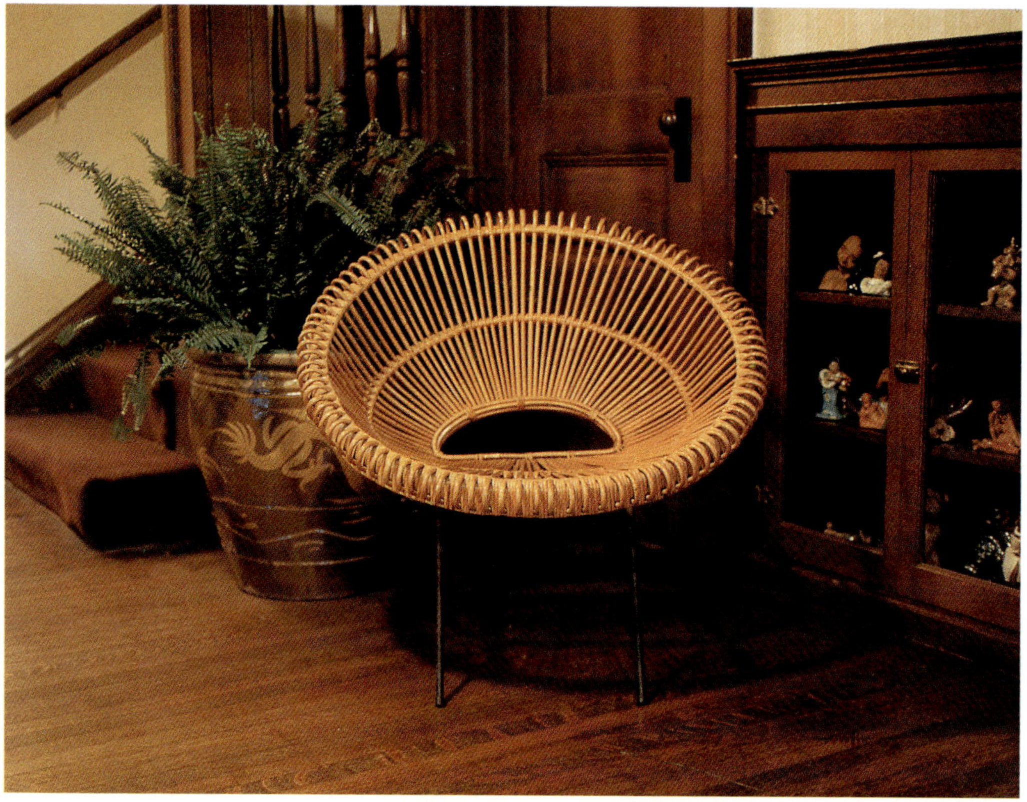

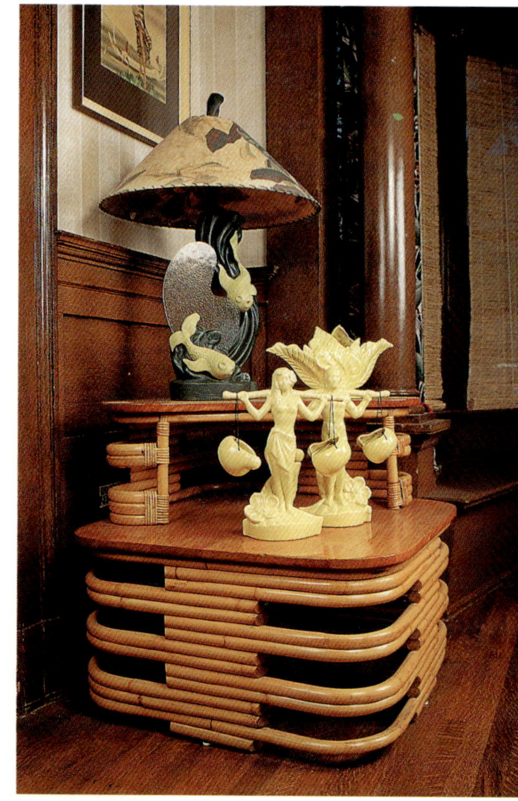

Very modern looking rattan chair on metal legs. *Courtesy: Tropical Sun Rattan, 20th Century Props.*

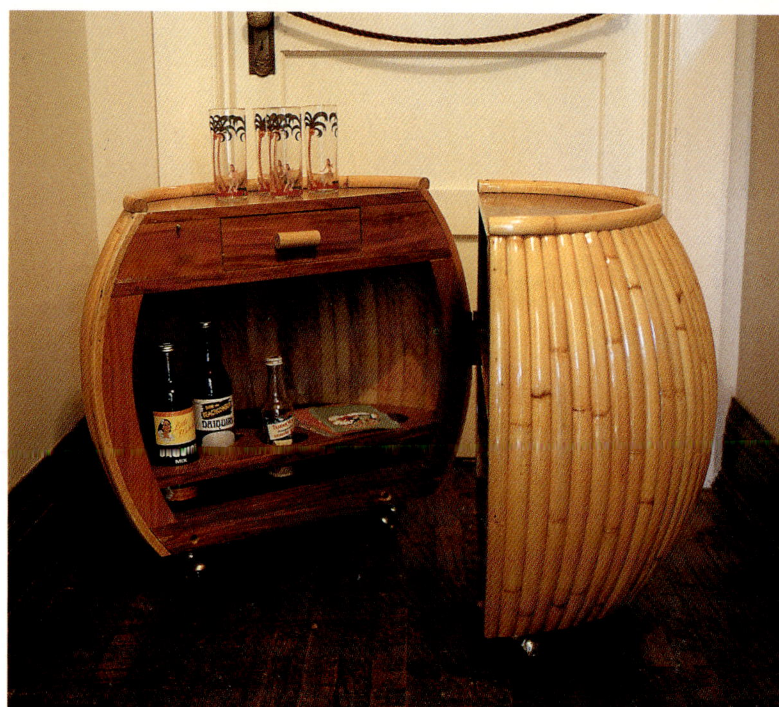

Above:
Rattan corner table. *Courtesy: Michael & Denise Queen.*

Left:
This rattan and koa wood rolling bar cabinet opens to reveal the storage area. A beautiful example of rattan work. *Courtesy: Michael & Denise Queen.*

Opposite left:
This small corner bar in rattan shows the design flexibility of the material. It is surrounded by rattan stools, knick-knack shelf, and lighting sconce.

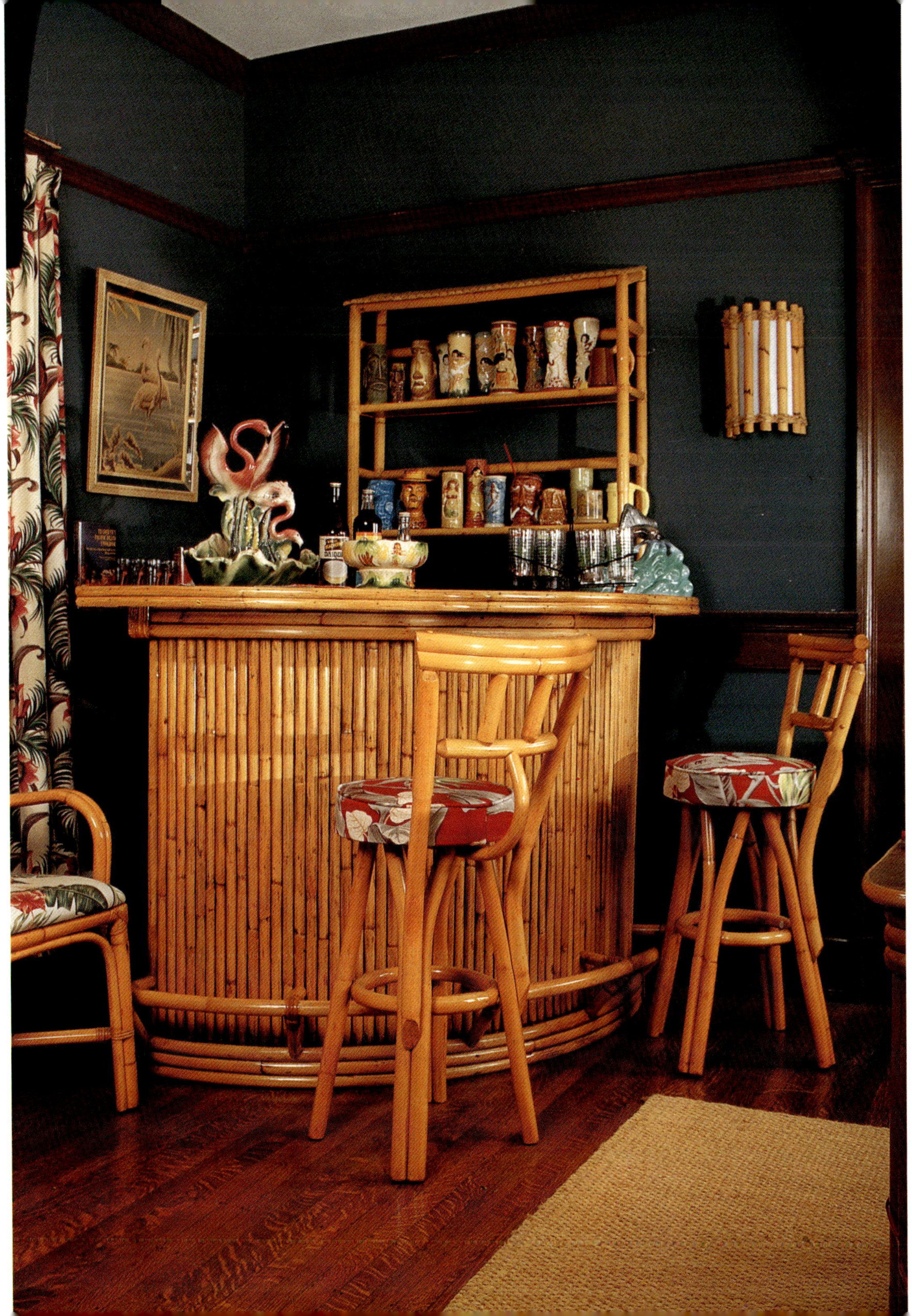

Close-up of the bar stool with its bark cloth cushion.
Courtesy: K.C. Heylin.

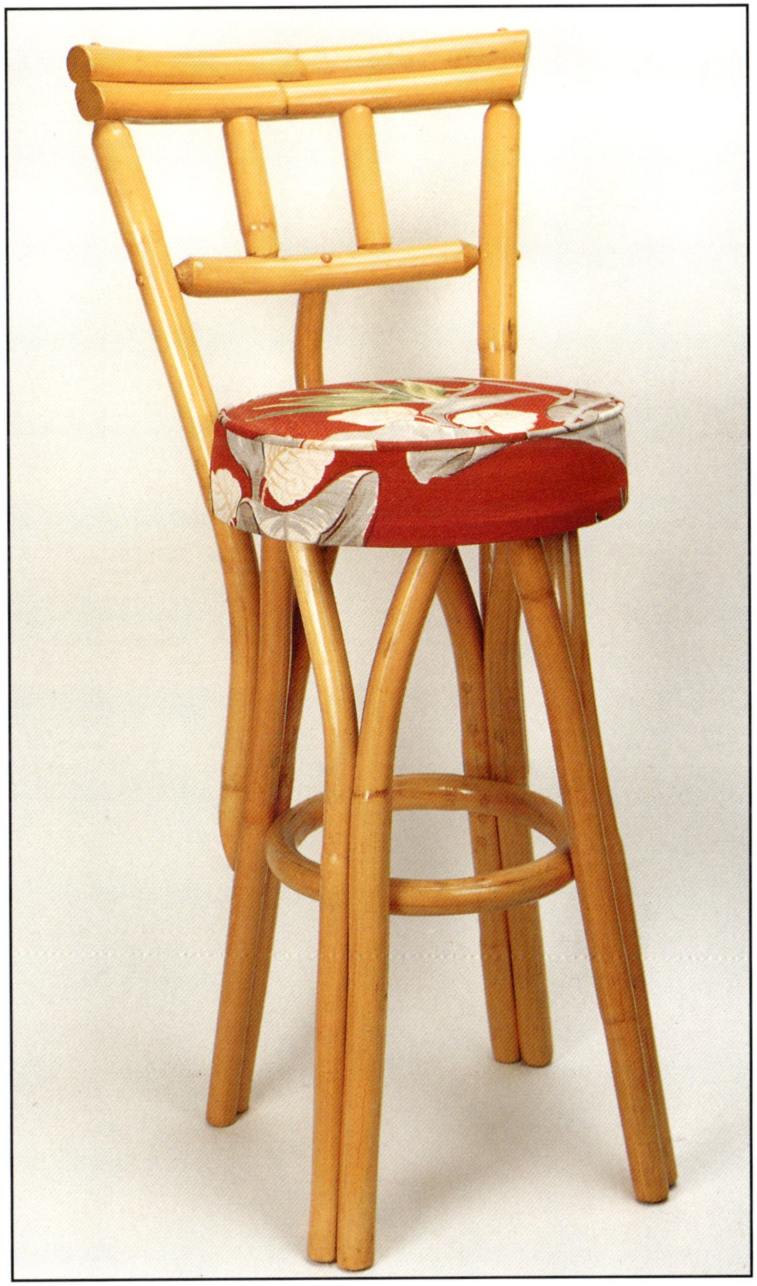

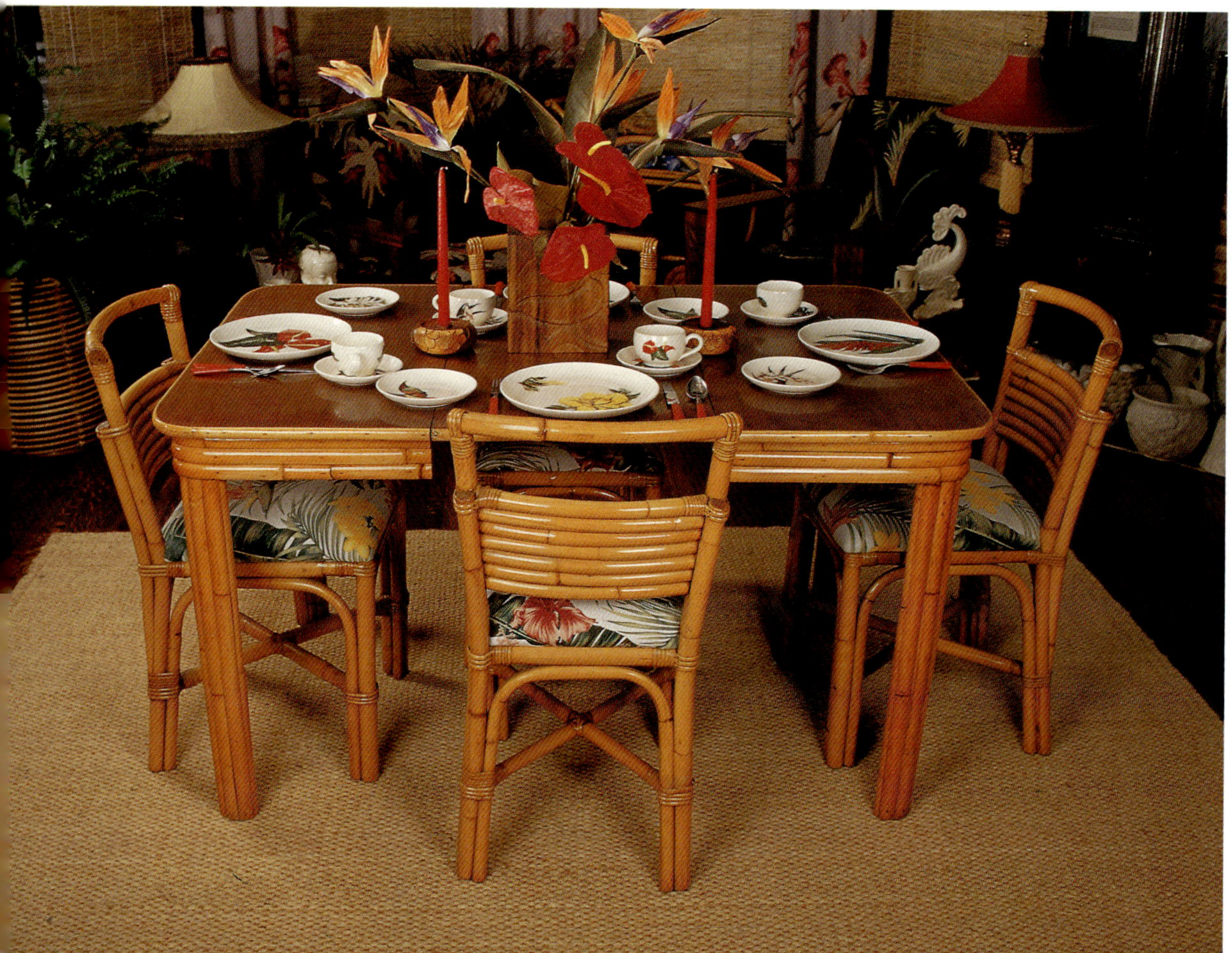

Dining room table and chairs.

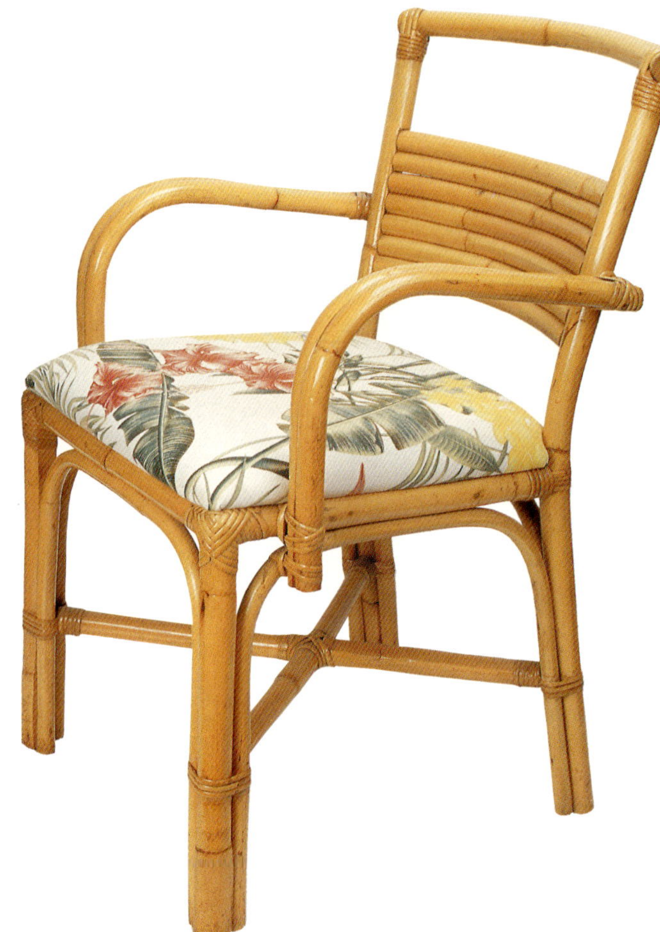

A dining room arm chair, matching the set.
Courtesy: Michele Leypoldt.

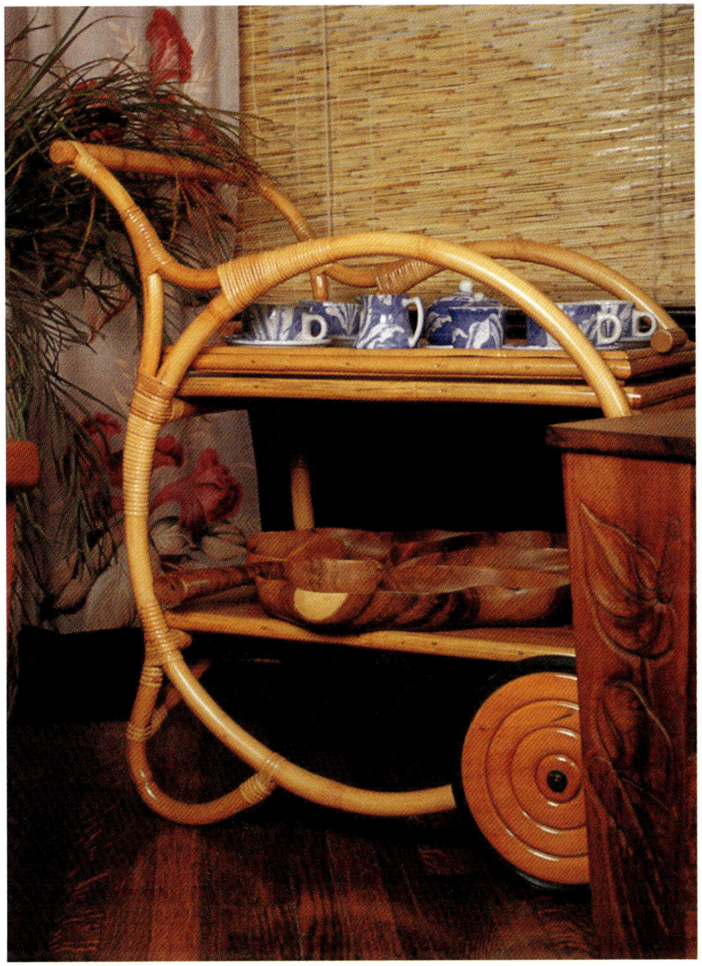

Wonderfully designed serving cart with two shelves and a removable serving tray. *Courtesy: Michael & Denise Queen*.

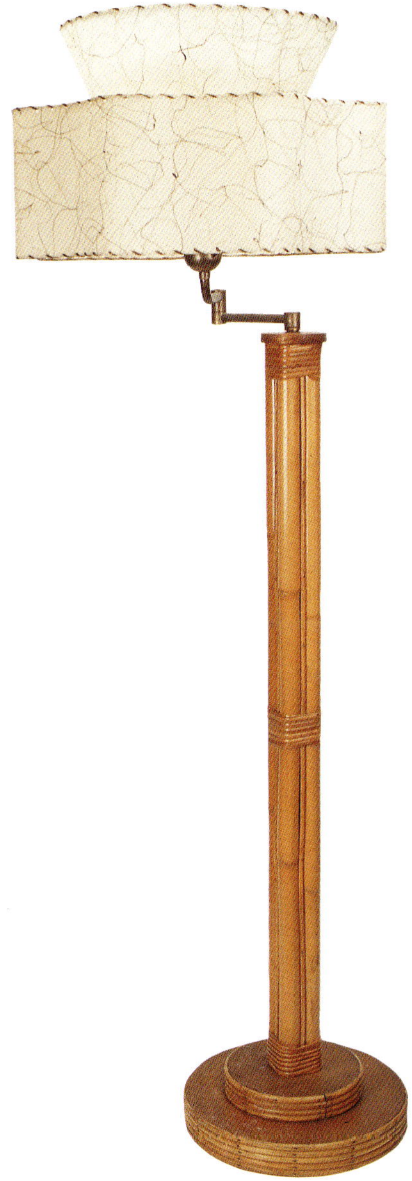

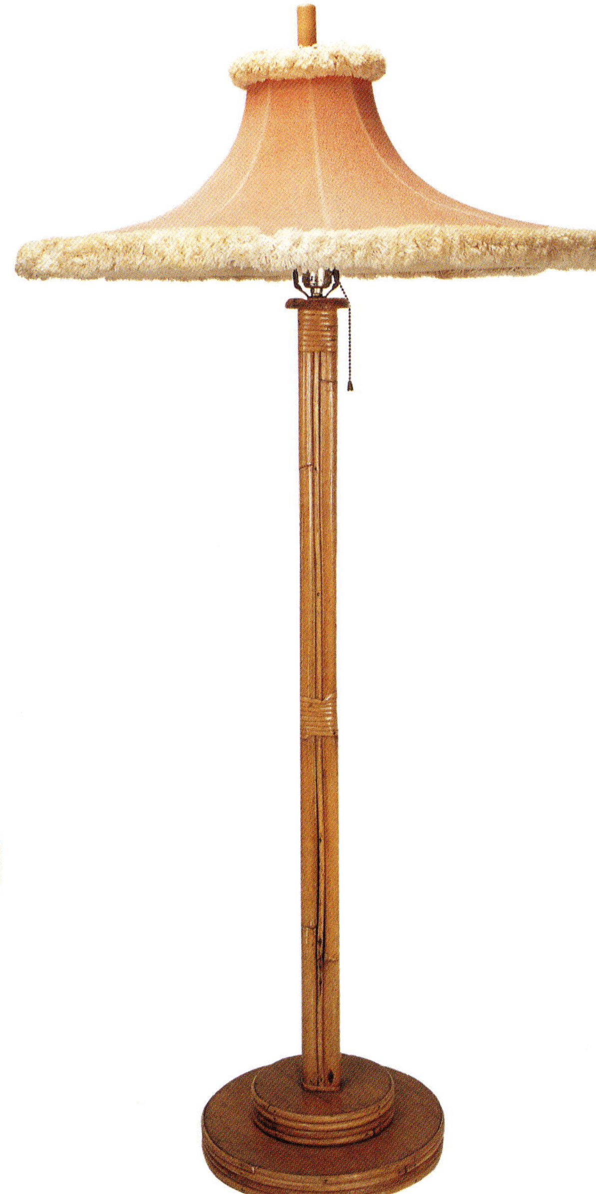

These two floor lamps have very similar rattan bases, but different shade treatments. *Courtesy: K.C. Heylin and Michele Leypoldt*.

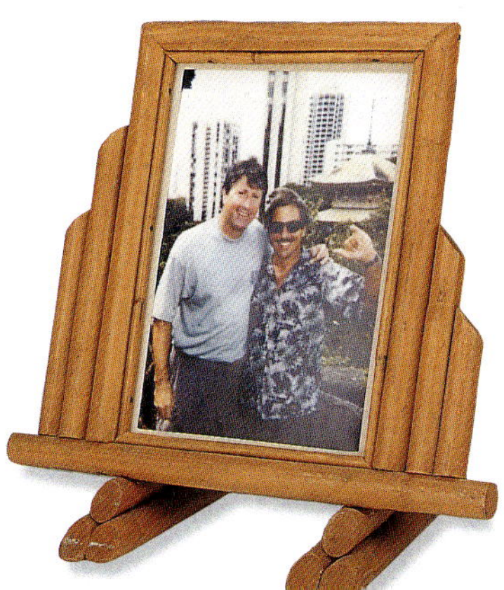

Matching accessories include this rattan picture frame for the table top. *Courtesy: the Collection of Brian Goddard & Gene Sweeney*.

Koa and Other Woods

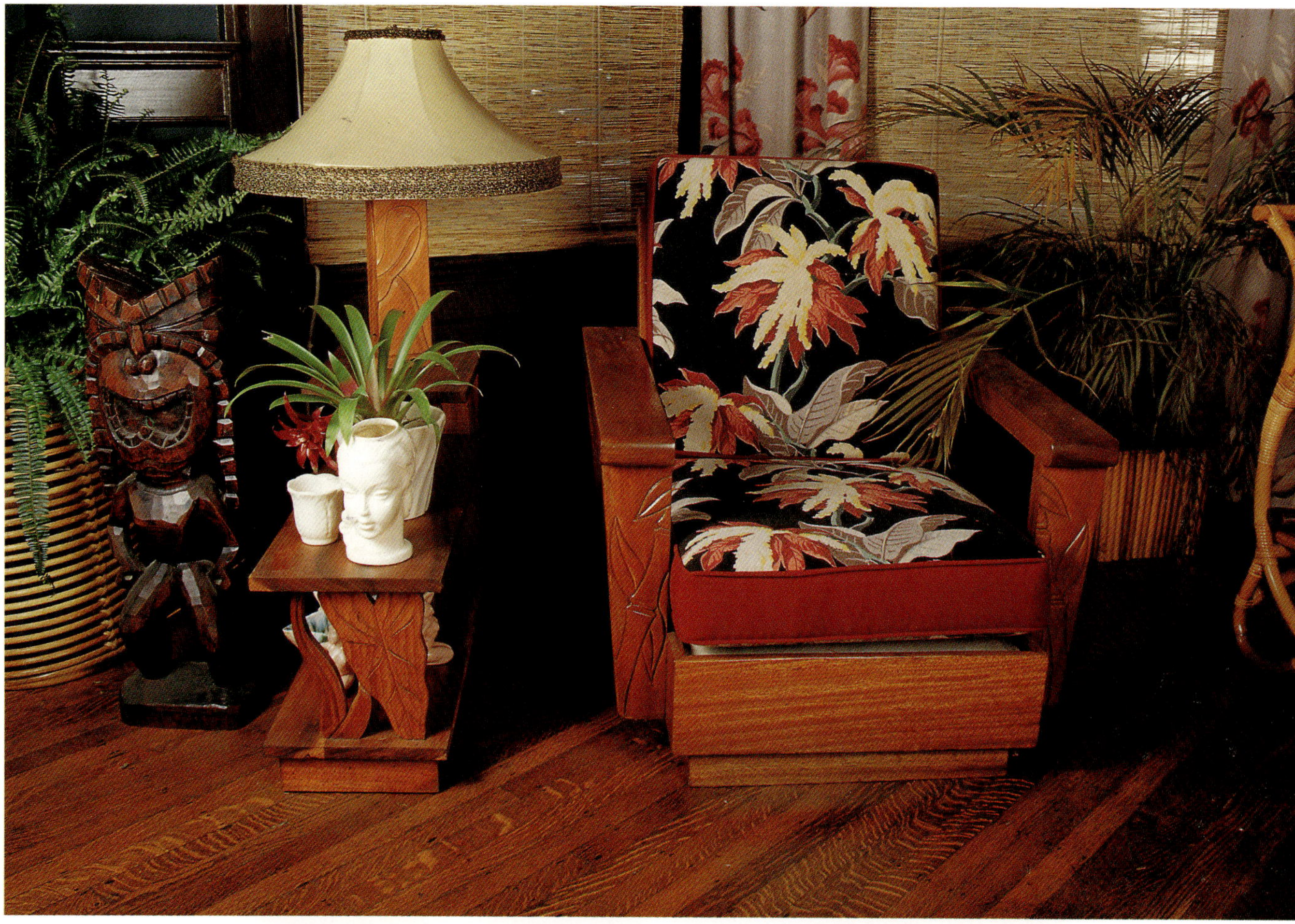

Carved koa wood easy chair, stepped end table, and lamp.

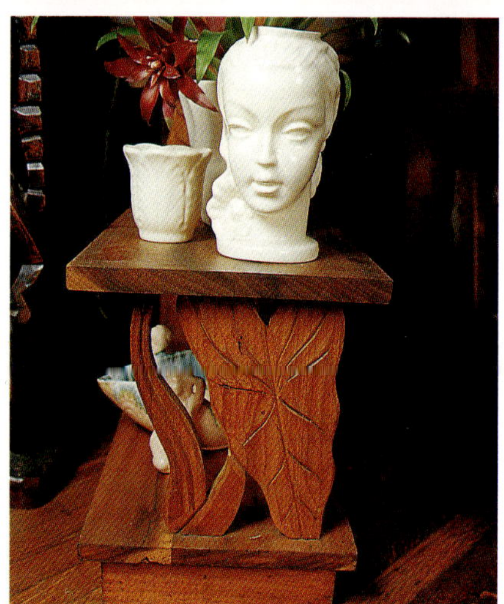

Close-up view of the carving of the end table.

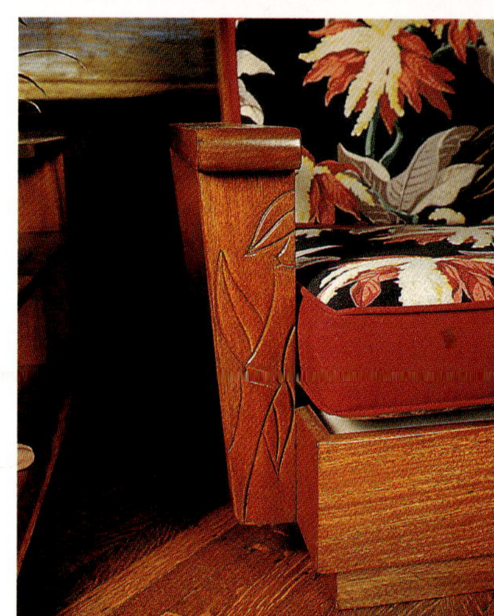

Close-up of the relief carving of bamboo on the chair's arm support. *Courtesy: Don Stewart*.

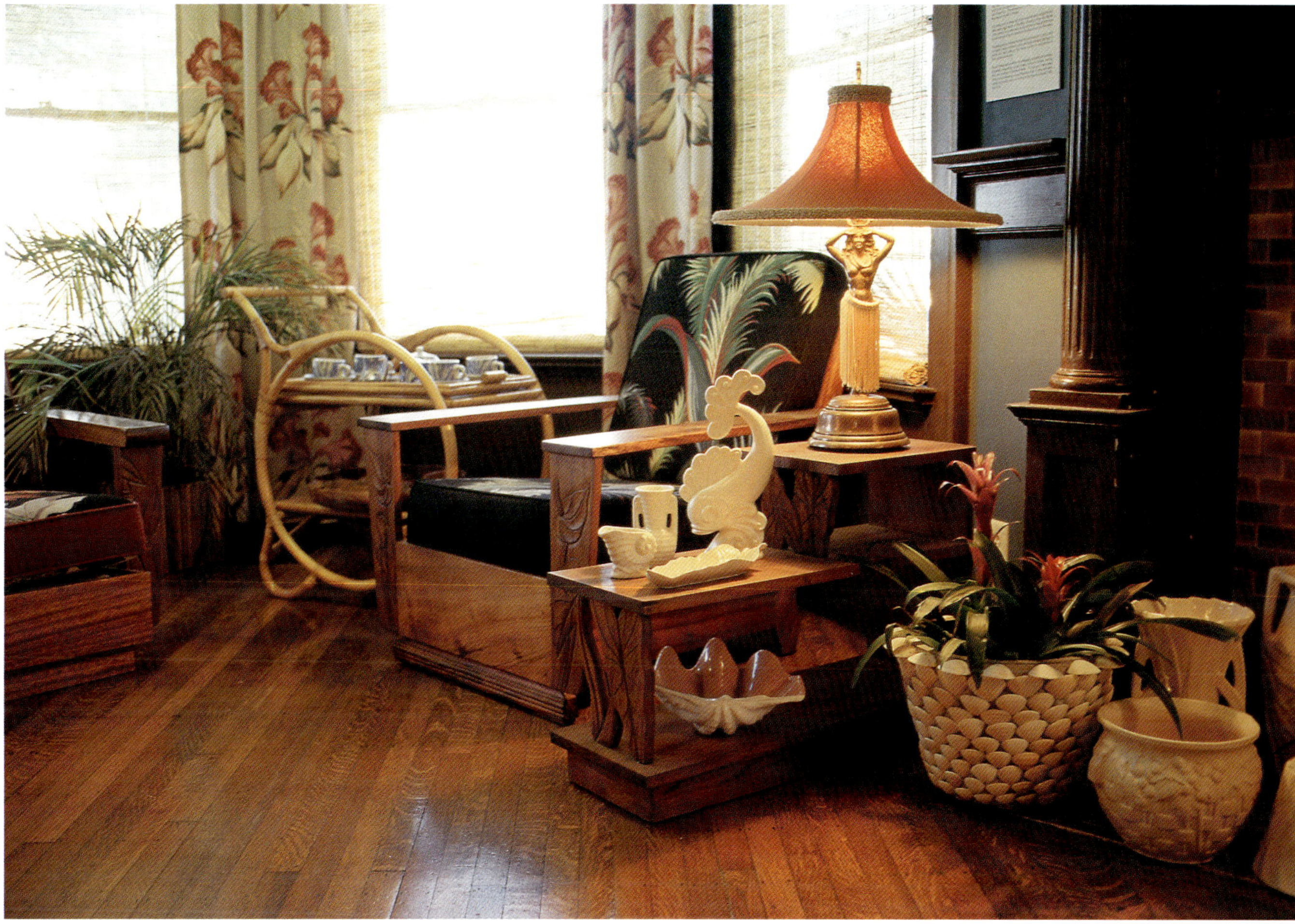

At the other side of the room is the mate to the previous end table and a similar arm chair.

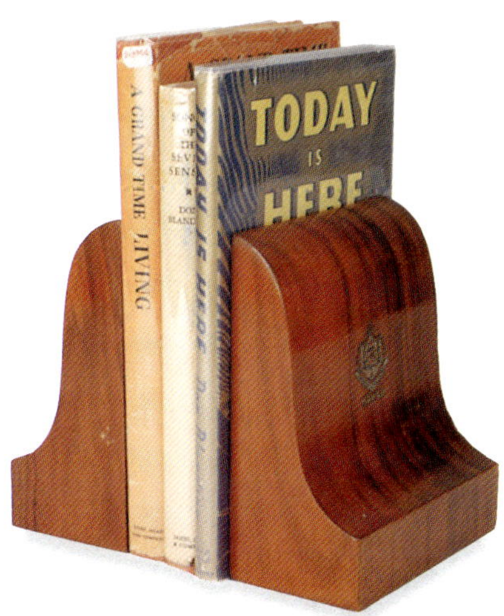

Koa wood bookends with coat of arms decal. *Courtesy: Don Stewart.*

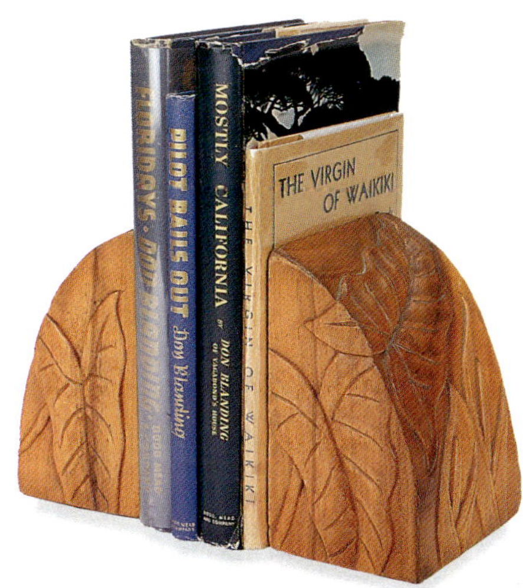

Carved monkey pod wood bookends with a selection of Don Blanding Books. *Courtesy: the Collection of Brian Goddard & Gene Sweeney.*

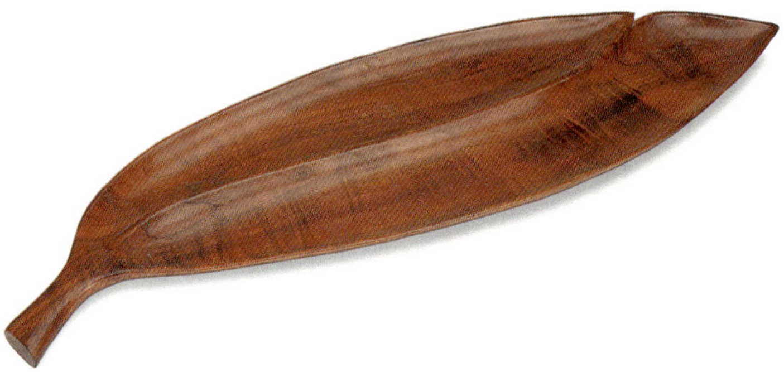

Carved tray, made in Hawaii. *Courtesy: Don Stewart*.

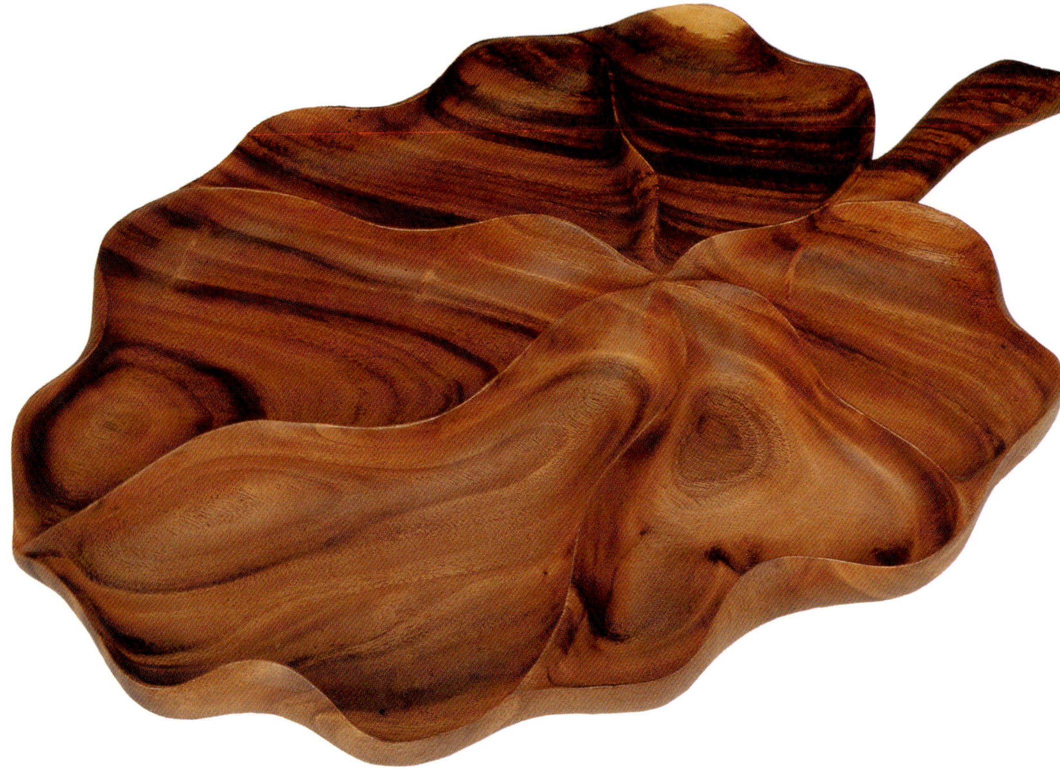

Large carved tray 28.5" wide. *Courtesy: the Collection of Brian Goddard & Gene Sweeney*.

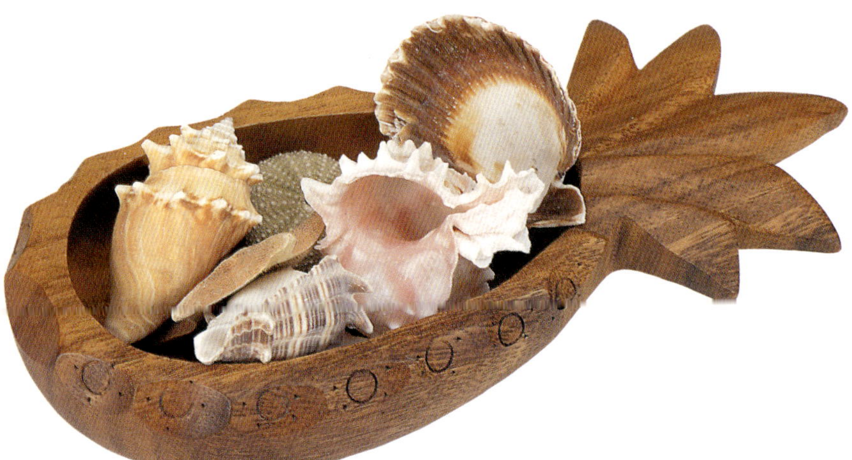

Nut bowl. 11" w. *Courtesy: the Collection of Brian Goddard & Gene Sweeney*.

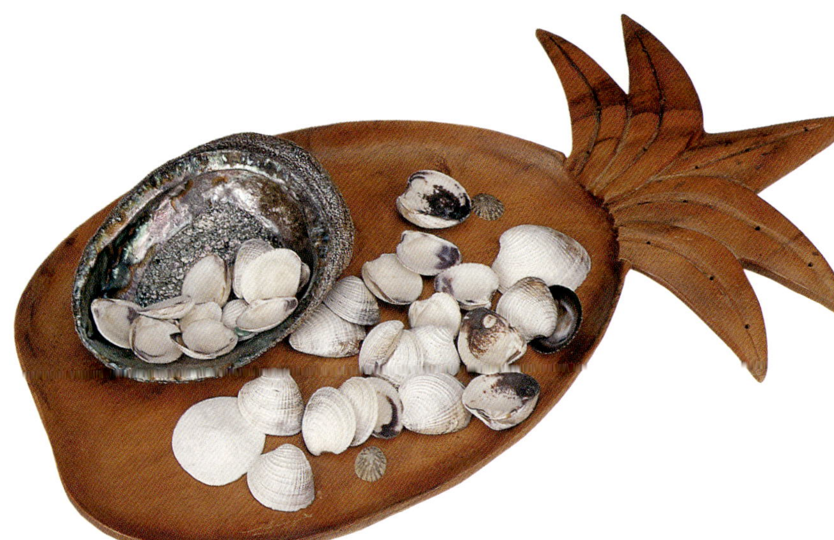

Hors d'oeuvre tray. *Courtesy: the Collection of Brian Goddard & Gene Sweeney*.

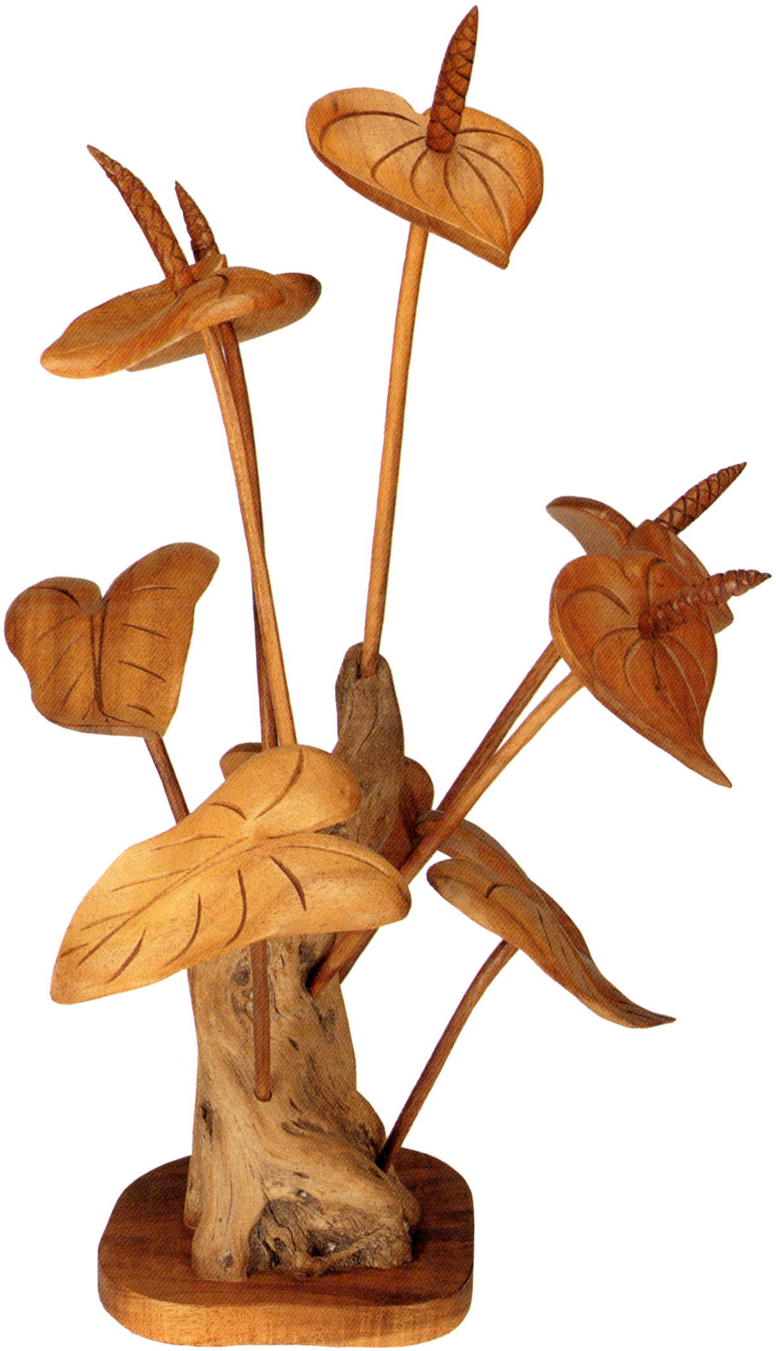

Monkeypod sculpture. 25" h. *Courtesy: the Collection of Brian Goddard & Gene Sweeney.*

Monkeypod vase. 8.5" h x 7.5" w x 4" d.
Courtesy: Michele Leypoldt.

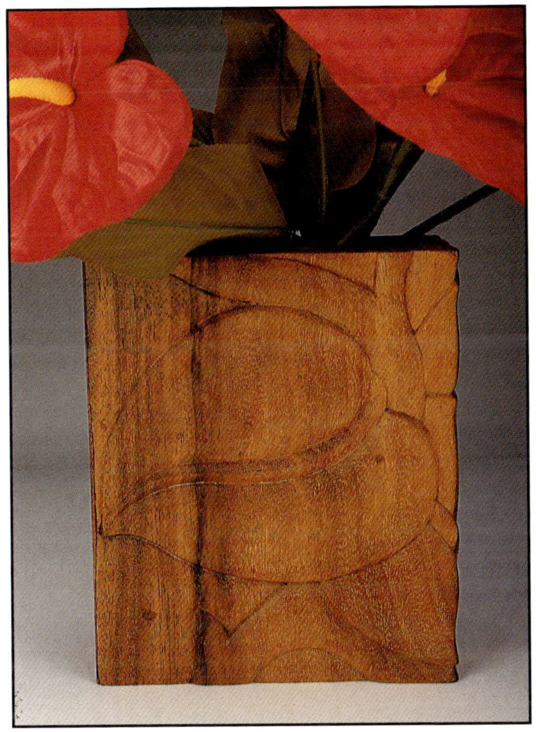

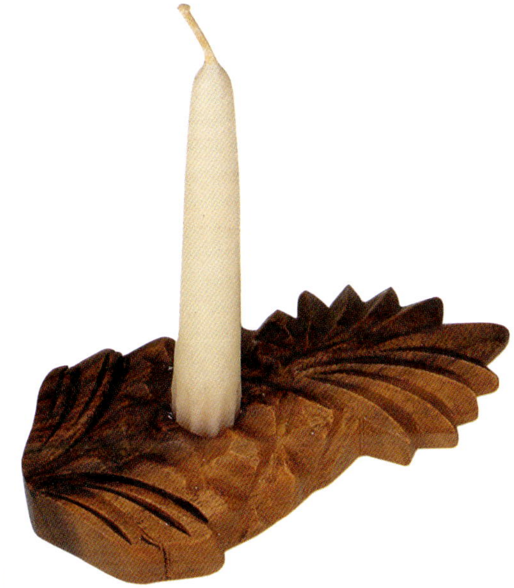

Candle holder. 6.75" w.
Courtesy: the Collection of Brian Goddard & Gene Sweeney.

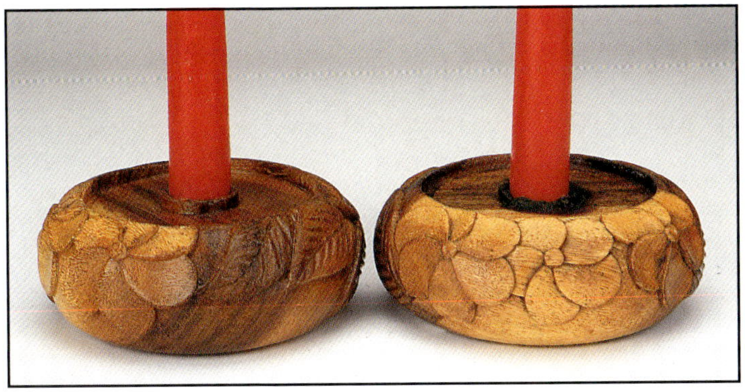

Monkeypod candle holders. 1.75" h., 4.75" d. *Courtesy: the Collection of Brian Goddard & Gene Sweeney.*

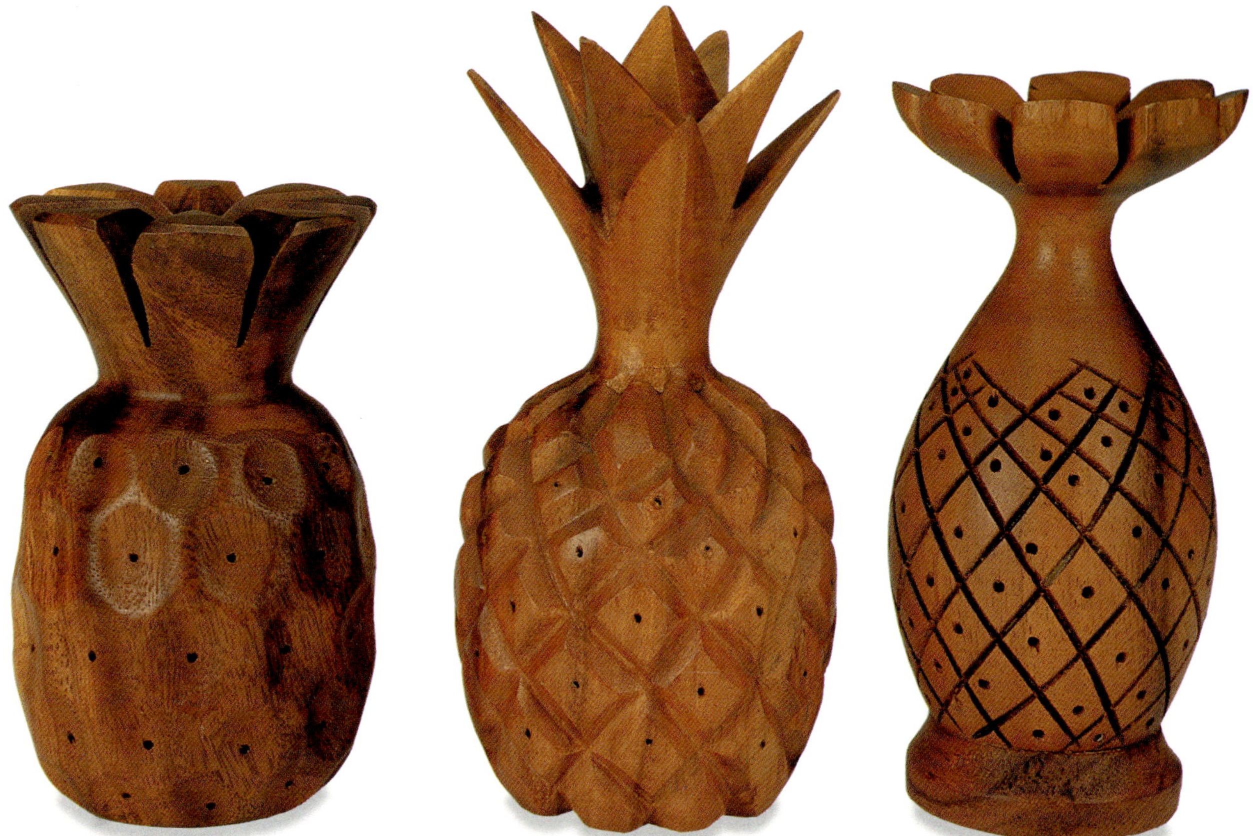

Left:
Monkeypod pineapple toothpick holders. 8" h. *Courtesy: the Collection of Brian Goddard & Gene Sweeney.*

Lower left:
Three smaller pineapple toothpick holders. 6" h. The middle one is marked House of Monkeypod. *Courtesy: the Collection of Brian Goddard & Gene Sweeney.*

Lower right:
Two other toothpick holders, one in full dress. 8" h. *Courtesy: the Collection of Brian Goddard & Gene Sweeney.*

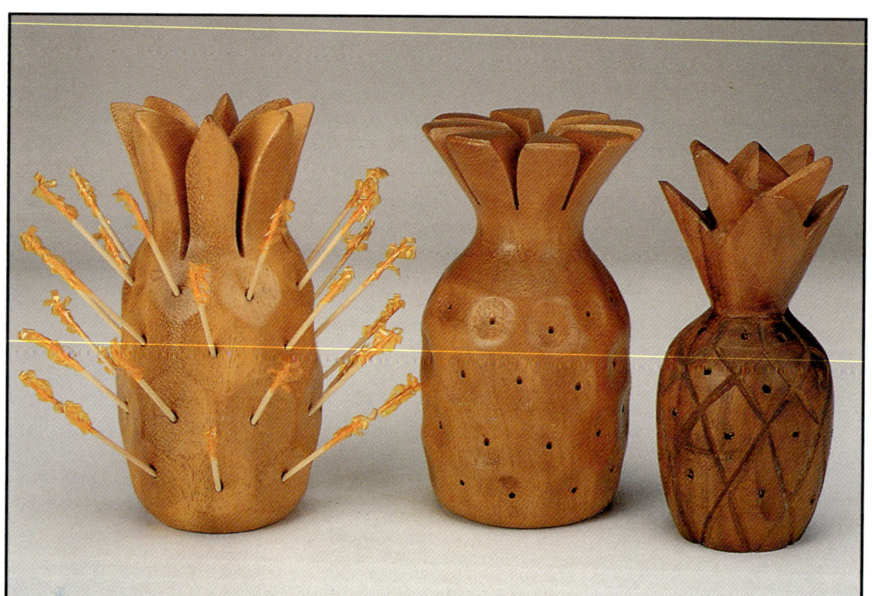

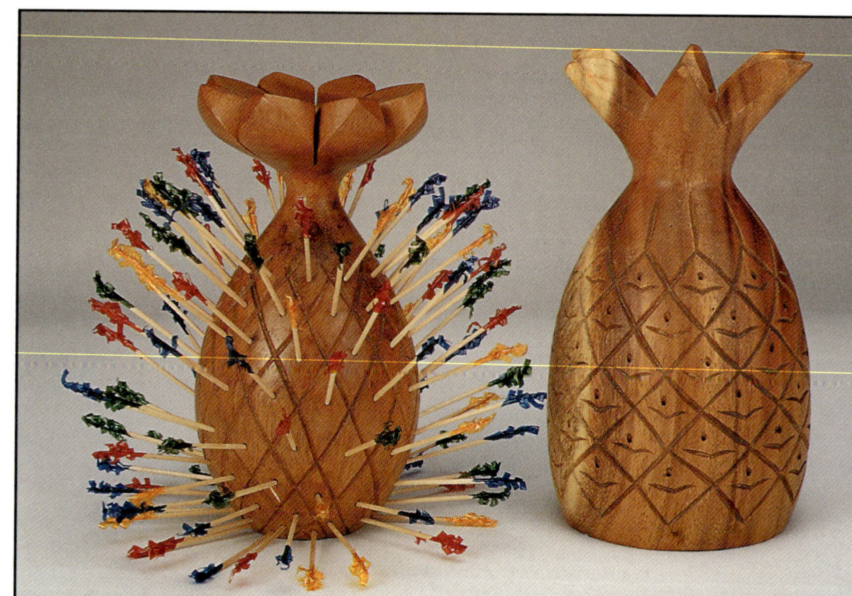

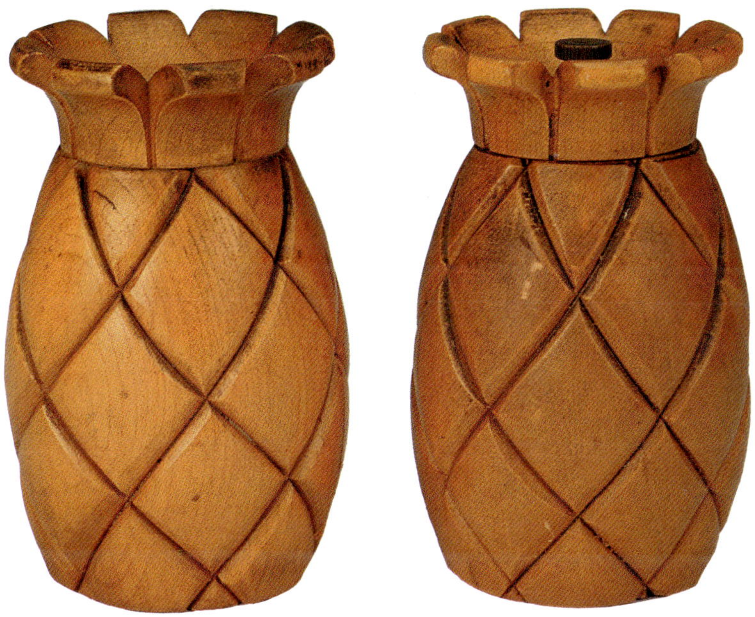

Salt shaker and pepper mill. 4" h. *Courtesy: the Collection of Brian Goddard & Gene Sweeney*.

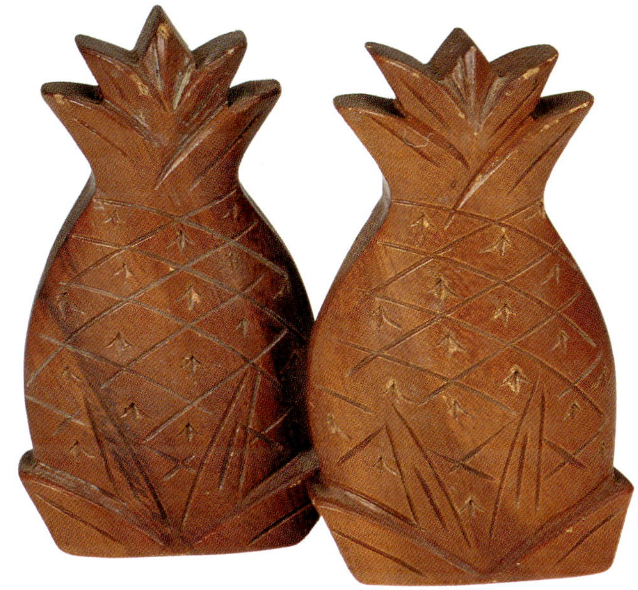

Salt and pepper shakers. 4" h. *Courtesy: Michael Trotter*.

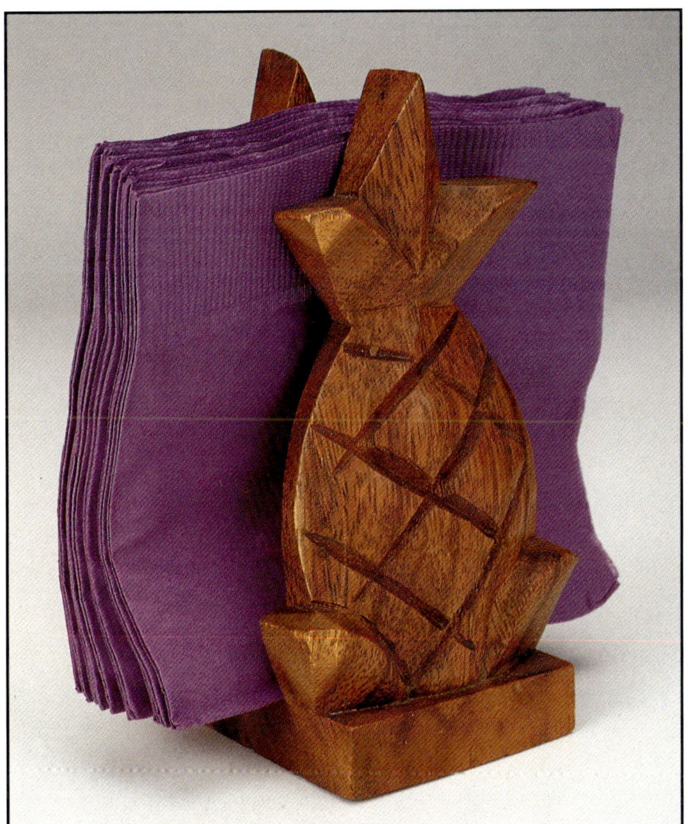

Napkin holder, 6.25". *Courtesy: the Collection of Brian Goddard & Gene Sweeney*.

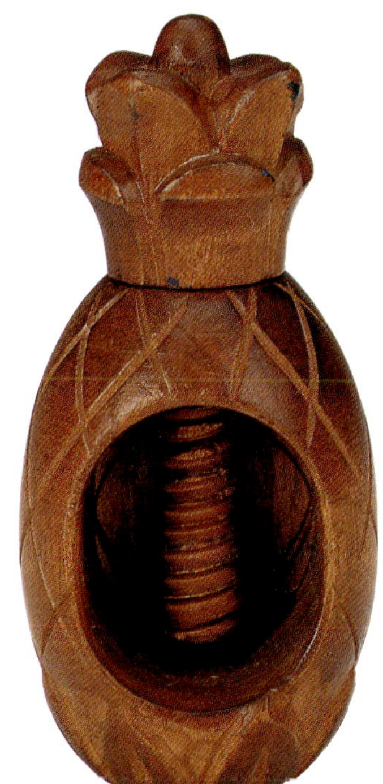

Nutcracker, 5" h. *Courtesy: the Collection of Brian Goddard & Gene Sweeney*.

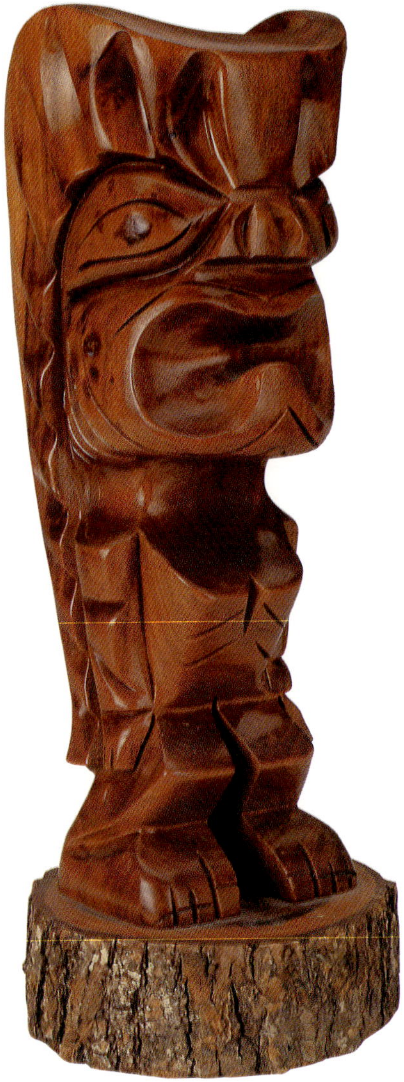

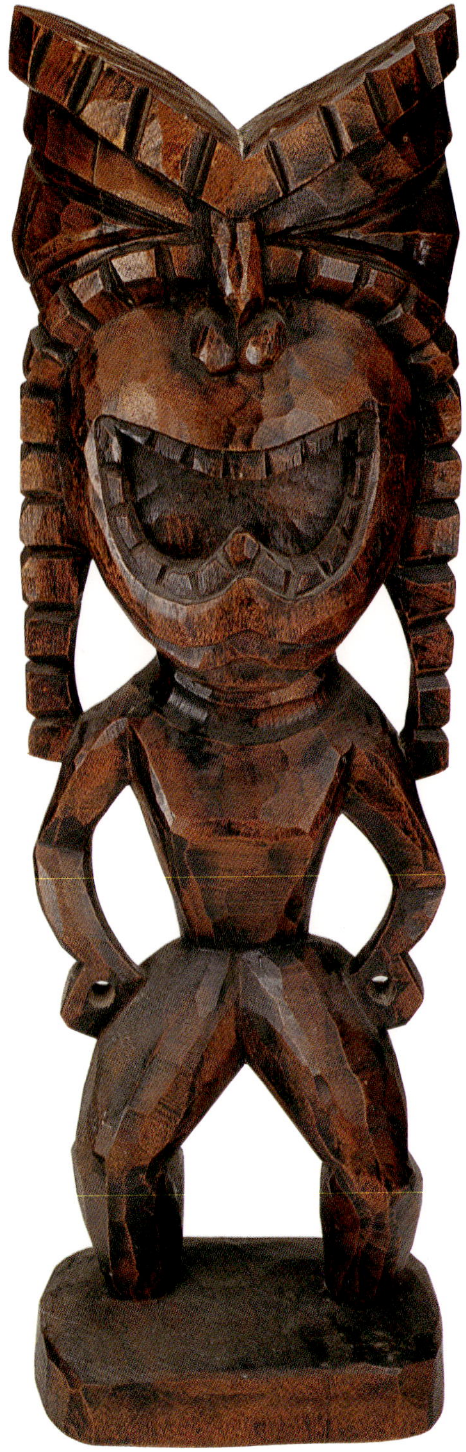

Large tiki carving. 30" tall. *Courtesy: Don Stewart*.

Carved wood Tiki figure, 16" tall. *Courtesy: Don Stewart*.

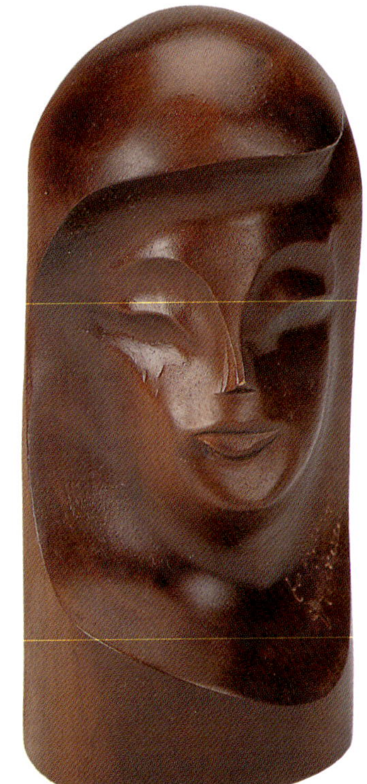

Carved face, signed By Briar, Hawaii, and marked Milo Wood, Made in Hawaii. 6.5" h. *Courtesy: the Collection of Sue White*.

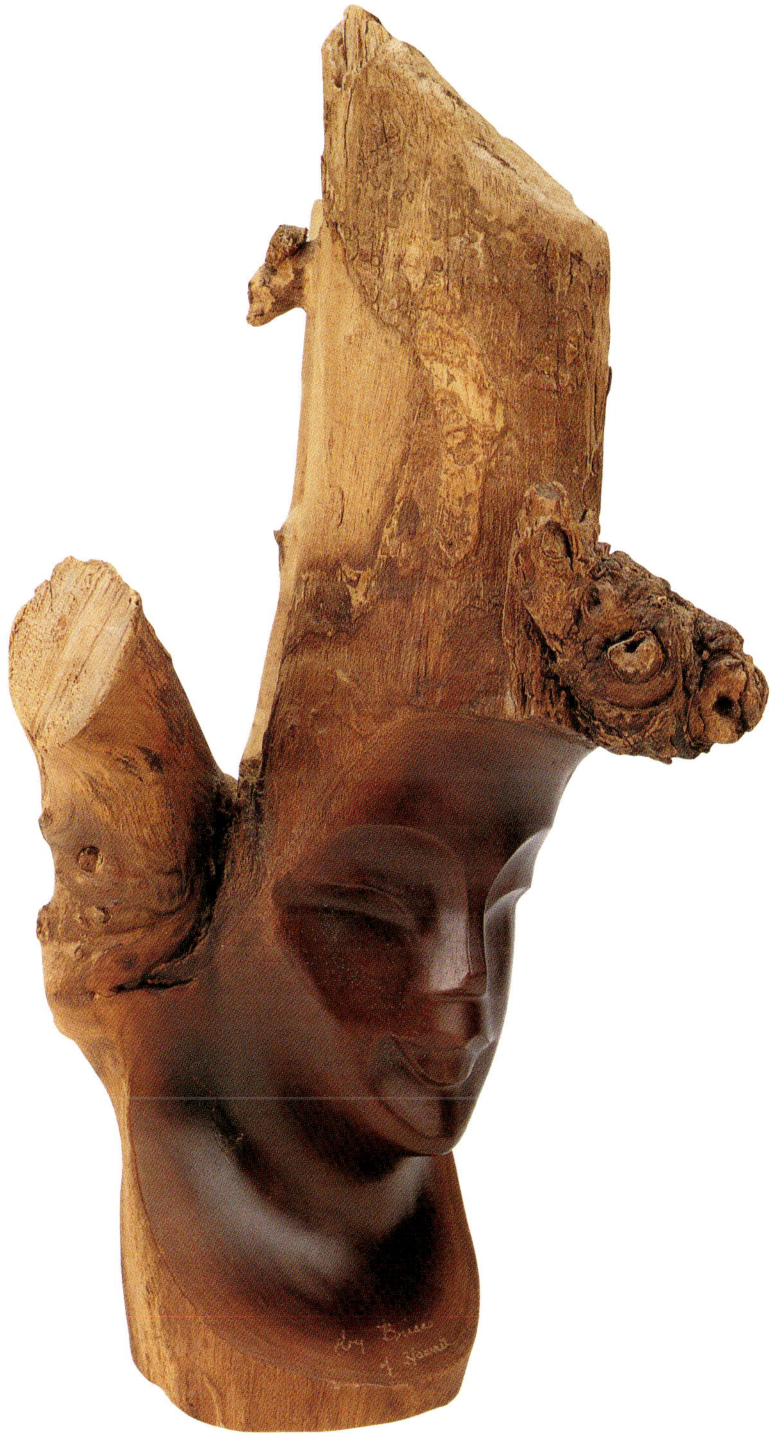

Carved face, signed By Briar, Hawaii, and marked Milo Wood, Made in Hawaii. 12" h. *Courtesy: the Collection of Sue White*.

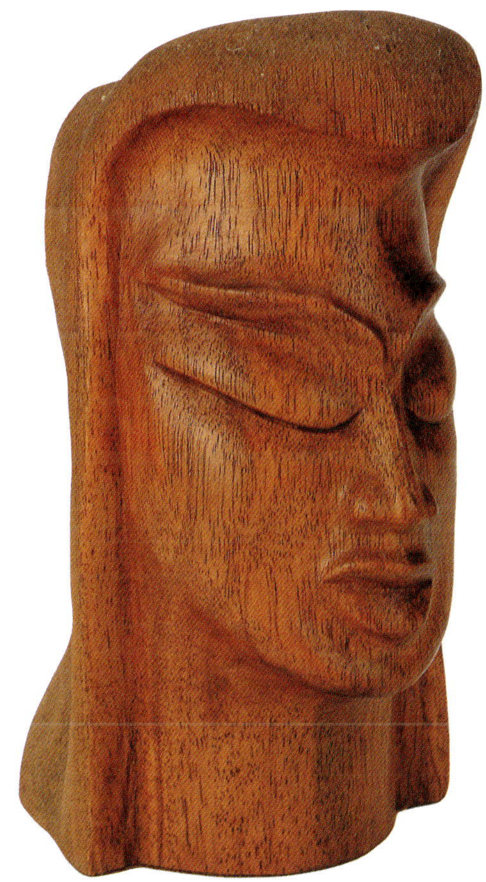

Carved head, 6" tall. *Courtesy: the Collection of Brian Goddard & Gene Sweeney*.

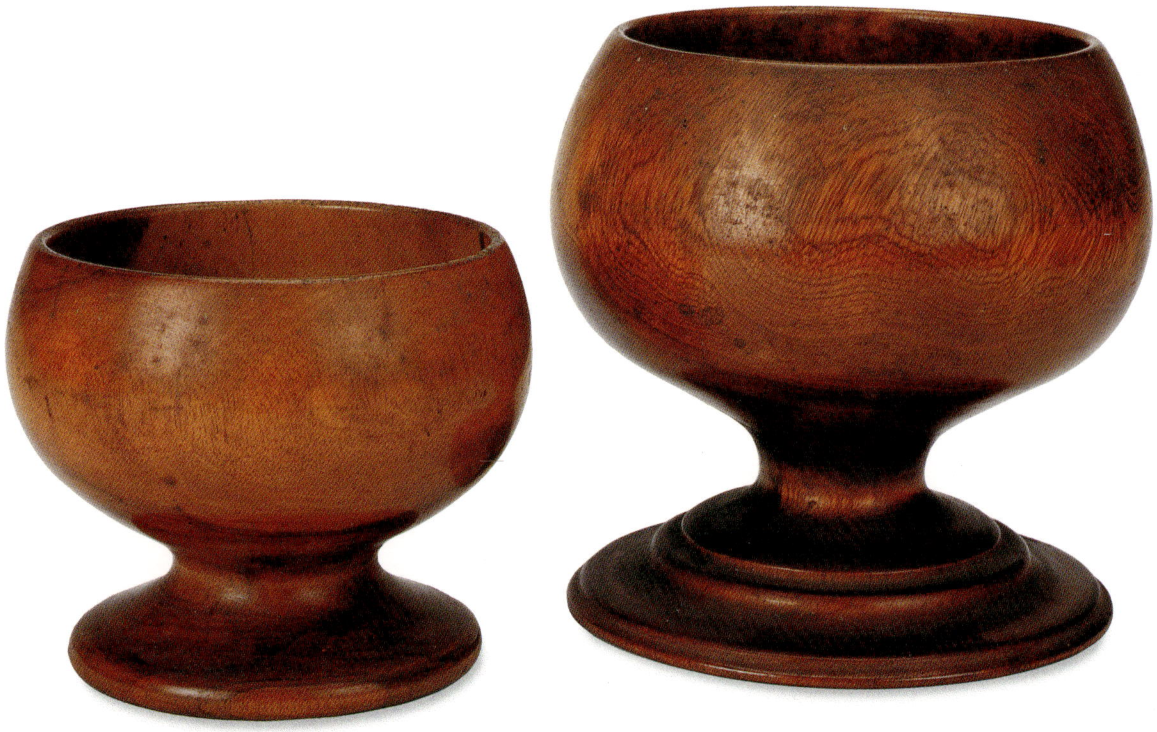

Left:
Koa wood footed goblets, left: 4.5" h., right 6" h. *Courtesy: Jim & Susie Stiso.*

Lower left:
Calabash bowl, 4.5" h., 7" d. *Courtesy: Jim & Susie Stiso.*

Lower right:
Very old calabash bowl, 8.5" h., 12" d. *Courtesy: Jim & Susie Stiso.*

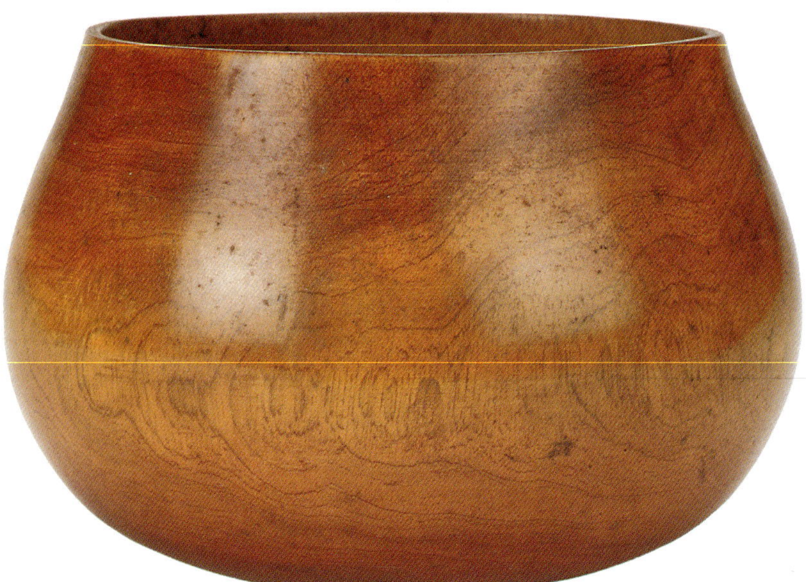

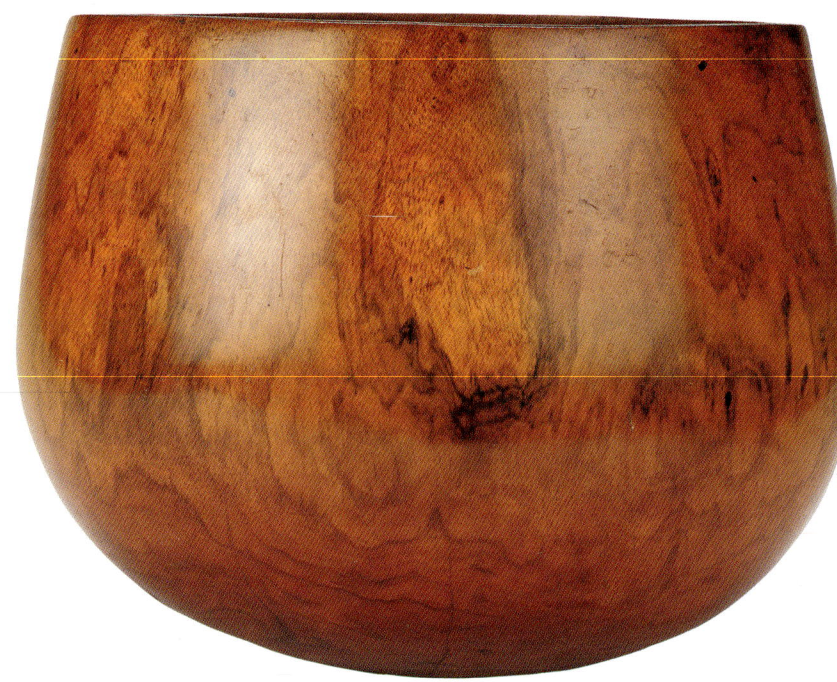

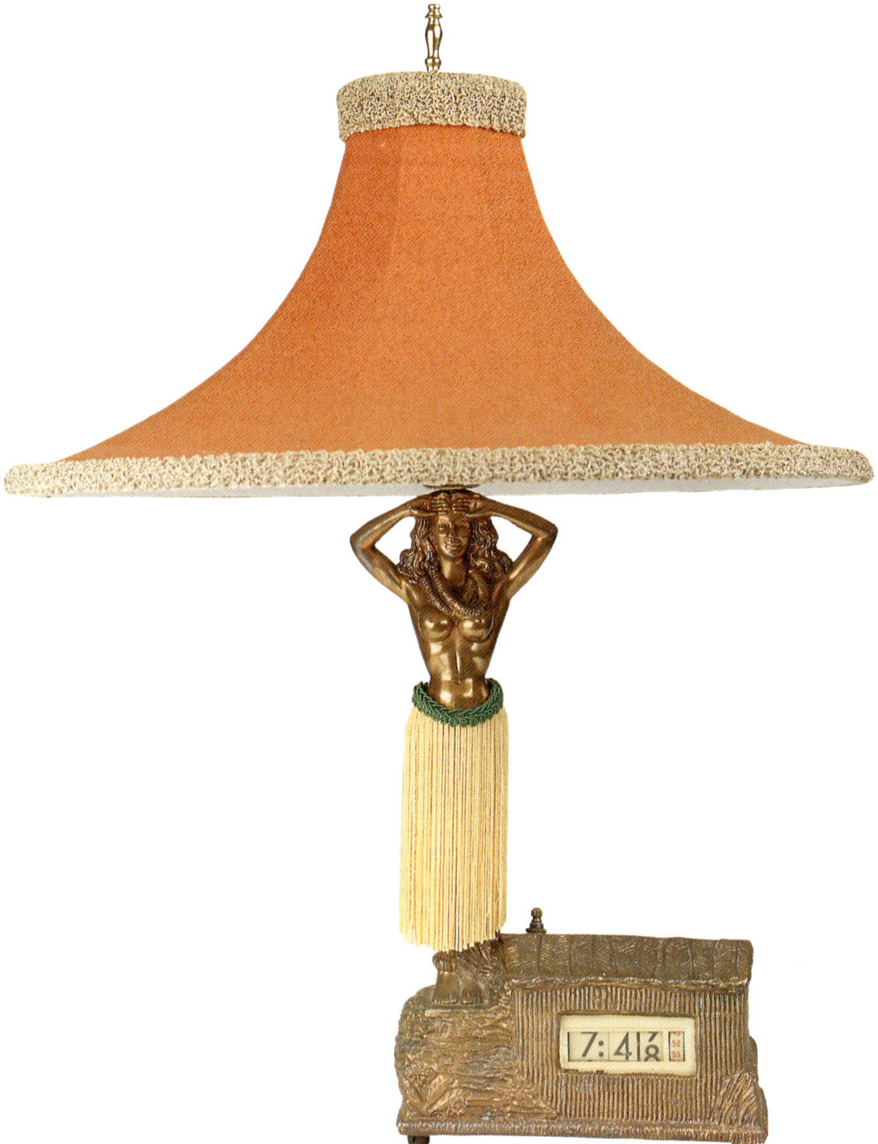

One of the popular hula lamps produced during the 1930s and 1940s. Blackburn shows a similar lamp without the digital clock. *Courtesy: Michael & Denise Queen*.

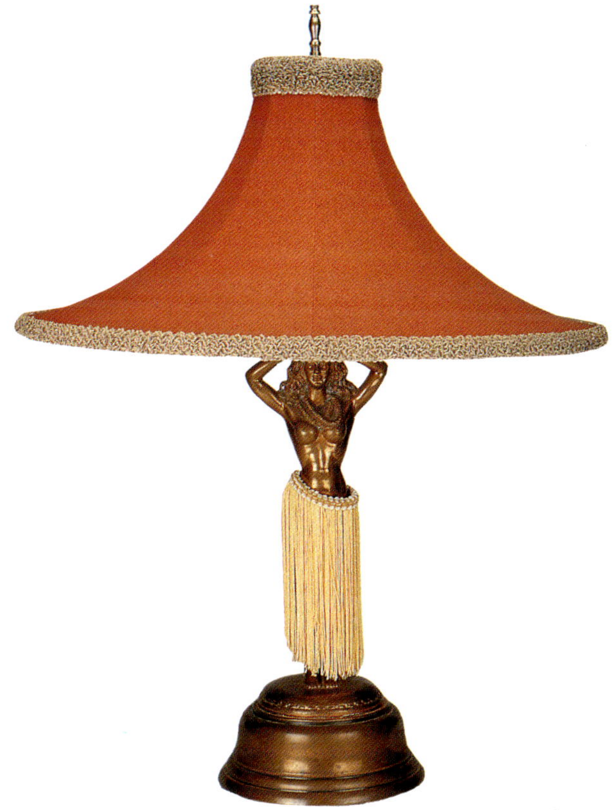

Hula lamp. *Courtesy: Michael & Denise Queen*.

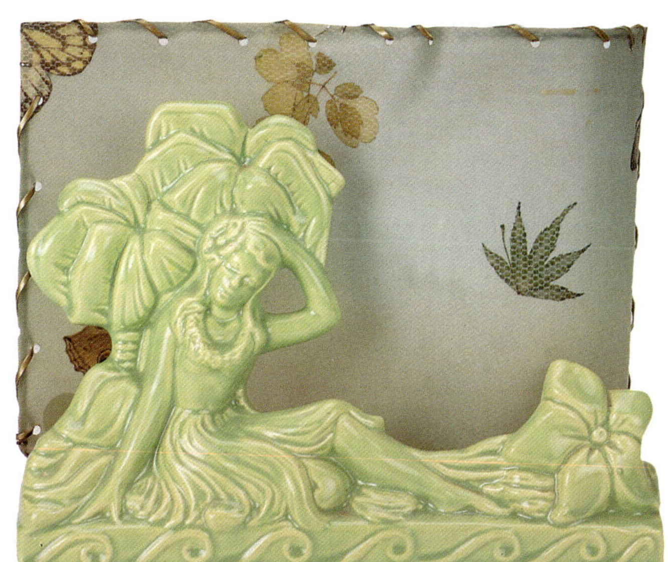

Ceramic lamp with fiberglass screen. 7.5" h. x 9" w. *Courtesy: Michele Leypoldt*.

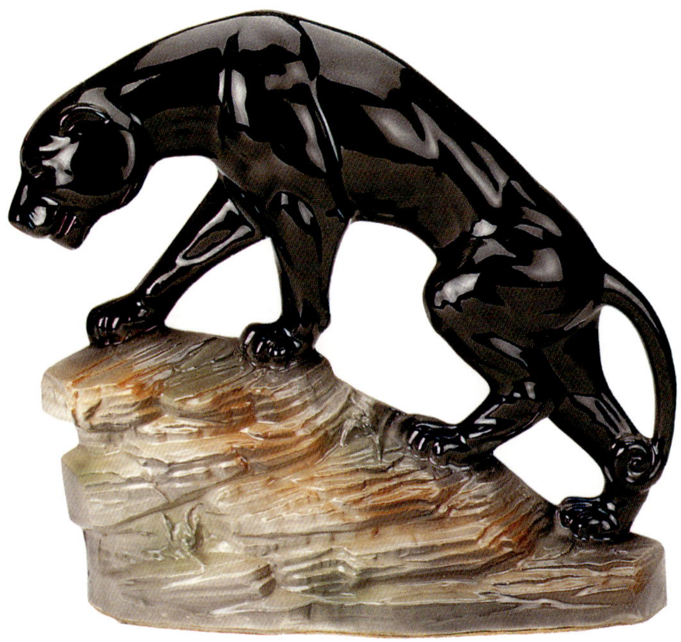

Panther lamp, ceramic. Lane & Company, Van Nuys, California. *Courtesy: Michael & Denise Queen*.

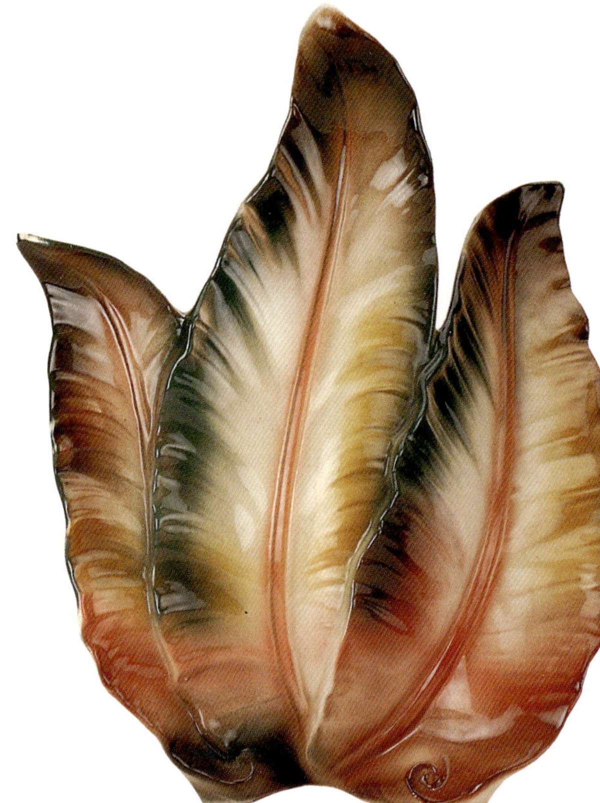

One of a pair of Lane Pottery lamps, 15" tall. *Courtesy: K.C. Heylin*.

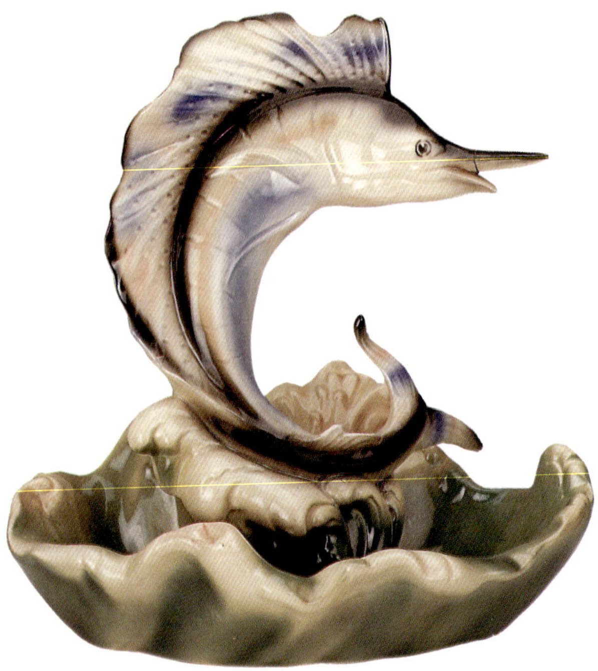

Ceramic lamp. *Courtesy: Michael & Denise Queen*.

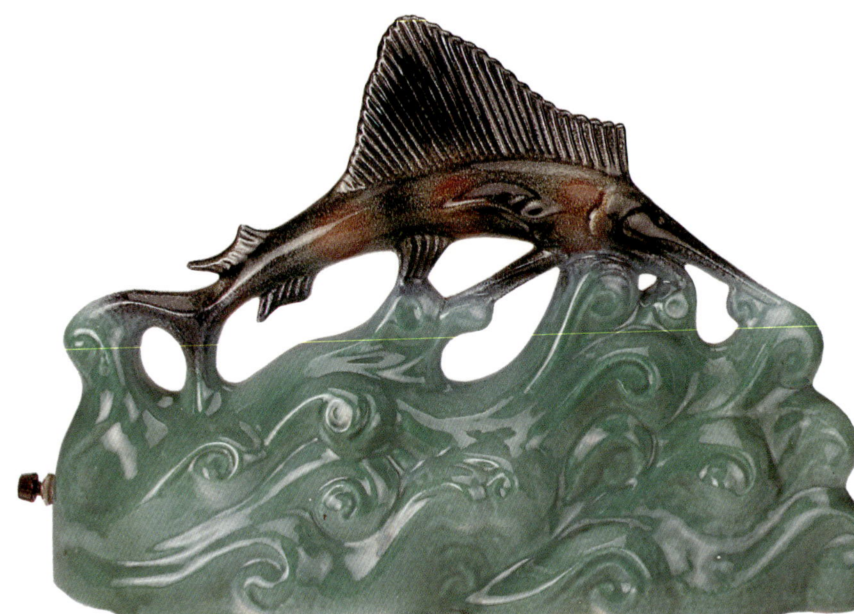

Ceramic lamp. 10.5" h. *Courtesy: Michael & Denise Queen*.

Right:
Large ceramic lamp. 16" h. *Courtesy: Michael & Denise Queen.*

Below:
Mermaid and shell lamp/ planter combination. Cali-Co of California. 8.5" h x 11" w.

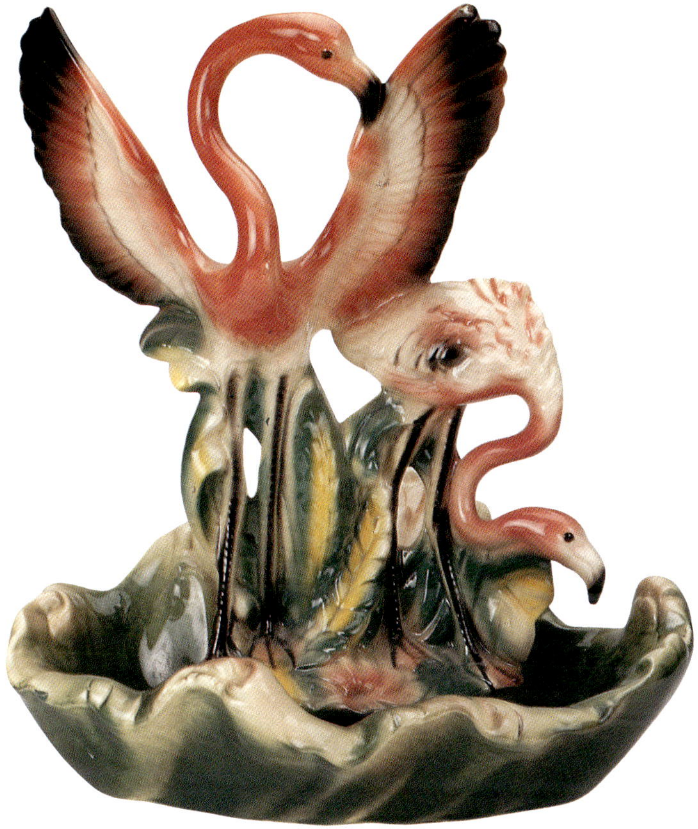

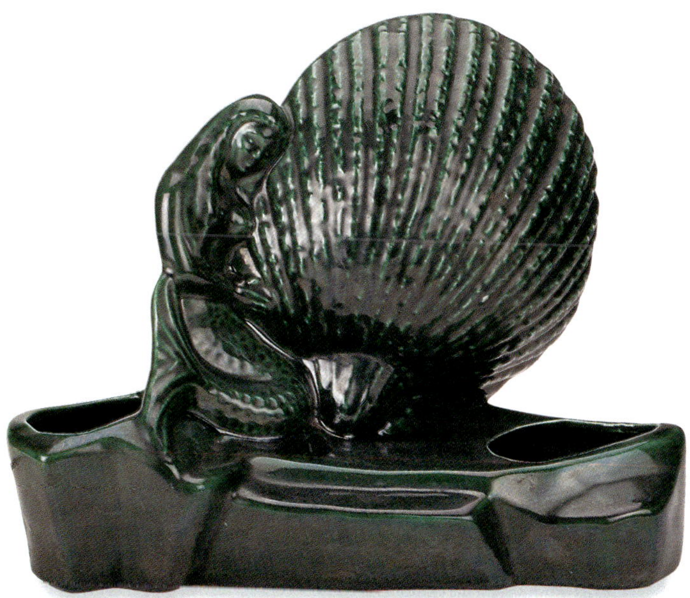

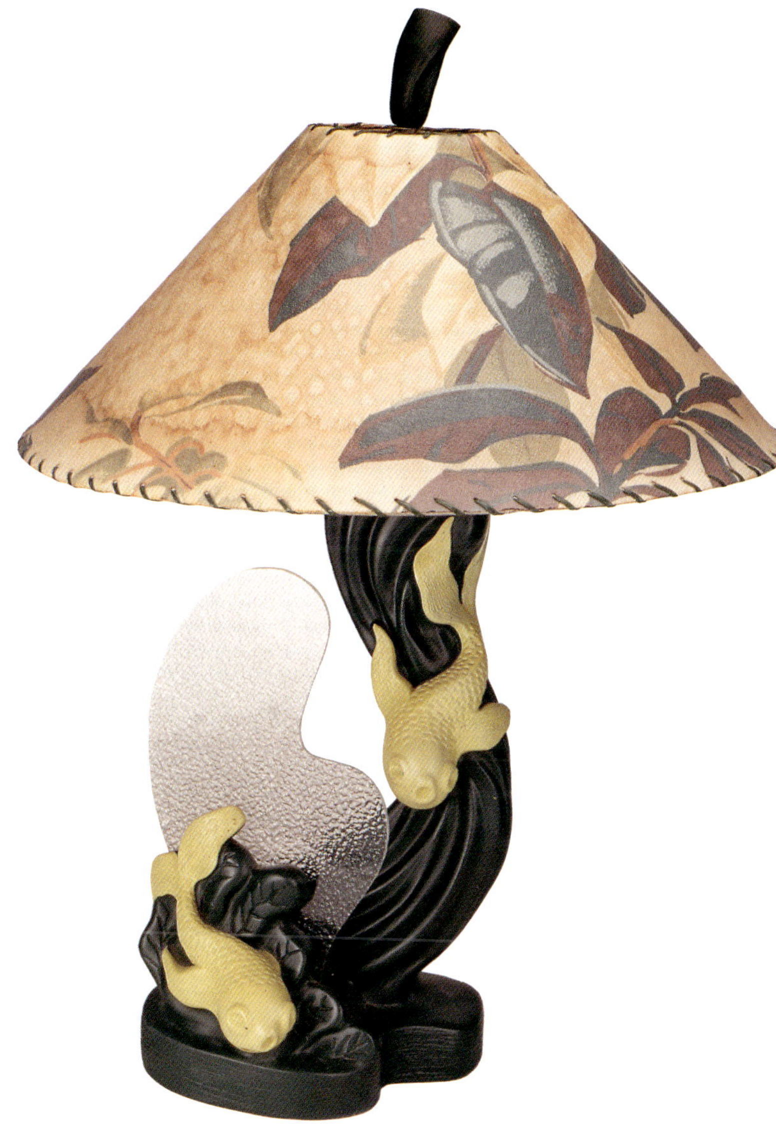

Ceramic and glass lamp with translucent shade. *Courtesy: K.C. Heylin.*

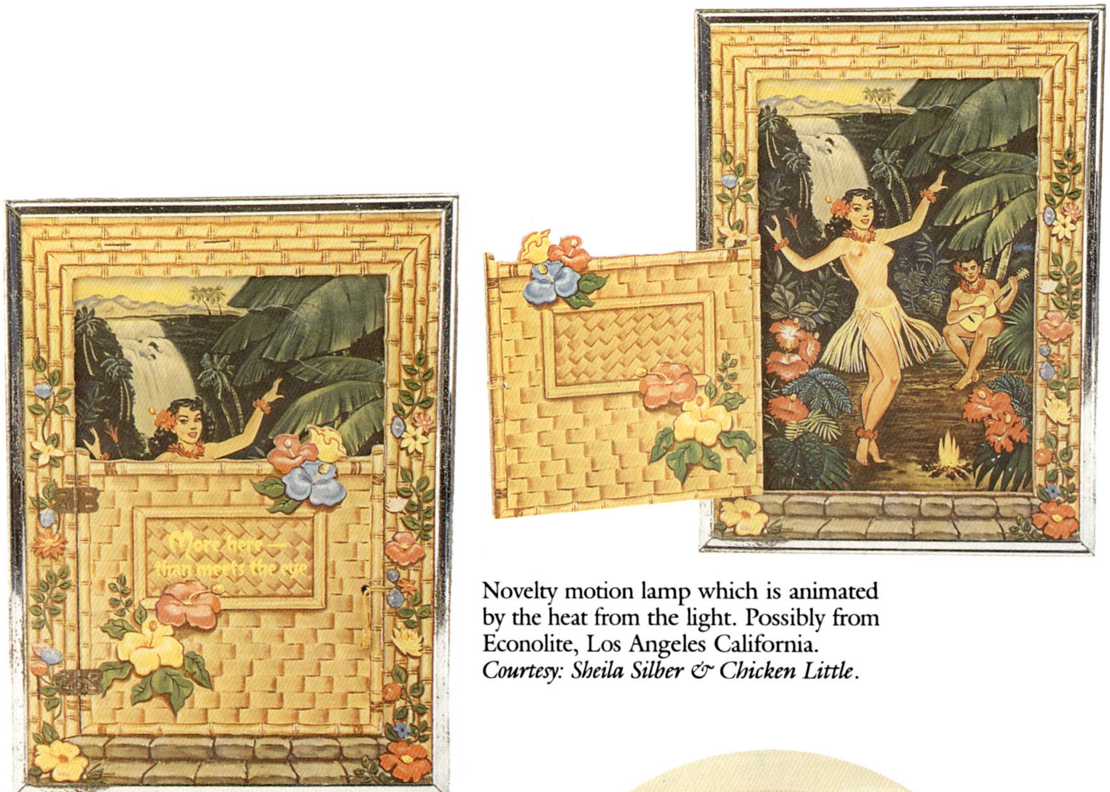

Novelty motion lamp which is animated by the heat from the light. Possibly from Econolite, Los Angeles California. *Courtesy: Sheila Silber & Chicken Little.*

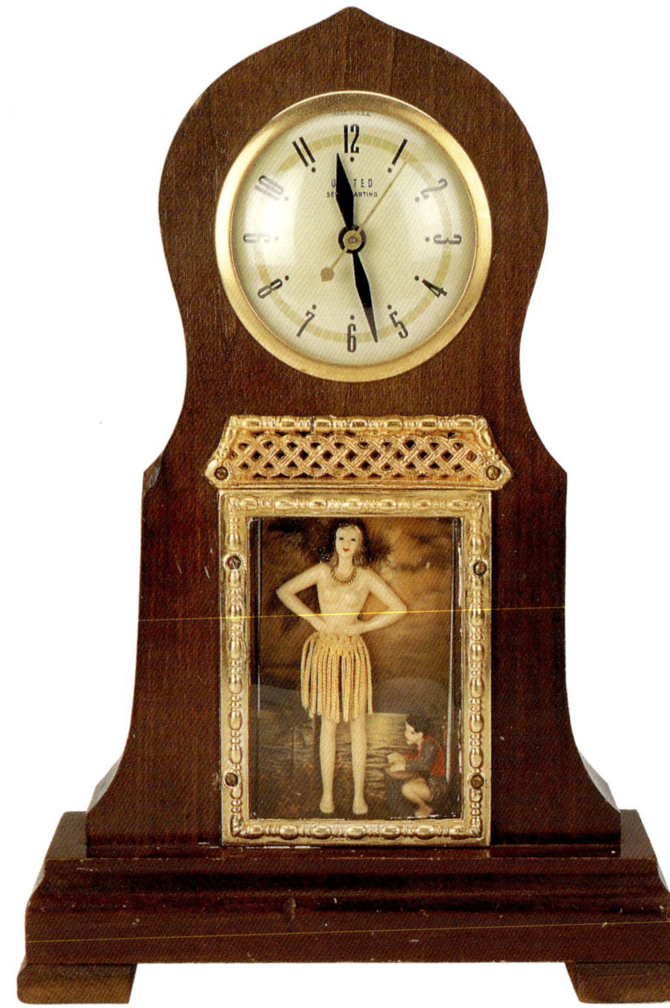

Hula clock. The figure in the bottom window dances. United Clock Co., "Self-starting." 14" h. *Courtesy: Sheila Silber & Chicken Little.*

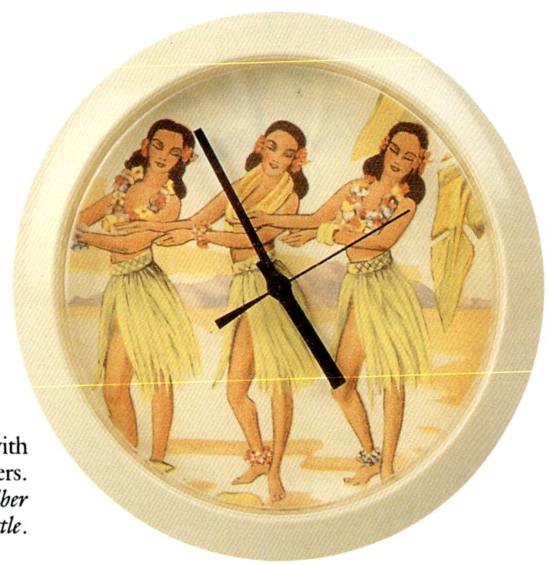

Plastic wall clock with hula dancers. *Courtesy: Sheila Silber & Chicken Little.*

Pillows

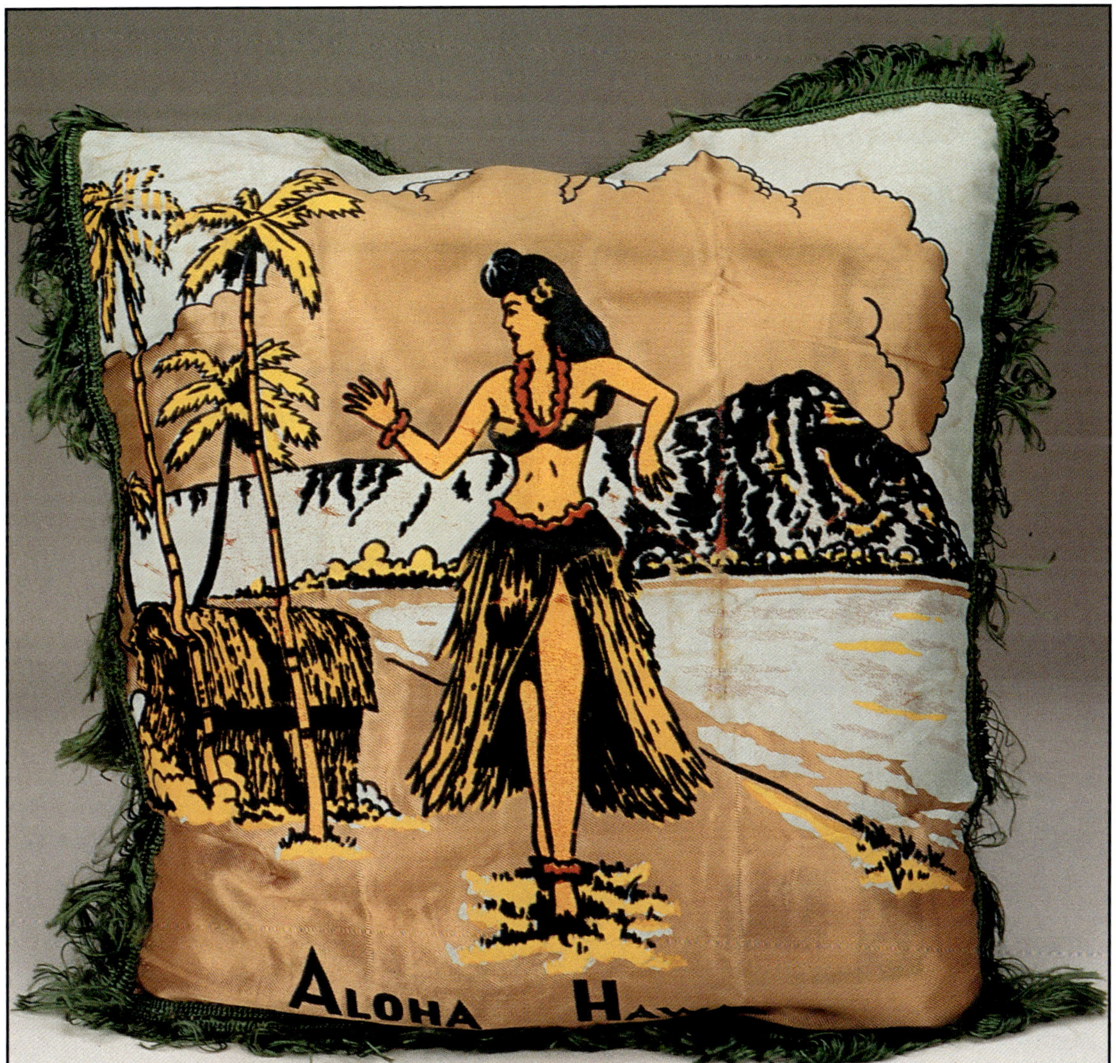

Aloha Hawaii pillow. 15" sq.
Courtesy: Jim & Susie Stiso.

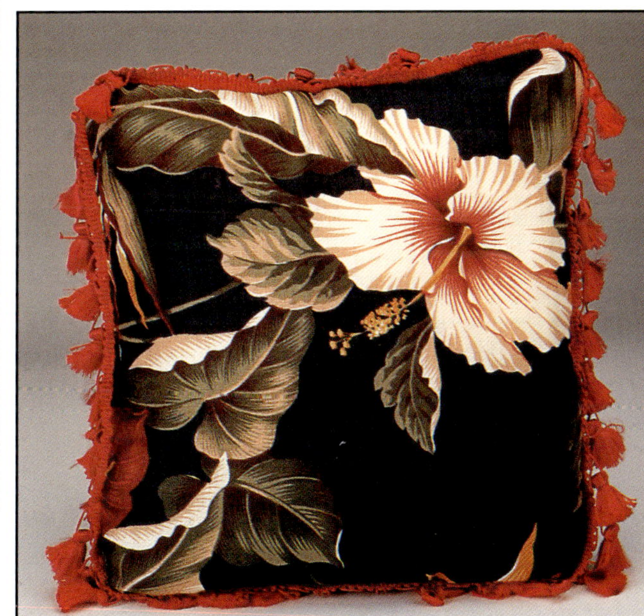

Stuffed pillow. 11" sq.
Courtesy: Tobi Smith.

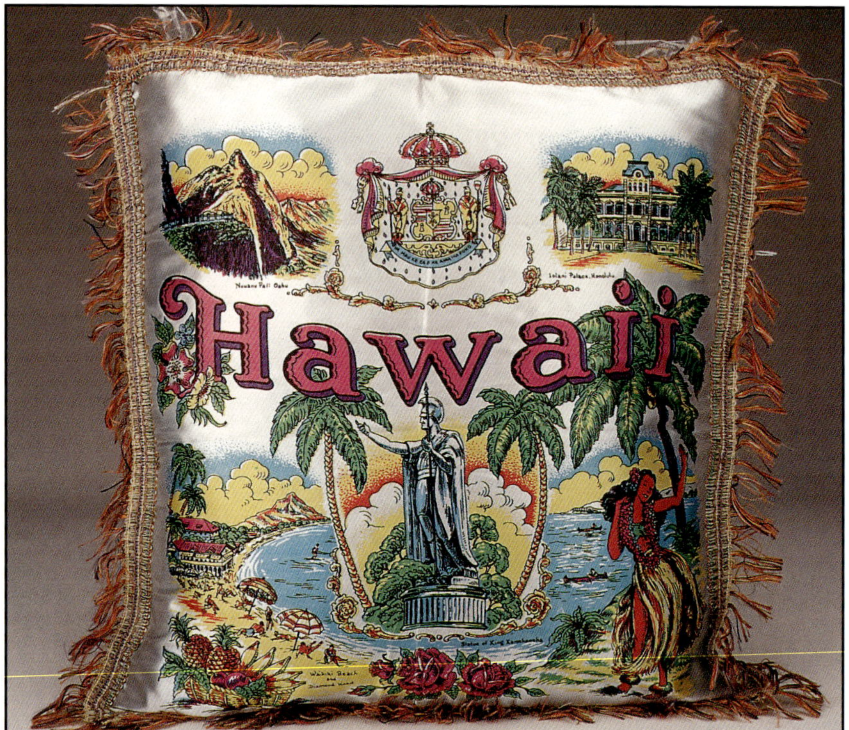

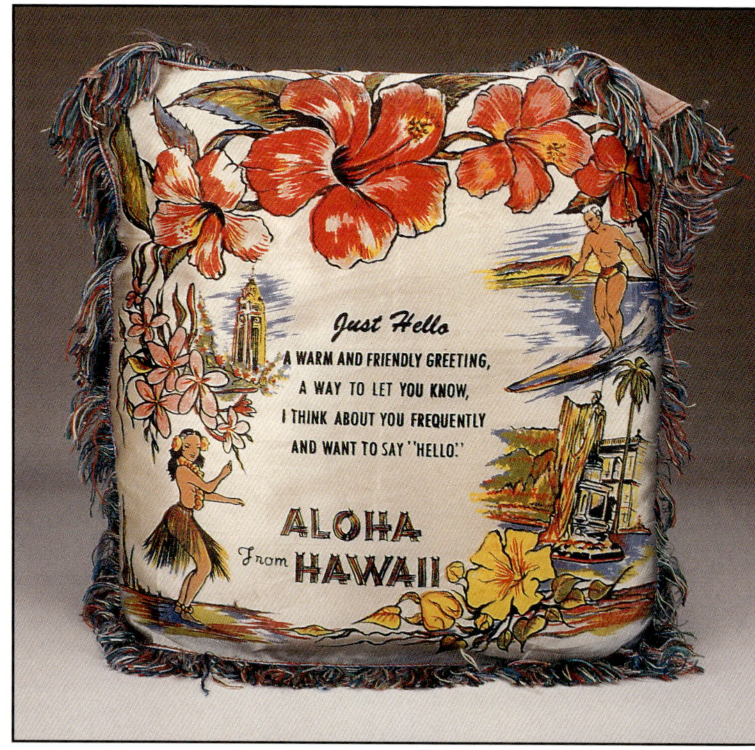

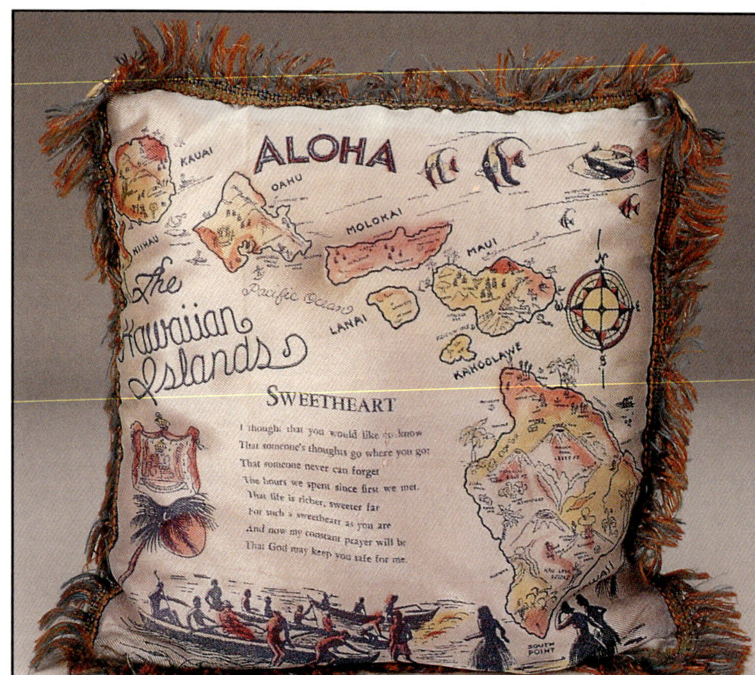

Above:
Souvenir pillow, 16" sq.
Courtesy: Sheila Silbert.

Above right:
Souvenir pillow. 18" sq.
Courtesy: Sheila Silber & Chicken Little.

Right:
A sweetheart pillow from the Islands. 10" sq.
Courtesy: Sheila Silber & Chicken Little.

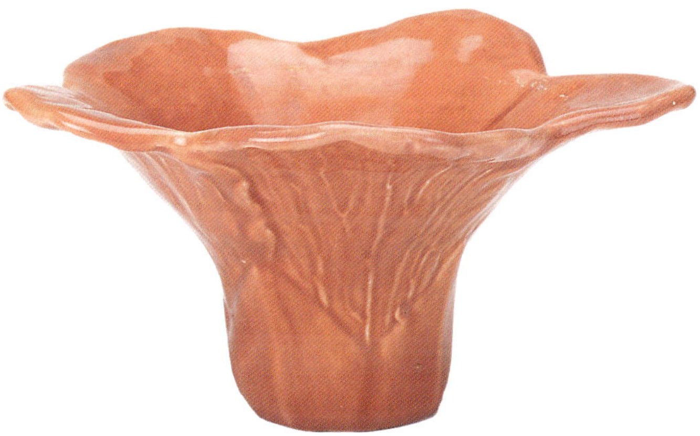

Hibiscus vase, marked Potters Guild (?). 3.5" h. *Courtesy: the Collection of Brian Goddard & Gene Sweeney.*

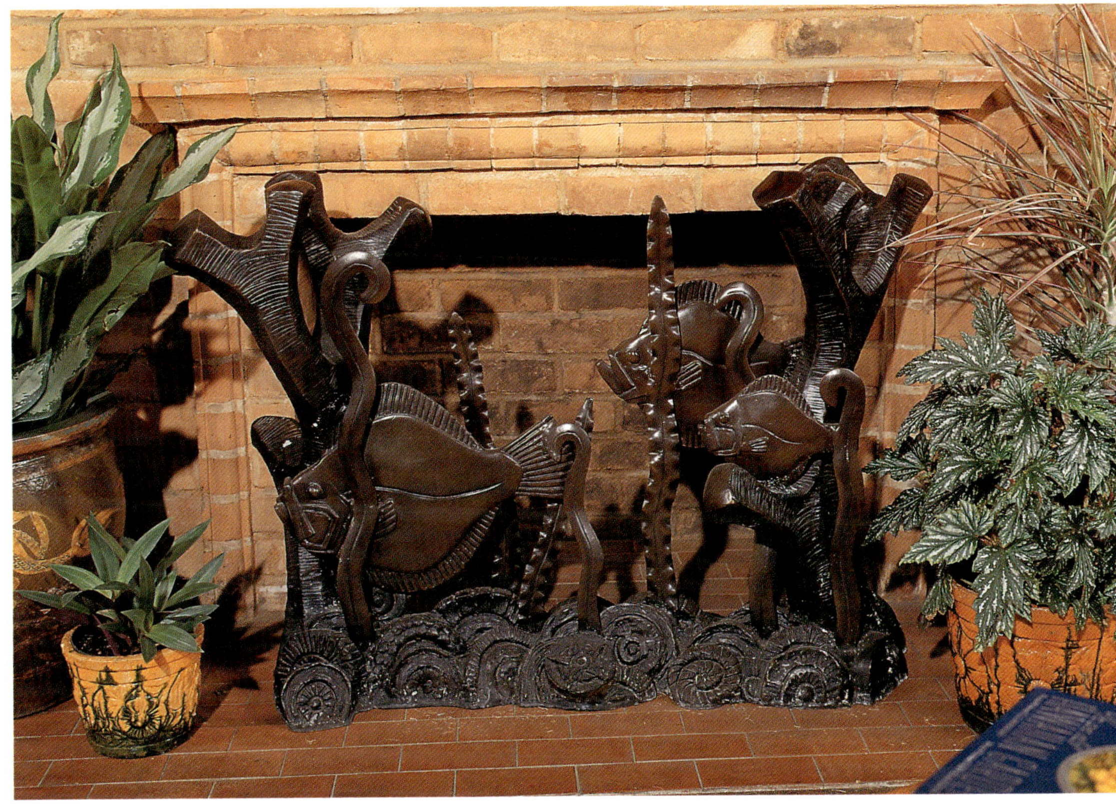

The front of the fireplace is decorated with colorful ceramic pots and a bronze aquatic scene. The bronze piece is actually the base for a glass top table. *Courtesy Sun Rattan, 20th Century Props.*

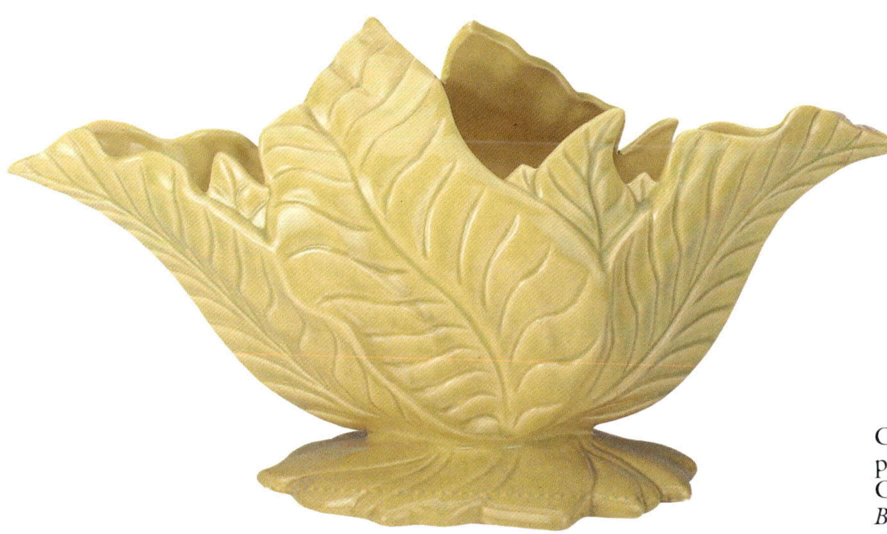

Ceramic flower arranger in leaf pattern. 8" h x 12" w. Marked Cemar 645. *Courtesy: the Collection of Brian Goddard & Gene Sweeney.*

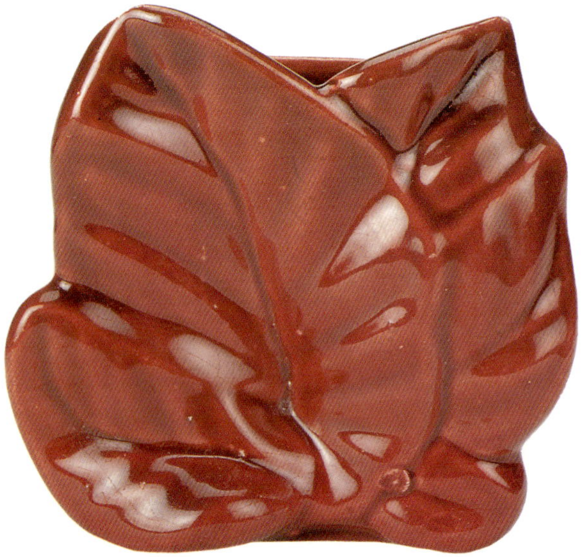

Hibiscus wall pocket, 3.5" h. *Courtesy: the Collection of Brian Goddard & Gene Sweeney*.

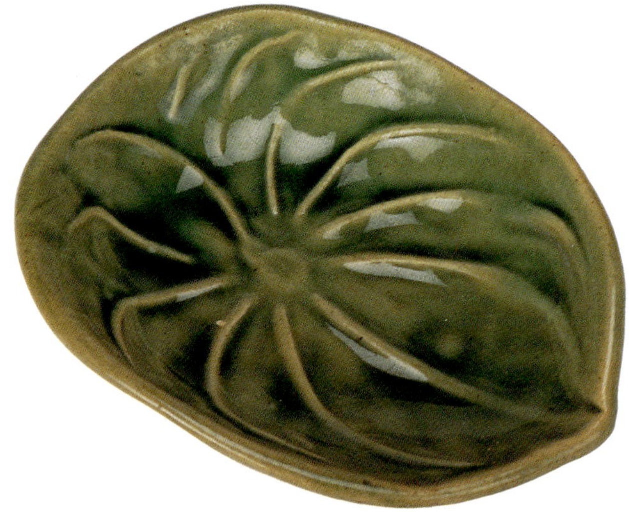

Left:
Small Anthurium dish, Hawaiian Potters' Guild, 3.5" w. *Courtesy: the Collection of Brian Goddard & Gene Sweeney*.

Below:
Leaf vase, 6.5" h. x 7.5" w. Made in U.S.A. *Courtesy: the Collection of Brian Goddard & Gene Sweeney*.

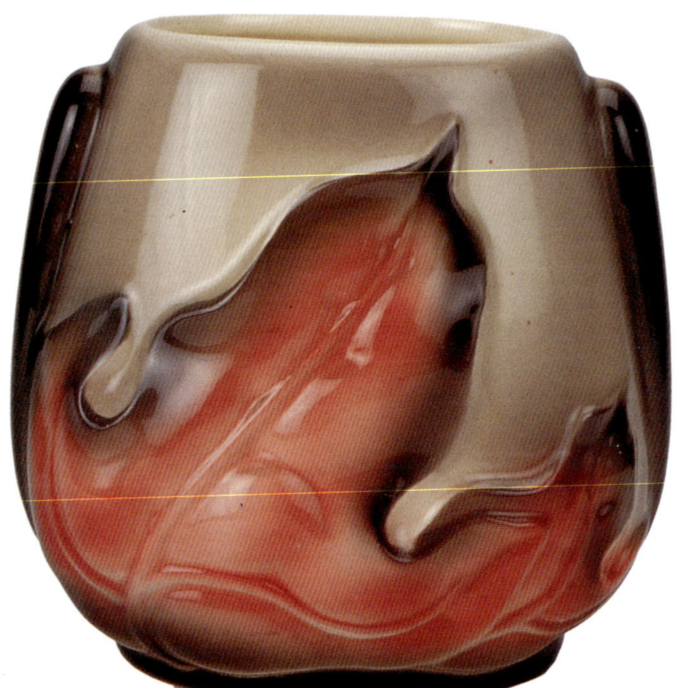

Royal Copley ceramic vase, 4.75" h. *Courtesy: the Collection of Brian Goddard & Gene Sweeney*.

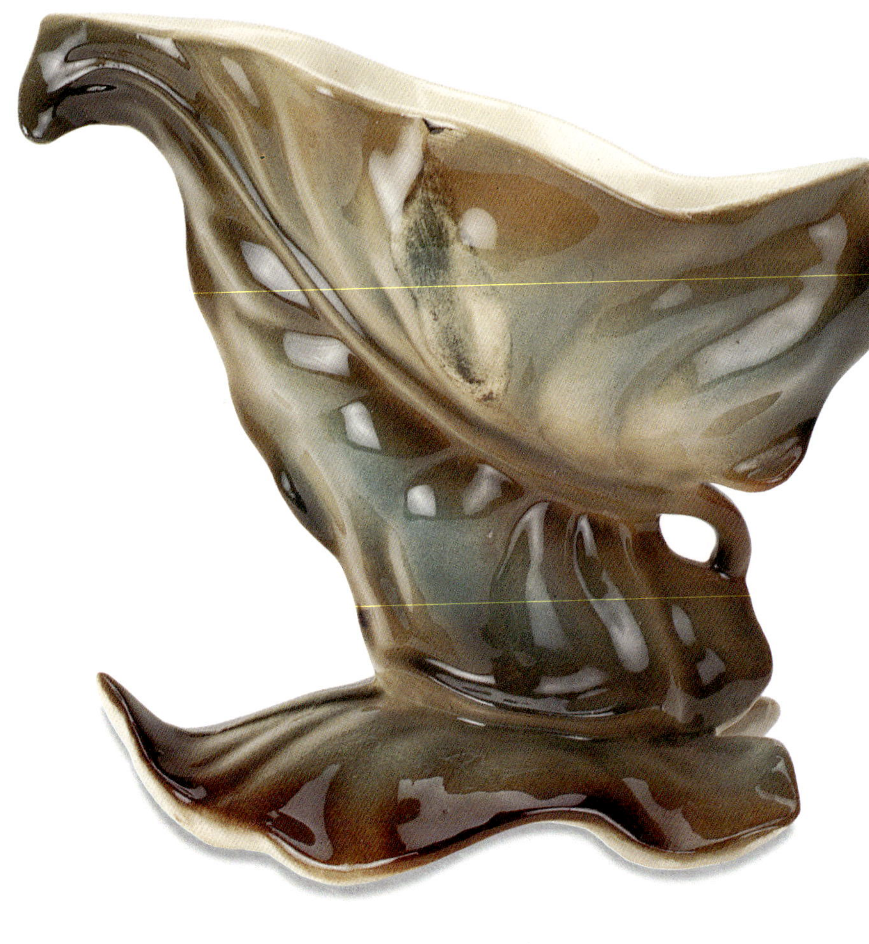

Taro leaf vase mark Sigfrid. 5.75" h. x 4.5" w. *Courtesy: the Collection of Brian Goddard & Gene Sweeney*.

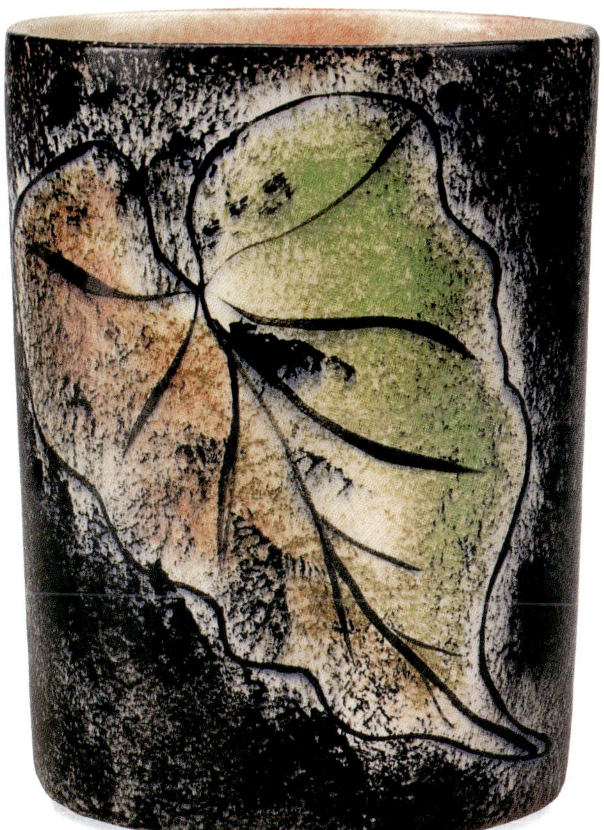

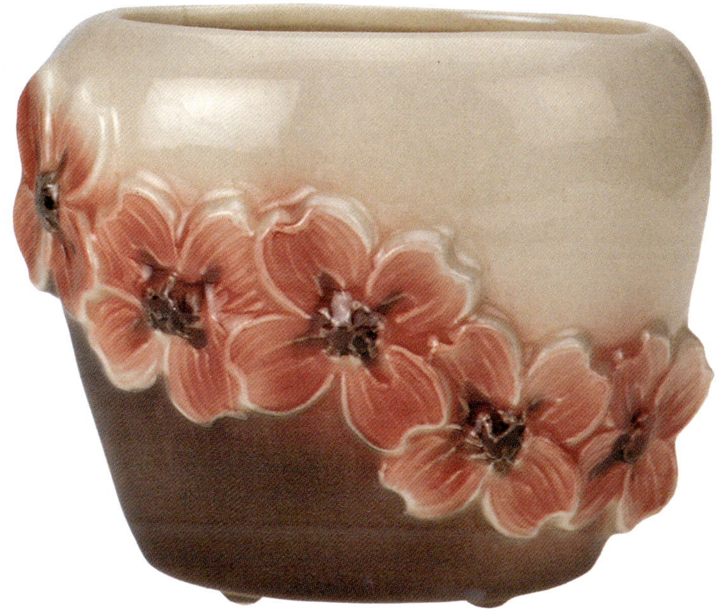

Left:
Royal Copley vase. 4" h. *Courtesy: the Collection of Brian Goddard & Gene Sweeney*.

Below:
Roseville conch shell vase. 5" h. *Courtesy: the Collection of Brian Goddard & Gene Sweeney*.

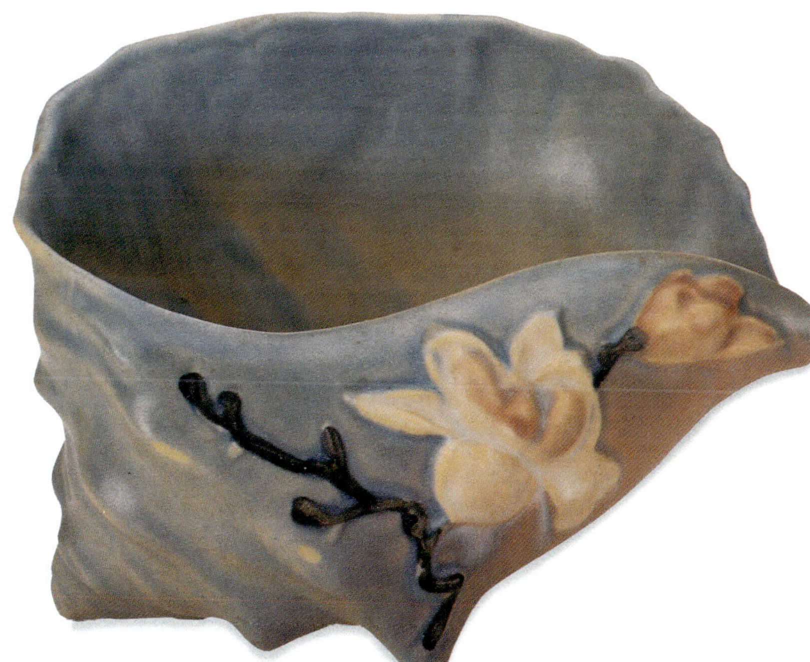

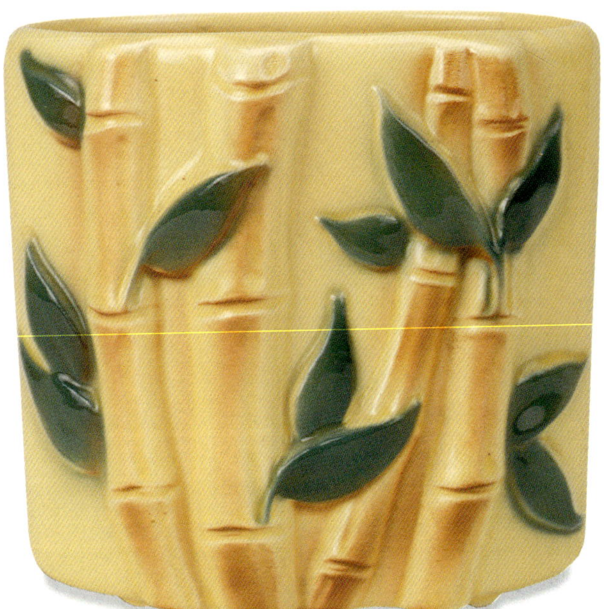

Bamboo vase. 4.75" h.
Courtesy: Michael Trotter.

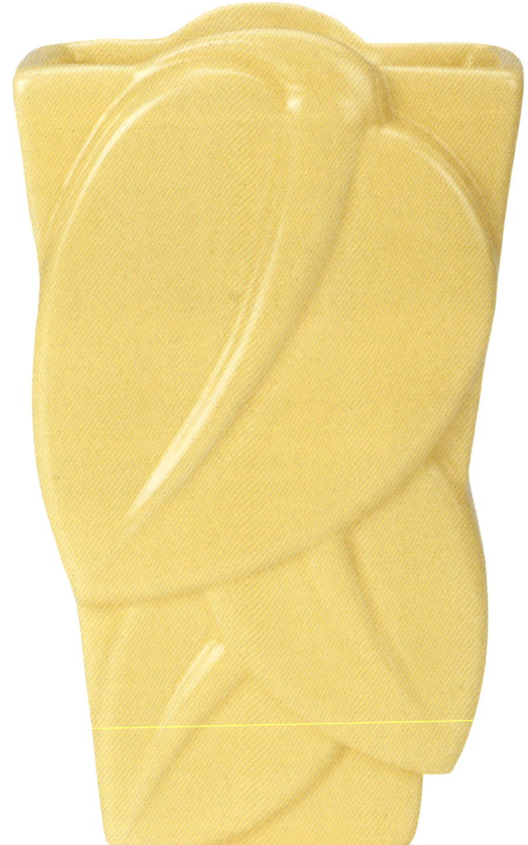

California Pottery vase, 6.25" h.
Courtesy: the Collection of Brian Goddard & Gene Sweeney.

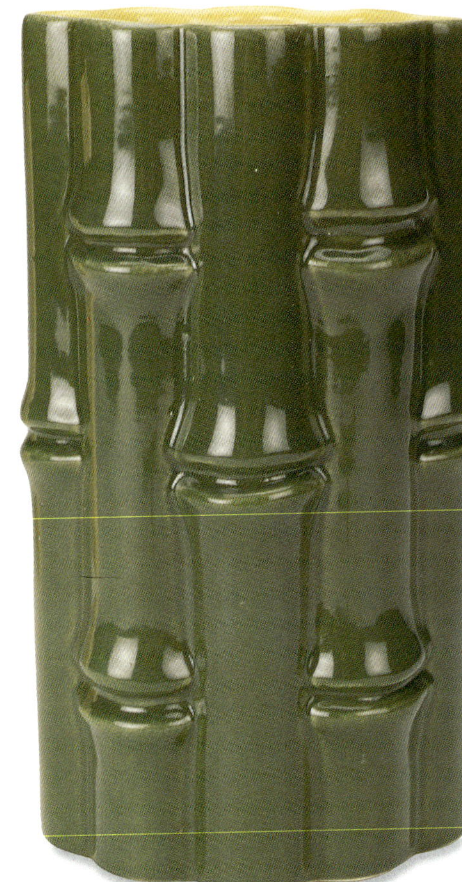

Redwing Pottery bamboo vase, 7.75" h.
Courtesy: the Collection of Brian Goddard & Gene Sweeney.

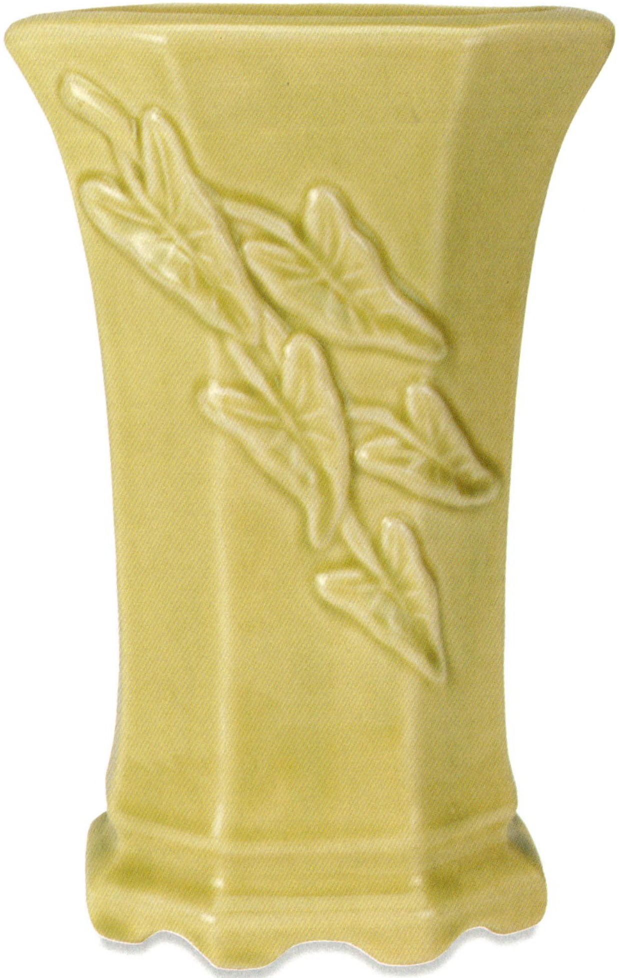

Flaring vase, 8" h. *Courtesy: the Collection of Brian Goddard & Gene Sweeney*.

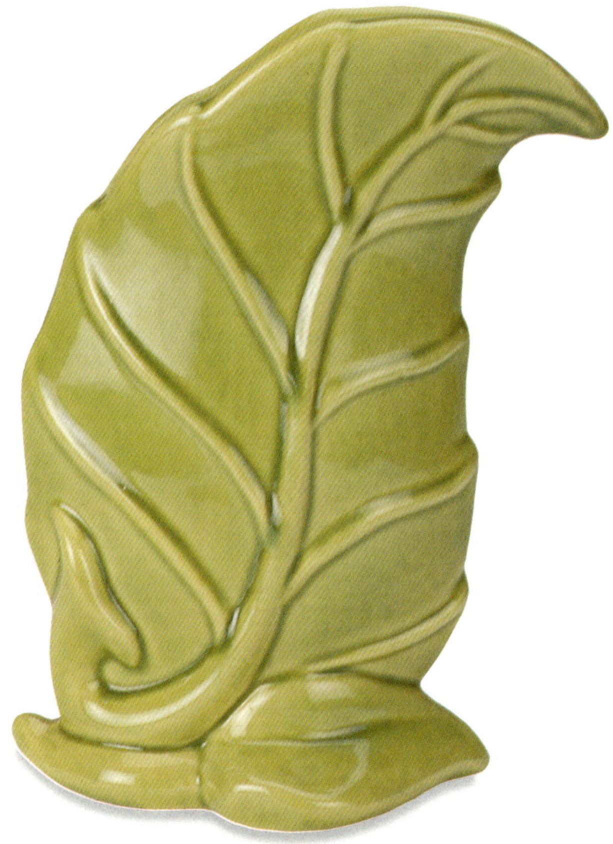

Leaf vase, 6.25" h. *Courtesy: the Collection of Brian Goddard & Gene Sweeney*.

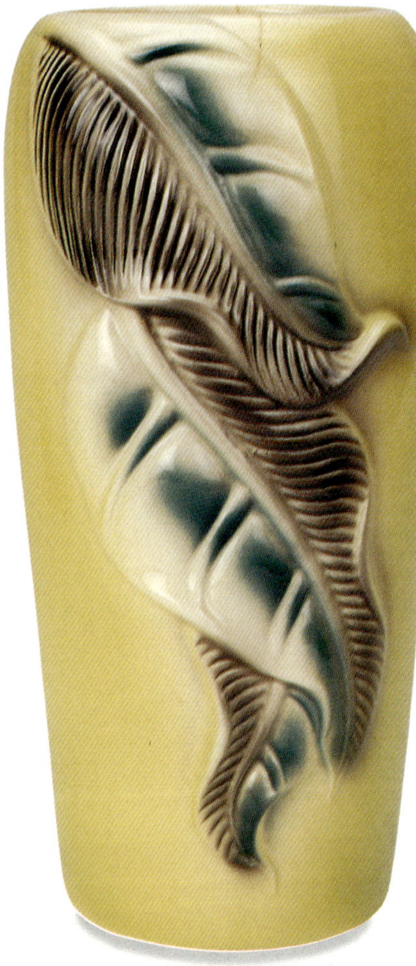

Royal Copley vase, 8.25" h. *Courtesy: the Collection of Brian Goddard & Gene Sweeney*.

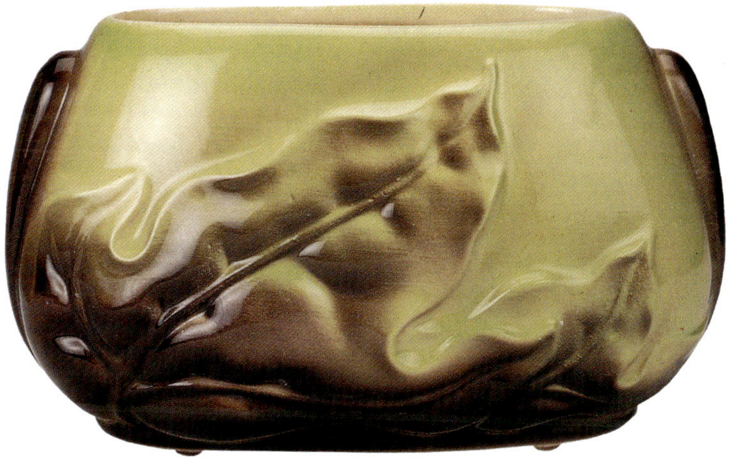

Royal Copley vase, 4.25" h. *Courtesy: the Collection of Brian Goddard & Gene Sweeney.*

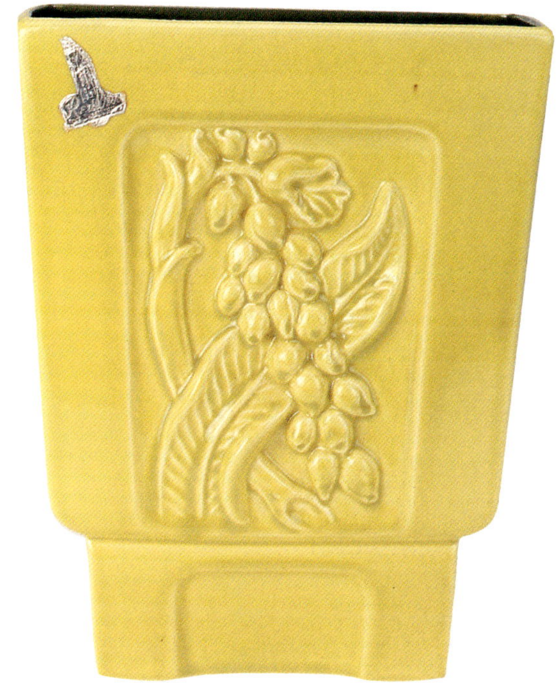

Opposite Upper Left: A pair of Potters' Guild candlesticks, 2.75" h. *Courtesy: the Collection of Susan White.*

Red Wing vase, 8.25" h. *Courtesy: the Collection of Brian Goddard & Gene Sweeney.*

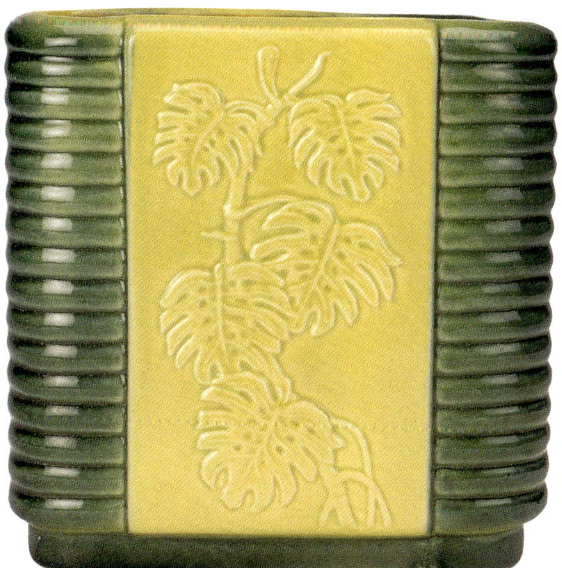

Aborn of California vase, 6.25" h. *Courtesy: the Collection of Brian Goddard & Gene Sweeney.*

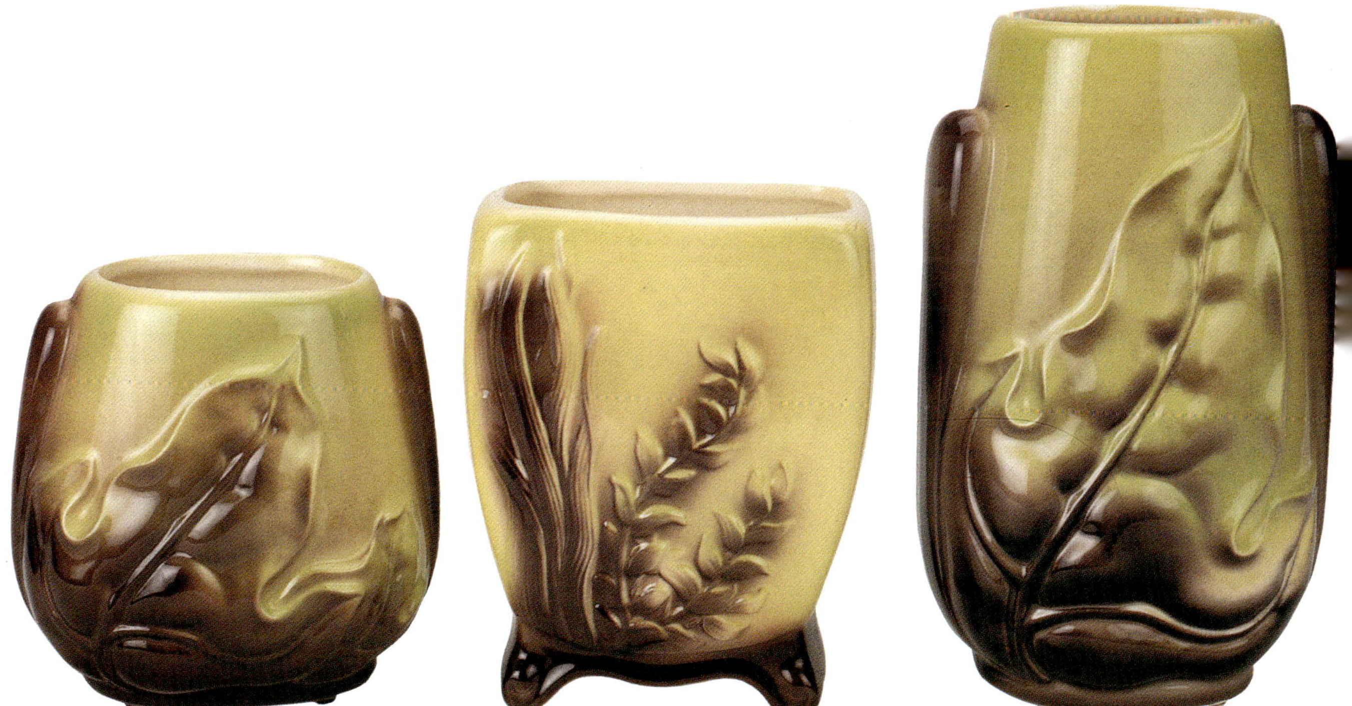

Three Royal Copley vases, 4.75", 5.5", and 7.5" h. *Courtesy: the Collection of Brian Goddard & Gene Sweeney.*

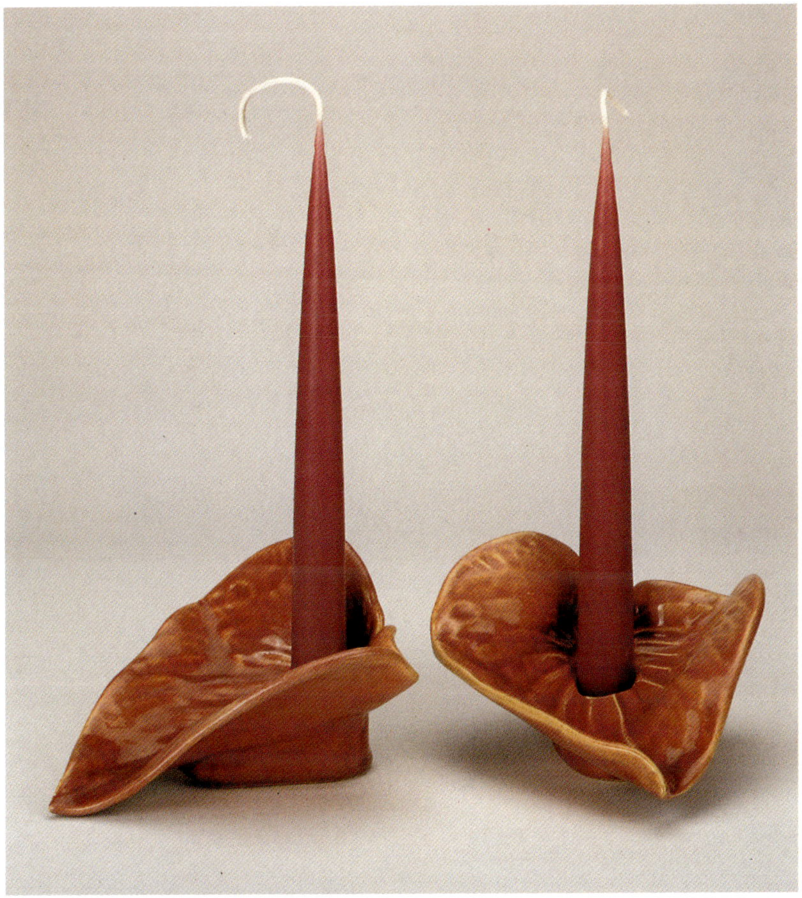

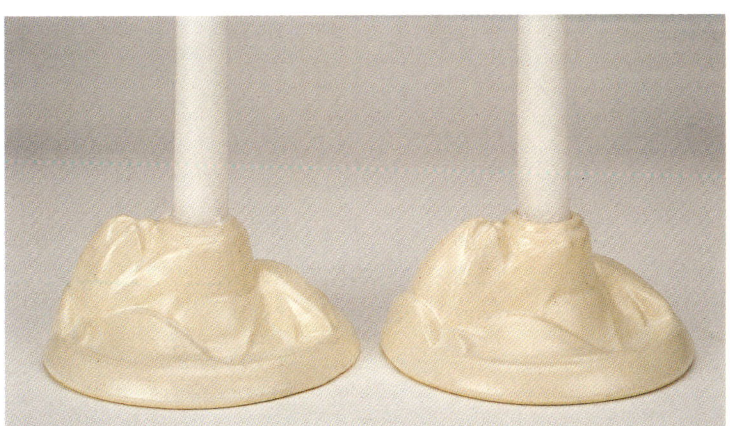

Candlesticks, 2.25". *Courtesy: Randy Hild*.

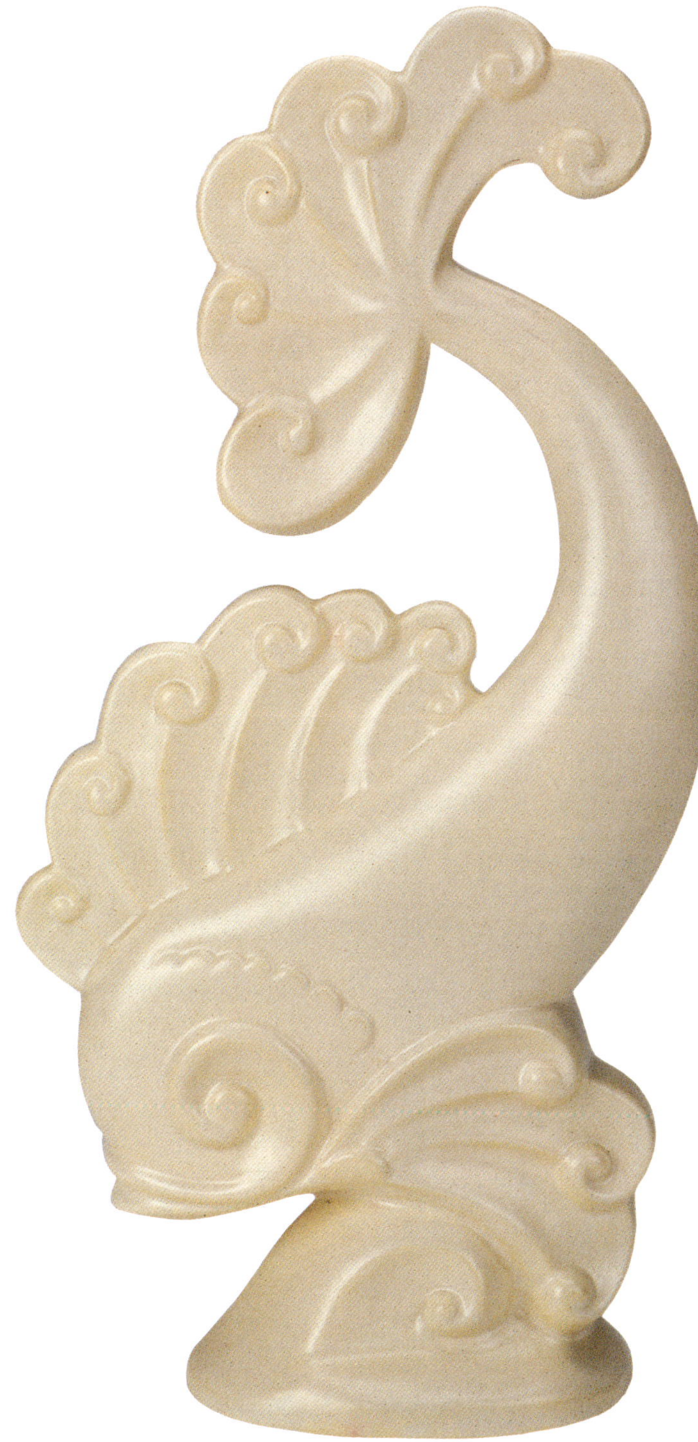

Cemar fish. 13" h. *Courtesy: the Collection of Brian Goddard & Gene Sweeney*.

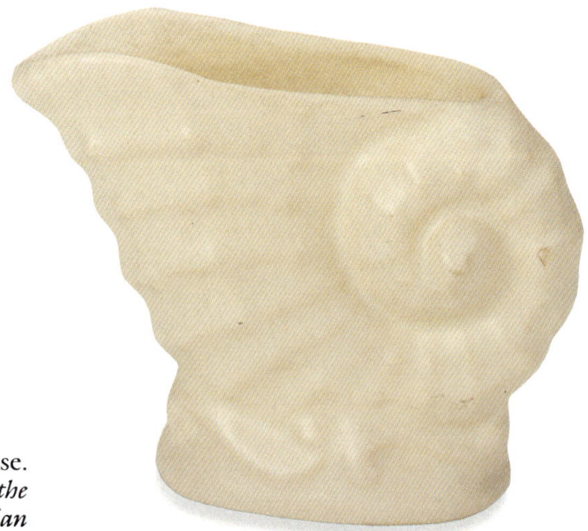

Royal Haeger shell vase. 3" h. *Courtesy: the Collection of Brian Goddard & Gene Sweeney.*

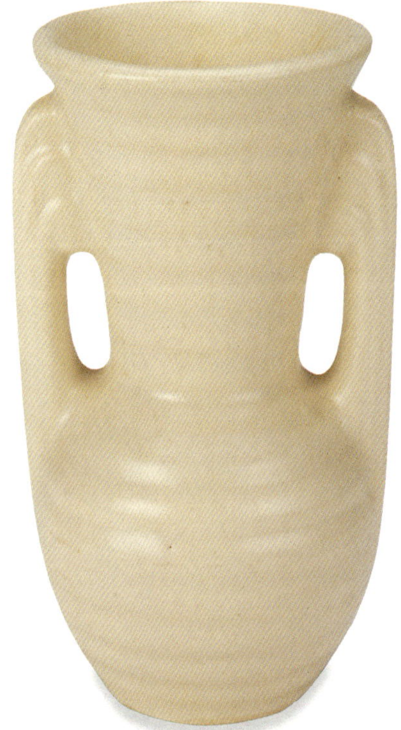

Handled vase, 5.25" h. *Courtesy: Michael Trotter*.

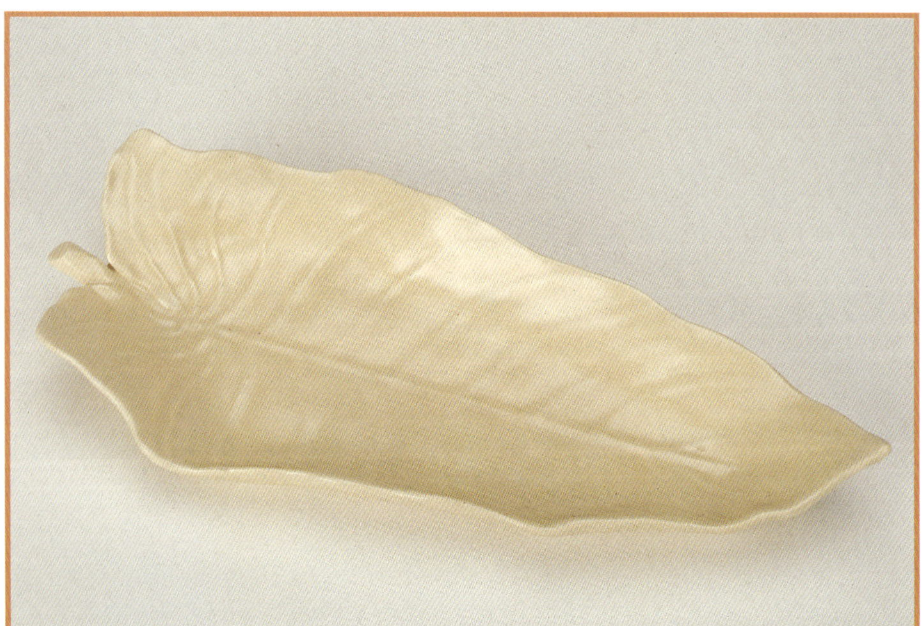

Metlox leaf dish, 10.5" w. *Courtesy: the Collection of Brian Goddard & Gene Sweeney.*

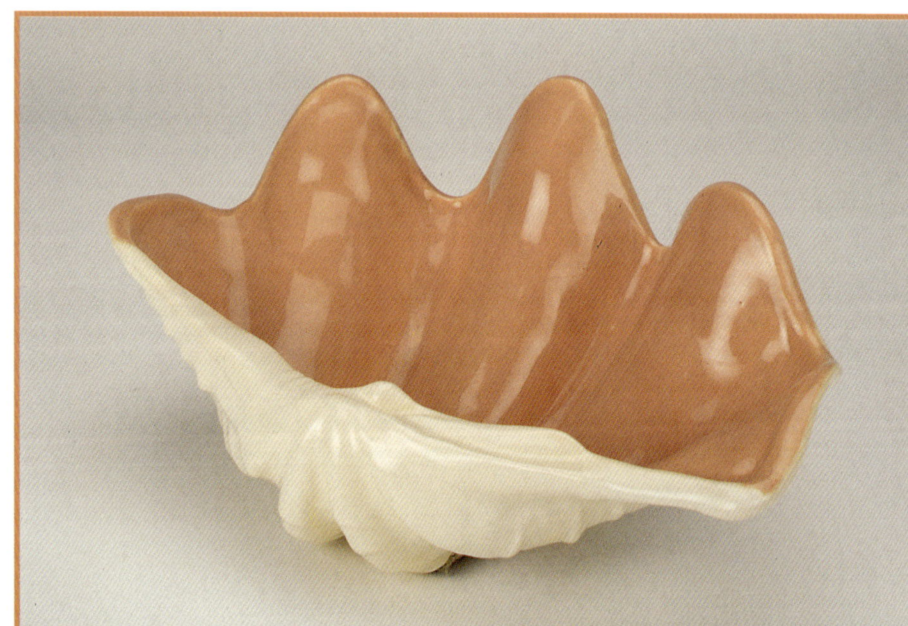

Metlox scallop shaped bowl, 5" h., 11" w. *Courtesy: the Collection of Brian Goddard & Gene Sweeney*.

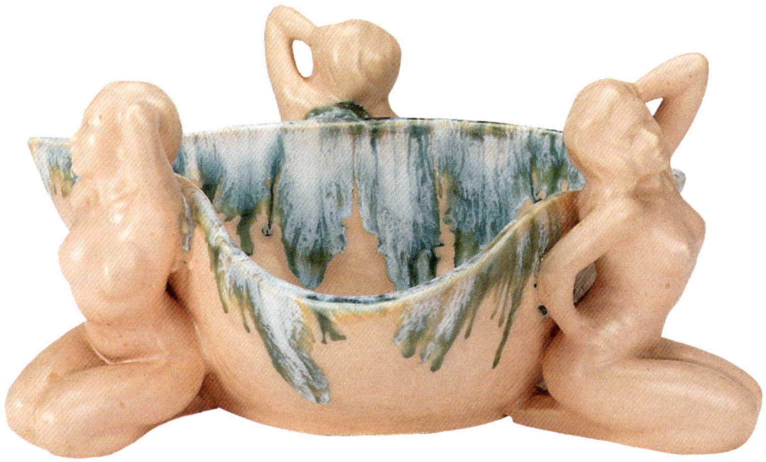

Triangular bowl with nude figures,. 4.75" h. *Courtesy: Oceanic Arts*.

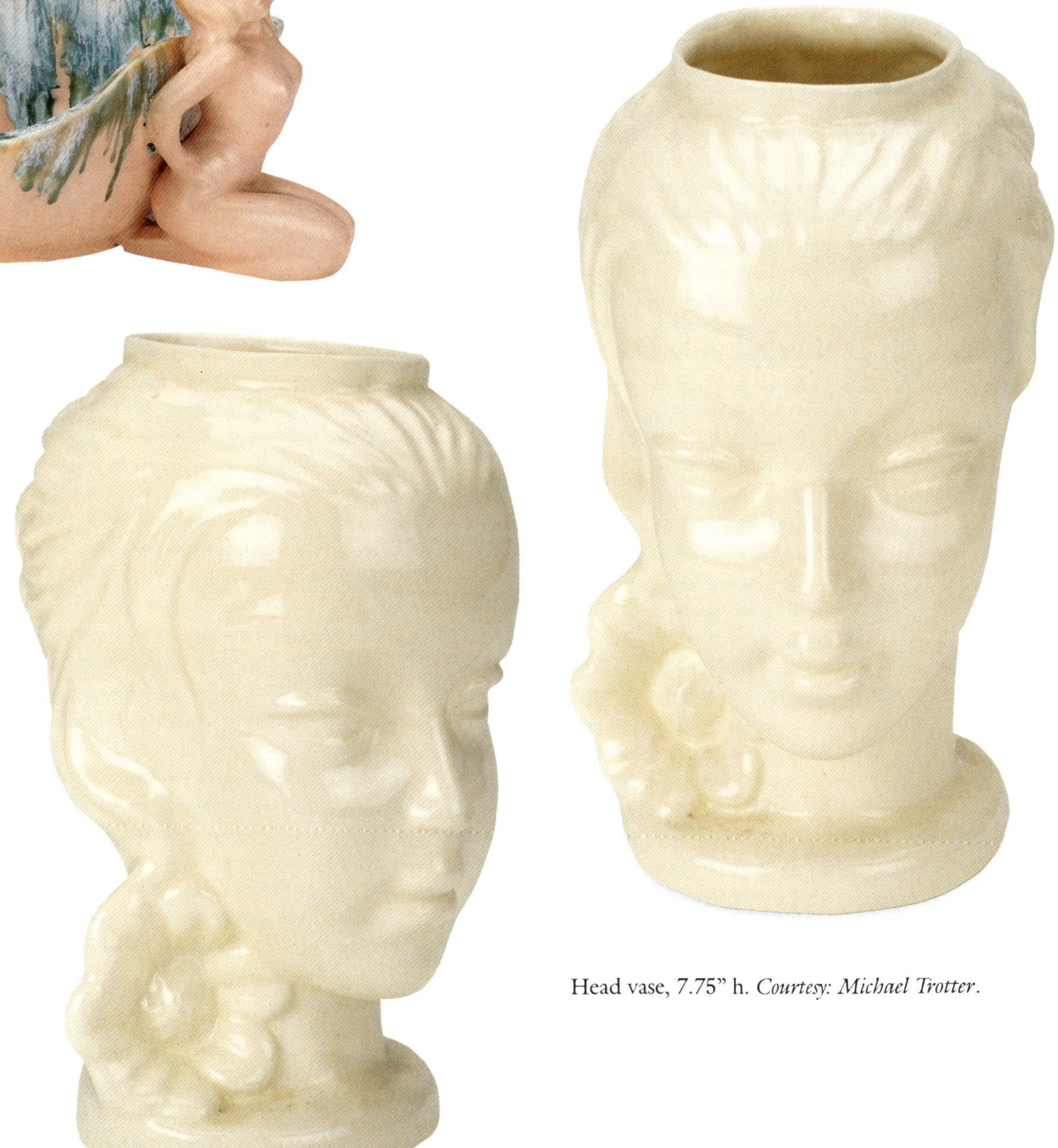

Head vase, 7.75" h. *Courtesy: Michael Trotter*.

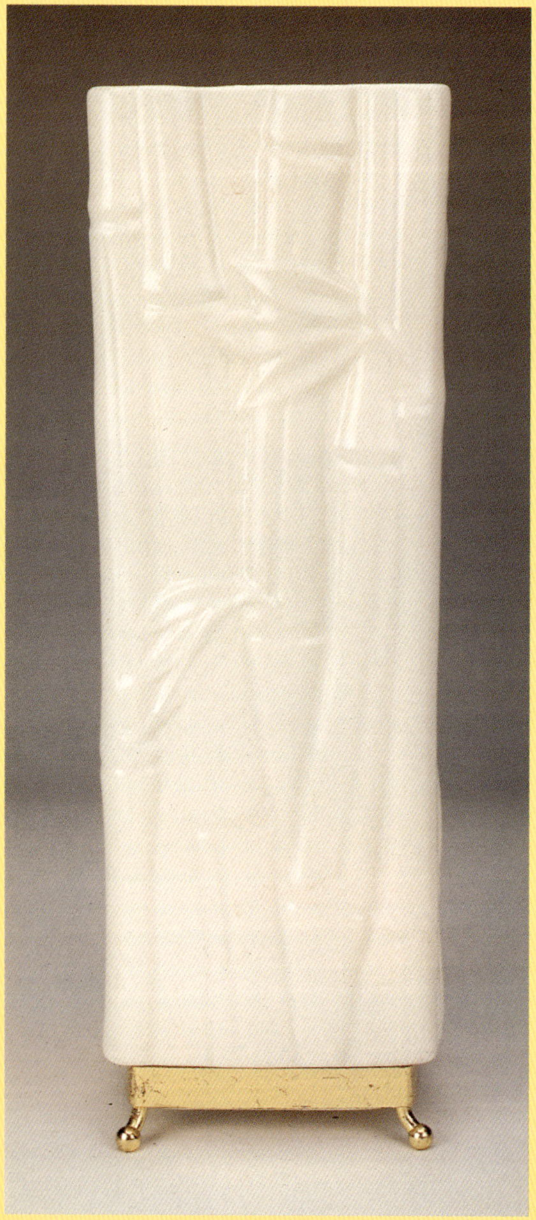

Miramar bamboo vase, 13" h. with brass stand. *Courtesy: the Collection of Brian Goddard & Gene Sweeney*.

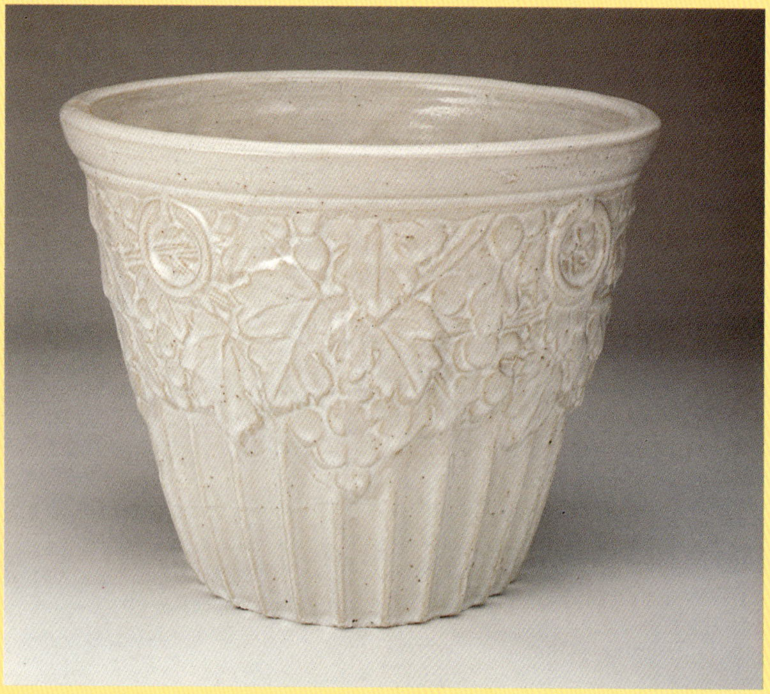

Planter. *Courtesy: Randy Hild*

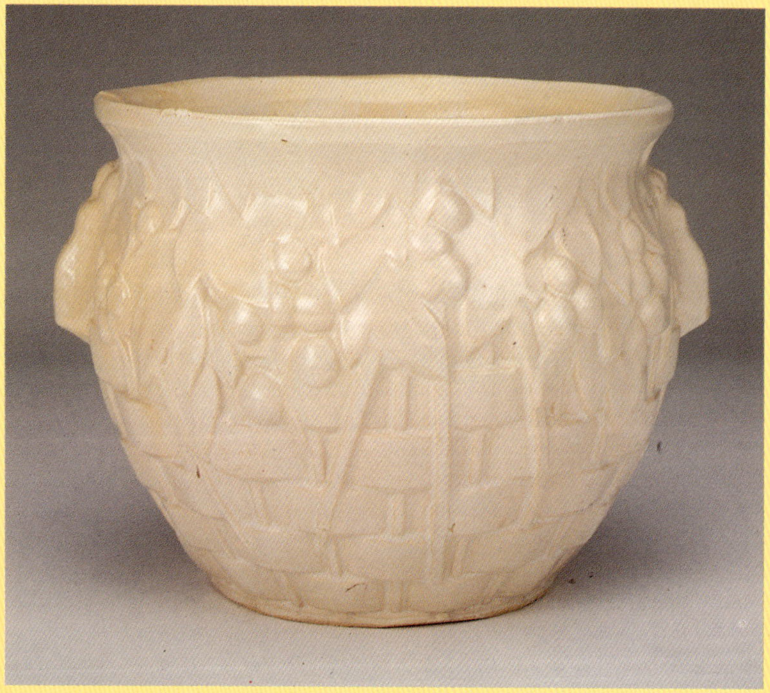

Planter. *Courtesy: Randy Hild*.

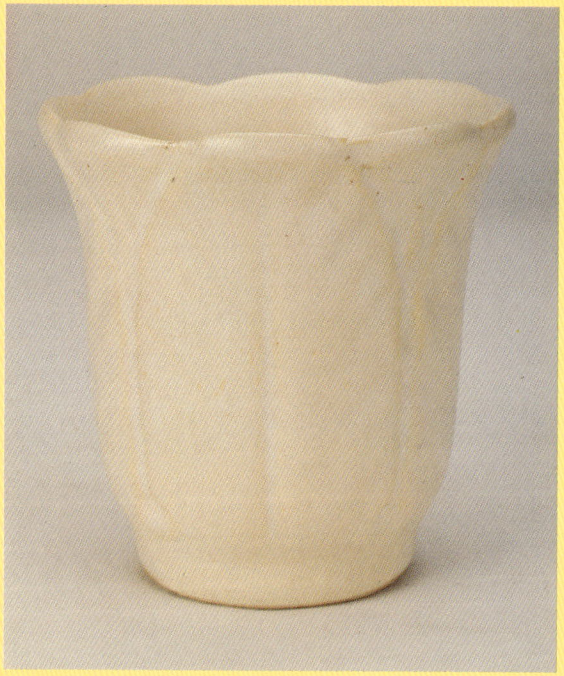

Shawnee Pottery vase, 3.5" h. *Courtesy: the Collection of Brian Goddard & Gene Sweeney*.

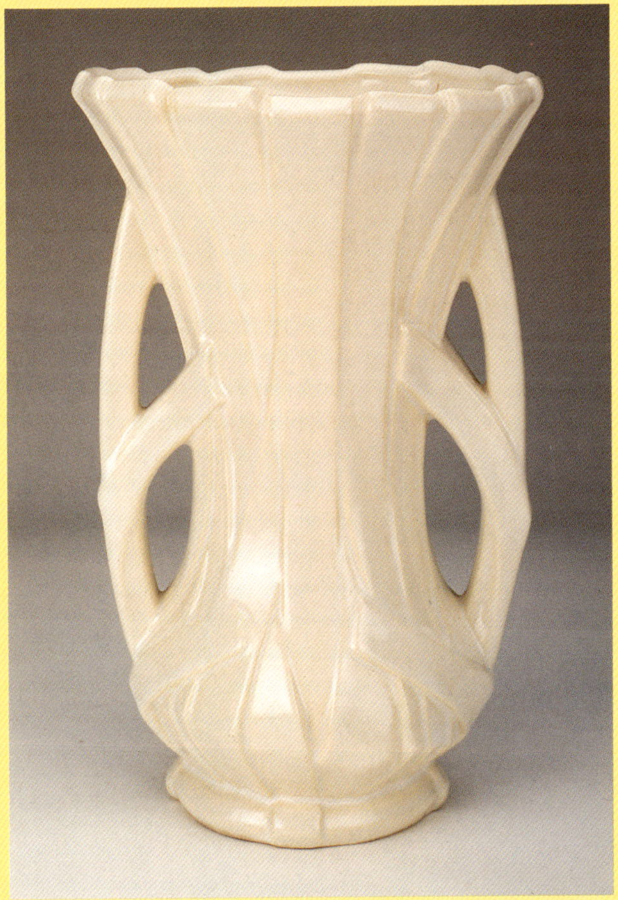

Right:
This McCoy vase shows a great deal of Hawaiian influence. 12" h. *Courtesy: Randy Hild.*

Below:
The wavy pattern Bauer flower pots came in a number of sizes. *Courtesy: Tobi Smith.*

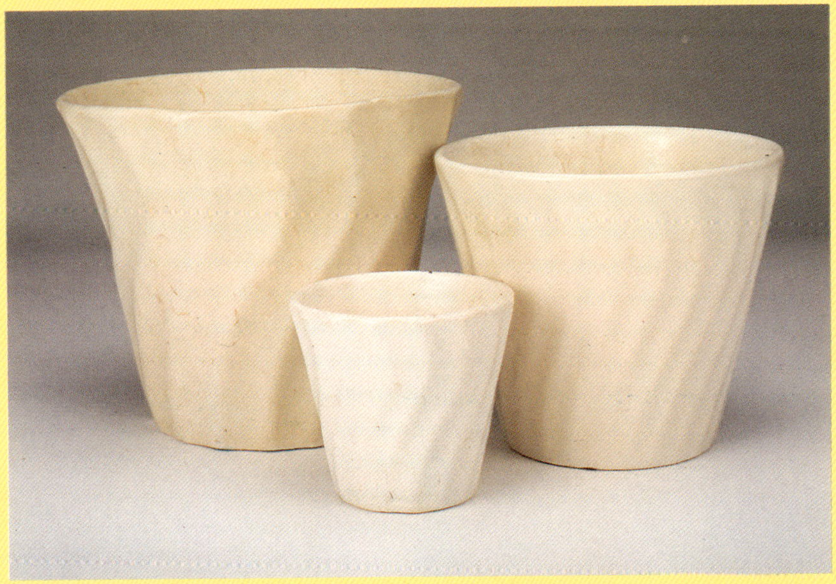

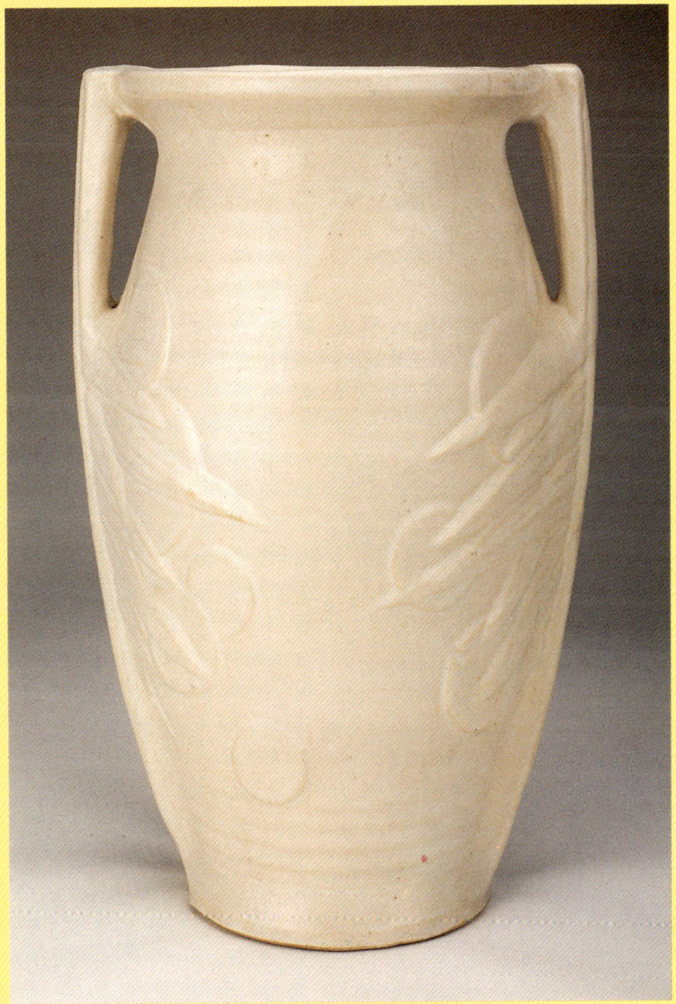

This handled pot has a combination of Art Deco and Hawaiian motifs. 14.5" h. *Courtesy: the Collection of Brian Goddard & Gene Sweeney.*

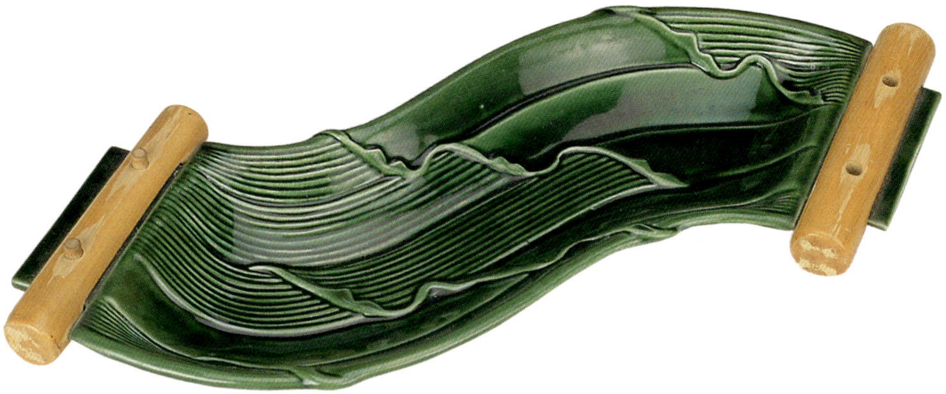

Ceramic and rattan dish. Cemar Trade Winds Lanai Ware. 18" w. *Courtesy: the Collection of Brian Goddard & Gene Sweeney.*

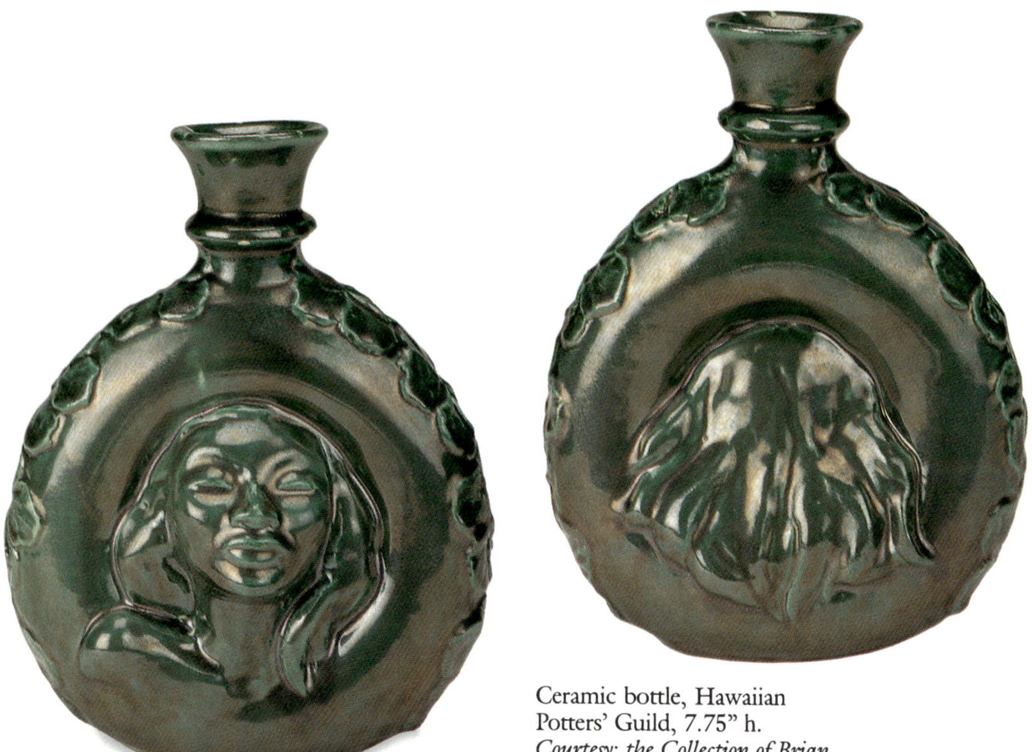

Ceramic bottle, Hawaiian Potters' Guild, 7.75" h. *Courtesy: the Collection of Brian Goddard & Gene Sweeney.*

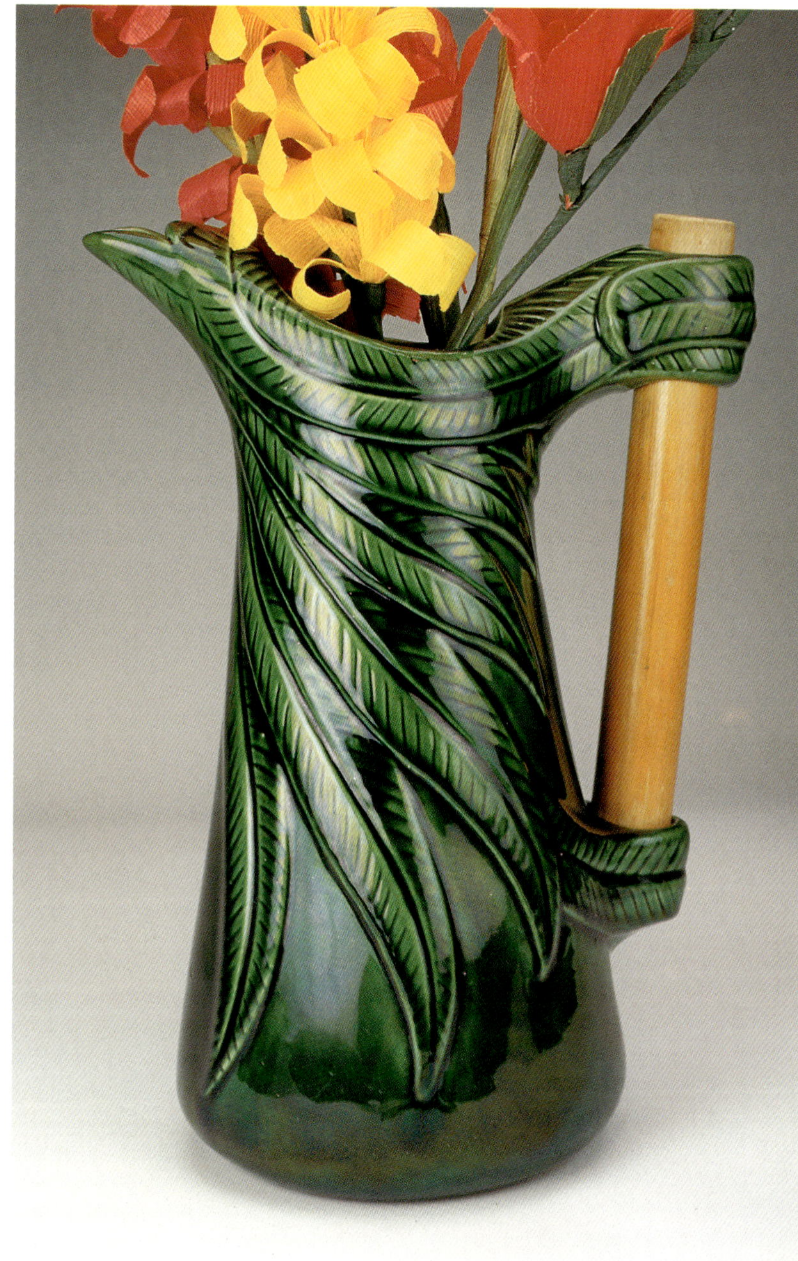

Ceramic and rattan pitcher. Cemar Trade Winds Lanai Ware. 14" h. *Courtesy: Michael & Denise Queen.*

Shell planter. 5" h. *Courtesy: Tobi Smith.*

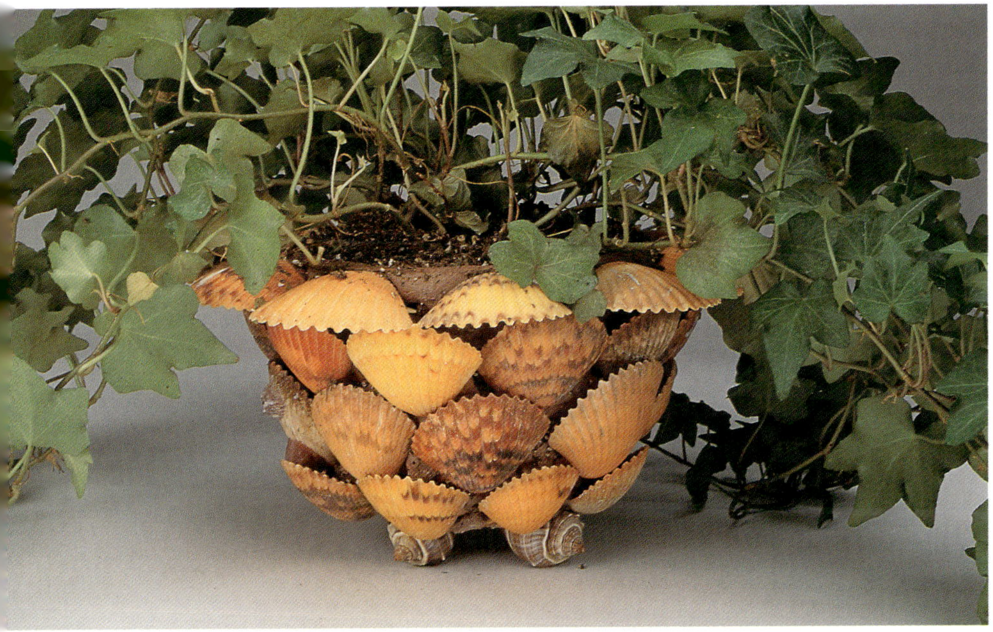

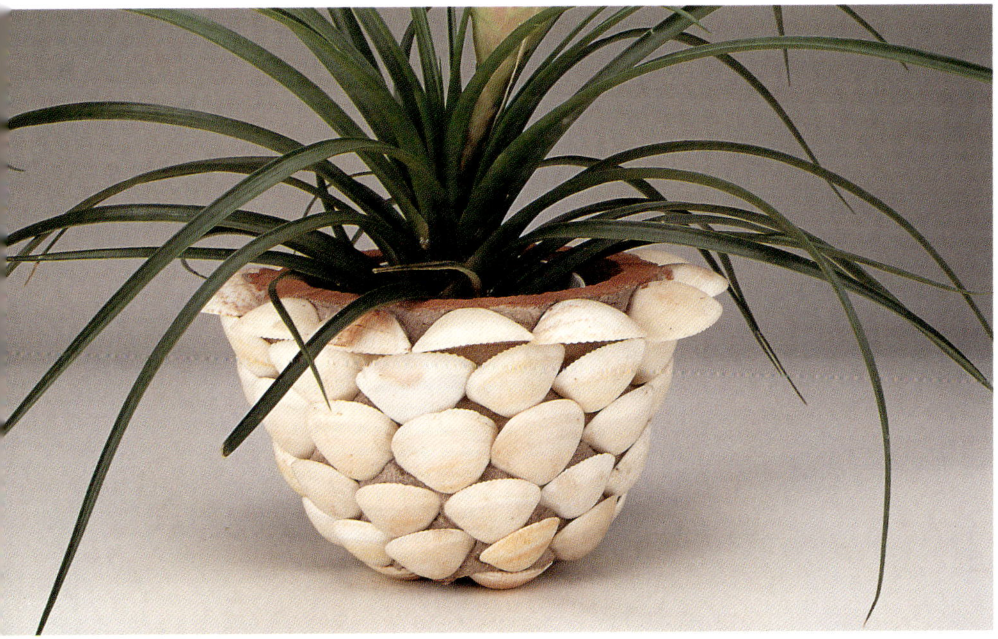

Shell covered pot, 5" h. *Courtesy: Michael Trotter.*

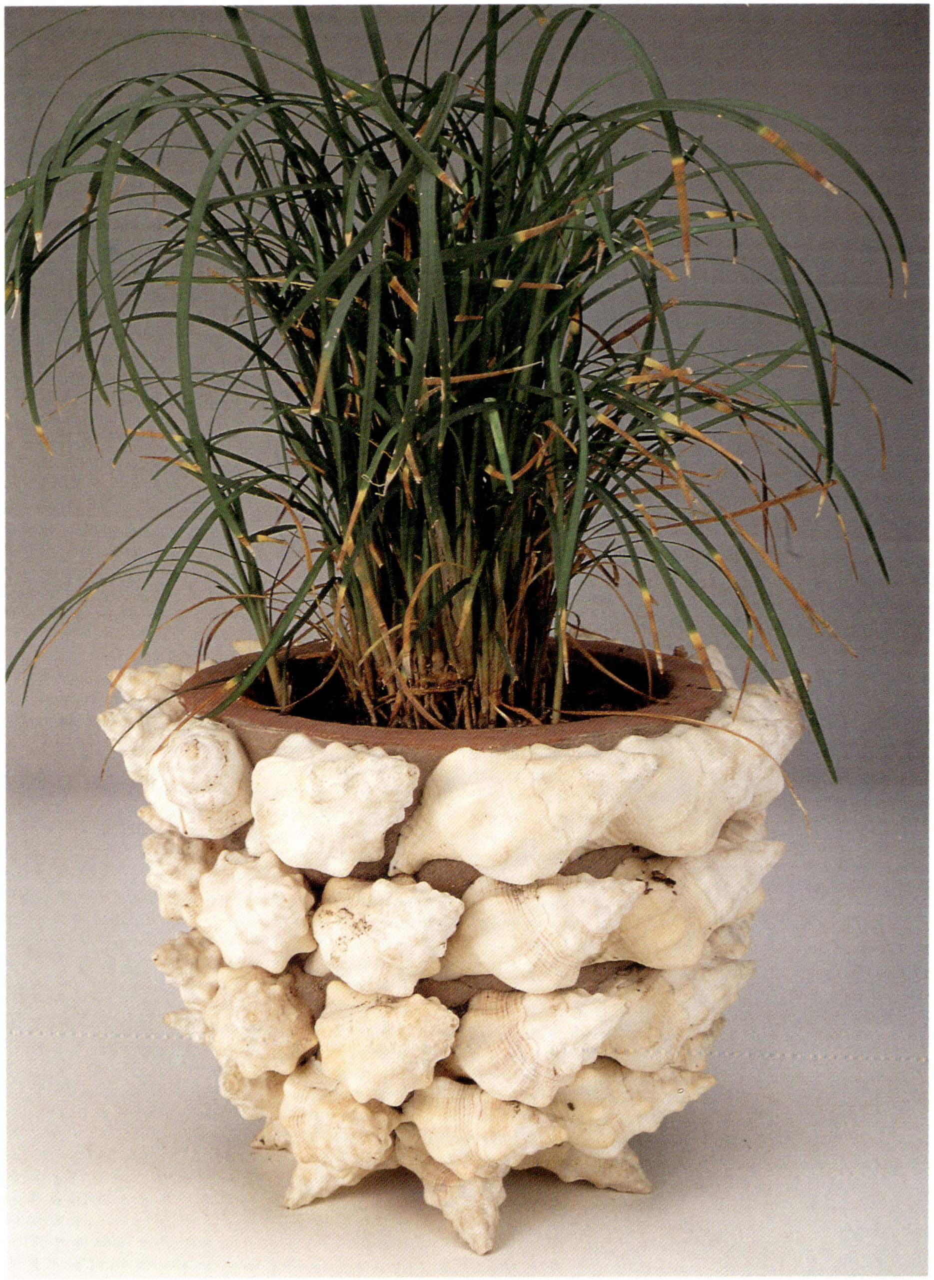

Shell planter, 5.25" h. *Courtesy: Michael Trotter.*

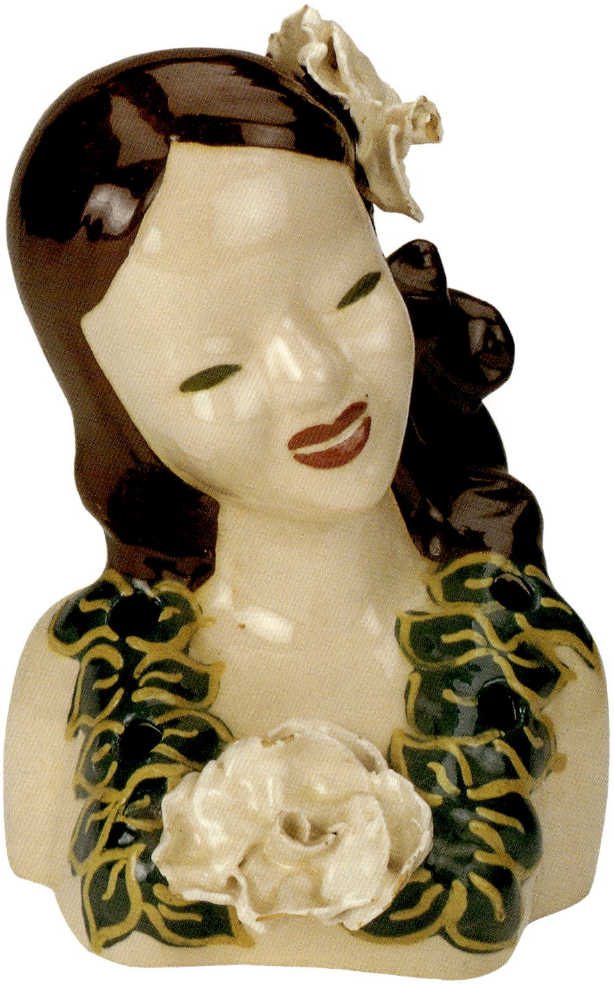

Ceramic vase, marked Kim Ward, Hollywood. *Courtesy: Michele Leypoldt*.

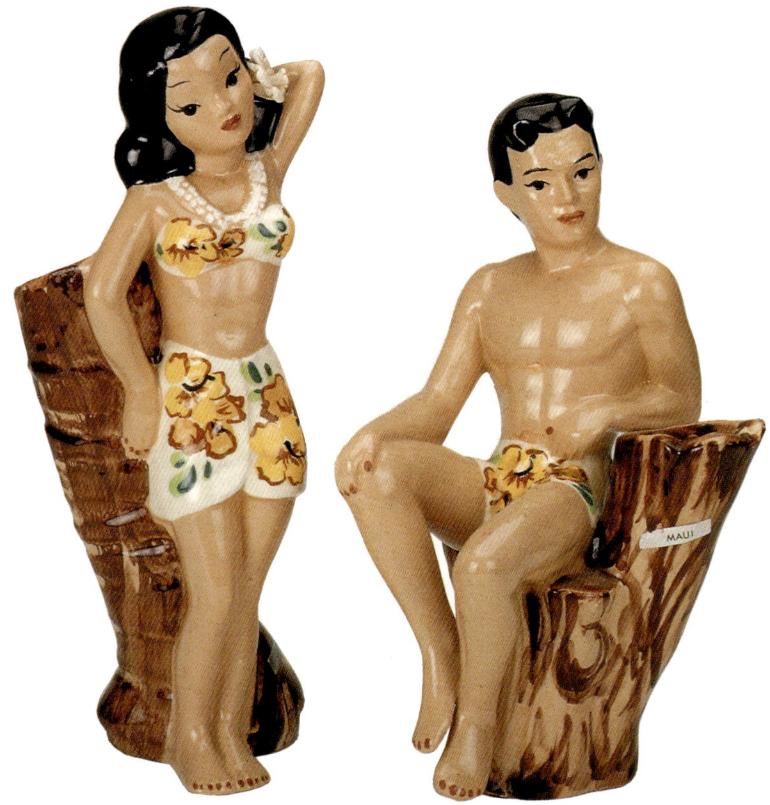

A pair of vases marked DeLee, Hollywood, 1949. The male figure has a sticker reading Maui, while the woman has one reading Luana. *Courtesy: Michele Leypoldt*.

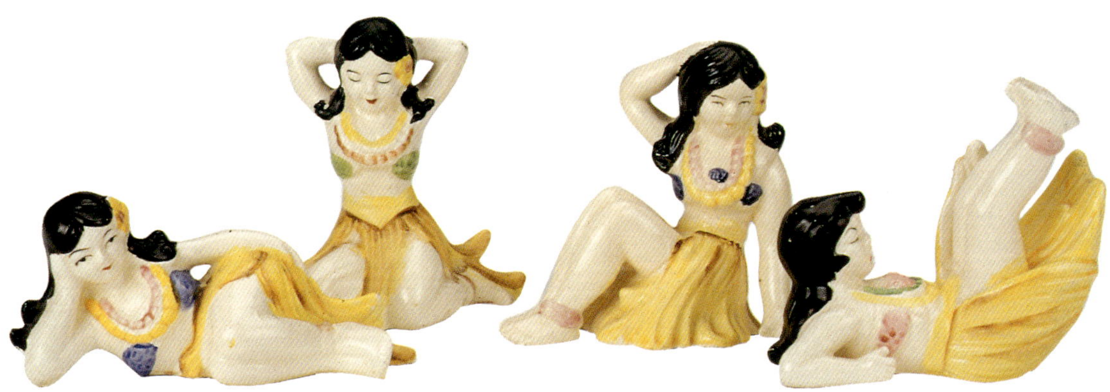

Four ceramic figures, marked c MK. *Courtesy: the Collection of Brian Goddard & Gene Sweeney*.

Unmarked vases of surfing figures.
Courtesy: Michele Leypoldt.

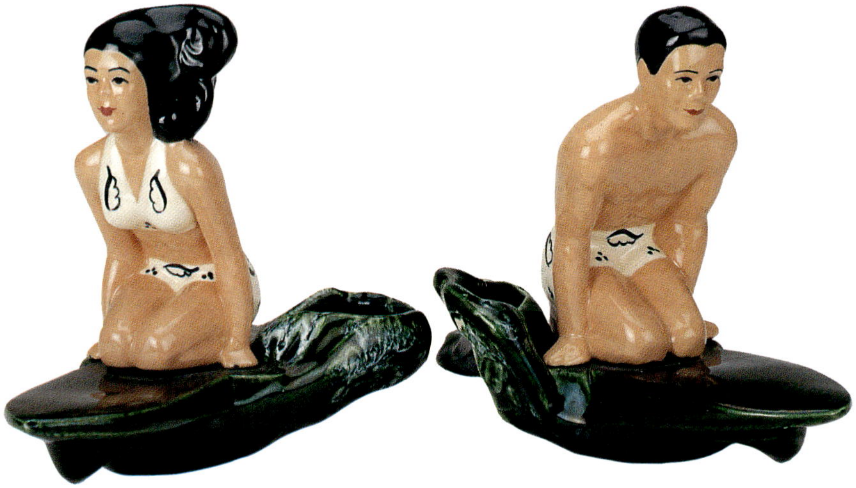

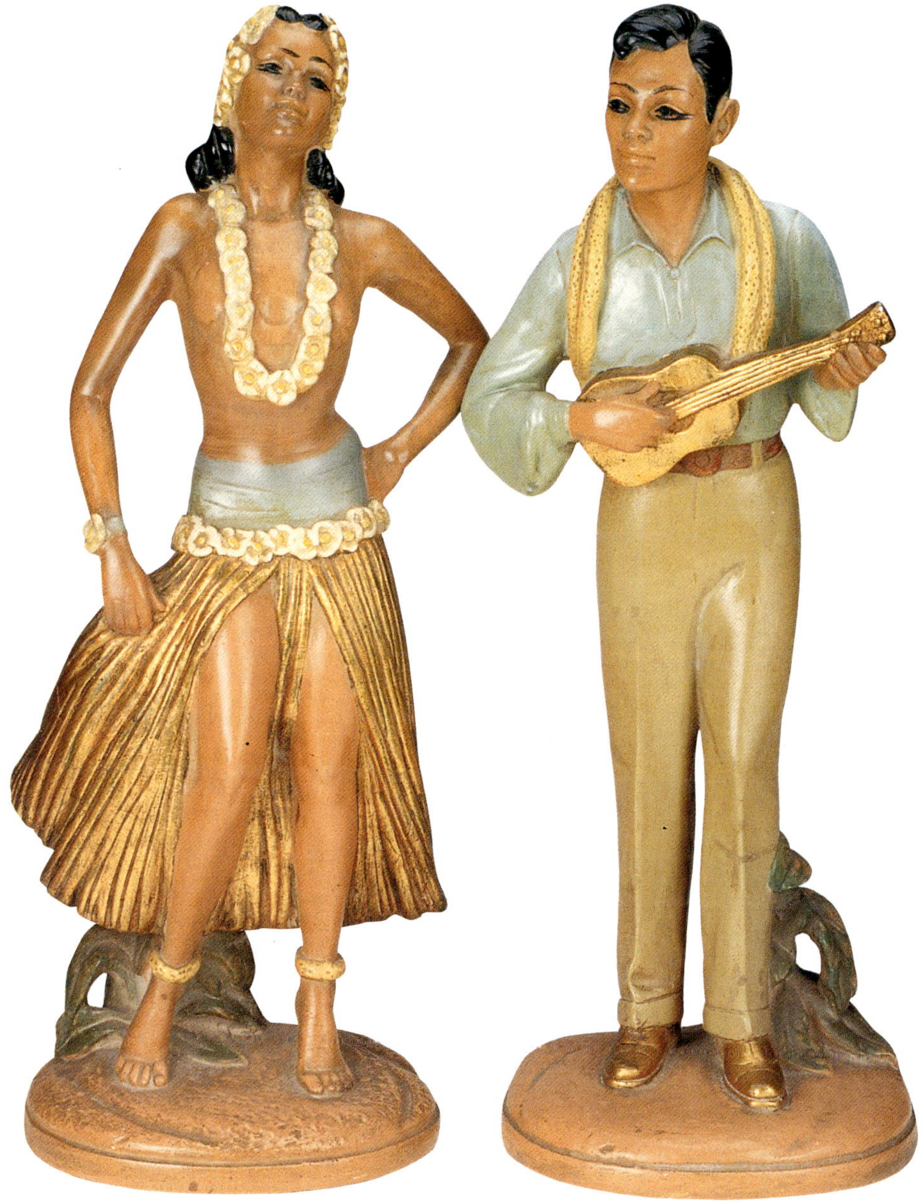

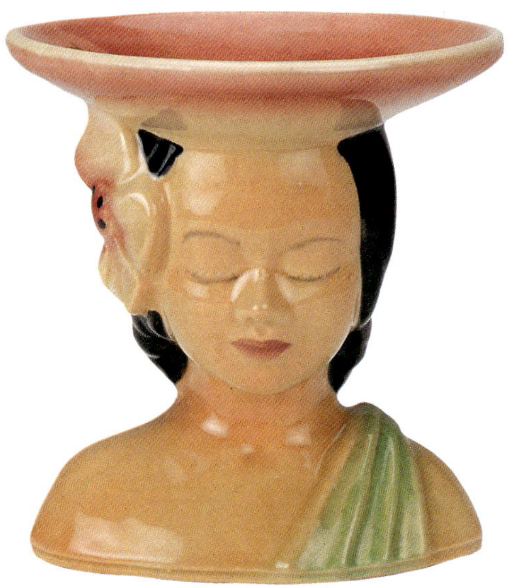

Shawnee vase, 6" h.
Courtesy: the Collection of Brian Goddard & Gene Sweeney.

Chalk figures of a ukelele player and a hula dancer. Marked Lindner. 18" h.
Courtesy: Michele Leypoldt.

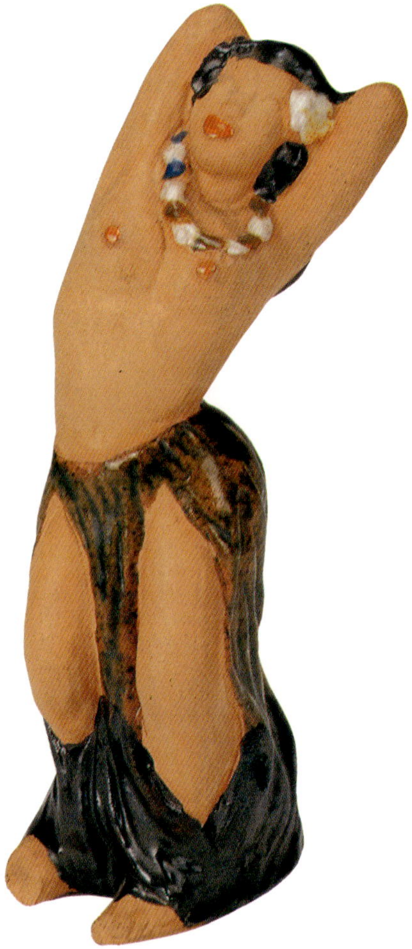

Dancing figure, 5.5" h. *Courtesy: the Collection of Brian Goddard & Gene Sweeney.*

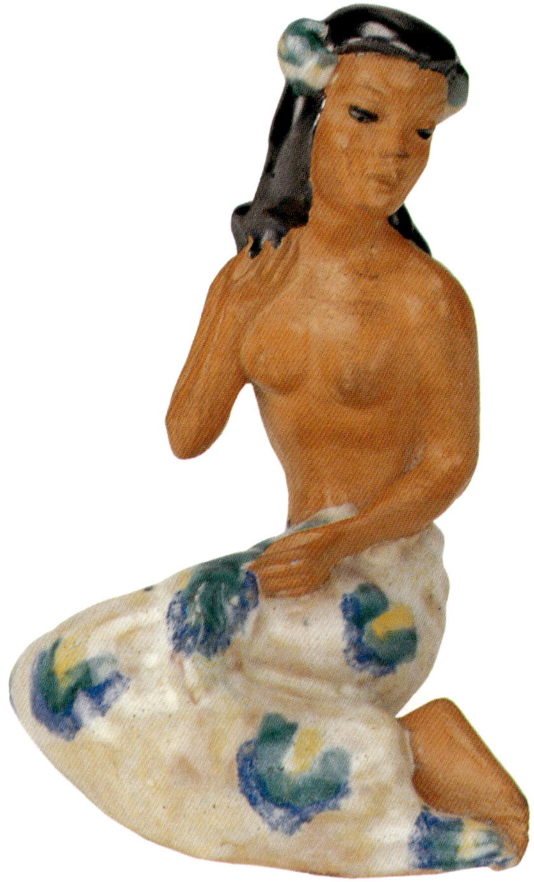

Seated figure, 6" h. *Courtesy: the Collection of Brian Goddard & Gene Sweeney.*

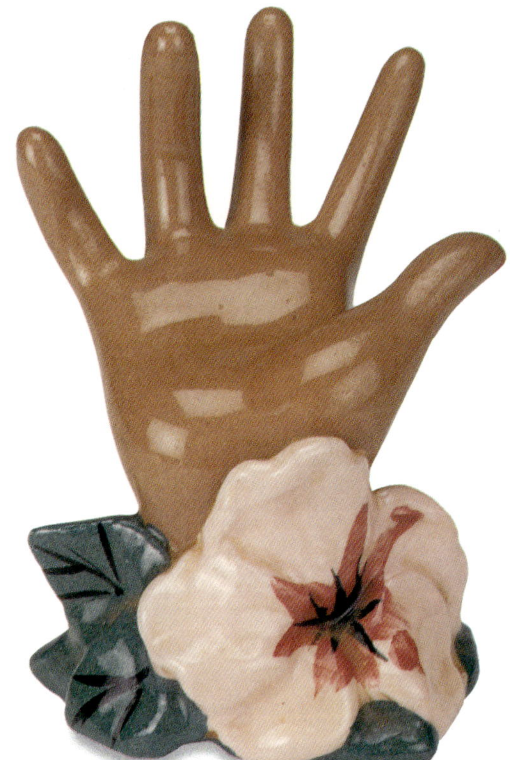

Clemuson hand figure, 3" h. *Courtesy: the Collection of Brian Goddard & Gene Sweeney.*

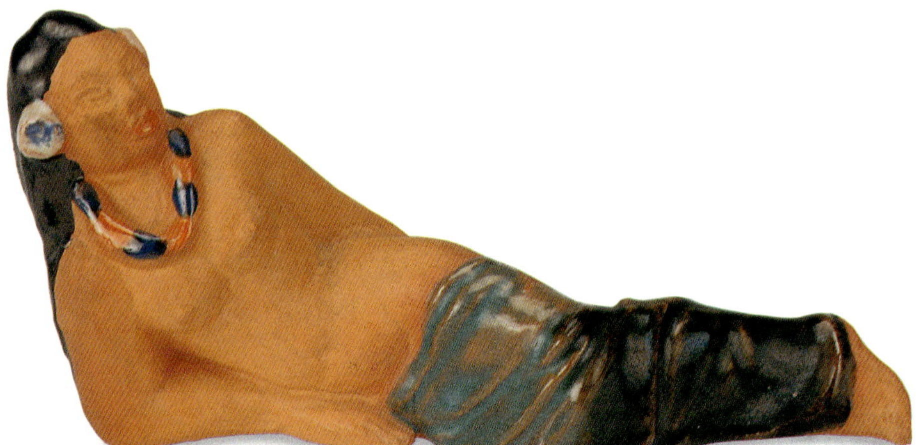

Reclining figure, 5.5" w. *Courtesy: the Collection of Brian Goddard & Gene Sweeney.*

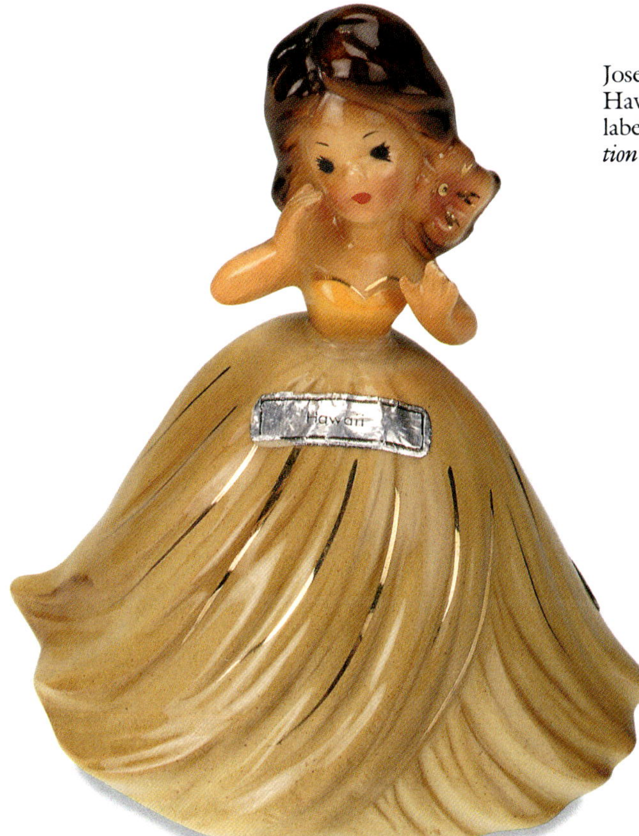

Josef original souvenir figure with Hawaii label on the skirt and Japan label underneath. *Courtesy: the Collection of Brian Goddard & Gene Sweeney*.

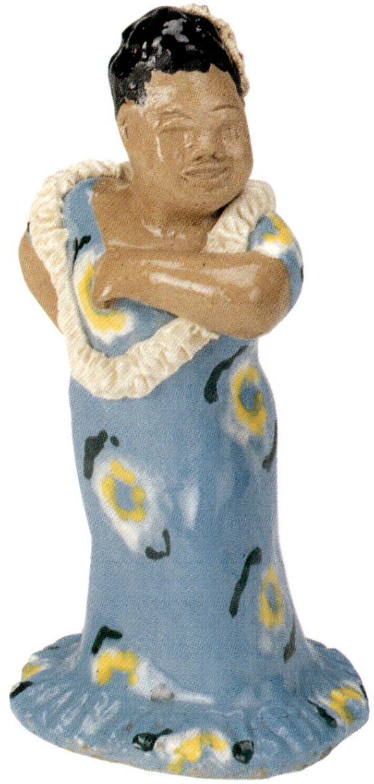

Ceramic figure marked Gertz, 5" h. *Courtesy: the Collection of Brian Goddard & Gene Sweeney*.

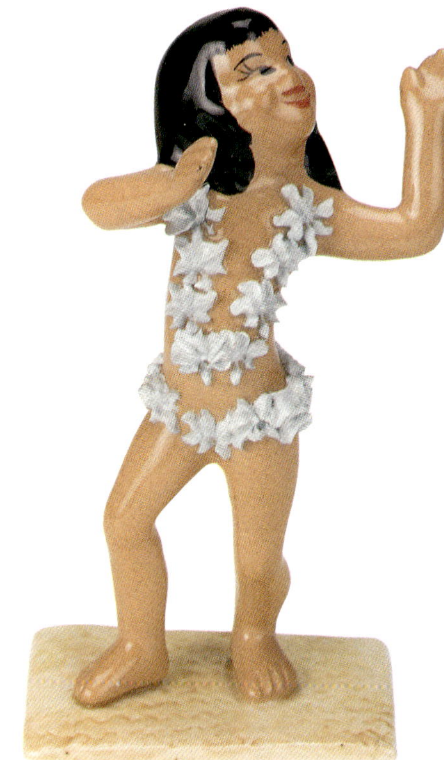

Figurine, marked copyright Millesan Drews Japan with Napco Originals Giftcraft label. 4" h. *Courtesy: the Collection of Brian Goddard & Gene Sweeney*.

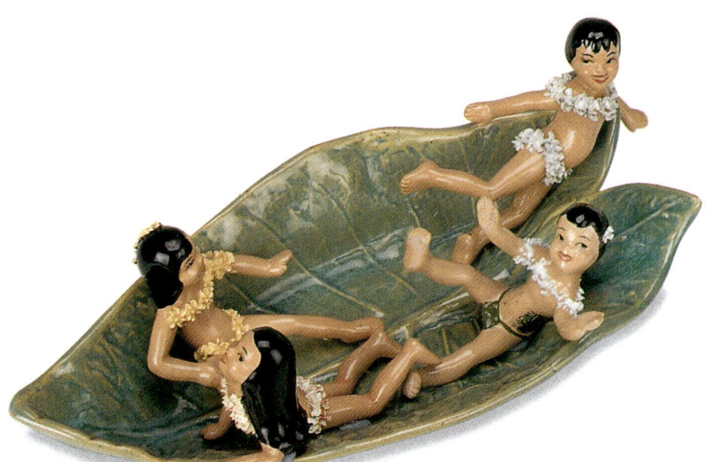

Four kids in a leaf. Marked Honolulu. 3.5" h, 1" w. *Courtesy: the Collection of Brian Goddard & Gene Sweeney*.

Ceramic water bearers, male and female. 14" h. *Courtesy: the Collection of Brian Goddard & Gene Sweeney*.

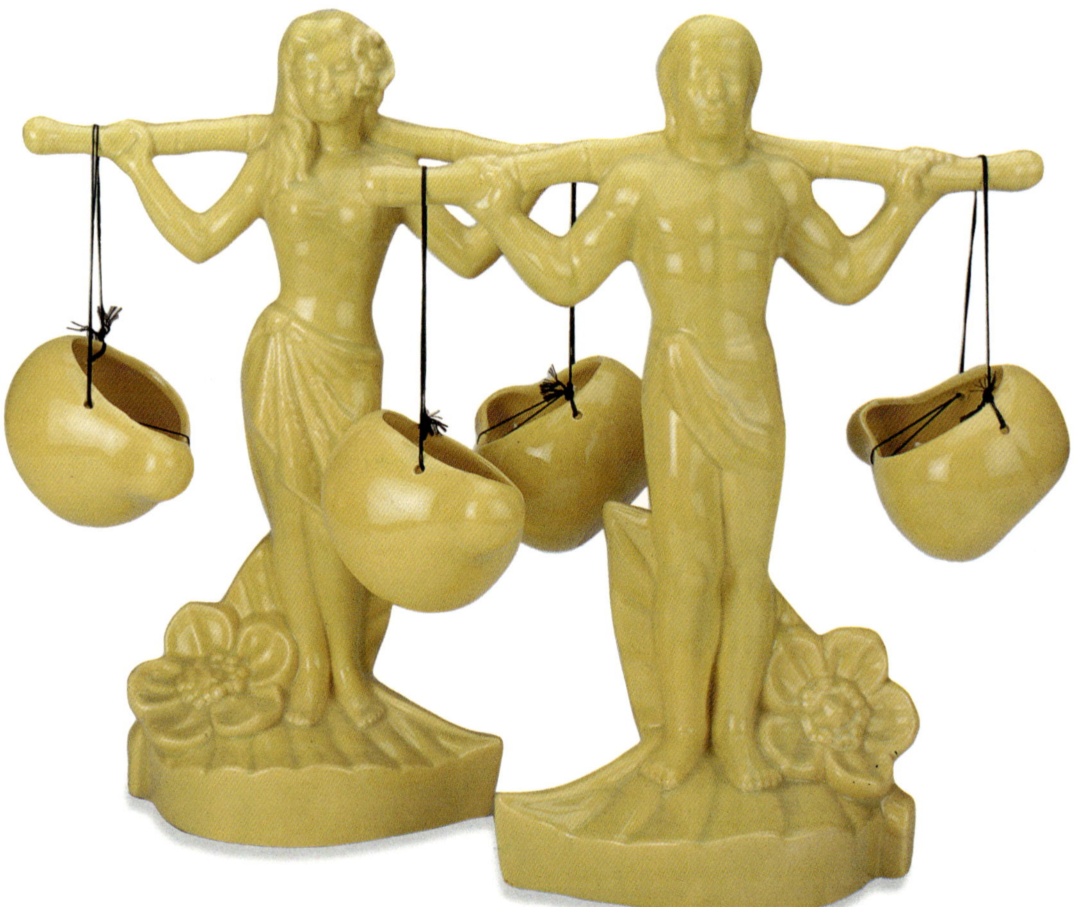

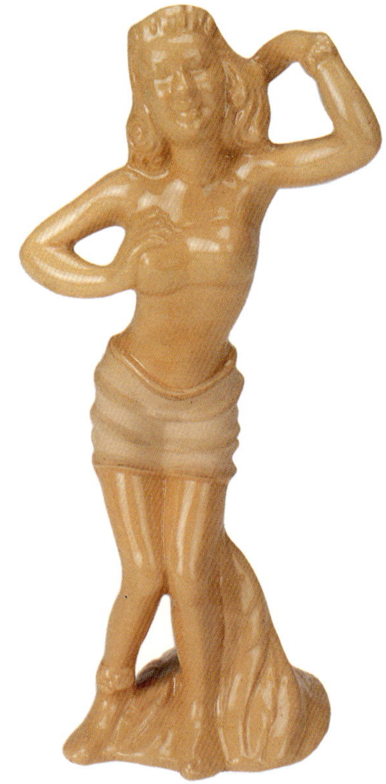

Left:
Figurine vase, marked Joseph Cossman Co., Hollywood. 7.5" h. *Courtesy: the Collection of Brian Goddard & Gene Sweeney*.

Below:
Dancer figurines by Treasure Craft. 7.75" h. *Courtesy: the Collection of Brian Goddard & Gene Sweeney*.

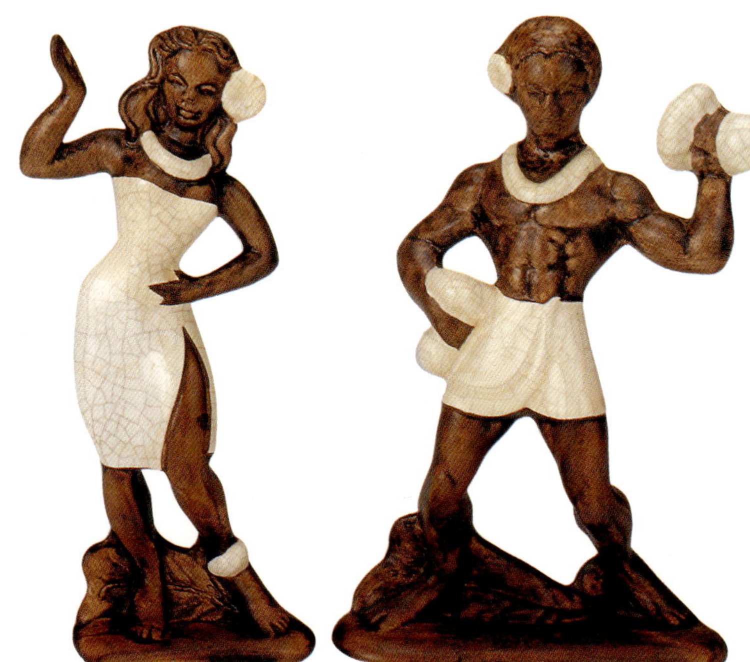

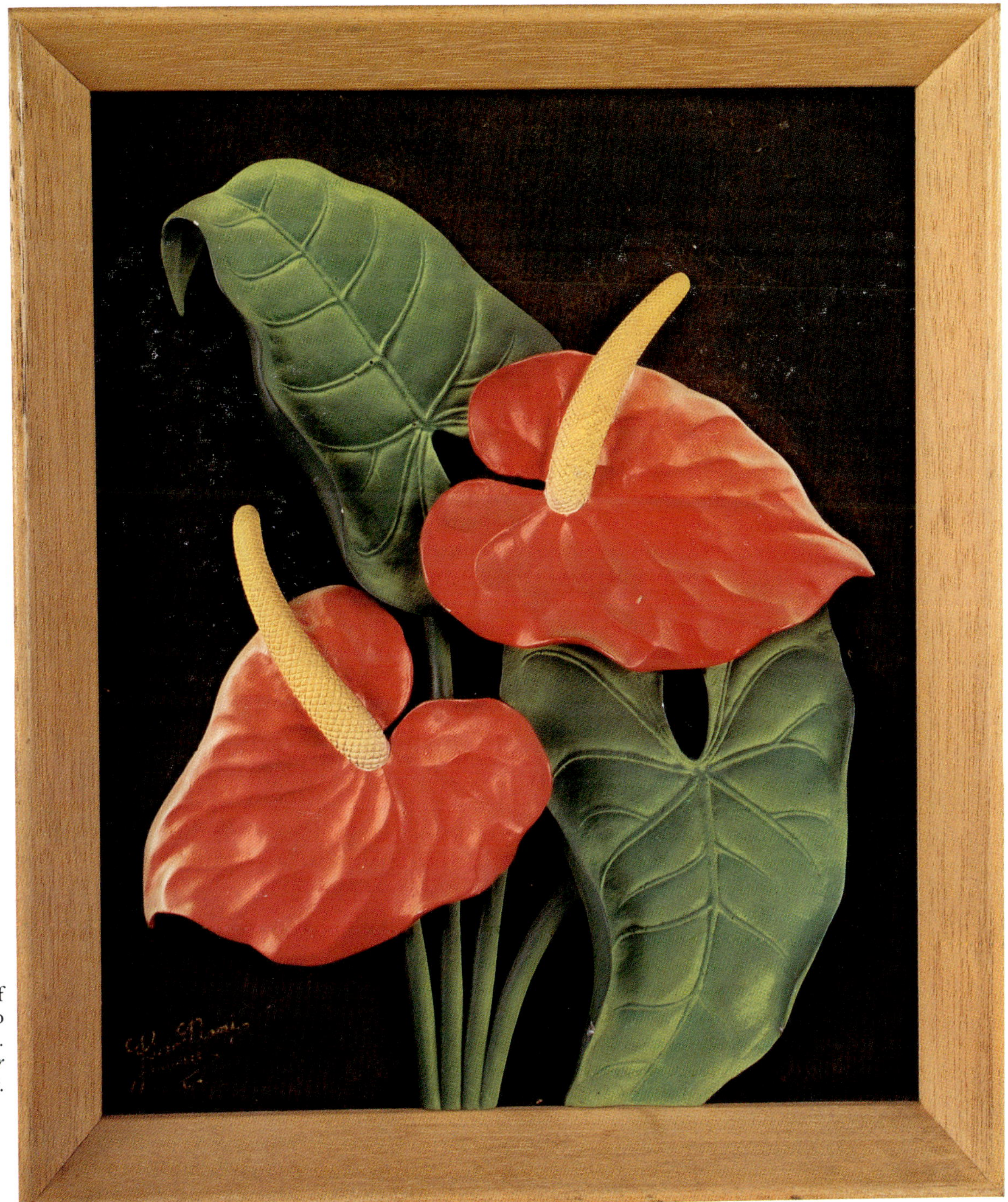

"Anthurium," relief ceramic, signed Kino Nani, Hawaii. *Courtesy: Sheila Silber & Chicken Little.*

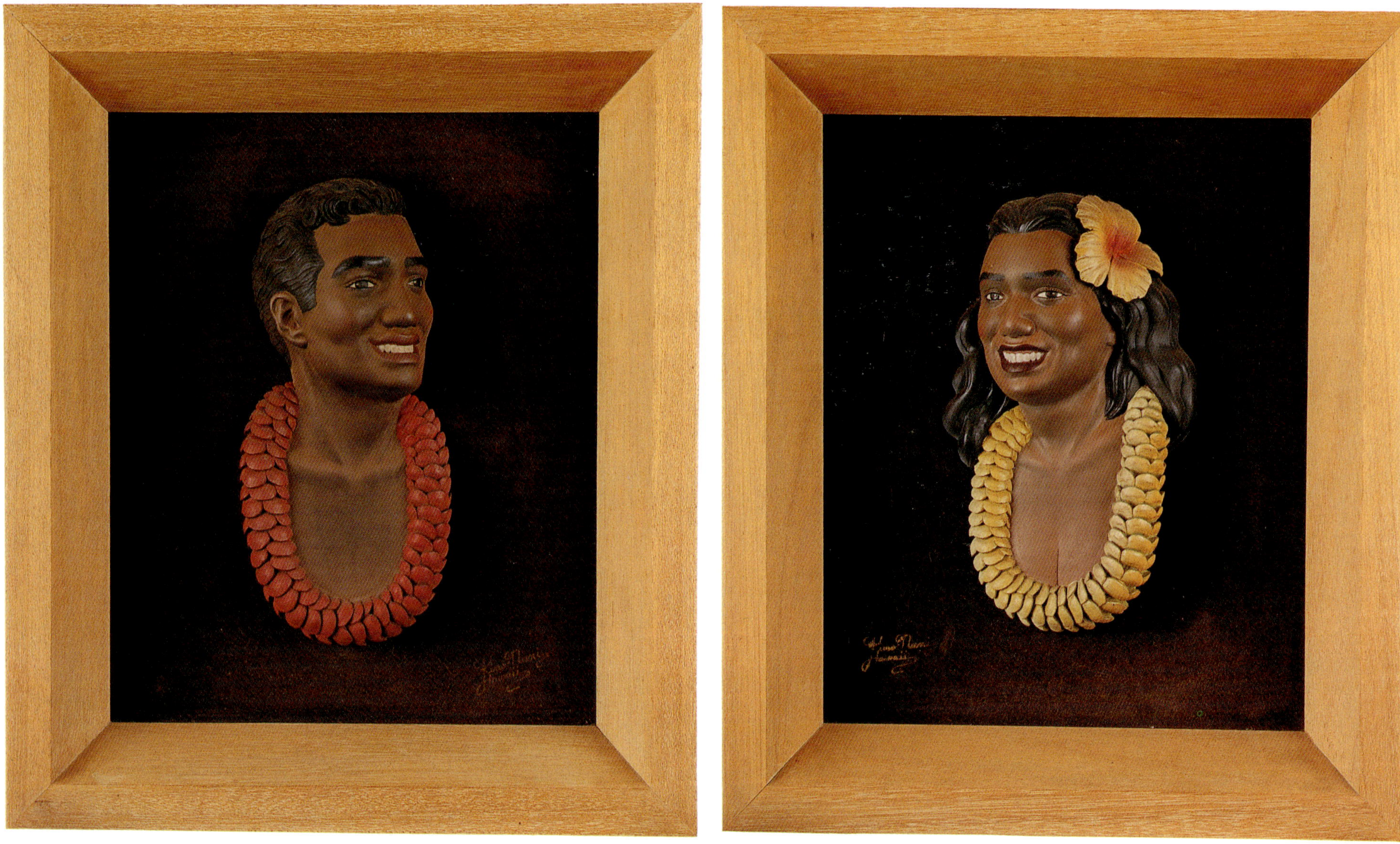

Ceramic heads with leis in relief, signed Kino Nani, Hawaii. *Courtesy: Jim & Susie Stiso*.

Ceramics by Julene

Started as a hobby by Julene and Harold Mechler, Julene ceramics originally consisted of a few figurines made as gifts for friends. A buyer from Liberty House placed an order for "heads" of Hawaiians and their business expanded to every conceivable form of ceramics that could be given a Hawaiian motif or decoration.

Harold, the handyman husband, built the original kiln, made the molds, and did the glazing. Julene designed the pieces and did the decorating. No two pieces are exactly alike. On each of the many thousands that have been made the features and pose have been changed so it is unique.

The Mechler-made collector's figures are works of art. Each detail is correct, from the ruffles of muumuus to the little monkeypod calabashes held by the grey-haired *kanes*. One mainland couple treasured their large King Kamehameha figurine so much that they made him a feather cloak.

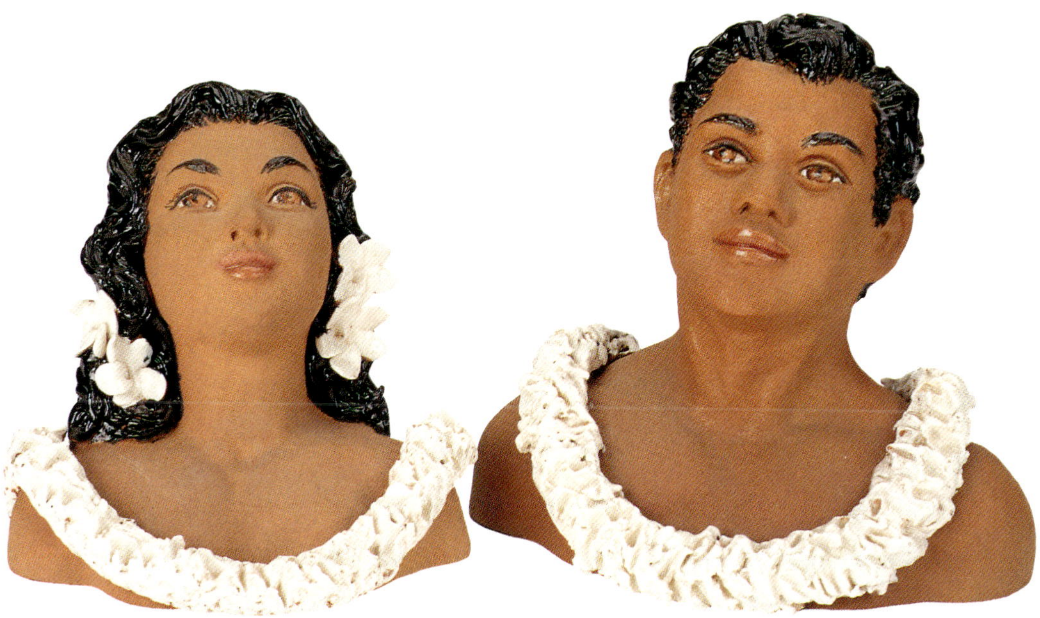

Julene ceramic busts.
Courtesy: Michele Leypoldt.

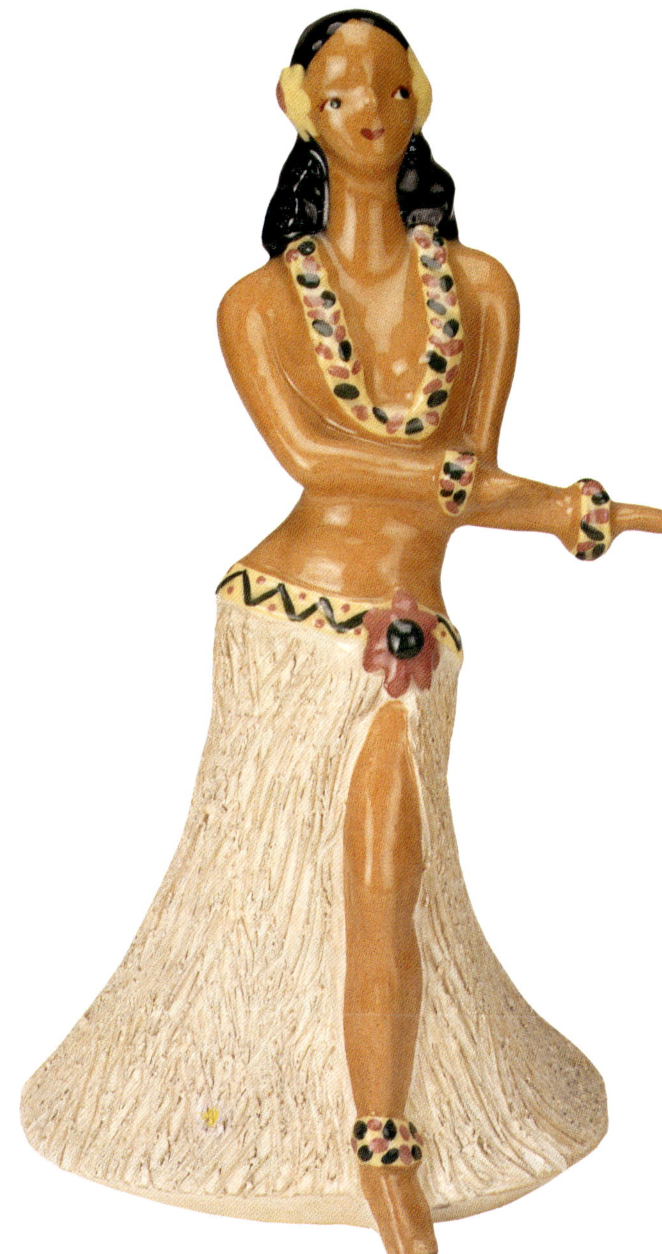

Yona, ceramic figurine by Julene. 10" h. *Courtesy: the Collection of Brian Goddard & Gene Sweeney.*

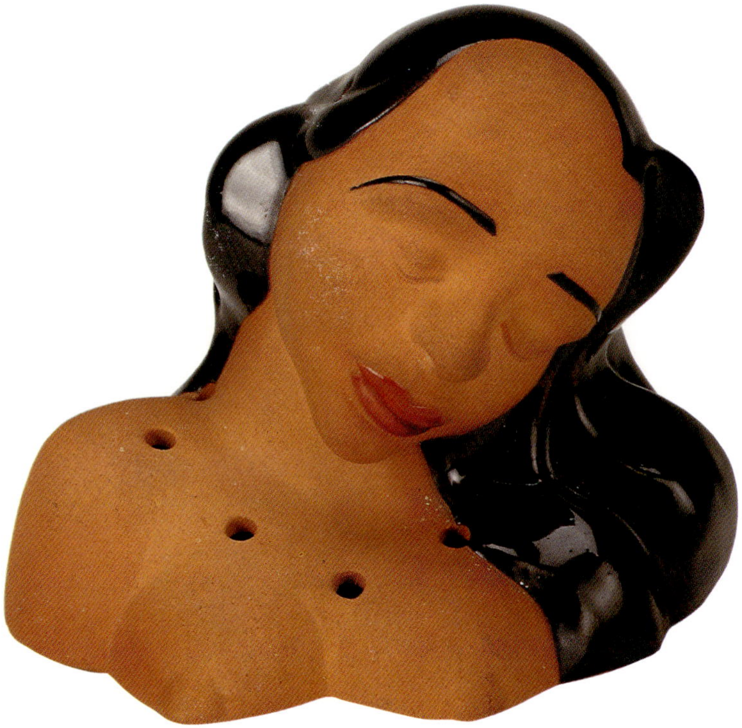

Julene bust, 4.5" h. *Courtesy: the Collection of Brian Goddard & Gene Sweeney.*

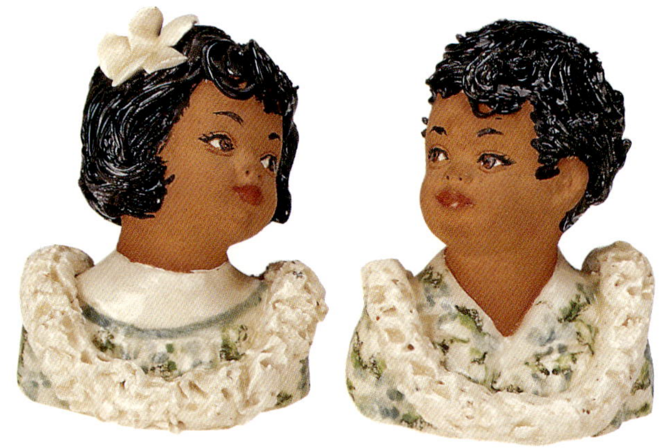

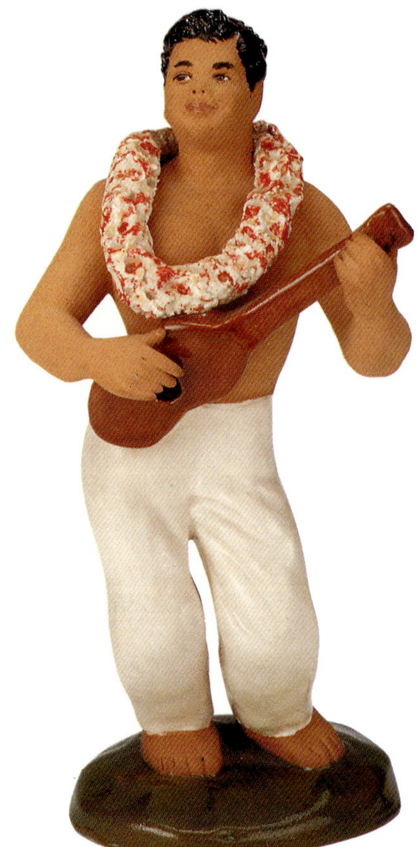

Above: A pair of Julene busts. 3" h. *Courtesy: the Collection of Brian Goddard & Gene Sweeney.*

Left: Julene ukelele player figurine. 7.25" h. *Courtesy: the Collection of Brian Goddard & Gene Sweeney.*

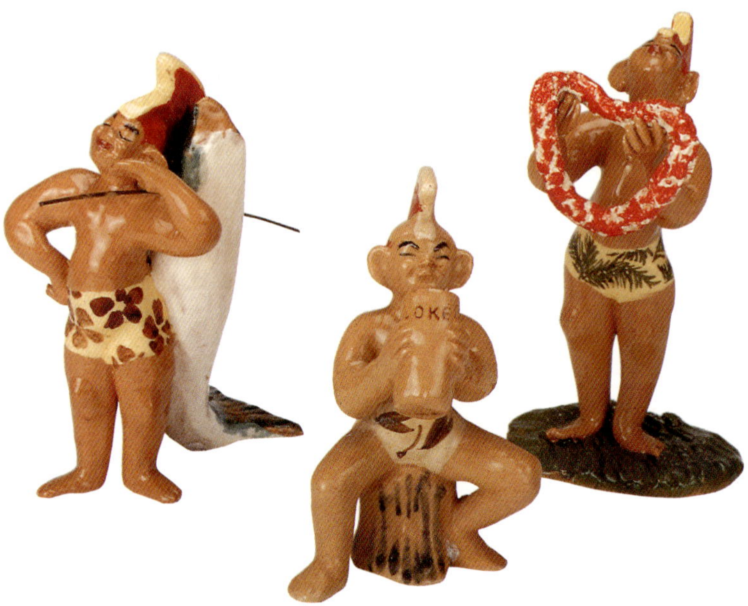

Group of figures by Julene. 4"-4.75" h. *Courtesy: the Collection of Brian Goddard & Gene Sweeney.*

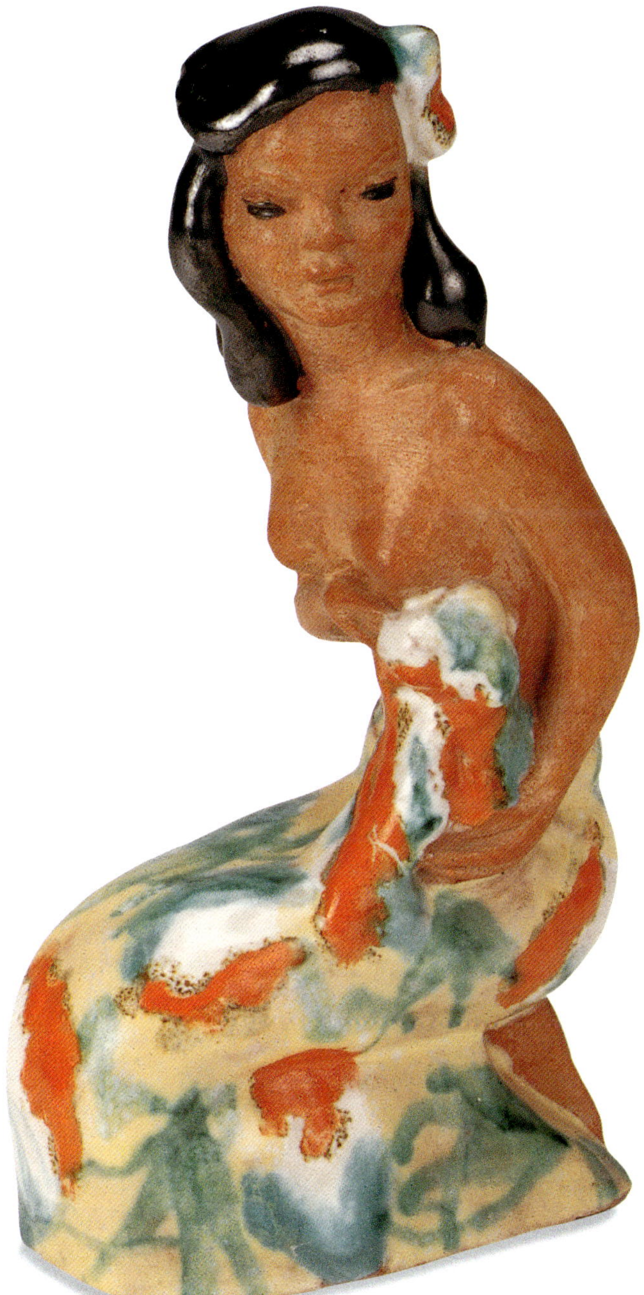

Julene figurine, 7" h. *Courtesy: the Collection of Brian Goddard & Gene Sweeney.*

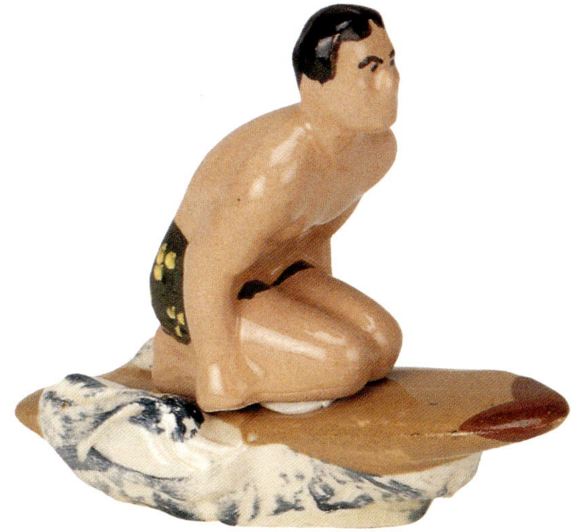

Julene surfing figurine, 2.75" h. *Courtesy: the Collection of Brian Goddard & Gene Sweeney.*

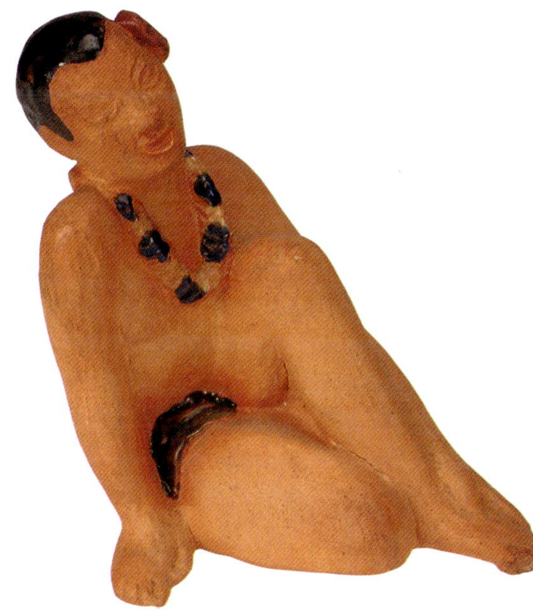

Julene sitting figure, 3.25" h. *Courtesy: the Collection of Brian Goddard & Gene Sweeney.*

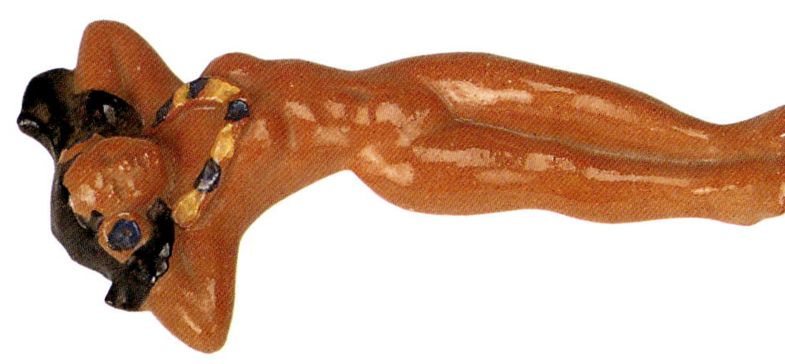

Reclining Julene figure, 4" w. *Courtesy: the Collection of Brian Goddard & Gene Sweeney.*

Hula Nodders

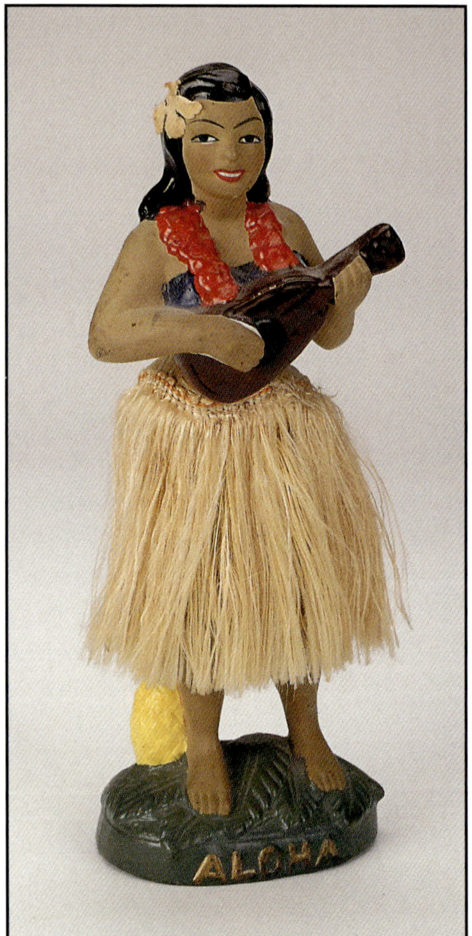

Aloha hula girl nodder, chalk. 7.75" h.
Courtesy: Susan Mast Enterprises.

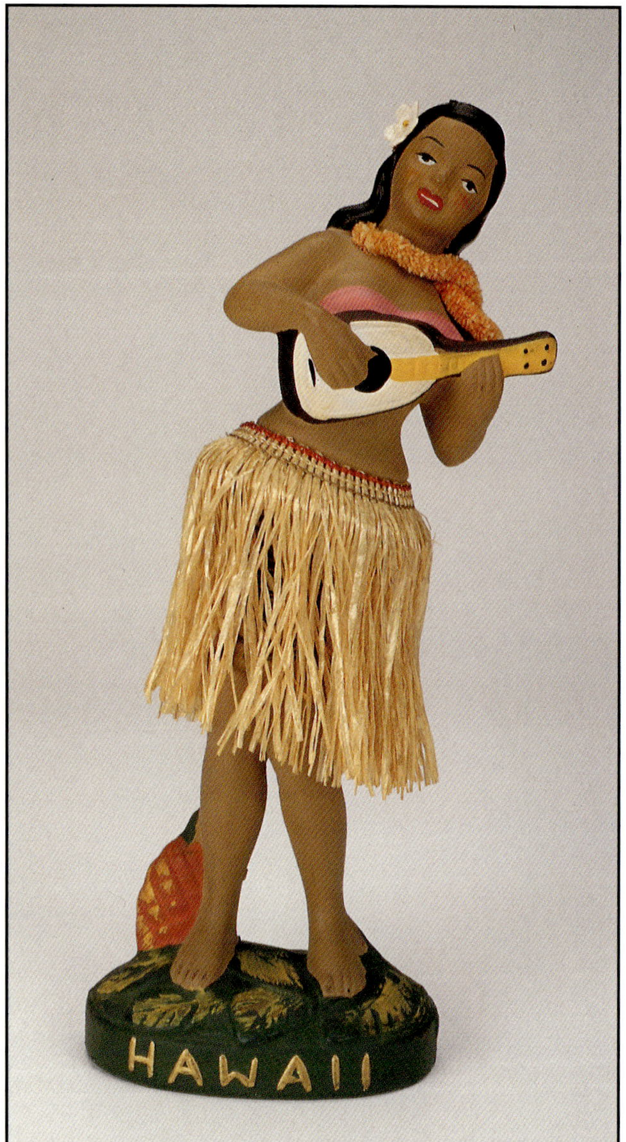

Large chalk hula girl nodder. 11" h.
Courtesy: Susan Mast Enterprises.

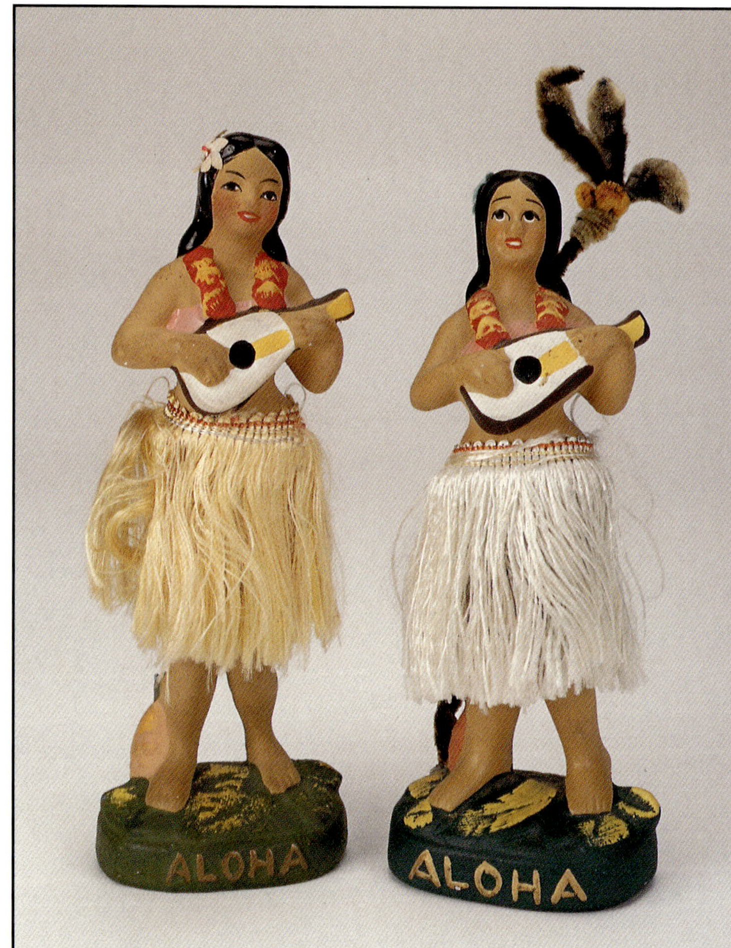

Two chalk hula girl nodders. 7.25" h.
Courtesy: Susan Mast Enterprises.

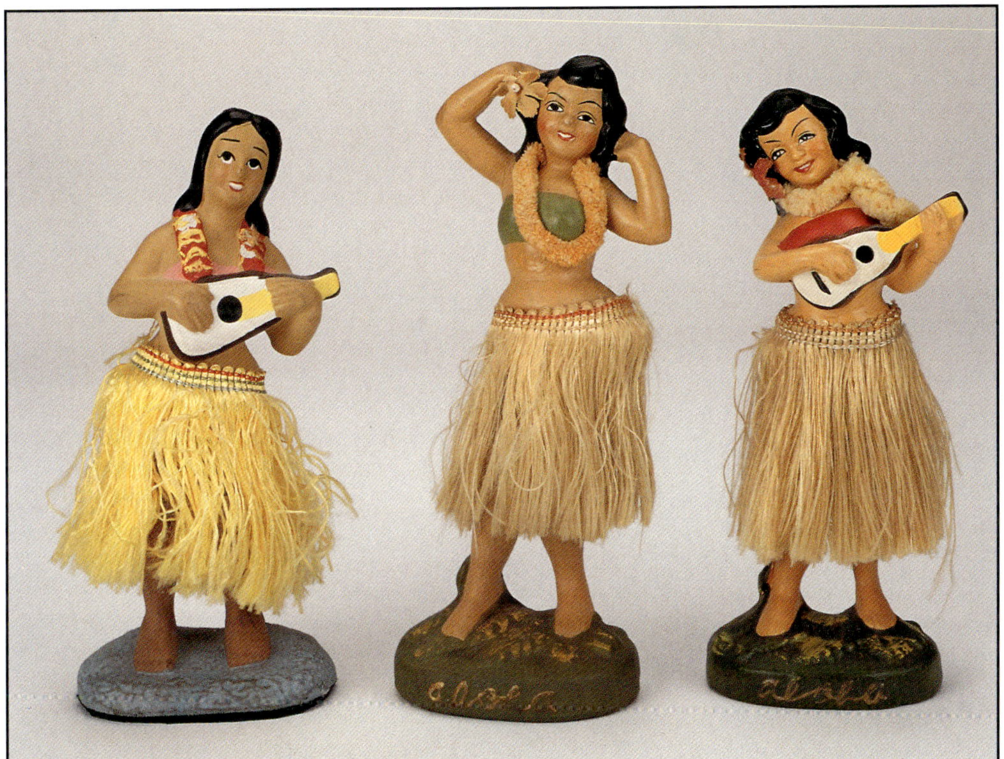

Three chalk nodders, 6.25"-6.75" h. The one on the left is marked Victoria Ceramics, made in Japan. The center figure is A Mark L Exclusive, also made in Japan. The right nodder is not marked.
Courtesy: Susan Mast Enterprises.

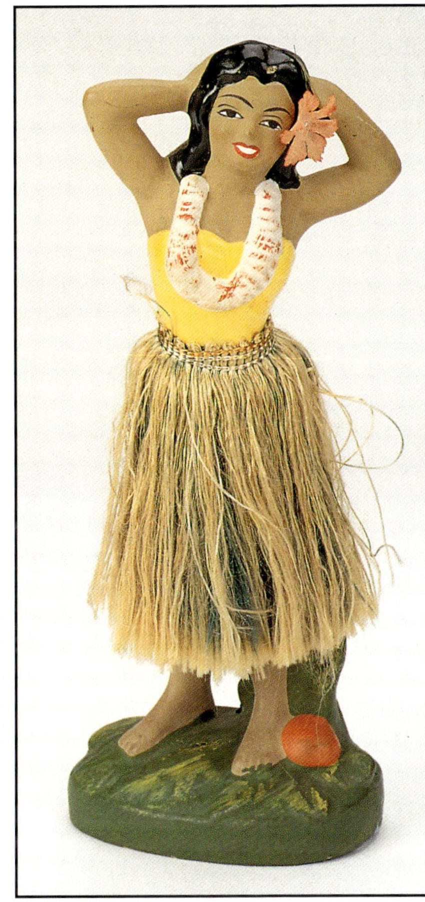

An unmarked nodder, 7.5" h.
Courtesy: Susan Mast Enterprises.

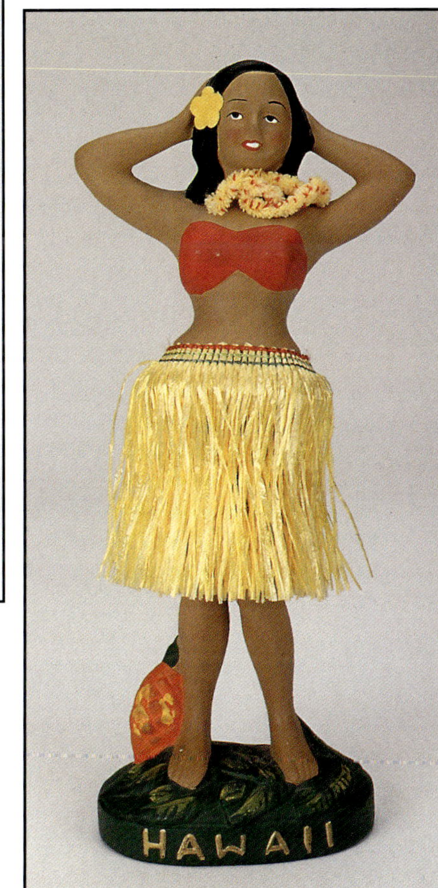

Another unmarked nodder. 7.5" h.
Courtesy: Susan Mast Enterprises.

Lava Figures

When Don Gallacher, a tuna boat captain, decided to leave the sea, he bought a small local gift shop in Hawaii. Housed in a little grass shack, it was called Cocojoe's Gifts. The tourists who frequented the store wanted small mementos of Hawaii to take home with them, so Don decided to see if he could come up with something.

Reflecting on the successful items he already sold, he decided to try his hand at making keyrings and magnets that resembled Hawaiian Tikis and artifacts. Working behind his shop he used a composition of resin and lava powder to make a few prototypes. They were an immediate hit with the tourists, and soon he was making all he could sell.

Seeing the success of the new product, the local salesmen told Gallacher that if he could supply them with the product, they could sell the lava items throughout the Islands. Before long Don opened a 22,000 square foot factory on Oahu's North Shore, employing 50 persons. Today Cocojoe's products are sold across Hawaii, Guam, Japan, as well as other mainland sites, including Disneyland and Disney World. The keychains and magnet souvenirs are still the best sellers.

Don is now retired and living on the island of Hawaii, growing Macadamia nuts. The products the company produces today contain no lava or wood, calling the composition "simulated" instead.

Some say the goddess Pele will put a curse on the person who takes lava from the Islands. Though many people have come to believe that this story is an ancient legend, in fact it was the product of a State Park Ranger in the early 1950s, who was simply trying to discourage people from taking lava from the parks. Legend or no, the popularity of "lava" items continues and other companies have joined Cocojoe's in their design and production, most notably Frank Schirman and Hip.

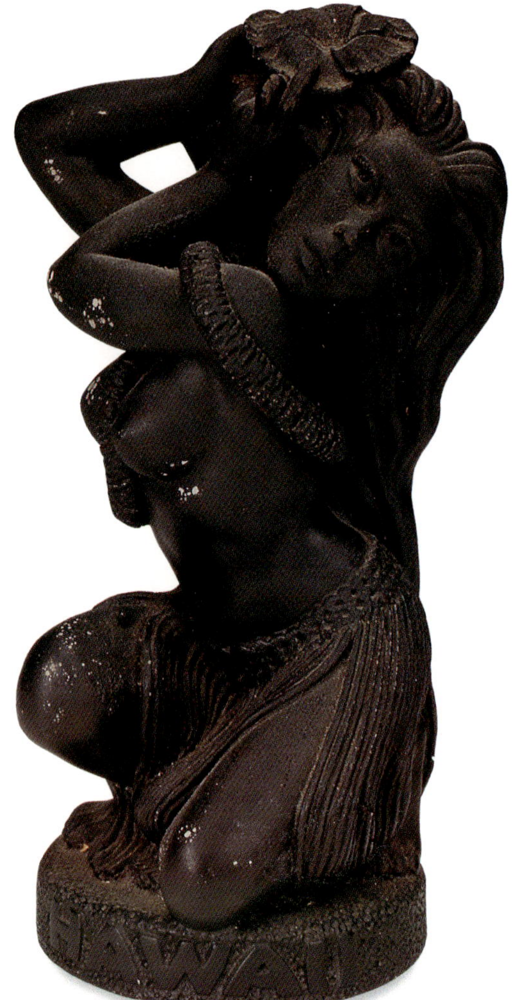

Left:
Polynesian Princess. A Hip Original, copyright 1973. *Courtesy: Michael Trotter.*

Below:
Pen holder. A Hip Original, Hawaiian Island Products. Copyright 1977. *Courtesy: Michael Trotter.*

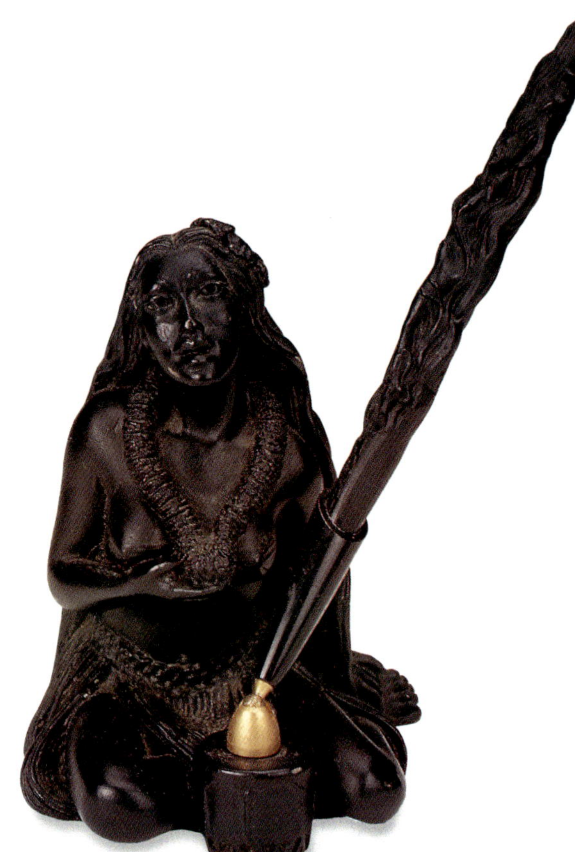

Momi, Exotic Black Coral designed by Frank Schirman. 4" h. *Courtesy: the Collection of Brian Goddard & Gene Sweeney.*

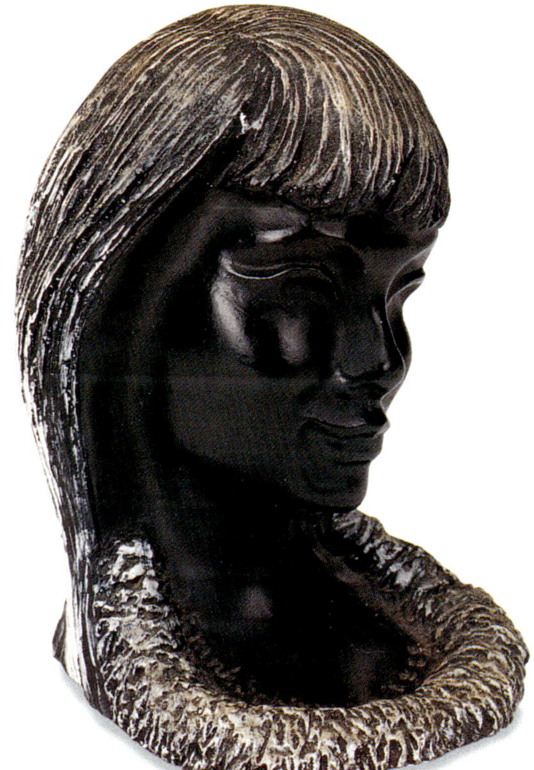

Another, smaller version of Napua, this marked Polyart #23, Hand made in Hawaii. 5.75" *Courtesy: Tiki Trader.*

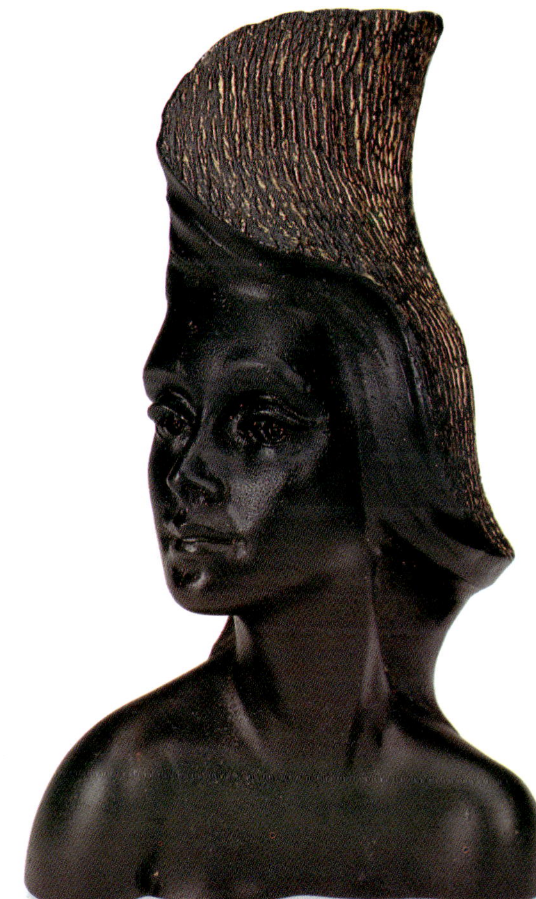

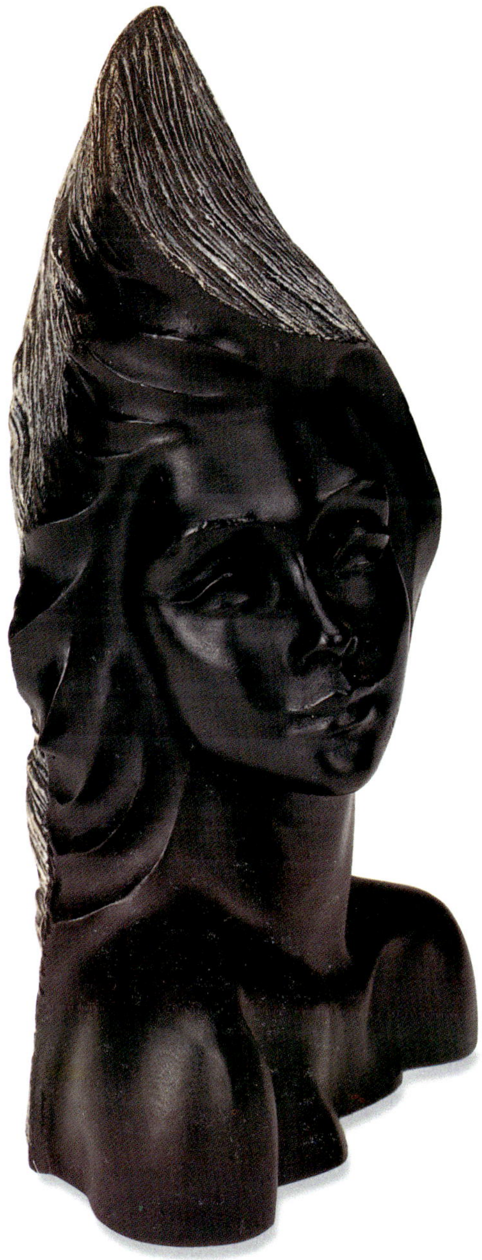

Napua. Exotic Black Coral designed by Frank Schirman. 7" h. *Courtesy: the Collection of Brian Goddard & Gene Sweeney.*

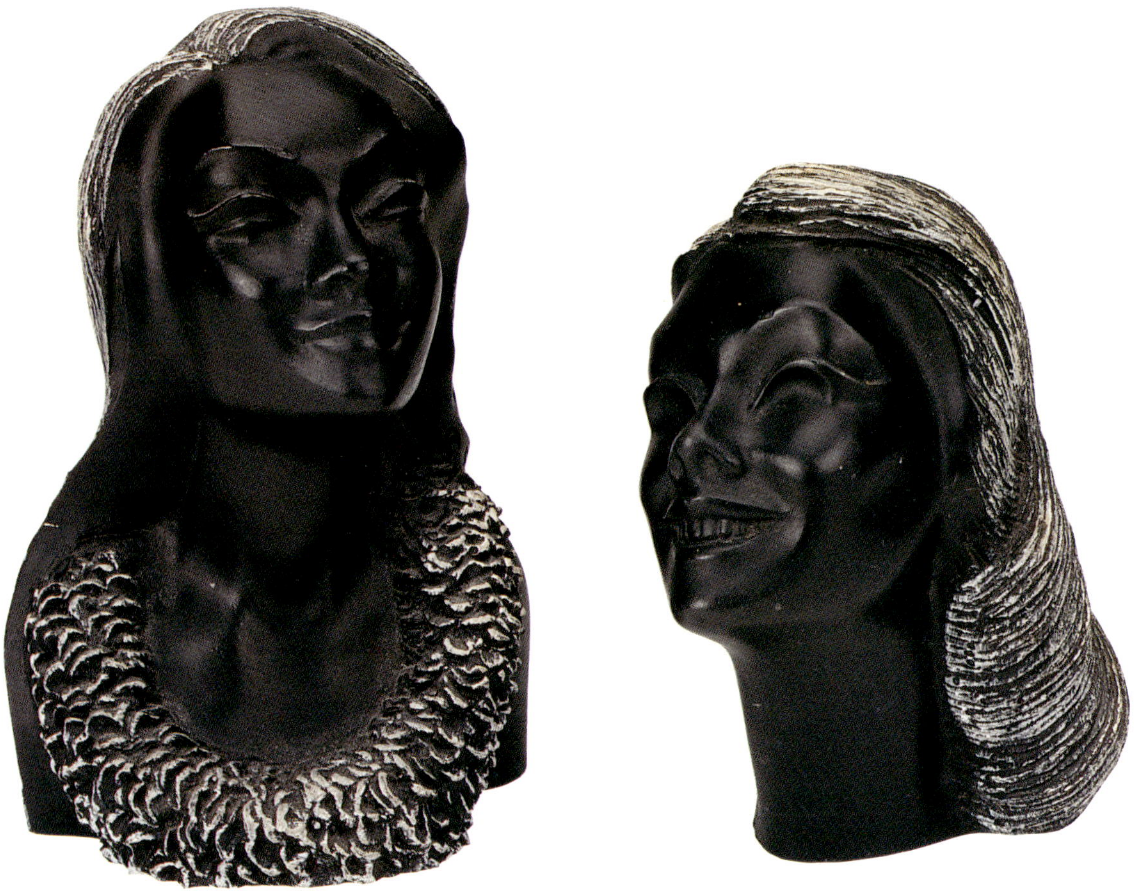

Left: Leialoha, designed by Frank Schirman, 5" h. Right: Kealoha, designer not indicated. Both by Exotic Black Coral. 4" h. *Courtesy: the Collection of Brian Goddard & Gene Sweeney*.

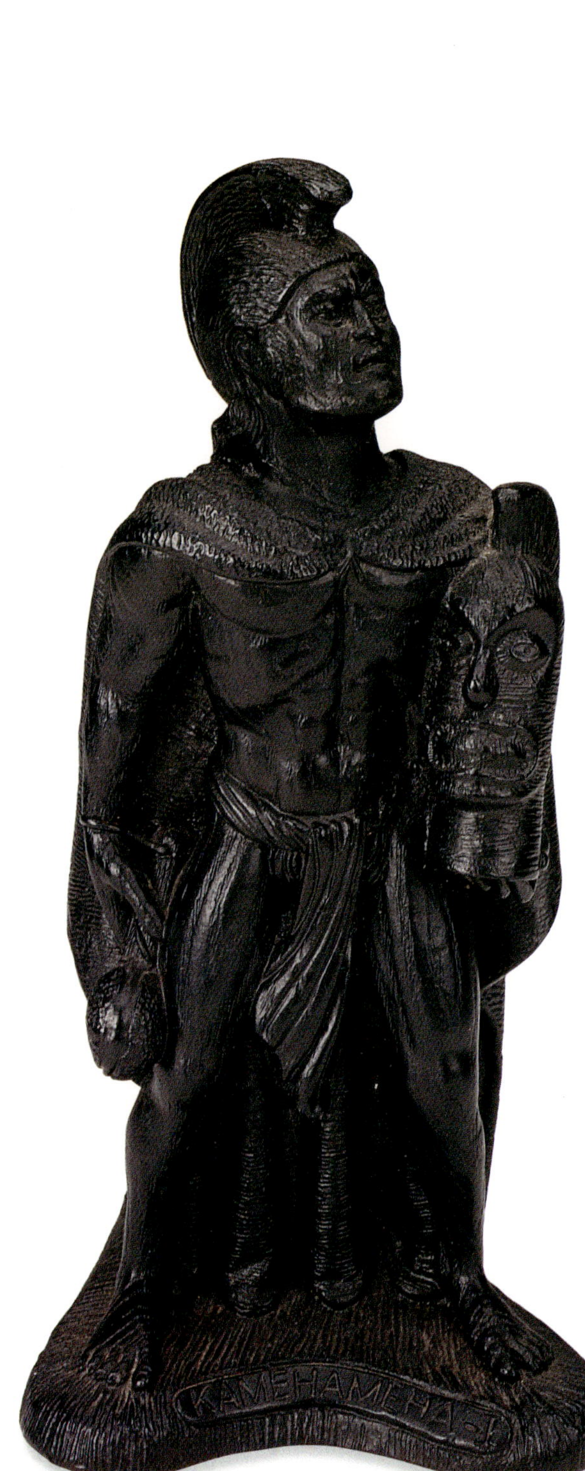

Kamehameha marked, 8" h. Cocojoe's, Made in Hawaii. *Courtesy: Michael Trotter*.

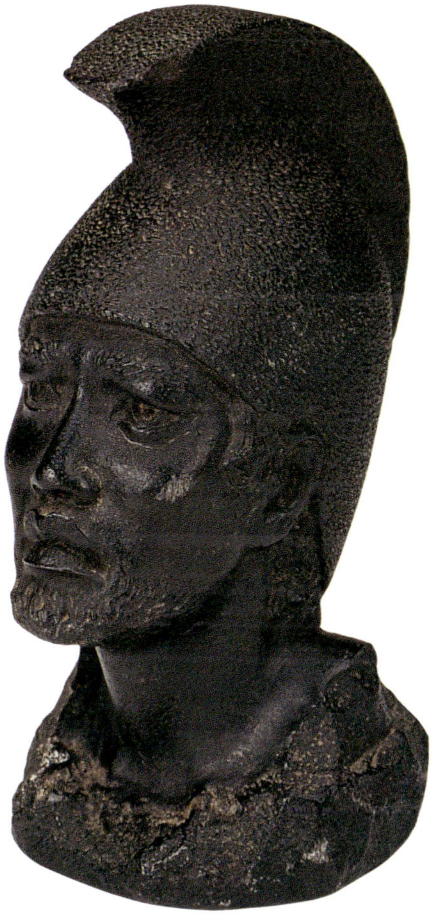

Hawaiian warrior, not marked. 4.5". *Courtesy: the Collection of Brian Goddard & Gene Sweeney.*

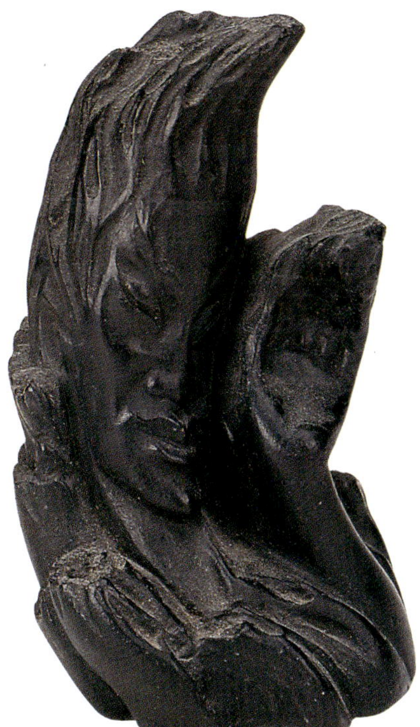

Pele Fire Goddess, from Cocojoe's, Made in Hawaii. 4". *Courtesy: Michael Trotter.*

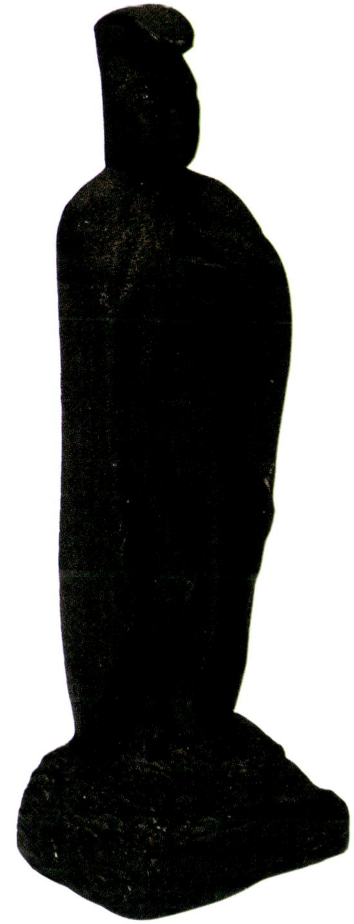

Small Kamehameha figurine. Cocojoe's. 5.5" h. *Courtesy Micheal Trotter*

Warrior, 6.5". Copyright 1970. *Courtesy: Tiki Trader.*

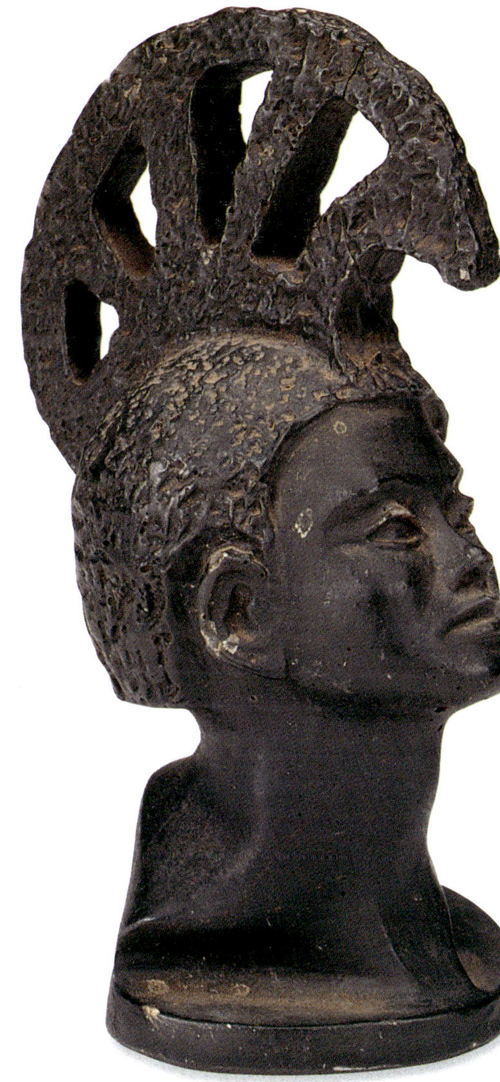

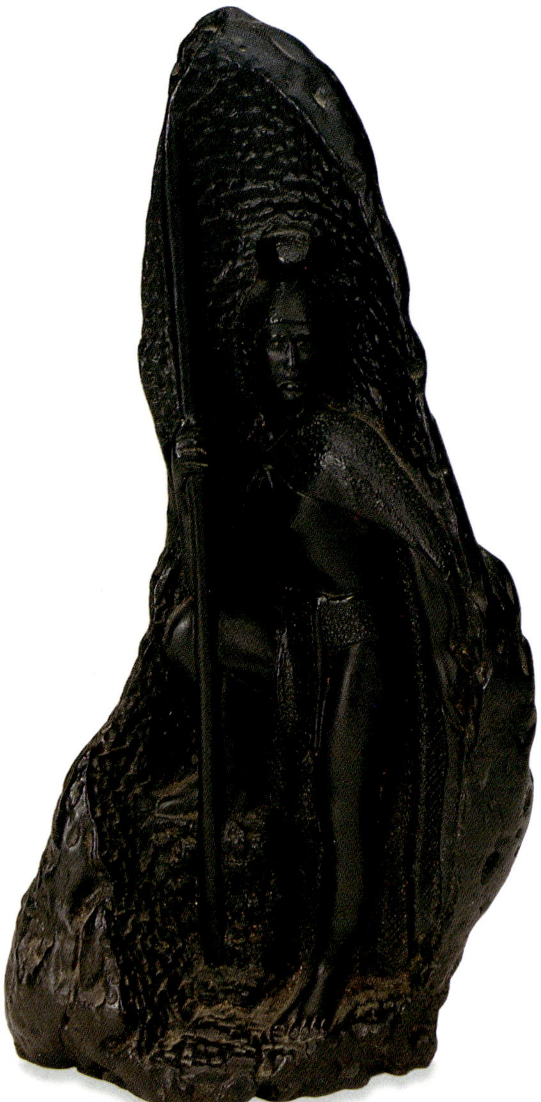

Left:
Kamehameha, 11.5". Cocojoe's.
Courtesy: Michael Trotter.

Below:
A Hip Original. 8" h., made in Hawaii.
Courtesy: Micheal Trotter.

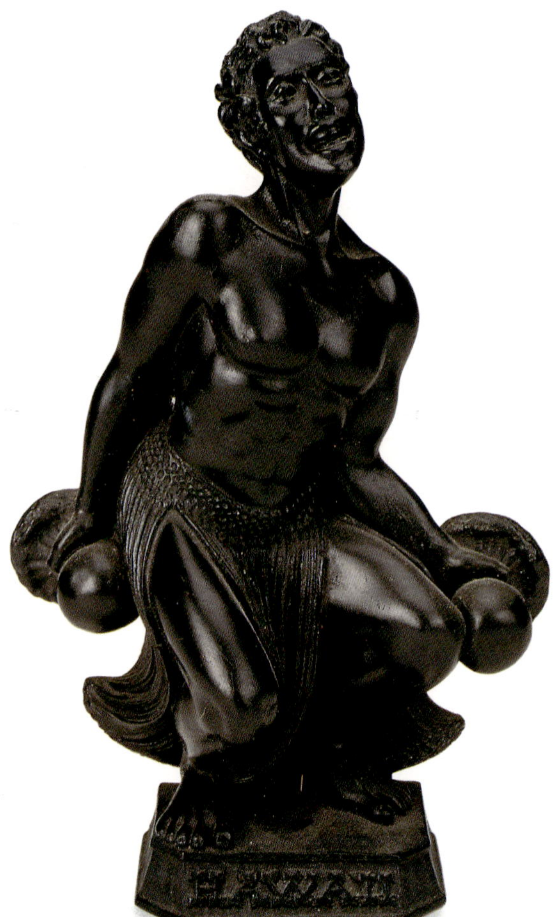

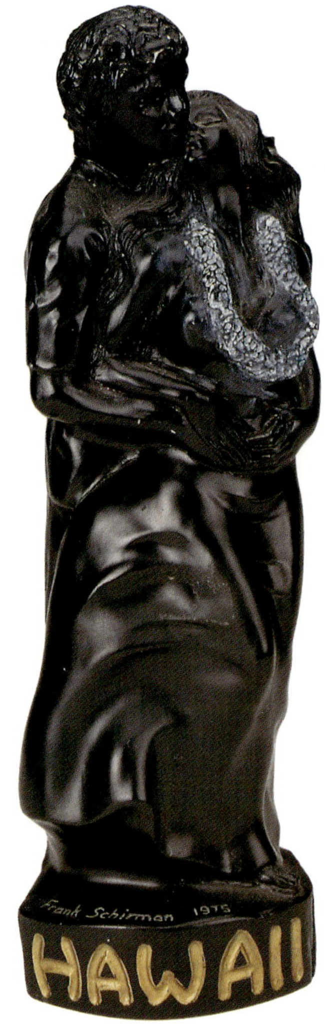

Pilialoha (Love Affair), Beauties with Black Coral, designs by Frank Schirman. Signed Frank Schirman, 1975. 10" h. *Courtesy: Michael Trotter*.

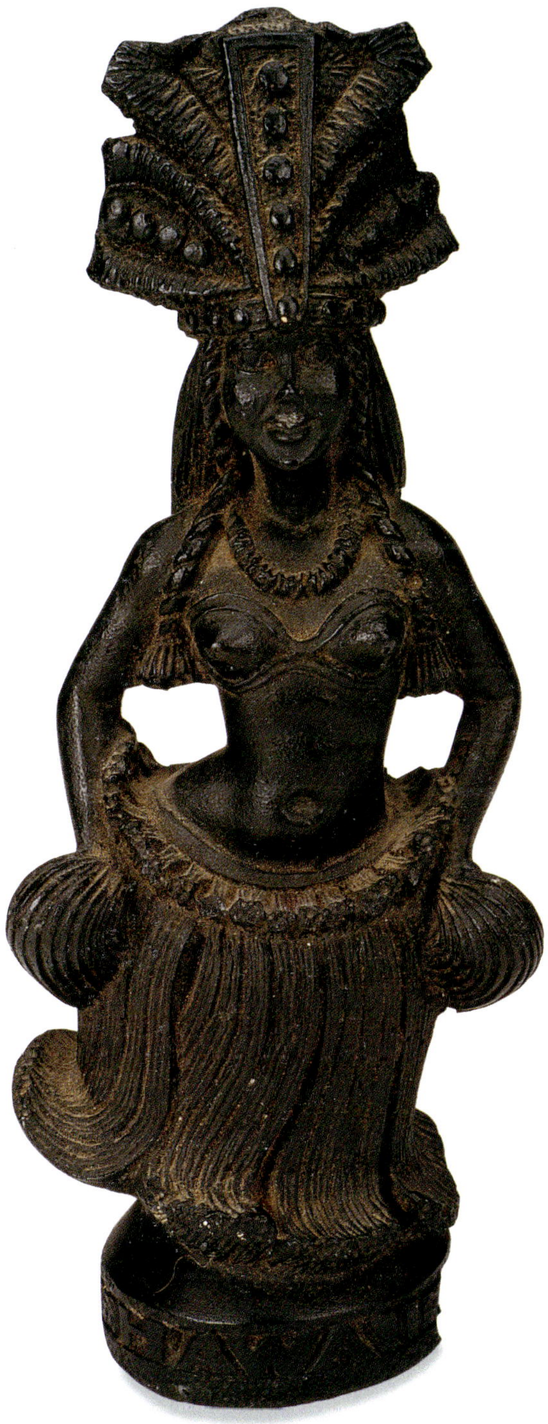

Left:
Hula Dancer. Maker unknown, 7.5" h. *Courtesy: Michael Trotter*.

Below:
Good Luck God, Exotic Black Coral, designed by Frank Schirman. 4" h. *Courtesy: Michael Trotter*.

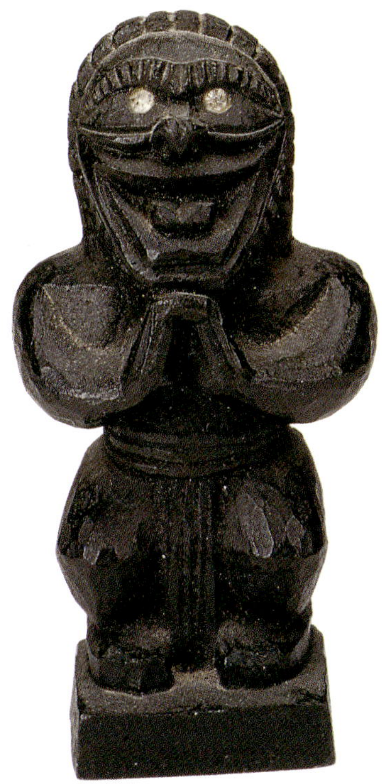

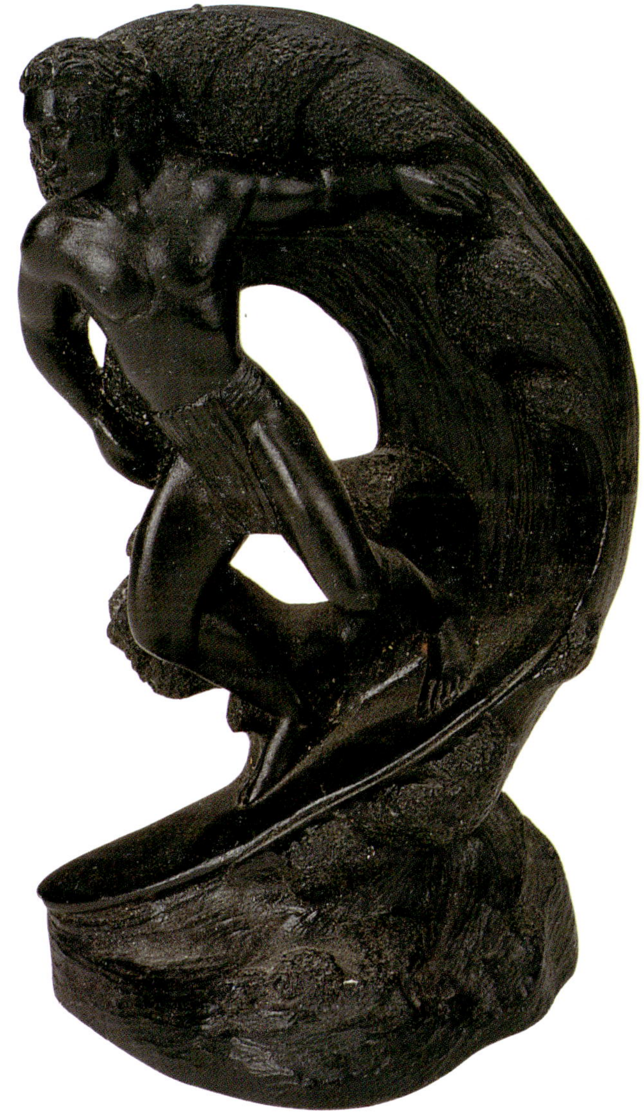

Surfer, 5.75" h. Cocojoe's. *Courtesy: Michael Trotter*.

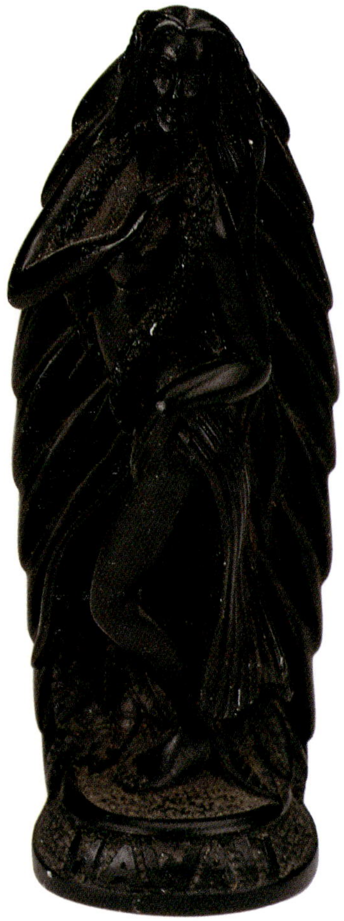

Hula dancer. Cocojoe's, 1980.
Courtesy: Michael Trotter.

Hula dancer. Polyart, 4.75".
Courtesy: Michael Trotter.

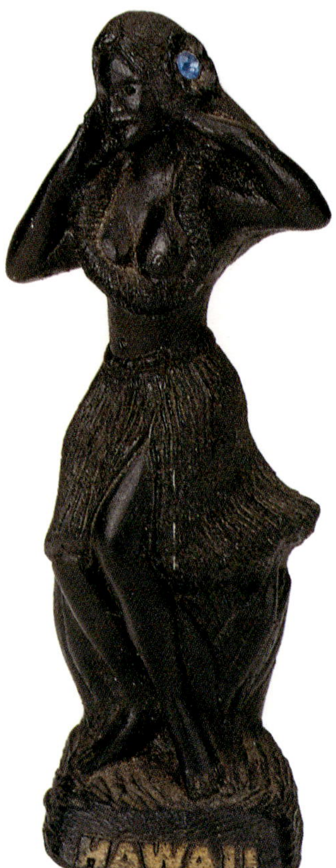

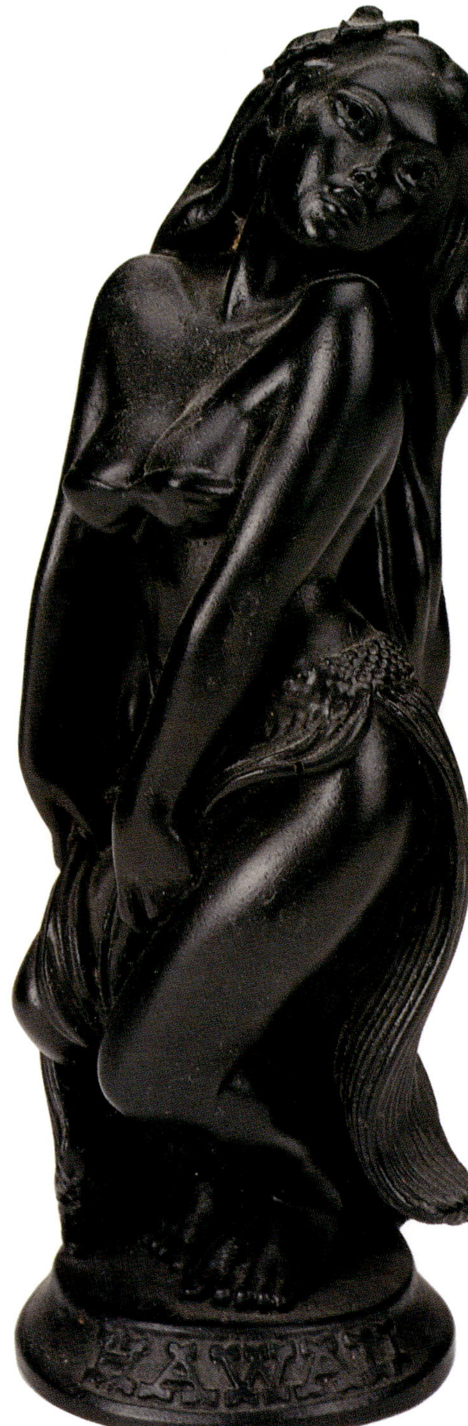

Left:
Hula dancer. Hip Original, 7.5".
Courtesy: Michael Trotter.

Below:
Easter Island Head. Cocojoe's, 4.5".
Courtesy: Michael Trotter.

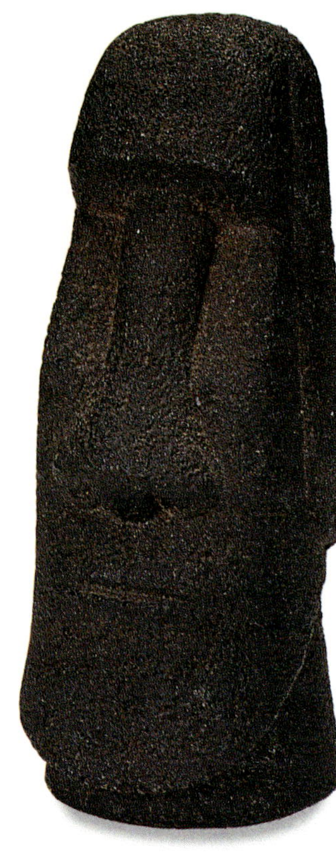

A pile of Menehunes against a surf board. Cocojoe's, copyright 1964. 7.75". *Courtesy: the Collection of Brian Goddard & Gene Sweeney*.

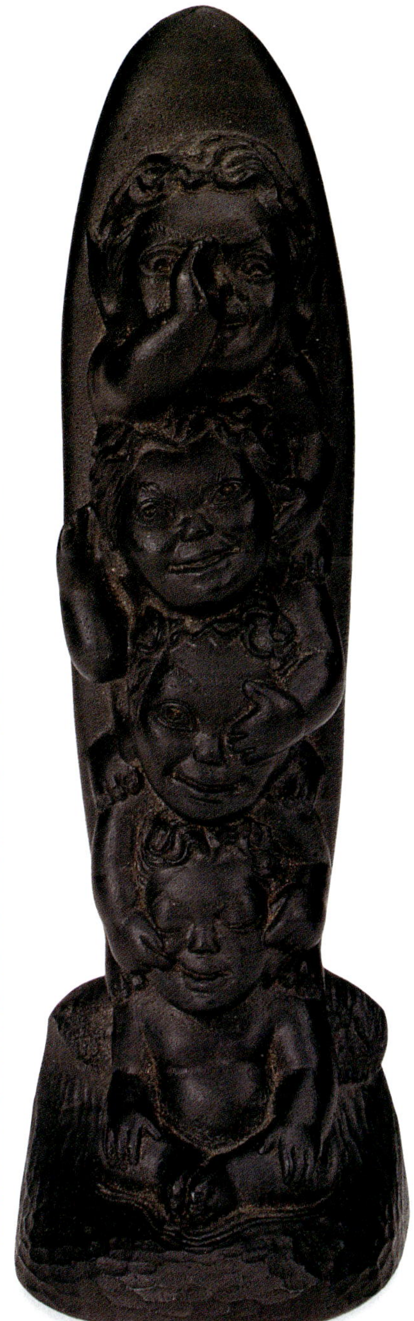

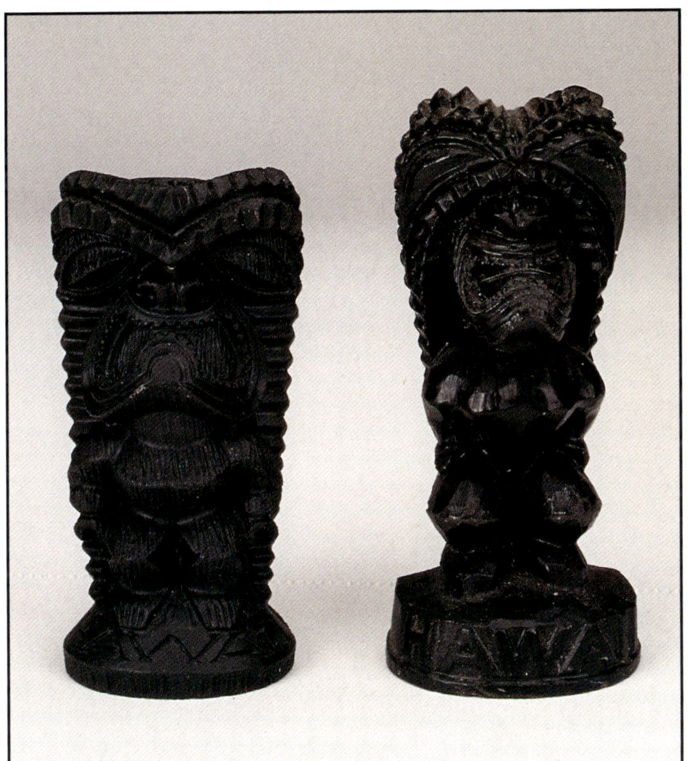

Two Lucky Tikis. The left is from Cocojoes, the right from Hip. 3.5" & 4.0". *Courtesy: Michael Trotter*.

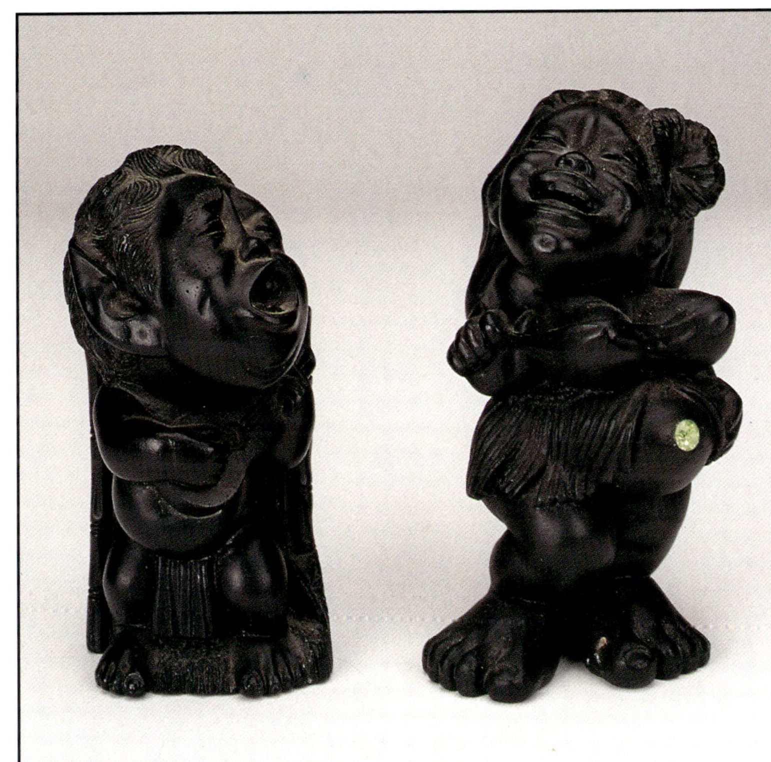

Caricature figures. On the left, the ukelele crooner from Cocojoe's, On the right, a fertility goddess from Hip. 4.25" & 4.75". *Courtesy: the Collection of Brian Goddard & Gene Sweeney and Michael Trotter*.

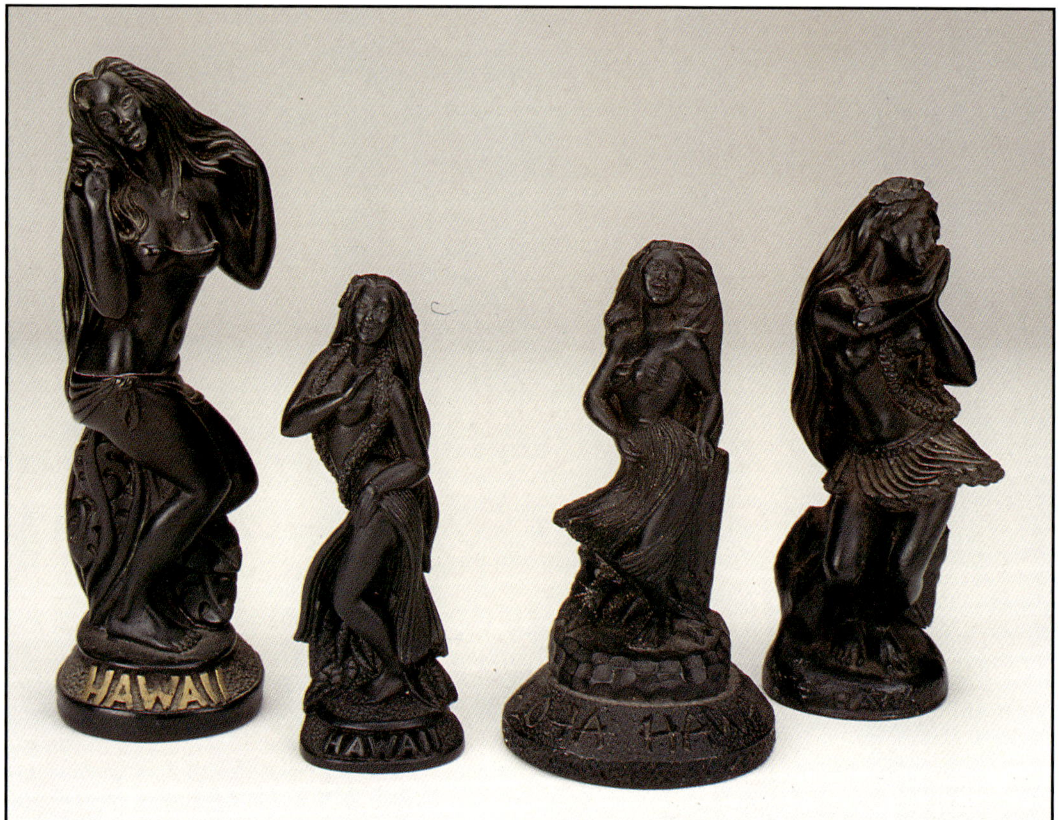

Hula dancers. Left to right: Cocojoe's, 7", Cocojoe's, 4.75", Cocojoe's, 5", Hip, 5.5". *Courtesy: Michael Trotter and the Collection of Brian Goddard & Gene Sweeney.*

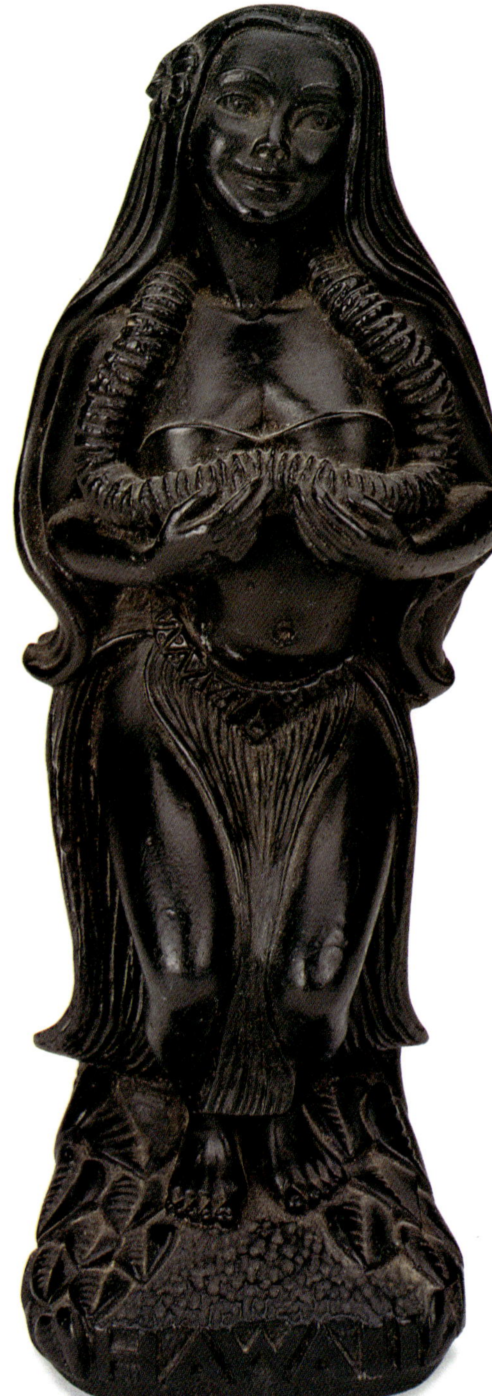

Unmarked hula dancer, sculpted in the round. 8.5" h. *Courtesy: Michael Trotter.*

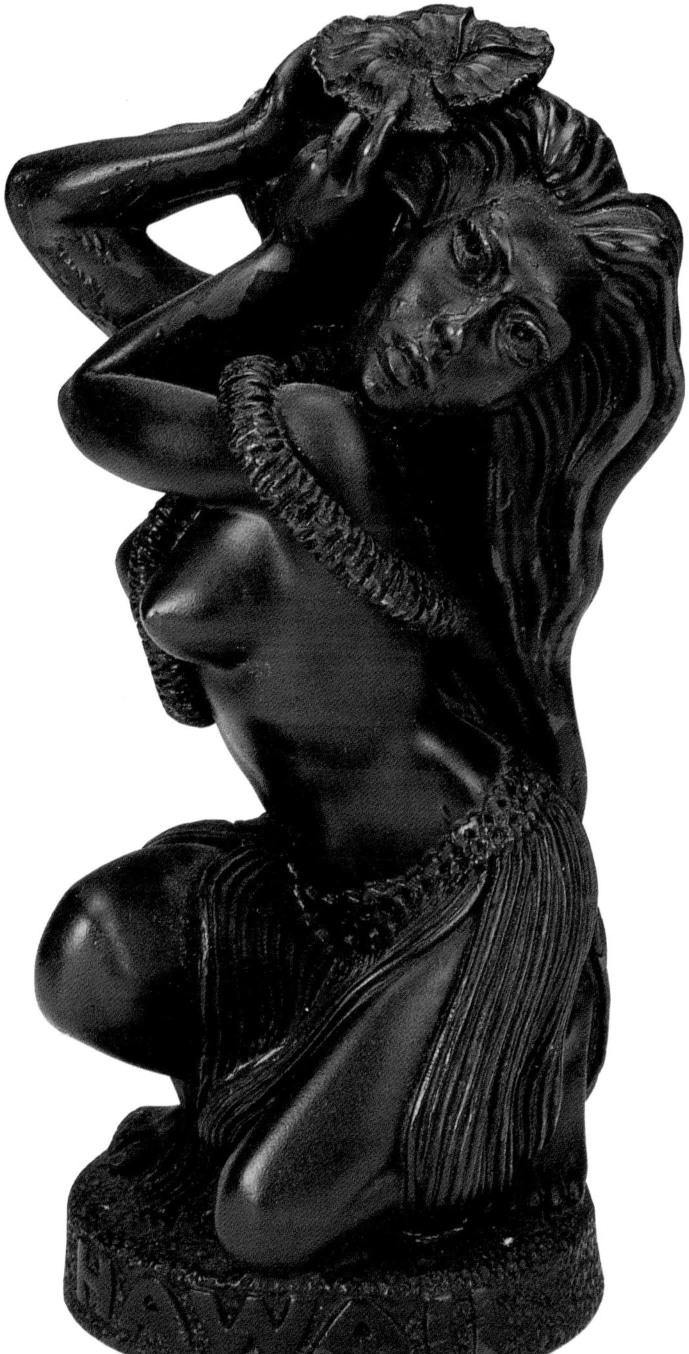

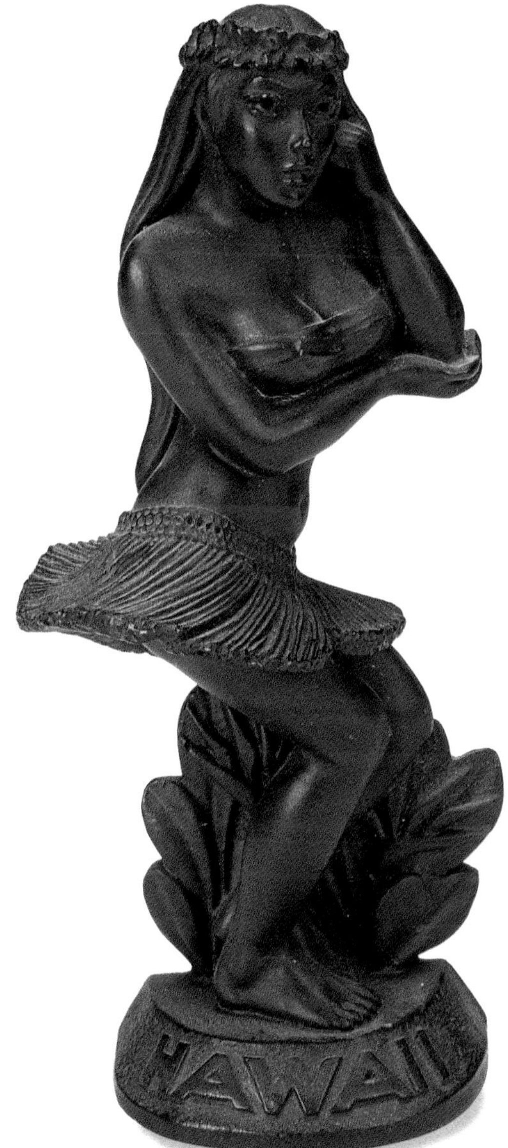

Left:
Hula Dancer by Hip, 7.25". *Courtesy: Michael Trotter*.

Below:
Caricature surfer by Cocojoe's. 5.75". *Courtesy: the Collection of Brian Goddard & Gene Sweeney*.

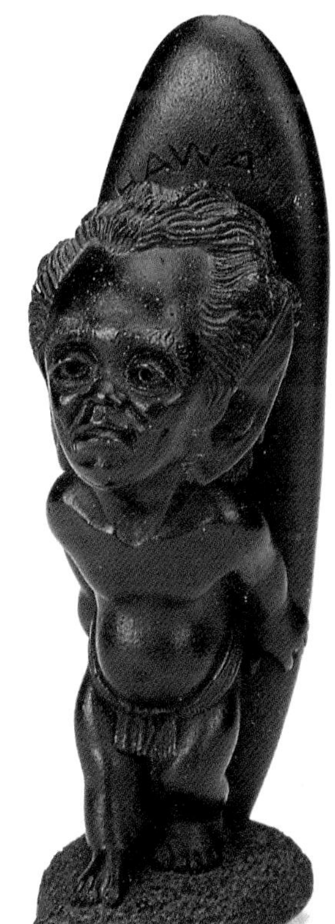

Large hula dancer. Hip copyright 1973. 10" h. *Courtesy: Michael Trotter*.

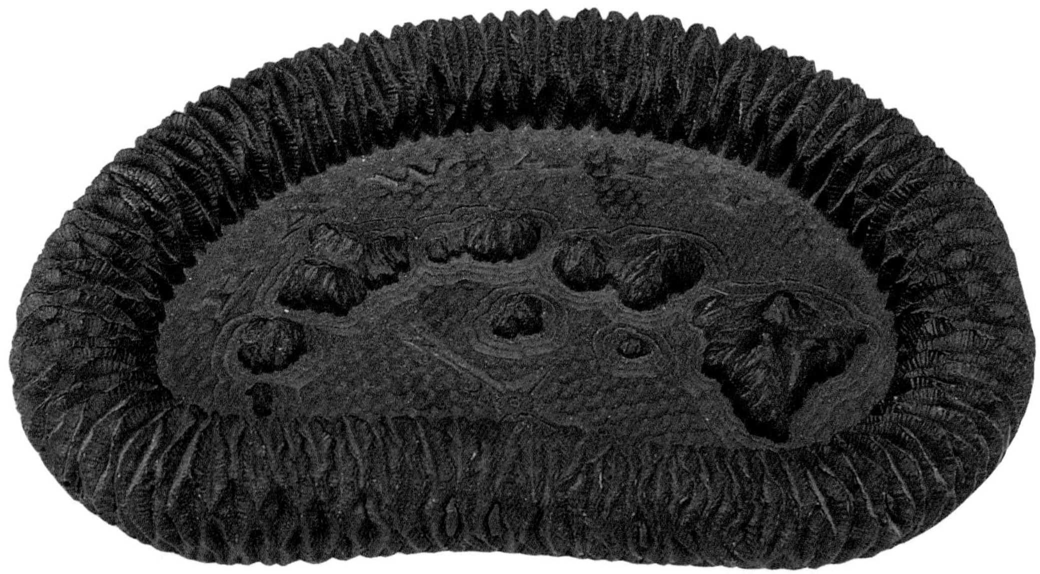

Left:
Hawaiian Islands ashtray, 6.5" w. *Courtesy: Michael Trotter*.

Below:
Aloha Hawaii ashtray, 7" sq. *Courtesy: the Collection of Brian Goddard & Gene Sweeney*.

Ashtray. Hip 5.25" d. *Courtesy: the Collection of Brian Goddard & Gene Sweeney*.

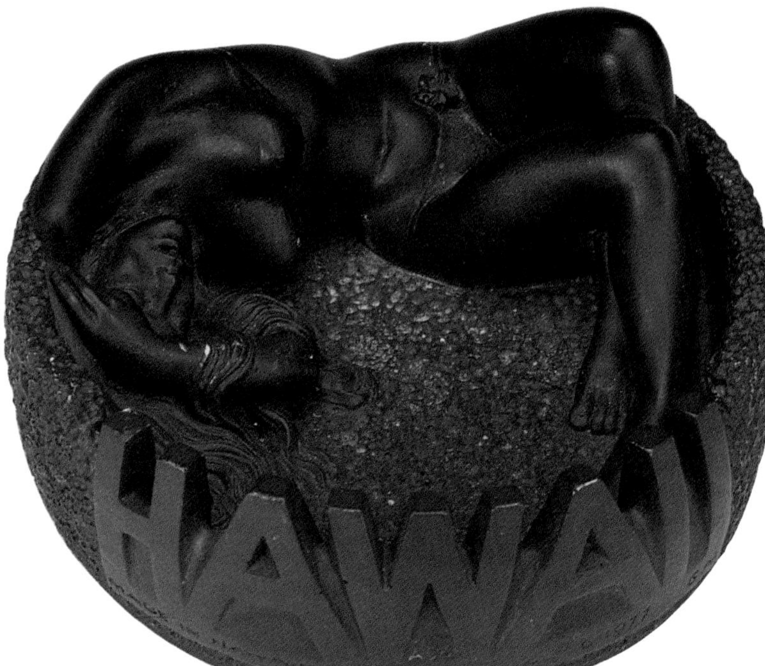

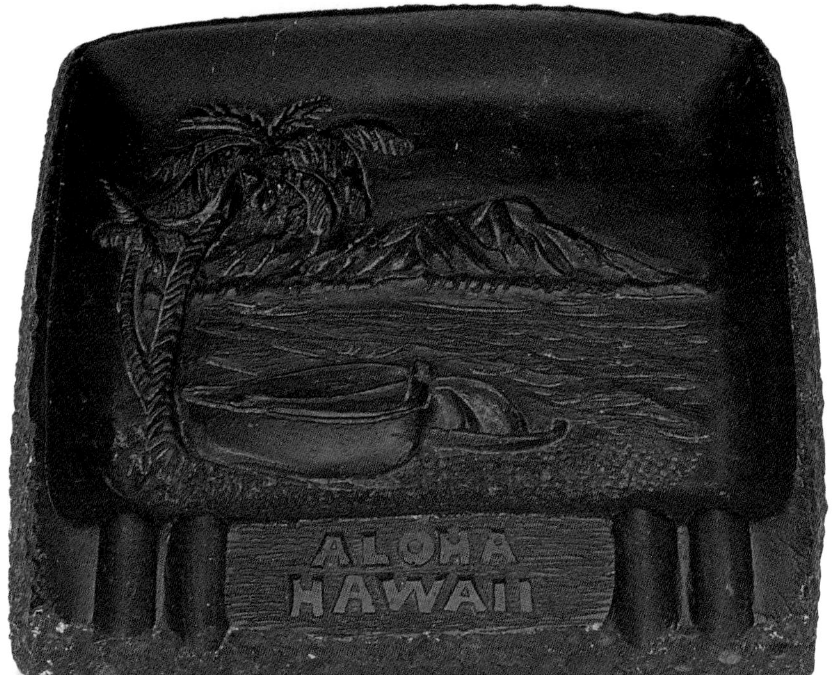

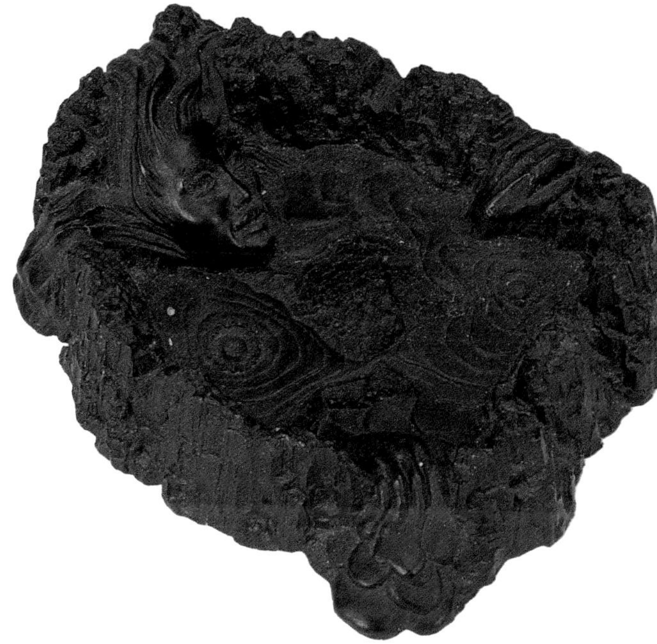

Left:
Pele ashtray from Cocojoe's. 5.75" w. *Courtesy: Michael Trotter*.

Below:
Aloha Hawaii ashtray. 8" wide. *Courtesy: Michael Trotter*.

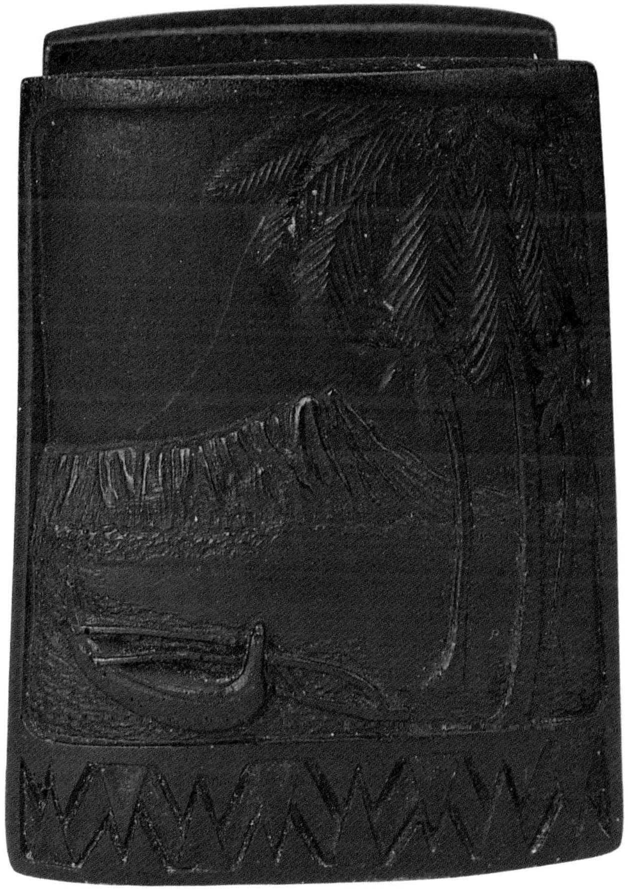

Napkin holder from Cocojoe's. 4" h. *Courtesy: the Collection of Brian Goddard & Gene Sweeney*.

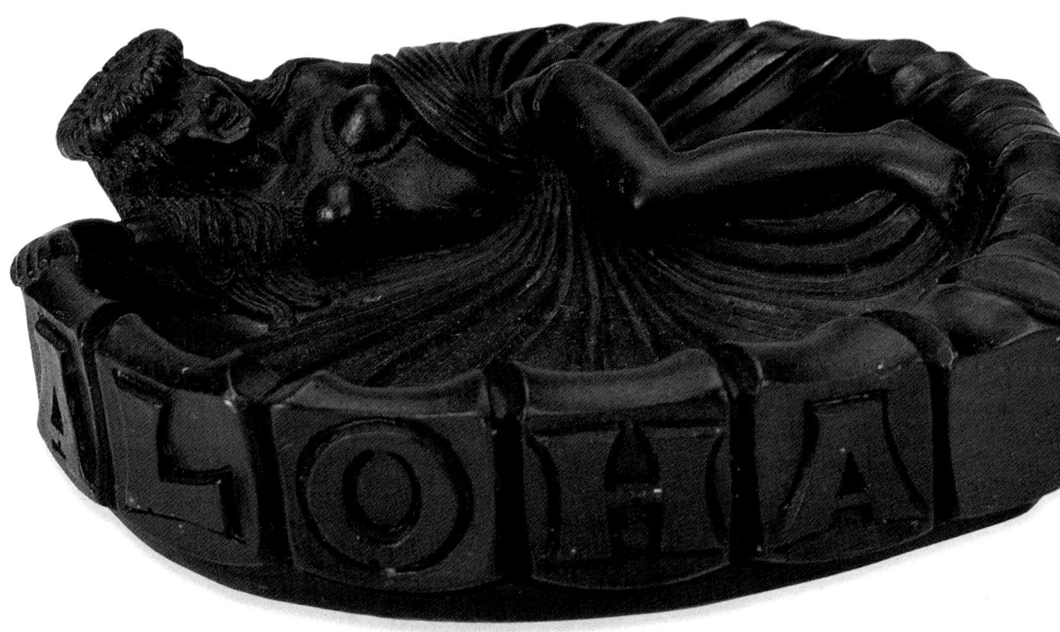

Food and Drink Hawaiian Style

Table and Kitchen Ware

Santa Anita Ware, copyright 1949, The Flowers of Hawaii styled by Iranda made in California. Red Anthurium. *Courtesy: K.C. Heylin.*

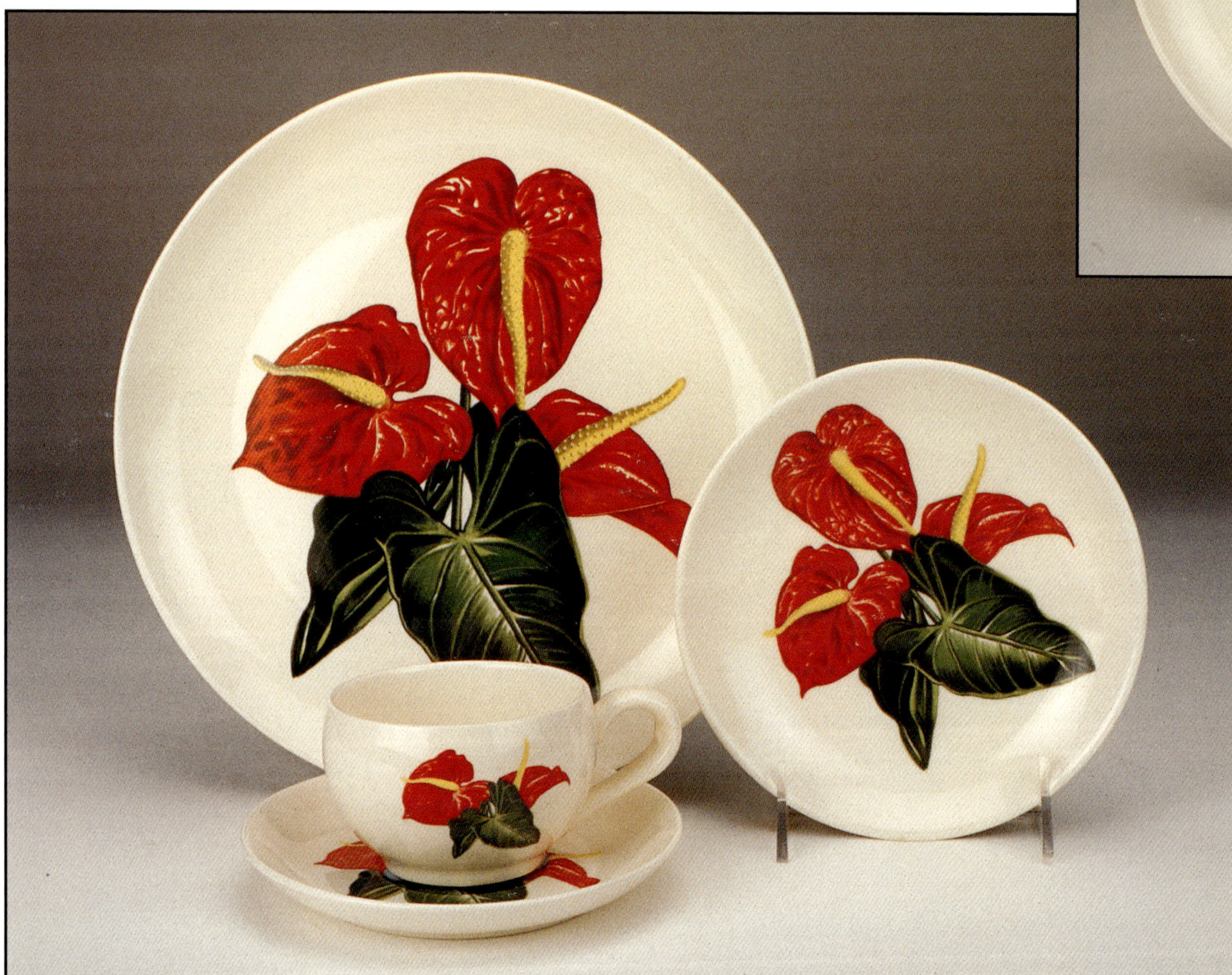

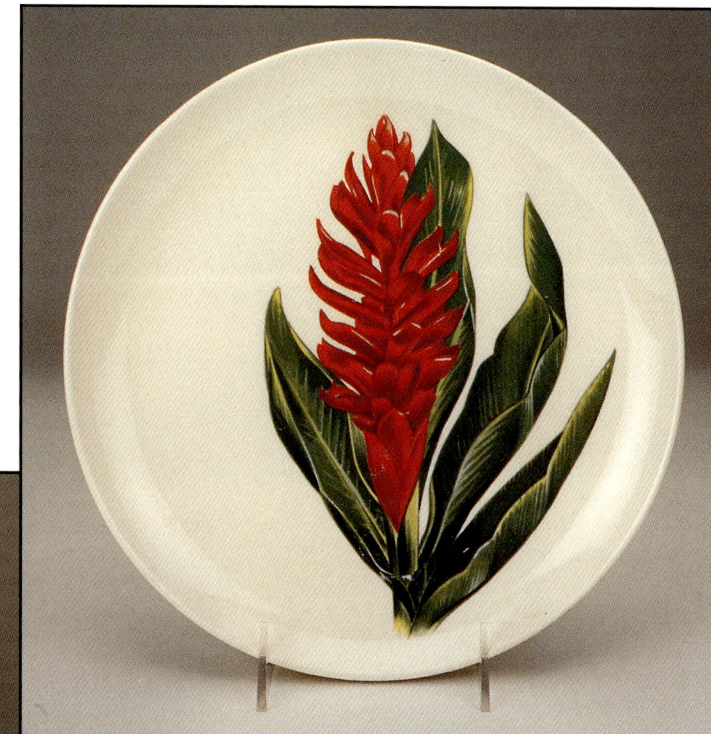

Red Ginger. *Courtesy: K.C. Heylin.*

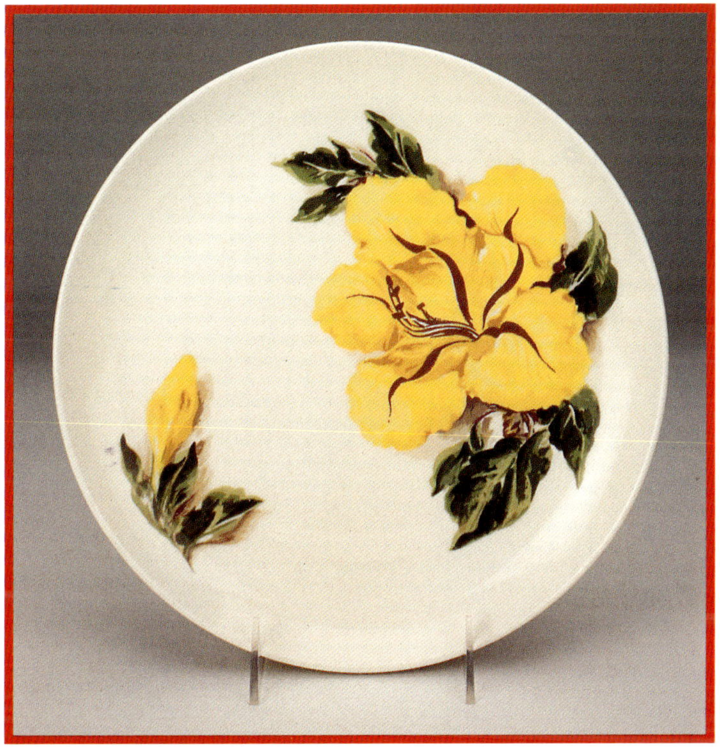

Cup of Gold. *Courtesy: K.C. Heylin*.

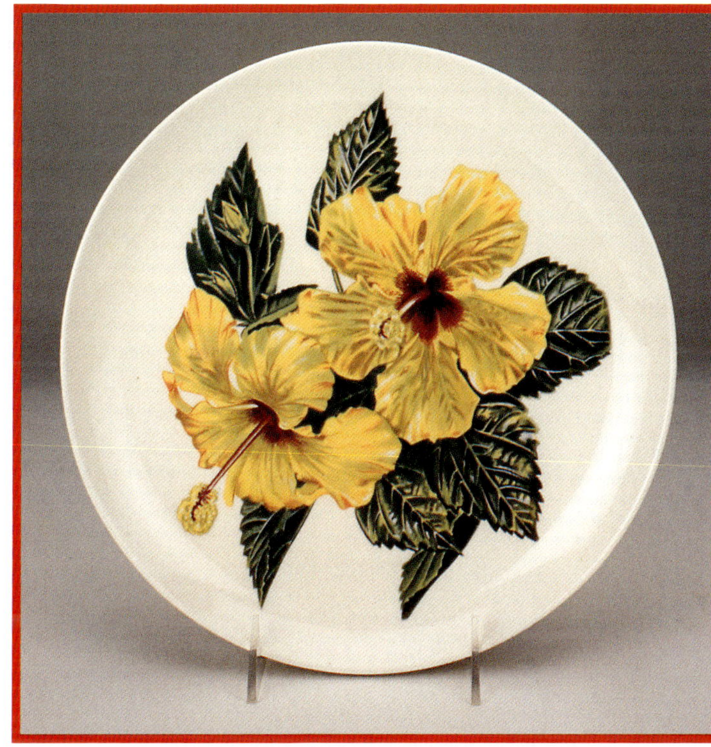

Yellow Hibiscus. *Courtesy: K.C. Heylin*.

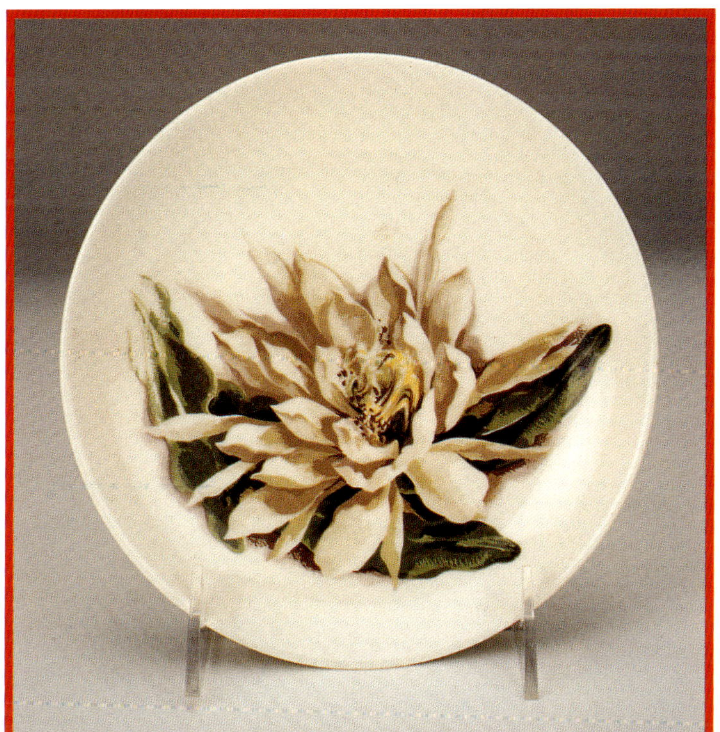

Night Blooming Cereus. *Courtesy: K.C. Heylin*.

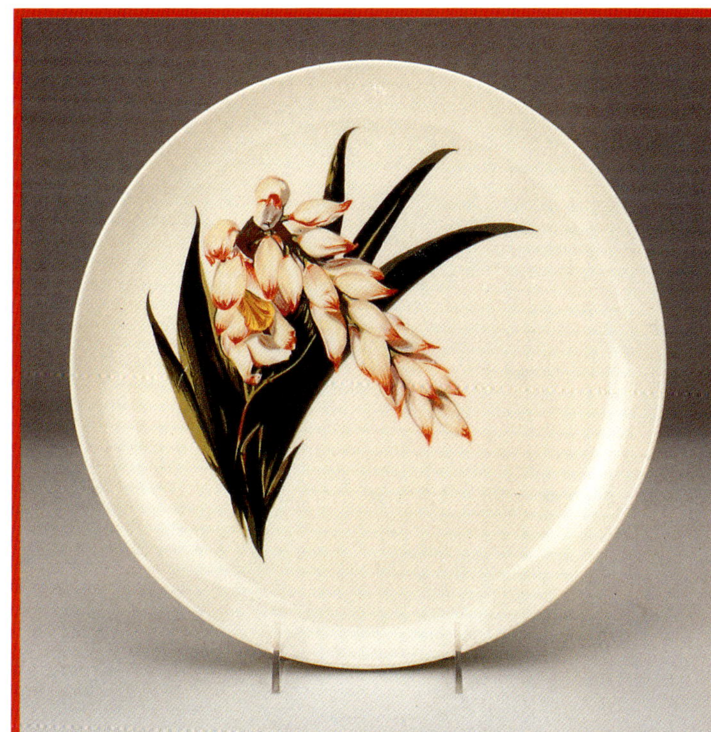

Shell Ginger. *Courtesy: K.C. Heylin*.

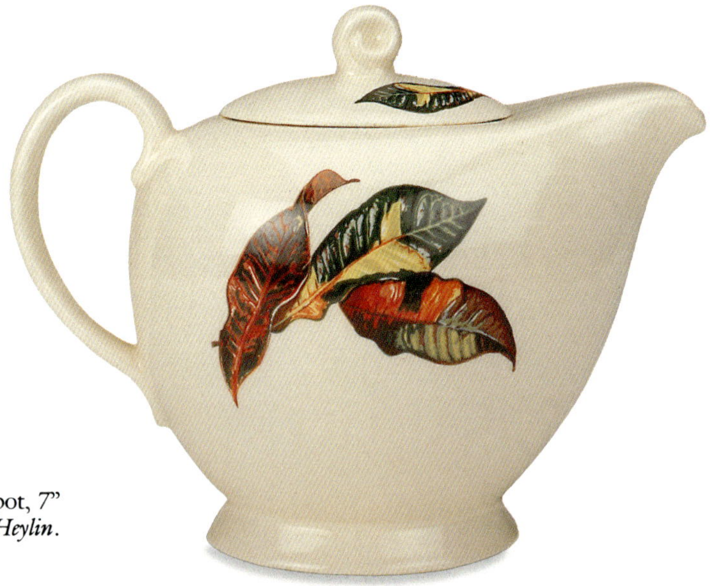

Croton Leaves teapot, 7" h. *Courtesy: K.C. Heylin.*

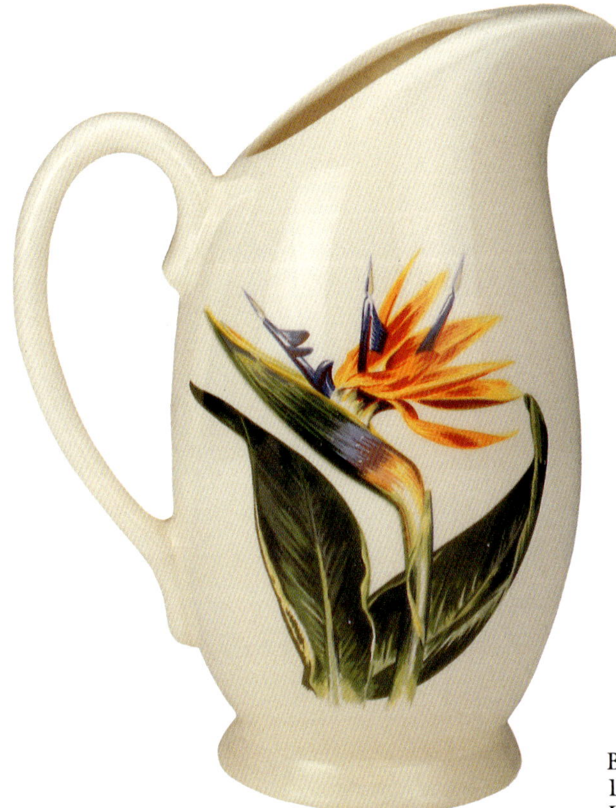

Bird of Paradise pitcher, 12" h. *Courtesy: K.C. Heylin.*

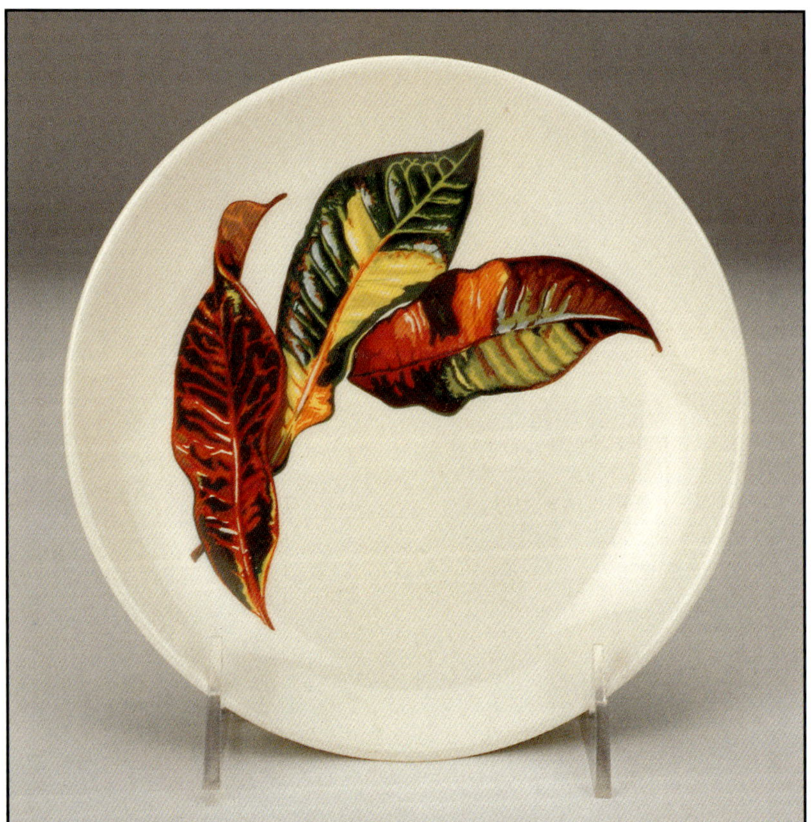

Croton Leaves. *Courtesy: K.C. Heylin.*

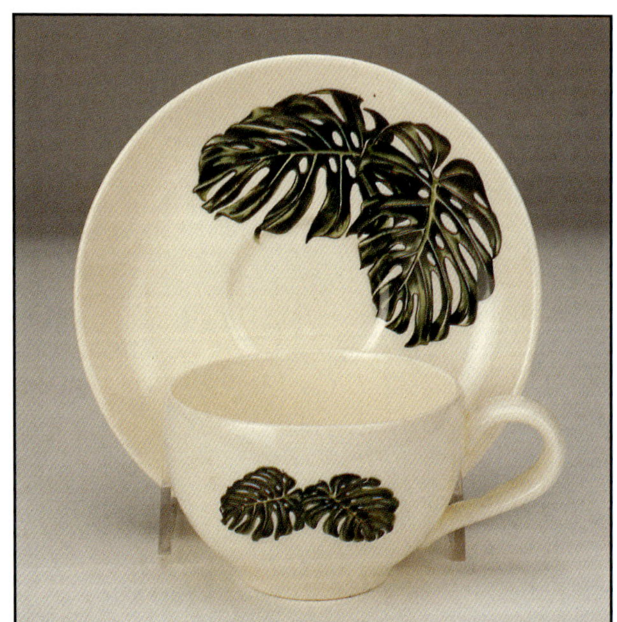

Monstera Leaves. *Courtesy: K.C. Heylin.*

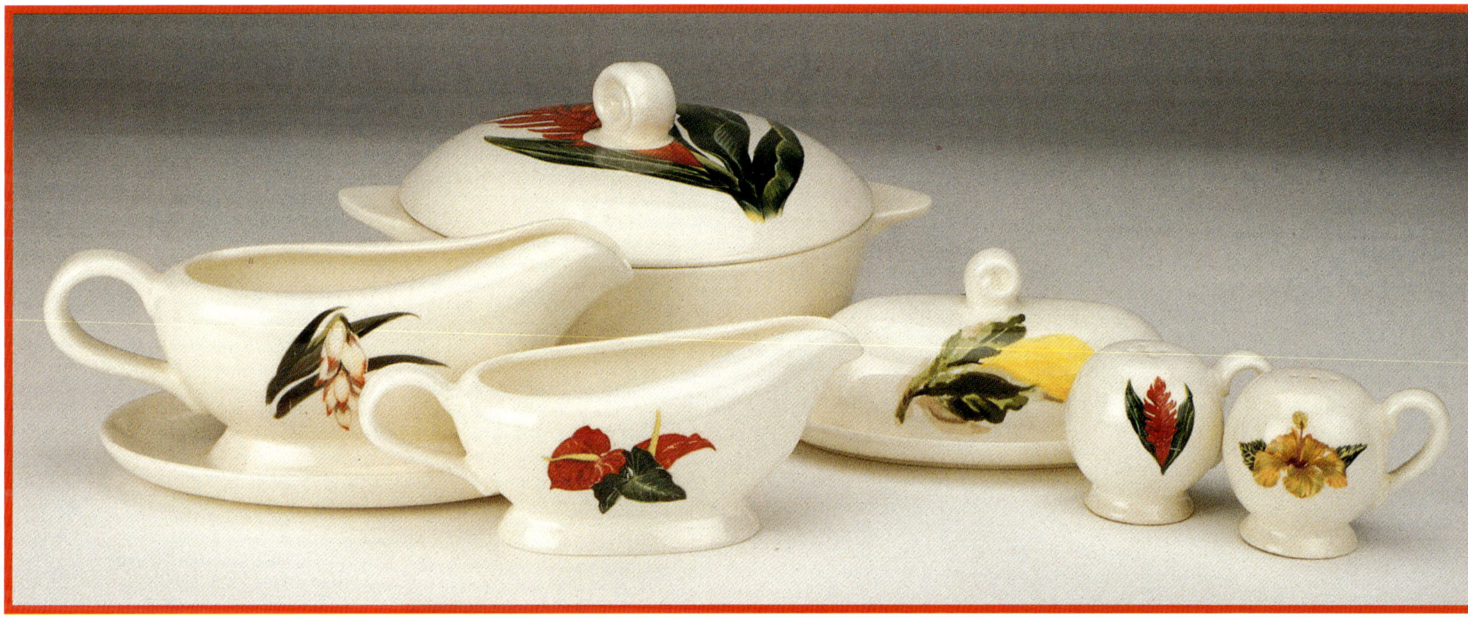

Santa Anita serving pieces in a variety of forms and patterns.*Courtesy: K.C. Heylin*.

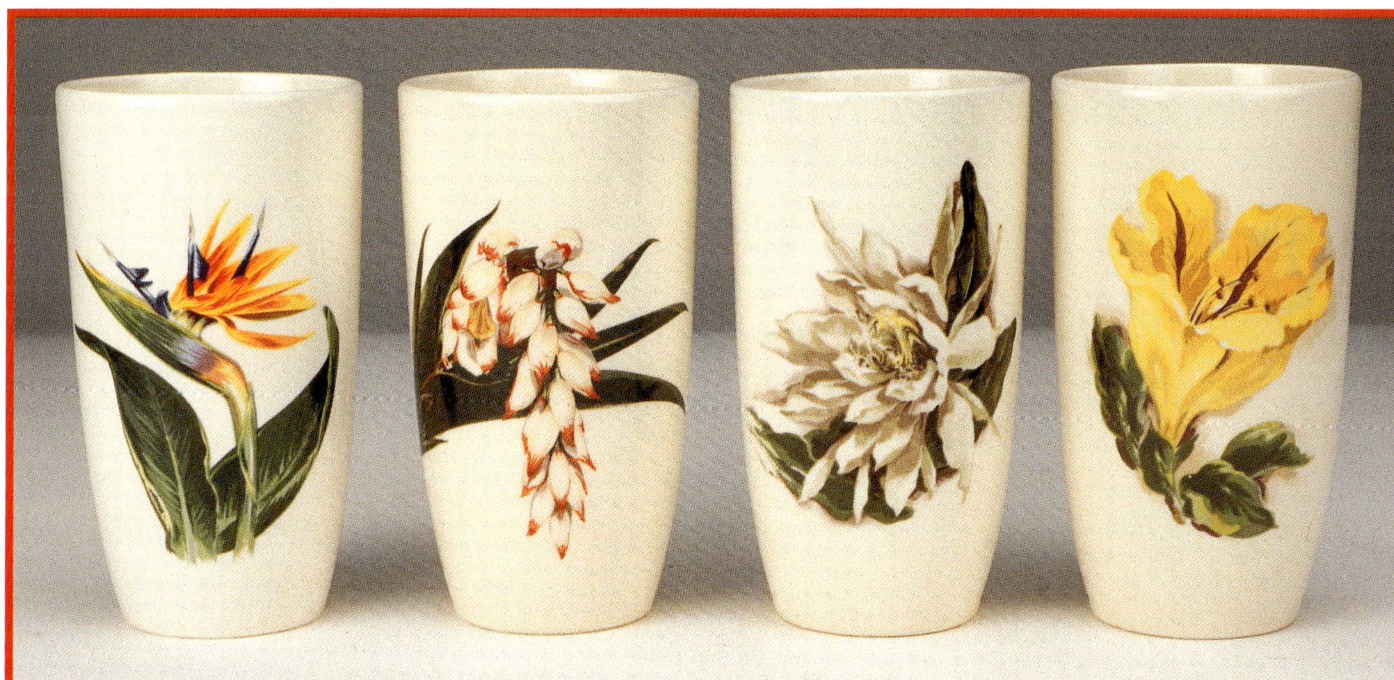

Set of four goblets with Santa Anita patterns. *Courtesy: Jim & Susie Stiso*.

Right:
Lei Lani by Vernon Kilns, produced from 1939-1955. Dinner plate, side plate, and cup and saucer. The design is by Don Blanding (1894-1957), known as the "Hawaiian Poet."He was the first artist to execute Hawaiian designs for Vernon Kilns. *Courtesy: K.C. Heylin.*

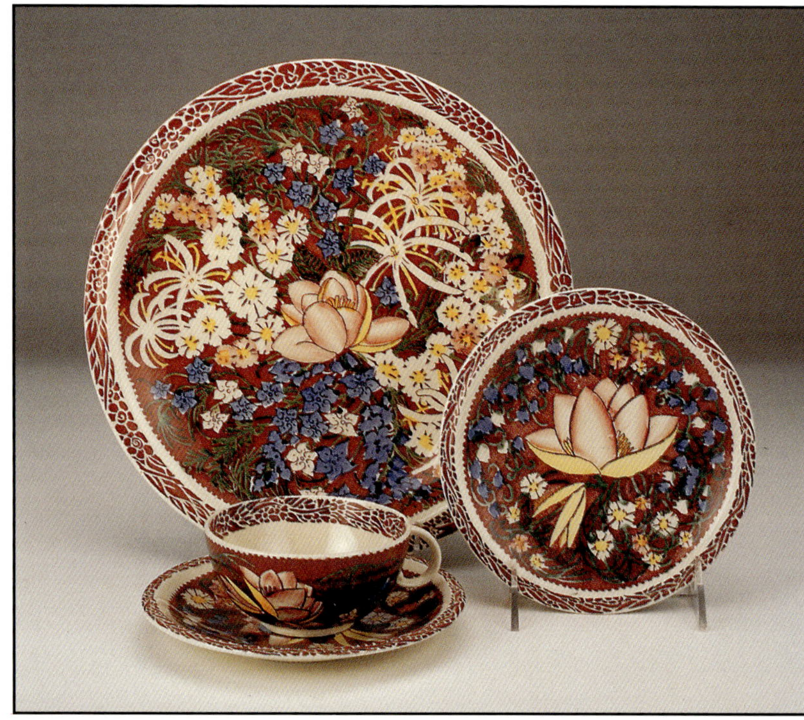

Below:
Coffee pot in Lei Lani. *Courtesy: Jim & Susie Stiso.*

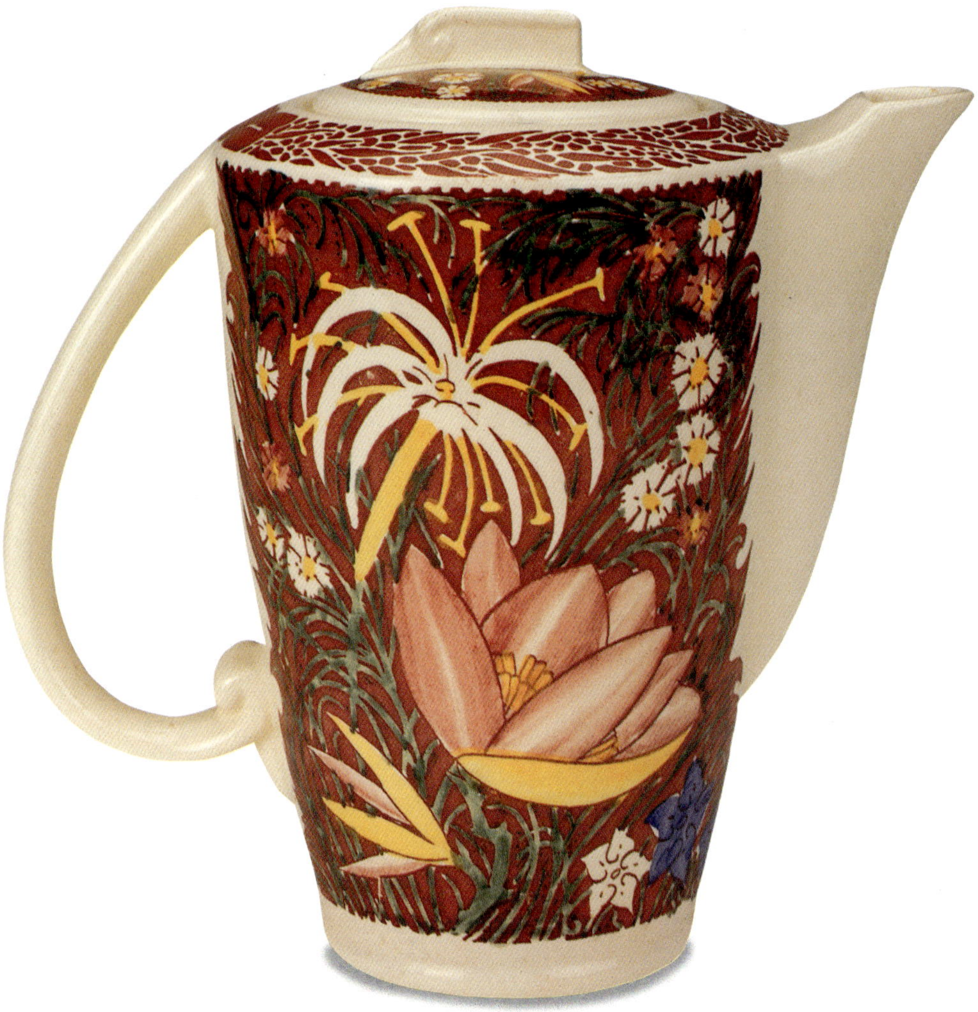

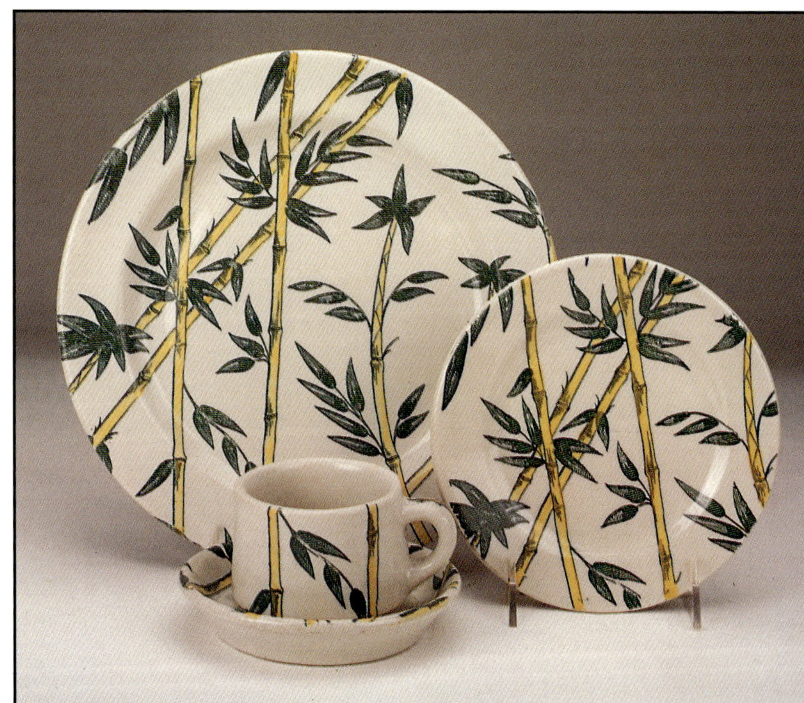

Tepco Bamboo pattern. *Courtesy: Michael & Denise Queen.*

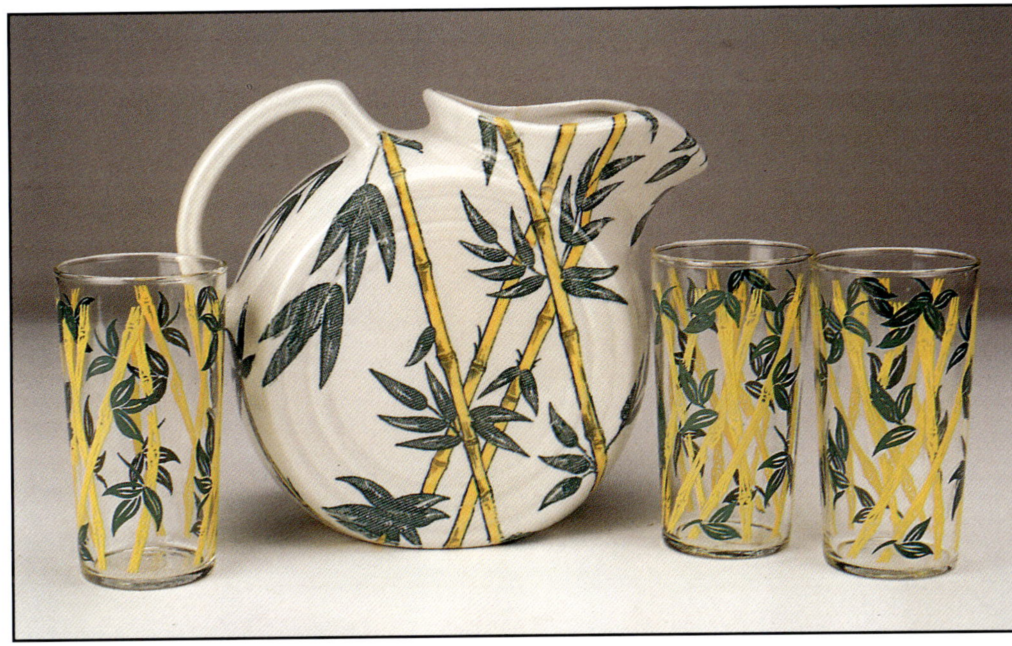

Pitcher and glasses in the Bamboo pattern. *Courtesy: Michael & Denise Queen.*

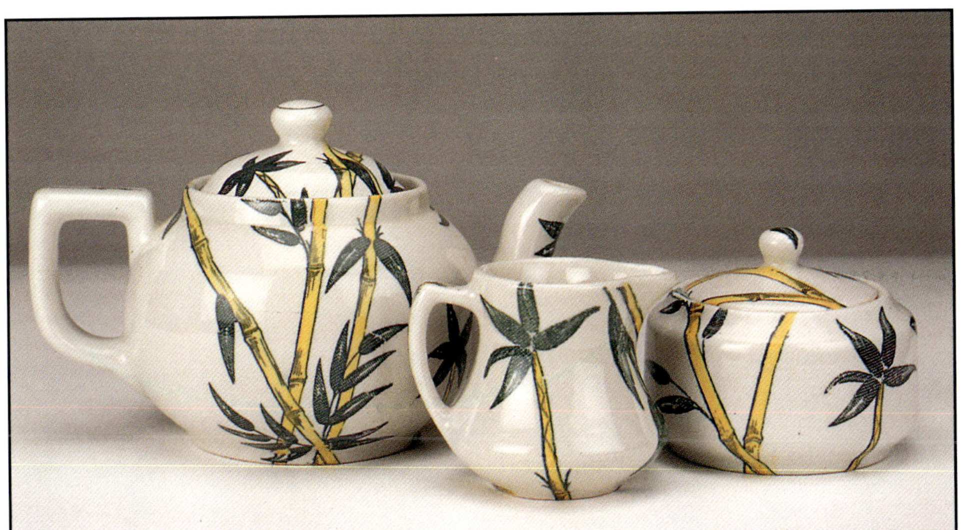

Bamboo teapot, creamer, and sugar. *Courtesy: Michael & Denise Queen.*

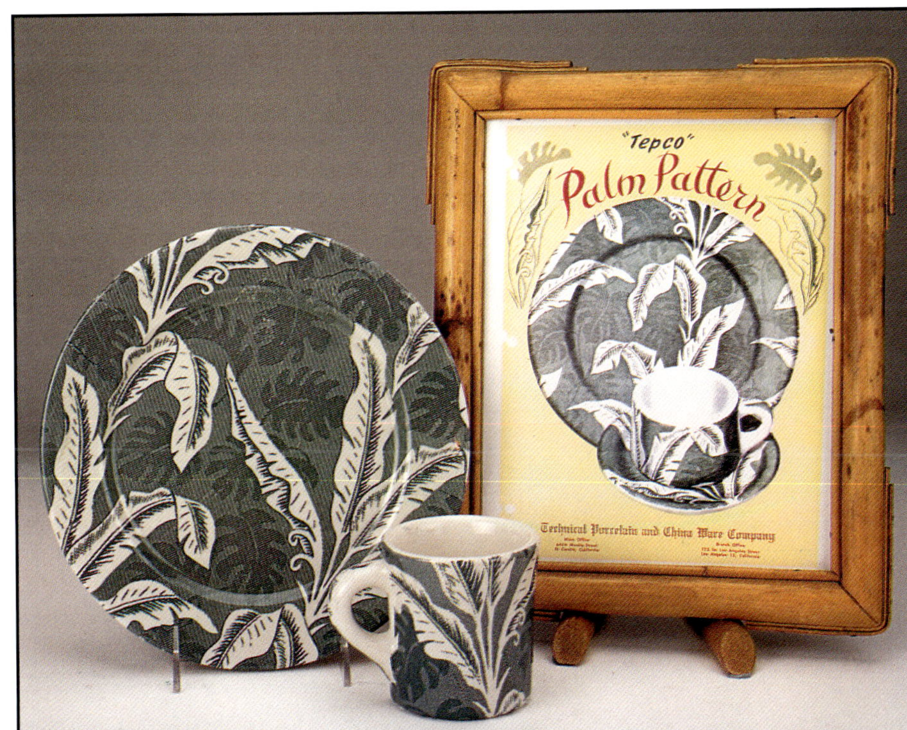

Tepco Palm Pattern with advertisement. *Courtesy: Michael & Denise Queen.*

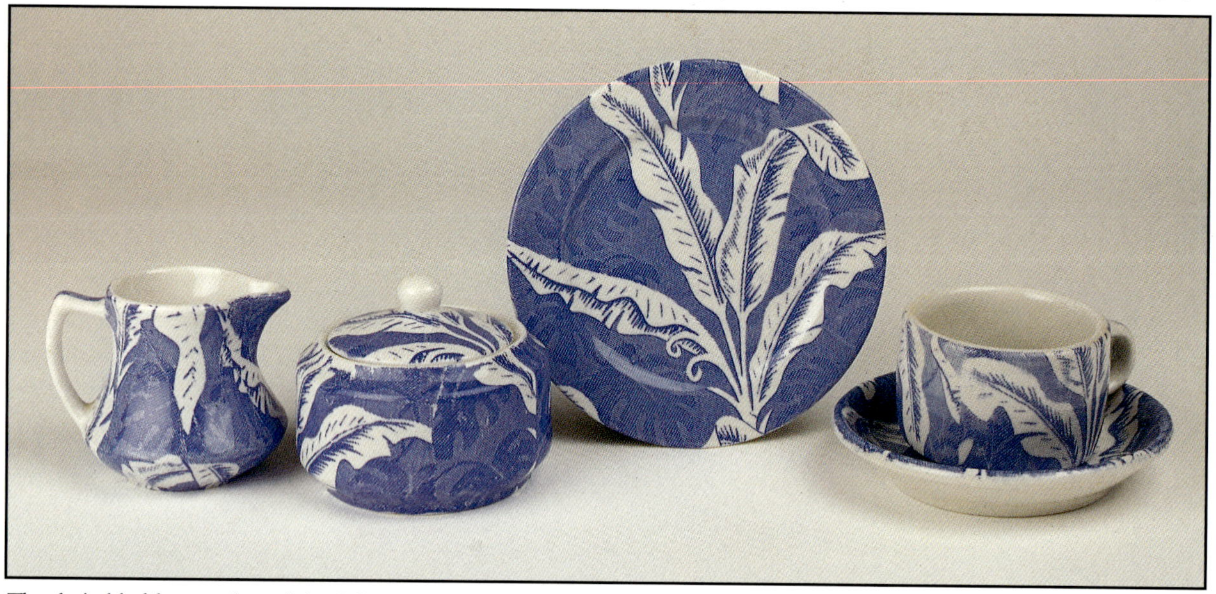

The desirable blue version of the Palm Pattern, shown here in the sugar and creamer, sandwich plate, and cup and saucer. *Courtesy: Michael & Denise Queen.*

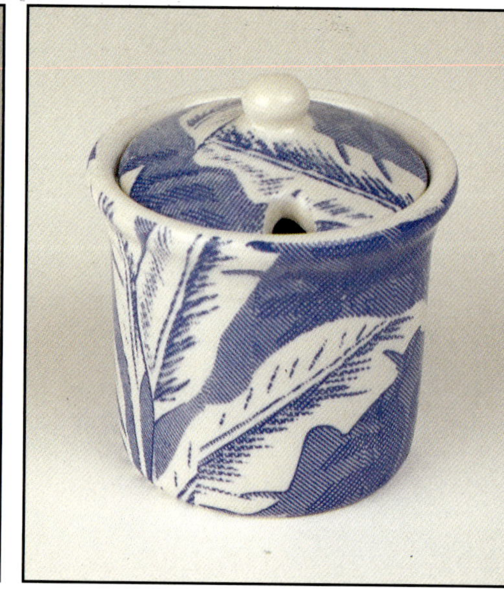

Covered jam jar in the blue Palm Pattern. *Courtesy: Michael & Denise Queen.*

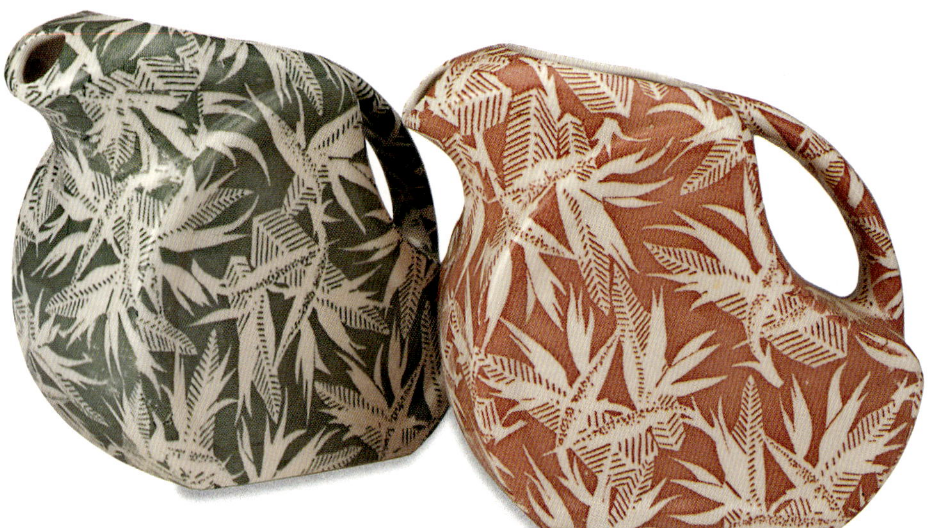

Pitchers by Wallace China, Los Angeles. 8" h. *Courtesy: Michael & Denise Queen.*

Pitchers by Wallace China. *Courtesy: Michael & Denise Queen.*

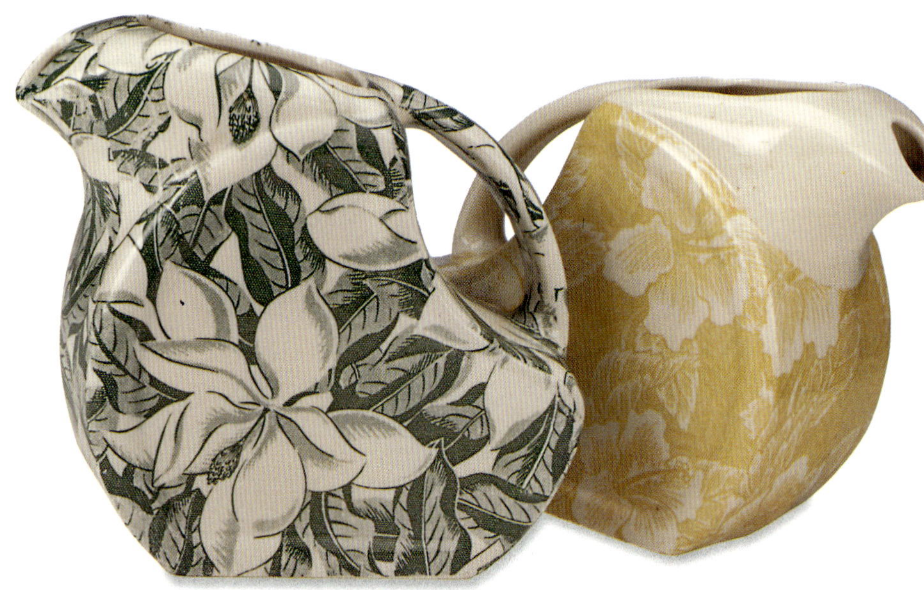

Right:
Tepco pitchers in the Palm Pattern. *Courtesy: Michael & Denise Queen*.

Below left:
Chop plate in lei design by Don Blanding for Vernon Kilns. *Courtesy: Jim & Susie Stiso*.

Below right:
Chop plate in fish design by Don Blanding for Vernon Kilns. *Courtesy: Jim & Susie Stiso*.

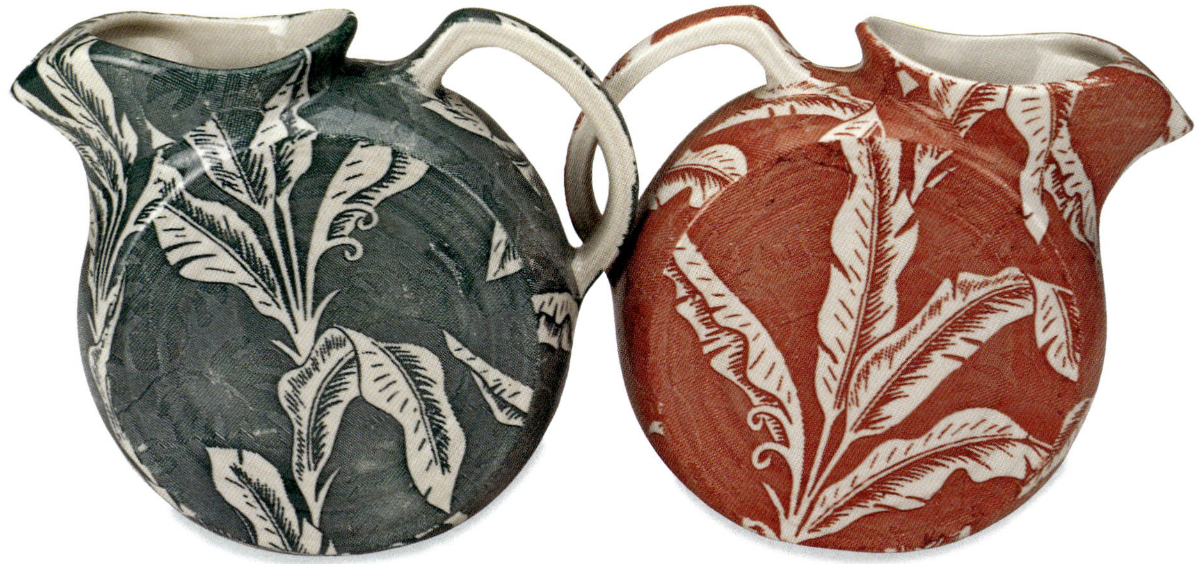

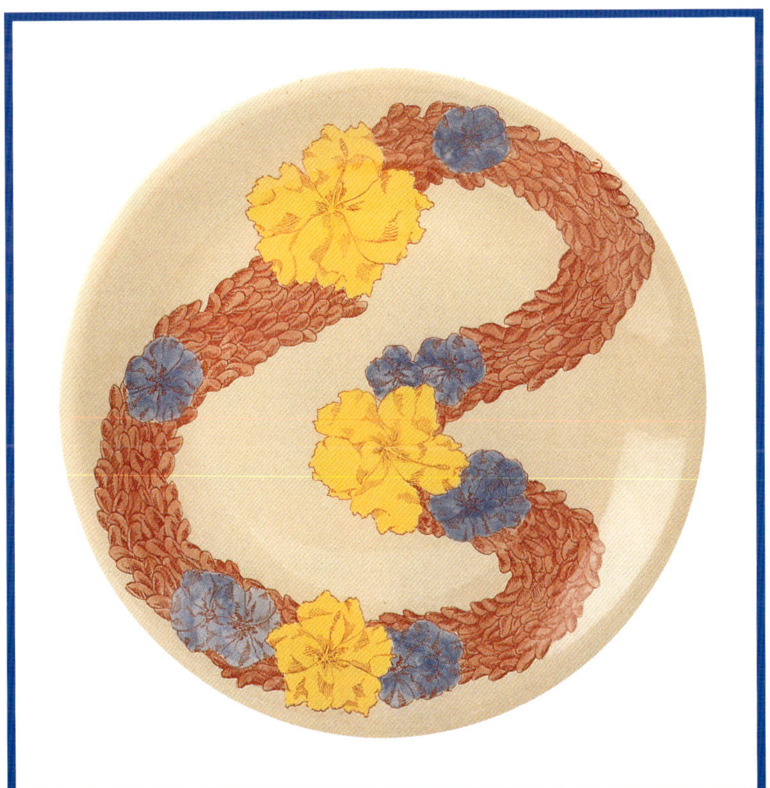

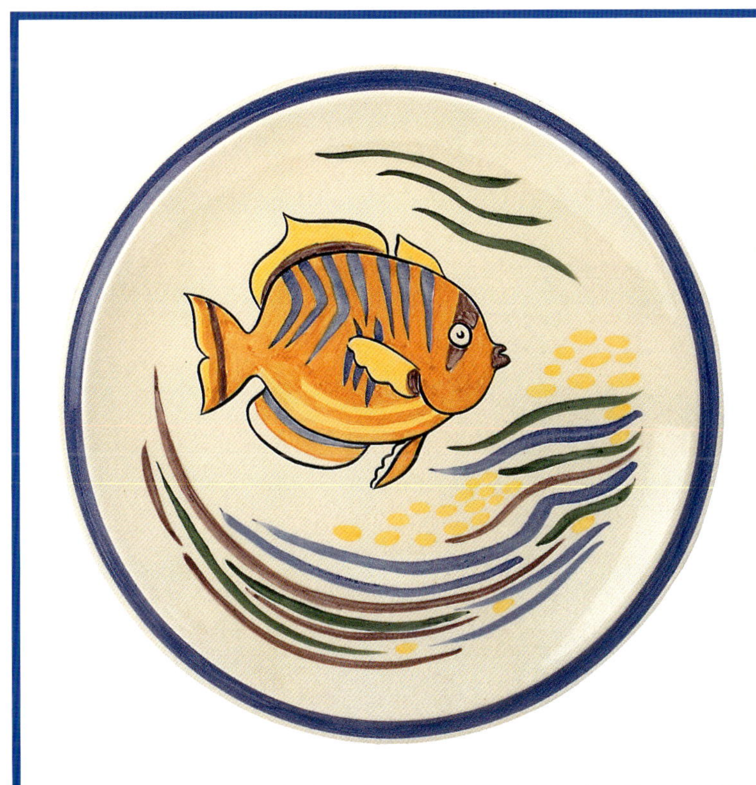

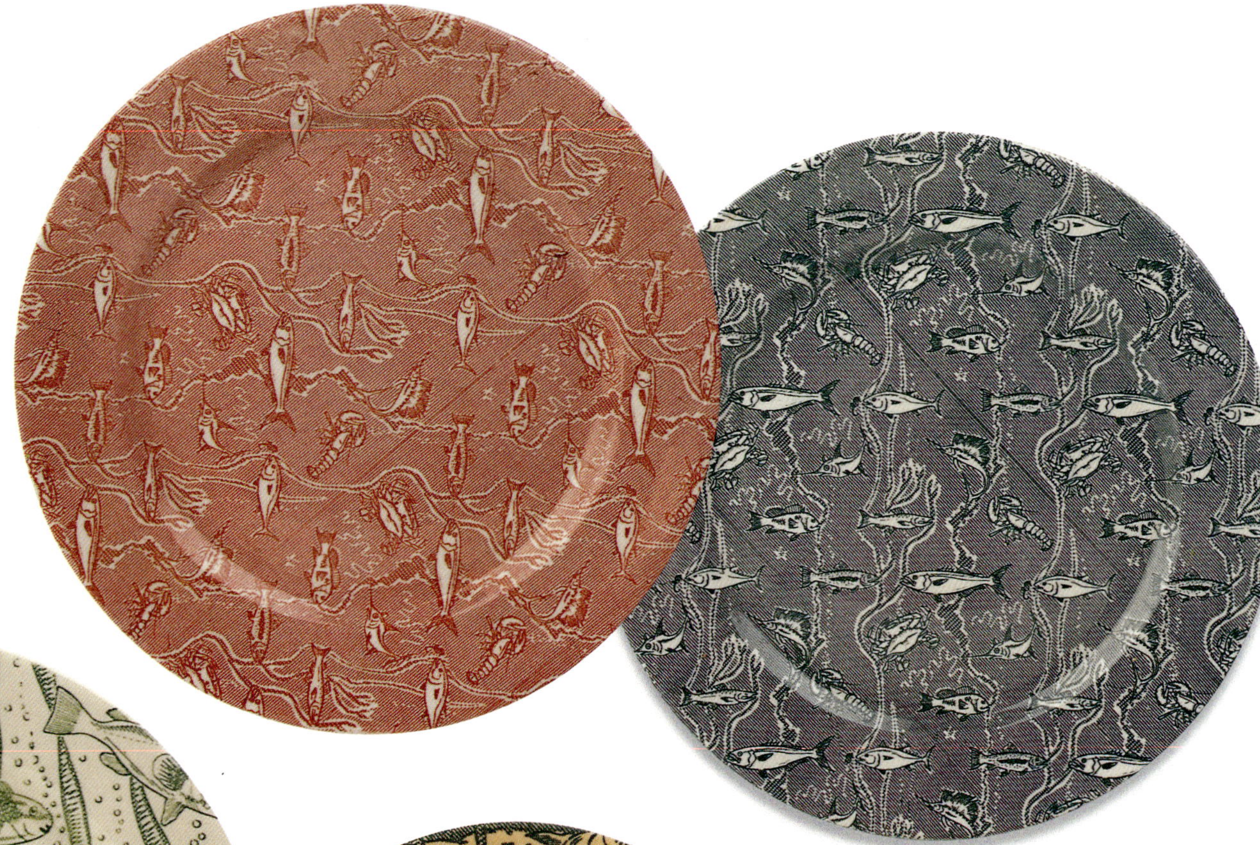

"Fish" design with pink and green backgrounds, Tepco. *Courtesy: Michael & Denise Queen*.

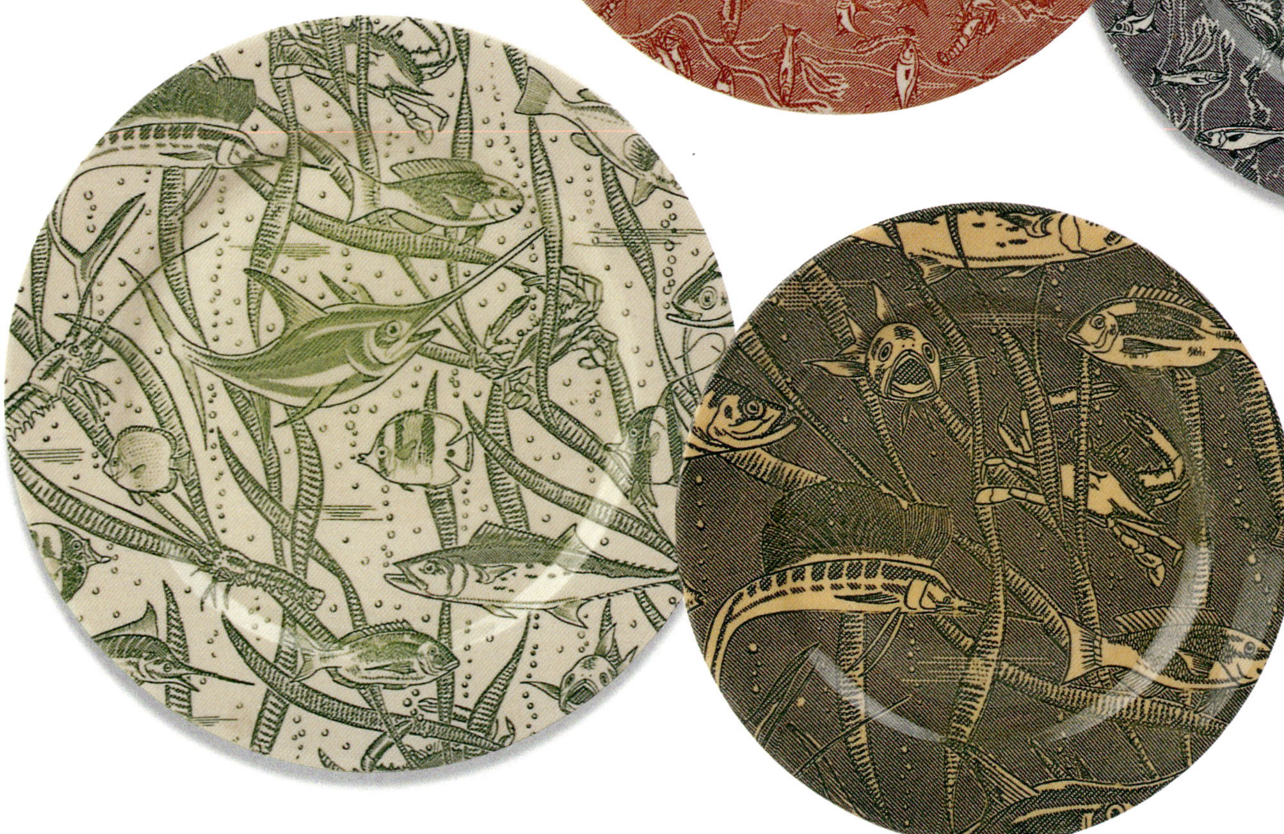

"Aquarium" design with green and white backgrounds, Tepco. *Courtesy: Michael & Denise Queen*.

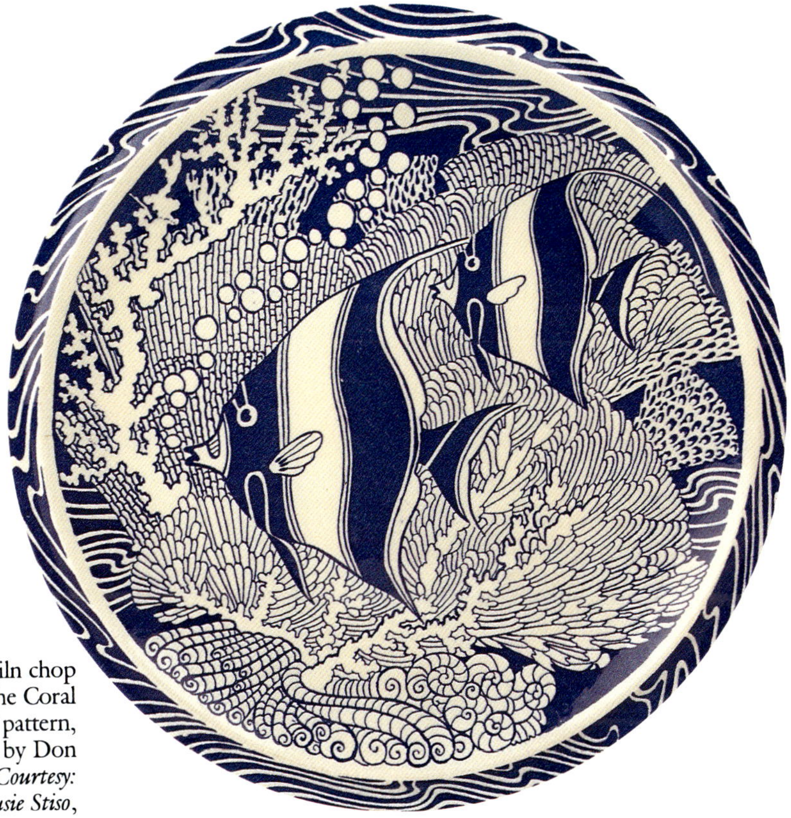

Vernon Kiln chop plate in the Coral Reef pattern, designed by Don Blanding. *Courtesy: Jim & Susie Stiso*,

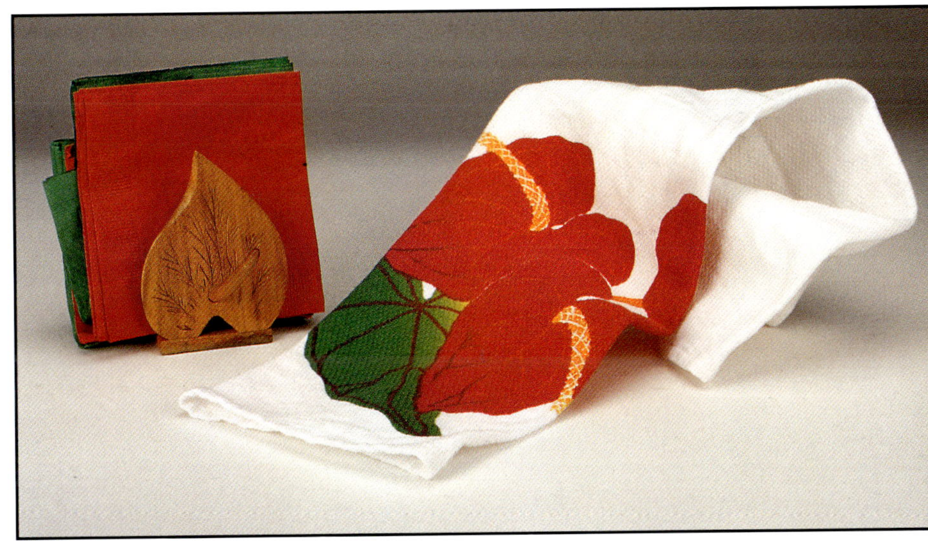

Left: carved wooden napkin holder. Right: silk-screened kitchen towel. *Courtesy: Tobi Smith and Michele Leypoldt*.

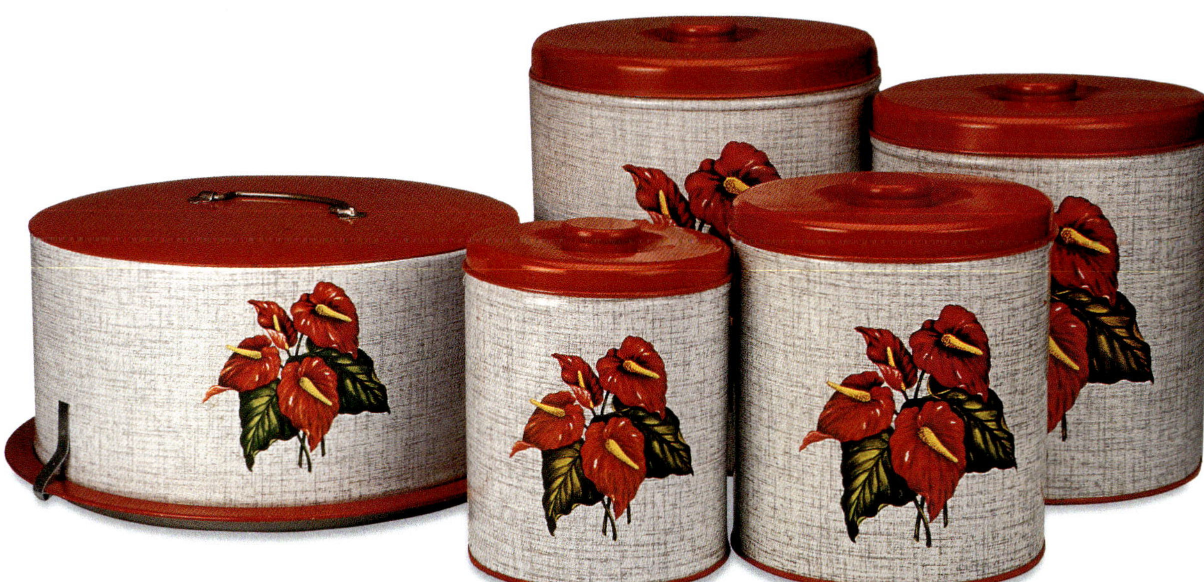

Canister set and cake tin by Decoware. *Courtesy: Michele Leypoldt*.

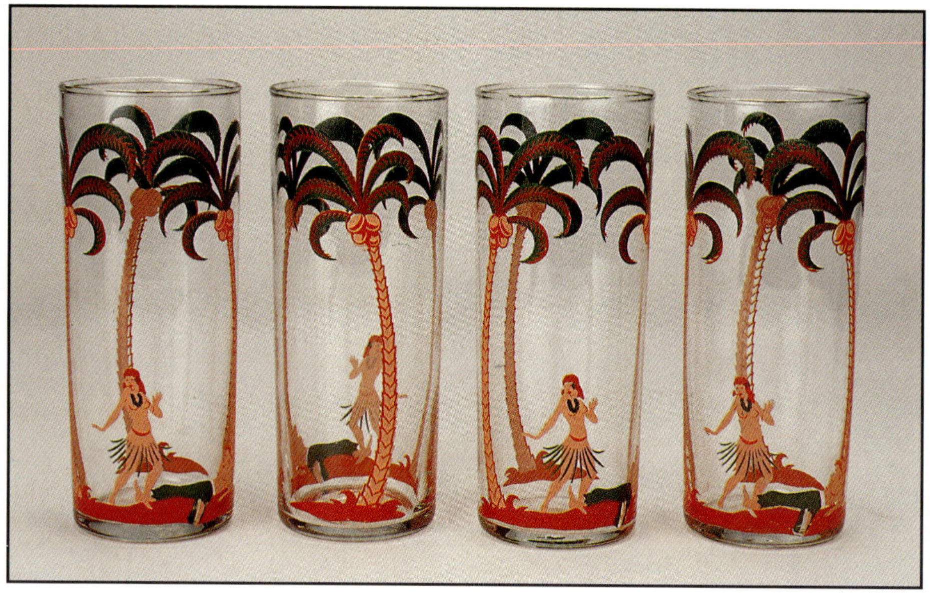

Set of four highball glasses with hula girl and palm tree motif. *Courtesy: Tiki Trader*.

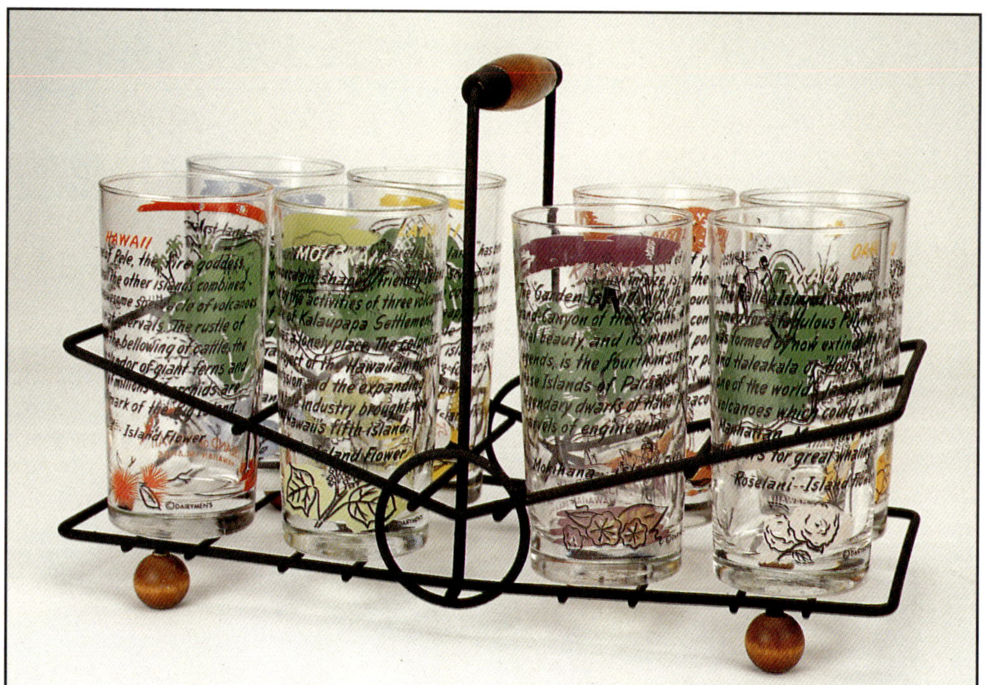

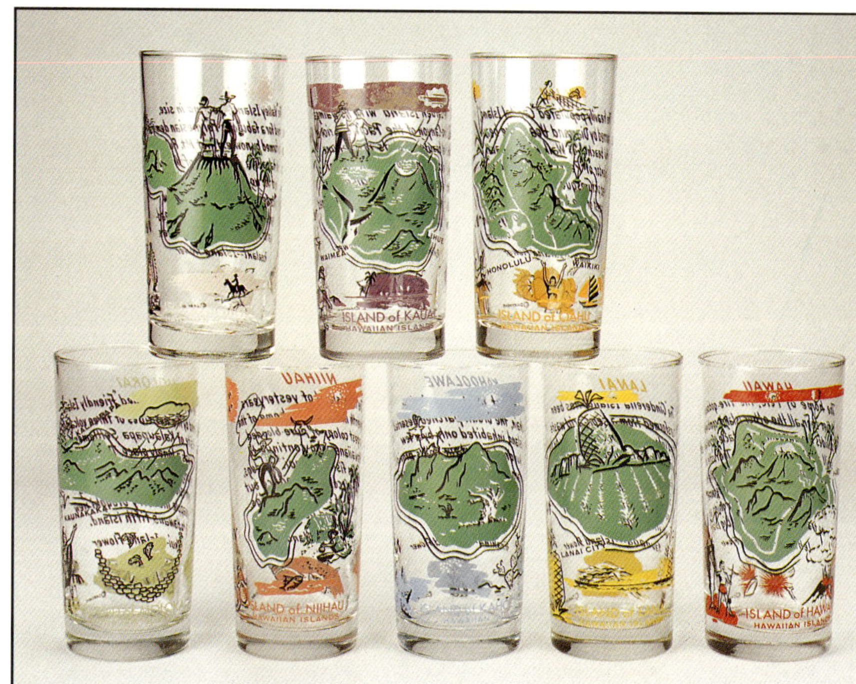

Set of eight highball glasses with descriptions of each of the islands. On the opposite side is a nice graphic portrayal of each island. Copyrighted by Dairymen's. *Courtesy: Michael Trotter*.

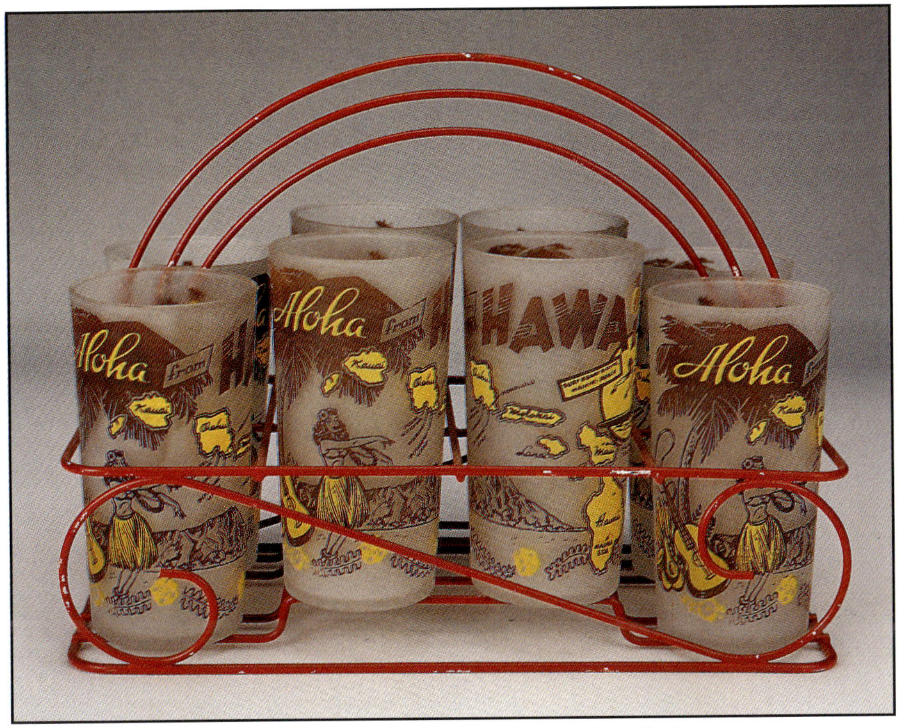

Set of eight Aloha Hawaii glasses in carrier. *Courtesy: the Collection of Brian Goddard & Gene Sweeney.*

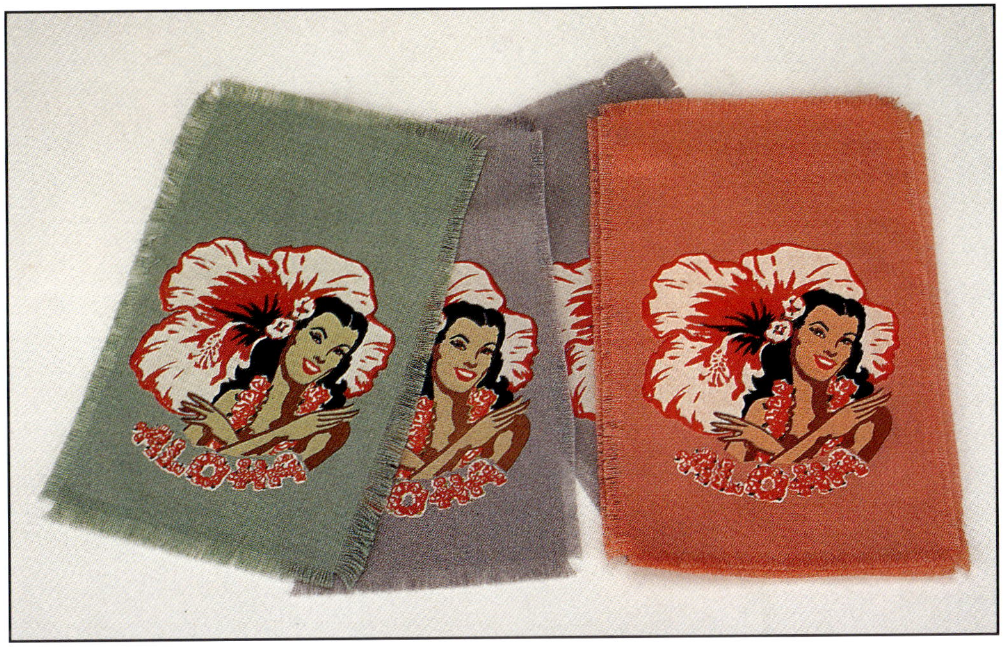

Aloha, silk-screened linen cocktail napkins. *Courtesy: Michele Leypoldt.*

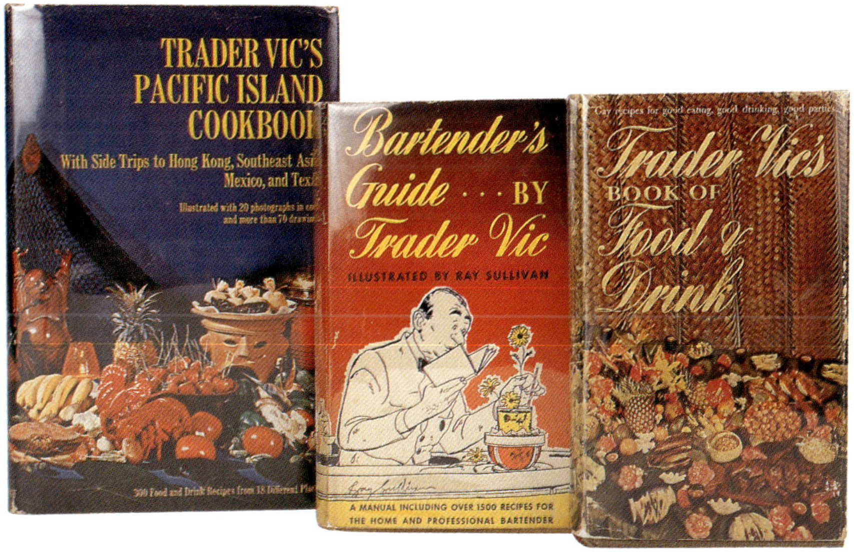

Trader Vic books. Left to right: *Trader Vic's Pacific Island Cookbook*, 1968; *Bartender's Guide...by Trader Vic*, 1947; and *Trader Vic's Book of Food and Drink*, 1946. *Courtesy: Michele Leypoldt.*

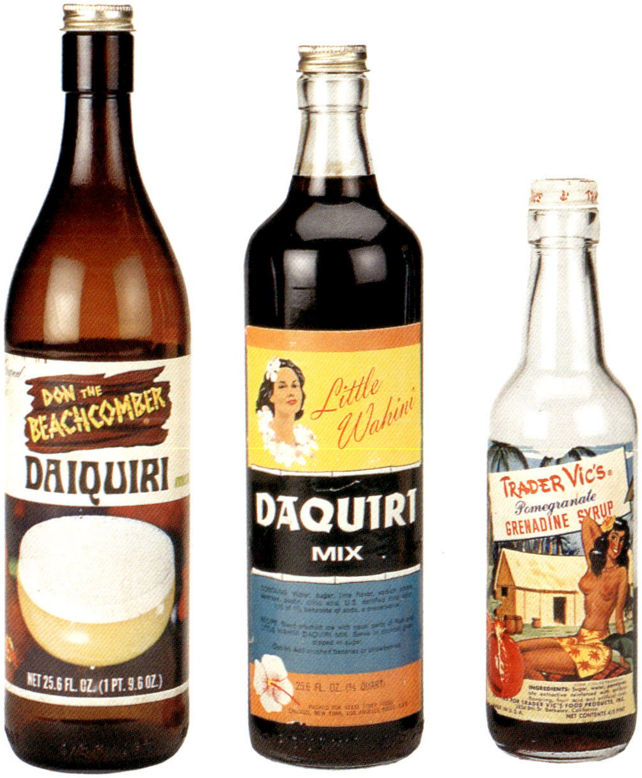

Bar bottles with Hawaiian themes. Left to right: Don the Beachcomber Daiquiri, Little Wahini Daiquiri Mix, and Trader Vic's Pomegranate Grenadine Syrup.

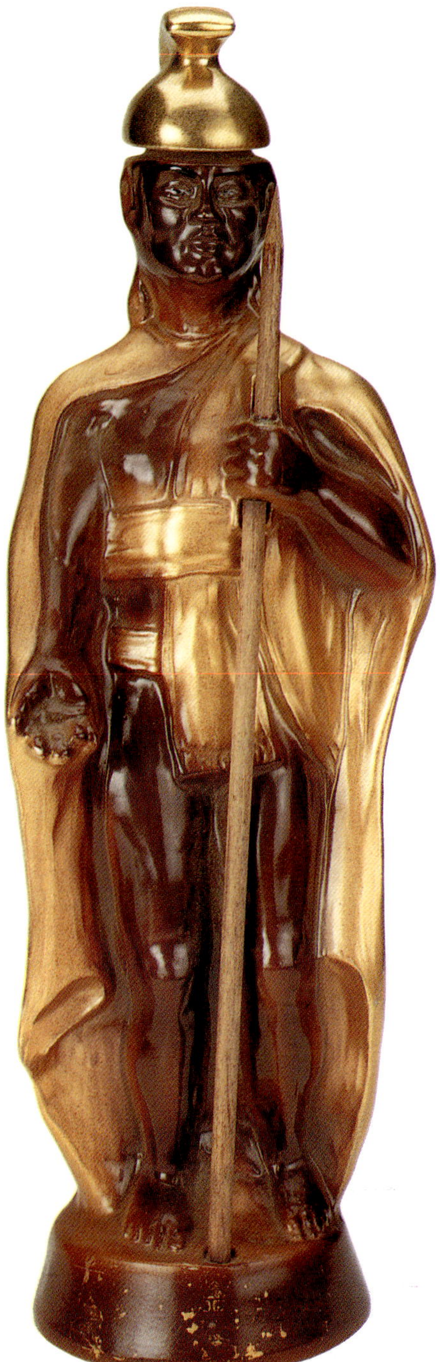

Jim Beam bottle, 1972. 15" h. *Courtesy: Oceanic Arts*.

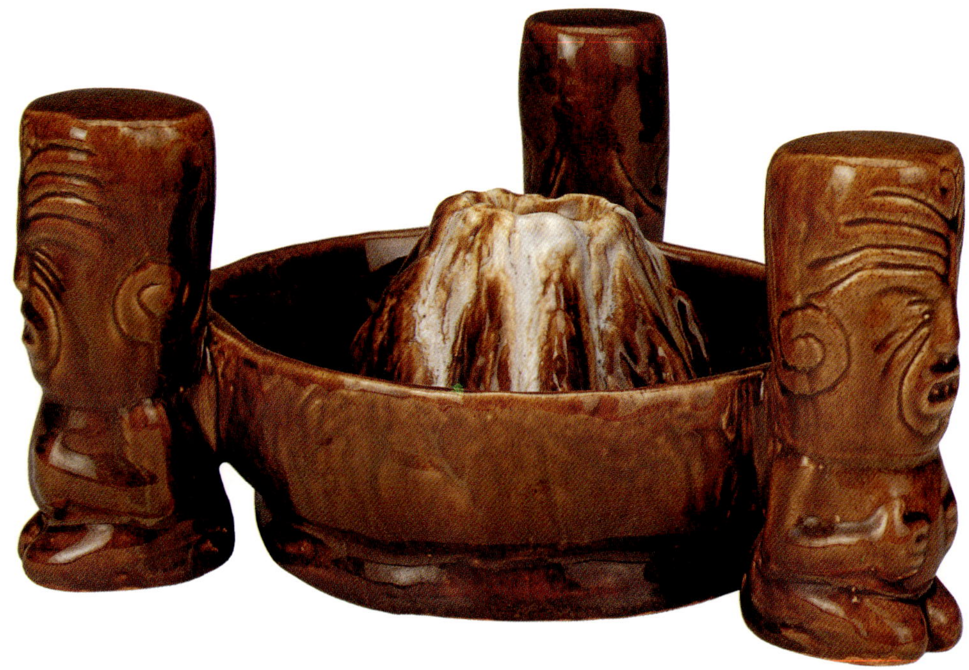

Volcano bowl, 4.5" h. *Courtesy: Oceanic Arts*.

Ceramic volcano bowl. 5" h. Marked Orchids of Hawaii and Made in Japan. *Courtesy: the Collection of Brian Goddard & Gene Sweeney*.

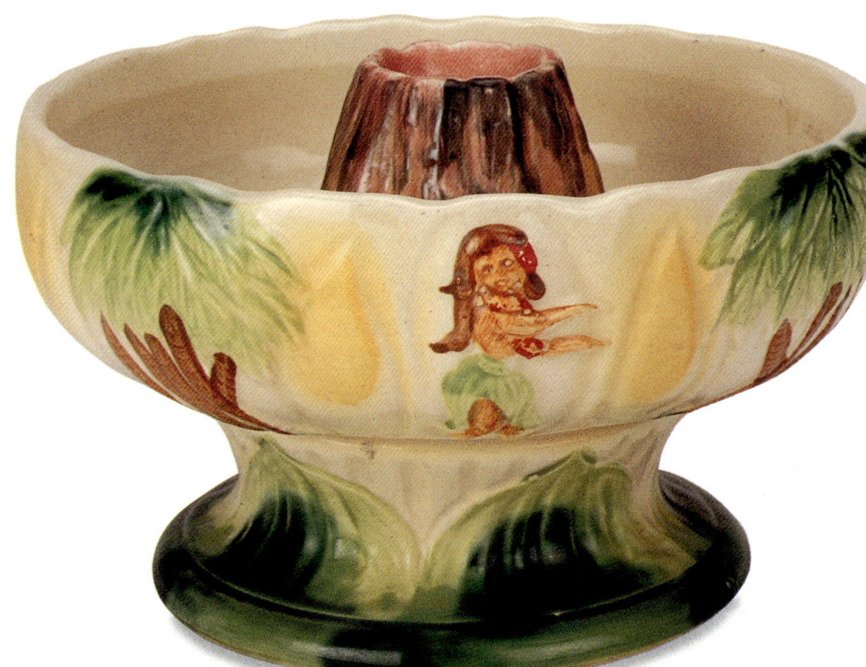

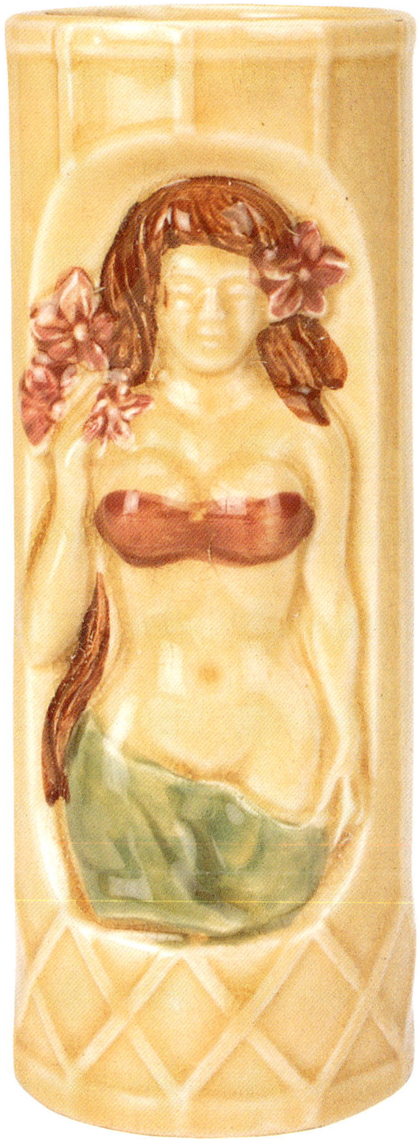

Orchids of Hawaii mug, made in Japan. 6.5" h. *Courtesy: the Collection of Brian Goddard & Gene Sweeney.*

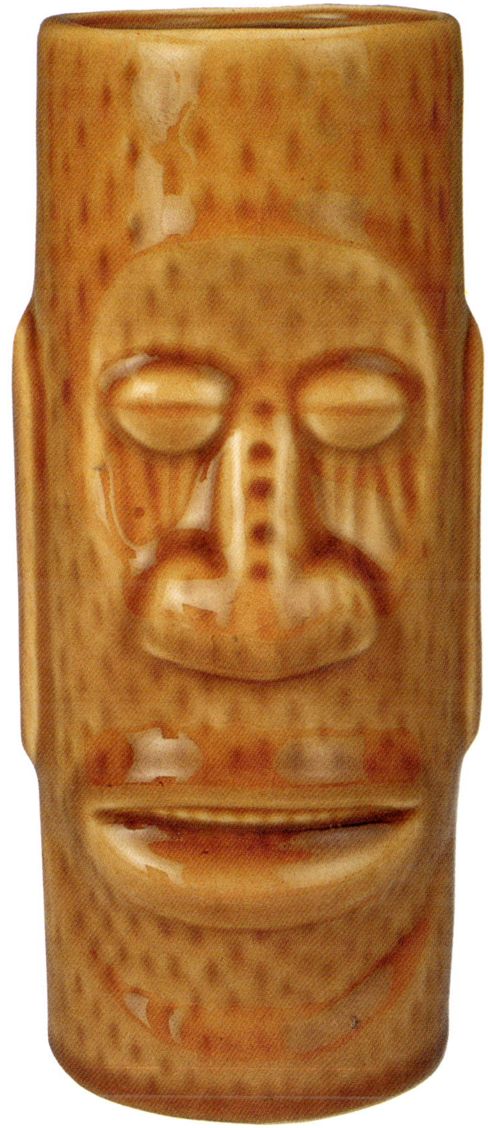

Orchids of Hawaii tiki glass. 6.75". *Courtesy: the Collection of Brian Goddard & Gene Sweeney.*

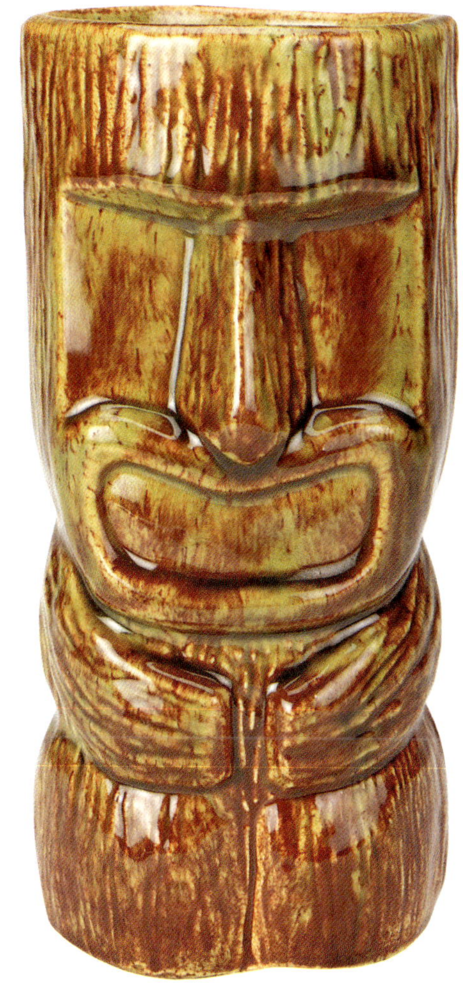

Tiki mug, Toby Designs, 1962. 5.25" h. *Courtesy: the Collection of Brian Goddard & Gene Sweeney.*

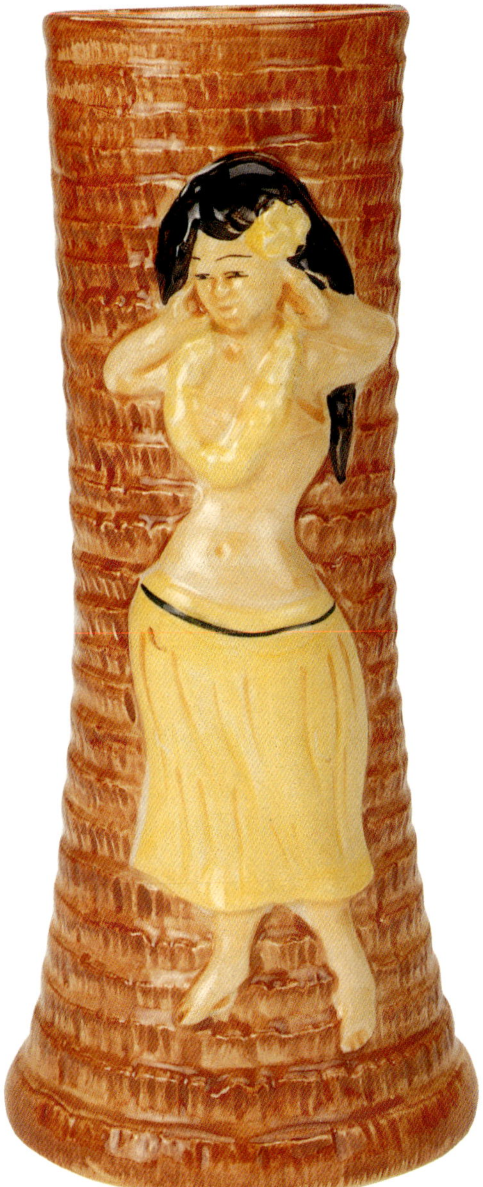

Hula girl mug with OMC Japan sticker underneath. 8.25" h. *Courtesy: the Collection of Brian Goddard & Gene Sweeney*.

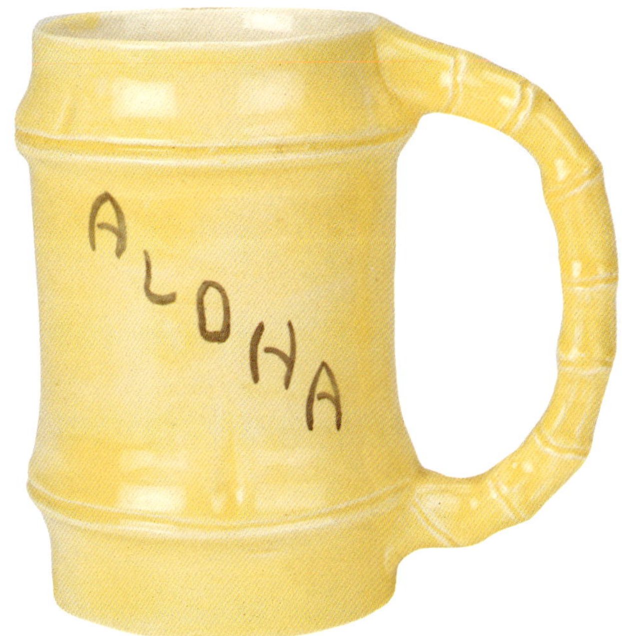

A handled Aloha mug. No marks, 4.75" h. *Courtesy: Oceanic Arts*

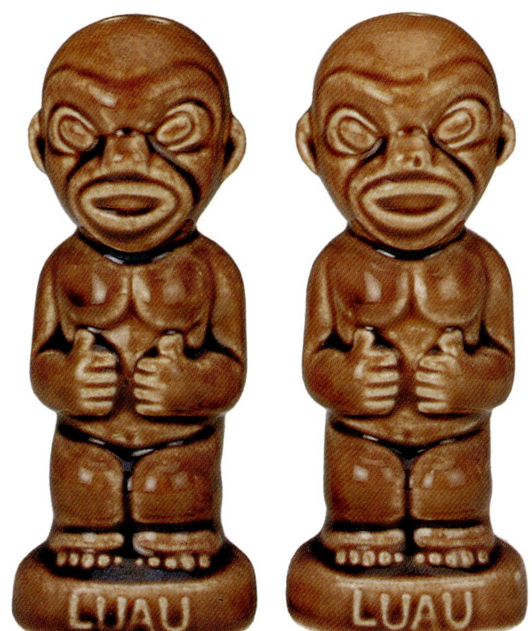

Luau salt and pepper shakers, OMC Japan. 4" h. *Courtesy: Michael Trotter*.

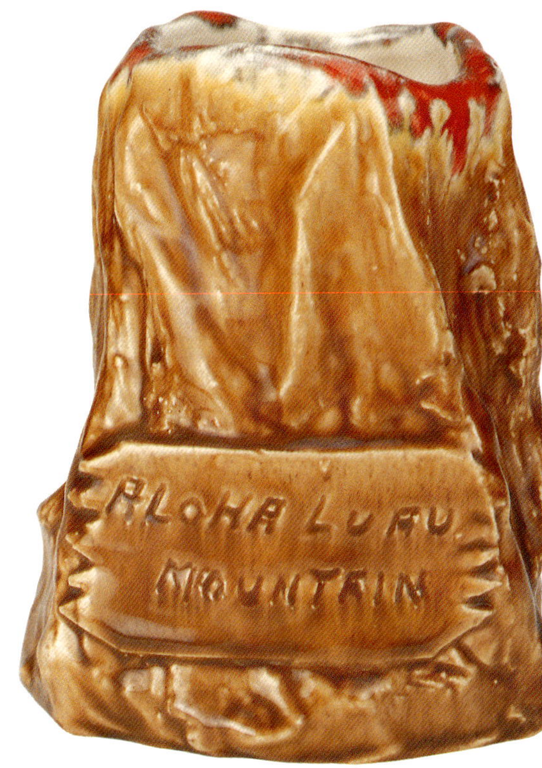

A souvenir mug from Aloha Luau Mountain, 4.25" h. *Courtesy: Oceanic Arts*.

Handled mug, marked Riddell, 1951. 6.25". *Courtesy: the Collection of Brian Goddard & Gene Sweeney*.

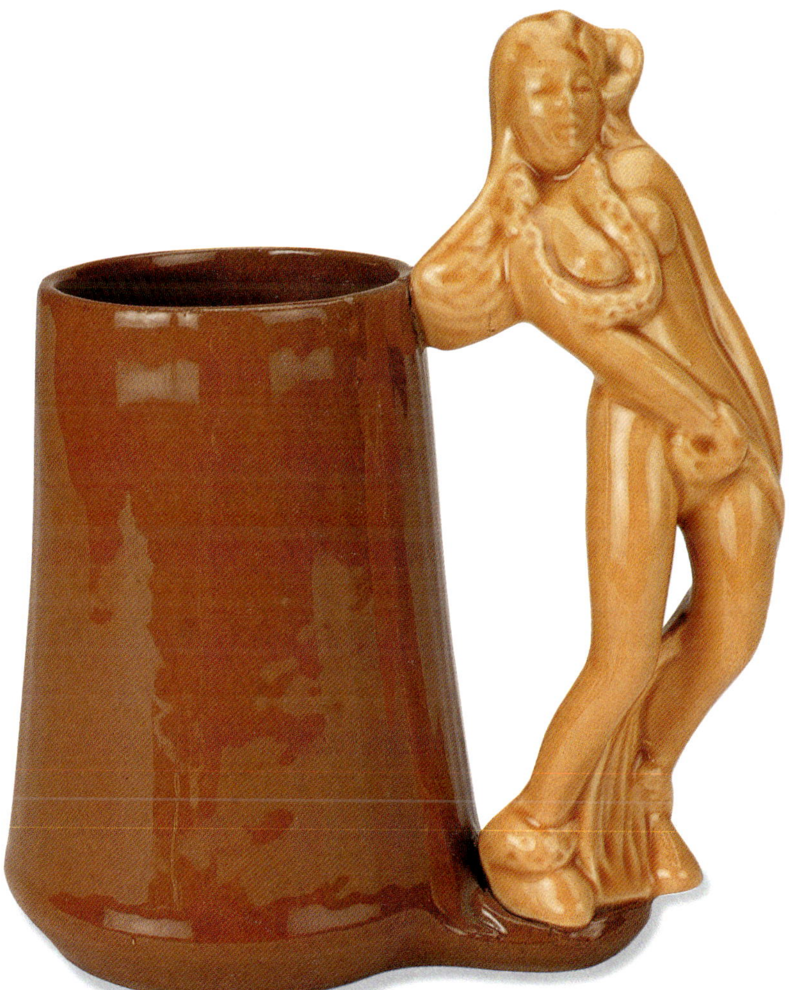

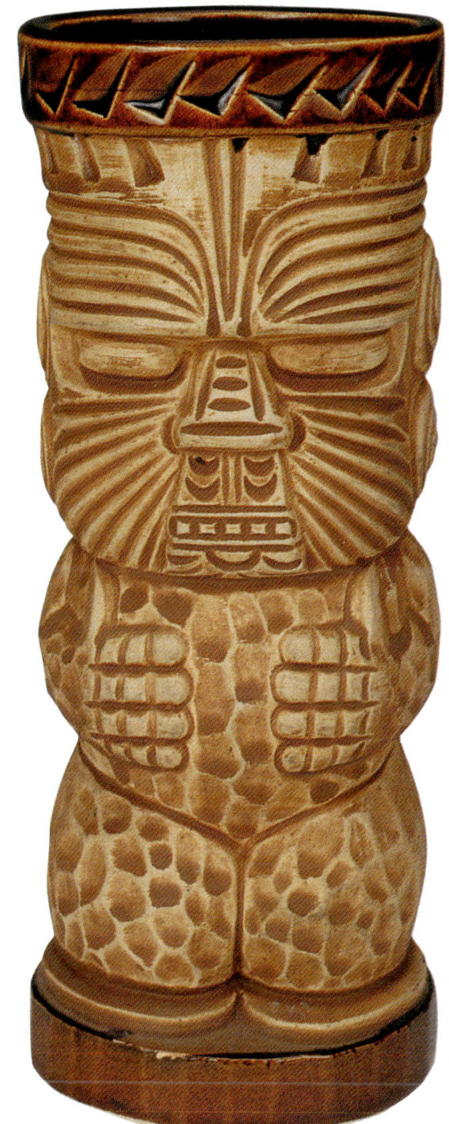

Tiki marked OMC Japan. 7" h. *Courtesy: Oceanic Arts*.

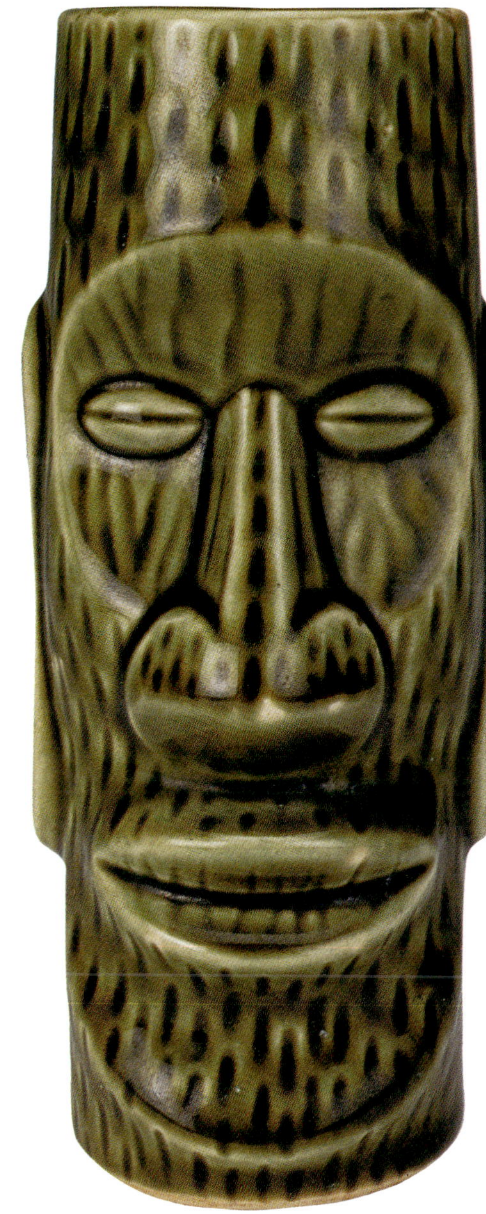

Made in Japan tiki mug. 6.75" h. *Courtesy: the Collection of Brian Goddard & Gene Sweeney*.

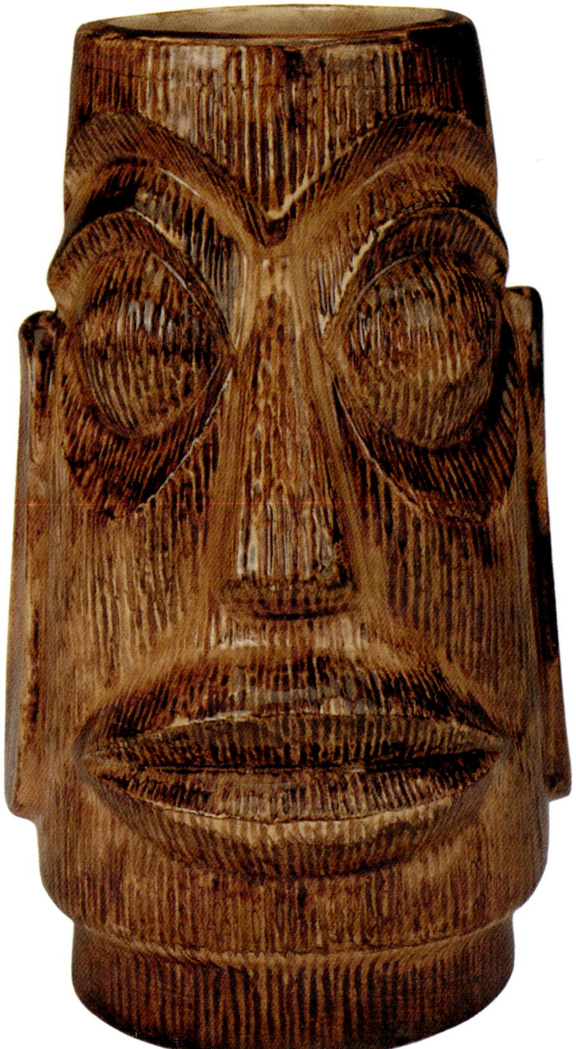

Otigiri tiki mug. 6" h.
Courtesy: the Collection of Brian Goddard & Gene Sweeney.

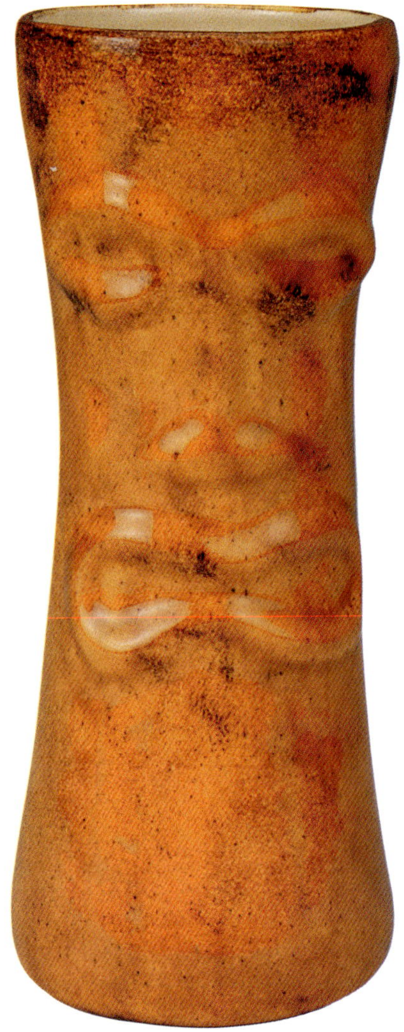

Unmarked tiki. 6.5". *Courtesy: the Collection of Brian Goddard & Gene Sweeney.*

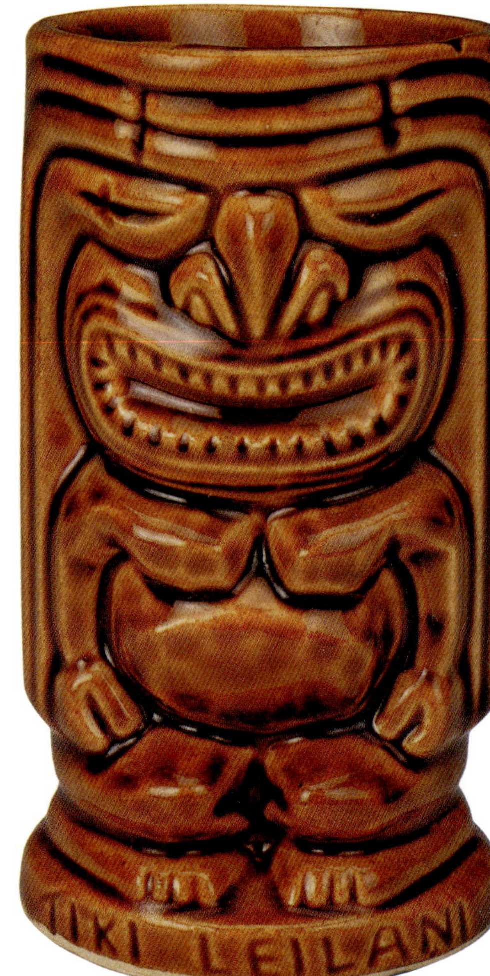

Leilani, marked USA. 5.25".
Courtesy: the Collection of Brian Goddard & Gene Sweeney.

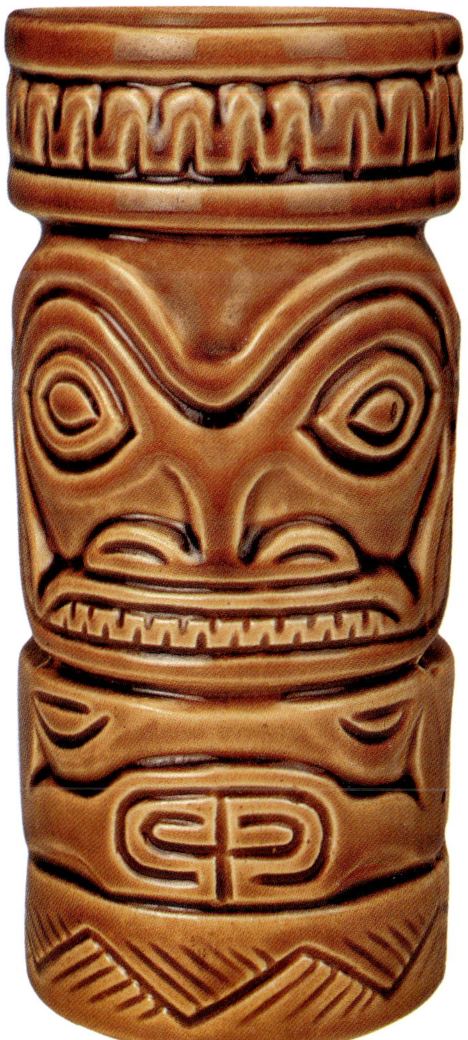

Tiki marked Hawaii. 7" h. *Courtesy: the Collection of Brian Goddard & Gene Sweeney.*

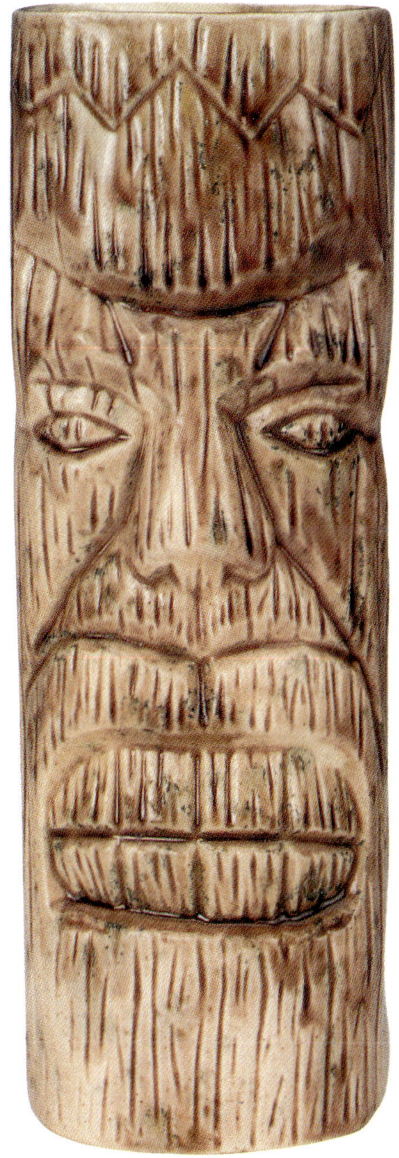

Tiki marked M.M. Studio. 8" h. *Courtesy: the Collection of Brian Goddard & Gene Sweeney.*

Tiki, 7.25". *Courtesy: the Collection of Brian Goddard & Gene Sweeney.*

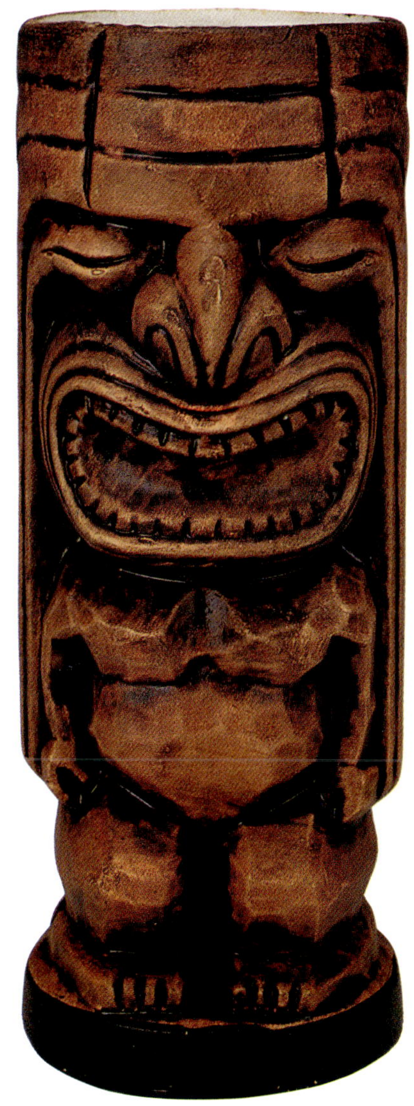

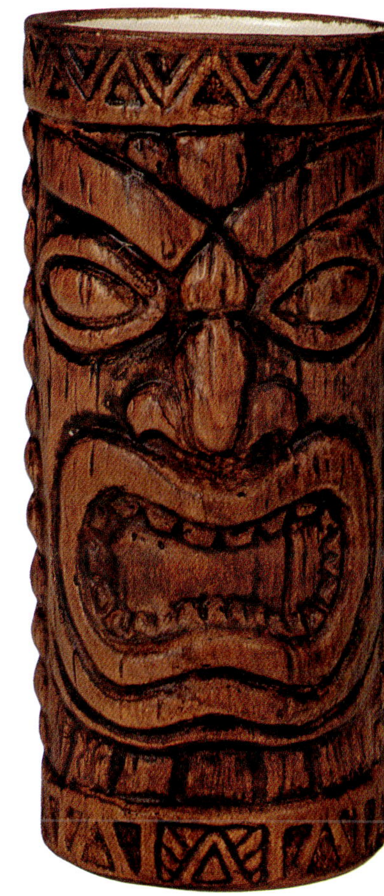

Treasure Craft tiki. 5.5". *Courtesy: the Collection of Brian Goddard & Gene Sweeney.*

Tiki marked Daga Hawaii. 5.25". *Courtesy: the Collection of Brian Goddard & Gene Sweeney.*

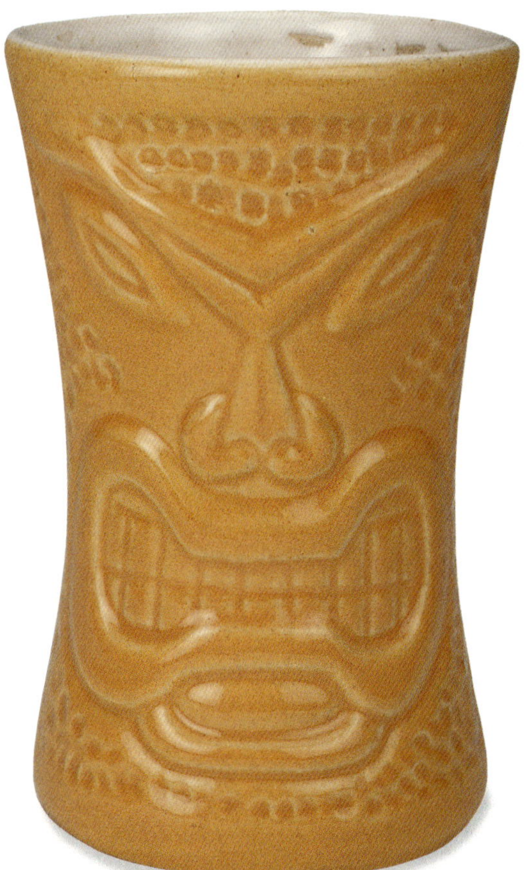

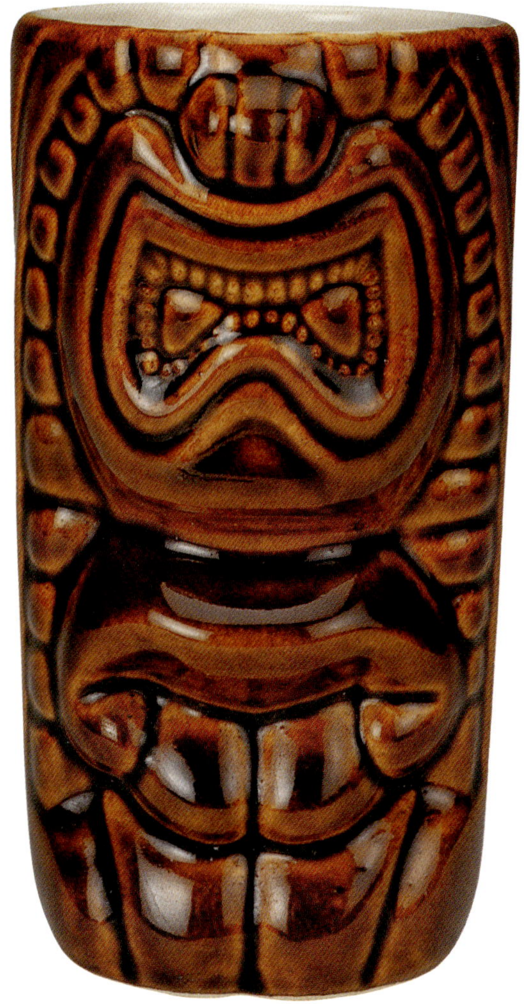

Tiki, no marks. 5.5". *Courtesy: the Collection of Brian Goddard & Gene Sweeney.*

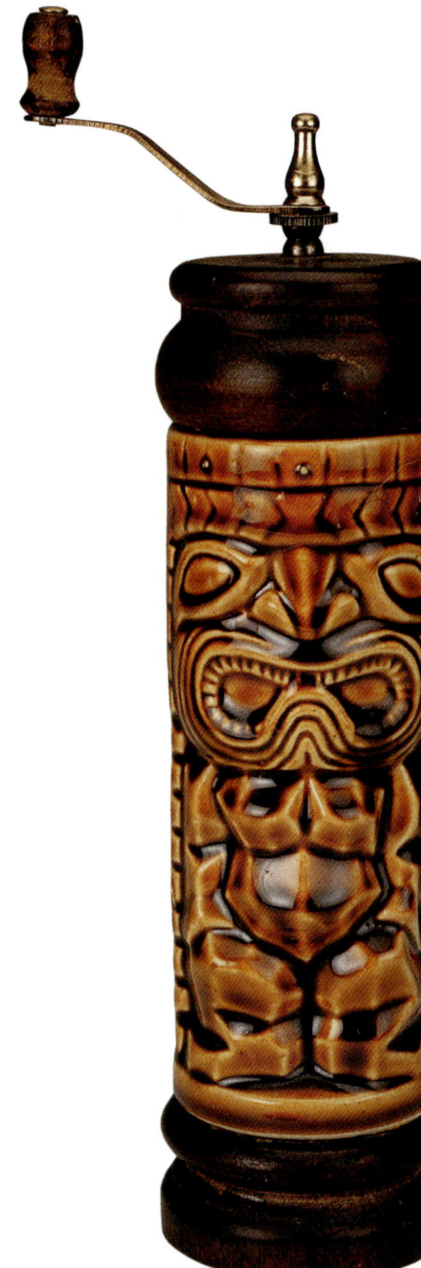

Tiki pepper mill, 11". *Courtesy: the Collection of Brian Goddard & Gene Sweeney.*

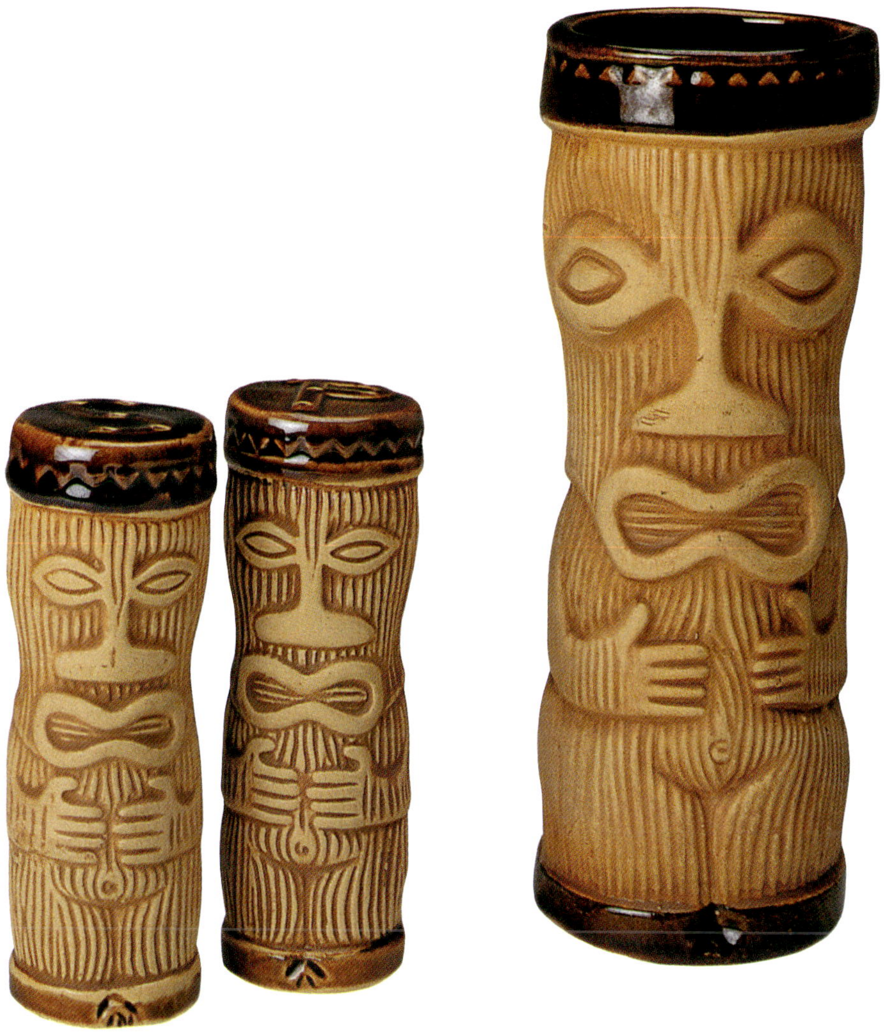

Tiki table set with vase and salt and pepper shakers. DMP designs, Japan. Shakers, 4.25", vase, 7". *Courtesy: the Collection of Brian Goddard & Gene Sweeney and Tiki Trader.*

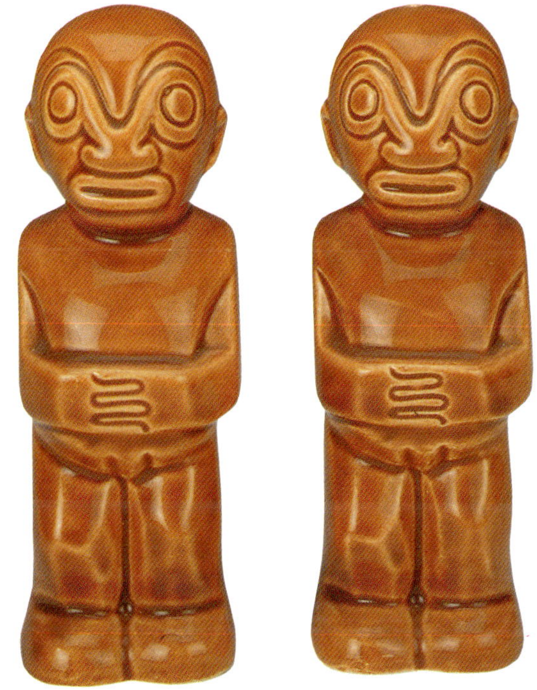

Salt and pepper shakers, 4.5" h. *Courtesy: Tiki Trader.*

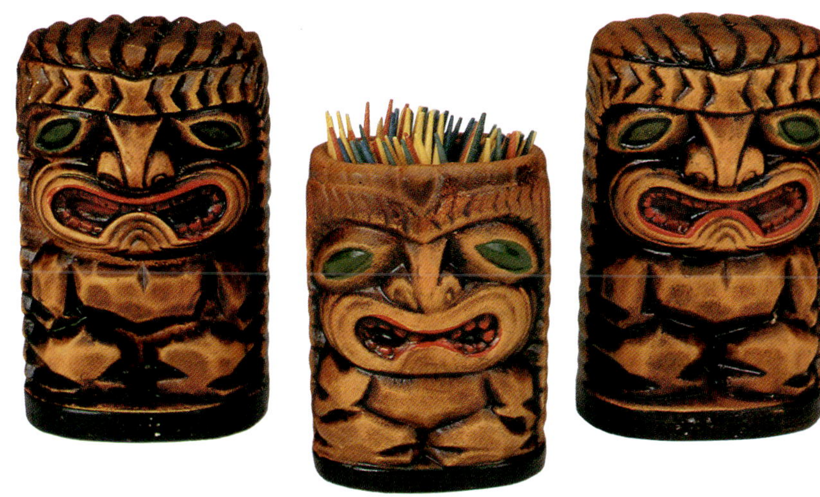

Salt and pepper shakers with matching toothpick holder. 3" h. *Courtesy: Tiki Trader.*

Tropical Restaurants

The romance and exotic ambience of the Islands was not lost on mainland business, and in particular, it seems on restaurants. Innkeepers around the country longed to create the same kind of relaxed, unpressured atmosphere for their customers that was experienced in Hawaii...the feeling that they never wanted to leave. Restaurants serving exotic drinks often served them in custom made tikis like those that follow. The menu also reflected the exotic fare within.

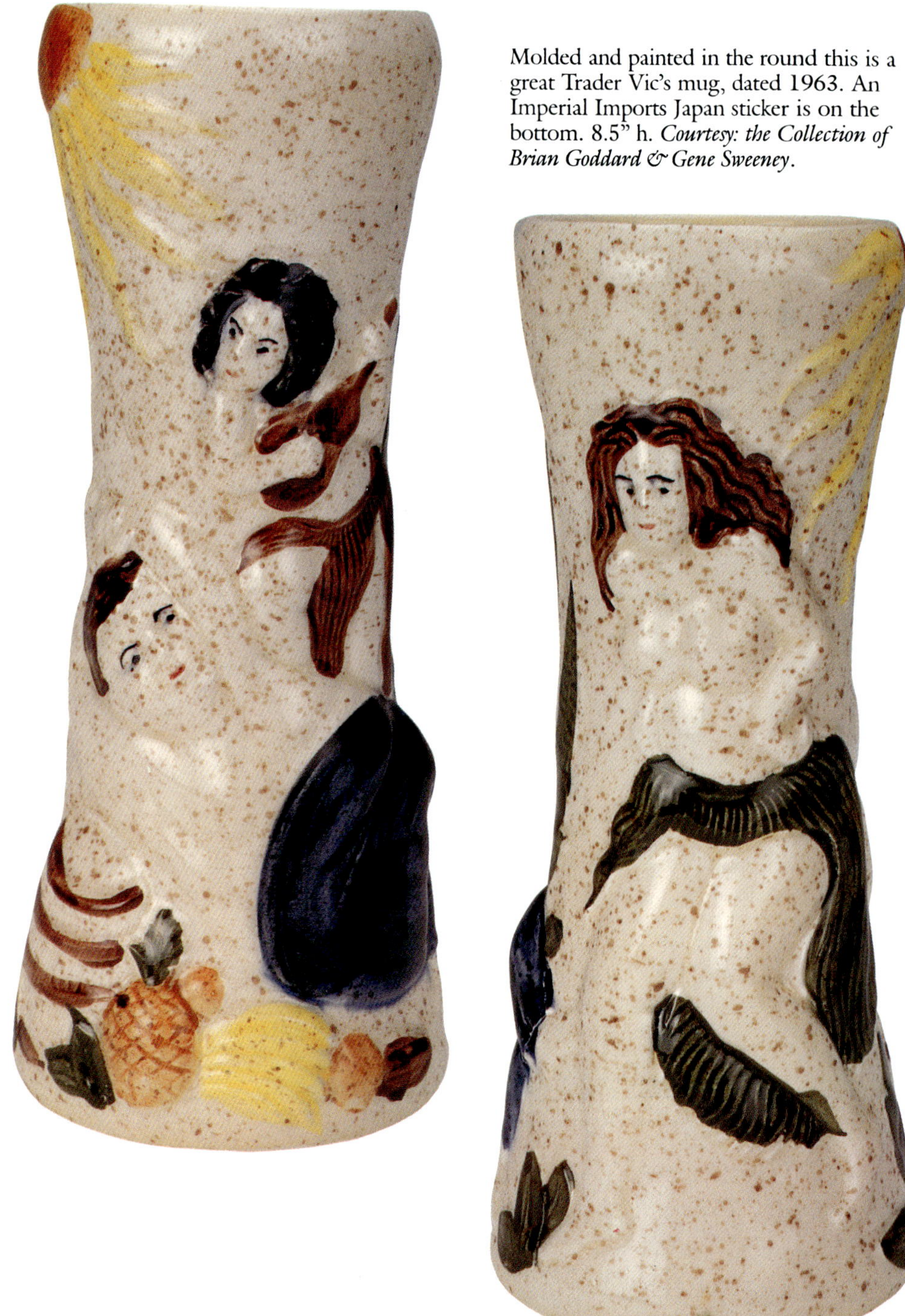

Molded and painted in the round this is a great Trader Vic's mug, dated 1963. An Imperial Imports Japan sticker is on the bottom. 8.5" h. *Courtesy: the Collection of Brian Goddard & Gene Sweeney*.

Trader Vic's

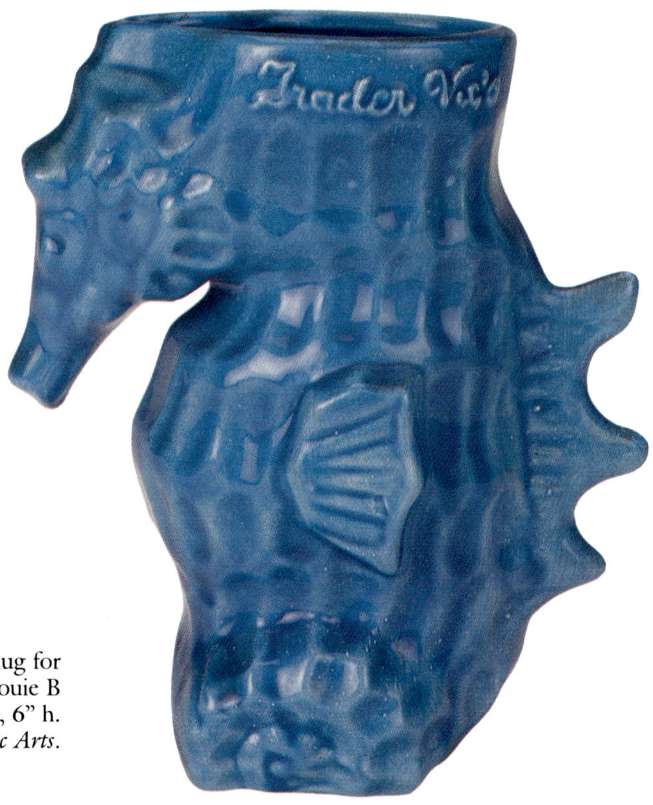

Seahorse mug for Trader Vic's, Louie B Ceramics, 6" h. *Courtesy: Oceanic Arts*.

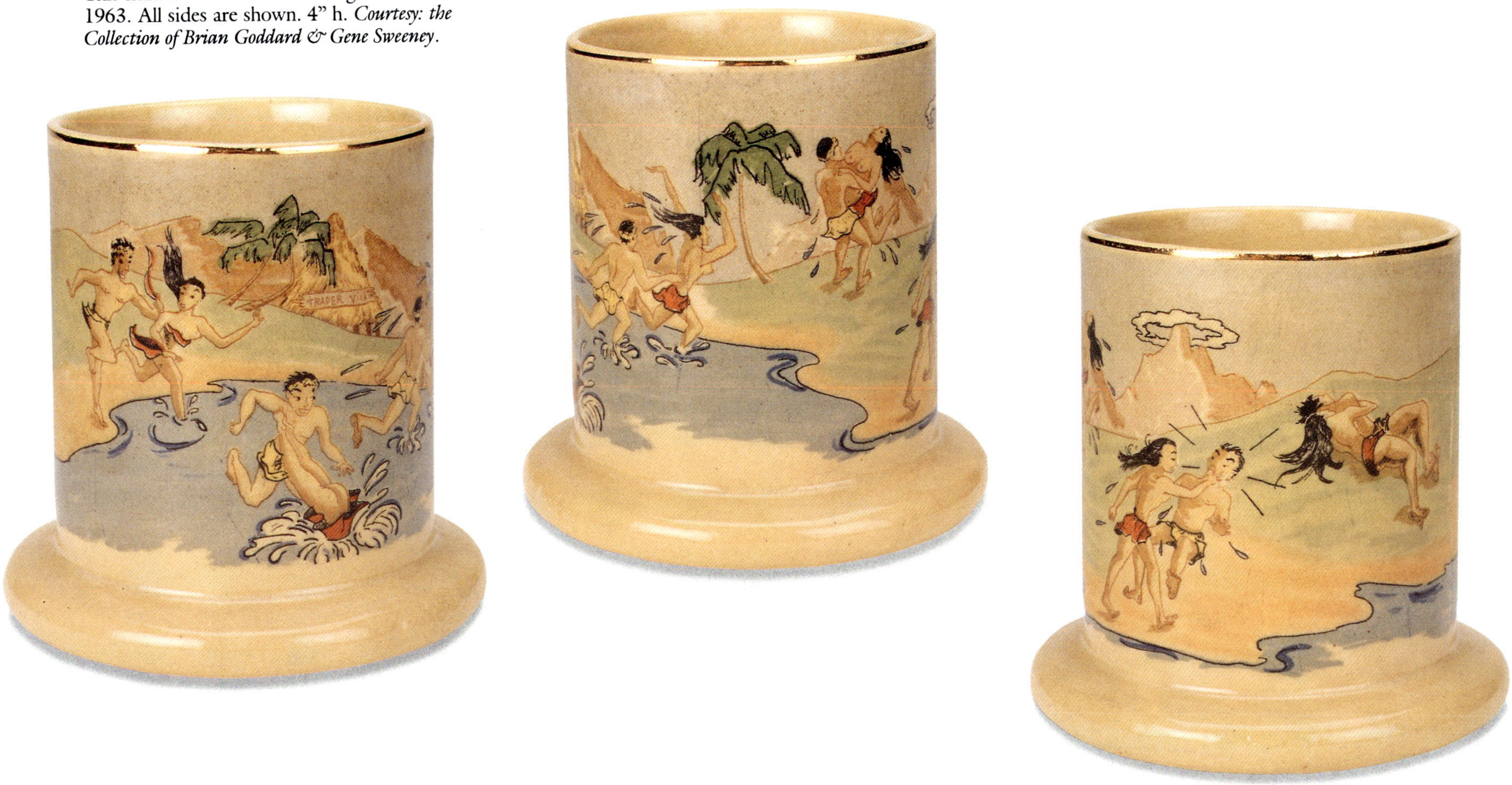

This humorous Trader Vic's mug dates to 1963. All sides are shown. 4" h. *Courtesy: the Collection of Brian Goddard & Gene Sweeney*.

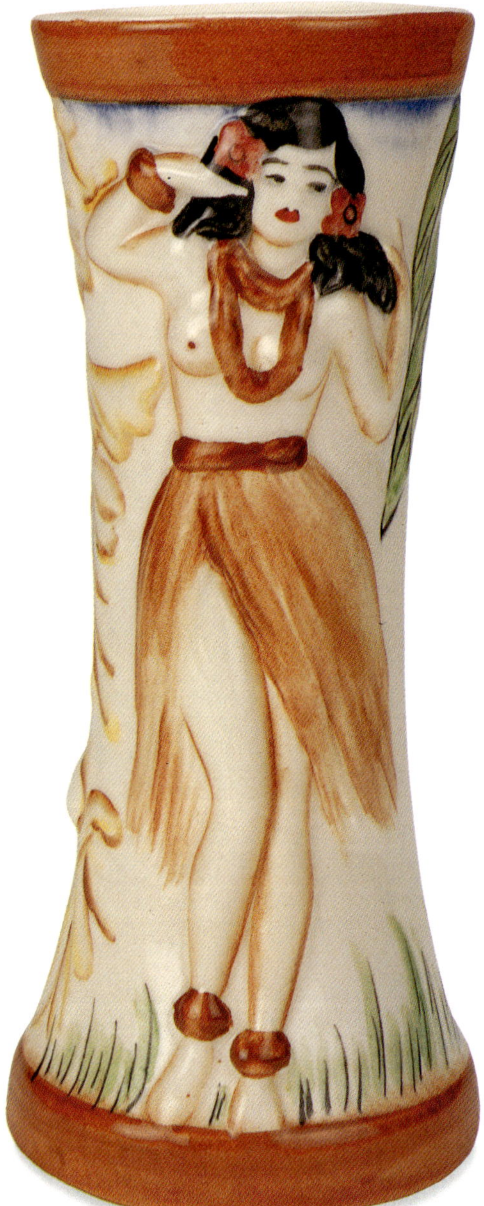

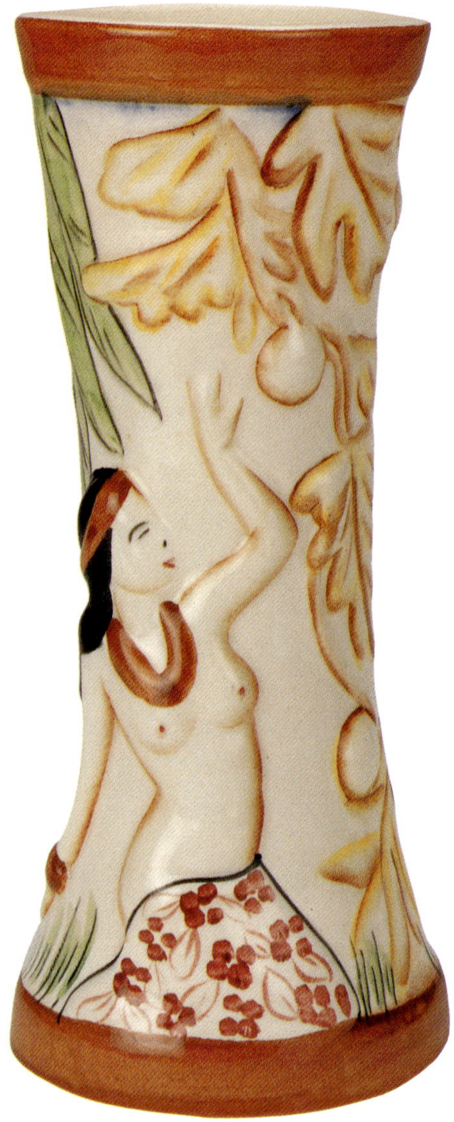

Trader Vic molded mug manufactured by Vernon Kilns. It is molded and painted in the round. Two views are shown. 8.5" h. *Courtesy: the Collection of Brian Goddard & Gene Sweeney*.

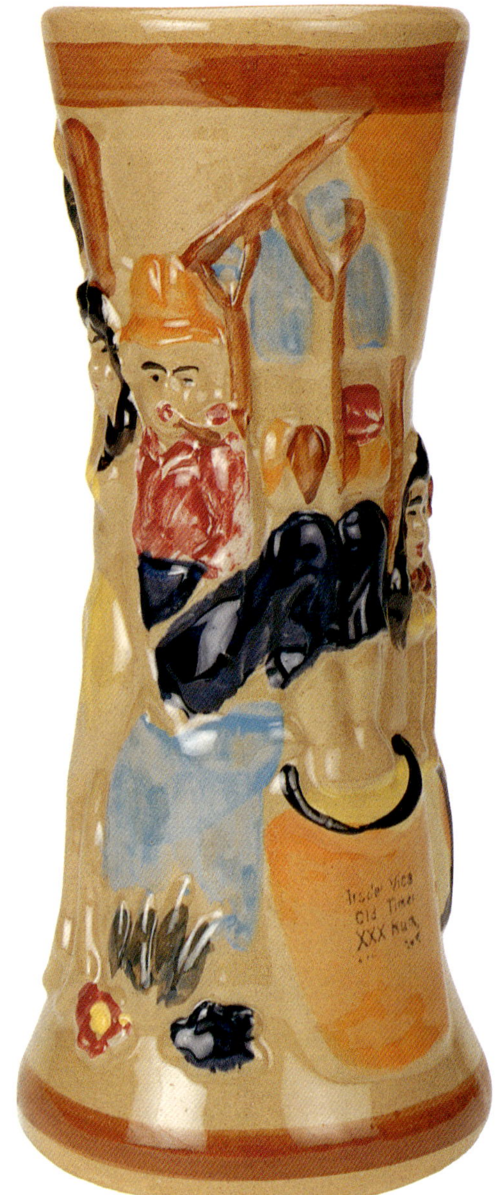

Trader Vic molded mug. 8.5" h.

Other Restaurant's Tikis

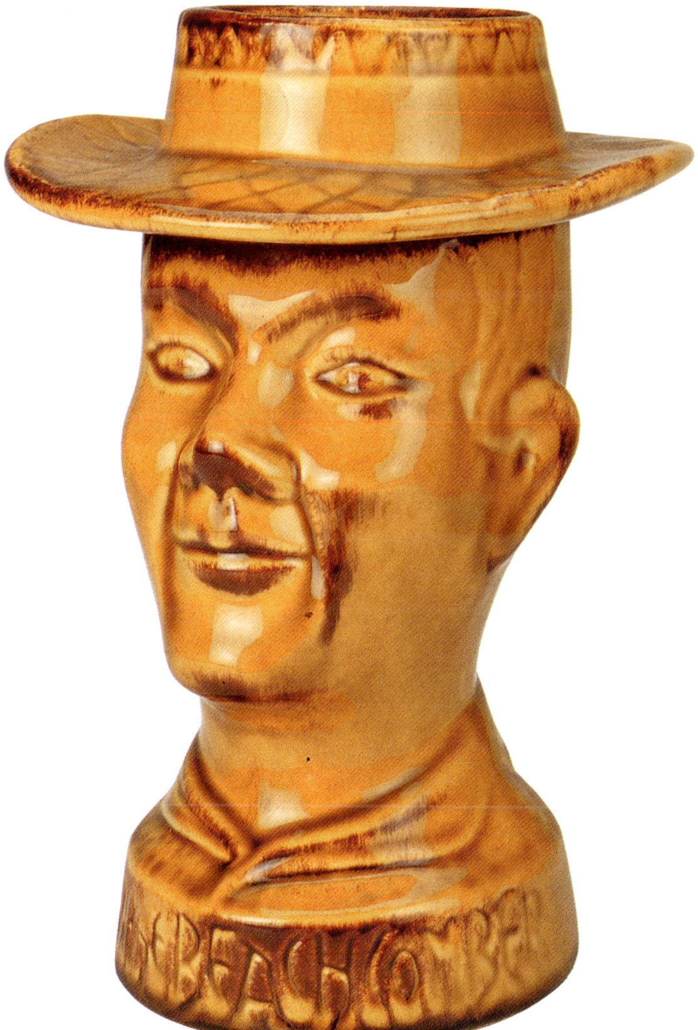

This wonderful figure is marker Don the Beachcomber on the base and Tiki Traders underneath. 7.25" h. *Courtesy: Tiki Trader.*

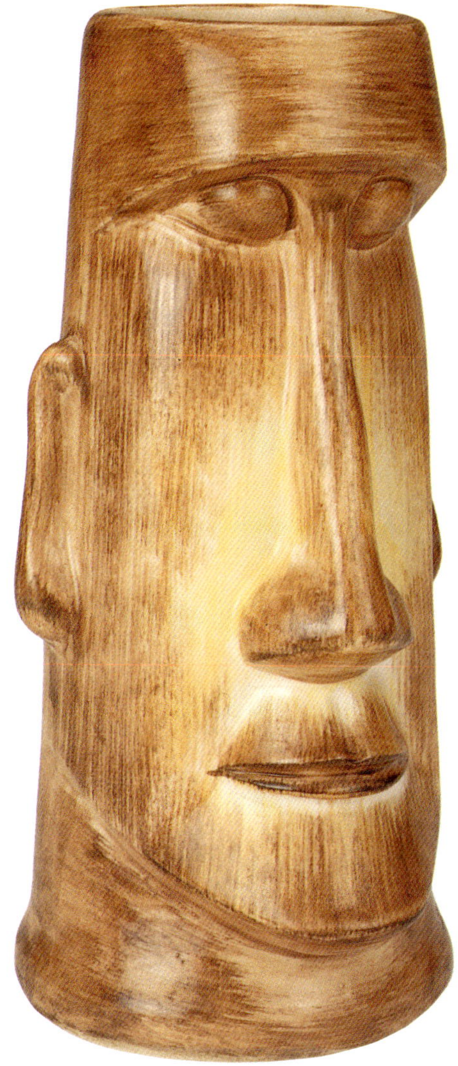

Easter Island like tiki mug made exclusively for Skipper Kent's in San Francisco and Kona. 8" h. *Courtesy: the Collection of Brian Goddard & Gene Sweeney.*

Fisherman's Wharf Honolulu, 7" h. *Courtesy: the Collection of Brian Goddard & Gene Sweeney.*

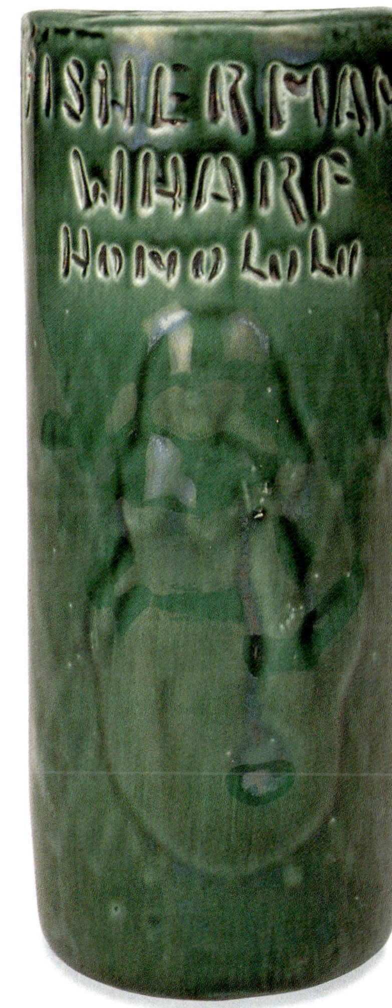

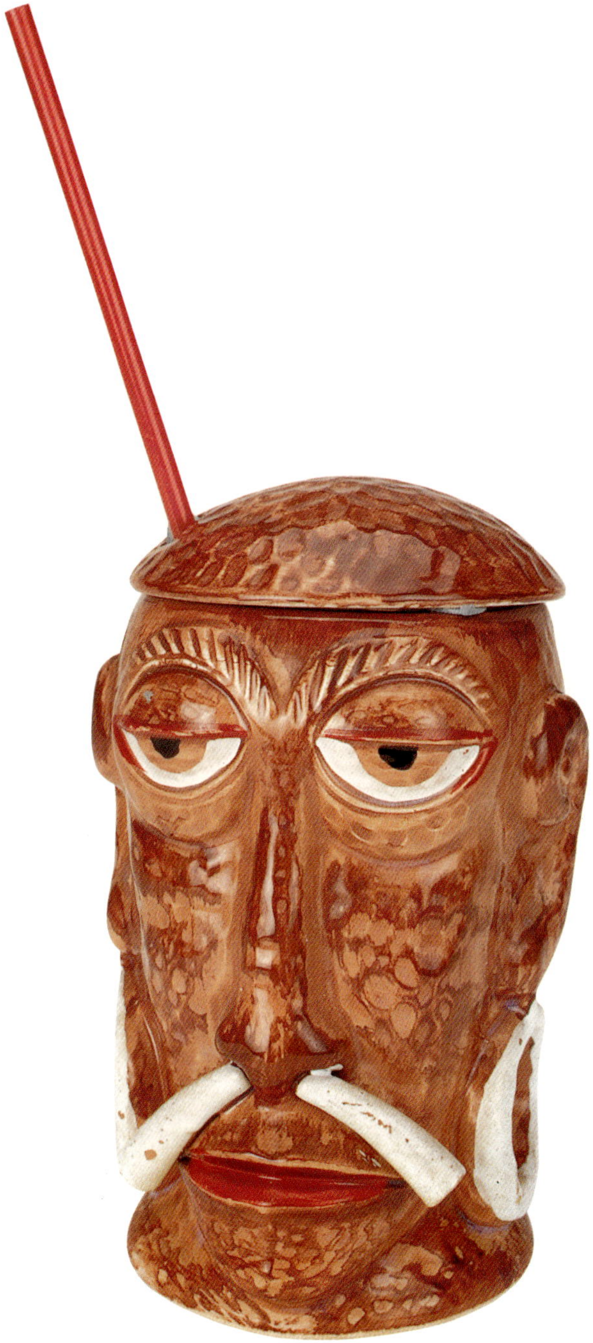

Three shakers. The outside shakers are from the Kahiki Supper Club and the middle is from Disneyland. 4" h. *Courtesy: Tiki Trader*.

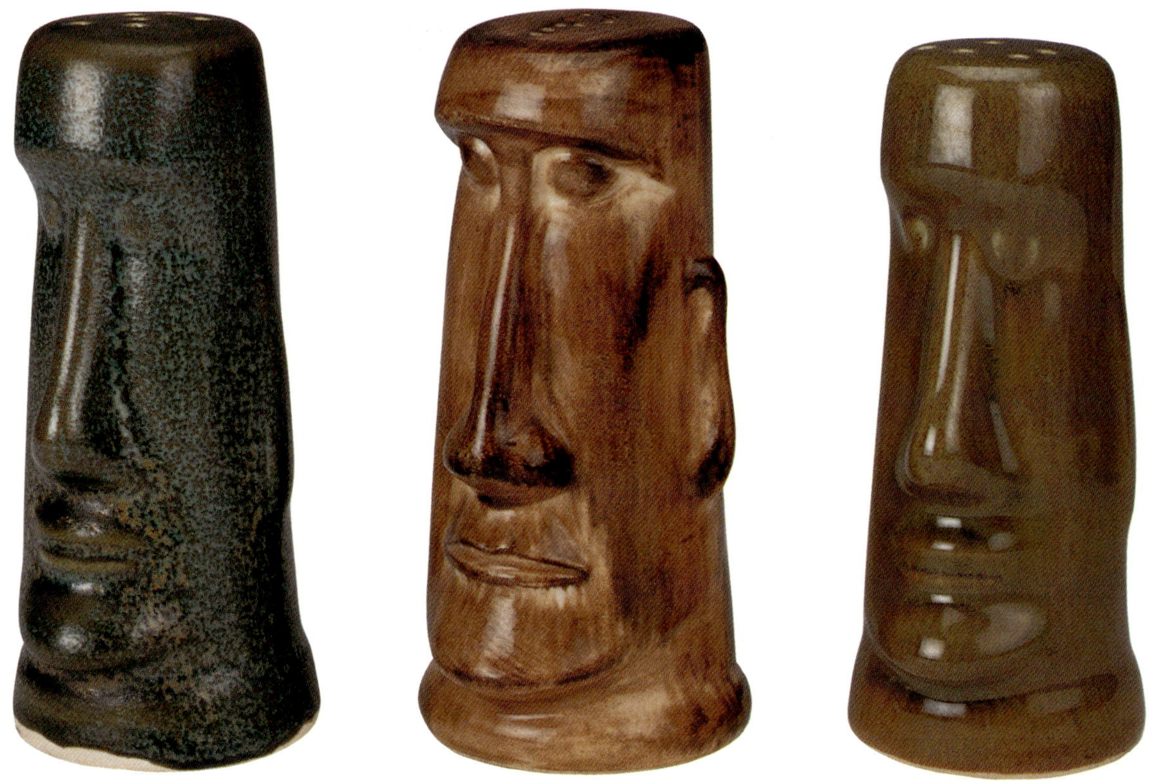

This lidded mug has holes for two straws so a couple can share a sip. Marked "Mr. Bali Hai," made Exclusively for the Bali Hai Restaurant, San Diego, Calif. 6.5" h. *Courtesy: Oceanic Arts*.

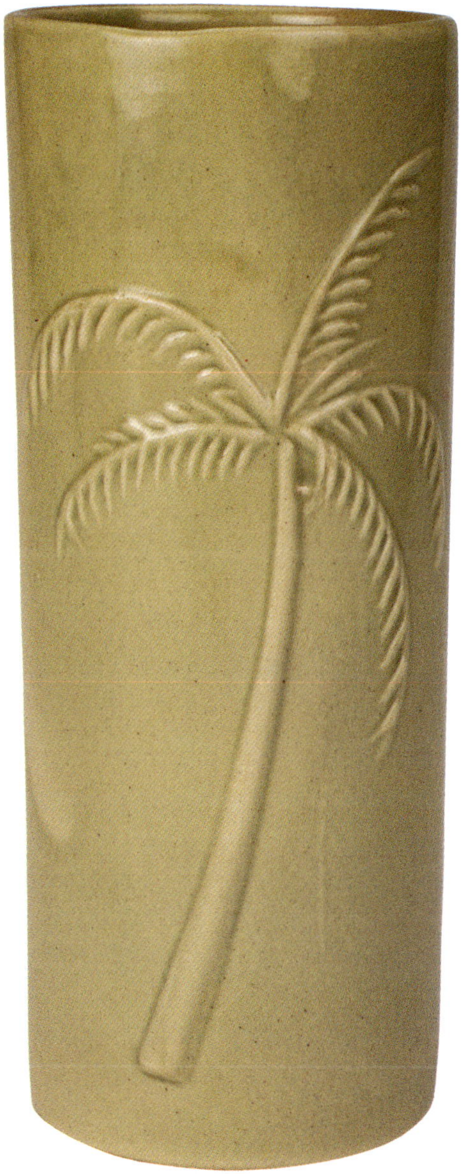

A palm tree adorns this mug from the Club Bonnie Rae. 6.75". *Courtesy: Oceanic Arts.*

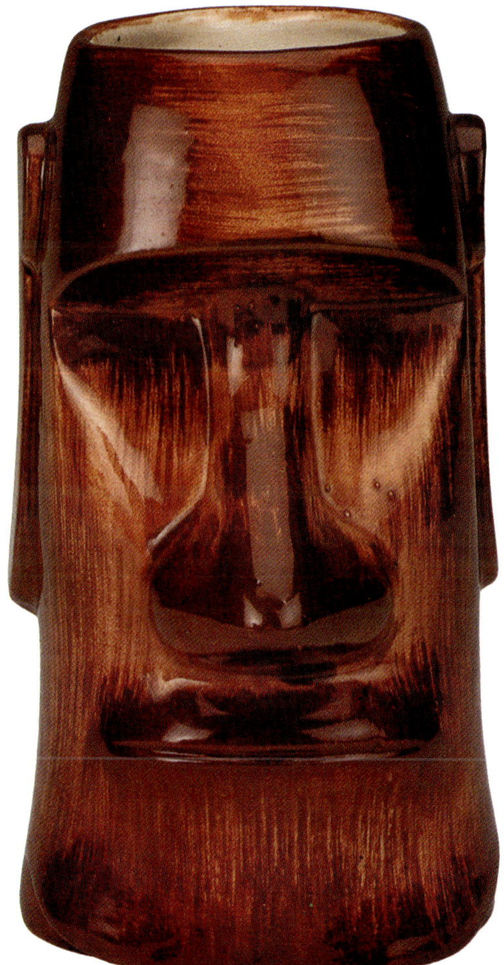

Tiki for Trader Dick's, Sparks, Nevada. 5.5" h. *Courtesy: the Collection of Brian Goddard & Gene Sweeney.*

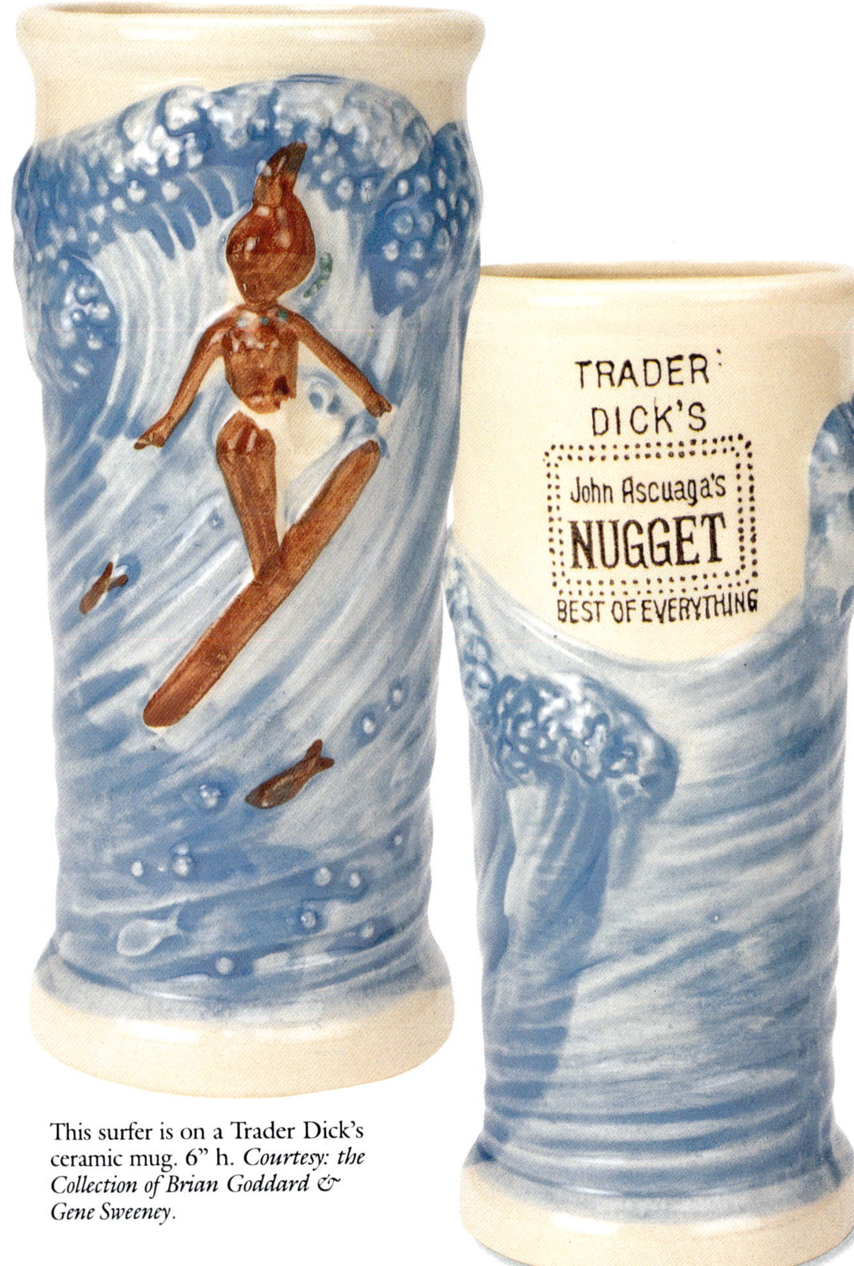

This surfer is on a Trader Dick's ceramic mug. 6" h. *Courtesy: the Collection of Brian Goddard & Gene Sweeney.*

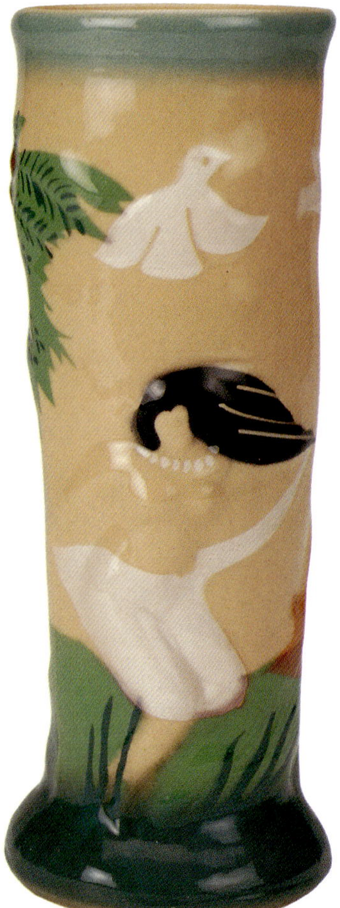

An experimental piece by Tepco, similar to those marked "Sail with Harvey." 8" h. *Courtesy: the Collection of Brian Goddard & Gene Sweeney*.

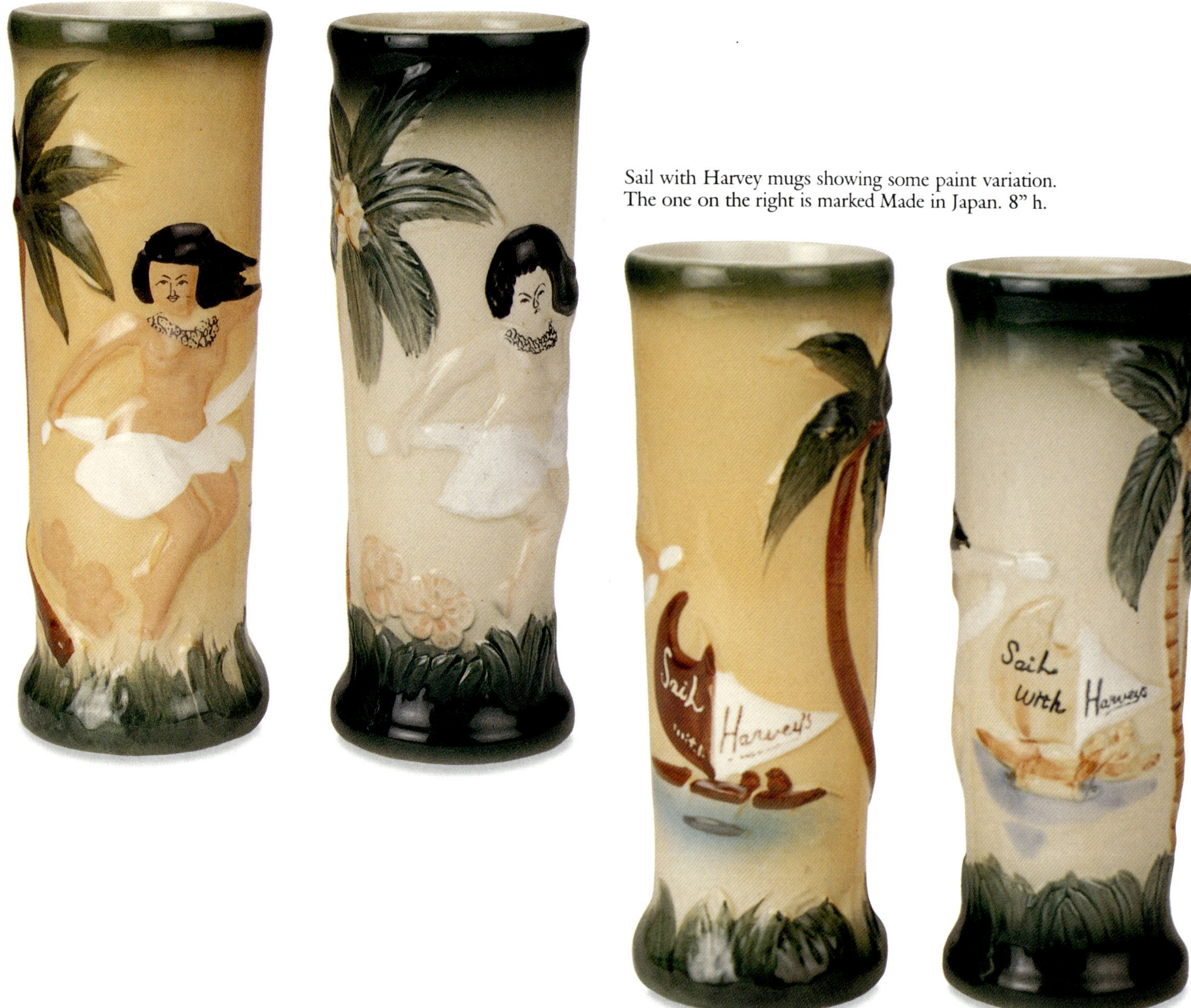

Sail with Harvey mugs showing some paint variation. The one on the right is marked Made in Japan. 8" h.

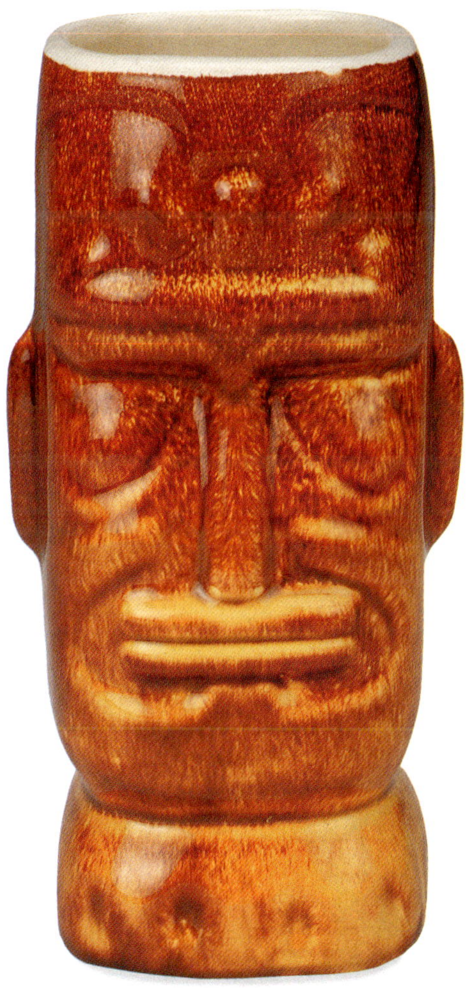

Tiki for the Kon Tiki Restaurant, Tucson, Arizona. 5.75" h. *Courtesy: the Collection of Brian Goddard & Gene Sweeney*.

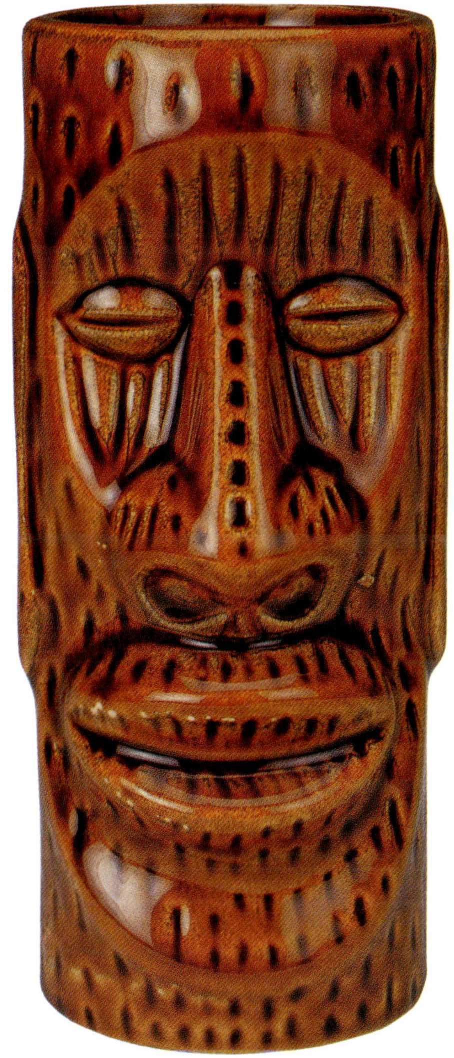

Kahiki tiki mug, made in Ohio. 6.75". *Courtesy: the Collection of Brian Goddard & Gene Sweeney*.

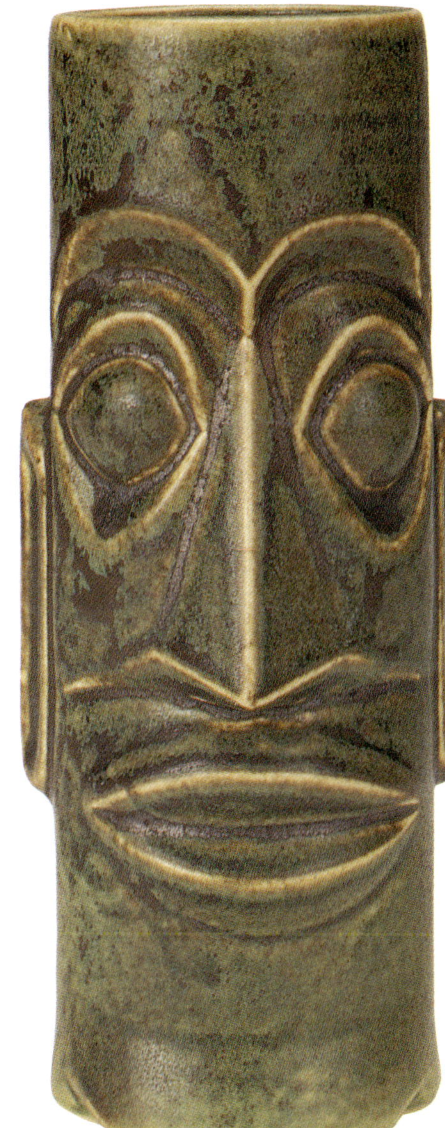

Outrigger mug, 7.75" h. *Courtesy: the Collection of Brian Goddard & Gene Sweeney*.

Restaurant Menus

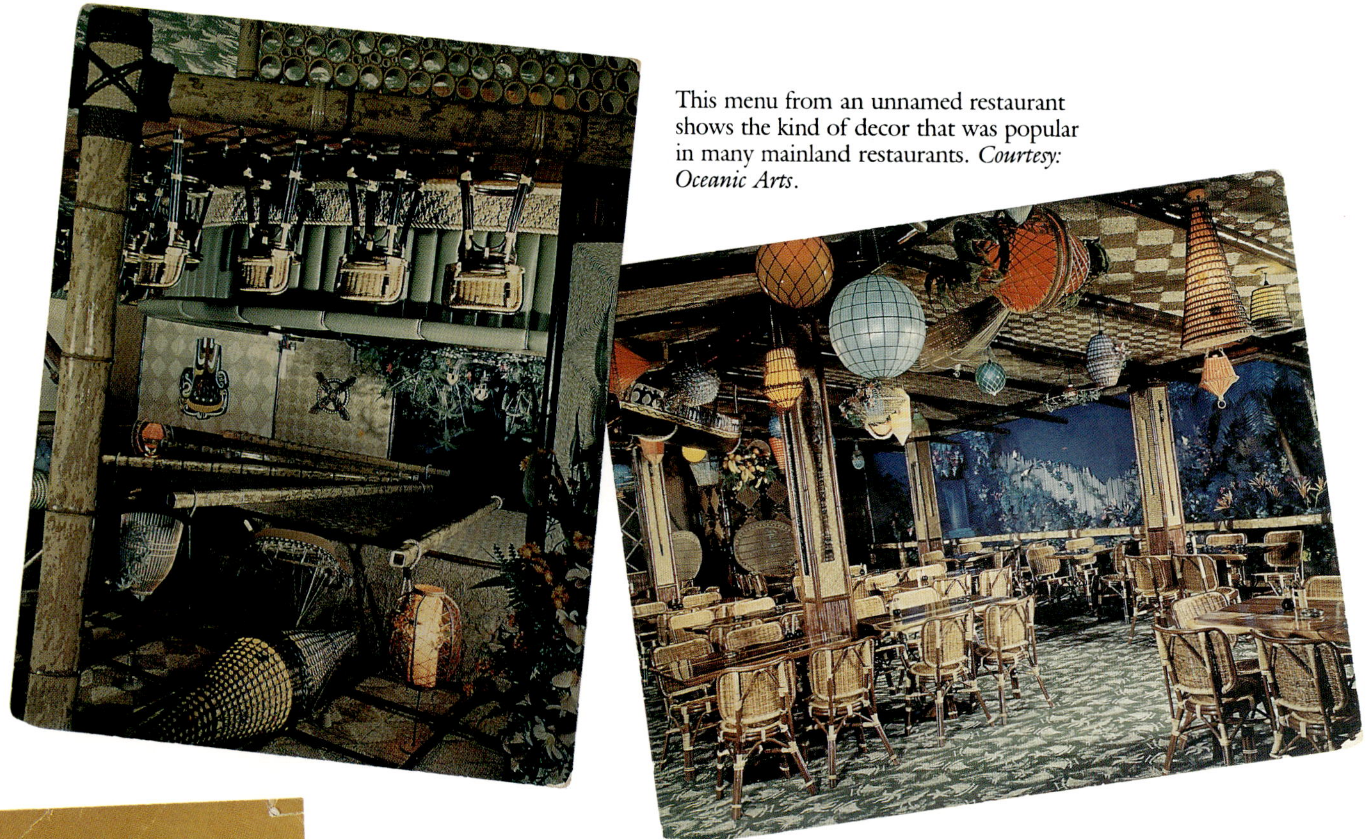

This menu from an unnamed restaurant shows the kind of decor that was popular in many mainland restaurants. *Courtesy: Oceanic Arts.*

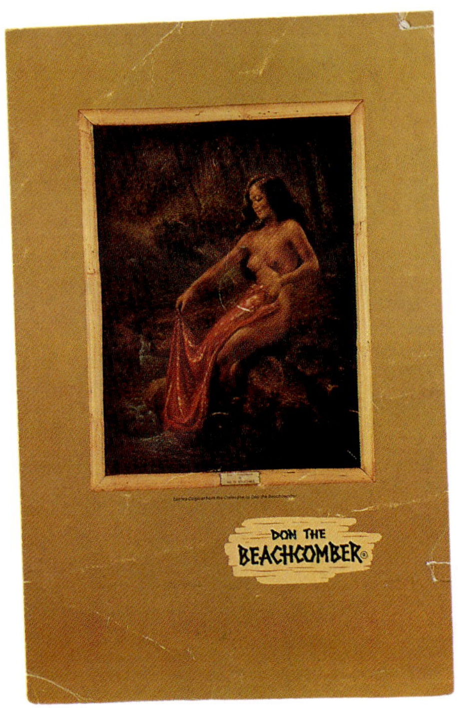

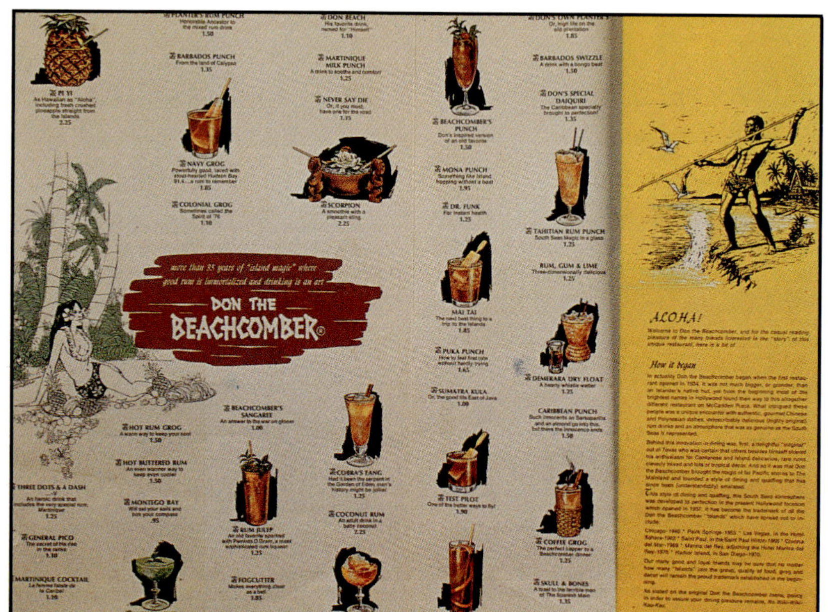

The first Don the Beachcomber was a small place on McCadden Place in Los Angeles, opened in 1934. It was small but popular for its Chinese and Polynesian cuisine, interesting bar offerings, and South Seas atmosphere. Its story is told on this menu, including its expansion into a chain of restaurants extending across the nation. *Courtesy: Oceanic Arts.*

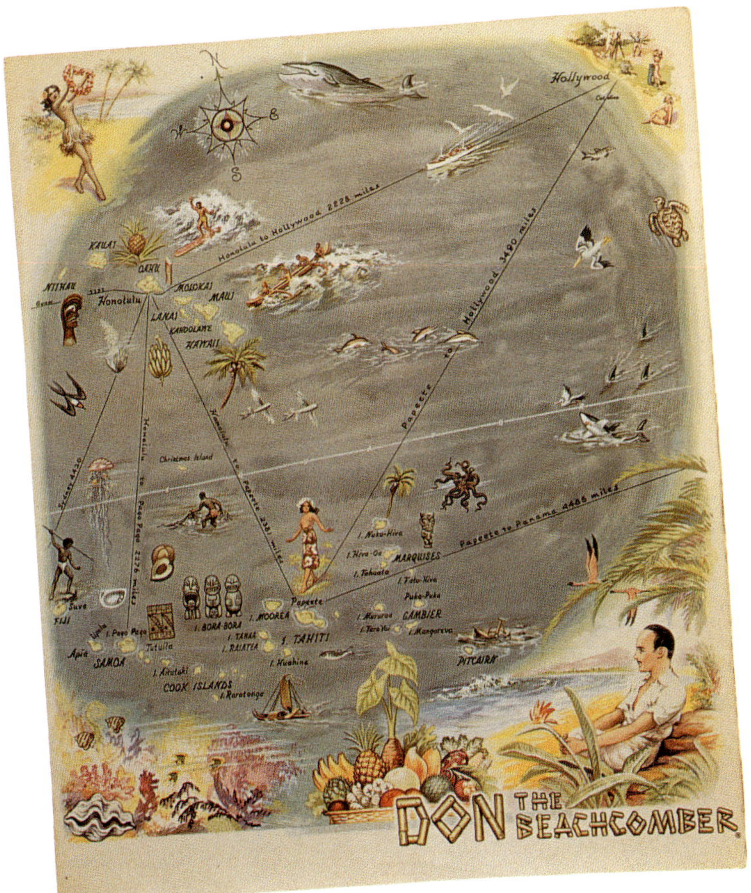

Another Don the Beachcomber menu with a map of the South Pacific. *Courtesy: Oceanic Arts.*

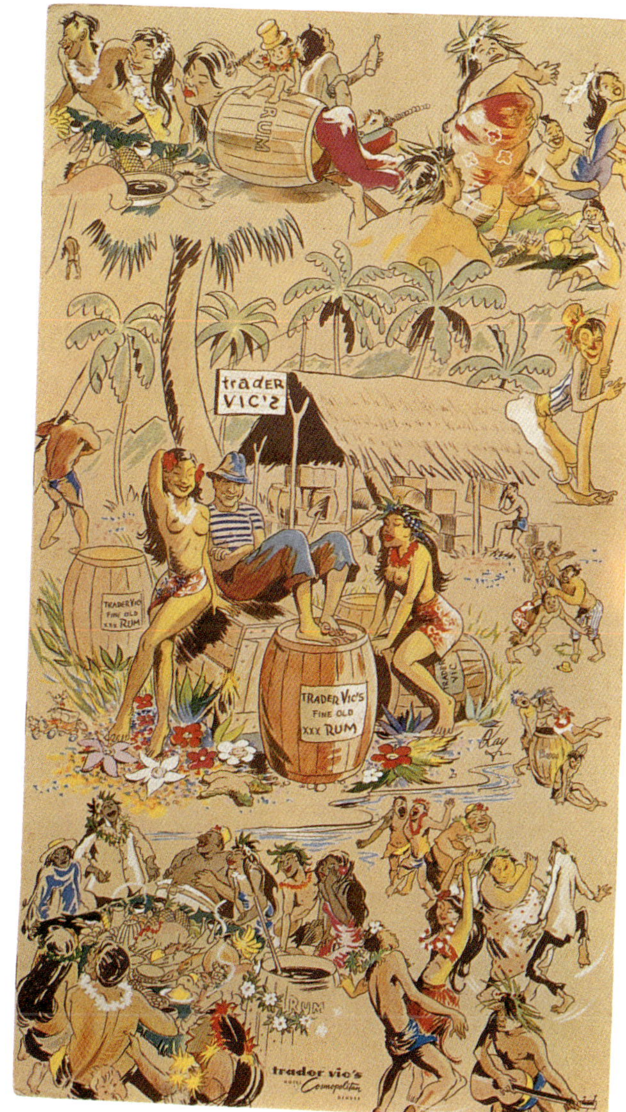

Trader Vic's has international locations, all known for their atmosphere and fine Polynesian cuisine. Their menus reveal a lighter side. *Courtesy: Oceanic Arts.*

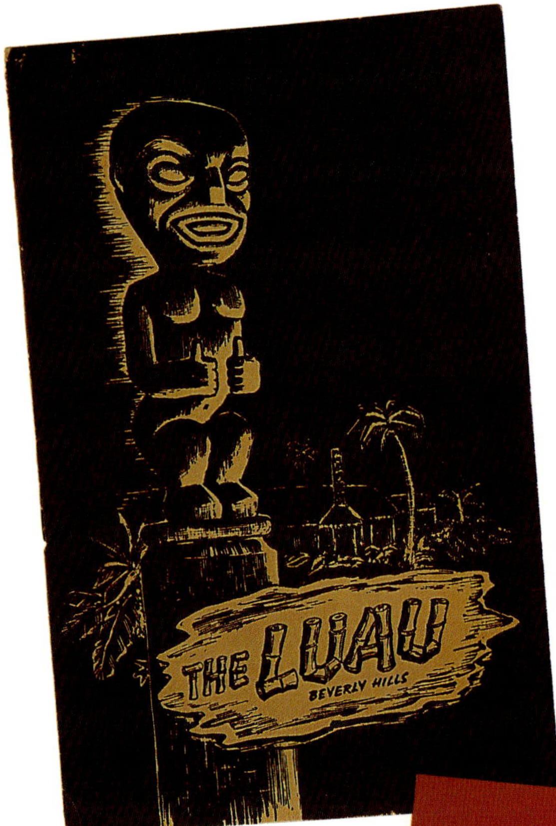

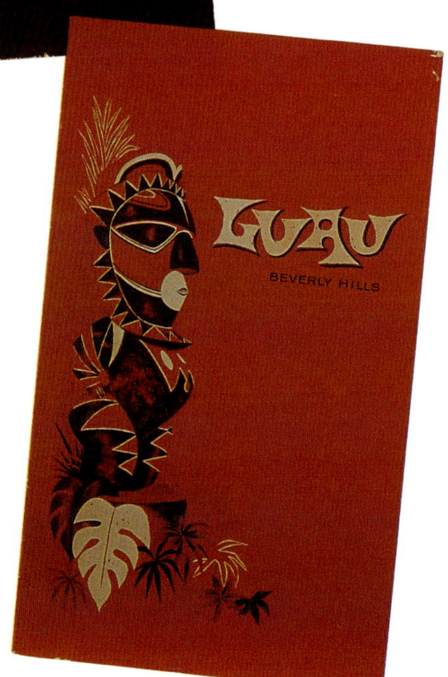

The Luau of Beverly Hills was a popular gathering spot. Here are two of its menus and the Tiki that used to adorn its decor. *Courtesy: Oceanic Arts.*

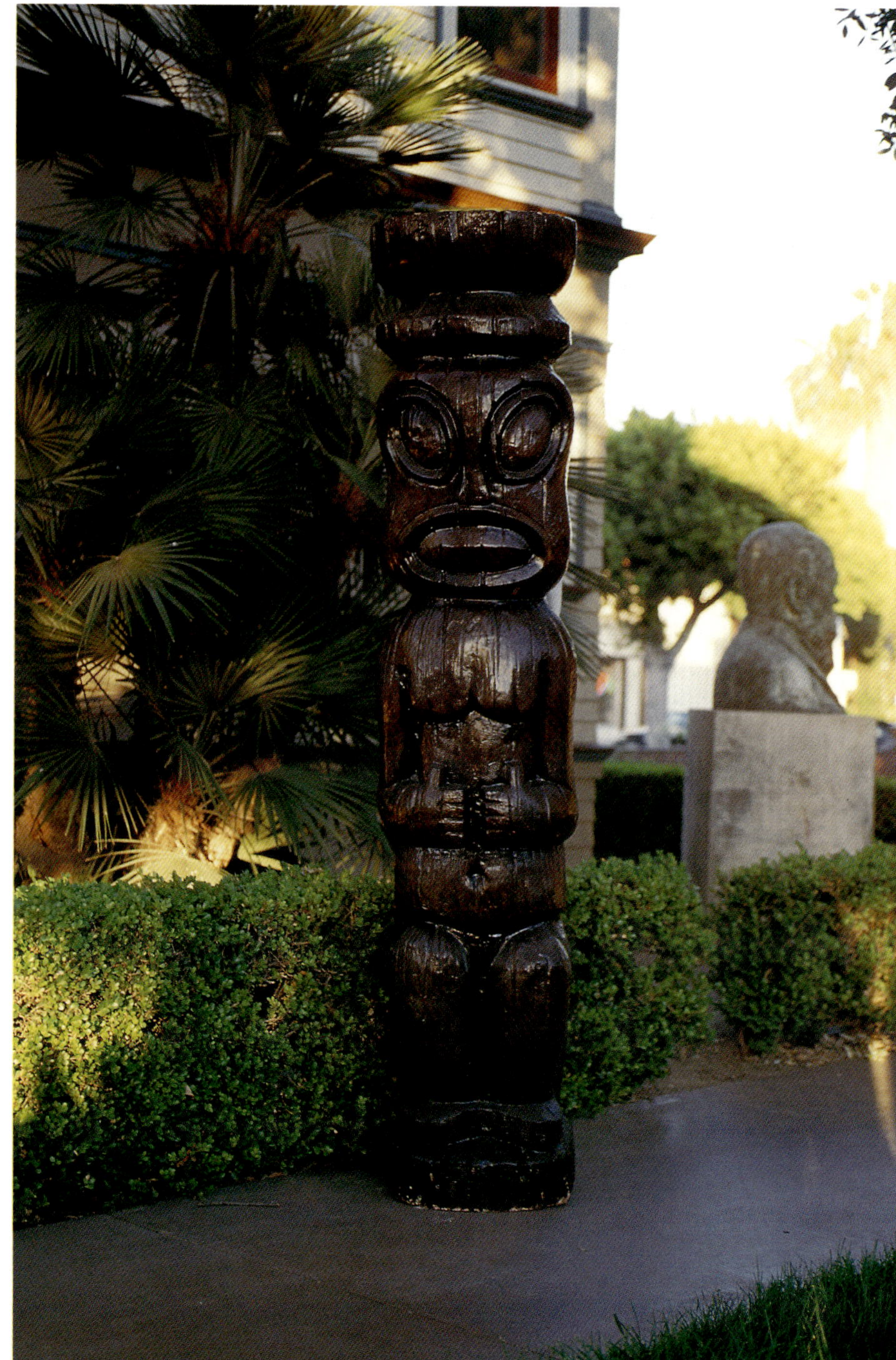

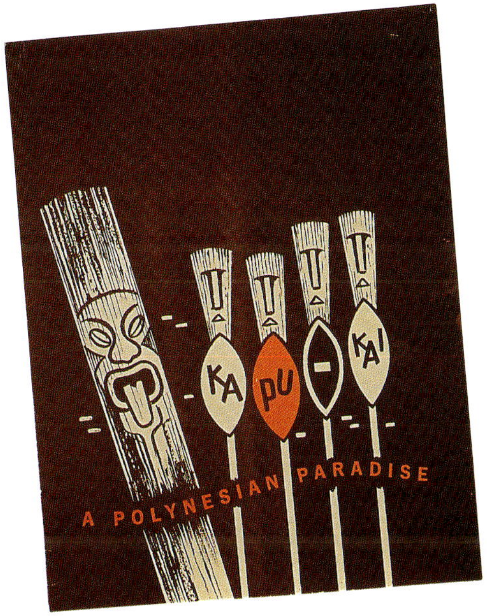

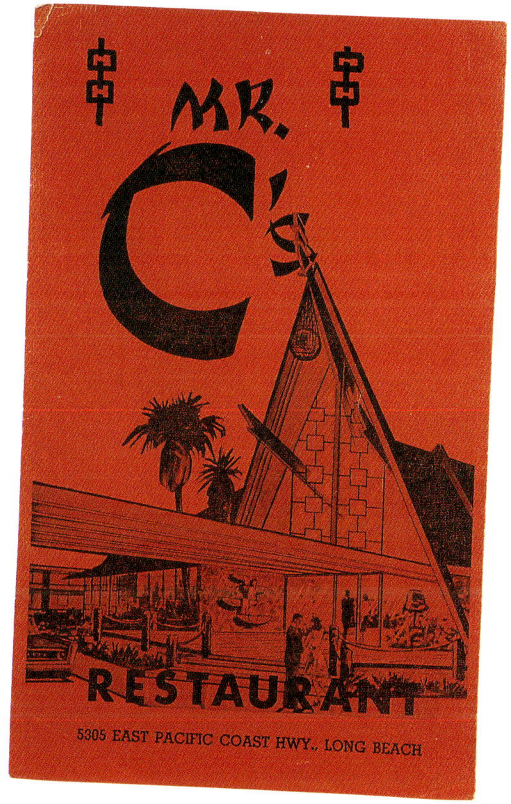

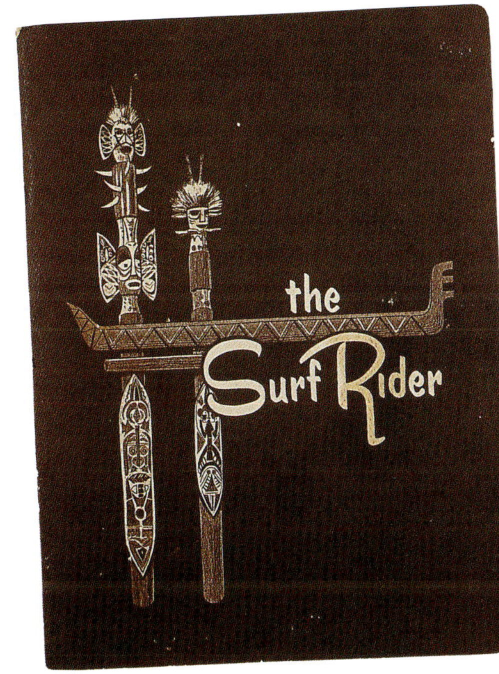

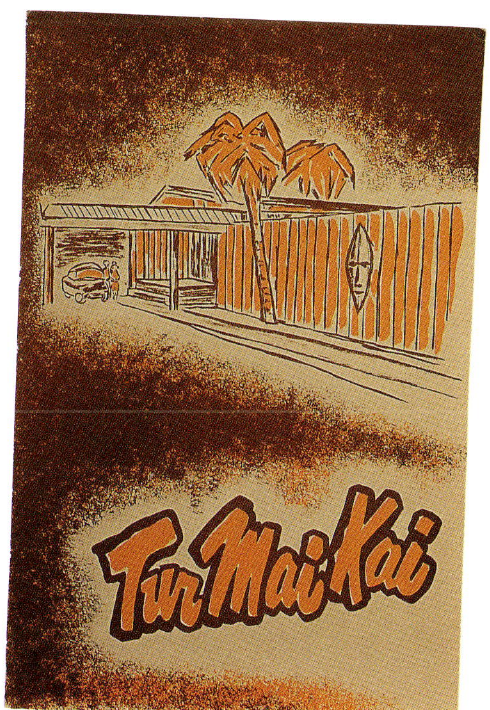

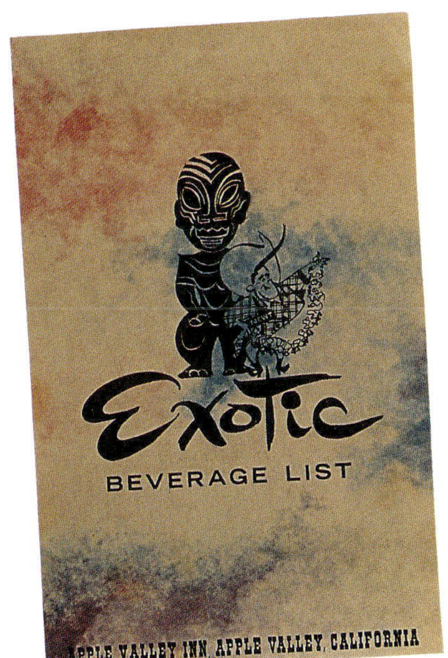

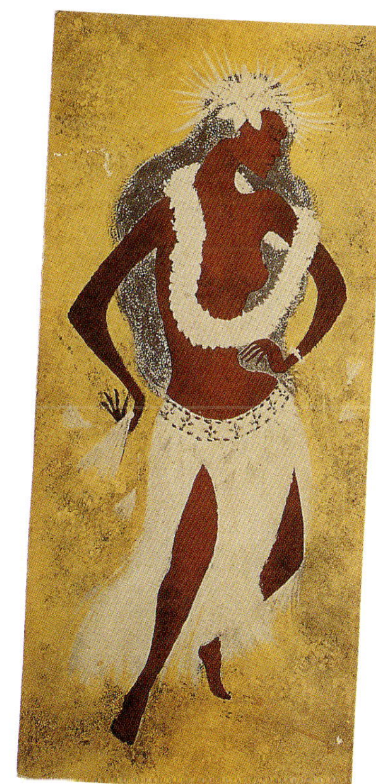

The extent of tropical fascination can be seen in this group of menus. *Courtesy: Oceanic Arts.*

Chapter 3

Personal Tropics

No visitor to the Islands would consider a trip complete without some personal memento, something that they could wear that would show the world where they had been. A shirt, a dress, a hat, jewelry, an exotic scent...each has come under the Hawaiian spell and has taken forms that are emblematic of the Aloha Spirit.

Fashion

The transforming power of the Aloha Spirit is evident in its fashions. They are the blending of the contributions of several cultures to create a new, unique product. That there are shirts and dresses at all is evidence of the influence of 19th century missionaries who taught sewing and introduced Western styles of dress—shirts, trousers, and dresses. The cotton and silk fabrics were introduced to the Islands by the Chinese and Japanese, who traded them for sandalwood, and gradually took the place of bark cloth.

Starting with individual tailor shops and gradually building into small manufacturers, a clothing industry developed on the Islands in the late 19th and early 20th centuries. Still, much of the clothing meant for local consumption was made at home.

In the 1920s Koichiro Miyamoto, a dry goods retailer, found himself with an abundance of English broadcloth, more than he could sell by the bolt. Taking the situation in hand he hired local seamstresses to transform the cloth into shirts, which he advertised locally as Musa-Shiya the Shirtmaker. Other fabrics were added to the line, including colorful patterned silks. Taking the traditional style of the palaka, a field hand's woven plaid shirt, and making it in colorful exotic fabrics, Musa-Shiya developed a shirt which he advertised as the Aloha Shirt in 1935. It has been known by this name ever since.

The bright, bold fabric patterns were also developed into women's styles of dress, including the muumuu, the holoku, pake muu, and tea-timers, as well as some newer innovations.

The clothing, made variously of silk, rayon, batik, and cotton, has become a visual symbol of the Hawaiian experience. Their popularity has spread throughout the world, and the bold floral and figural designs are imitated by fabric designers everywhere.

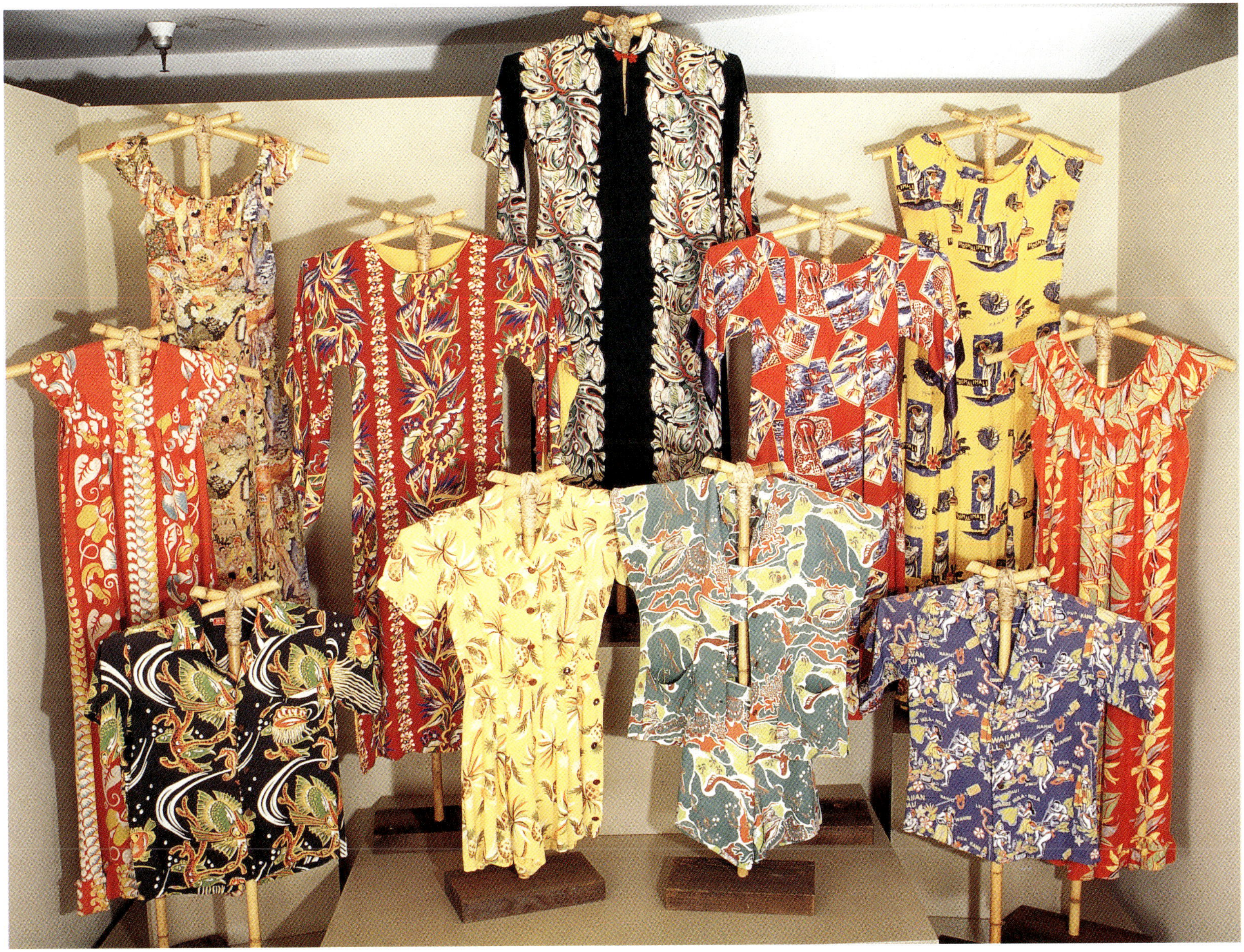

Left to right. Back row: Savages's "Island Feast" design adorns this holomu with scooped neckline; a wonderful pake muu in paneled ape leaf pattern with black background and richly colored leaves; Pacific Sportswear muu featuring a stylized lei seller. Middle row: Traditional muu-muu in red with alternating panels of foliage and abstract pattern; pake muu in deep red with wide panels of Birds of Paradise alternating with narrower panels of smaller blossoms *(see detail)*; postcard-like views of typical Hawaiian scenes adorn this pake muu *(see detail)*; traditional muu-muu in floral paneled pattern *(see detail)*. Front row: A wonderfully colorful aquatic scene adorns this shirt *(see detail)*; pineapples and palm trees grace this one piece woman's jump suit *(see detail)*; wonderful three piece outfit with bra, shorts, and jacket in scenic pattern; hulas, luaus, and other Hawaiian scenes make this a wonderful tourist's memento *(see detail)*.

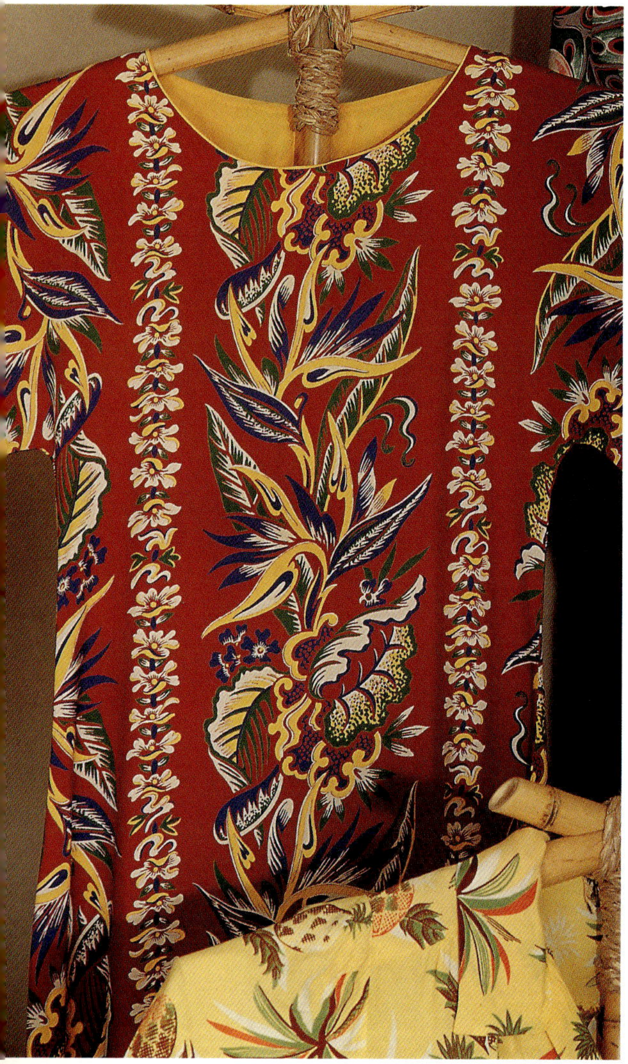

Detail of Bird of Paradise paneled fabric. *Courtesy: M. Miller*.

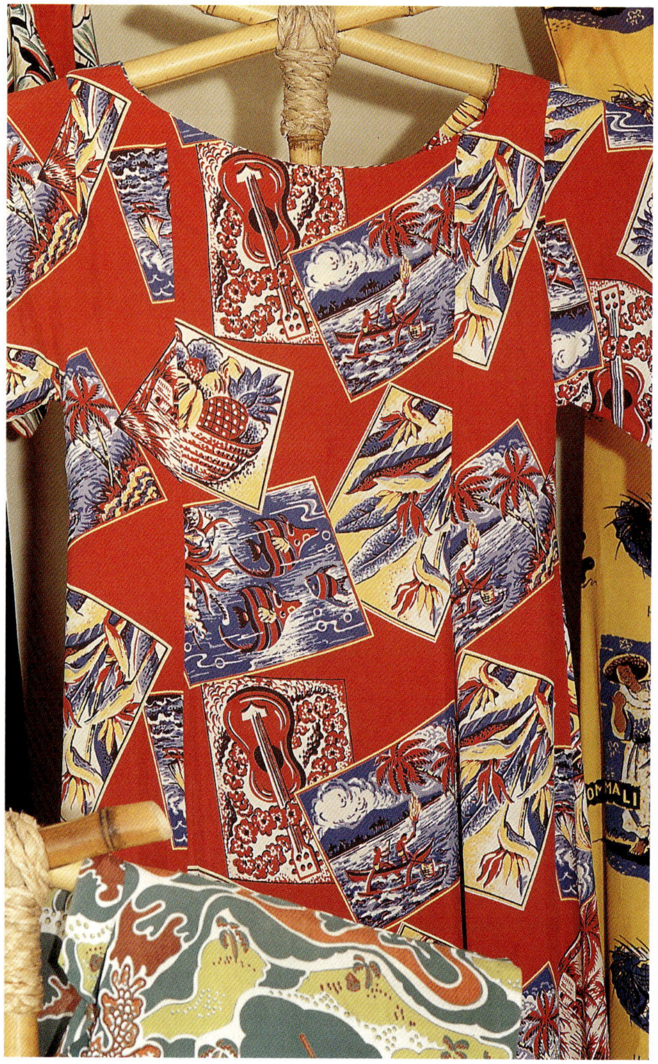

Detail of postcard fabric. *Courtesy: Locals Only, Laguna Beach*.

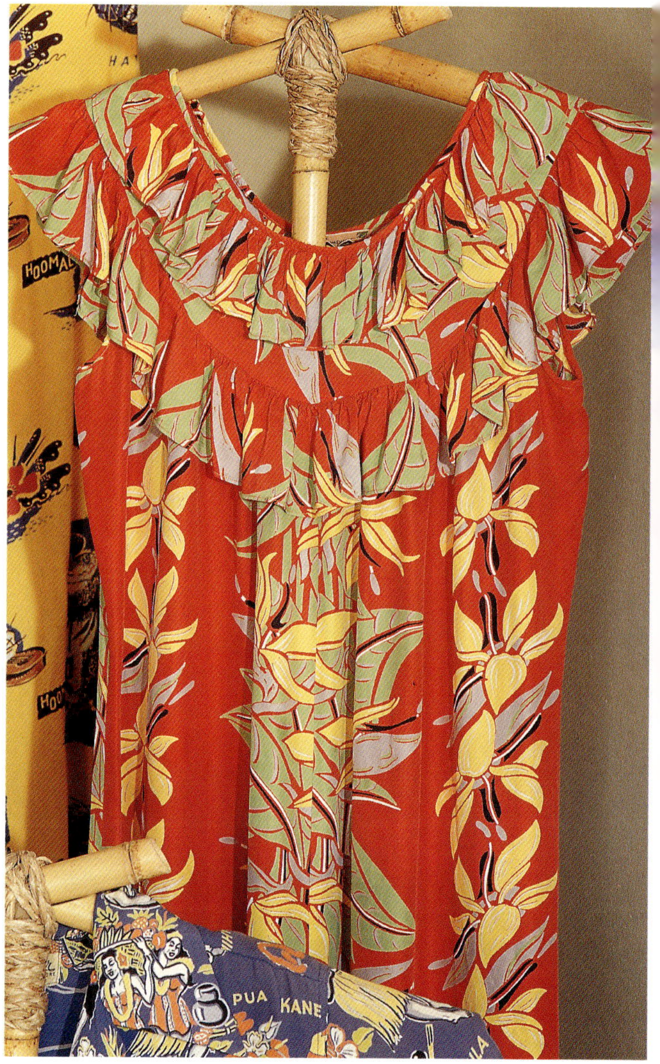

Detail of floral panel pattern. *Courtesy: Dyana Sasse, Sante Fe, NM*

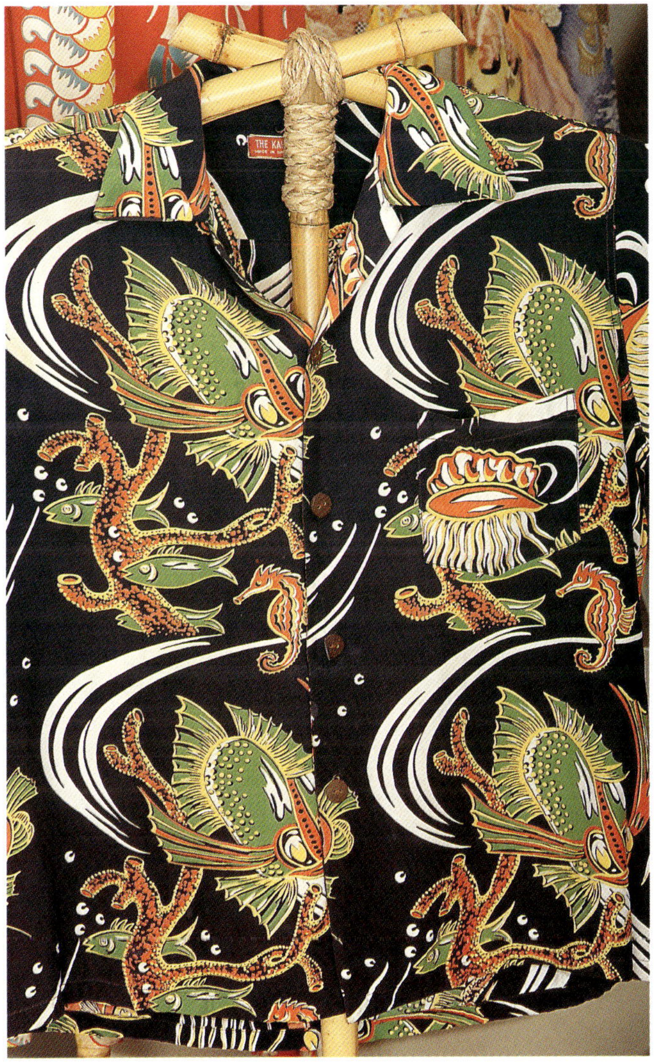

Detail of aquatic scene pattern.
Courtesy: Cary B. Weiss.

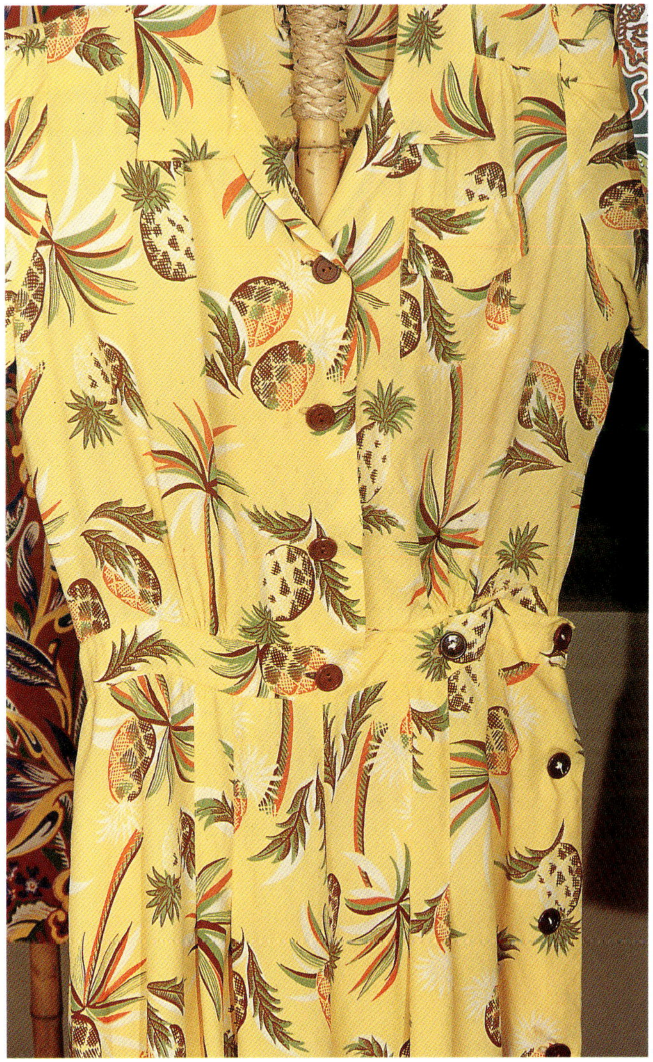

Detail of jump suit pattern.
Courtesy: Dyana Sasse, Sante Fe, NM.

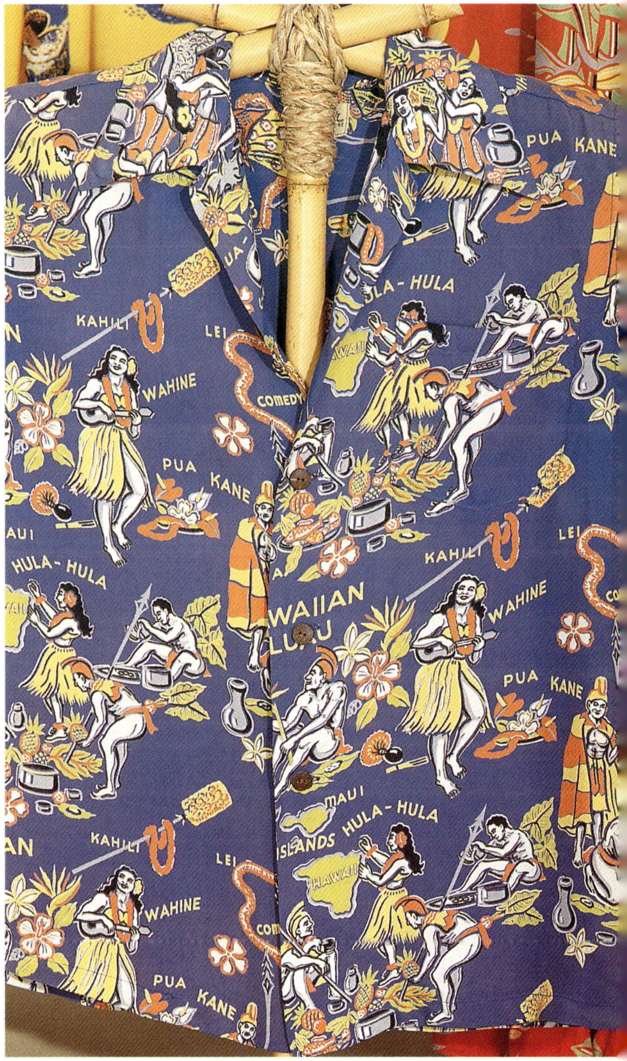

Detail of scenic pattern.
Courtesy: Cary B. Weiss.

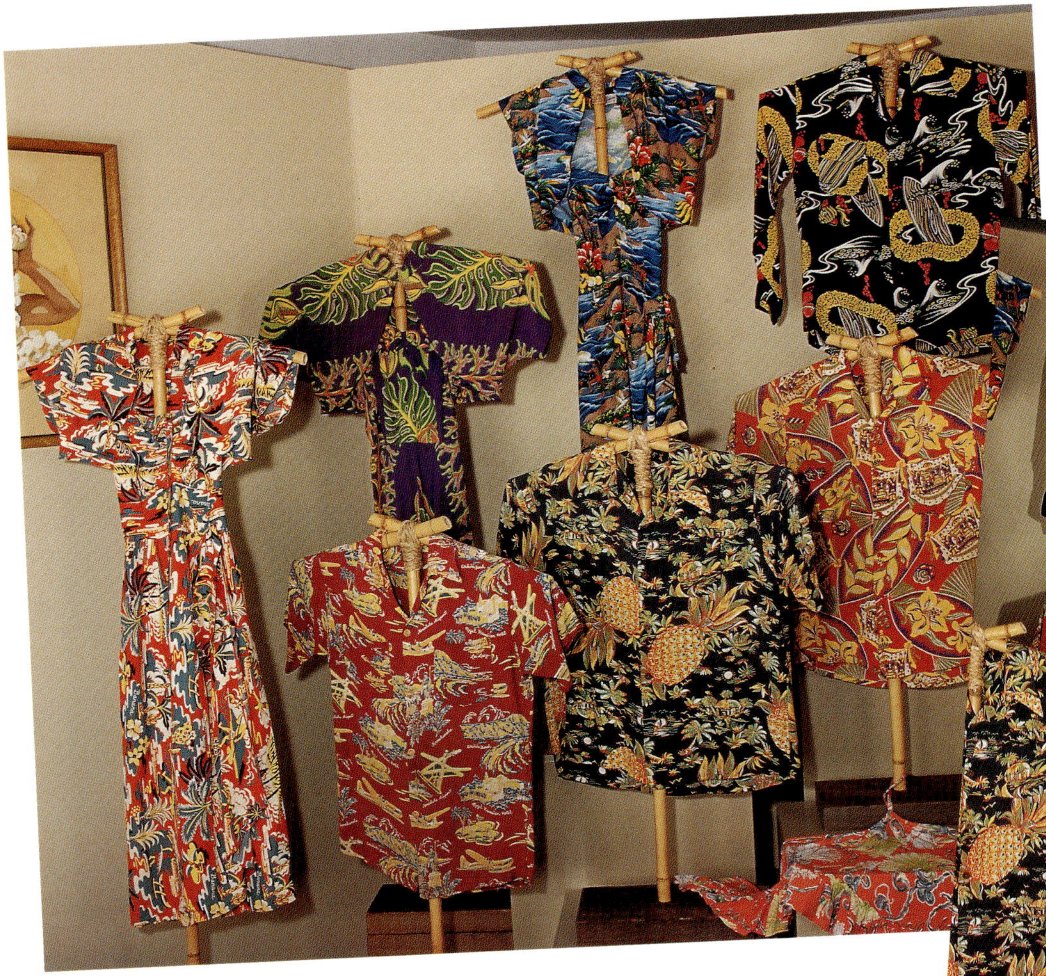

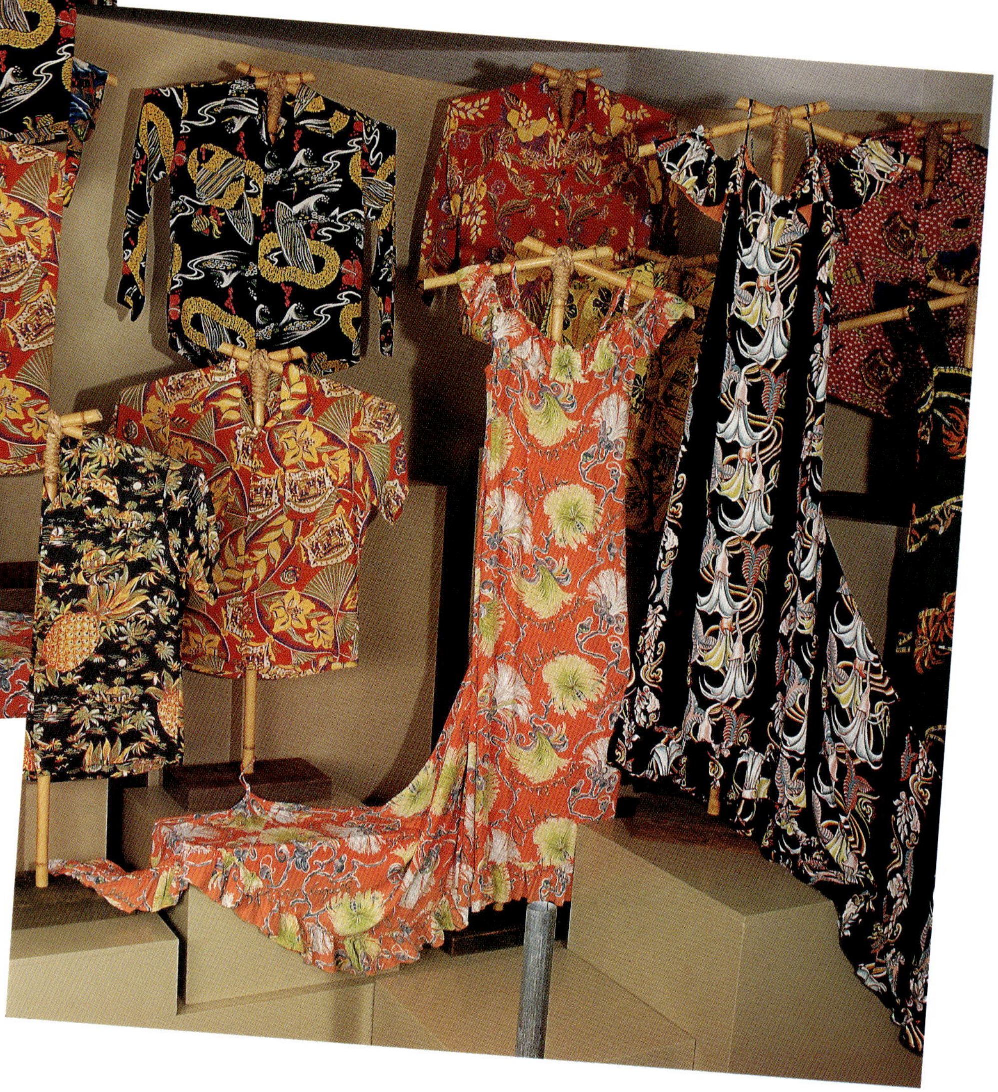

Left to right. Back row: Dress with short jacket in a rich paneled fabric of grape leaves on a deep purple background; jacketed dress with scenic print featuring the blue ocean, islands, flowers and ukuleles; long sleeve shirt with colorful surfboards and leis on a black background *(see detail)*; long sleeve shirt with an all-over floral pattern on a deep red background Front row: Jacketed dress in a scenic fabric of palm trees and water on a red background; scenic short sleeve shirt featuring well-known tourist sites including the Royal Hawaiian Hotel, Honolulu Airport, the Lei Lady, and the statue of Kamehameha *(see detail)*; pineapples are the prominent image on this scenic shirt in black *(see detail)*; embedded among the floral sprays on this short sleeved shirt is the Royal shield *(see detail)*; a holoku or formal muumuu in a floral pattern featuring bombax blossoms and the word Aloha.

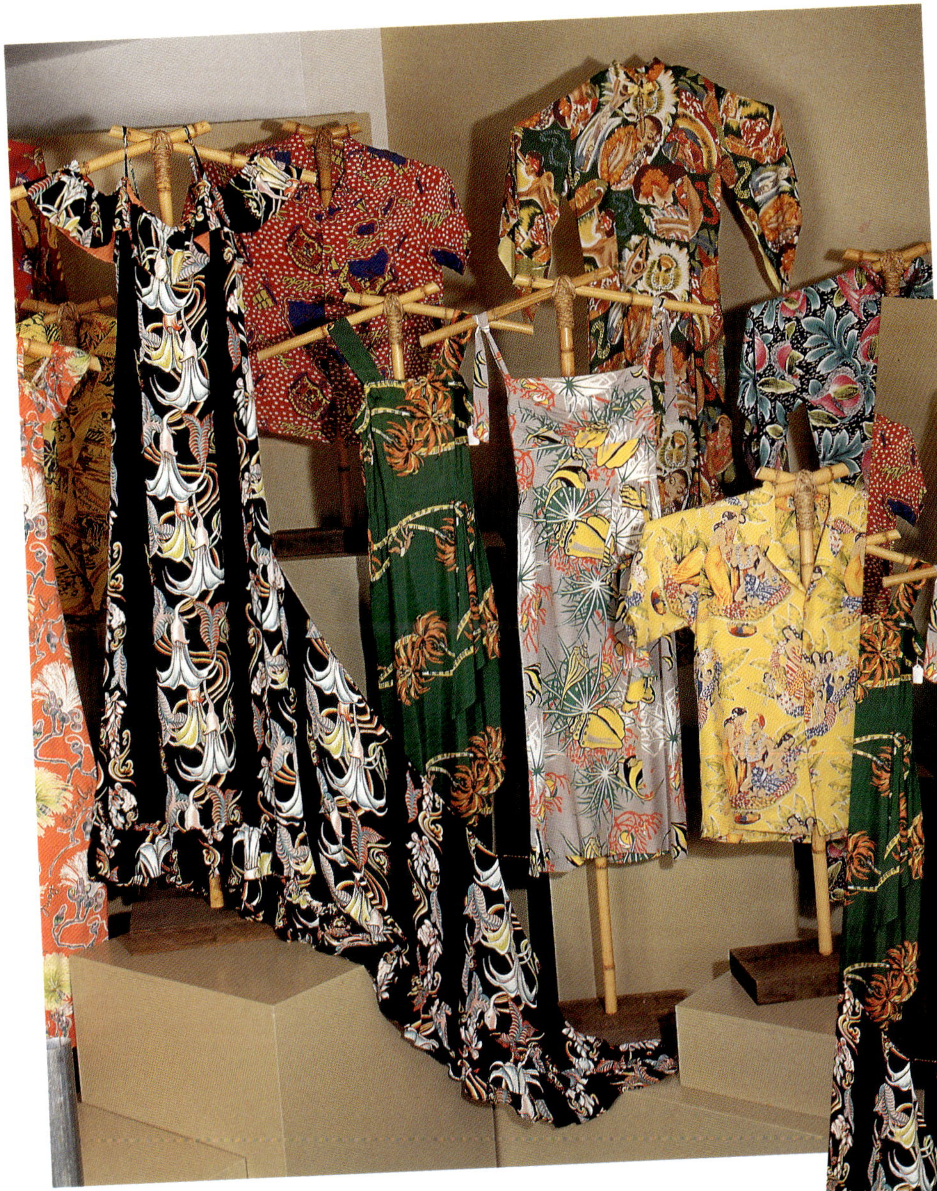

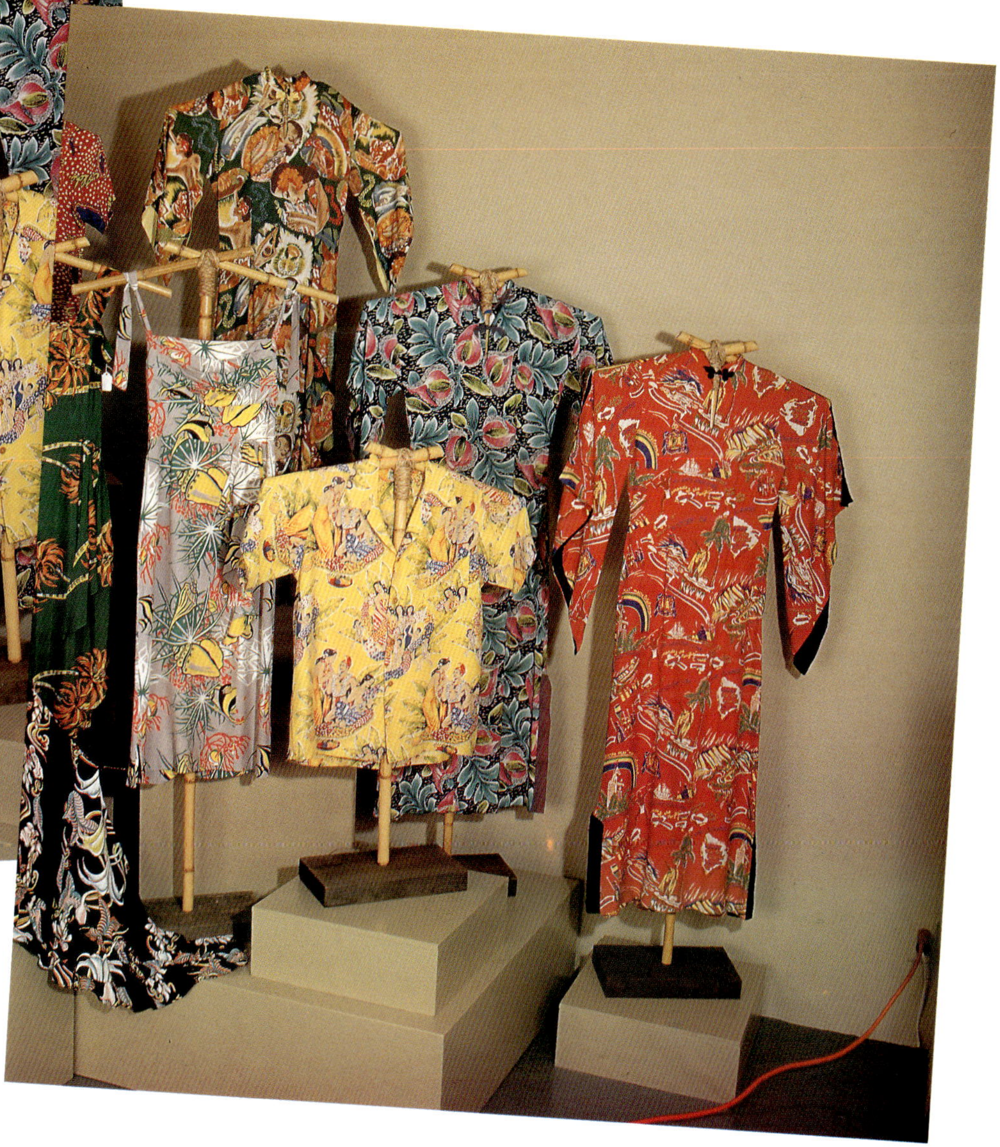

Left to right. Back row: Holoku in black and floral panels (see detail); shirt in a pattern of Island maps, Royal shields, and "Alohas"; pake muu in a pattern reminiscent of Frank MacIntosh's style *(see detail)*; pake muu in a wonderful floral print in turquoise and pink on a black background *(see detail)*. Front row: bias cut sundress with graphic print of a boy climbing a palm tree *(see detail)*; strapped dress in an unusual fabric with sea life pattern on a gray background *(see detail)*; Yellow shirt with images of Hawaiian people frolicking in leis *(see detail)*; pake muu in red fabric with scenes from the history of the Hawaiian Islands.

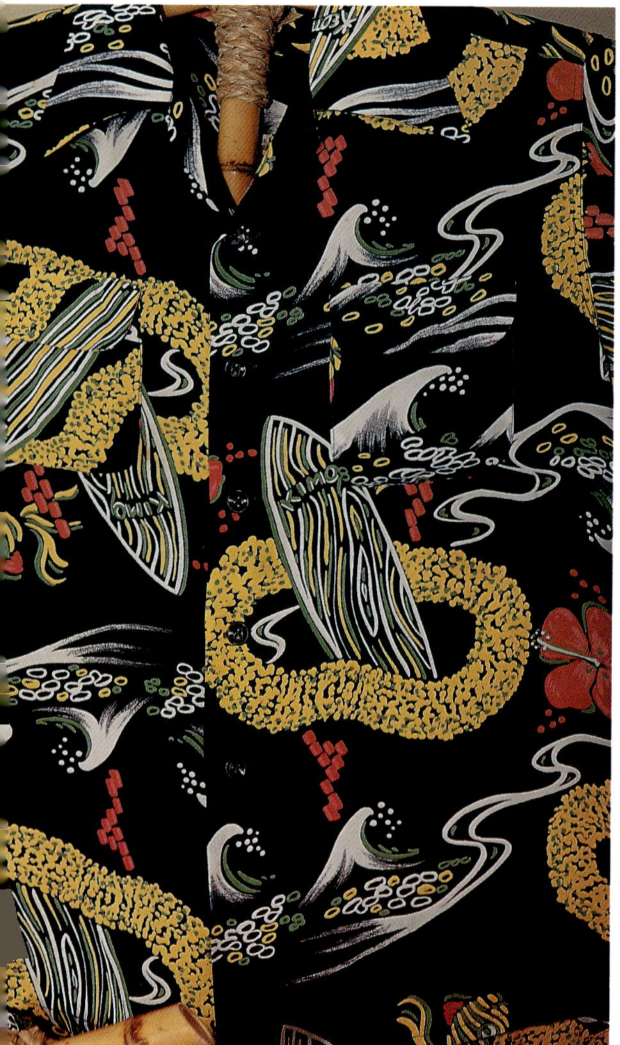

Detail of the surfboard and lei pattern.
Courtesy: Cary B. Weiss.

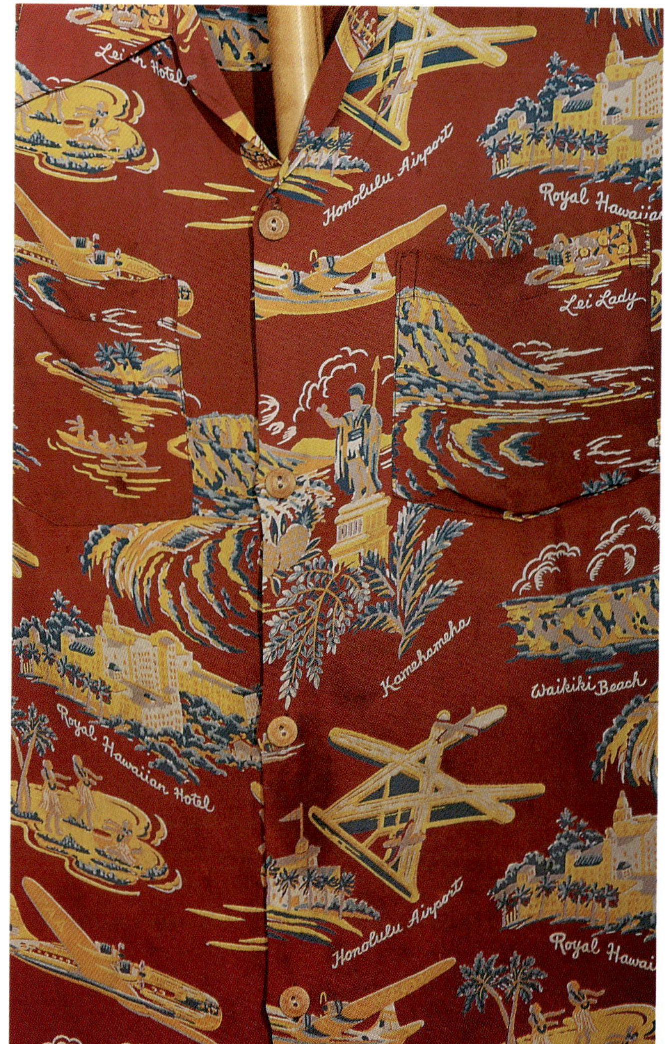

Detail of the scenic landmarks fabric.
Courtesy: Cary B. Weiss.

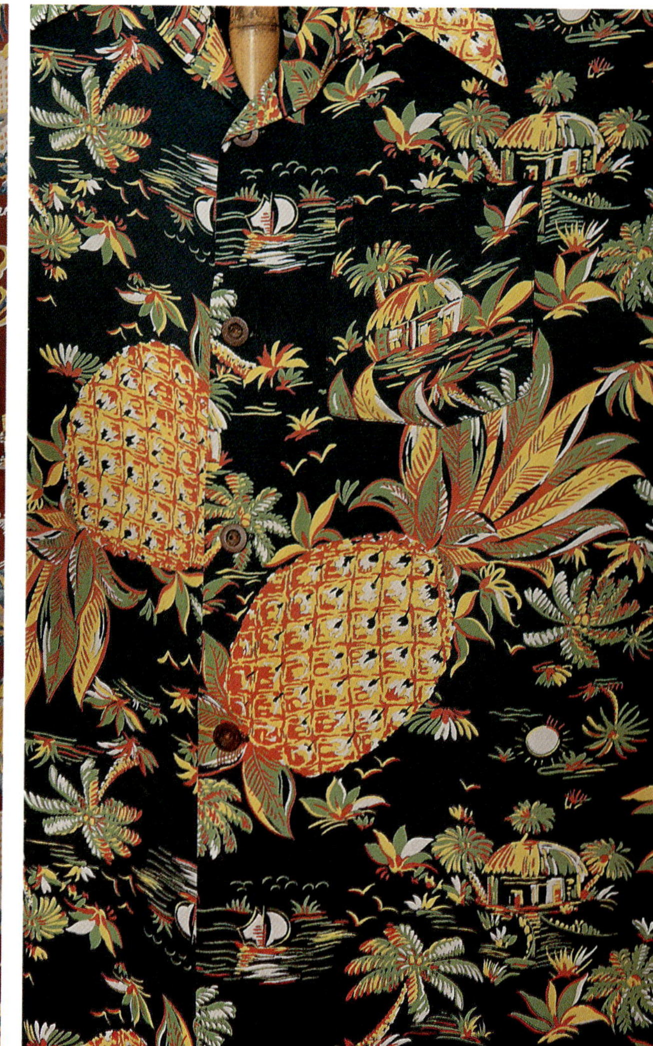

Detail of the scenic pineapple pattern.
Courtesy: Cary B. Weiss.

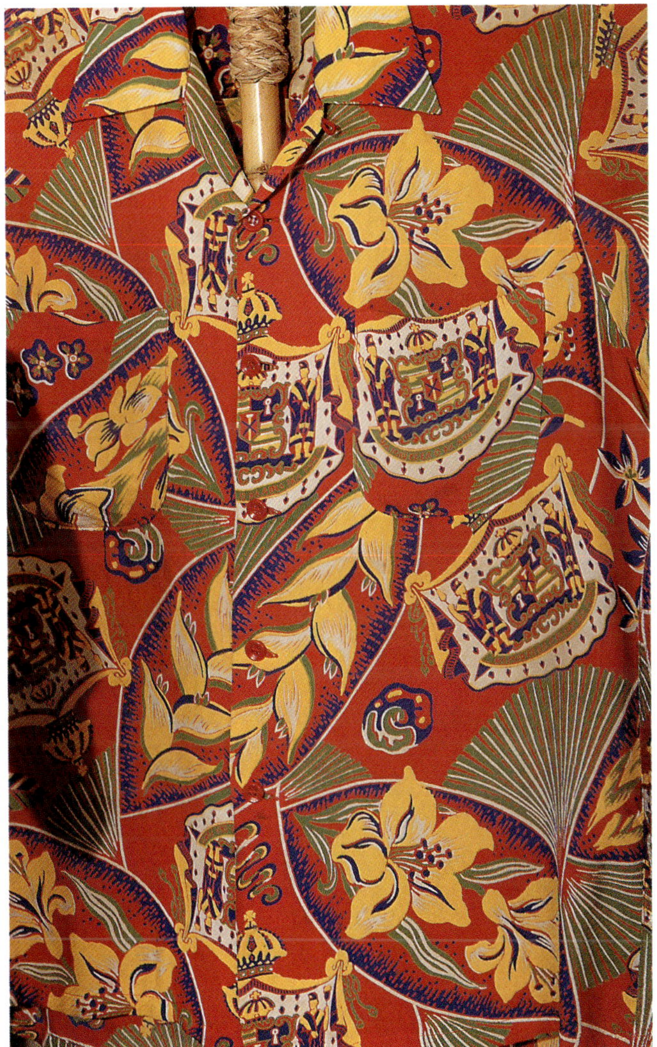

Detail of the Royal shield floral fabric. *Courtesy: Cary B. Weiss.*

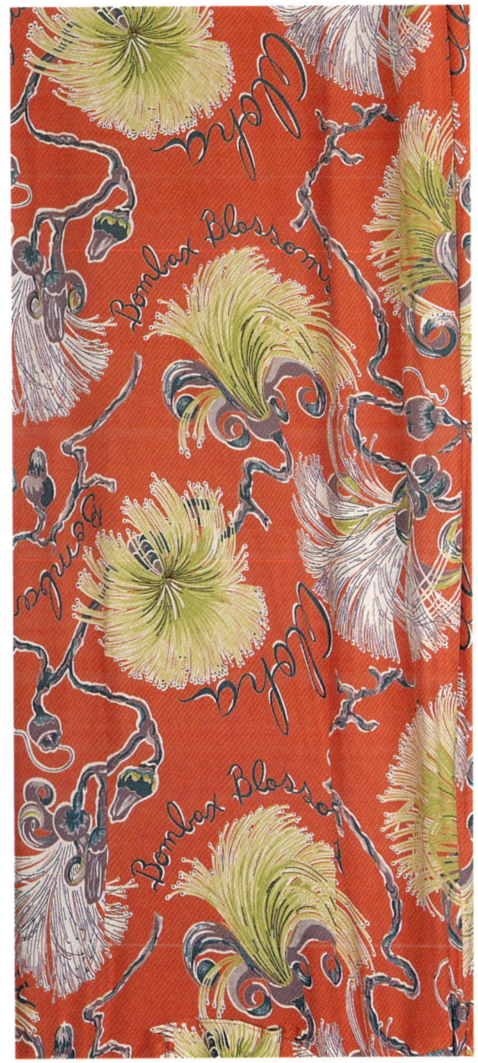

Detail of the bombax/Aloha fabric. *Courtesy: Laurie Haslund.*

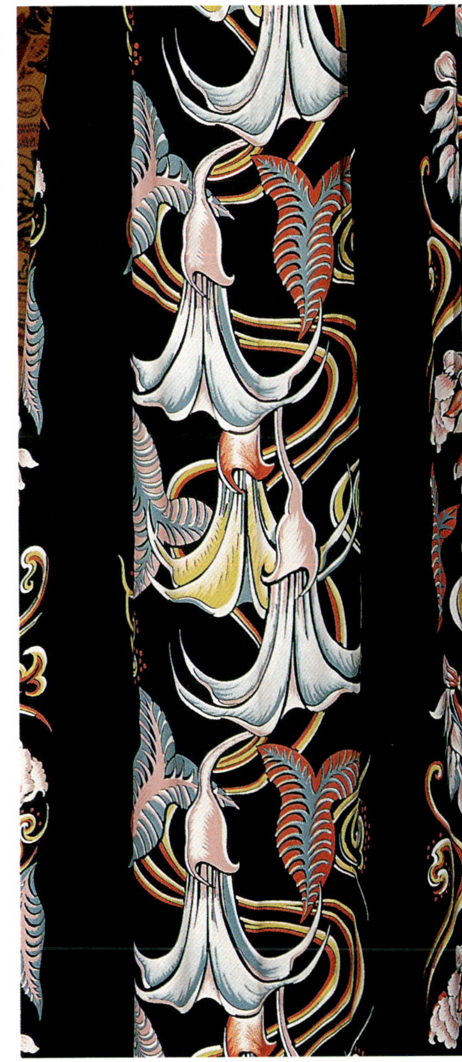

Detail of the black and floral patterns of the holoku. *Courtesy: James O'Mahoney, S.B.S.M.*

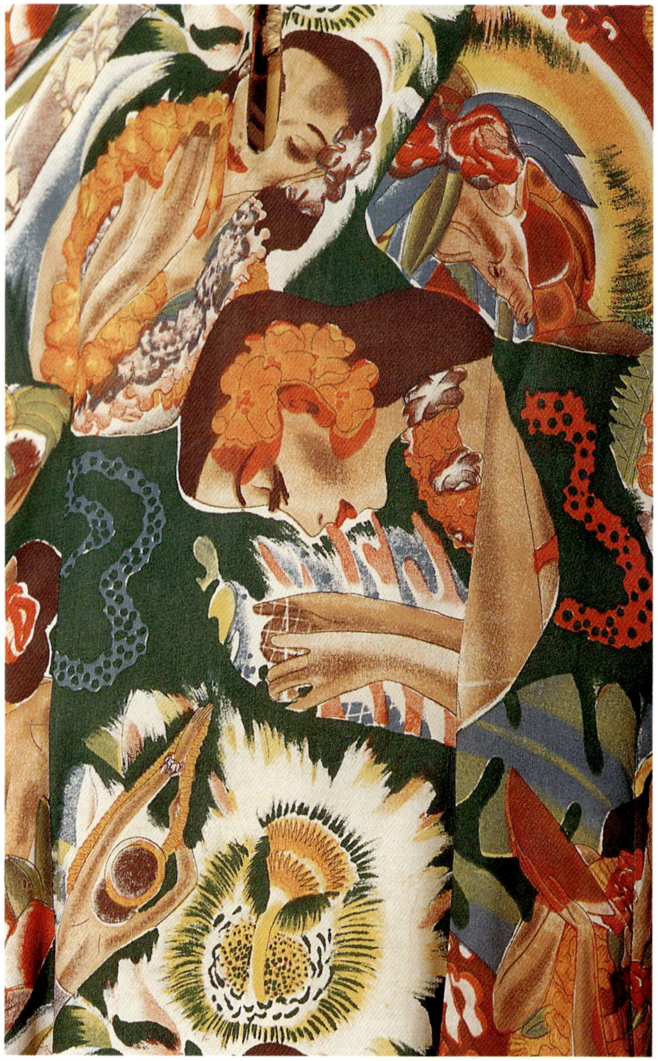

Detail of the MacIntosh-like pattern. *Courtesy: Locals Only, Laguna Beach.*

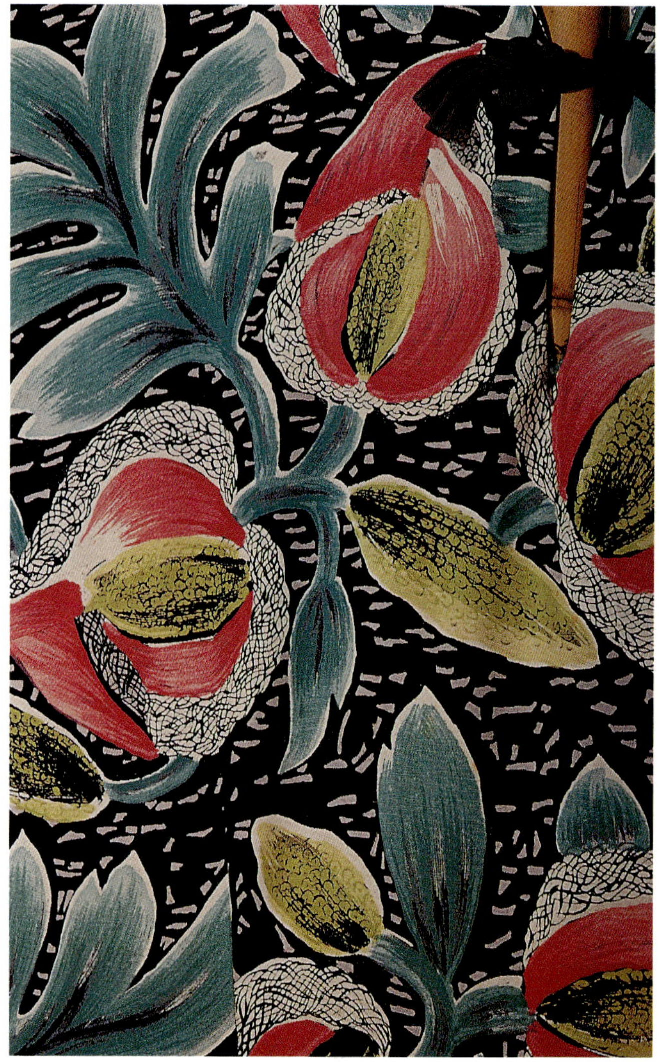

Detail of the turquoise and pink floral pattern. *Courtesy: Locals Only, Laguna Beach.*

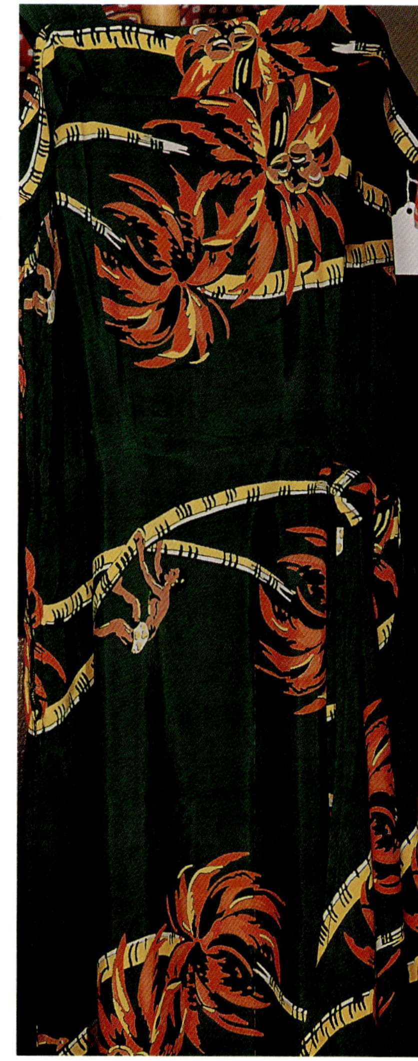

Detail of the graphic print on the sundress. *Courtesy: Dyana Sasse, Sante Fe, NM.*

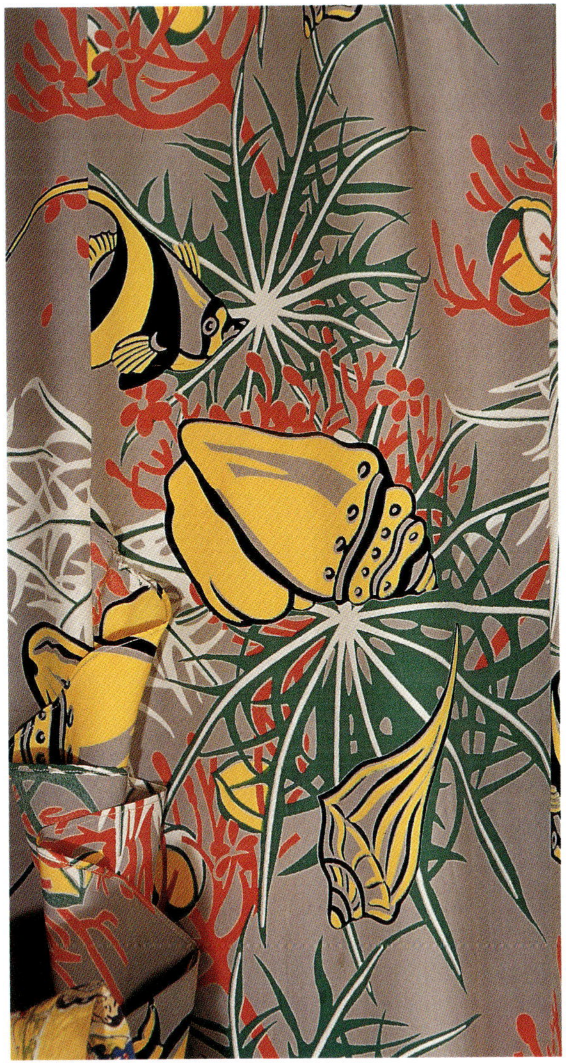

Detail of the sea life pattern.
Courtesy: Locals Only, Laguna Beach.

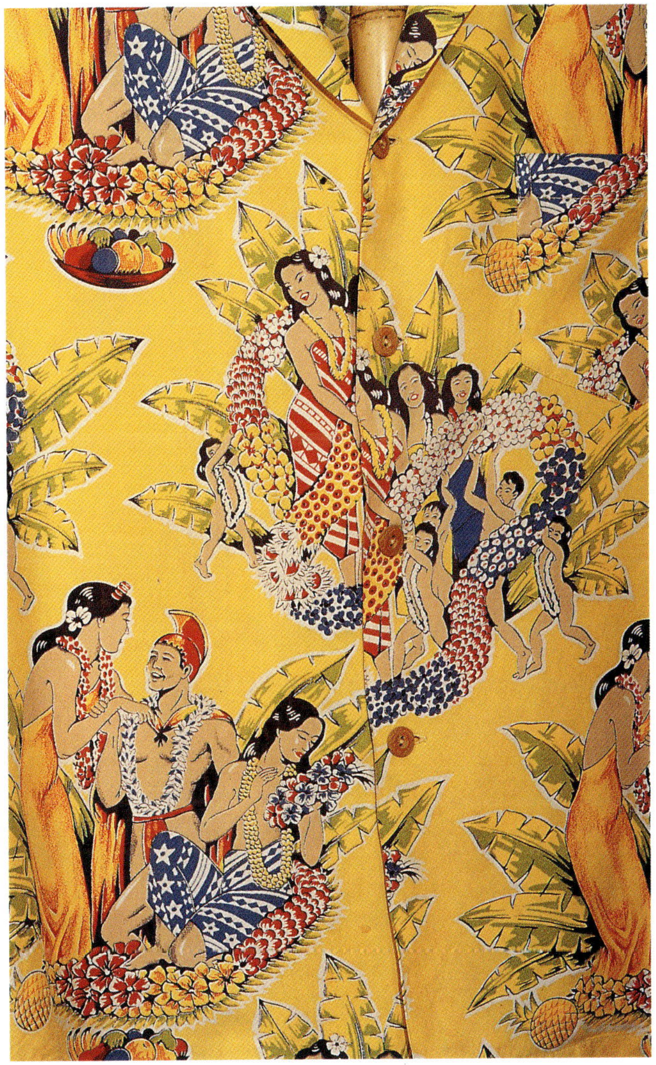

Detail of the Hawaiian people pattern.
Courtesy: Cary B. Weiss.

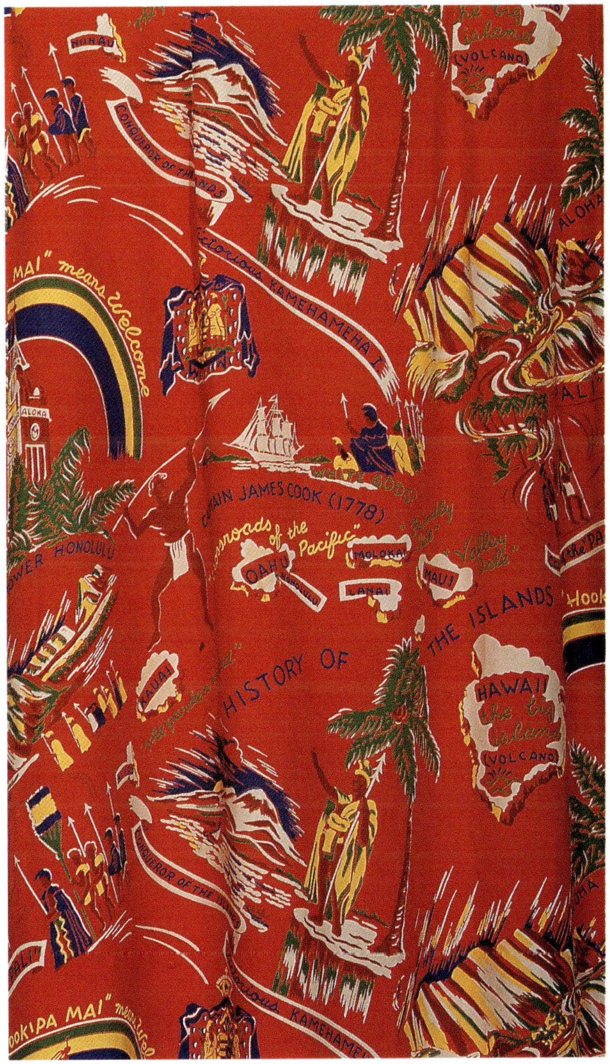

Detail of the historical print. *Courtesy: Locals Only, Laguna Beach.*

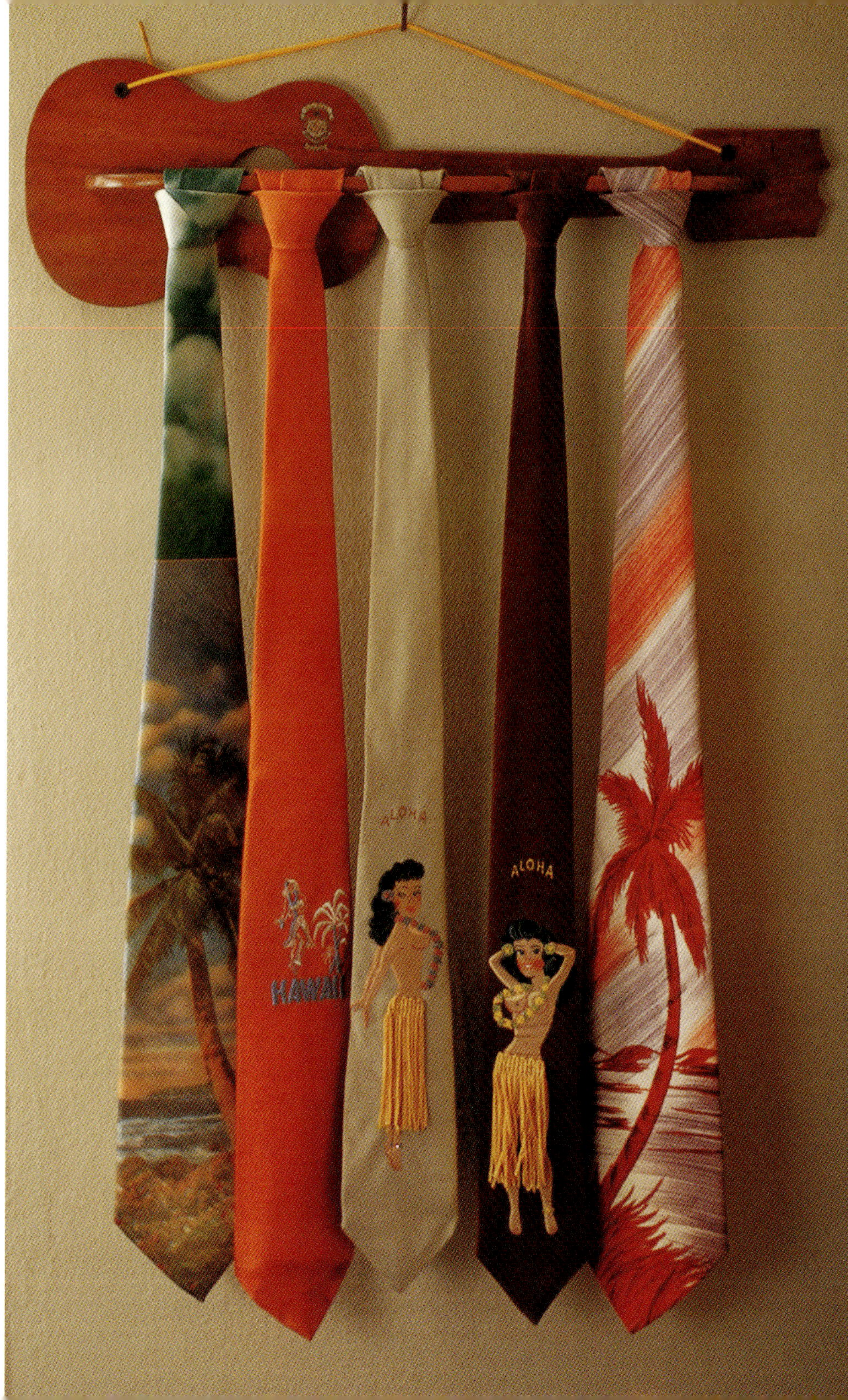

A few of the many neckties manufactured to capture the Hawaiian experience. Many were probably kept in the closet as a secret memento, but some were undoubtedly worn with pride. *Courtesy: Jim & Susie Stiso*.

Jewelry

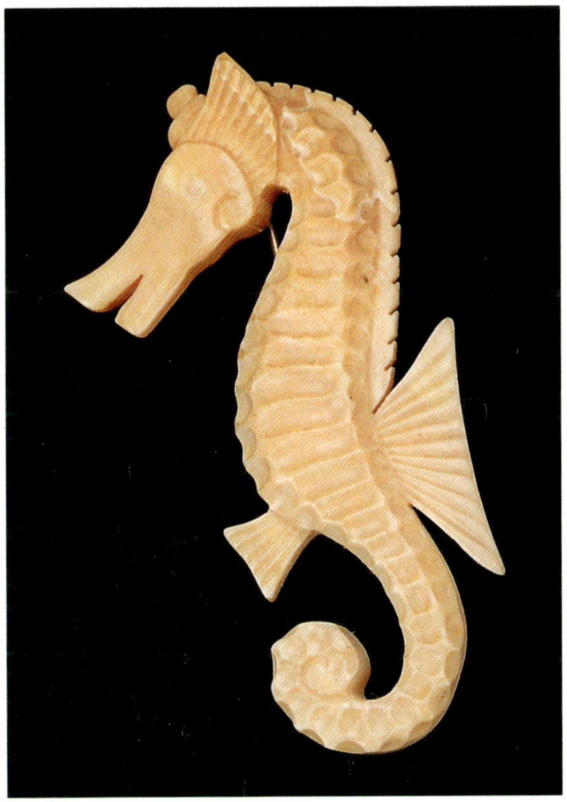

Ming sea horse, 3". *Courtesy: Locals Only, Laguna Beach.*

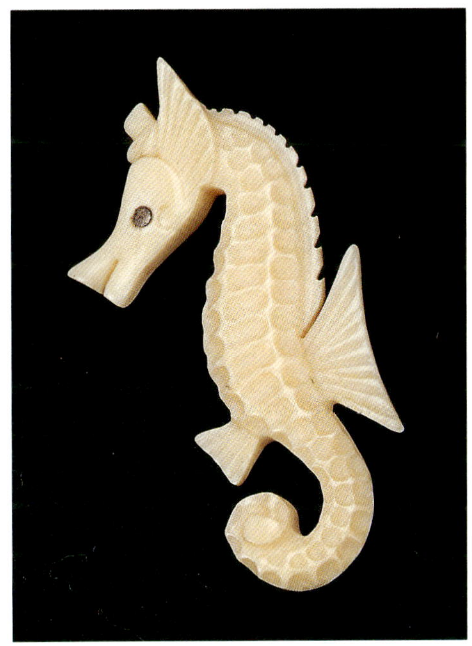

Ming sea horse, 2.25" h. *Courtesy: Susan Mast Enterprises.*

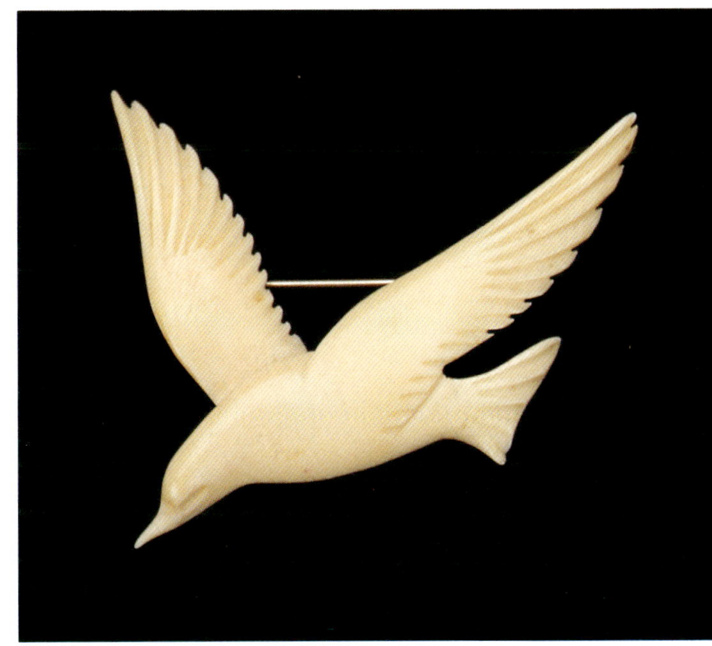

Ivory bird pin, 3.25". *Courtesy: Susan Mast Enterprises.*

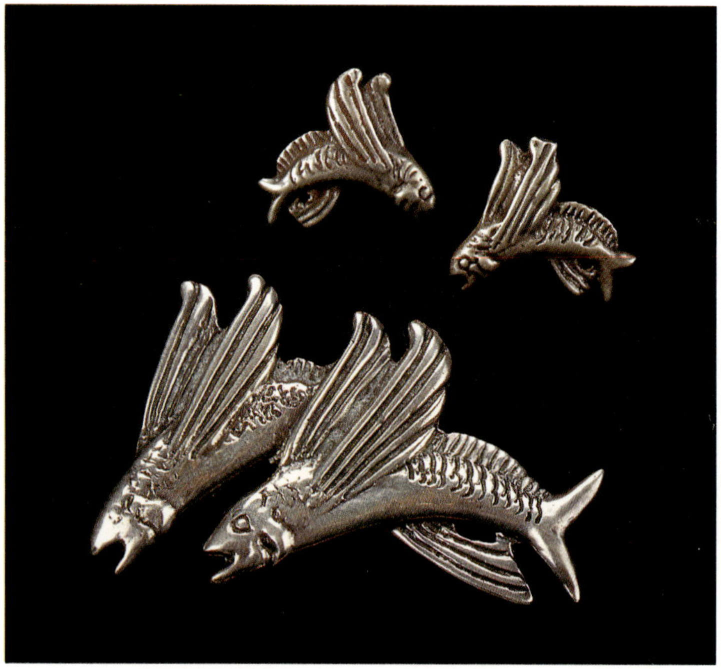

Ming's Flying Fish pin and earrings. Pin 2.75" w.
Courtesy: Locals Only, Laguna Beach.

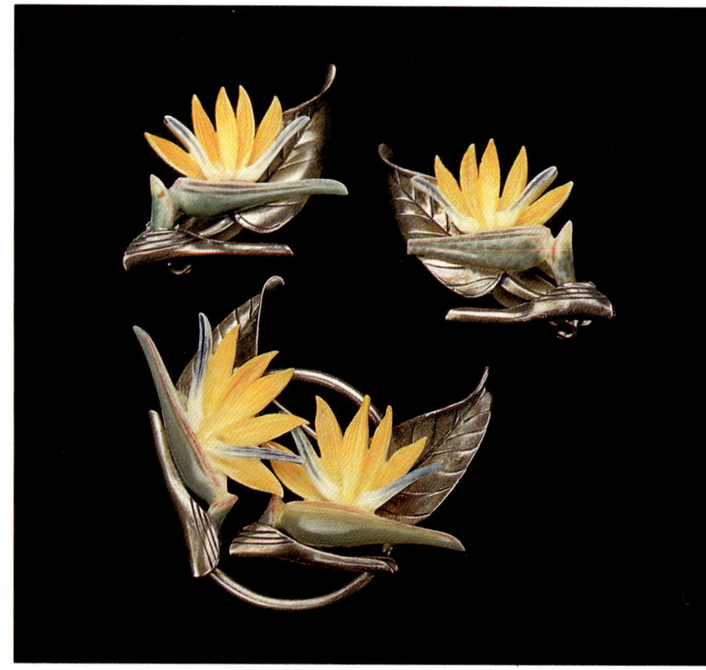

Ming's Bird of Paradise pin and earrings. Pin 2" w.
Courtesy: Michael & Denise Queen.

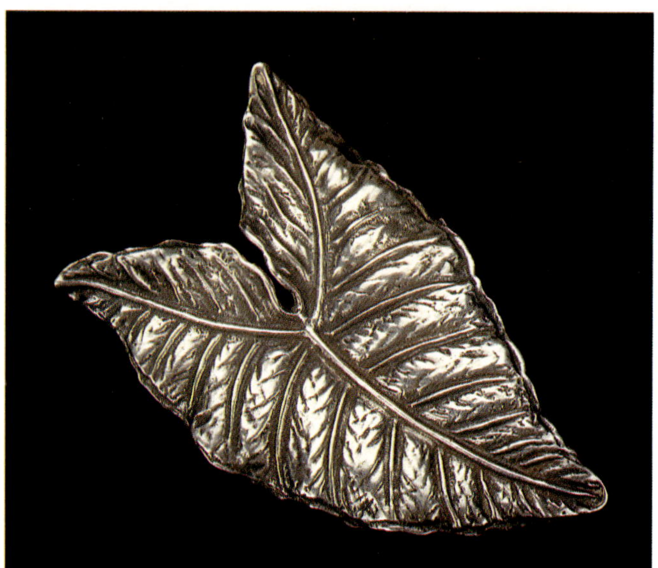

Monstera leaf pin 2.75" w. *Courtesy: Locals Only, Laguna Beach.*

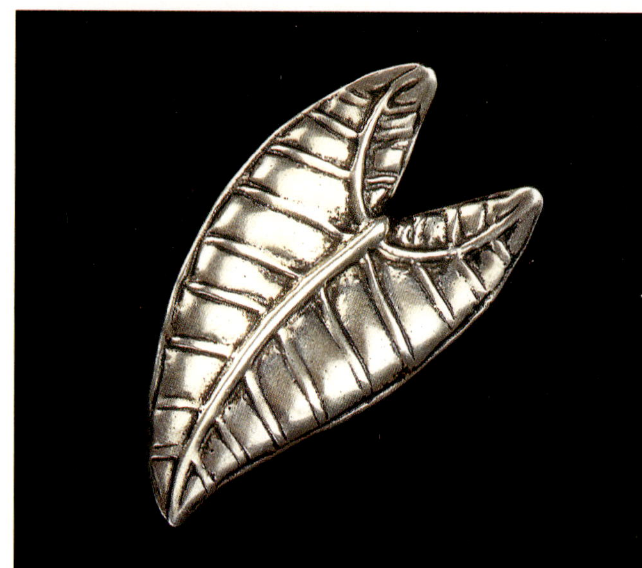

Ming's monstera leaf pin, 2.25" w.
Courtesy: Locals Only, Laguna Beach.

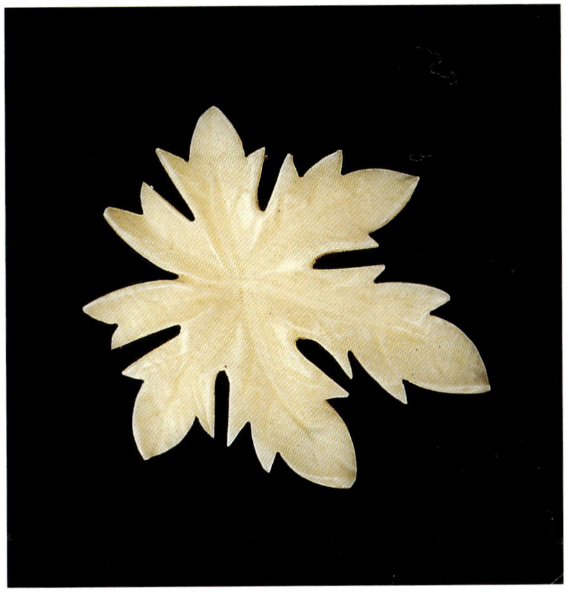

Ming's ivory papaya leaf pin, 1.25".
Courtesy: Laurie Haslund.

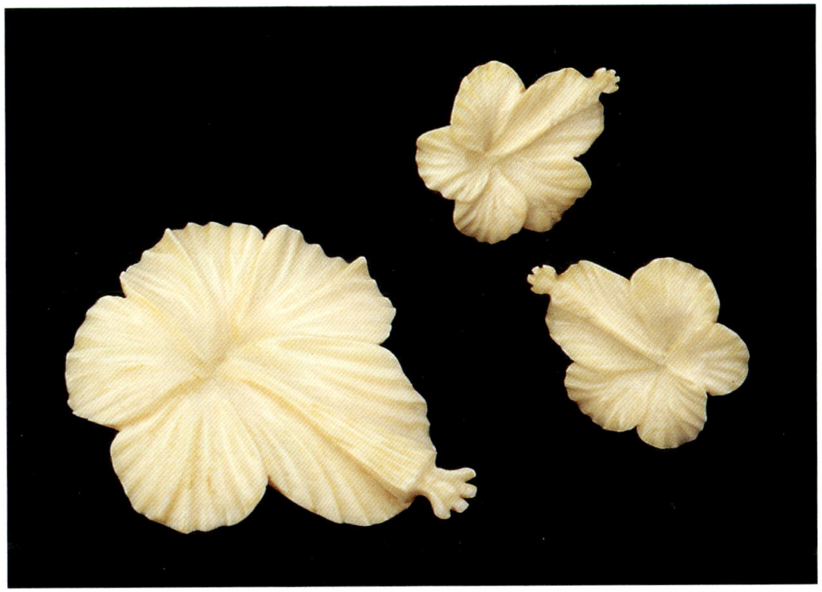

Ivory hibiscus blossom pin and earrings. Pin 1.75"
Courtesy: Laurie Haslund.

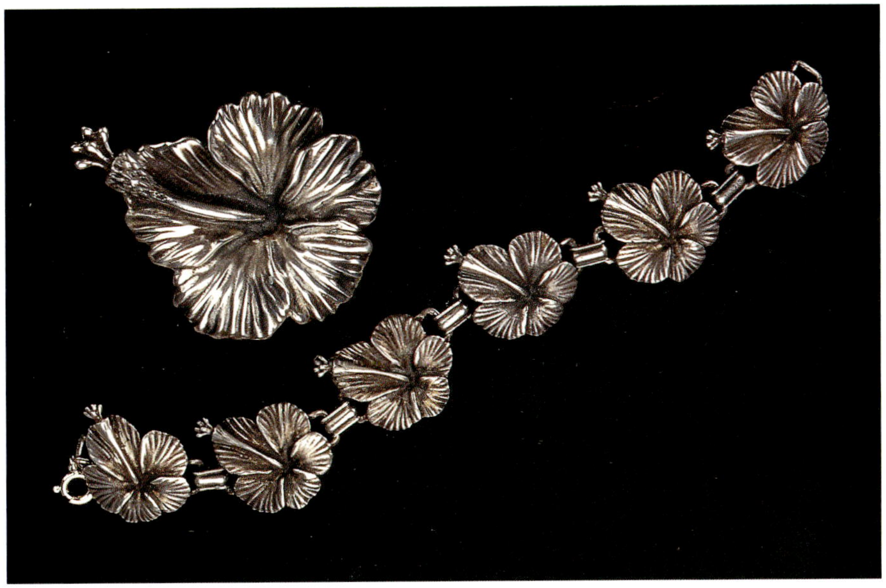

Ming's hibiscus pin and bracelet. Silver.
Courtesy: Laurie Haslund.

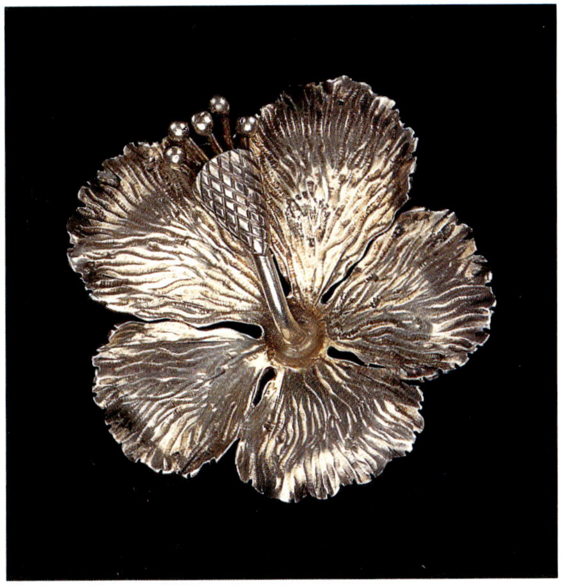

Ming hibiscus pin. Silver. *Courtesy: Locals Only, Laguna Beach.*

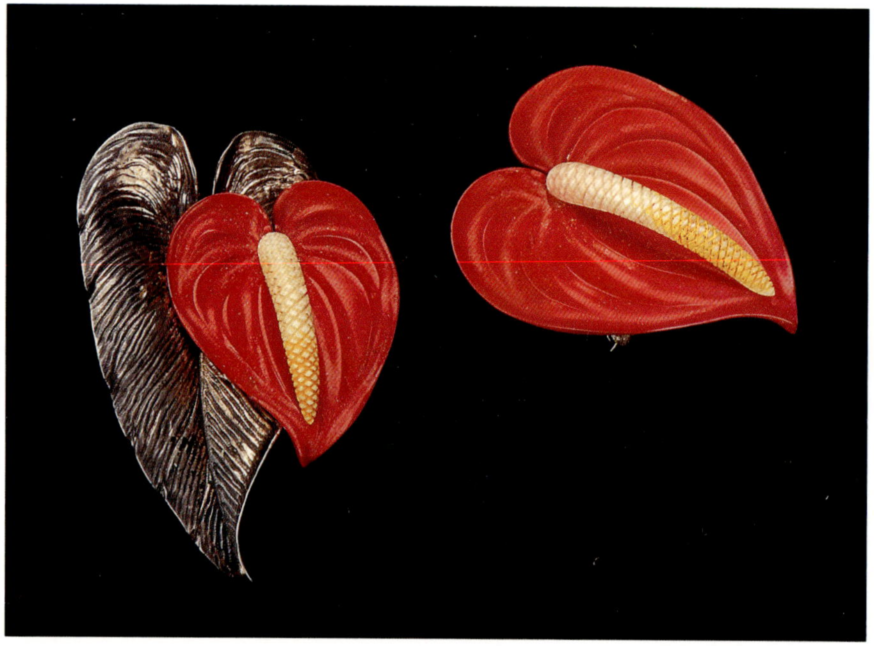

Ming pins. Left: silver and ivory red Anthurium pin; right: red Anthurium pin. *Courtesy: Locals Only, Laguna Beach.*

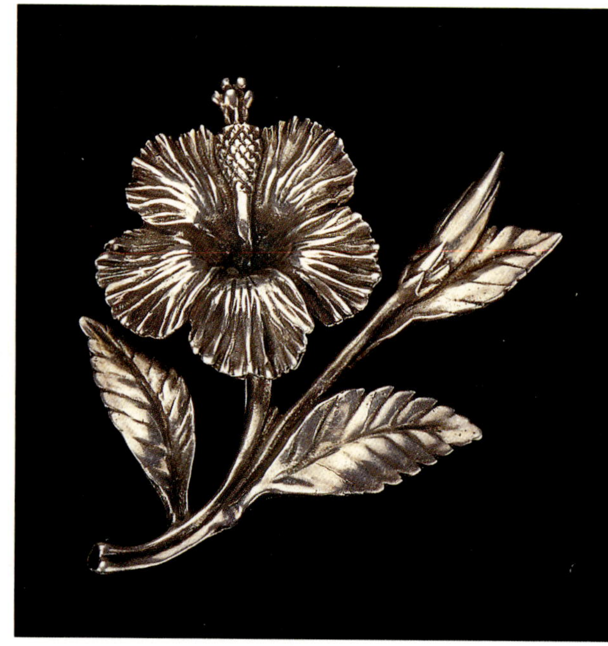

Ming hibiscus silver pin with branch. *Courtesy: Locals Only, Laguna Beach.*

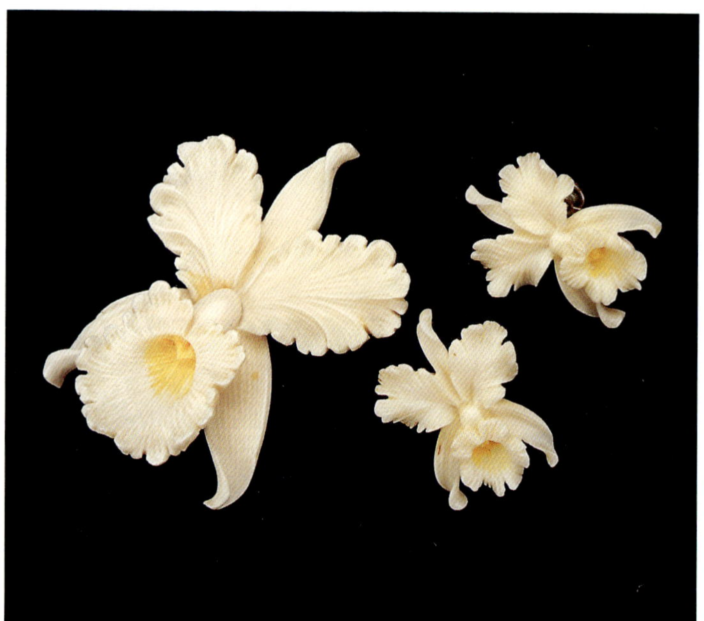

Ivory orchid set. Ming. *Courtesy: Laurie Haslund.*

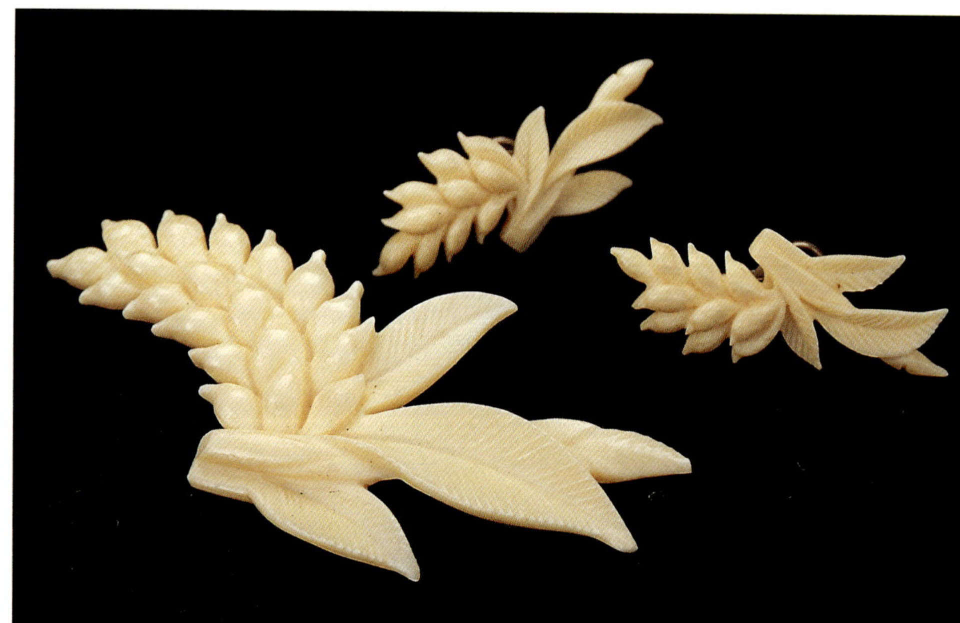

Ivory rice flower set. *Courtesy: Laurie Haslund.*

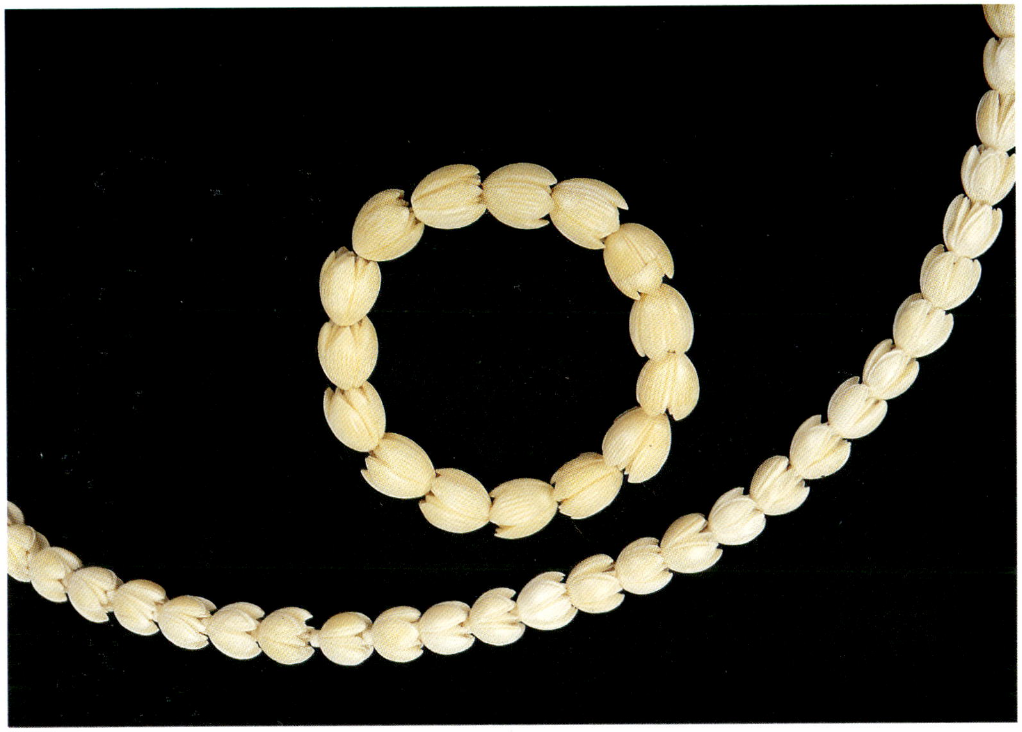

Gumps ivory pikake bracelet and necklace. *Courtesy: Laurie Haslund.*

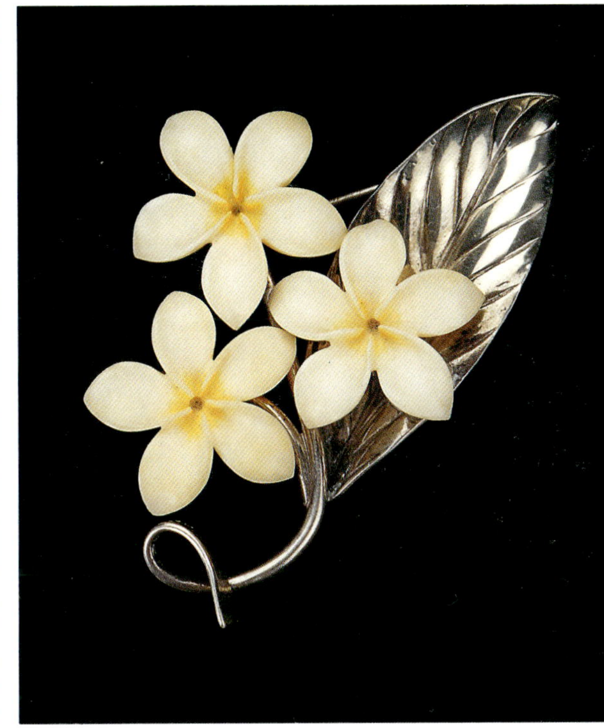

Silver and rose plumeria pin. *Courtesy: Locals Only, Laguna Beach.*

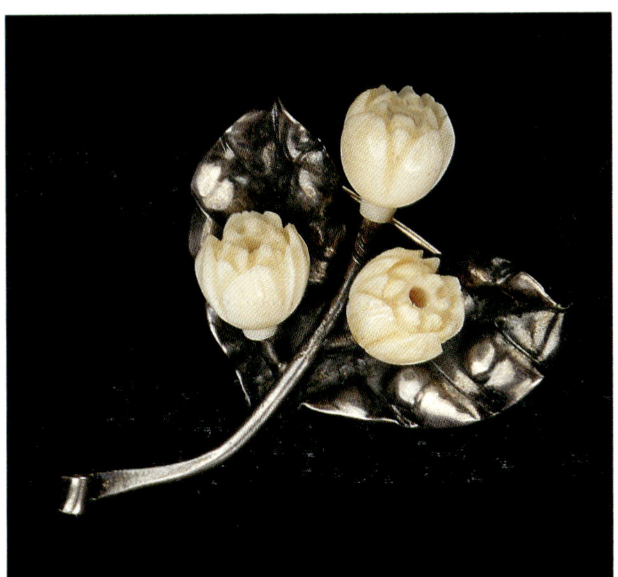

Silver and ivory kahiki floral spray pin. *Courtesy: Michele Leypoldt.*

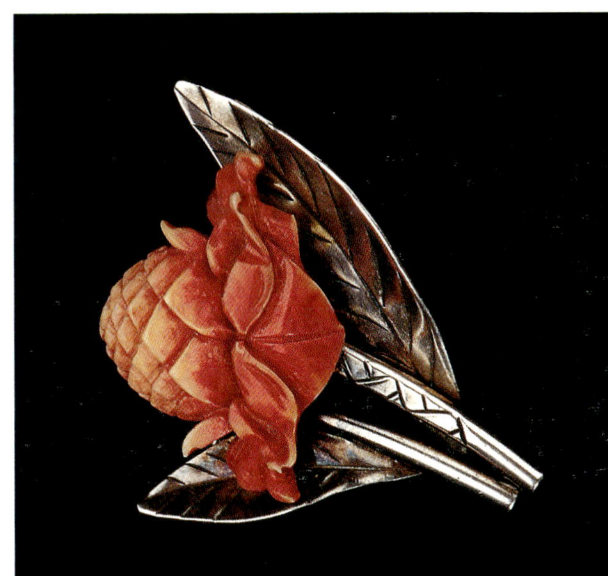

Silver and red dyed ivory red ginger pin. *Courtesy: Laurie Haslund.*

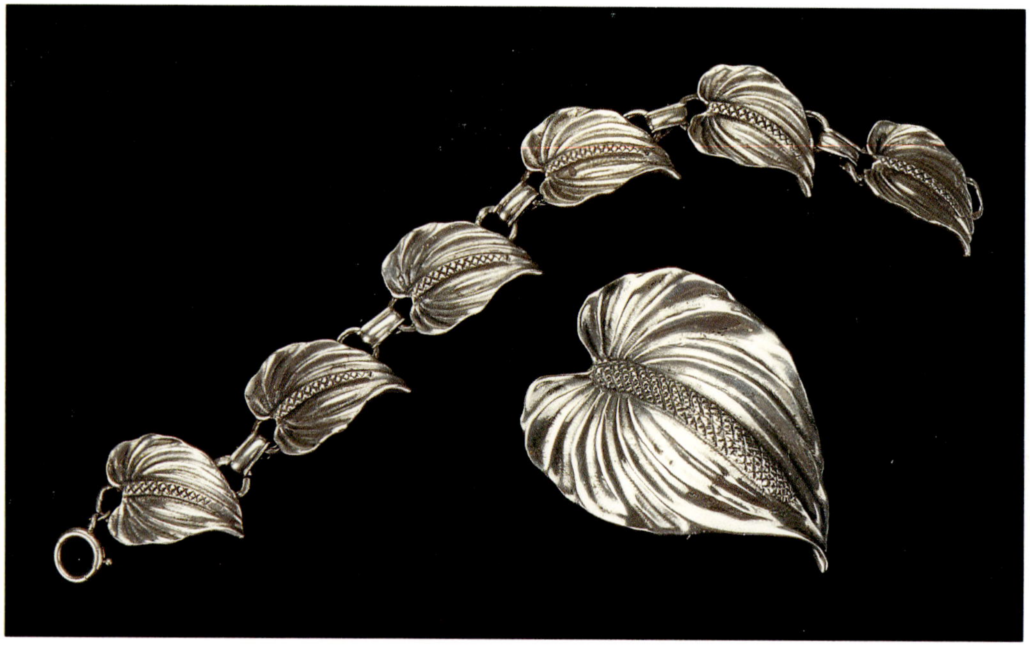

Ivory anthurium pin. *Courtesy: Laurie Haslund.*

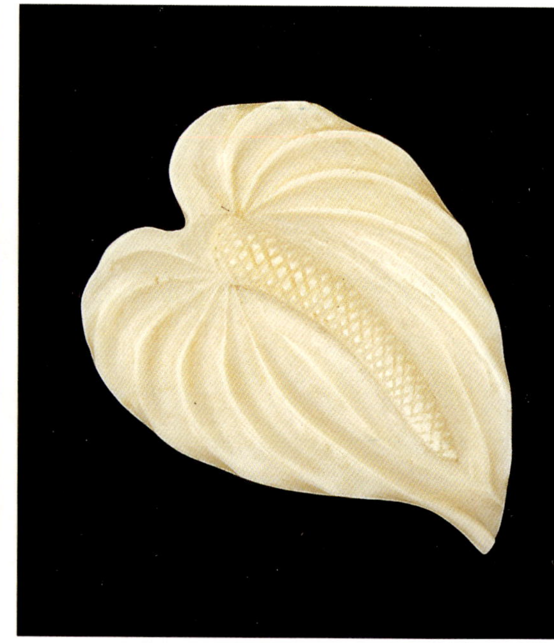

Ming silver anthurium bracelet and pin. *Courtesy: Laurie Haslund.*

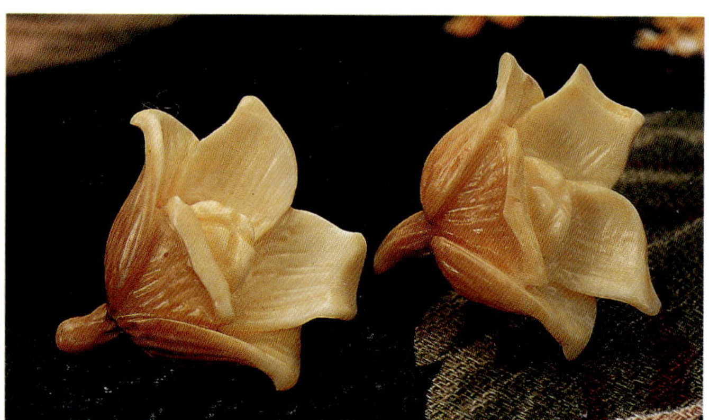

Ivory rose earrings. *Courtesy: Laurie Haslund.*

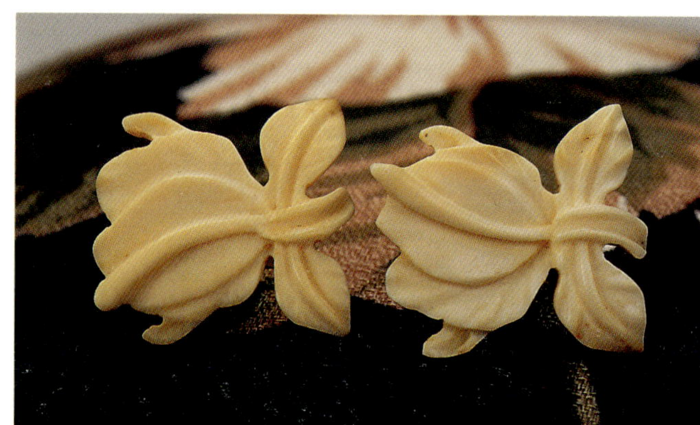

Ivory orchid pins. *Courtesy: Laurie Haslund.*

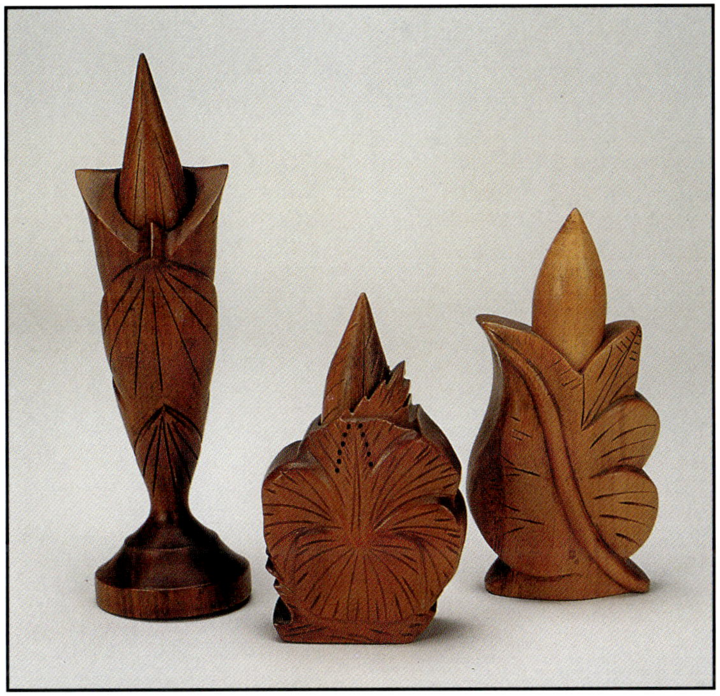

Perfume bottles. *Courtesy: Tiki Trader and Michele Leypoldt*.

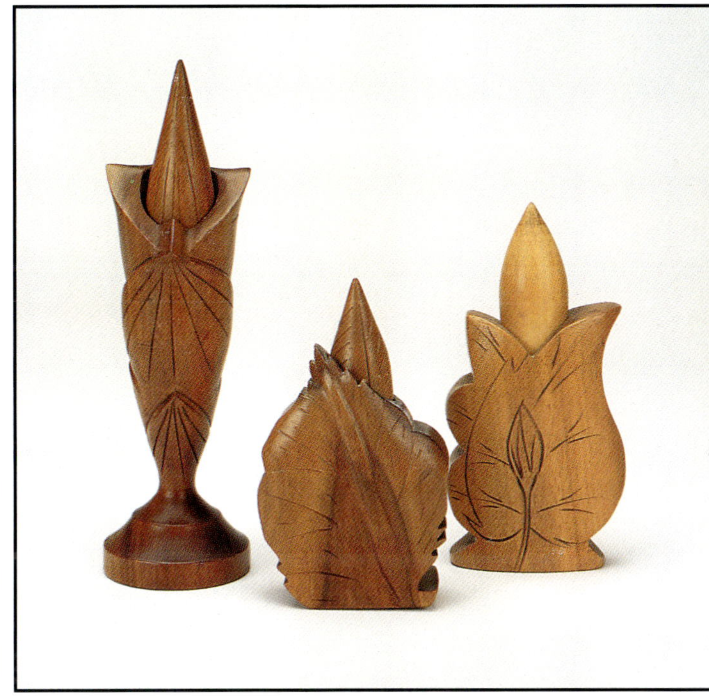

The reverse of the right two bottles.

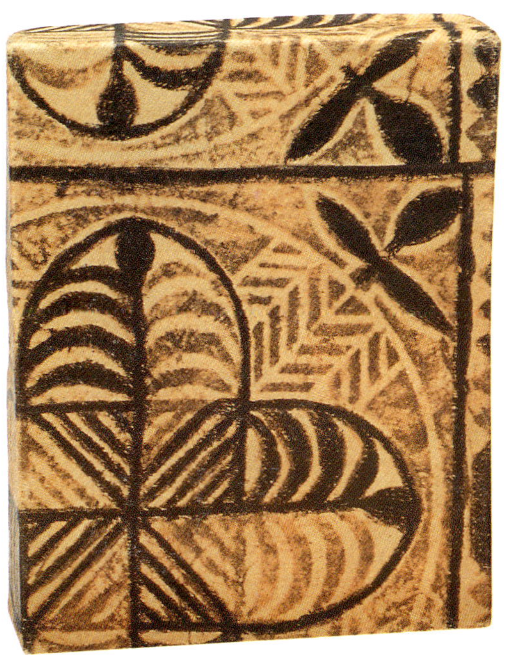

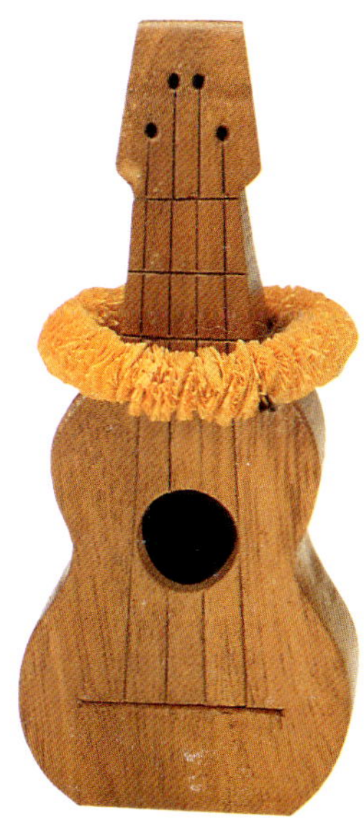

Uke bottle with box. Ka-lae, Hawaii. *Courtesy: Michele Leypoldt*.

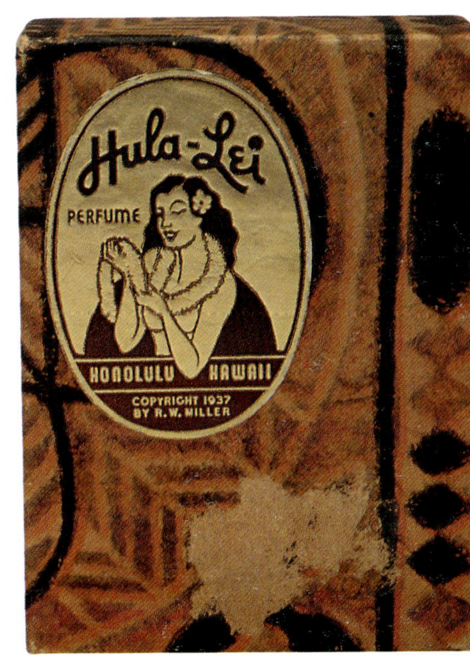

Hula-Lei Perfume box for Pikaki fragrance. Hula-Lei Products, Honolulu, 1937. *Courtesy: Michele Leypoldt*.

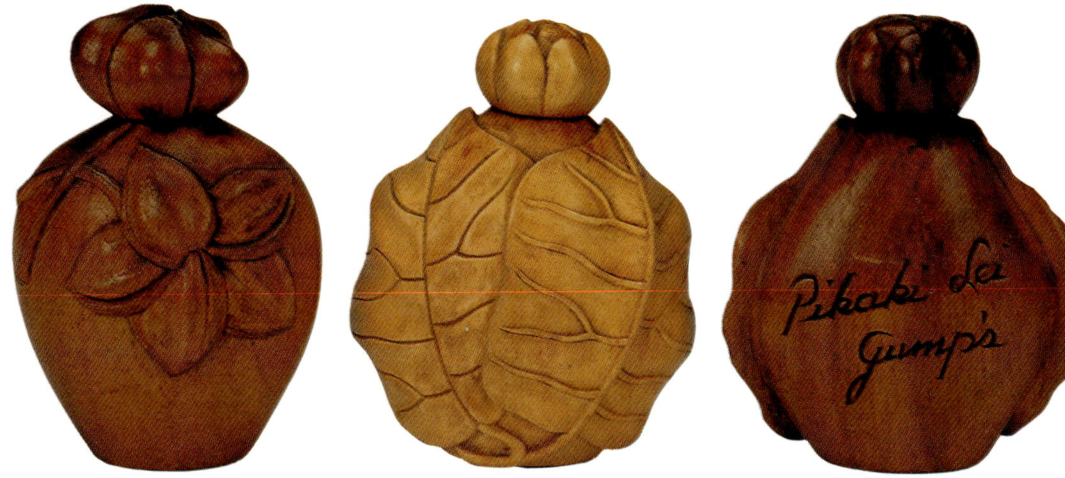

Three bottles from Gump's. Left: Plumeria Lei, center and right: Pikaki Lei. *Courtesy: Michele Leypoldt and the Collection of Brian Goddard & Gene Sweeney.*

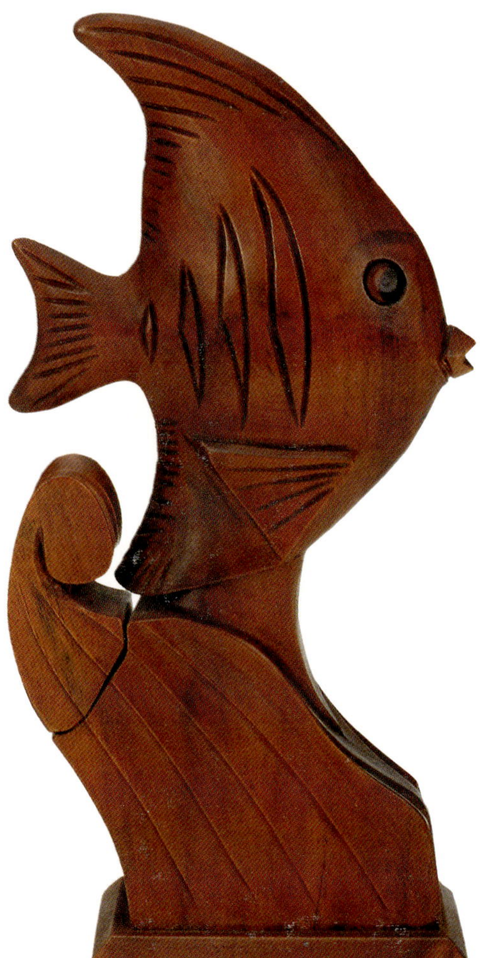

Nicely designed Sunfish on a wave. John A. Oya. *Courtesy: Michele Leypoldt*

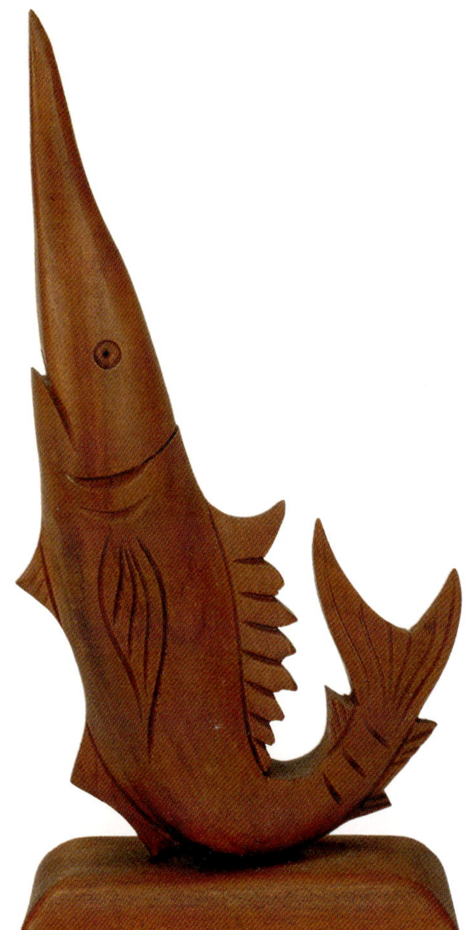

Carved Marlin perfume bottle. *Courtesy: Jim & Susie Stiso.*

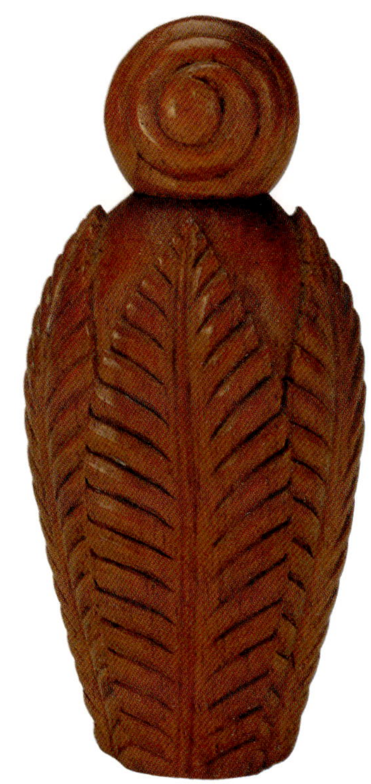

Fern Lei Perfume from Gump's. *Courtesy: Jim & Susie Stiso.*

A group of carved foliage bottles. Note the unusual cap to the bottle on the right. *Courtesy: Michele Leypoldt and Susan Mast Enterprises.*

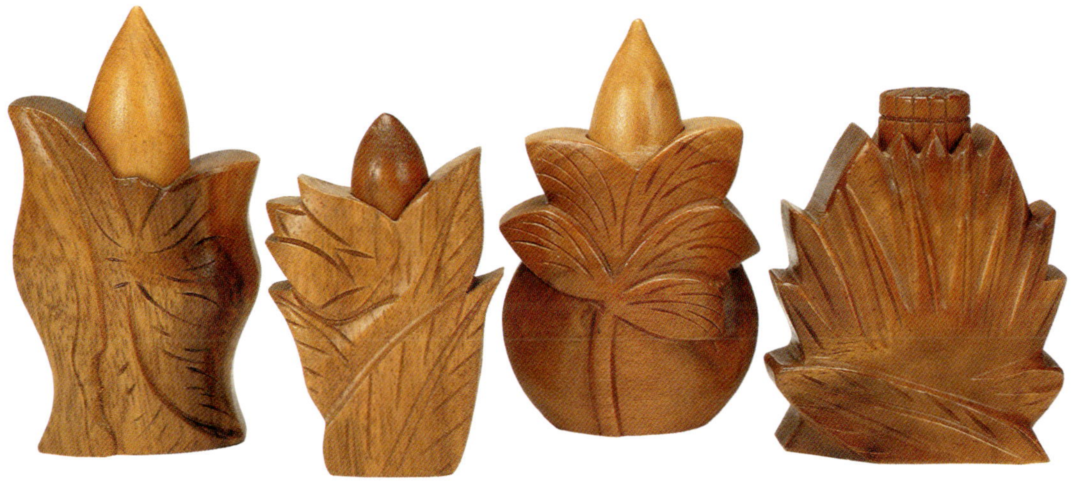

The horn of this unicorn is the opener for the perfume bottle. *Courtesy: Jim & Susie Stiso.*

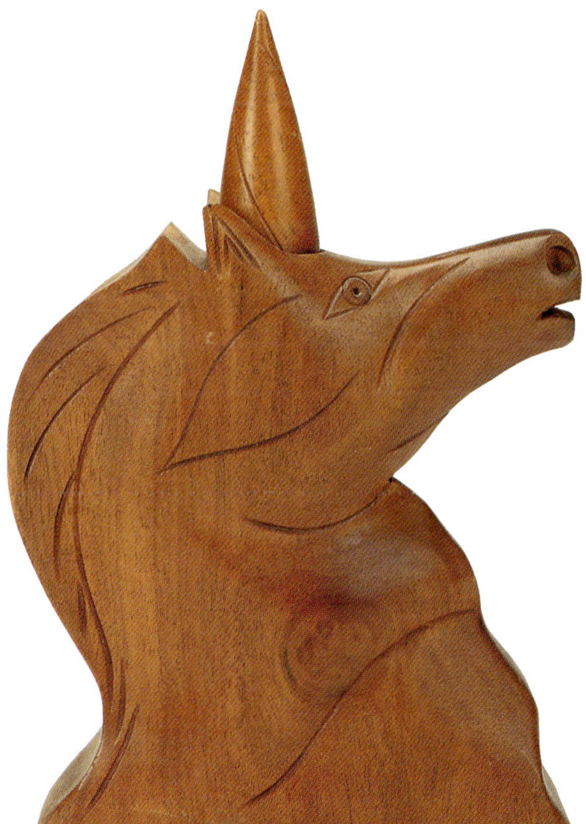

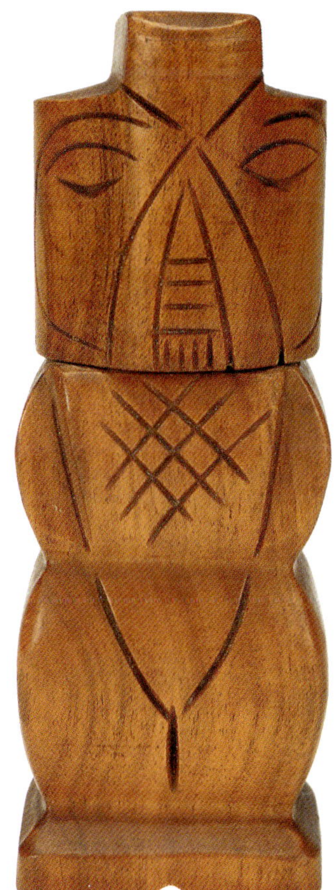

A simple tiki figure. Probably John A. Oya. *Courtesy: Michele Leypoldt.*

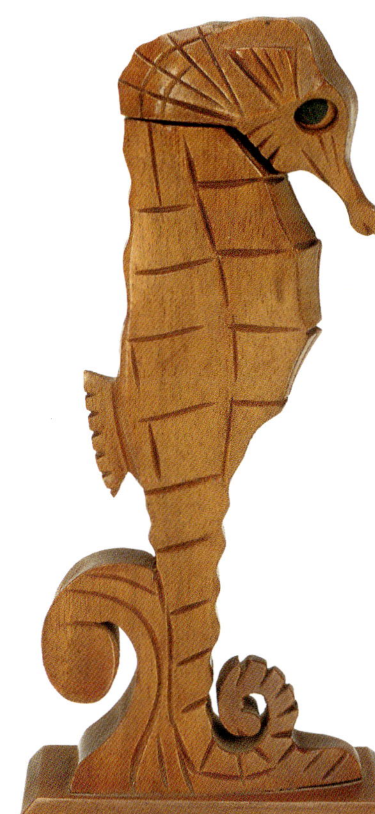

A Seahorse bottle. John A. Oya. *Courtesy: Michele Leypoldt.*

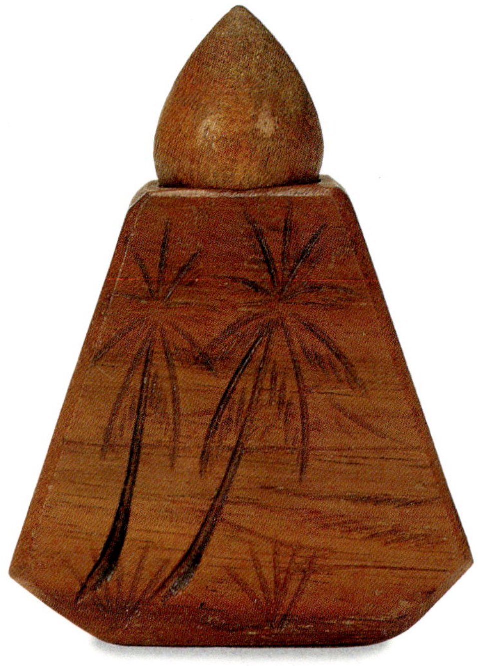

This pyramid-shaped bottle has incised carving of palm trees. *Courtesy: Michele Leypoldt*.

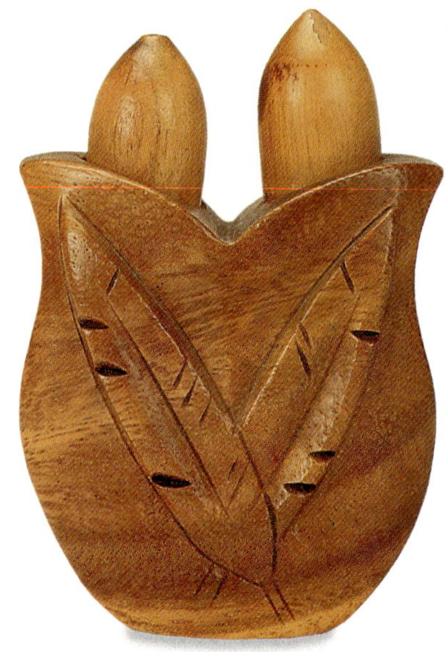

A double bottle with carved banana leaves. Hula-Lei. *Courtesy: Michele Leypoldt*.

Two foliage bottles. *Courtesy: Michele Leypoldt and Susan Mast Enterprises*.

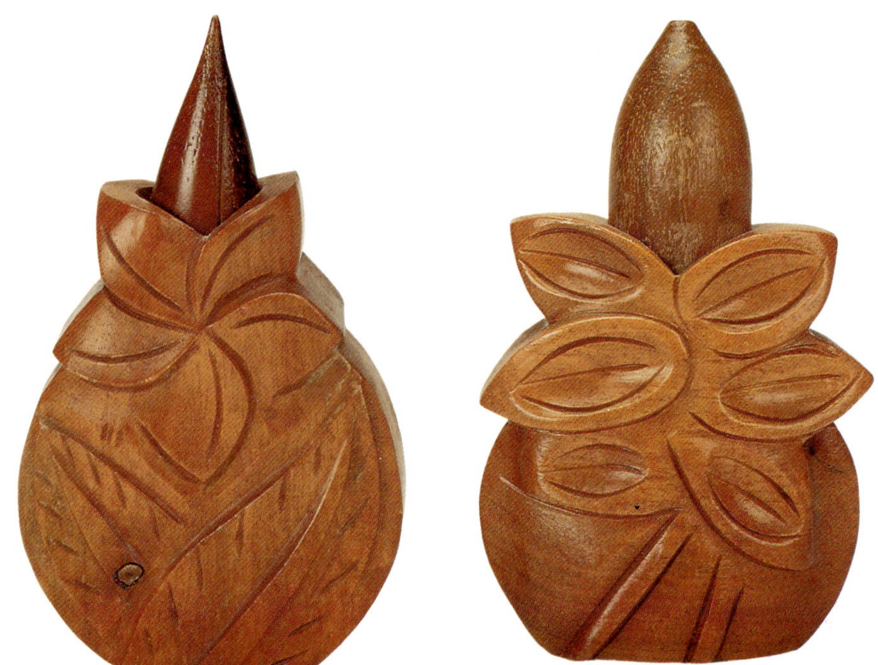

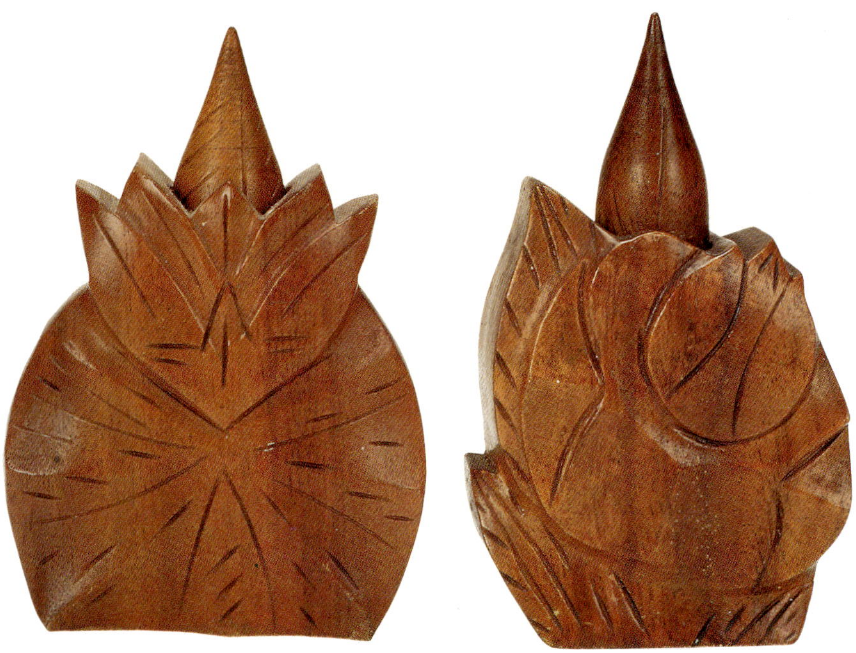

Two foliage bottles. John A. Oya. *Courtesy: Gwen & Evan Olins, Hula Heaven and Michele Leypoldt*.

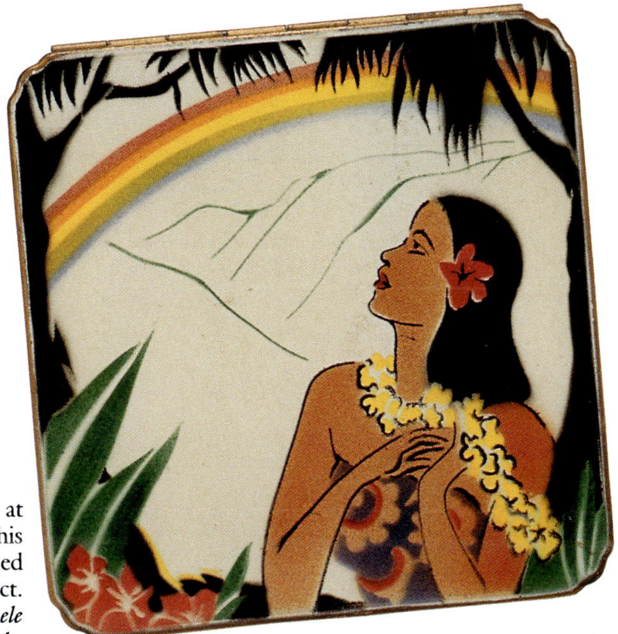

A dreamy look at a rainbow on this colorful enameled compact. *Courtesy: Michele Leypoldt.*

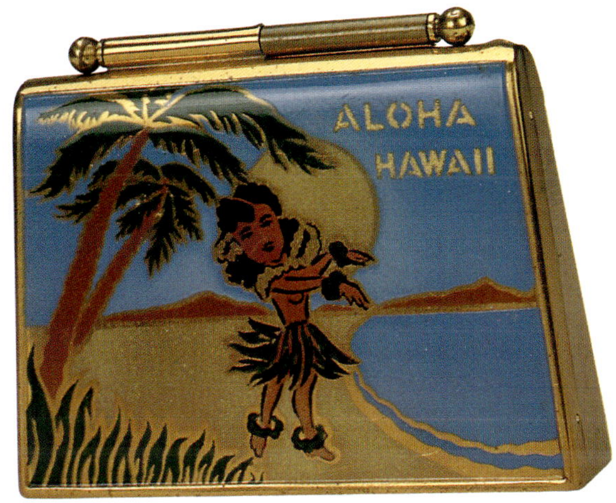

Caricature hula girl on valise-shaped enameled compact. *Courtesy: Michele Leypoldt.*

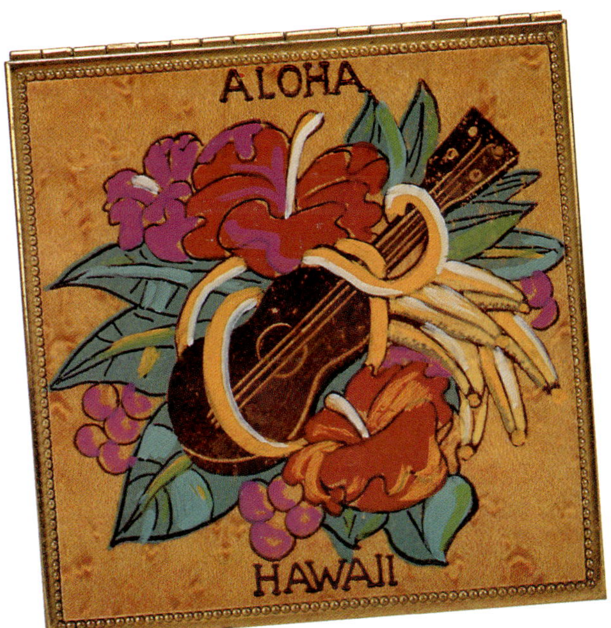

A ukelele entwined in tropical foliage strikes the theme for this Aloha Hawaii compact. *Courtesy: Michele Leypoldt.*

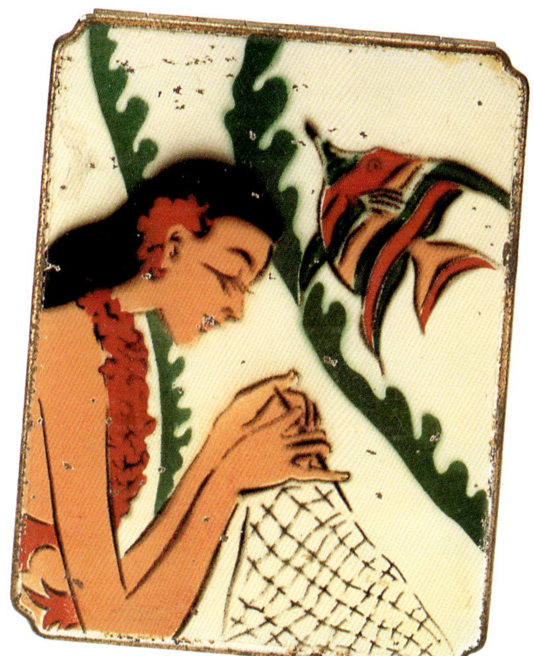

Enameled compact featuring a woman mending a net. *Courtesy: Michele Leypoldt.*

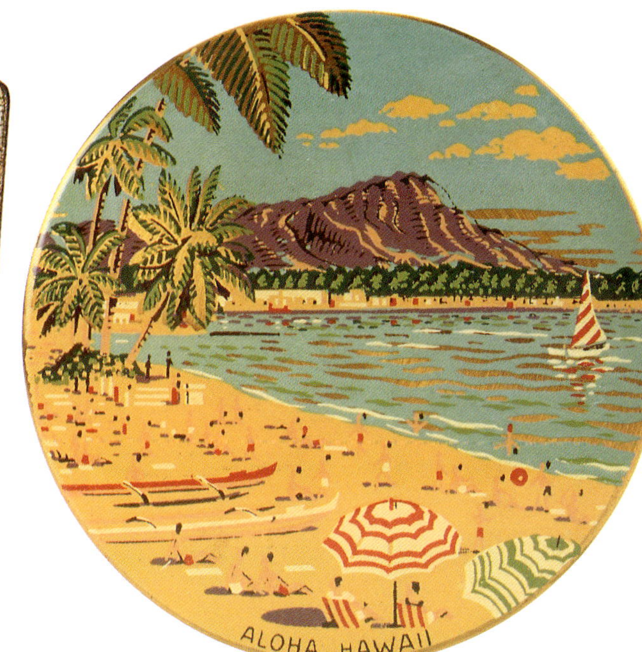

This enameled compact has an intricate and colorful design of the beach near Diamond Head. Aloha Hawaii. *Courtesy: Michele Leypoldt.*

An eight-sided compact with a view of Diamond Head. Enameled, it also came with a blue background. *Courtesy: Michele Leypoldt.*

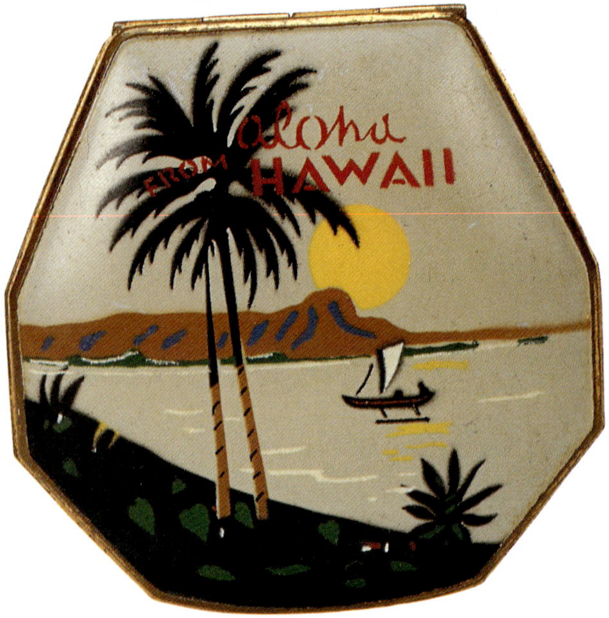

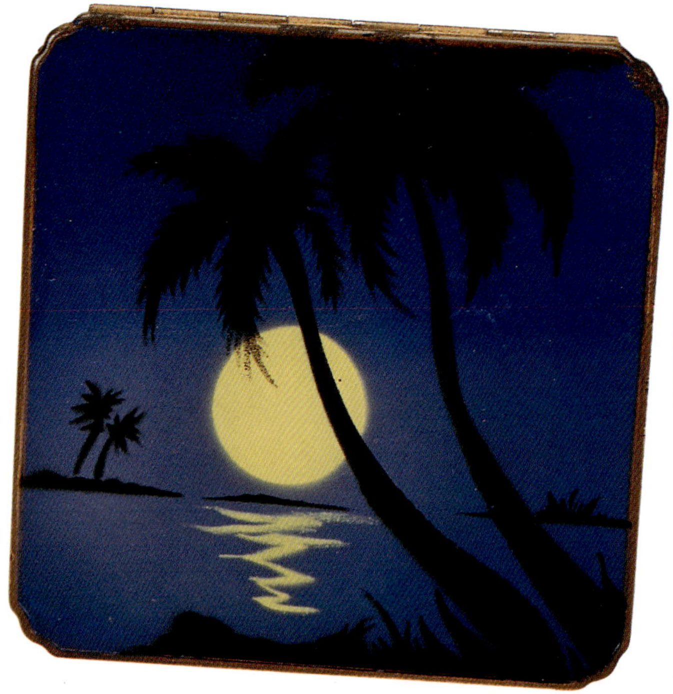

A romantic moon and palm trees would make this a welcome memento. Enameled metal. *Courtesy: Michele Leypoldt.*

"Aloha Hawaii" enameled compact. *Courtesy: Michele Leypoldt.*

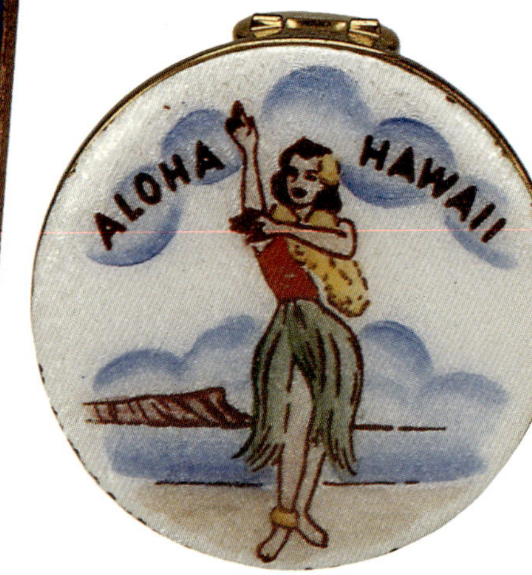

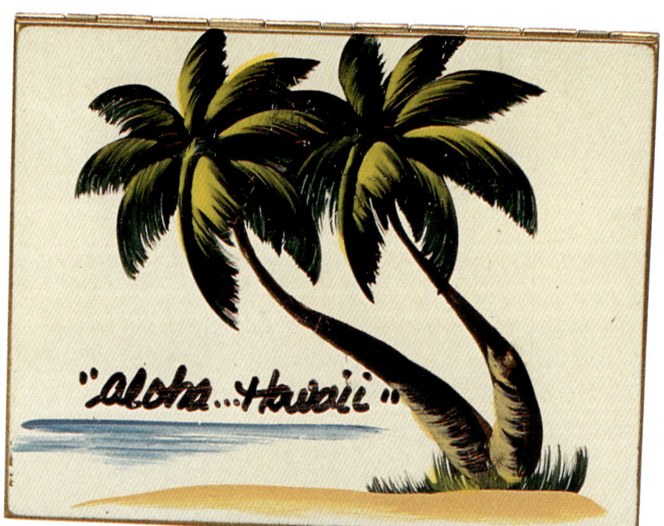

"Aloha...Hawaii" enameled compact. *Courtesy: Michele Leypoldt.*

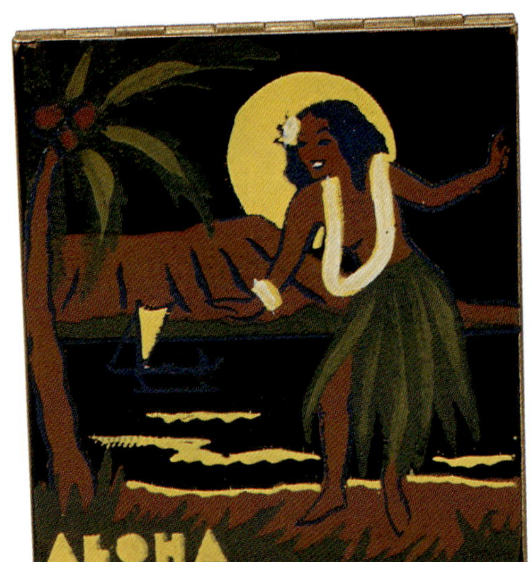

"Aloha." Enameled compact with moonlit hula girl. *Courtesy: Michele Leypoldt.*

Another romantic evening, this time with a rosy sky and a grass shack and outrigger in the foreground. Enameled. *Courtesy: Michele Leypoldt.*

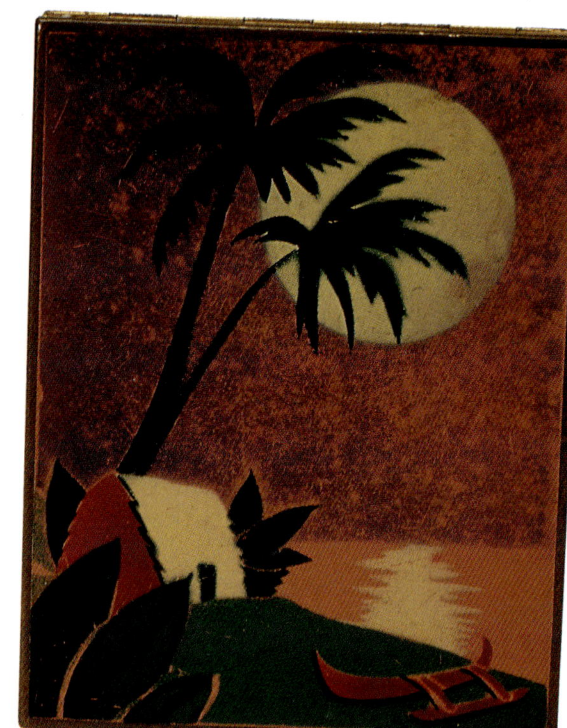

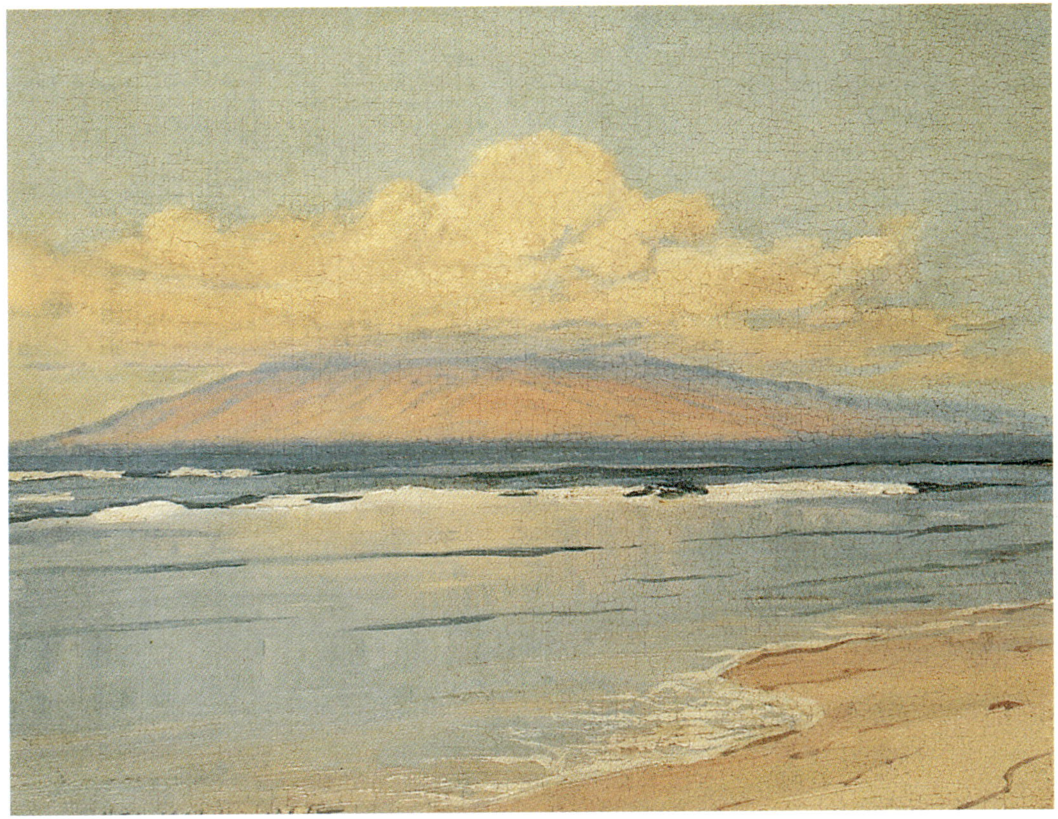

Chapter 4

Art

David Hitchcock, "Lanai from Lahaina, Maui," c. 1913, oil on artist's board, 12" x 16". A sunny day over the usually calm channel between Lanai and Maui. See Pages 169-172. *Courtesy: Douglas A. Frazer Fine Art*.

Popular Art

Air Brush Art

The forms of popular art are as varied on the Islands as anywhere else, ranging from the rich Maxfield Parrish-like colors of Pressler to simple prints or tinted photographs.

Among the most widely recognized are the works popularly known as "air brush art." This beautiful medium is actually created using several stencils, one after the other. According to Mark Blackburn in *Hawaiiana,* the art form began with itinerant Honolulu artists in the late 1930s, selling to the tourist trade. With the increased demand from military personnel during World War II, many artists set up studios where their work could be mass produced. The lack of quality materials during the war meant that works surviving from that era may be in less than fine condition. Post-war works, made with finer materials, have fared better, and because of the demand from an increased tourist trade, they are also more plentiful.

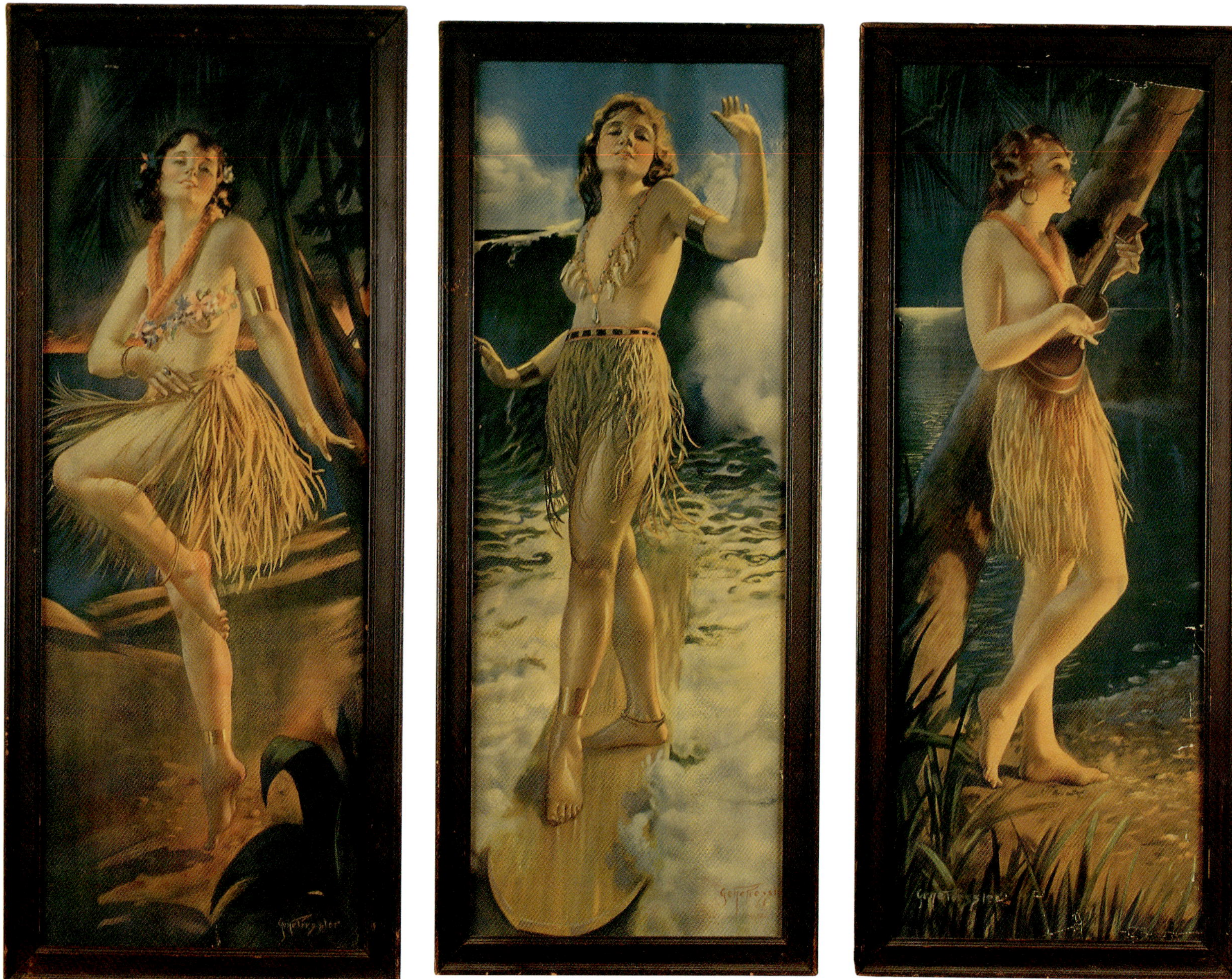

This trio of beauties are rarely seen together, but illustrate Gene Pressler's command of color, the human figure, and the Aloha Spirit. *Courtesy: Michele Leypoldt*.

Gill

The airbrush art signed Gill was created from the 1930s to early 1950s. According to Blackburn, the artist is as yet unidentified, except that he worked in San Francisco.

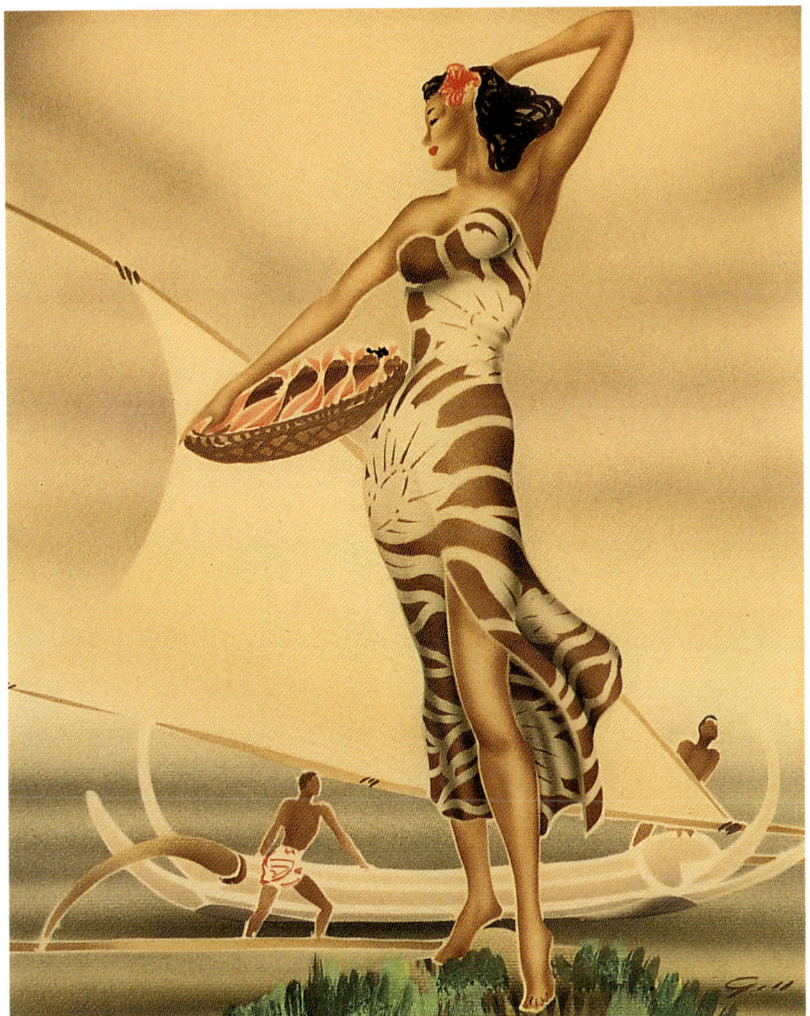

"Woman in Sarong with Calabash of Flowers and Outrigger Canoe." Signed Gill. *Courtesy: Jim & Susie Stiso*.

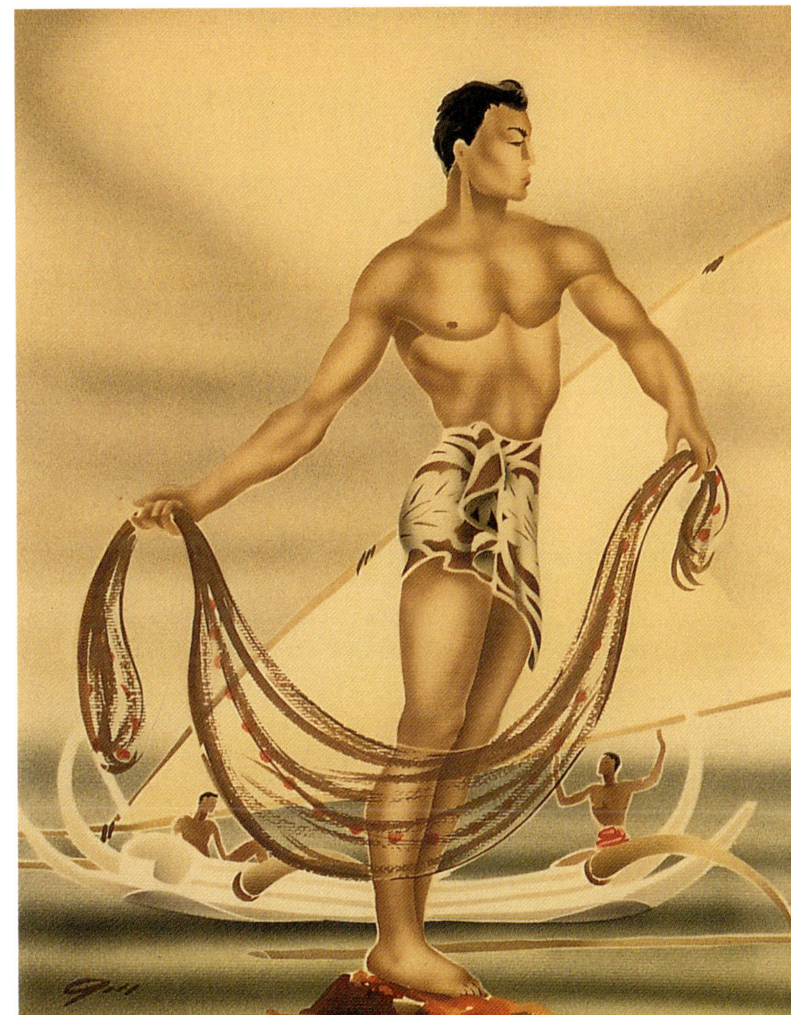

"Net Fisherman and Outrigger." Signed Gill. *Courtesy: Jim & Susie Stiso*.

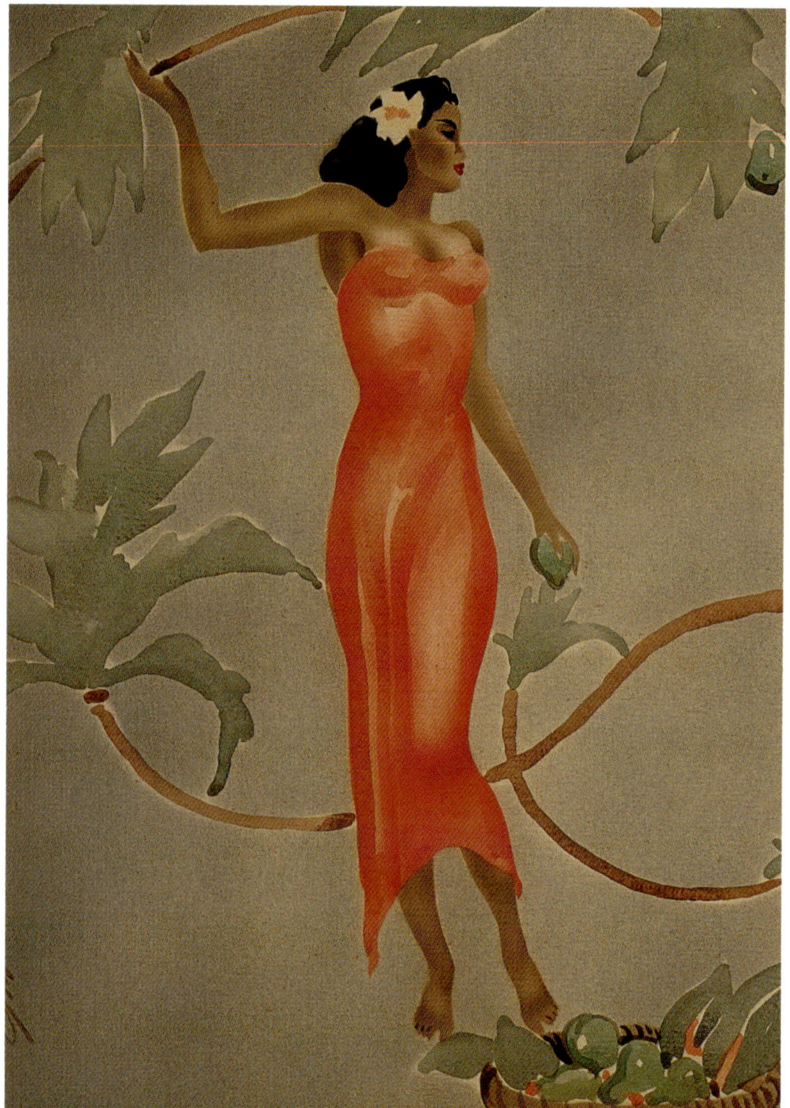

"Woman in Sarong with Basket of Fruit." Signed Gill.
Courtesy: Jim & Susie Stiso.

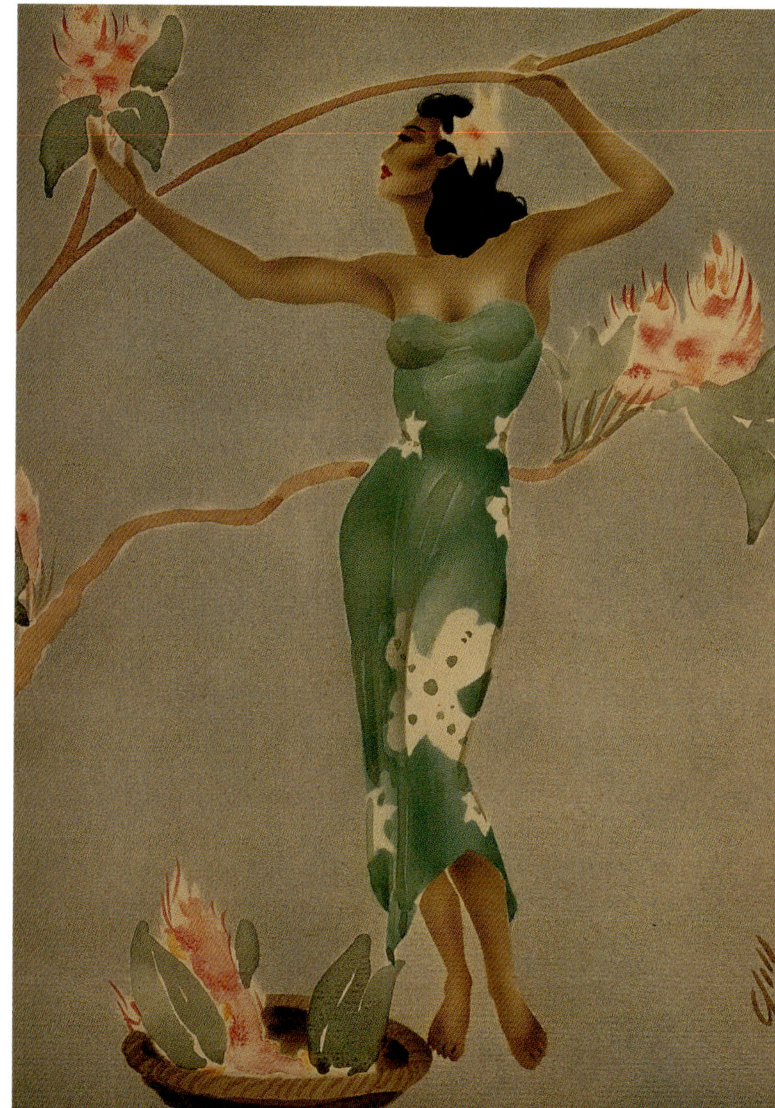

"Woman in Sarong with Basket of Flowers." Signed Gill.
Courtesy: Jim & Susie Stiso.

Mundorff

Born in Pittsburgh, Pennsylvania, in 1910, Ted Mundorff was educated in Honolulu. He left the Islands for a time, only to return and open a gallery in Honolulu called the Hawaiian Pallet. Primarily known for his floral prints and illustrations, he also ventured into other subjects. Mundorff died in 1969.

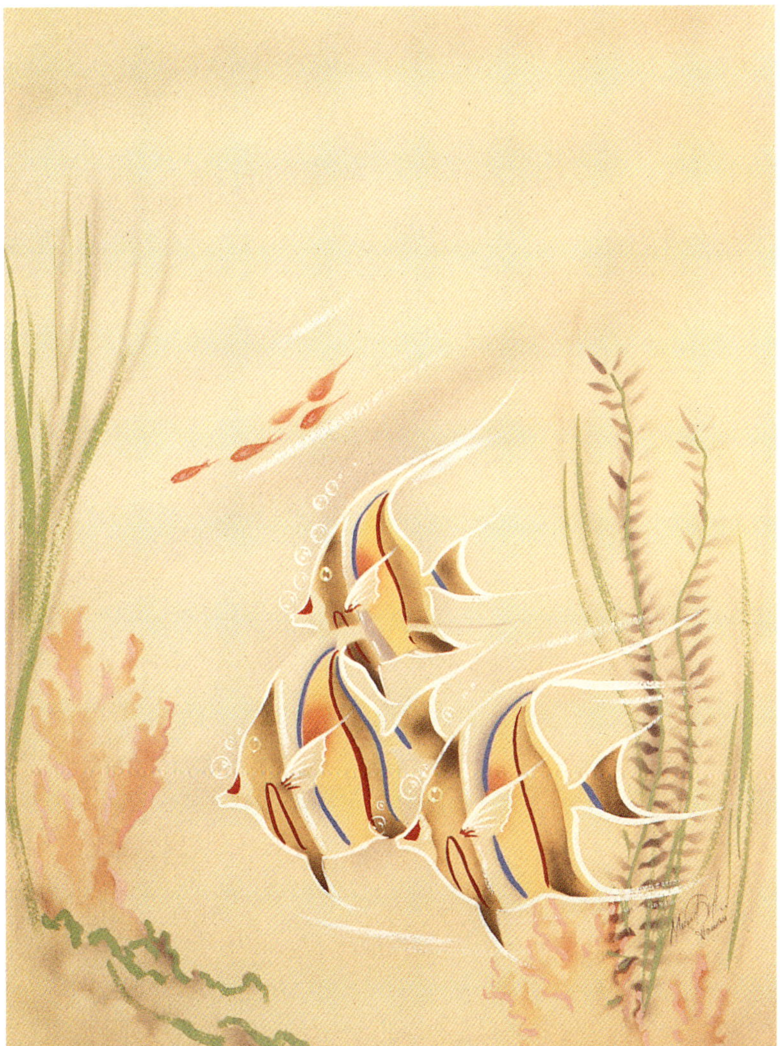

"Kihi Kihi" signed Mundorff, Honolulu.
Courtesy: Jim & Susie Stiso.

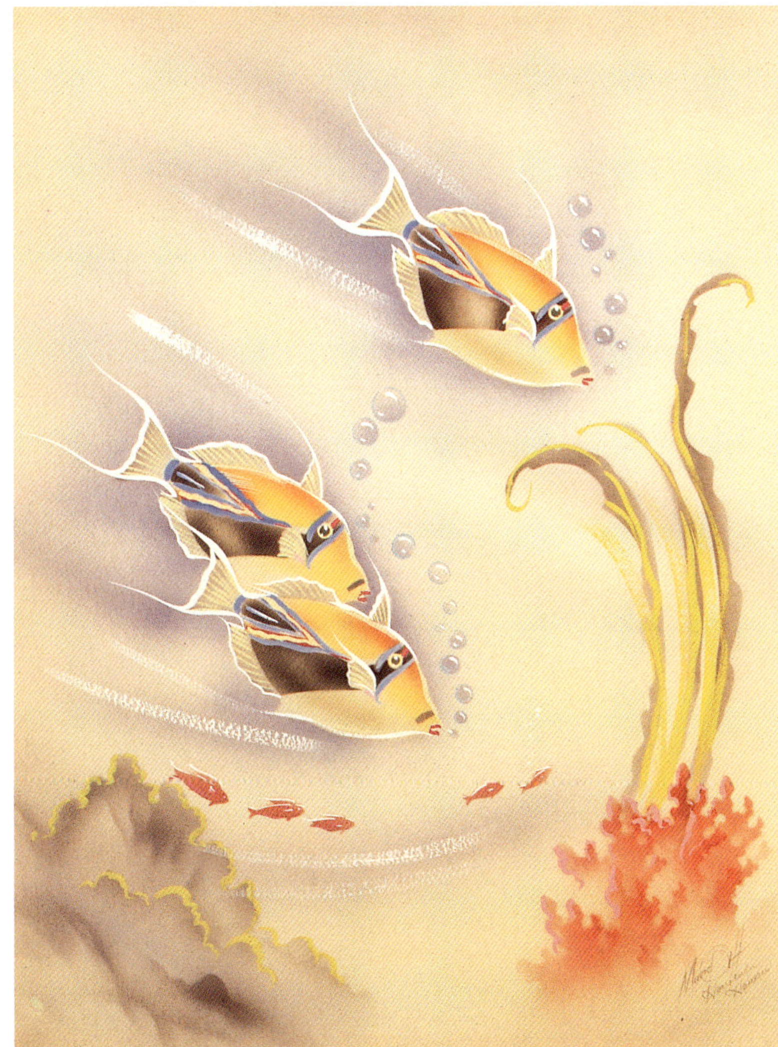

"Sealife" signed Mundorff, Honolulu, Hawaii.
Courtesy: Jim & Susie Stiso.

Freeman

Born in 1910, Clifford "Tip" Freeman moved to the Islands in the 1930s and opened his studio in 1943. He died in 1995 in Florida.

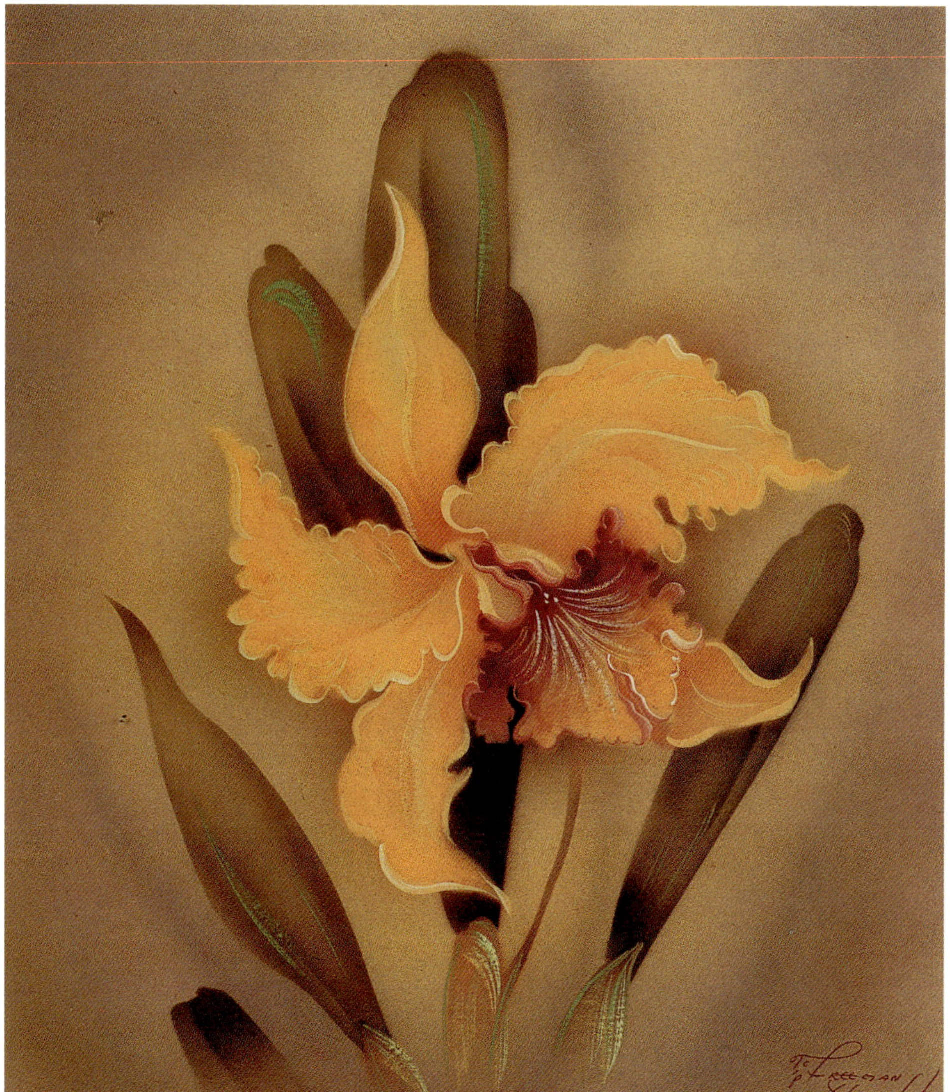

"Cattleya Orchid." Signed Tip Freeman, Honolulu. *Courtesy: K.C. Heylin.*

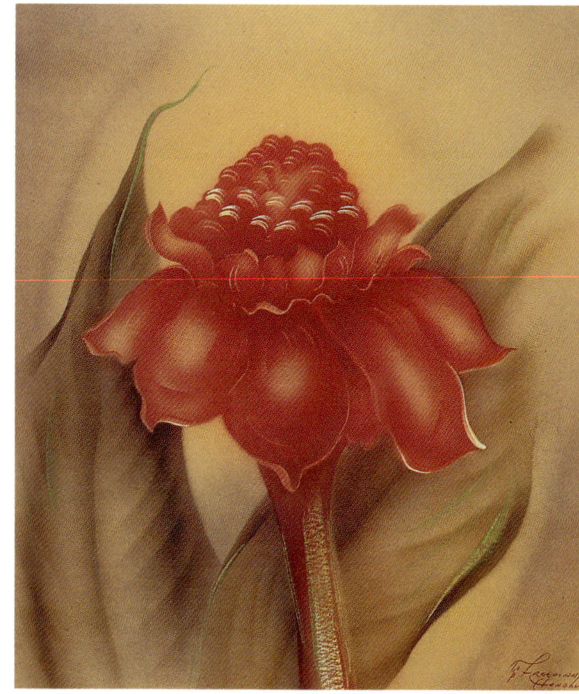

"Torch Ginger." Signed Tip Freeman, Honolulu. *Courtesy: K.C. Heylin.*

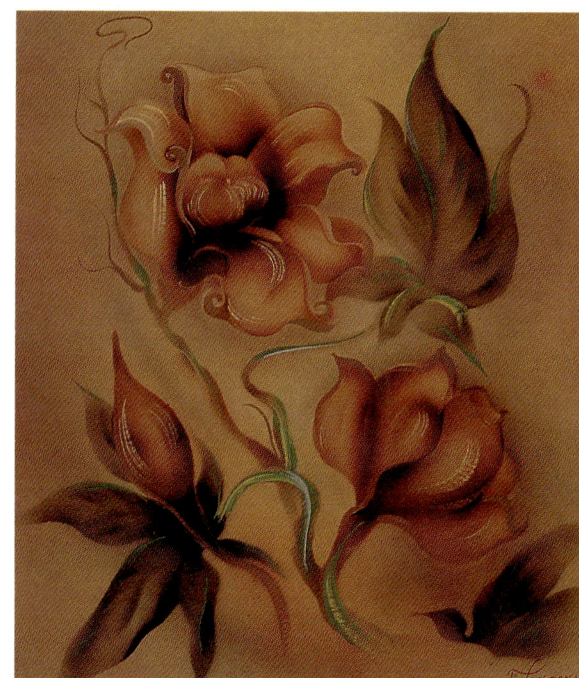

"Flowers." Signed Tip Freeman, Honolulu. *Courtesy: K.C. Heylin.*

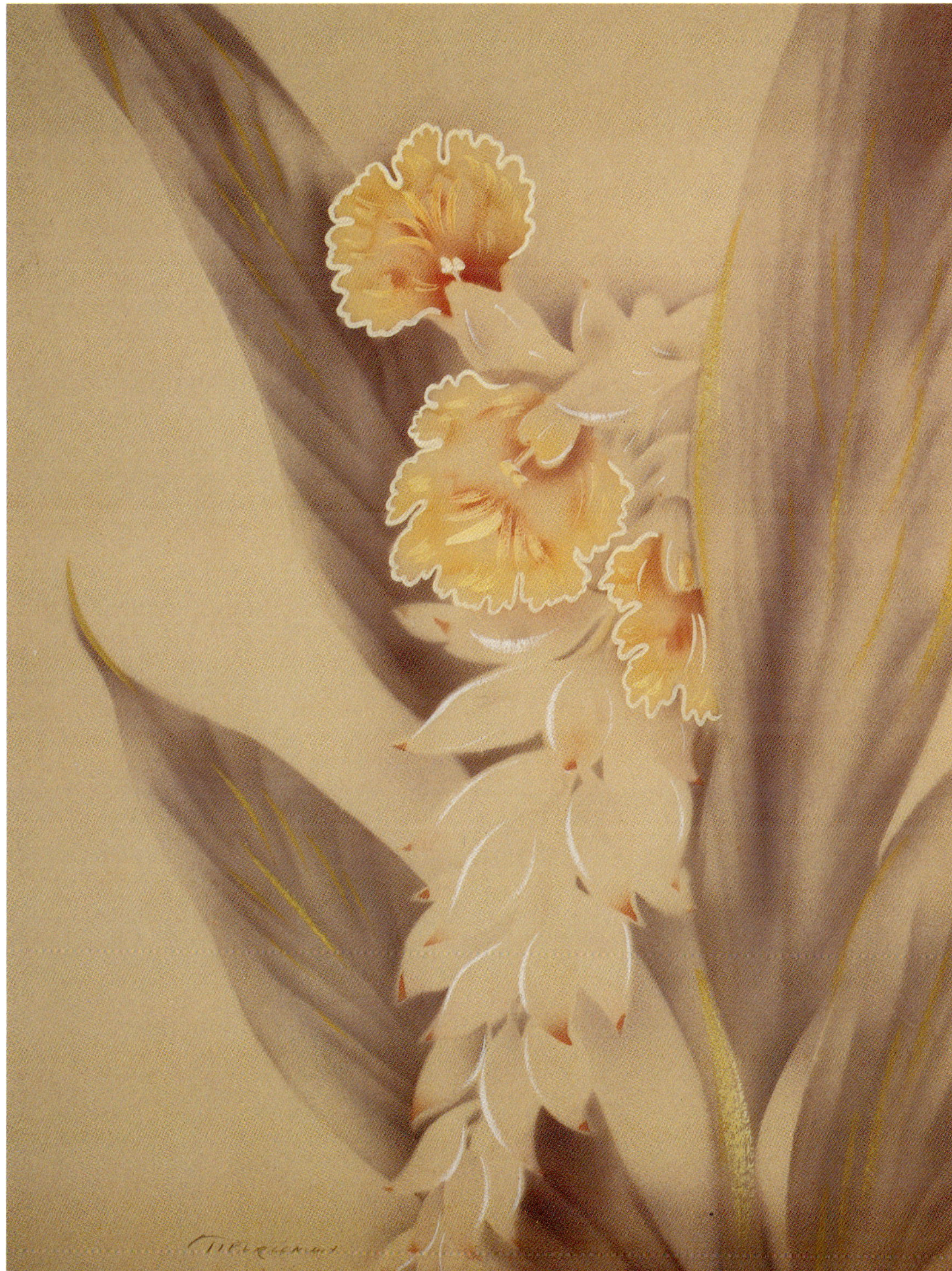

"Shell Ginger." Signed Tip Freeman, Honolulu. *Courtesy: the Collection of Brian Goddard & Gene Sweeney.*

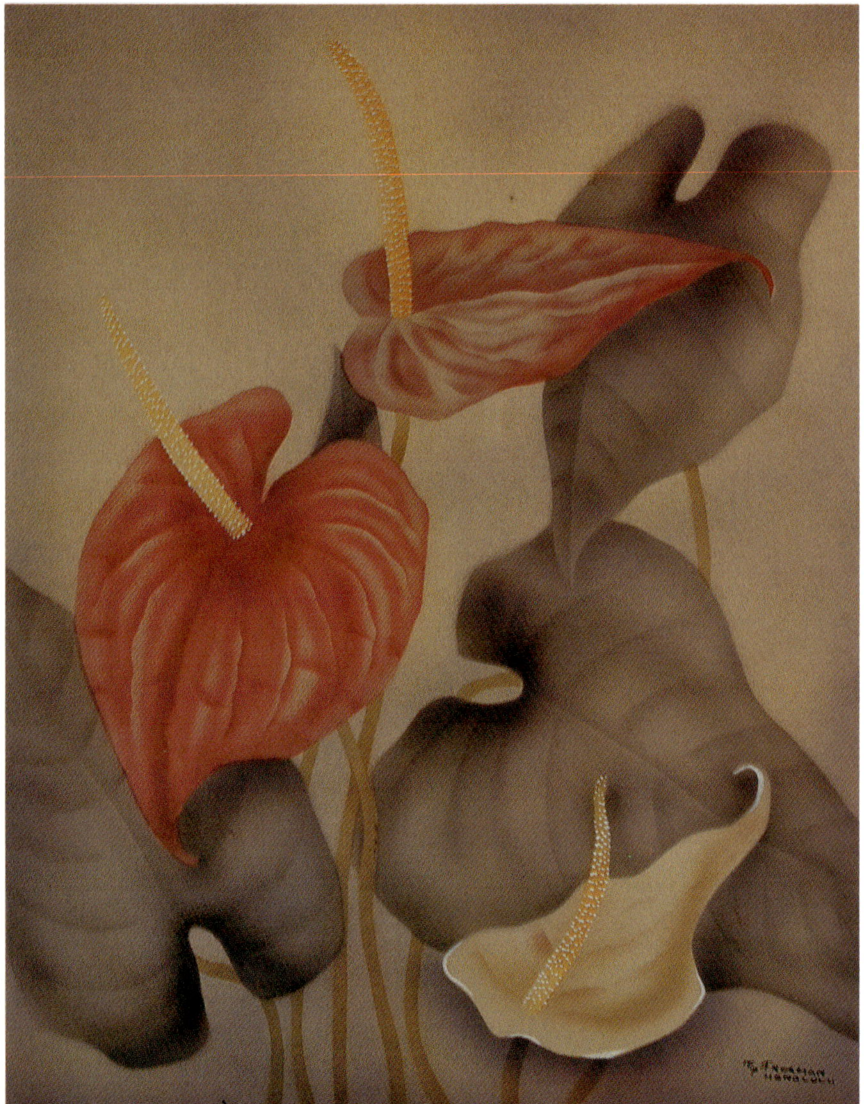

"Anthurium." Signed Tip Freeman, Honolulu.
Courtesy: Jim & Susie Stiso.

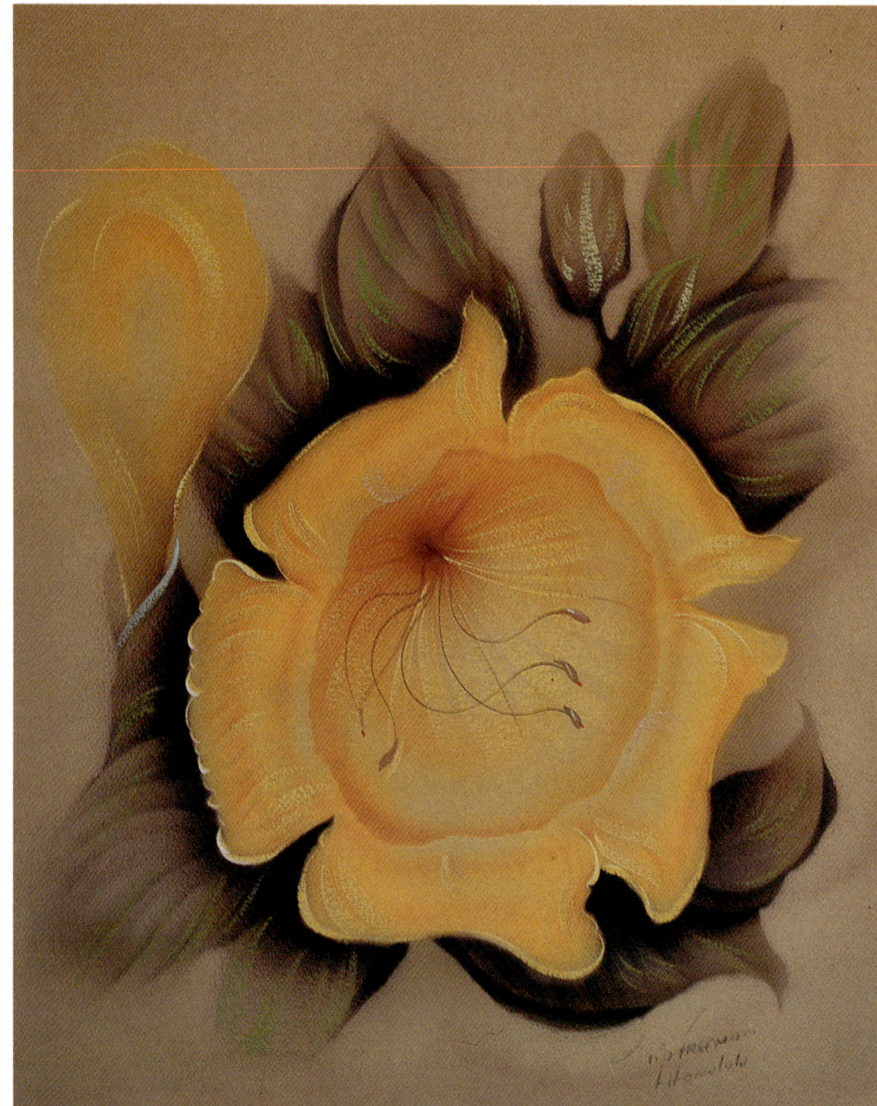

"Night Blooming Cereus." Signed Tip Freeman, Honolulu.
Courtesy: the Collection of Brian Goddard & Gene Sweeney.

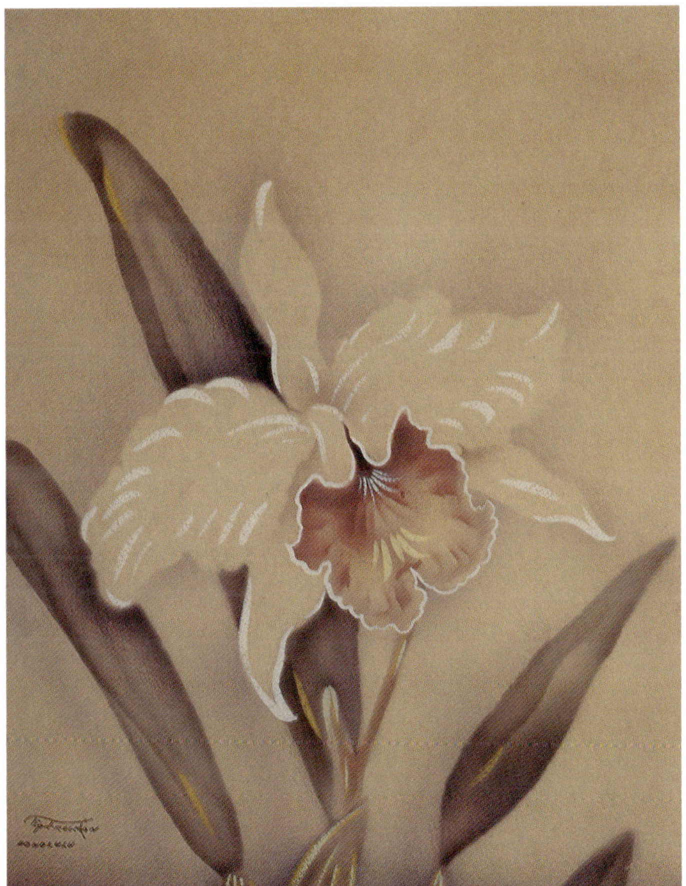

"White Cattleya Orchid." Signed Tip Freeman, Honolulu.
Courtesy: the Collection of Brian Goddard & Gene Sweeney.

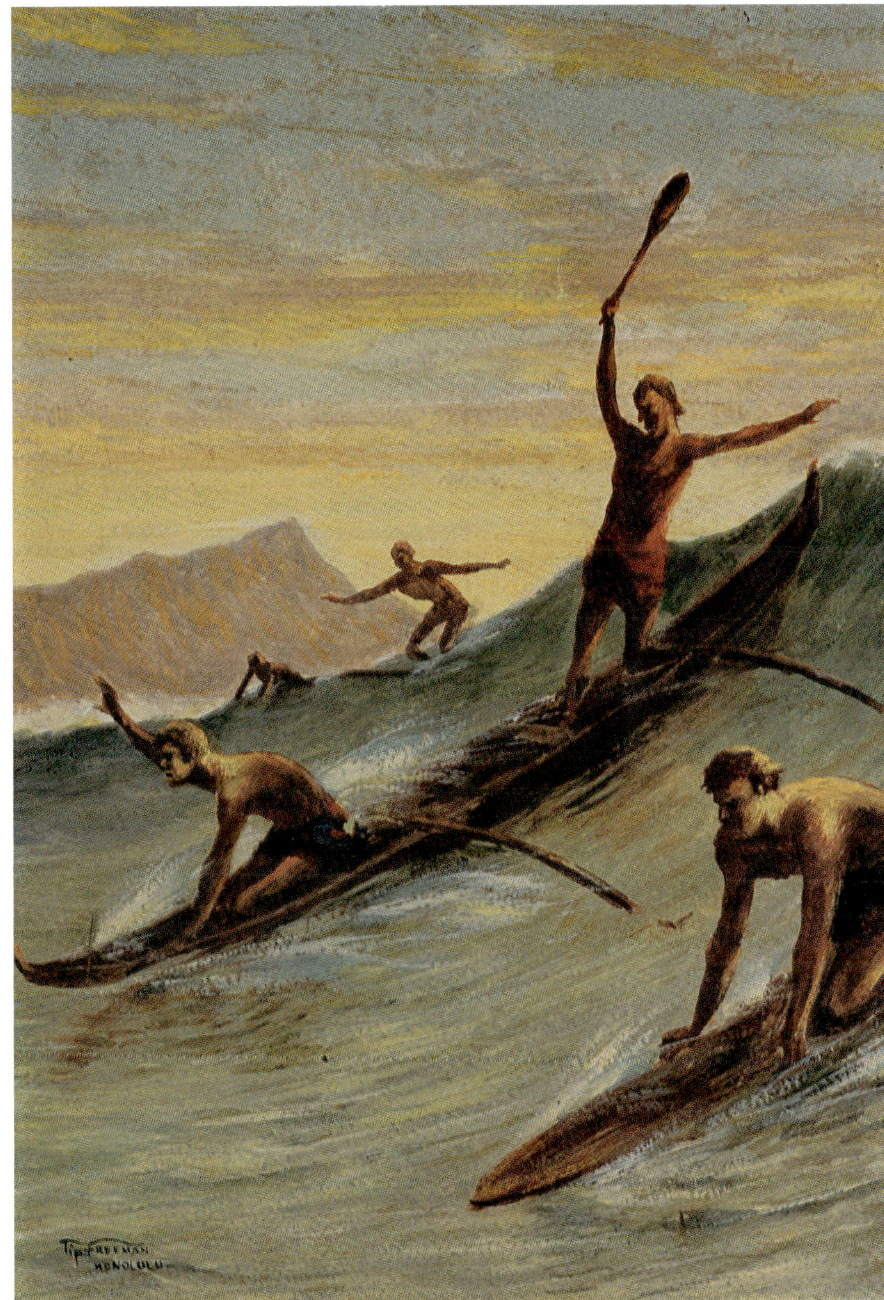

"Surfers." Signed Tip Freeman, Honolulu. *Courtesy: Stephen & Sandy Arterburn.*

Oda (Hale Pua)

Hale Pua was born in Honolulu in 1914 with the name Frank Yasutaro Oda. Sent to Japan for his education, he developed artistic skills early in his childhood. After receiving formal art training he returned to Hawaii, where he produced images of flowers, trees, and volcanoes. In the 1940s he added the medium of engraved glass to his list of accomplishments, opening a studio which in 1951 became known as Arts Hawaii, Inc.

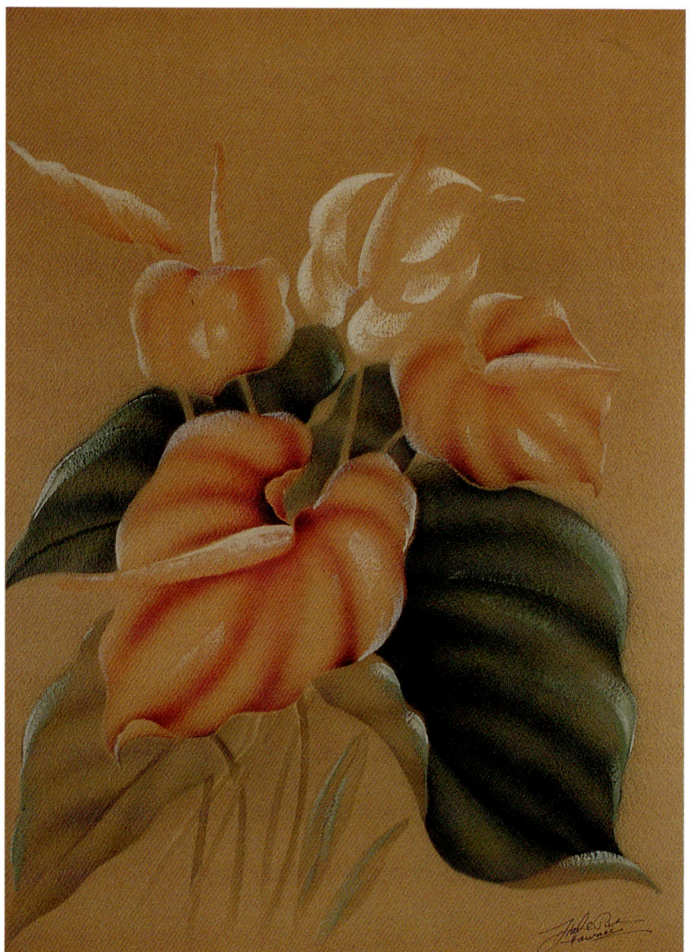

"Anthurium." Signed Hale Pua Hawaii. *Courtesy: the Collection of Brian Goddard & Gene Sweeney.*

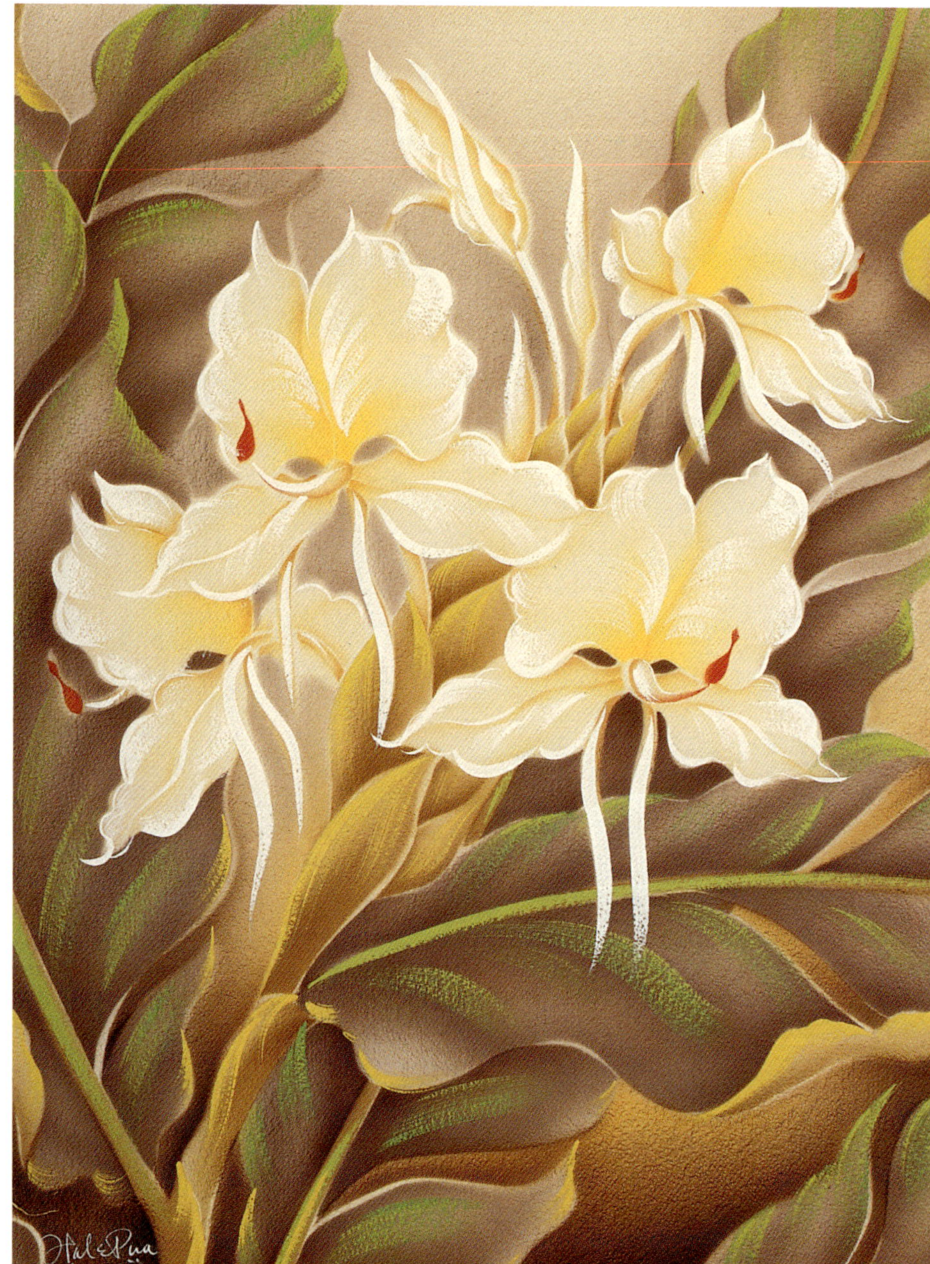

"Orchid." Signed Hale Pua Hawaii. *Courtesy: Randy Hild.*

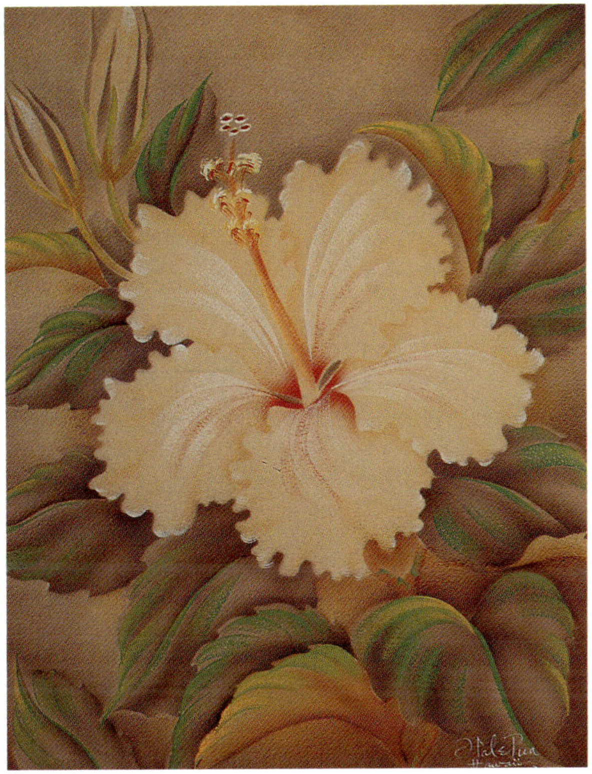

"White Hibiscus." Signed Hale Pua Hawaii. *Courtesy: Randy Hild*.

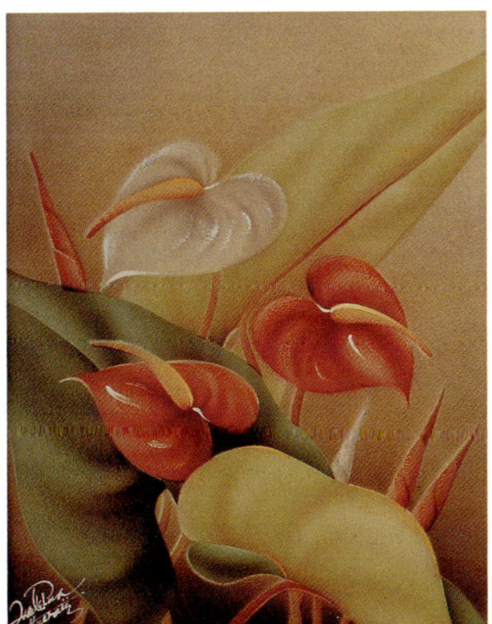

"Mixed Anthurium." Signed Hale Pua Hawaii. *Courtesy: Jim & Susie Stiso*.

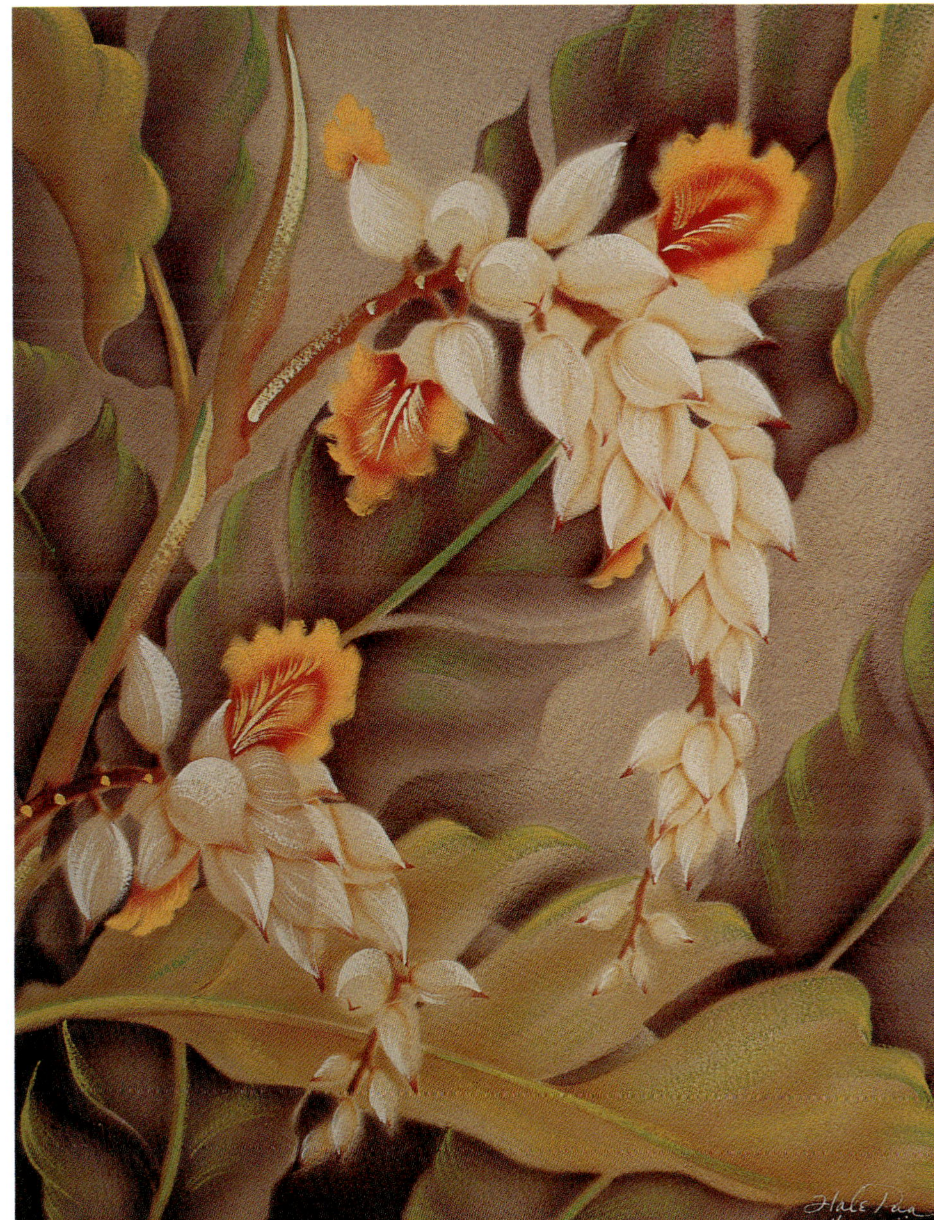

"Shell Ginger." Signed Hale Pua Hawaii. *Courtesy: Randy Hild*.

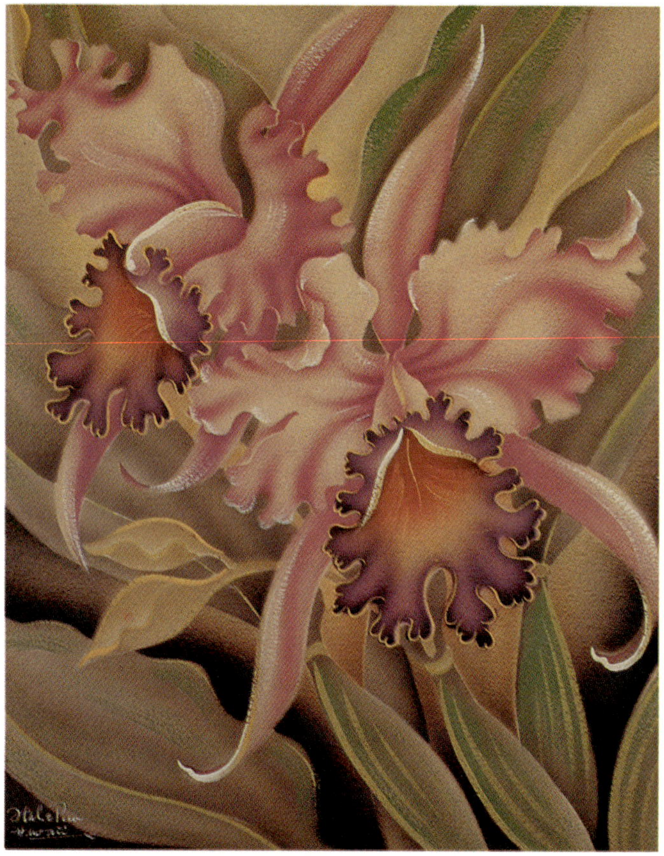

"Pink Orchids." Signed Hale Pua Hawaii. *Courtesy: the Collection of Brian Goddard & Gene Sweeney*.

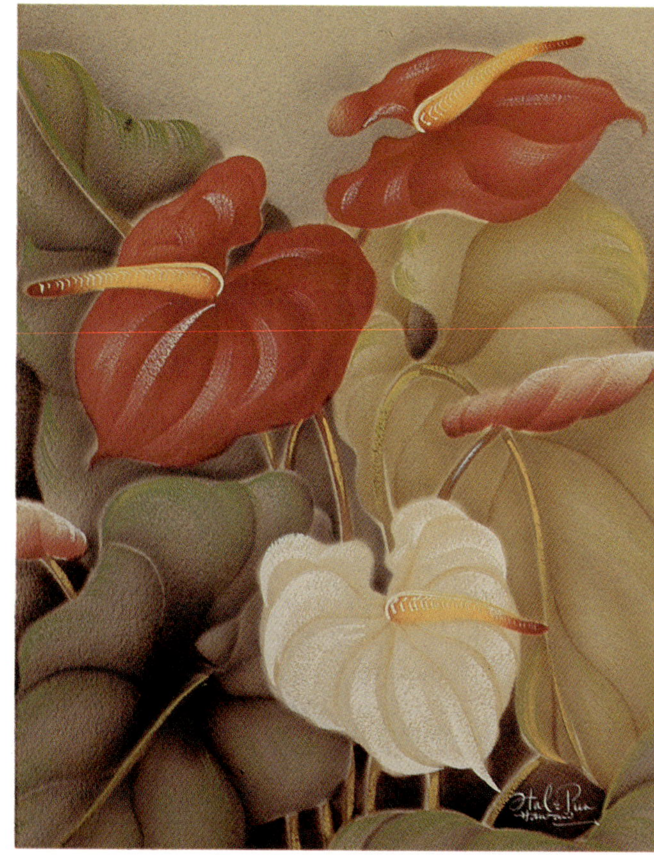

"Mixed Anthurium." Signed Hale Pua Hawaii. *Courtesy: the Collection of Brian Goddard & Gene Sweeney*.

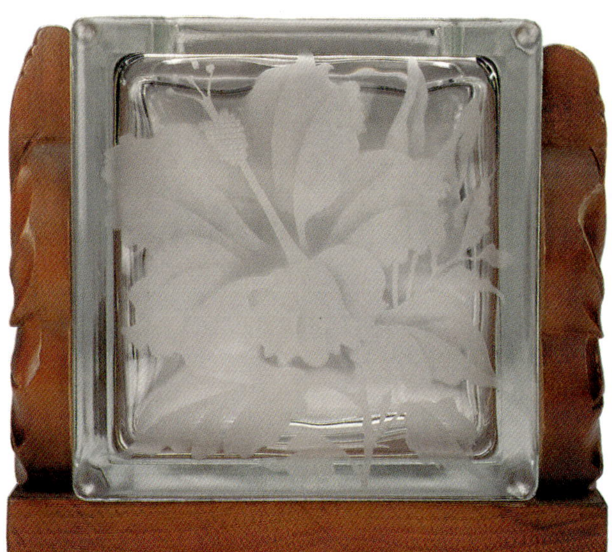

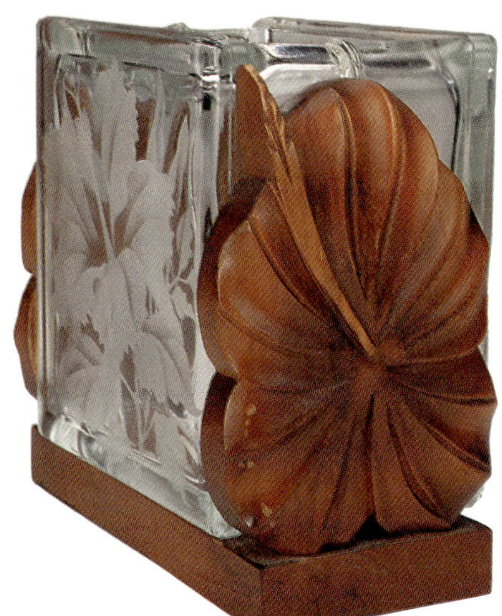

"Hibiscus." Frank Oda etched glass design in carved koa wood stand. *Courtesy: the Collection of Susan White*.

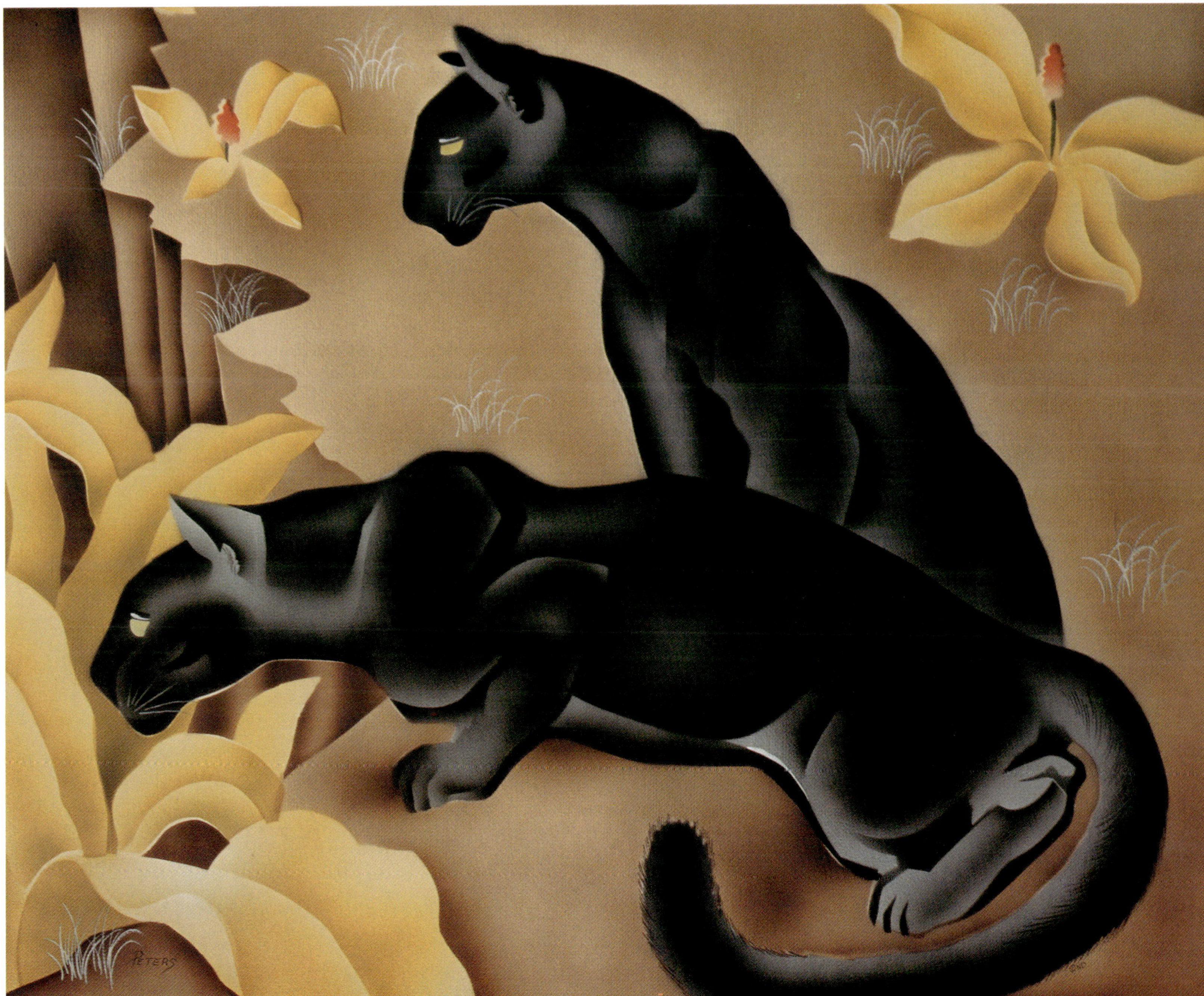

"Panthers," Peters. *Courtesy. Michael & Denise Queen.*

Sunset Magazine Covers

Many magazines from the early 1900s to the present have used tropical images on their covers to captivate their readers and engage their imaginations. *Sunset, The Magazine of the West* produced several of these, three of which are shown here.

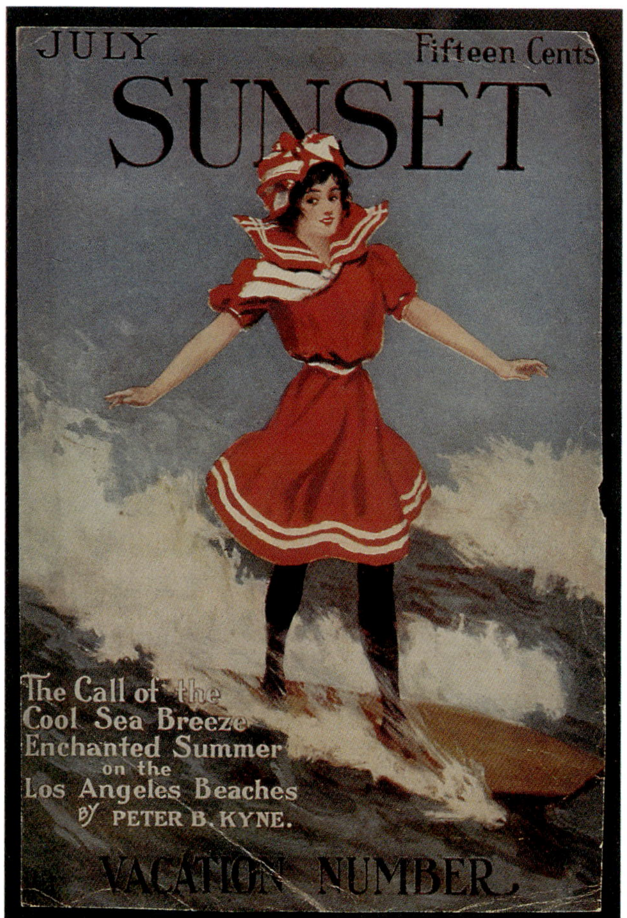

Sunset magazine with art by A. Cahill. The surf boarding bathing beauty on a cover promoting Los Angeles beaches is a clear indication of the influence Hawaii was having in California in the early 1900s. *Courtesy: Dan Pincetich.*

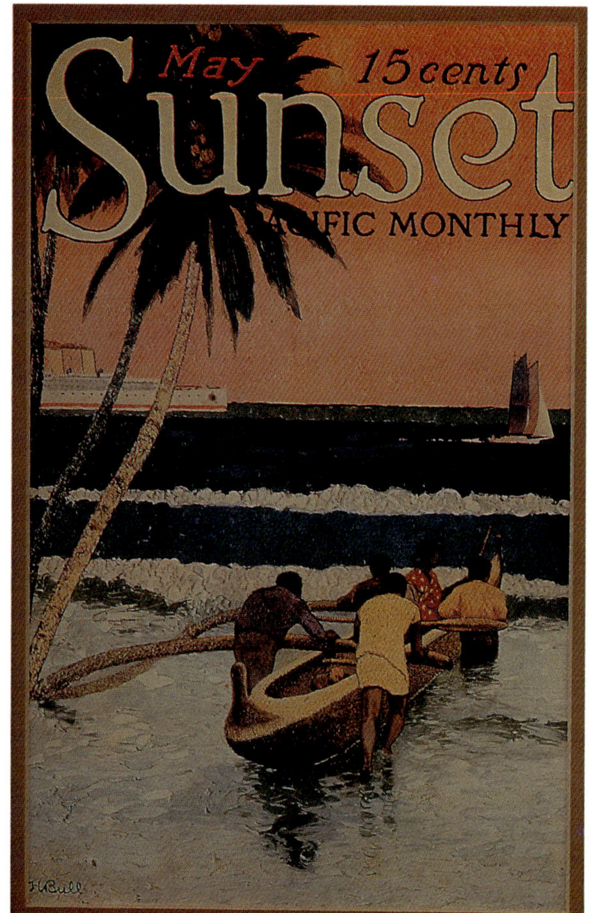

Pushing the outrigger into the surf just as the tourist ship appears tells part of the story of the Islands' romantic atmosphere for vacationers. The image is signed Bull. *Courtesy: Dan Pincetich.*

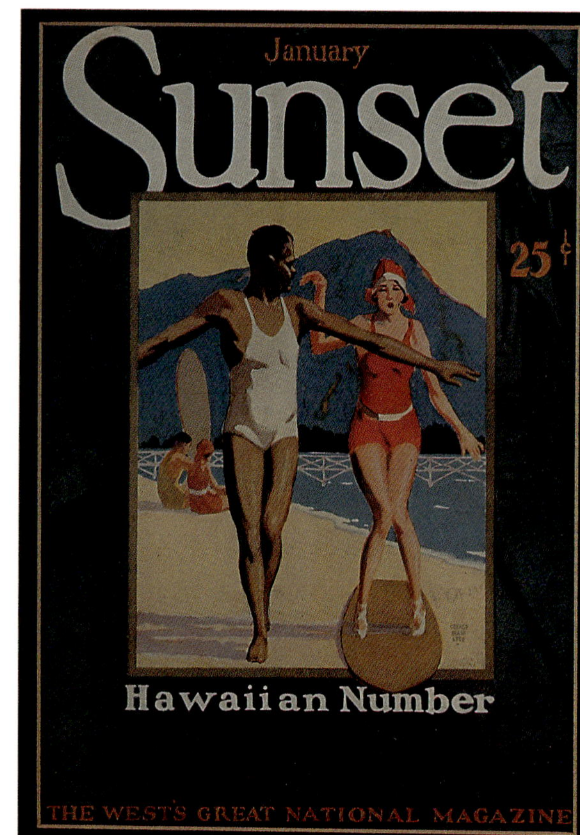

A later *Sunset* cover by George Blake Lyle. *Courtesy: Dan Pincetich.*

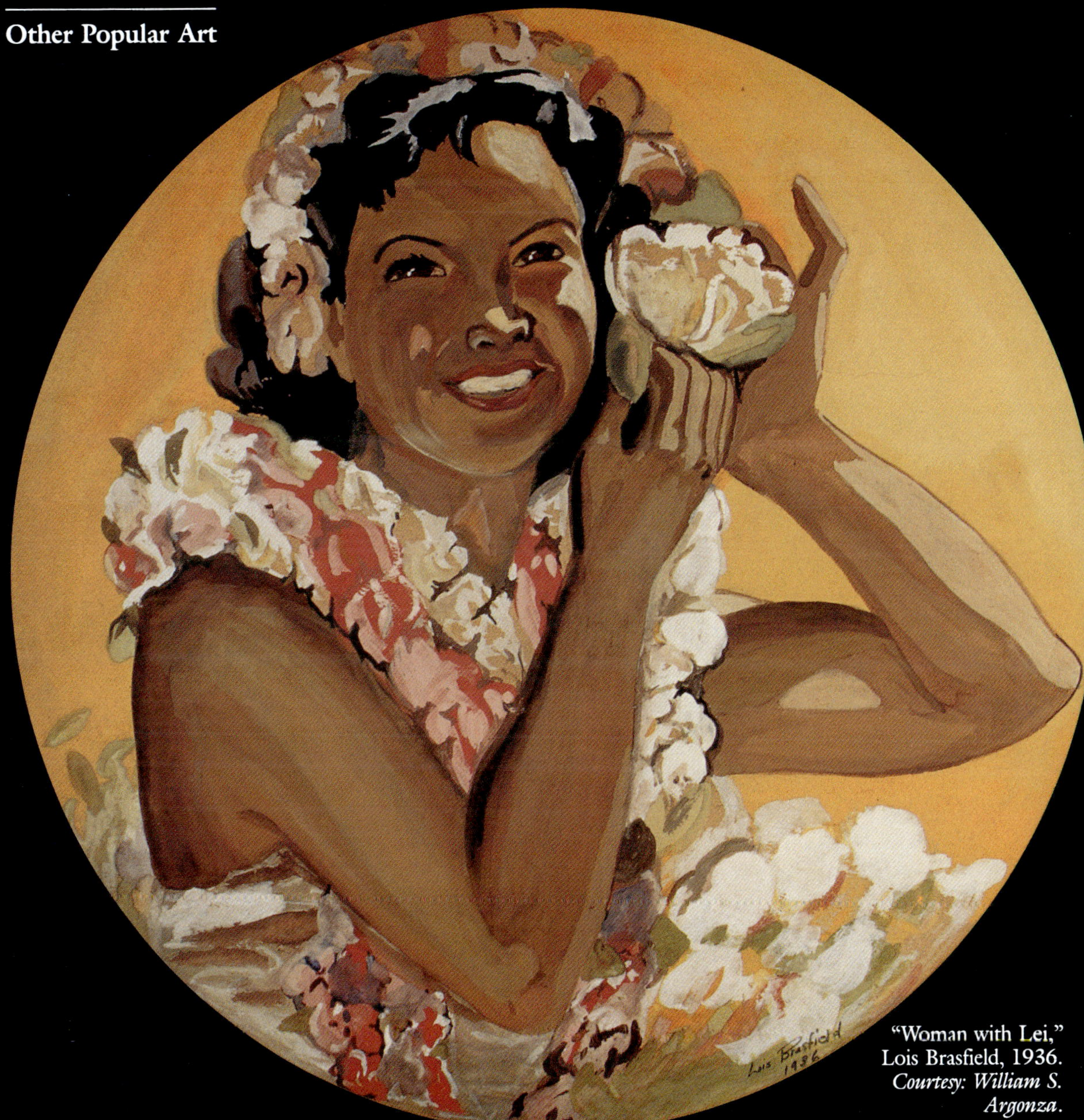

"Woman with Lei,"
Lois Brasfield, 1936.
Courtesy: William S. Argonza.

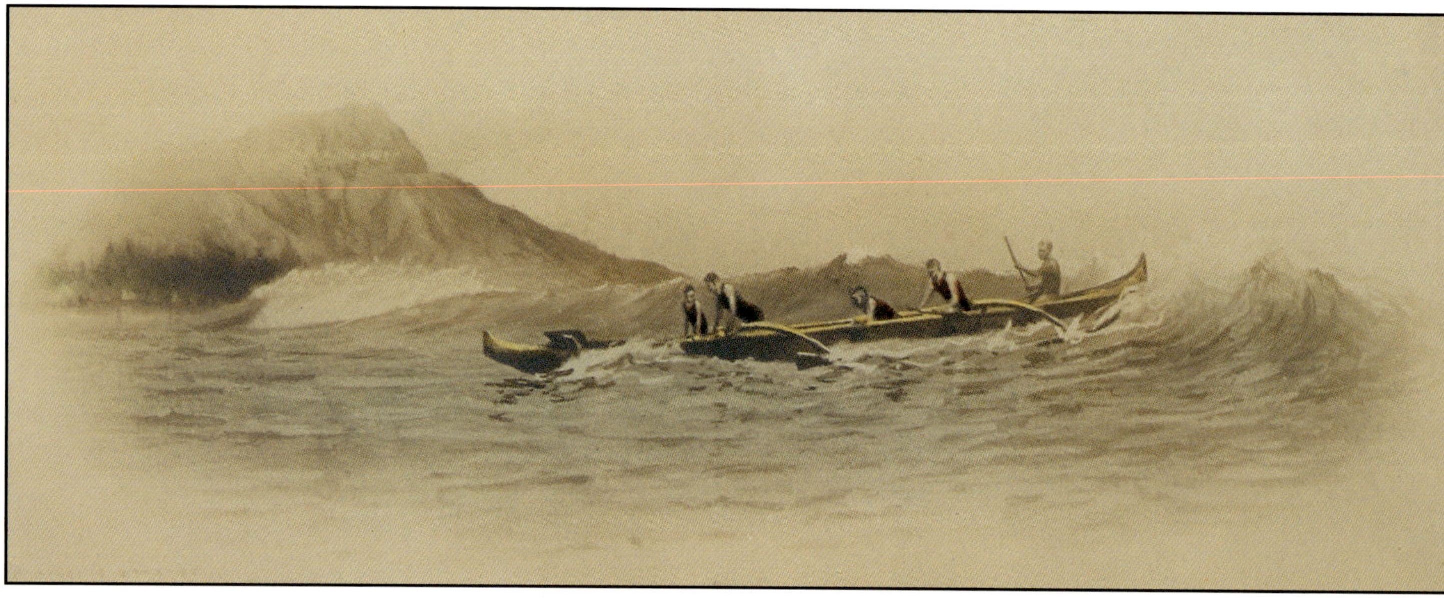

"Outrigger," tinted photograph. *Courtesy: Michele Leypoldt*.

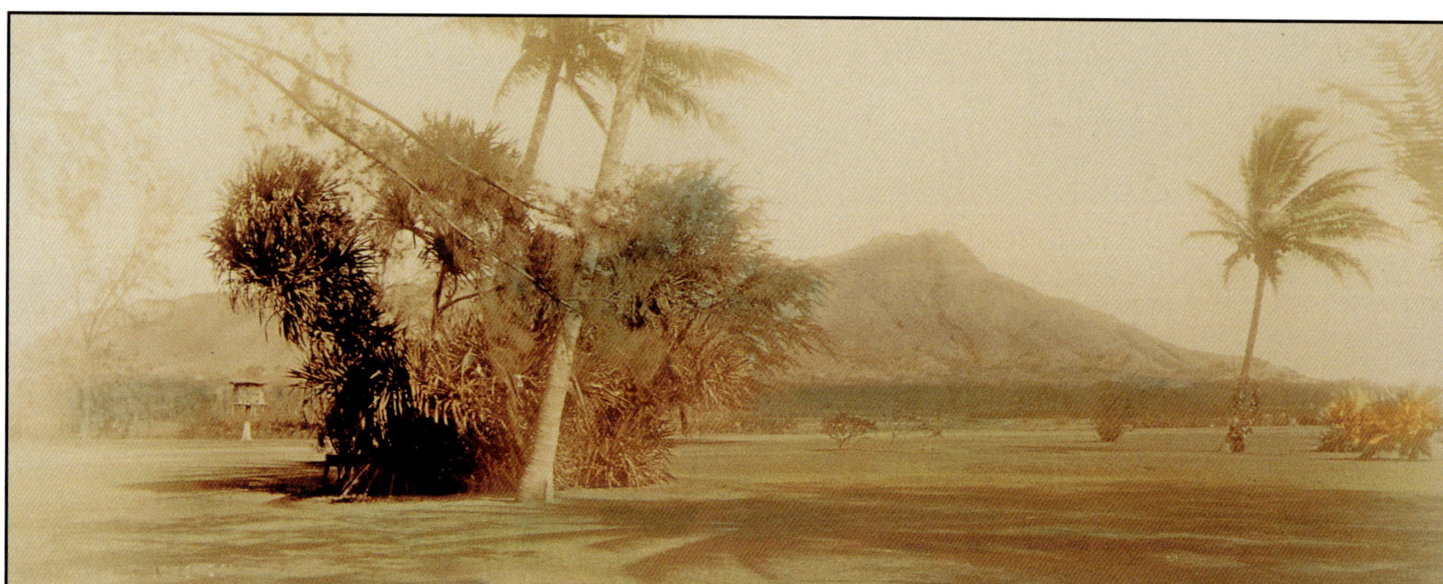

"Diamond Head," tinted photograph. *Courtesy: Michele Leypoldt*.

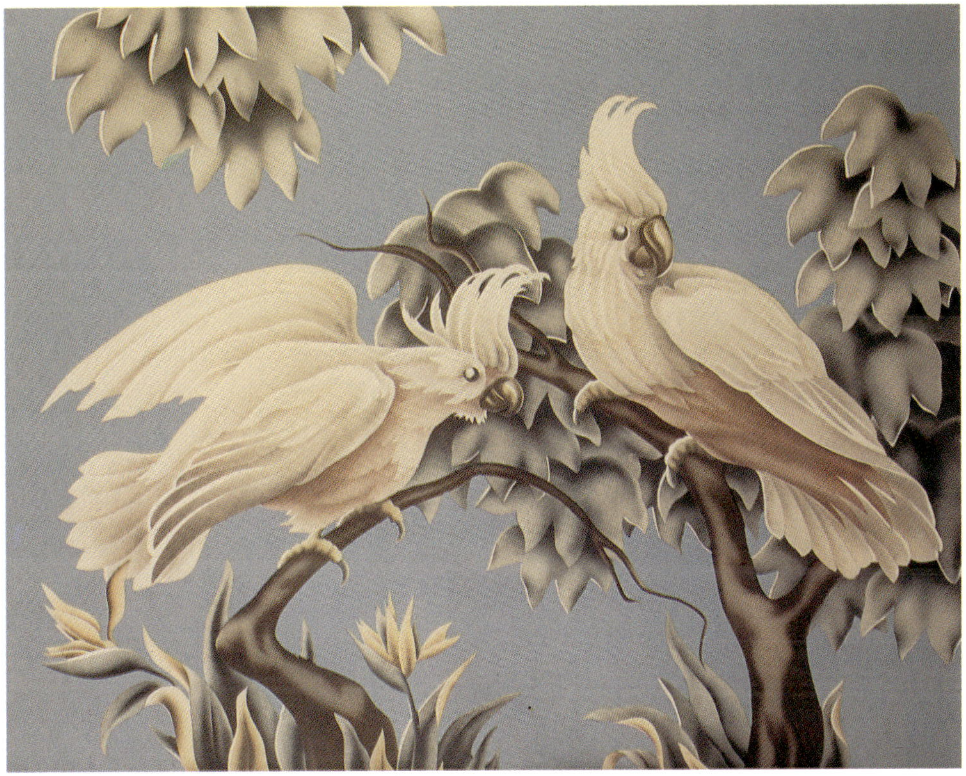

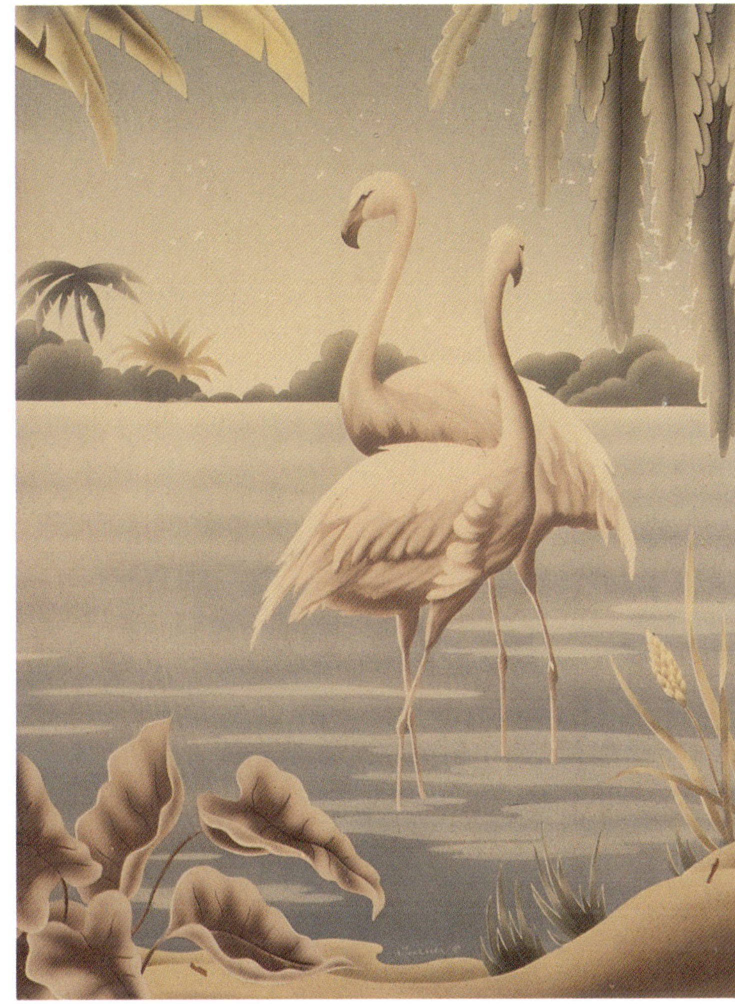

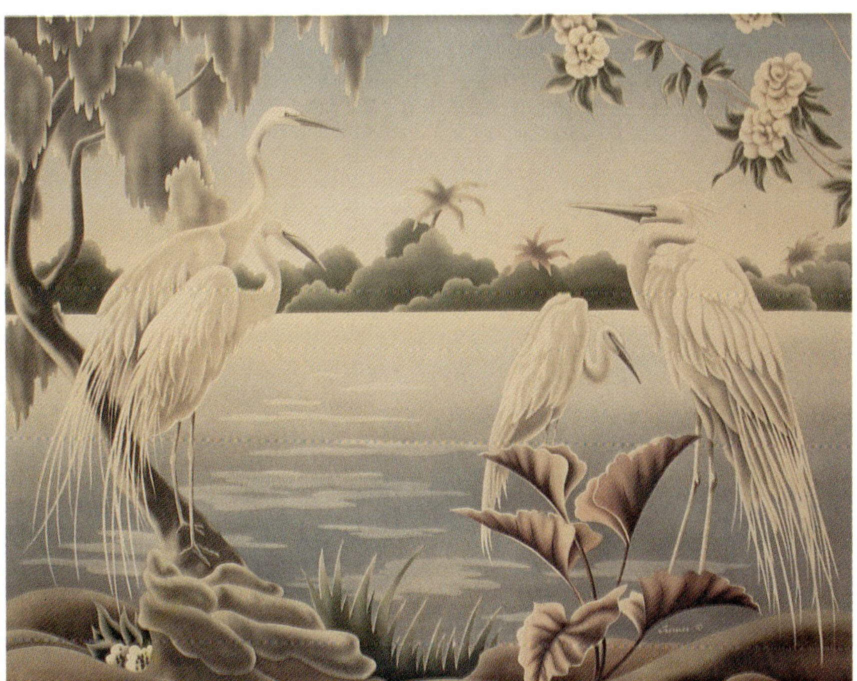

Above:
"Flamingoes," Turner. *Courtesy: Michael Trotter.*

Above left:
"Cockatoo," Turner. *Courtesy: Michael & Denise Queen.*

Left:
"Cranes," Turner. *Courtesy: Michael & Denise Queen.*

Fine Art

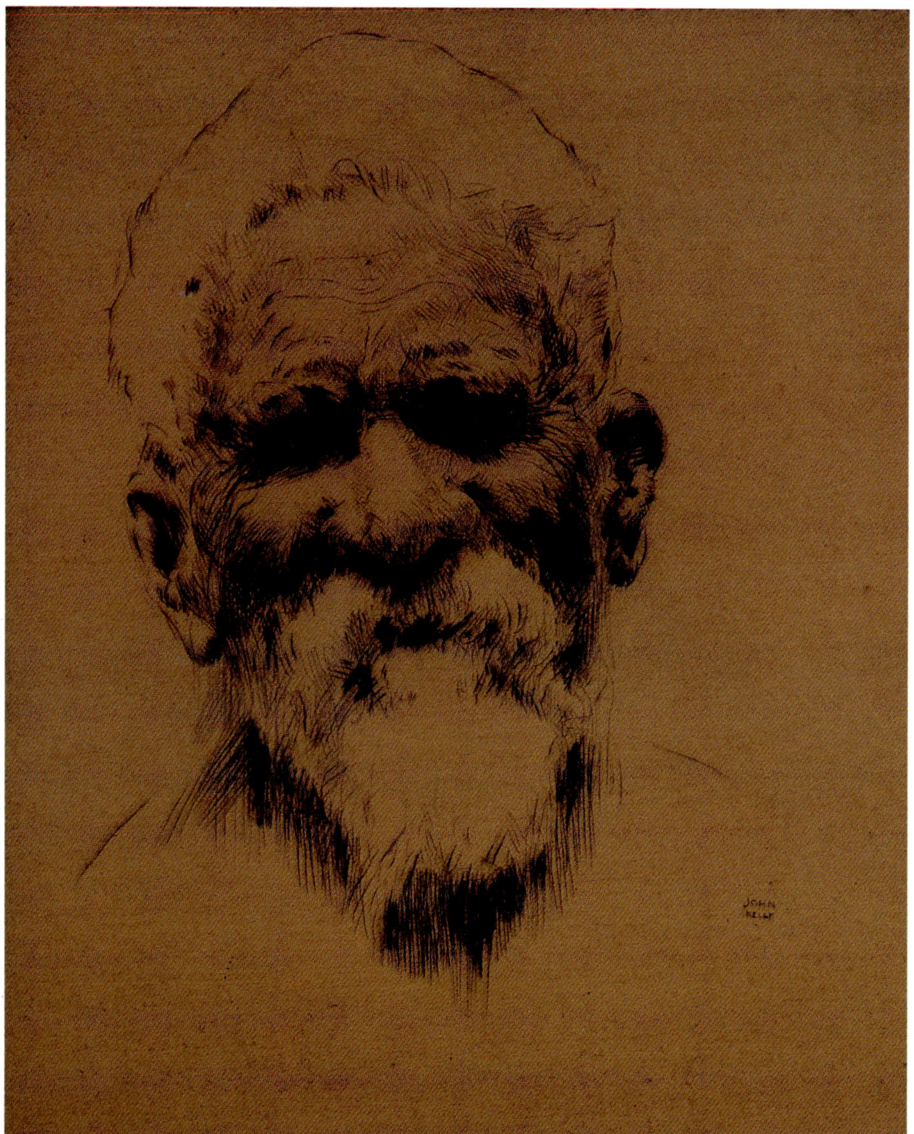

Kelly

John Melville Kelly (1878-1964) was born in Arizona. Raised on a ranch, his formal education extended only through the third grade. In his youth he was an accomplished bicycle racer and boxer, but as he matured he turned to art. He attended art school in San Francisco, where he met and married Kathryn Harland. He worked as an artist on the staff of the *San Francisco Examiner.*

His art took him to Hawaii in 1923 where he was commissioned to create promotional art for land in Lanikai which was being developed by Charles Frazier. It was a one year contract so Kelly took his family with him. They never left.

He landed a job as an illustrator for the *Honolulu Star-Bulletin*, and as the Depression struck the economy he moved into the area of fine arts. His talent served him well. Both he and his sculptor wife received worldwide recognition and acceptance for their work.

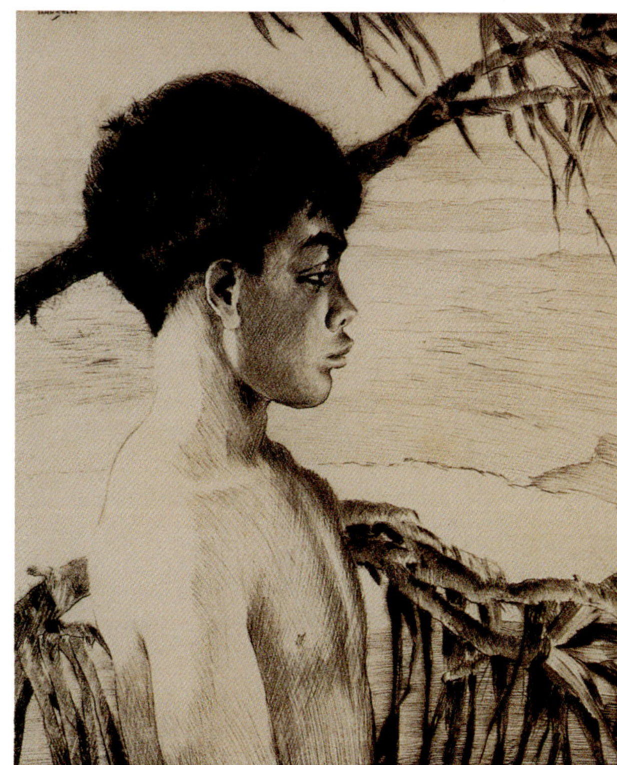

Left:
"Kaipo," c. late 1930s, drypoint. 8" x 9.5". *Courtesy: Douglas A. Frazer Fine Art.*

Far left:
"Old Kalama," 1939, drypoint, 6.2" x 7.625". *Courtesy: Douglas A. Frazer Fine Art.*

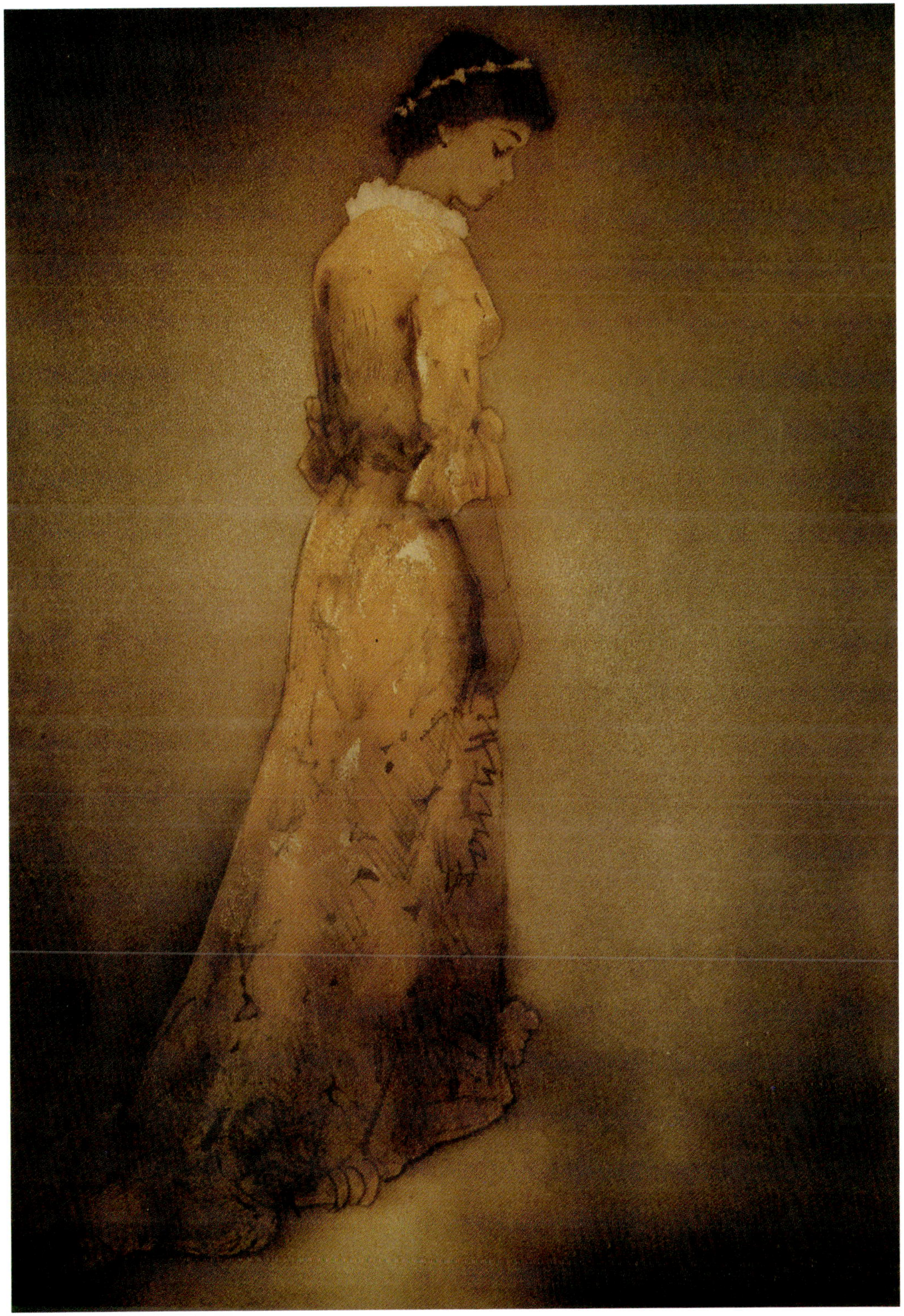

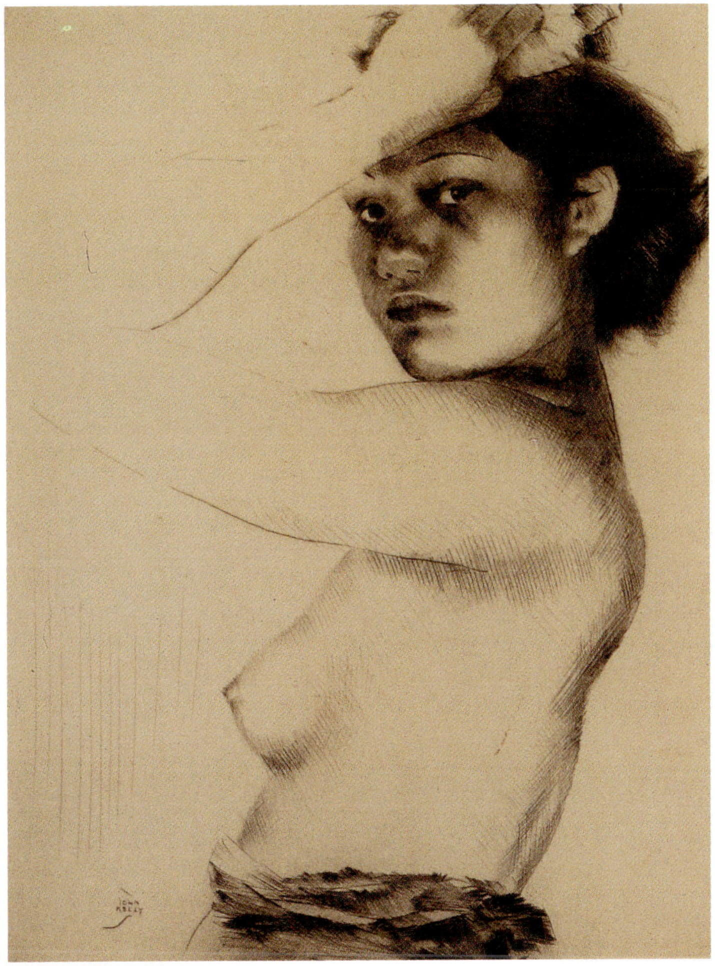

Above :
"Kanani," c. 1938, drypoint, 8.375" x 11.25". The model lived across the street from the artist and was adored by some of the male customers. *Courtesy: Douglas A. Frazer Fine Art.*

Left:
"Yellow Holoku," no date available, polychrome aquatint, 9.9" x 15.125". *Courtesy: Douglas A. Frazer Fine Art*

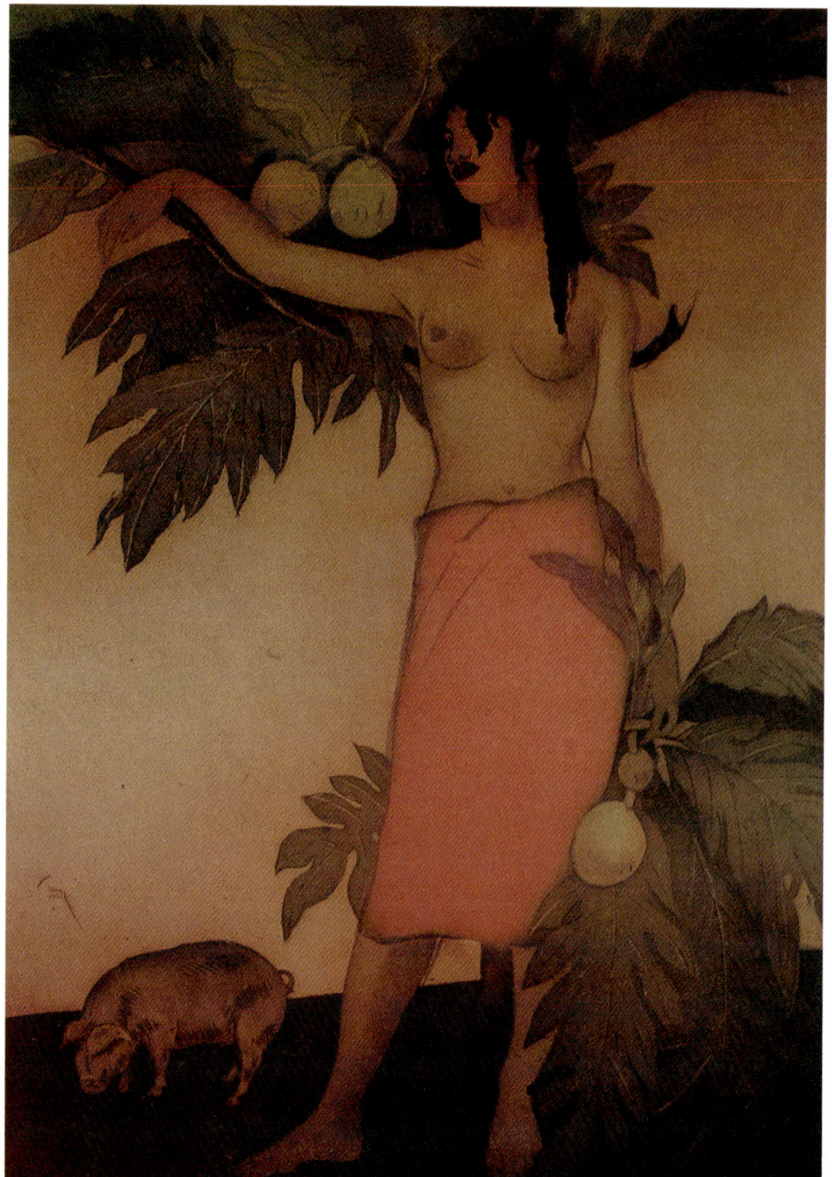

"Breadfruit Girl," c. 1940, Aquatint, 10.75" x 15". *Courtesy: Douglas A. Frazer Fine Art.*

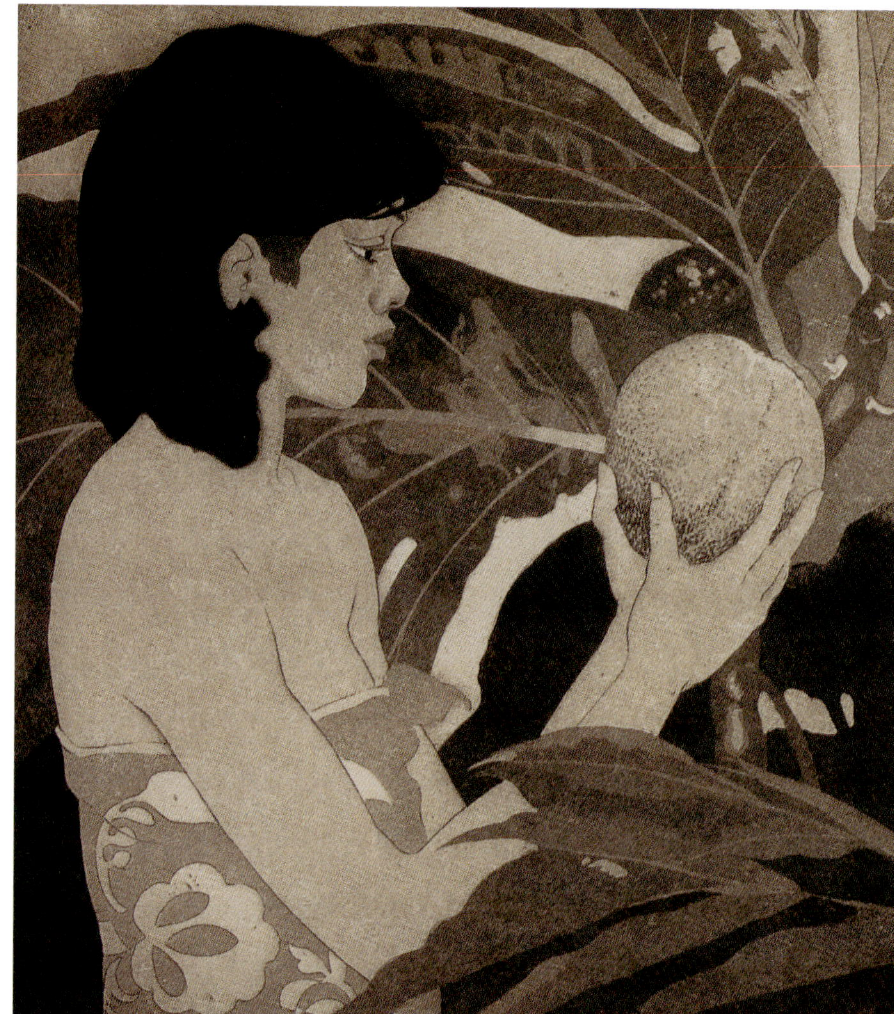

"Breadfruit," c. 1936, polychrome aquatint, 10" x 10.875". *Courtesy: Douglas A. Frazer Fine Art.*

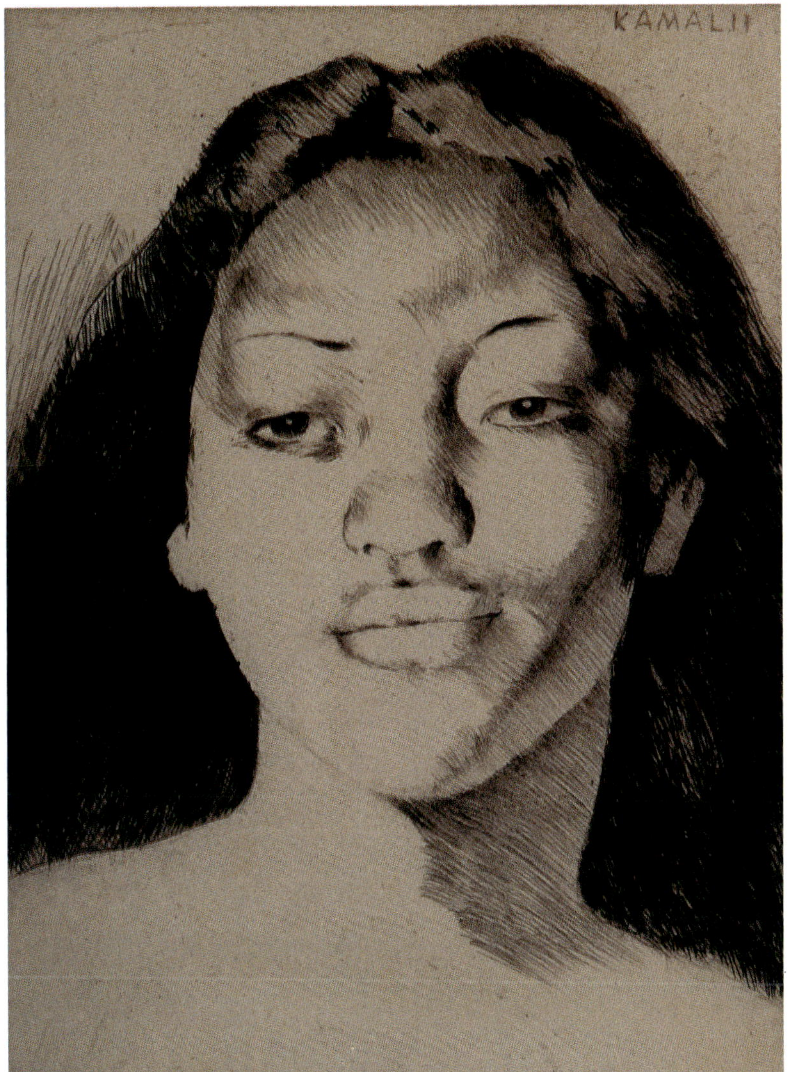

"Kamalii," c. 1940, drypoint, 6.875" x 7.875", from an edition of over 100. This print was one of the gift prints of the Honolulu Printmakers Society. *Courtesy: Douglas A. Frazer Fine Art.*

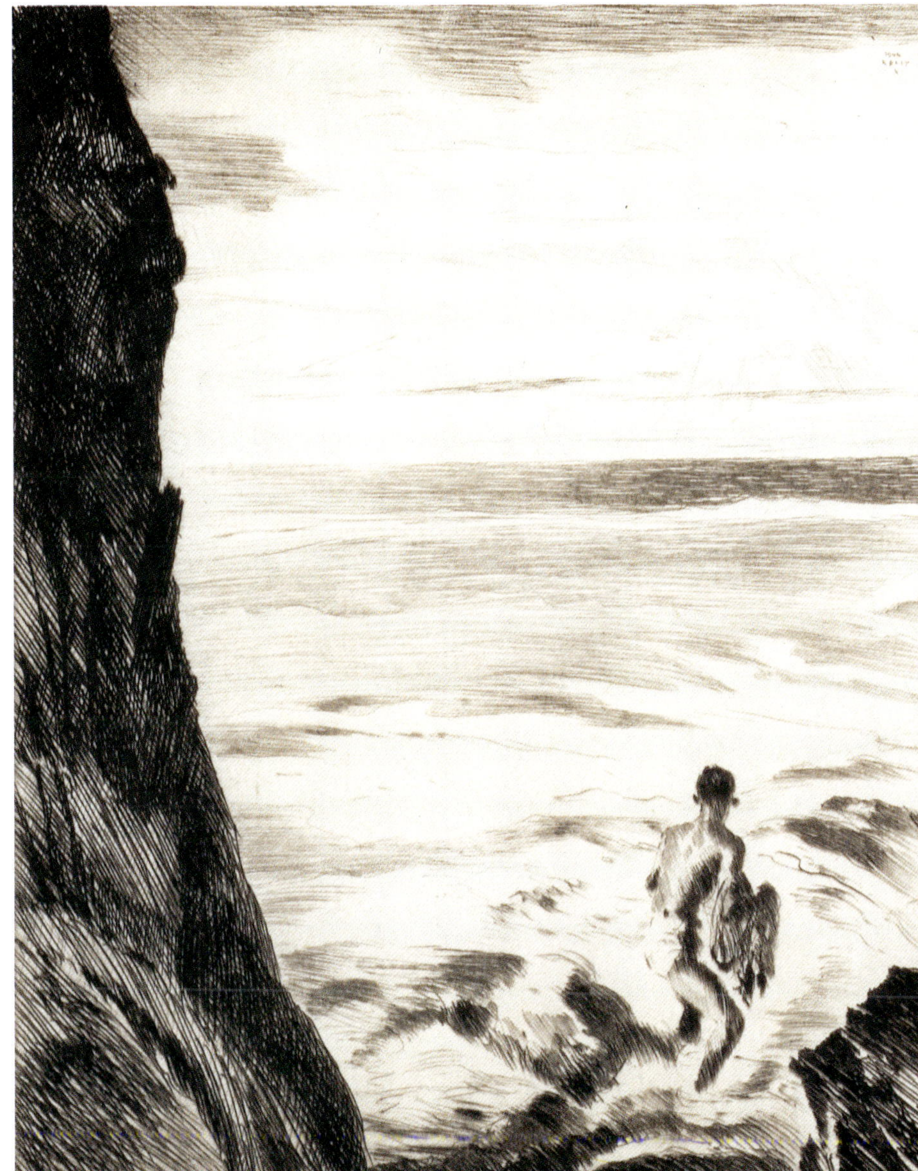

"Moi Water," c. 1939, drypoint, 8" x 10". The model for this print was the son of the artist, John Kelly, Jr. *Courtesy: Douglas A. Frazer Fine Art.*

Luquiens

Born in Auburndale, Massachusetts, Huc Mazelet Luquiens (1881-1961) spent his youth in New Haven, Connecticut, where his father chaired the Romance Languages Department at Yale University. Luquiens received his B.A. and Master of Fine Arts degrees from Yale before continuing his studies at the Ecole des Beaux Arts and the Academie Julien in Paris. Upon returning to the United States he established a strong reputation as portraitist.

His first visit to Hawaii, in 1917, was to see his sister, who had married into the Kama'aina Judd family, and to paint some commissioned portraits. He was smitten by the beauty of the Islands and decided to make his home in Hawaii.

During the 1920s he spent his summers recording the landscapes of the big island of Hawaii. He did this so well that after his death, some forty years later, his images continued to be the standard by which the changes in the landscape were measured. In 1924 he became the first art teacher at the University of Hawaii, where he organized the department and set high standards, both as a teacher and as the head of the department until his retirement in 1946.

In 1948, Luquiens, along with Alice N. Poole, founded the Honolulu Printmakers, the oldest professional art organization in Hawaii.

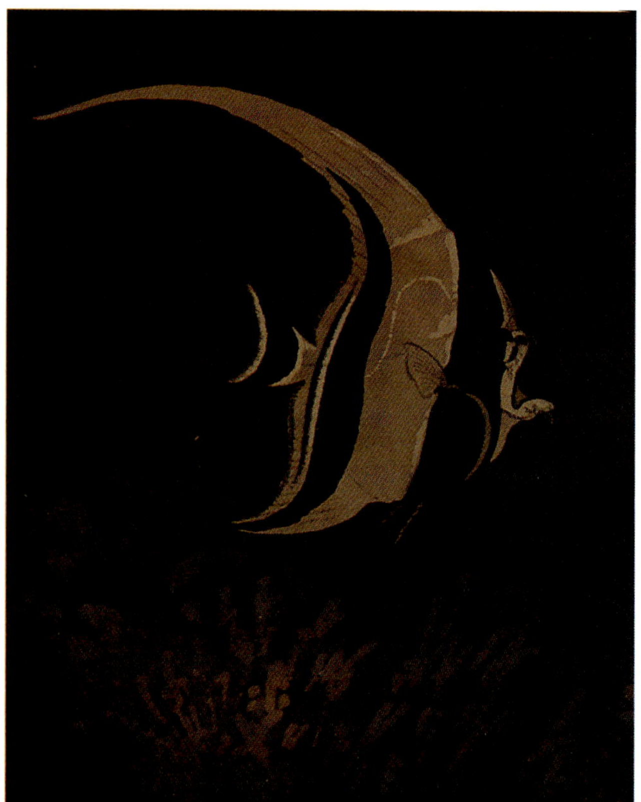

Right:
"Playfellows," not dated, aquatint, 7.75" x 5.875". *Courtesy: Douglas A. Frazer Fine Art.*

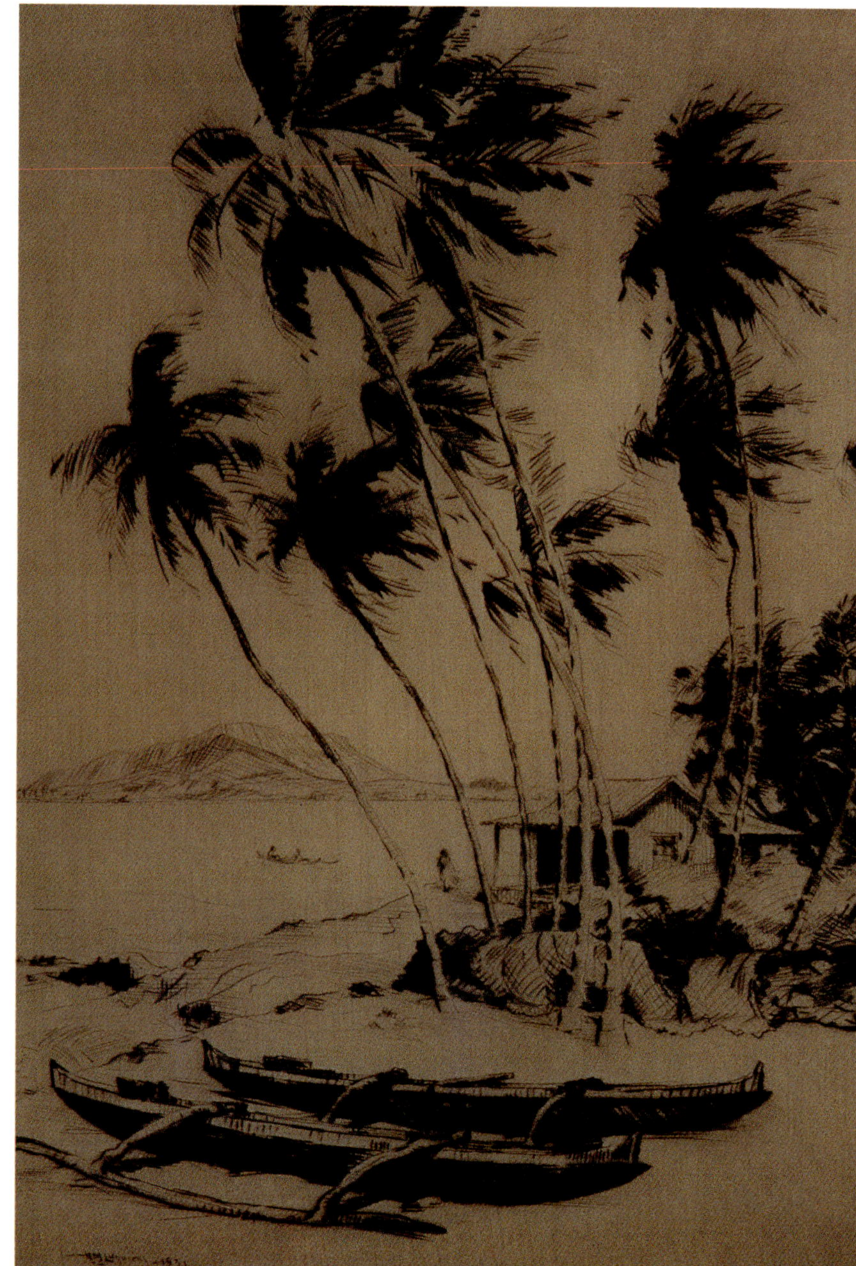

Far right:
"Trade Wind," not dated, drypoint, 5.875" x 8.5". *Courtesy: Douglas A. Frazer Fine Art.*

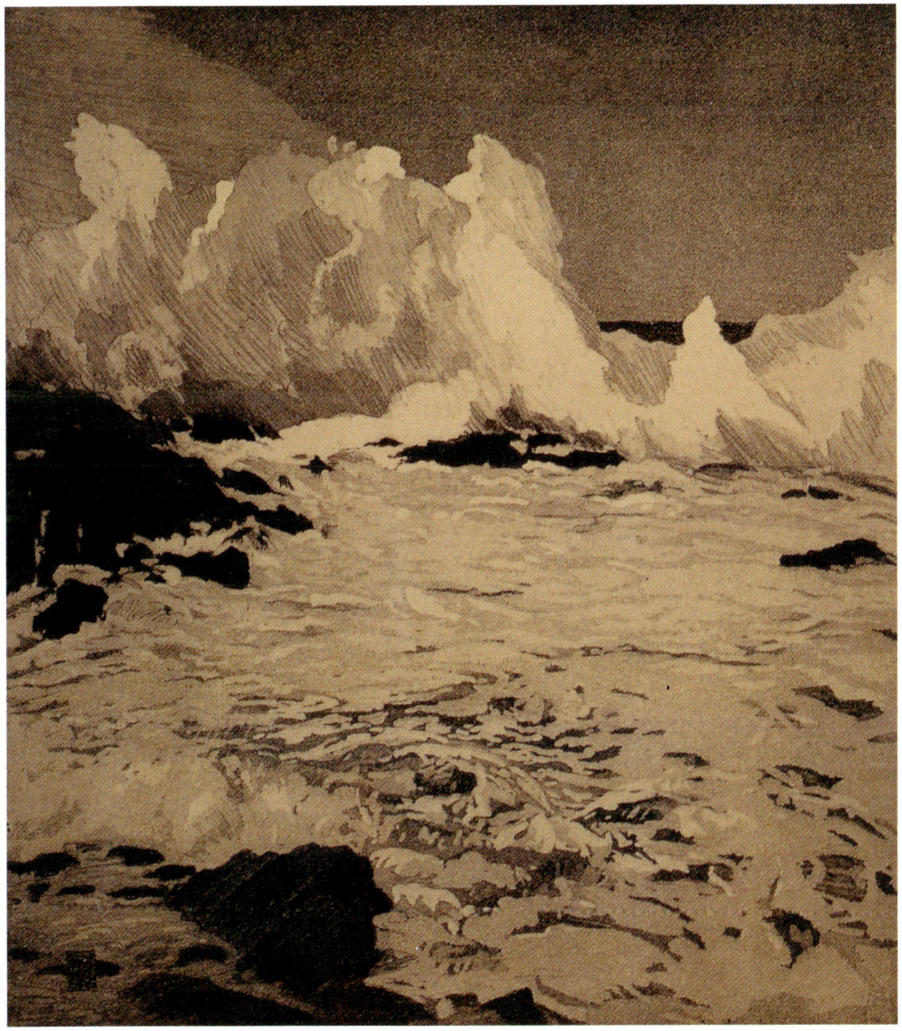

"The Roar of the Surf," not dated, aquatint with soft ground etching, artist's monogram in image at lower left, 9.75" x 9".
Courtesy: Douglas A. Frazer Fine Art.

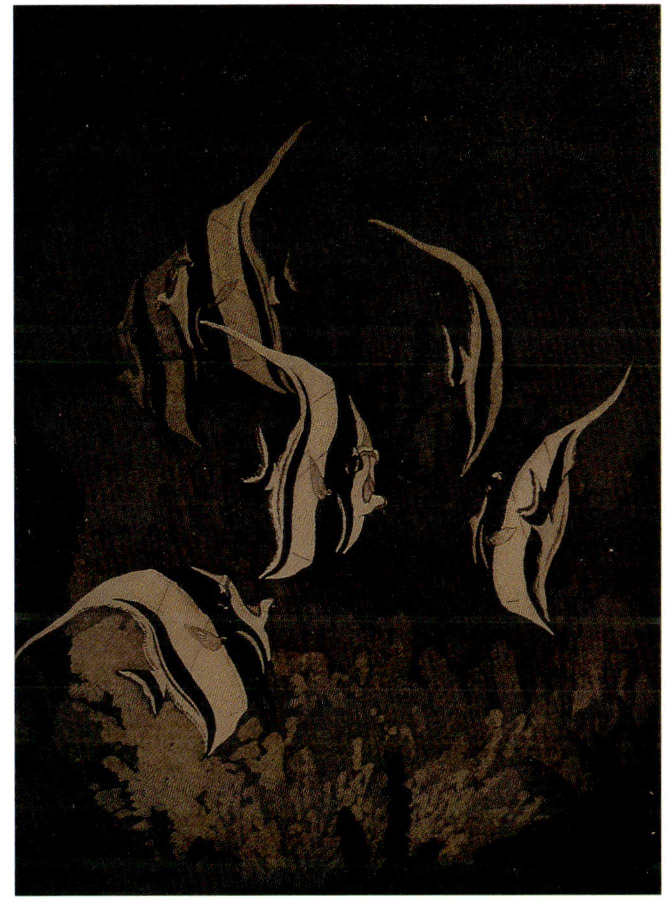

"Moorish Idol," not dated, aquatint, 6" x 5".
Courtesy: Douglas A. Frazer Fine Arts.

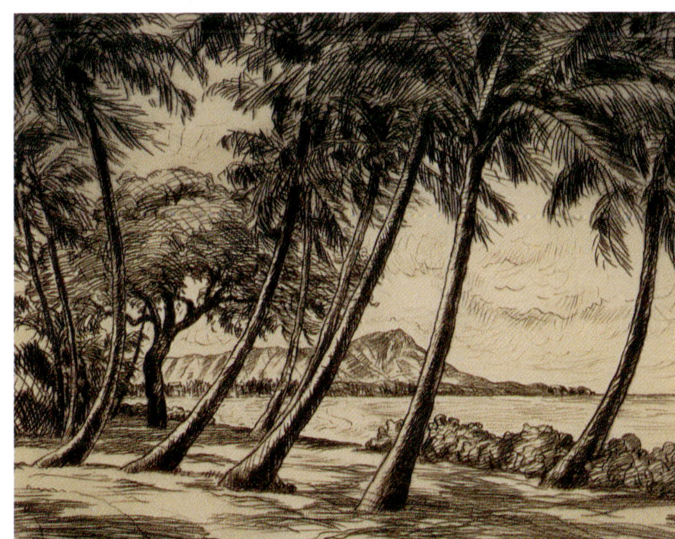

"Halekylani," not dated, drypoint, 9.875" x 7.875".
Courtesy: Douglas A. Frazer Fine Art.

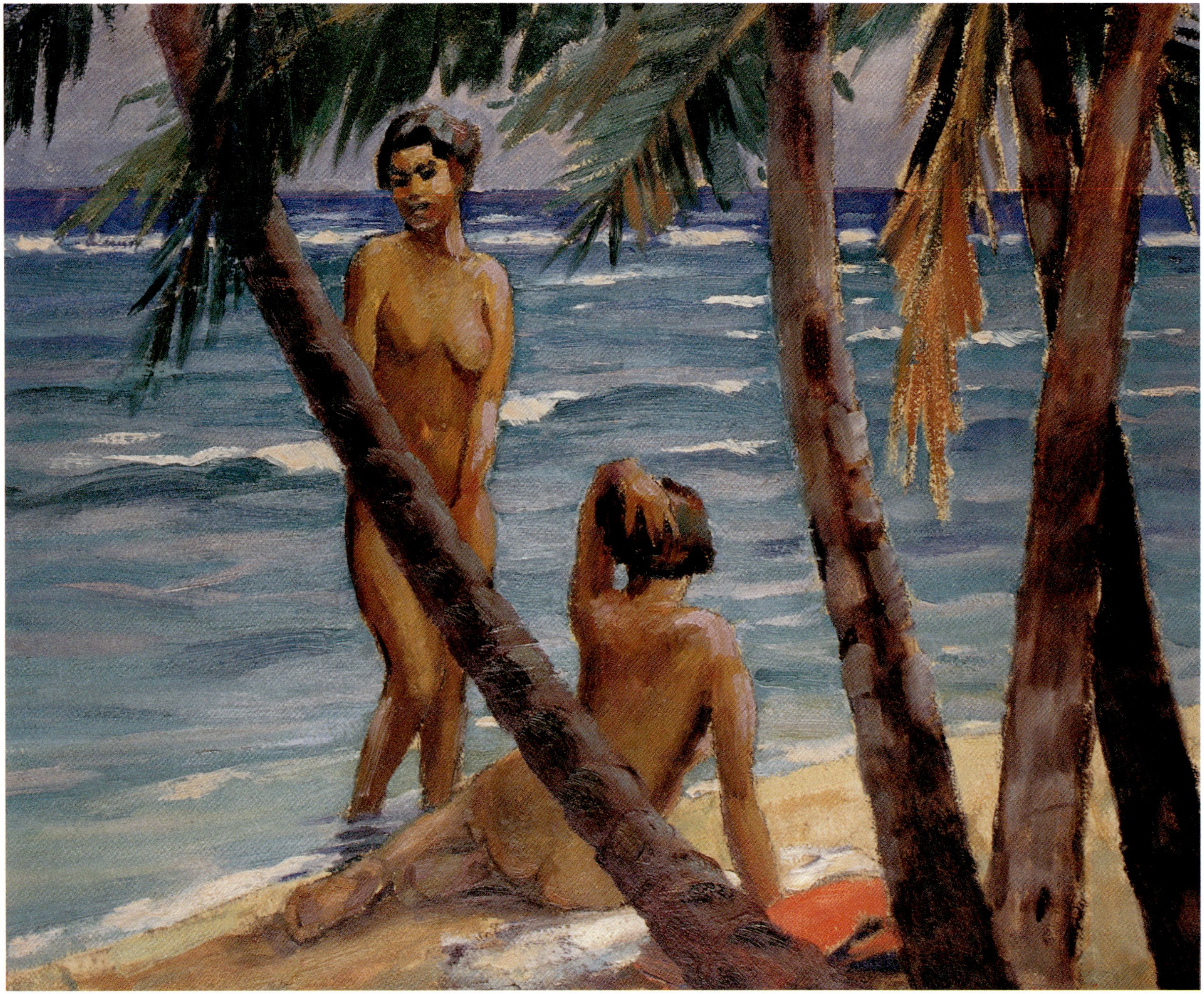

"Coral Sea," ca. 1929, oil on board, 20" x 24". *Courtesy: Douglas A. Frazer Fine Art.*

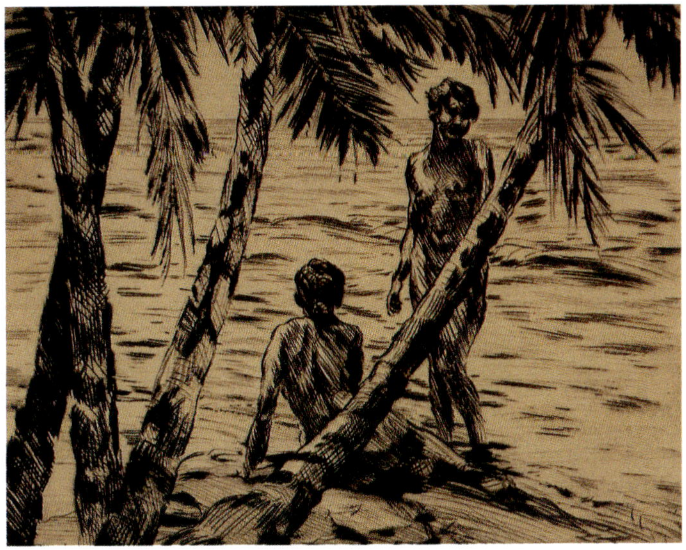

Left:
"Coral Sea," 1929, drypoint (1st state), 8" x 9.875". *Courtesy: Douglas A. Frazer Fine Art*.

Below:
"Surf Riders Waikiki," 1918, drypoint (1st state). *Courtesy: Dan Pincetich*.

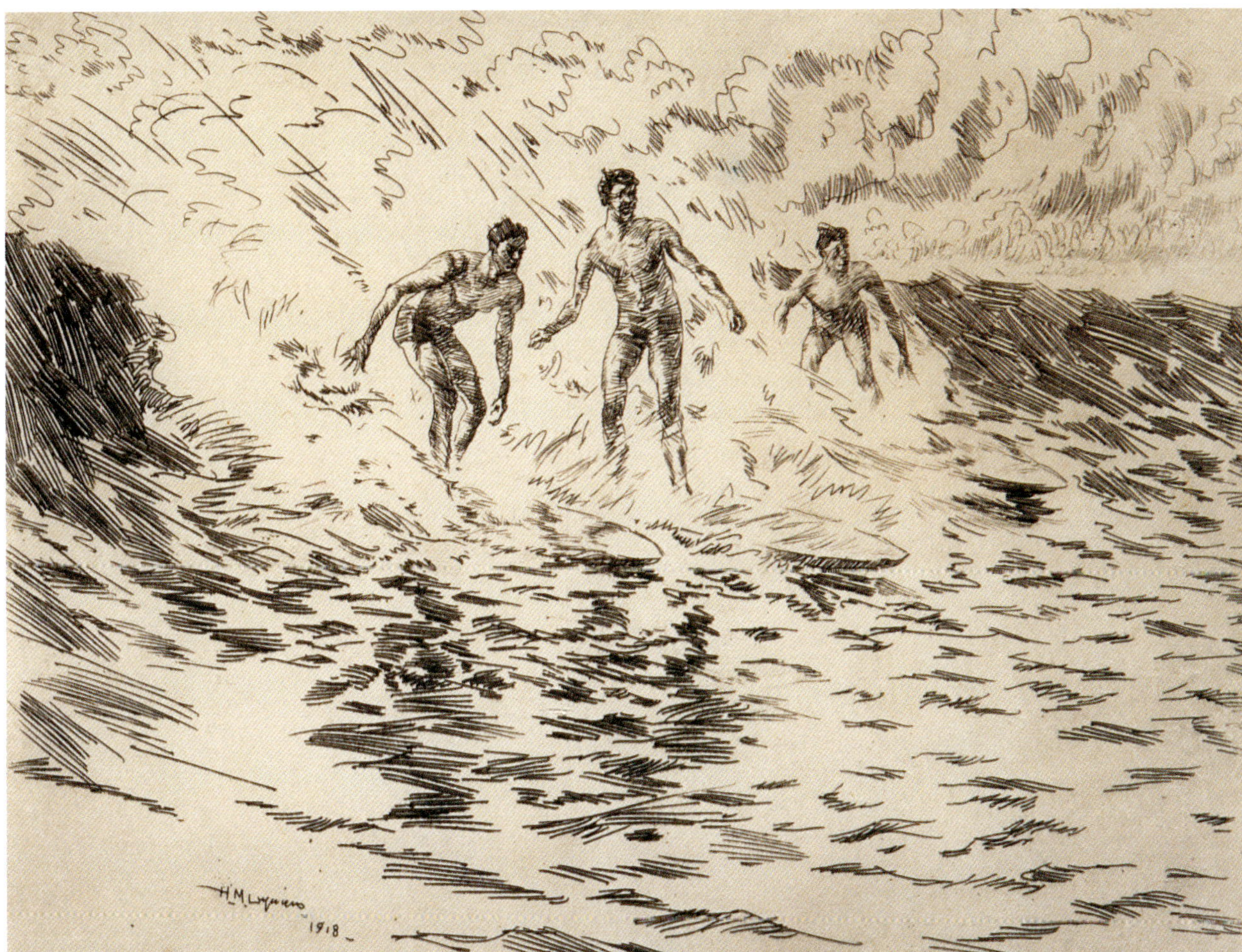

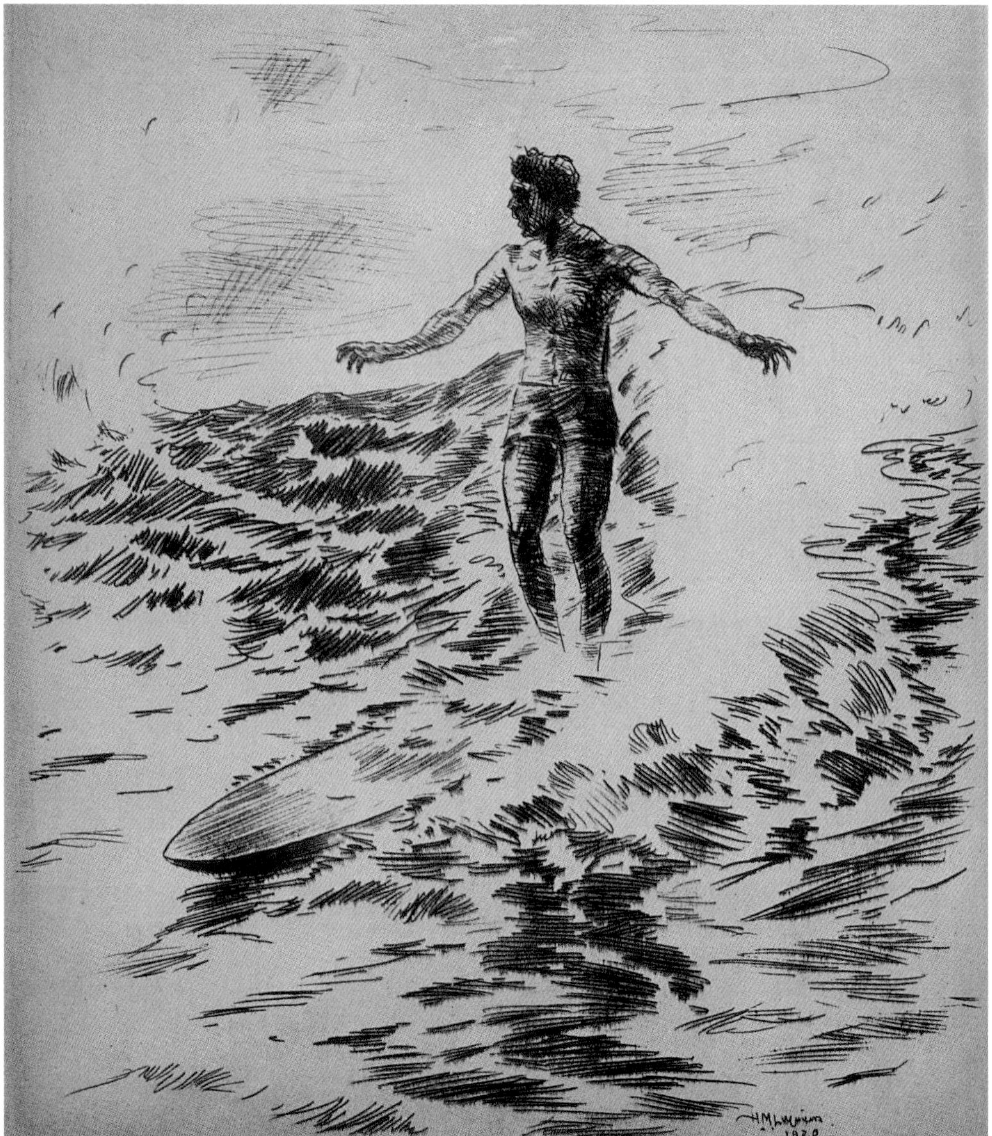

"Surfer," 1920, drypoint. *Courtesy: Dan Pincetich.*

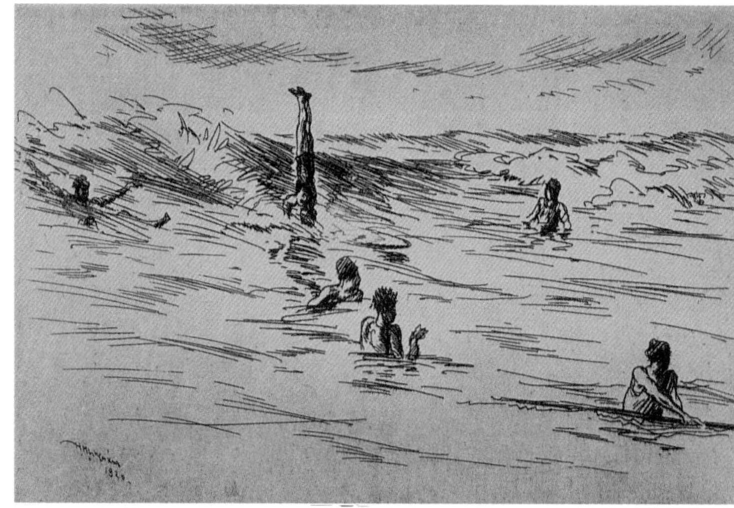

"Surfers," c. 1920, drypoint. *Courtesy: Randy Hild.*

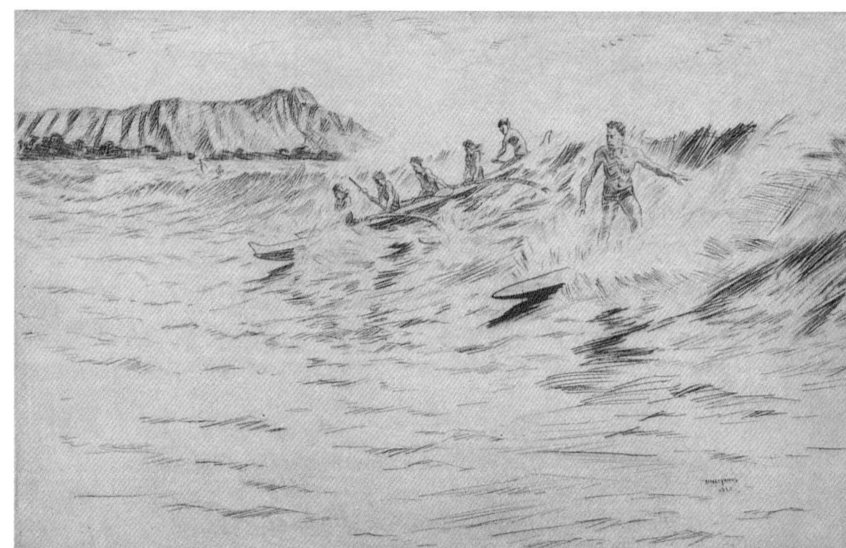

"Surf Riders," c. 1920, drypoint. *Courtesy: Dan Pincetich.*

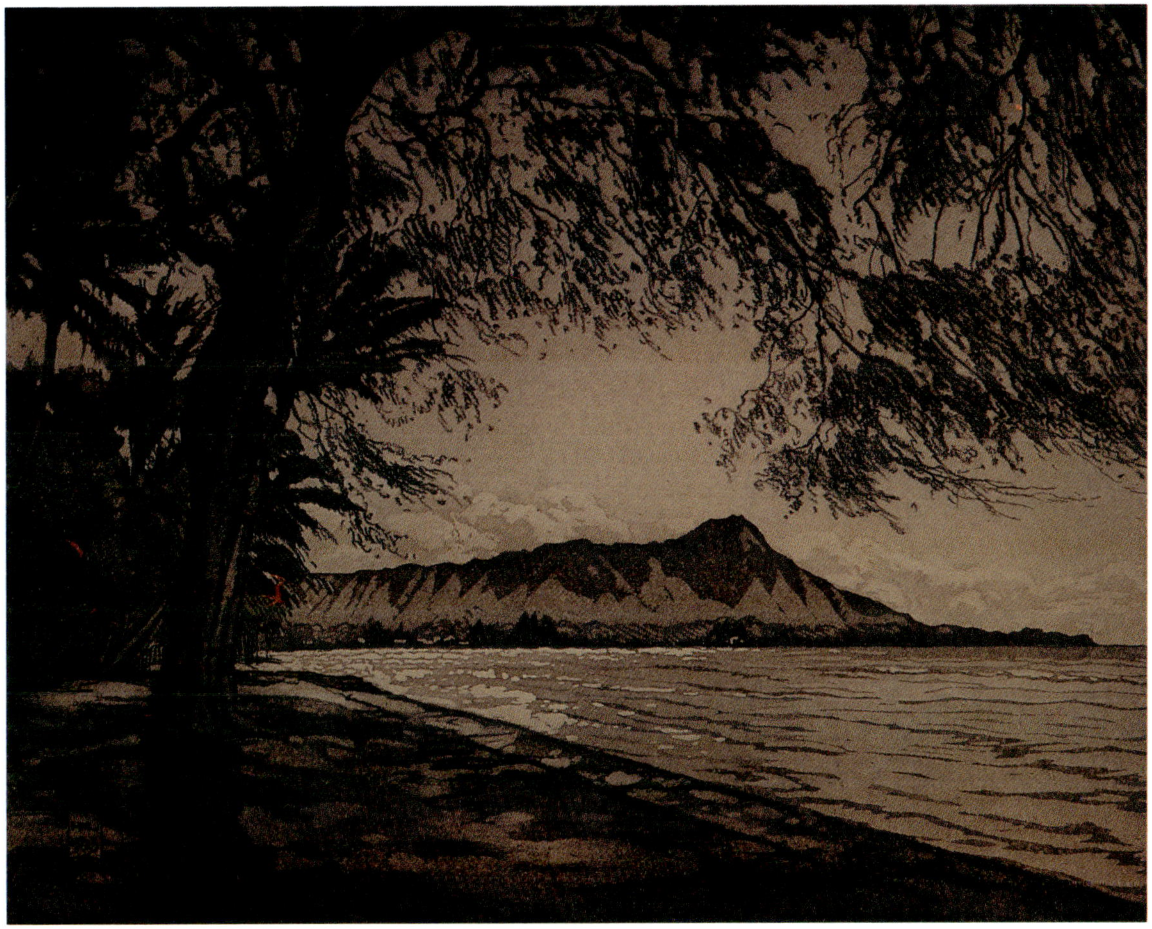

"Diamond Head," c. 1923, drypoint, marked with artist's monogram in lower left. *Courtesy: Randy Hild*.

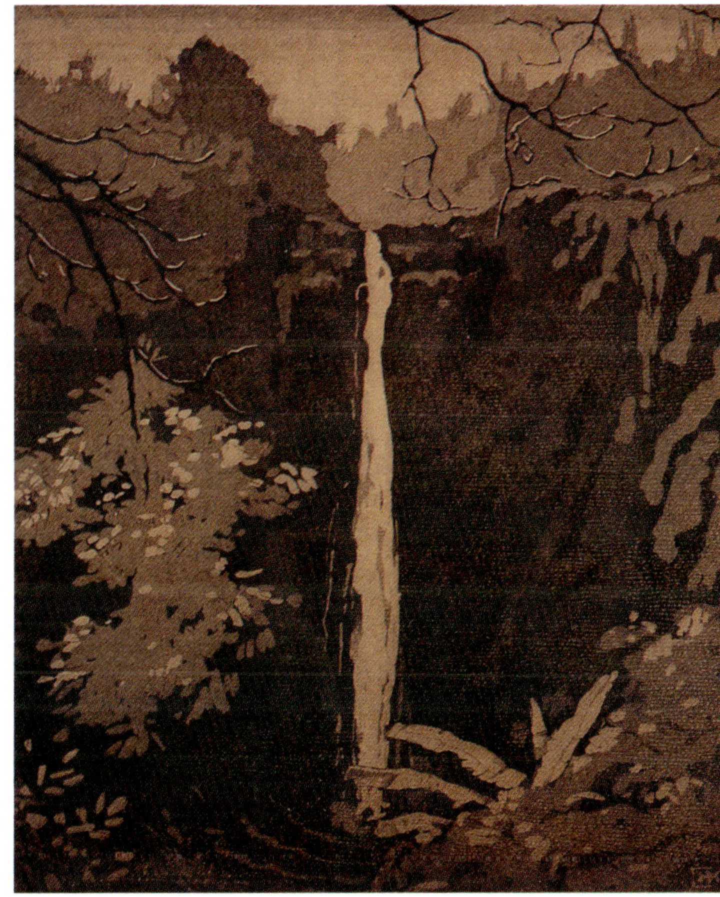

"Akaka Falls," drypoint, marked with artist's monogram in image at lower right. *Courtesy: Douglas A. Frazer Fine Art*.

Foley

Cornelia Macintyre Foley (b. 1909) was born in Honolulu to a well-established Kama'aina family with an unusual creative background. Foley's great grandfather, Edwin O. Hall, arrived on the Islands in 1837 with Amos Cooke, and served as a printer for the early missionaries. Her grandmother, Elizabeth Van Cleeve Hall, was one of Hawaii's pioneer photographers and Foley's mother, Florence Hall Macintyre, was an amateur woodcarver.

Foley studied at the University of Hawaii with Huc Luquiens, who had a strong influence on her, then attended the University of Washington. After two more years of classes at the Slade School in London (1928-29) she returned to Honolulu. There she studied with Madge Tennent and became a successful artist and printmaker.

1934-37 were the most productive printmaking years for Foley. She produced a variety of wood engravings, wood block prints, linocuts, and an unusual series of color wood block monotypes embellished with watercolor applied to the surface of the blocks.

In 1936 her painting "The Blue Sweater" won the grand prize at the exhibit of the Association of Honolulu Artists. Solo shows of her works were held at the Honolulu Academy of Arts in 1934 and 1937. Also in 1937 she married Lieutenant Paul Foley, Jr. and moved to the mainland, where she continued to paint and make prints. She became intrigued with acrylic painting, using hard edge approaches, and turned her attention more fully to this medium. In recent years she has lived on Long Island, New York.

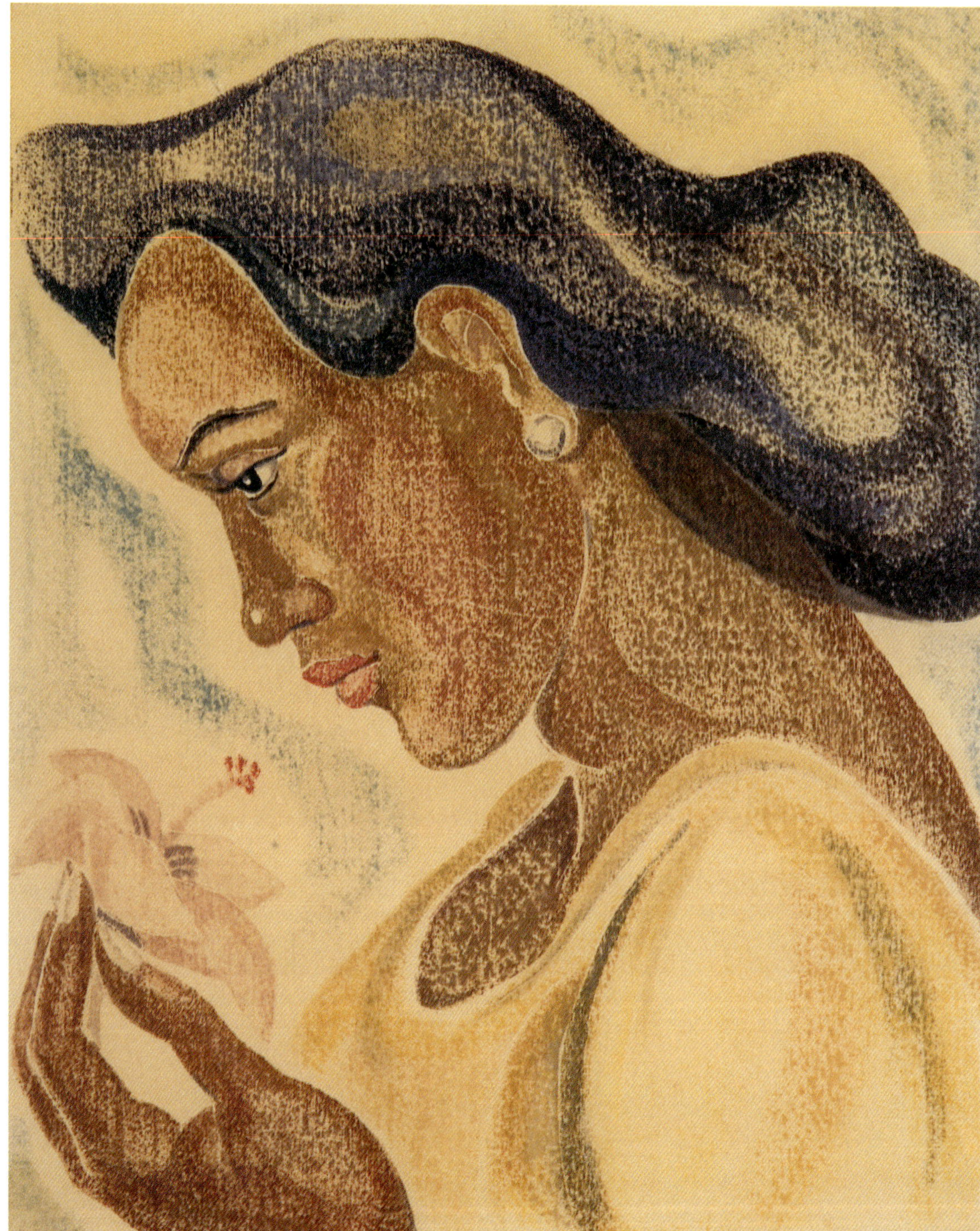

"The Pink Hibiscus," c. 1938, color wood block print, reduction process, 6.5" x 8". Each application of color required a separate hand application of color to the block. *Courtesy: Douglas A. Frazer Fine Art.*

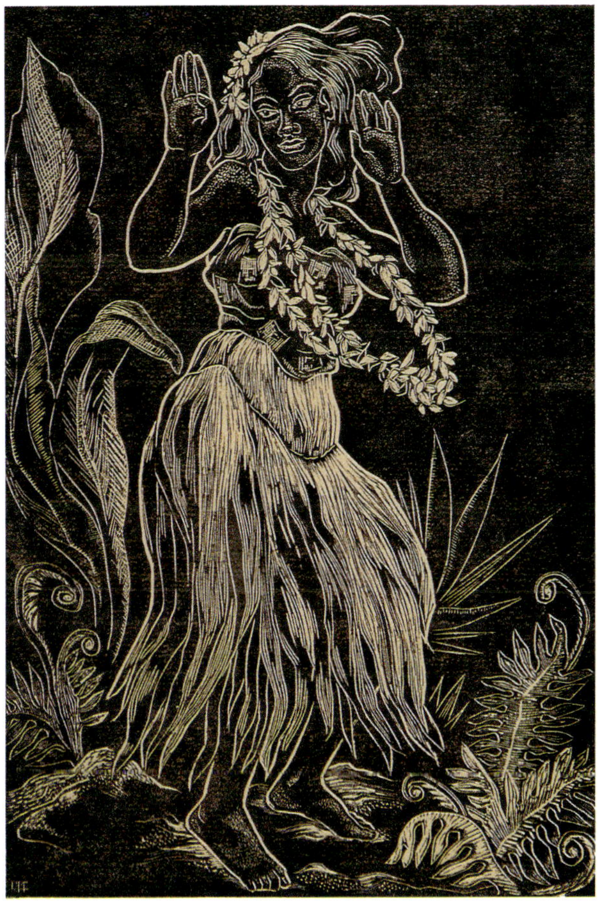

"Hawaiian Dancer," c. 1940, wood engraving, 5.5" x 8". Collection of the Honolulu Academy of the Arts, Library of Congress. *Courtesy: Douglas A. Frazer Fine Art.*

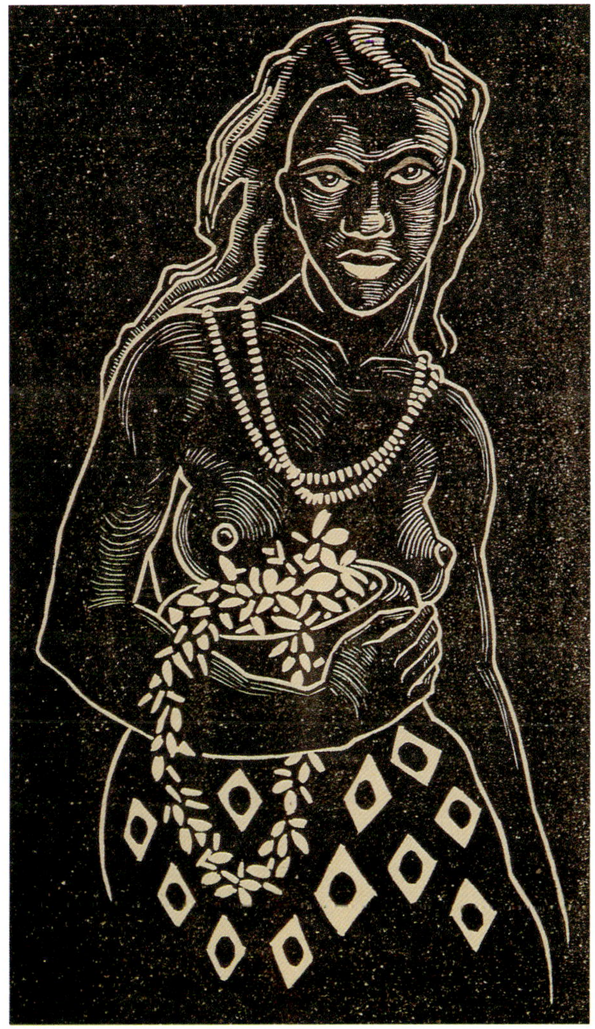

"Maile," c. 1939, linocut, 5.25" x 9". *Courtesy: Douglas A. Frazer Fine Art.*

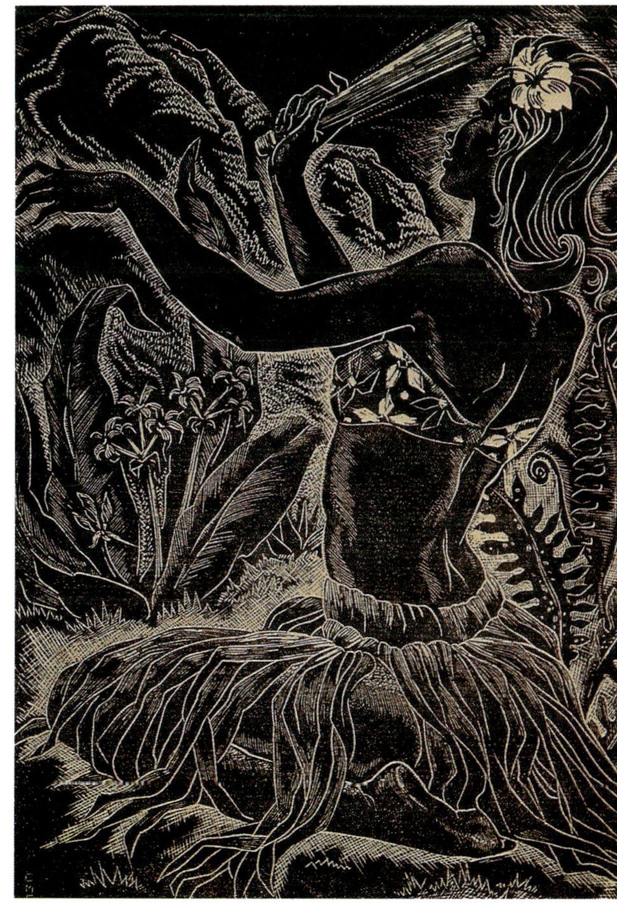

"Bamboo Hula," c. 1940, wood engraving, 5.5" x 8". *Courtesy: Douglas A. Frazer Fine Art.*

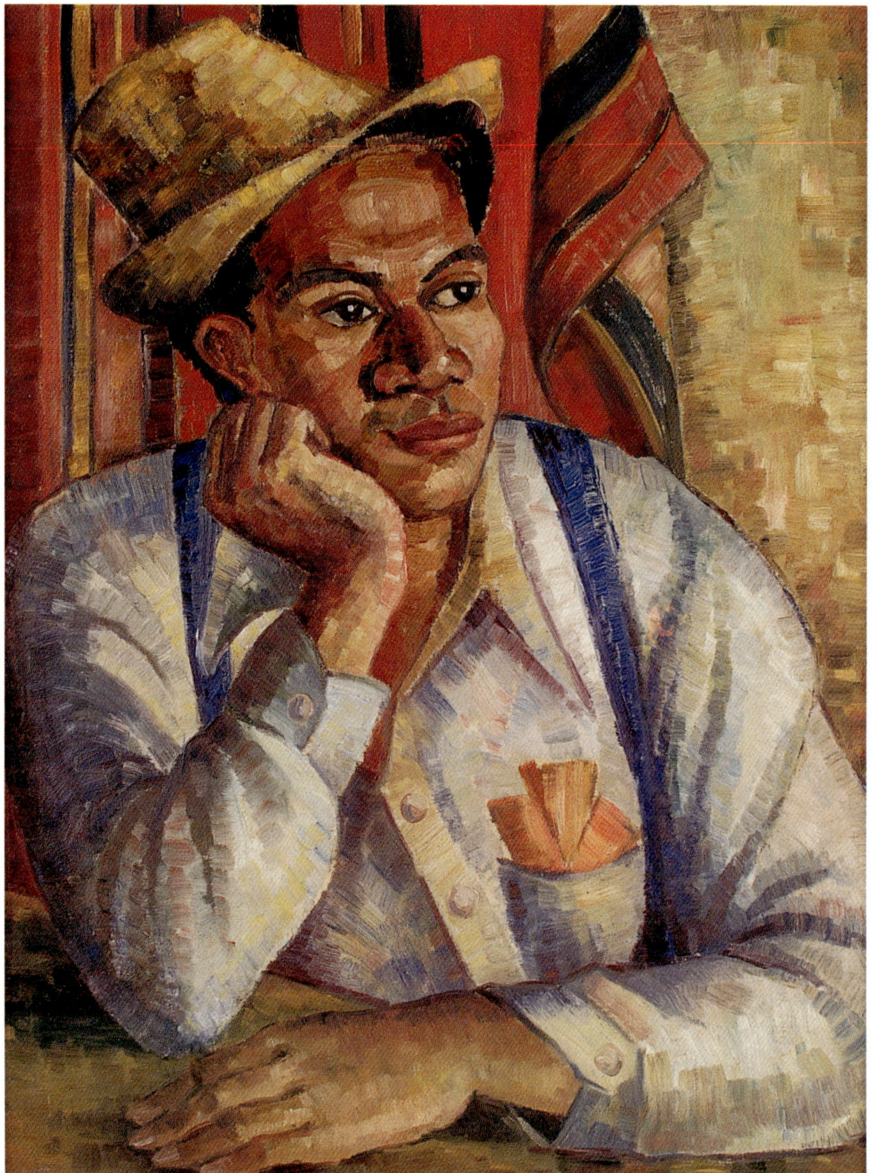

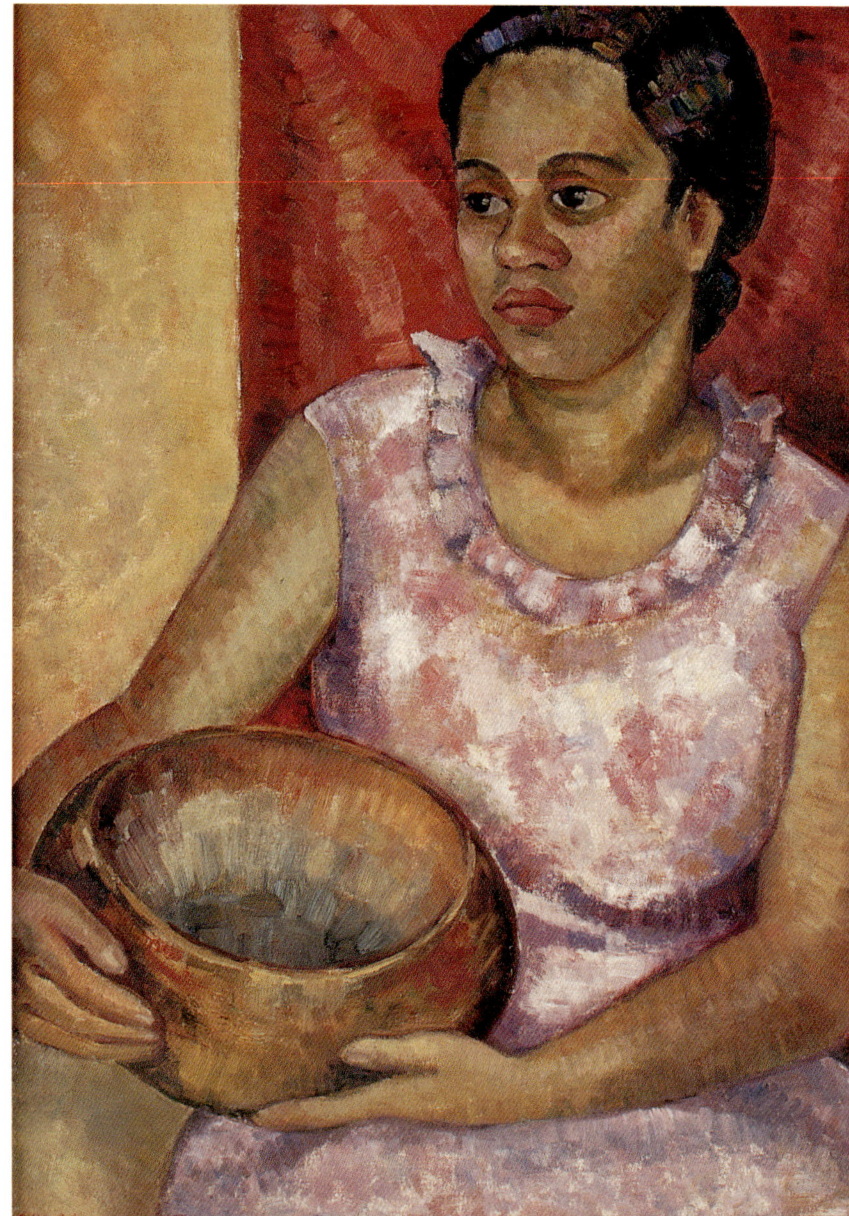

Titles unknown, c. 1937, oil on canvas, 19" x 26".
Courtesy: Douglas A. Frazer Fine Art.

Hitchcock

David Howard Hitchcock (1861-1943) was born in Hilo, Hawaii on May 15, 1861. Trained in Paris, he returned to the Islands in 1893 and devoted himself to capturing their exotic landscapes. Traveling extensively Hitchcock explored the volcanic regions of Hawaii and became one of the earliest artists to paint the Waimea Canyon on Kauai on his first visit there in 1907. In 1915 and 1916 he toured Maui, producing a series of views of the island.

Hitchcock was recognized for his large dioramas and mural-size paintings of the Islands. He also created representations of Hawaiis' dramatic scenery to be displayed on the vessels of the Inter-Island Steam Navigation Company.

After being exposed to other artists' contemporary work in New York and Hawaii, Hitchcock tried introducing some new ideas into his work in the late 1920s. The public's reaction was less than favorable, causing him to revert to his old style, one he once called "conservative-impressionistic."

Hitchcock exhibited widely, particularly at the Honolulu Academy of Arts, where a 1936 retrospective of his work was held in honor of his 75th birthday. In 1939 his works were exhibited at both the Golden Gate International Exhibition in San Francisco and at the World's Fair in New York. He was on of the forces behind the founding of the Kilohana Art League in 1894. Hitchcock died in Honolulu on January 1, 1943.

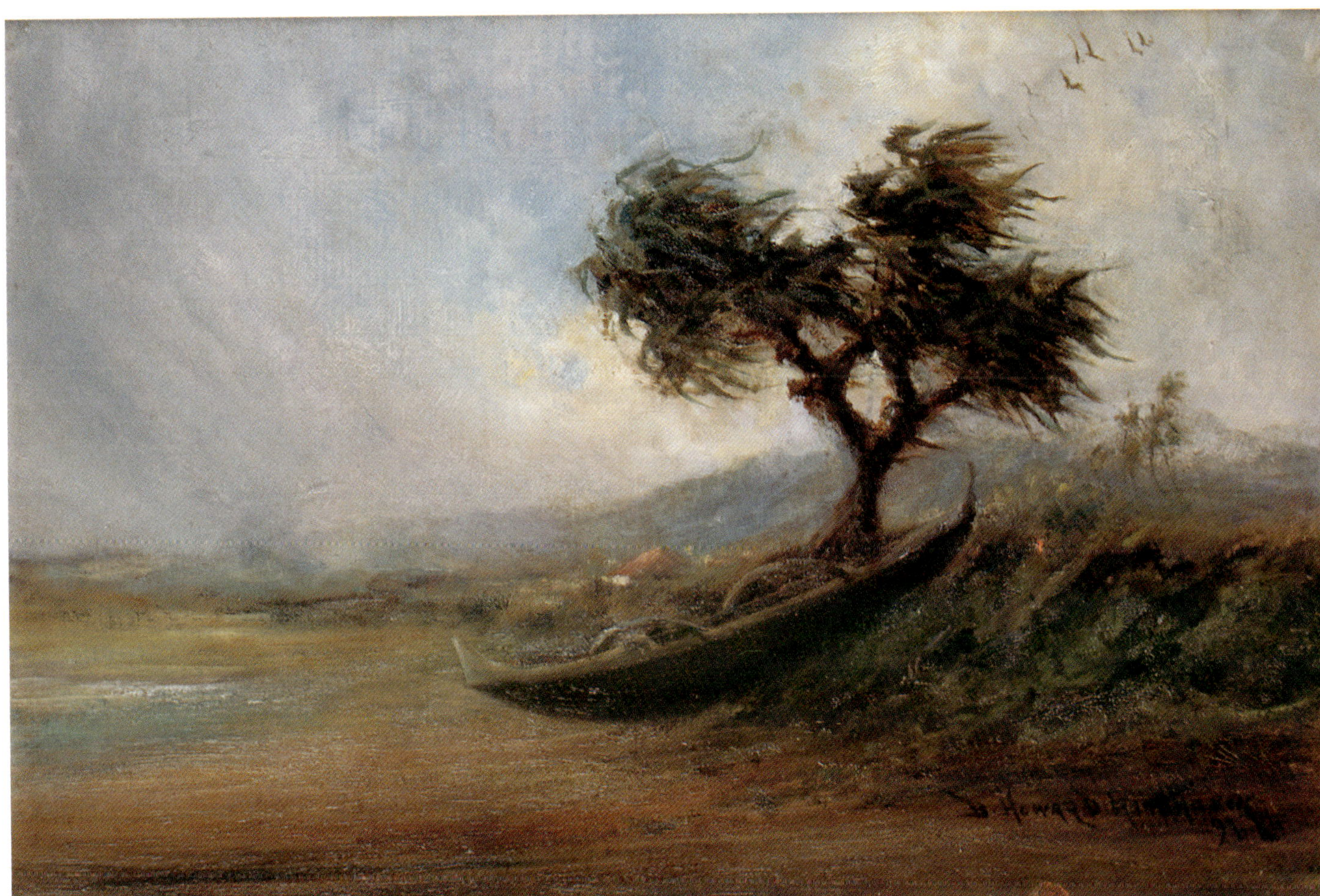

"Beached Canoe with Lauhala," 1896, oil on canvas, 12" x 18". Hitchcock resided on the Big Island at this time, making occasional trips to Oahu to visit family and do business. At this point in his career Hitchcock was only a few years removed from his academic training in France. An incoming squall has made the weather unfavorable for fishing, thus the beached canoe and the blowing Lauhala tree. *Courtesy: Douglas A. Frazer Fine Art.*

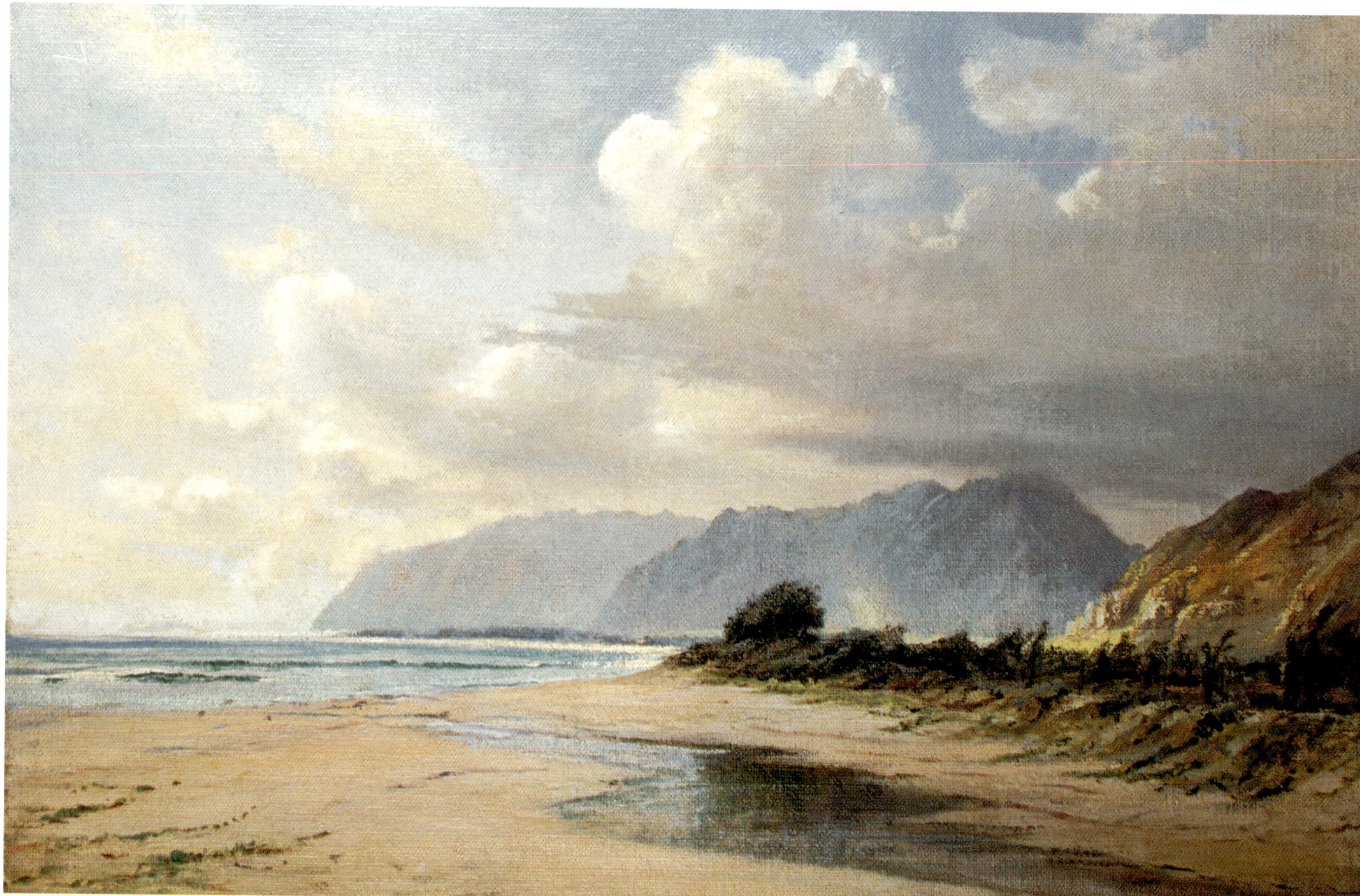

"Punaluu," c. 1915, oil on Masonite, 20" x 30". A painting of this same view graces the cover of Helen Maxon's book, *Islander*. This painting was formerly in the collection of the Hawaii Visitor's Bureau. *Courtesy: Douglas A. Frazer Fine Art*.

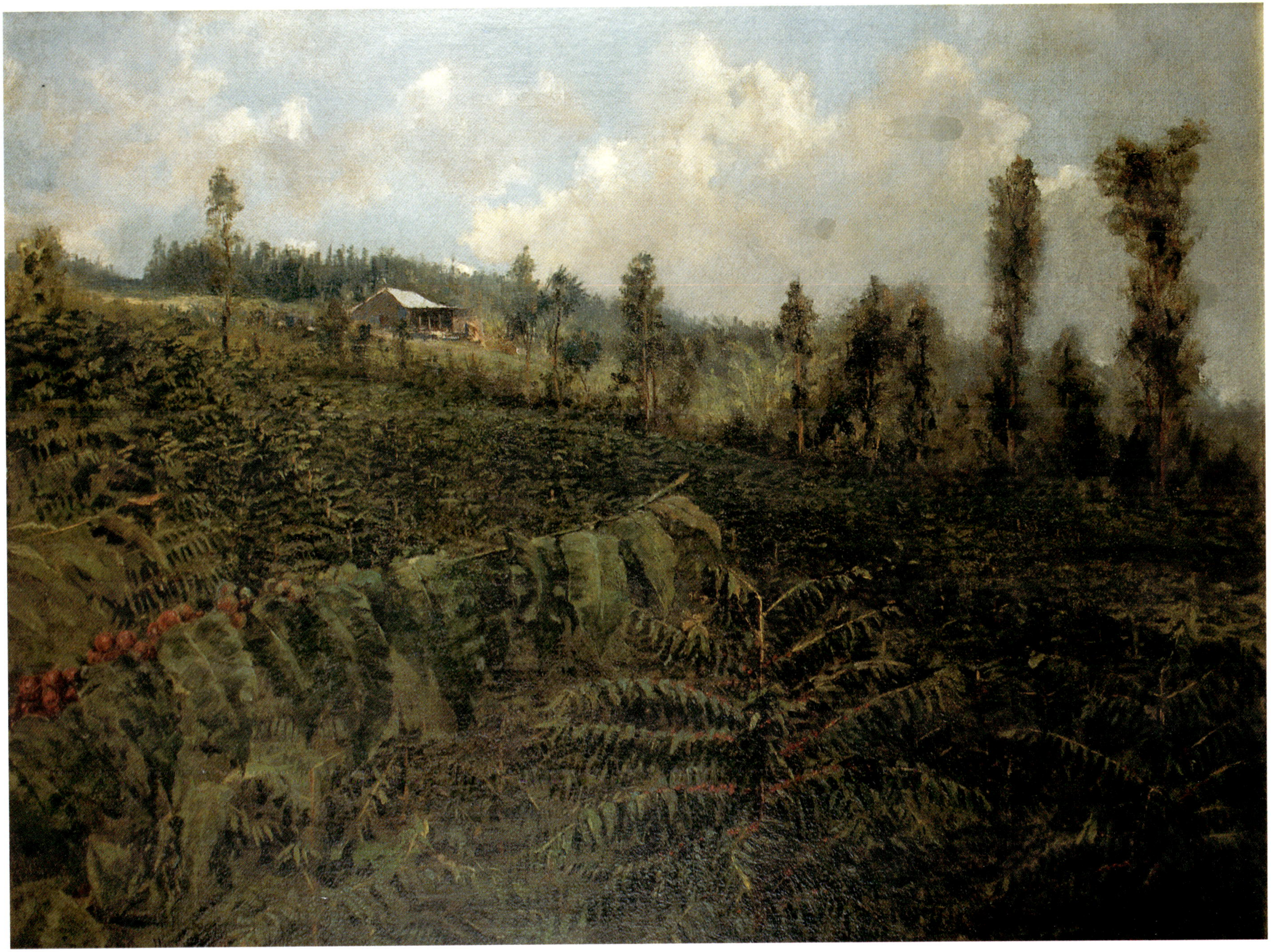

"Puna 1897," 1897, oil on canvas, 25" x 27". This painting is unusually large for a work this early. Puna, which lies east of Hilo on a porous volcanic slope, was the original seat of the coffee industry on the Big Island. A blight wiped out the crops after this was painted, and coffee farming moved to Kona, where it thrives today. The Puna area is now devoted to raising Anthuria, orchids, macadamia nuts, and papaya. *Courtesy: Douglas A. Frazer Fine Art.*

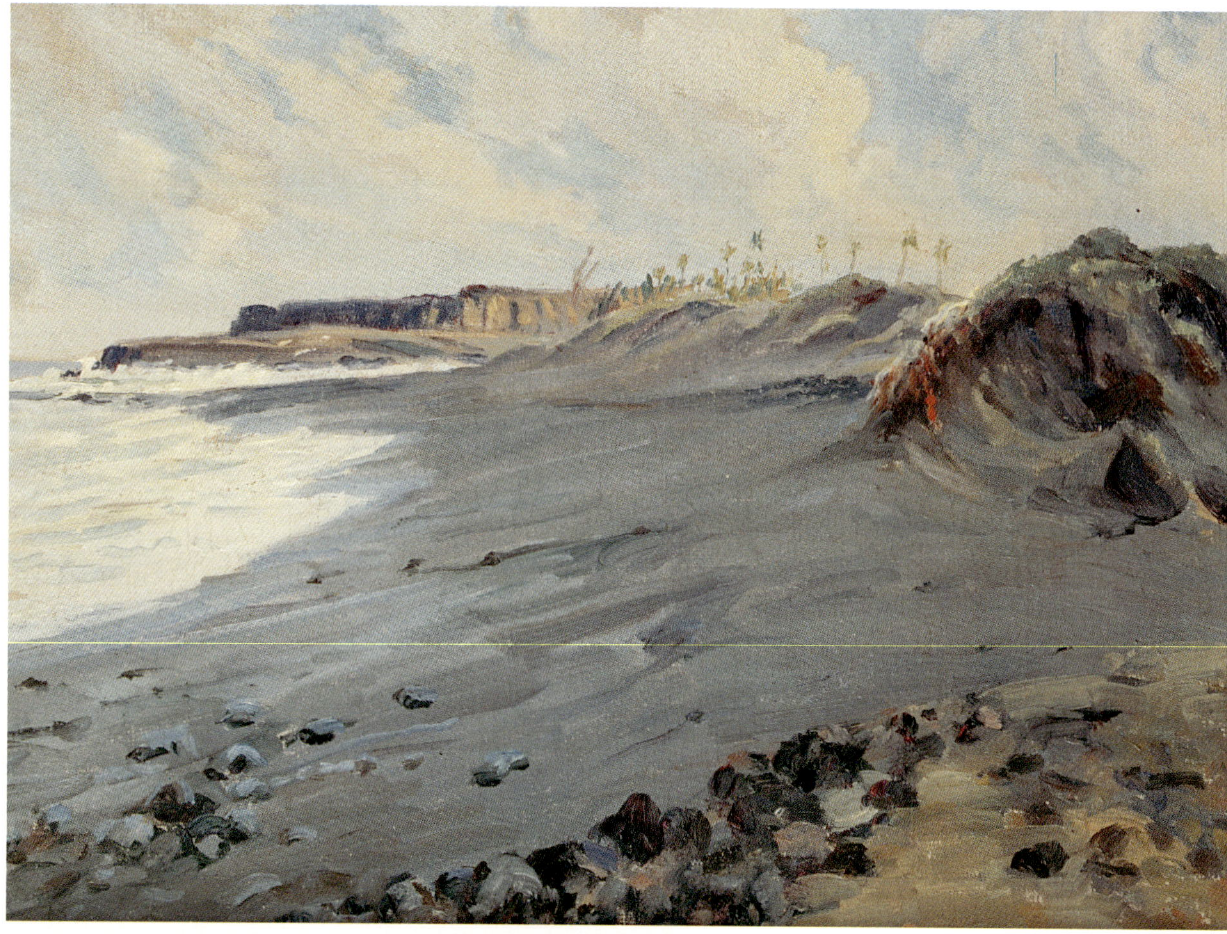

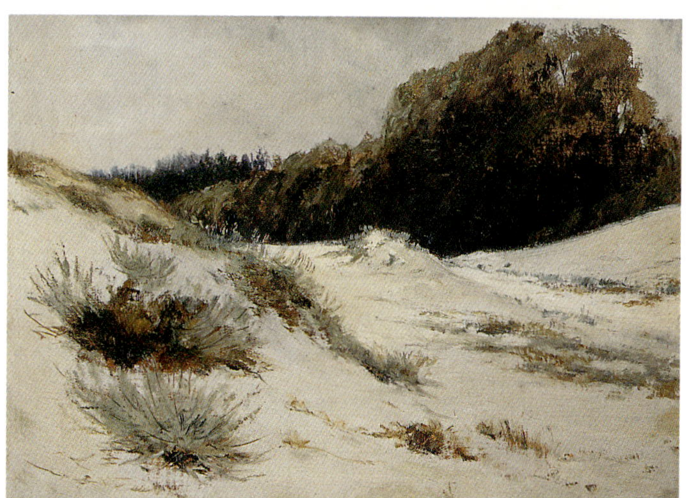

Above:
"Grey Sands, Monterey," c. 1910, oil on canvas, 12" x 16". *Courtesy: Douglas A. Frazer Fine Art.*

Left:
"Big Island Beaches and Escarpments," c. 1910, oil on canvas board, 12" x 16". *Courtesy: Douglas A. Frazer Fine Art.*

Sheets

Born in Pomona, California, in 1907, Millard Sheets was a designer, painter, and graphic artist. He enrolled at the Chouinard Art Institute in Los Angeles in 1925. His affinity for the medium of watercolor led the school to hire him as an instructor while still a student. His early works were rooted in impressionism and the styles of his Chouinard instructors, Clarence Hinkle and F. Tooles Chamberlin.

His working for *Life* magazine in India and Burma, during World War II, helped his work mature, taking on a more somber nature. Following the war he organized an architectural firm designing commercial and residential buildings in California and Texas.

Throughout his career Sheets was involved in art education, directing the Fine Arts Exhibition at the Los Angeles County Fair, teaching or directing at Scripps College, Claremont Graduate School, and Otis Art Institute in Los Angeles.

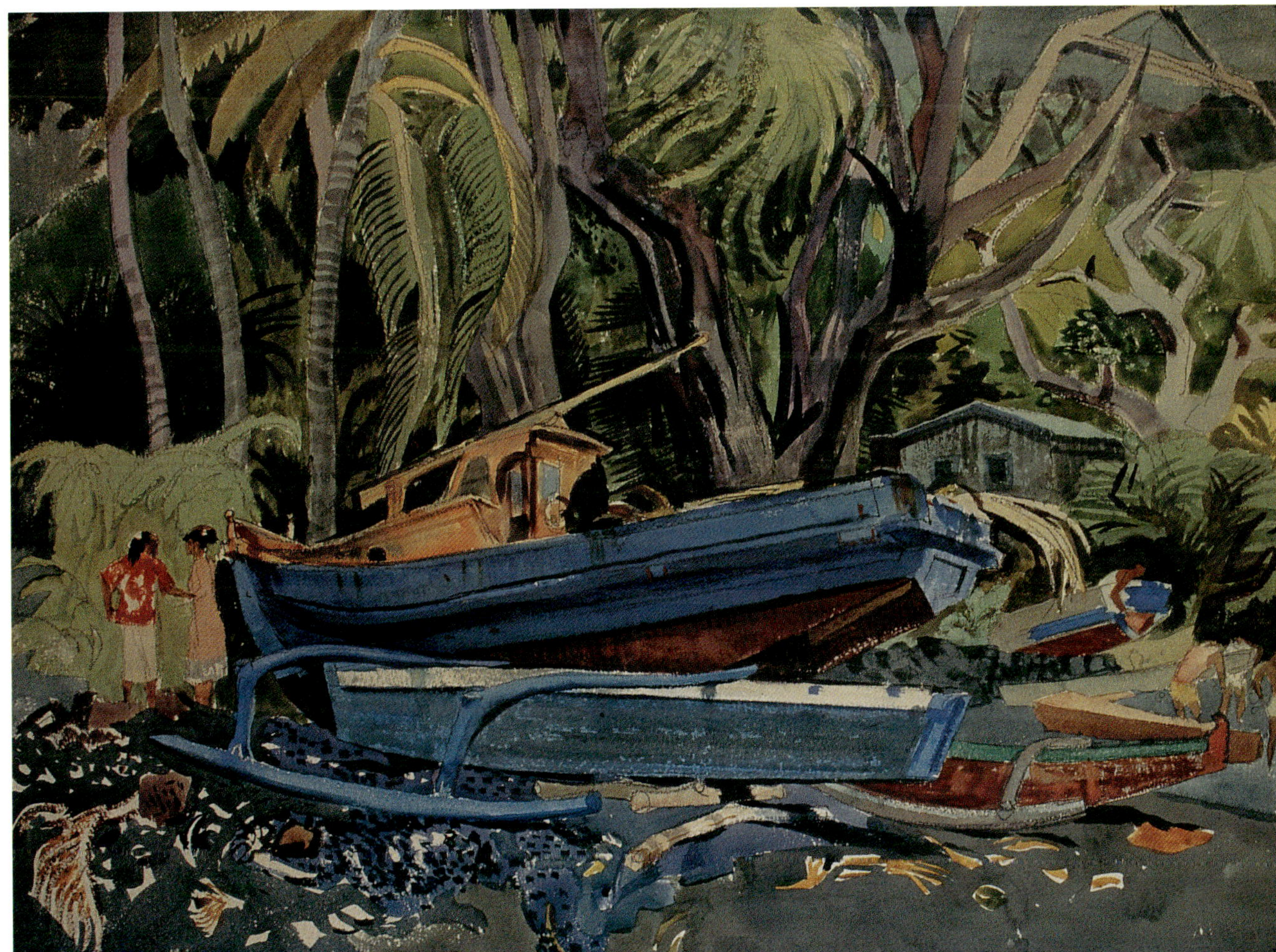

"Sampan Keahau," after Millard Sheets *Courtesy: Douglas A. Frazer Fine Art.*

Robert Lee Eskridge moved to Honolulu late in 1932, having lived for four years in the South Pacific, including Tahiti and Mangareva. He wrote a popular account of Mangareva entitled *Mangareva: The Forgotten Islands* while there. After arriving in Hawaii he wrote and illustrated a children's book, *Umi, The Hawaiian Boy Who Became King*, which also won widespread acclaim.

Eskridge was born in Philipsburg, Pennsylvania, in 1891. He studied at the University of Southern California, the Chicago Institute of Art, and in Paris, where he came under the influence of Andre Lhote and Bernard Boutet de Monvel.

From 1932 on Eskridge lived on the Islands periodically for the rest of his life. He taught at the University of Hawaii from 1939 to 1941, and spent the war years teaching in Florida and Los Angeles. His work was exhibited in Chicago, New York, San Francisco, Paris, as well as in Hawaii. He died in Honolulu on April 14, 1975.

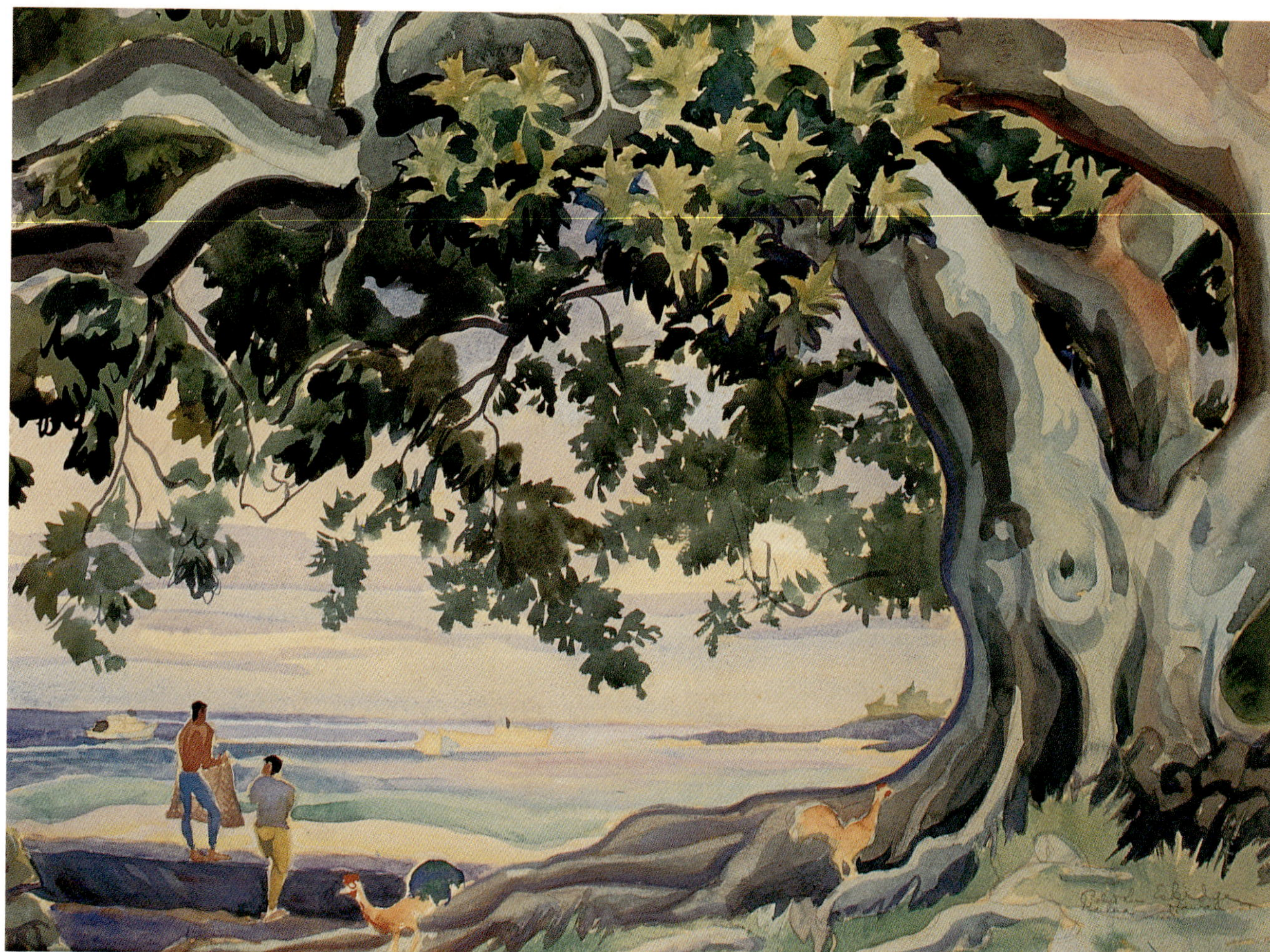

"Kailua," 1951, watercolor, 22" x 30". *Courtesy: Douglas A. Frazer Fine Art.*

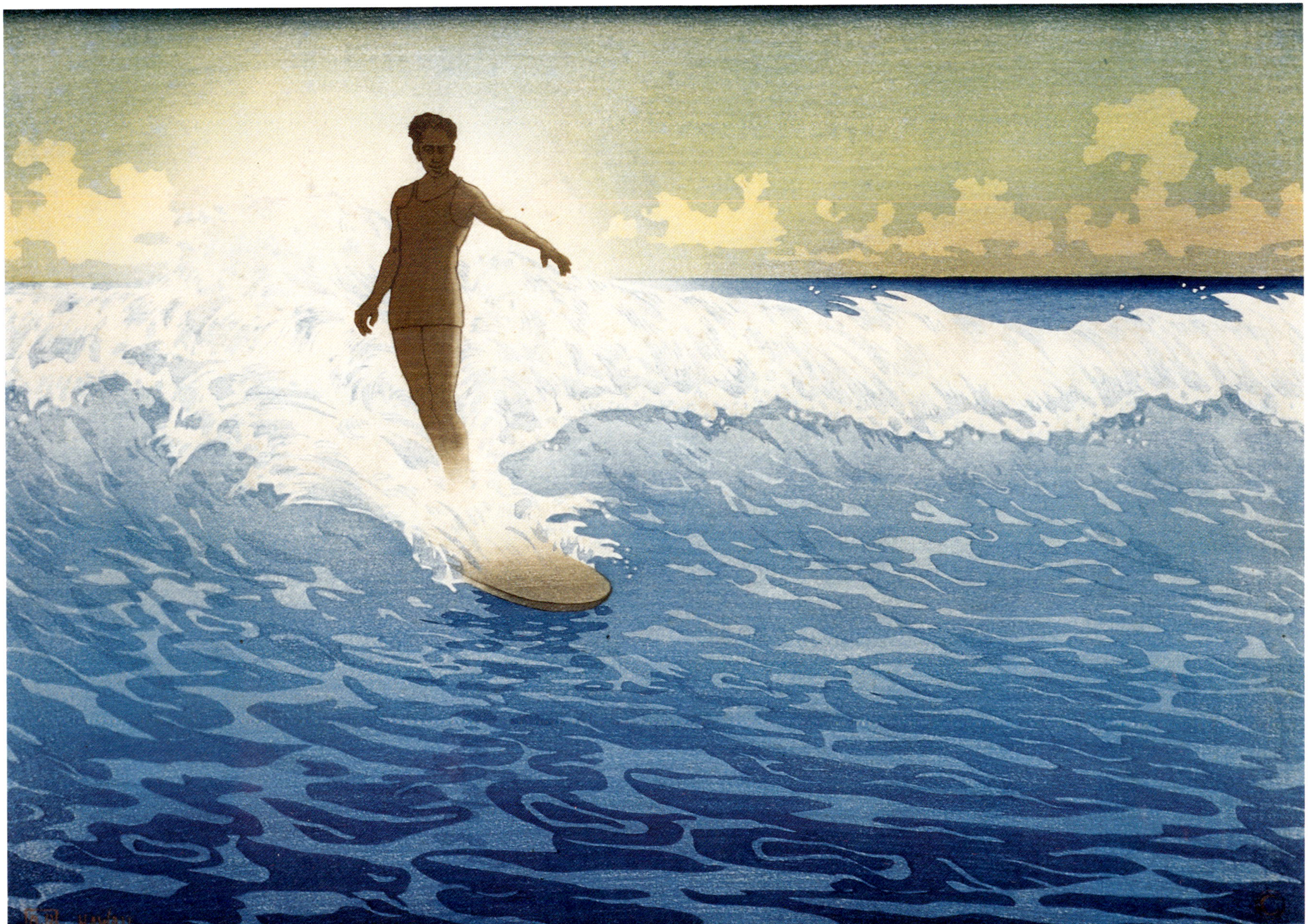

"Hawaii." Charles W. Bartlett. *Courtesy: Dan Pincetich*.

Riggs

Robert Riggs was born in Decatur, Illinois, and studied art there at the James Millikin University before transferring to the Art Students League in New York City. After two years in the military during World War I, he studied at the Academie Julien in Paris. His experience was broadened by travel in North Africa, China, Thailand, and the West Indies, during which he gathered artifacts and recorded his observations.

In the 1930s Riggs returned to the United States where he developed a reputation as a fine commercial artist, illustrator, and graphic artist. His lithographic work tends to focus around the circus, prize fighting, and street scenes. The three Hawaiian images exhibited here were commissioned by the Dole Pineapple Company. They show his dynamic use of contrasting darks and lights to create a sense of action.

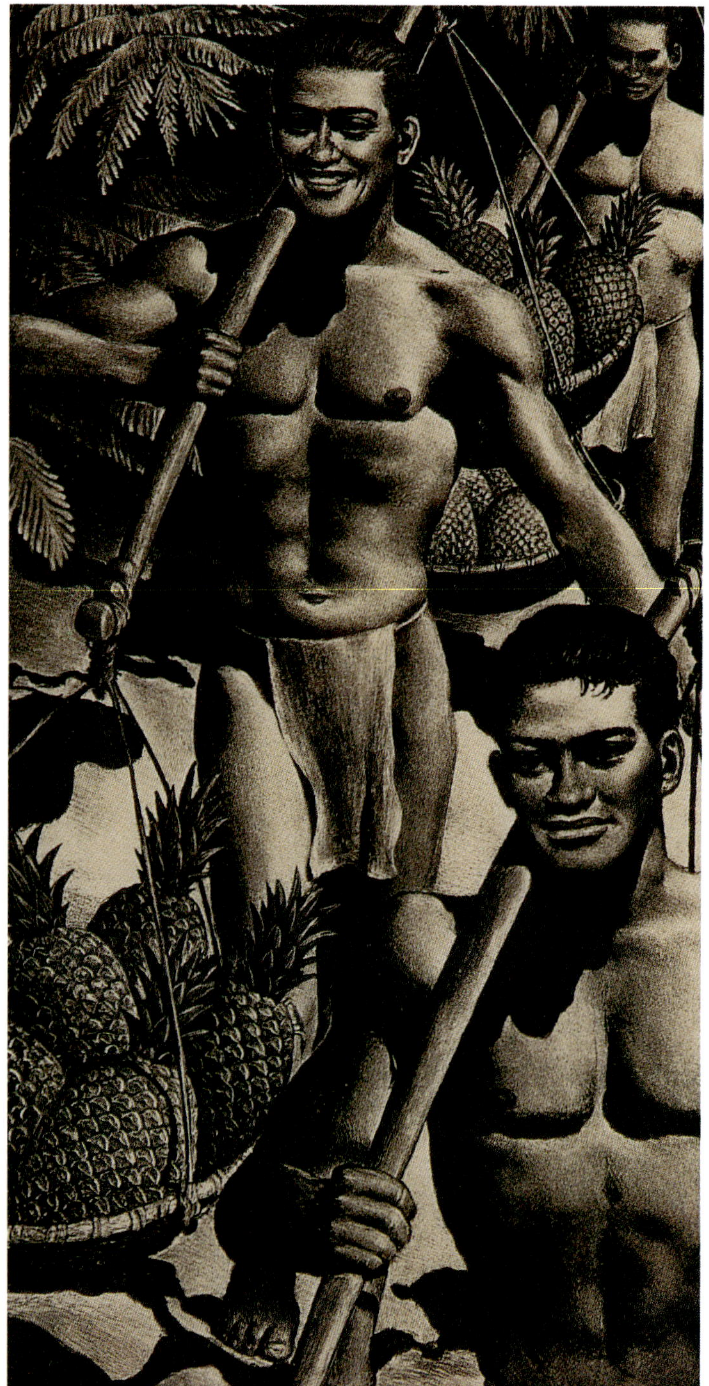

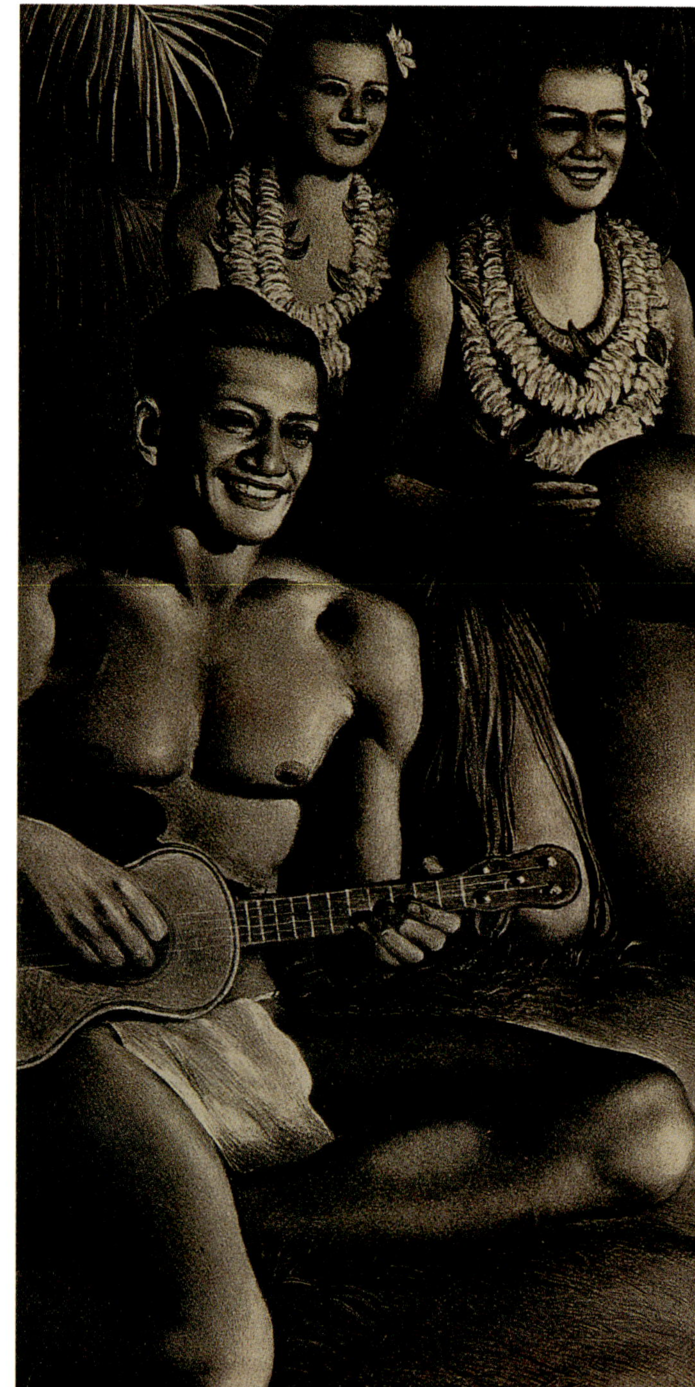

Three lithographs, c. 1930, 4.625" x 6.125". *Courtesy: Douglas A. Frazer Fine Art.*

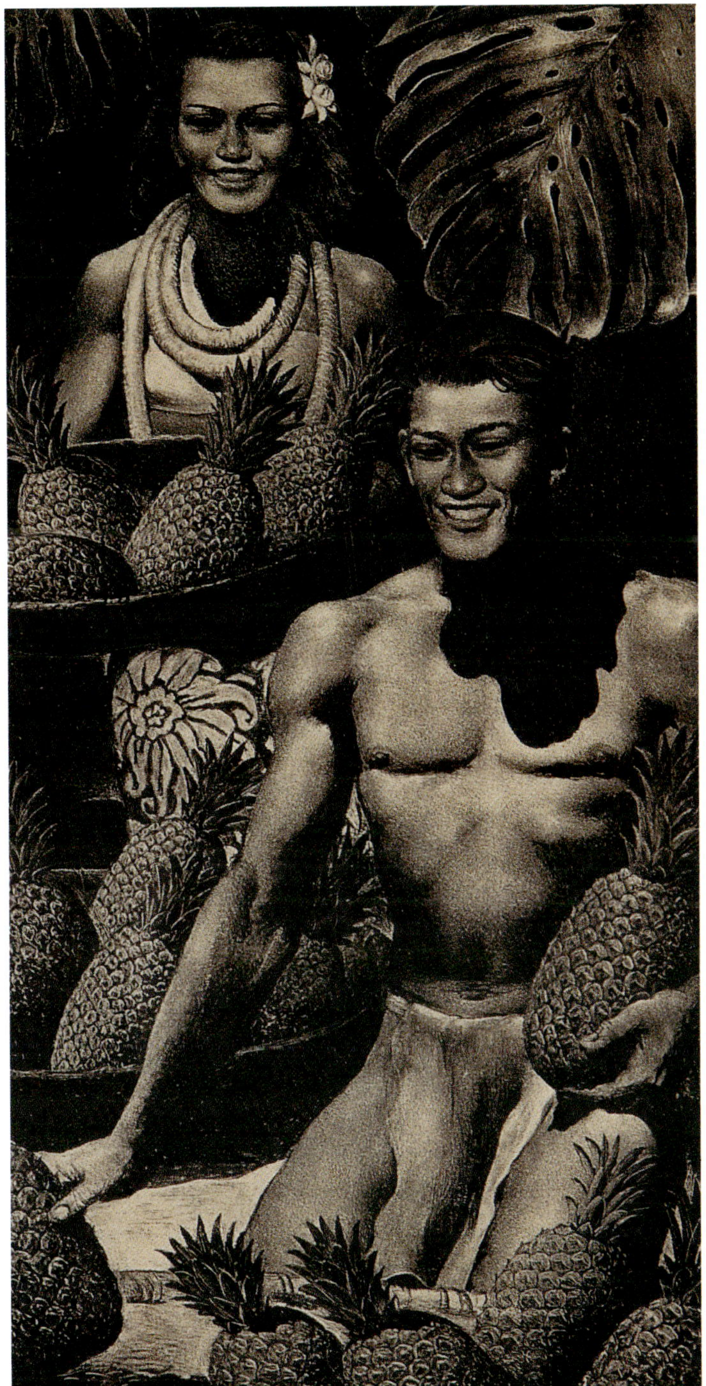

Patterson

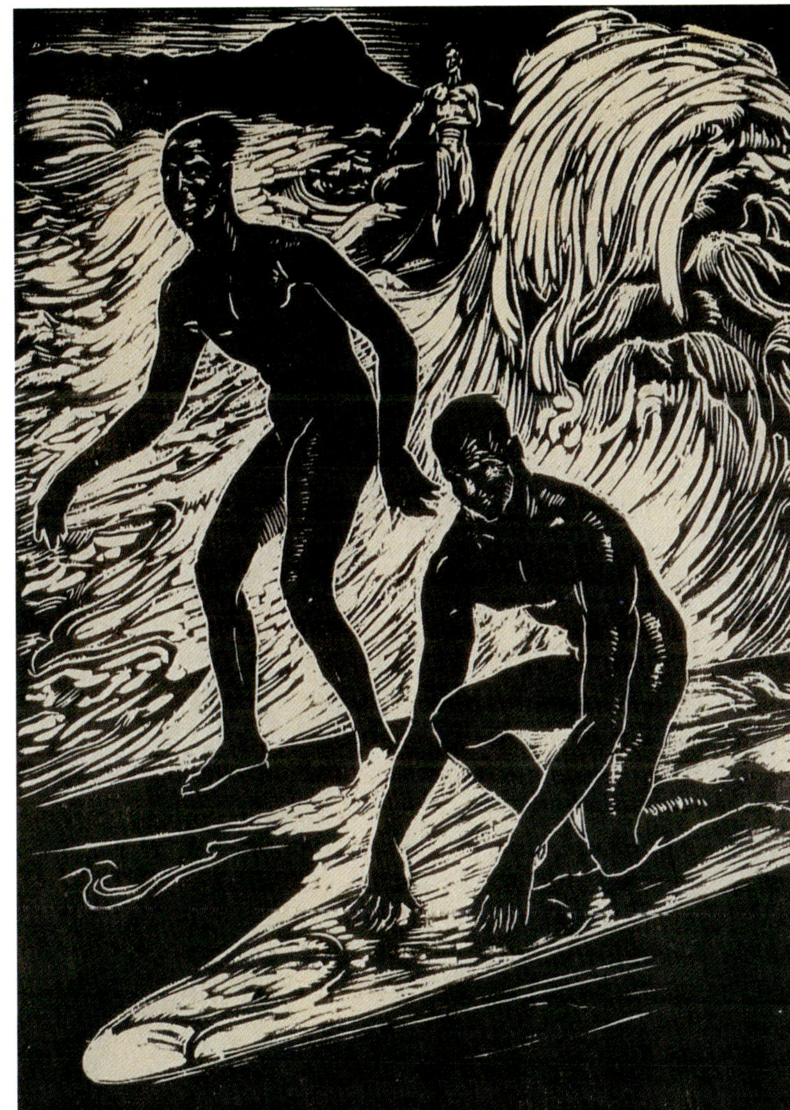

"Surf Riders Honolulu," woodcut, Ambrose Patterson.
Courtesy: Dan Pincetich.

Chapter 5

Music

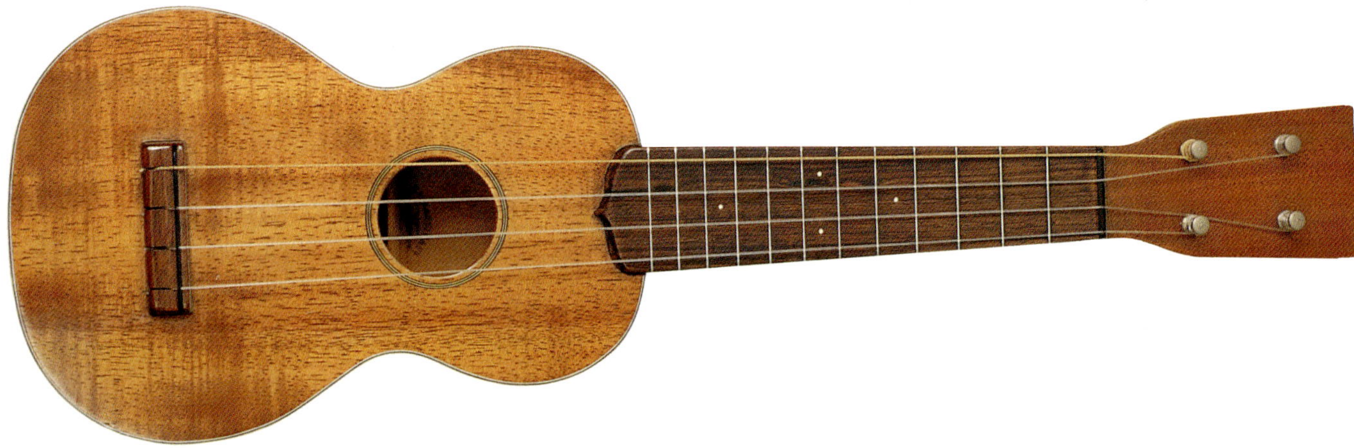

Martin Ukulele K-2, koa wood, c. 1940s. *Courtesy: Don Stewart.*

Ukuleles

The ukulele is another example of how a new arrival on the Islands found itself transformed by the Aloha Spirit. The story goes that Augusto Dias, with his wife and four children, came to Hawaii from Funchal in the Madeira Islands of Portugal in 1879 on the English ship *Ravenscrag*. Dias was a cabinet maker by trade and a musician by advocation. The contract that brought him to the Island required that he spend a certain period of time doing agricultural labor. When that was complete he resumed his trade.

Dias opened a shop on King Street where he made and improved a Portuguese instrument called the Braginha. He introduced it into the Hawaiian culture, where it found great acceptance. A visiting musician/entertainer admired the instrument and began to play it. As he did so, he leapt about from place to place, reminding people of a jumping flea, which is "ukulele" in the Hawaiian language.

Ukuleles soon became a symbol of the Islands, and closely identified both with Hawaiian music and dance. It is no surprise, then, that tourists brought them back from the Islands as mementos of their vacations. During the decade of the 1920s, the Martin Guitar Company produced nearly 30,000 of the instruments, according Mark Blackburn's *Hawaiiana*. In the 1940s and 1950s Arthur Godfrey, a Hawaii-phile and entertainer, brought renewed publicity and interest in the ukulele. Its reputation may have suffered, however, when another entertainer, Tiny Tim, used it to accompany his singing of "Tip Toe through the Tulips."

The unique and beautiful quality of the instrument's sound when masterfully played, often accompanies a traditional hula or an accomplished group of Hawaiian singers.

Early ukuleles were made in the Islands using the Spanish style of construction. Most were made of koa wood. According to Blackburn, after the Pan Pacific International Exposition of 1915, mainland companies began to produce ukuleles. They usually used mahogany or birch and a different construction method than the Hawaiian makers. Nevertheless, to distinguish their work from the imitators, Hawaiian ukulele makers devised a brand which would tell the would-be buyer that this was the genuine article. It consisted of a crown, an inverted crescent, the word "tabu," two crossed tabu or kapu sticks, and the words "Made in Hawaii." According to Blackburn this brand was used from the late teens through the mid-1920s.

Right:
Hawaiian Guitar Radio Tone, student model, square neck, c. 1940s.
Courtesy: Don Stewart.

Center:
Hawaiian Resonator, student model, probably licensed by Dobro, c. late-1940s-early 1950s.
Courtesy: Don Stewart.

Far right:
Oahu Hawaiian, student model, square neck, 1940s.
Courtesy: Don Stewart.

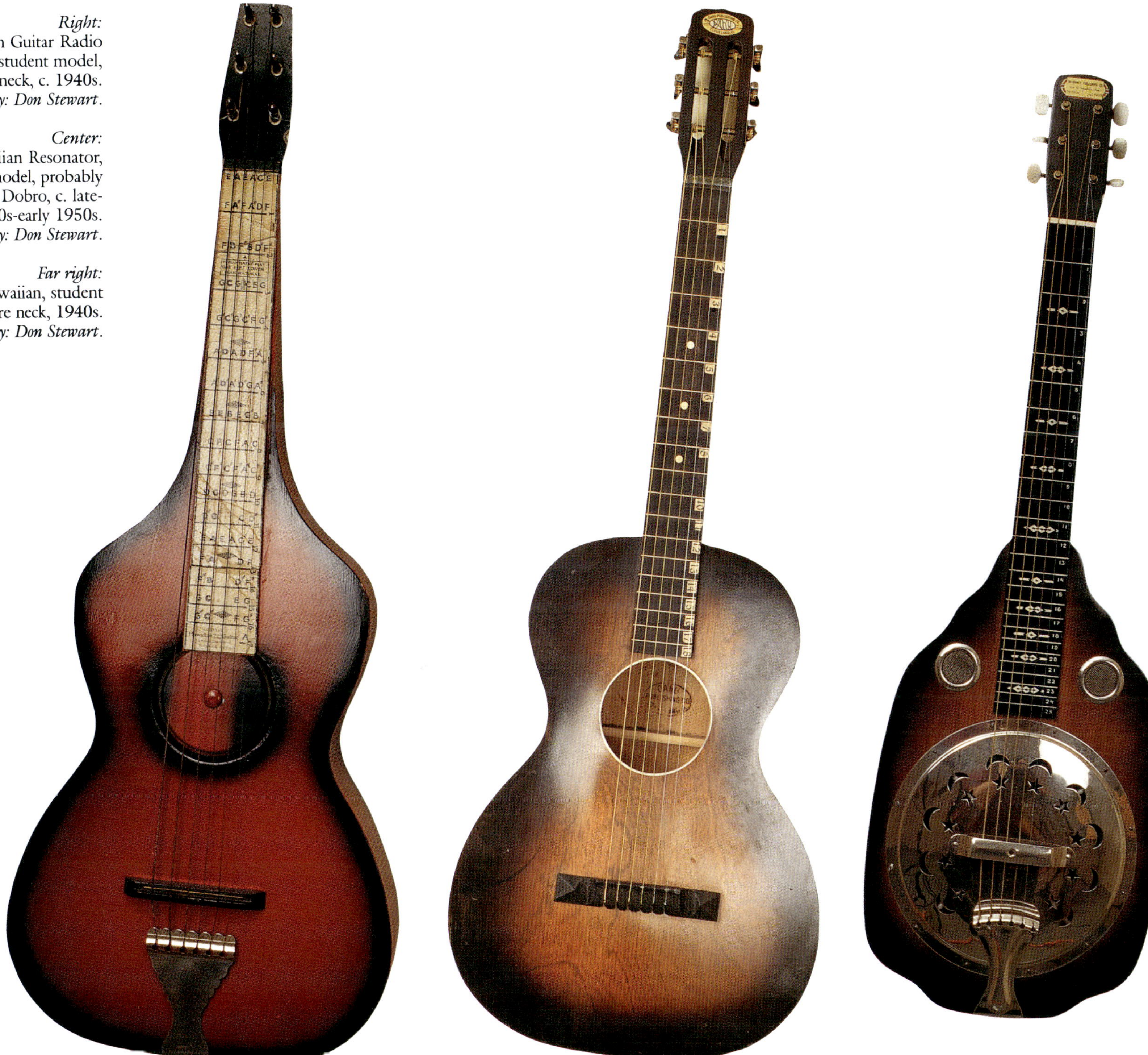

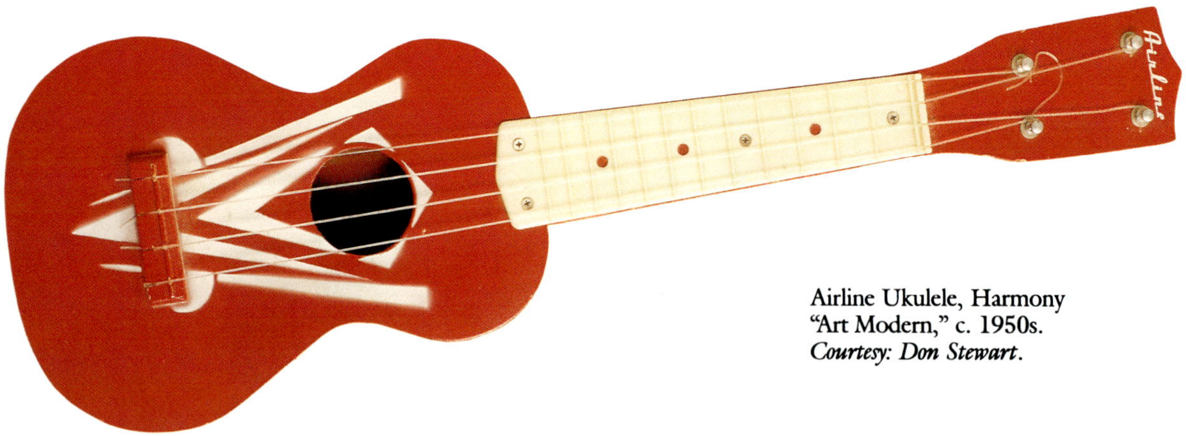

Airline Ukulele, Harmony "Art Modern," c. 1950s. *Courtesy: Don Stewart.*

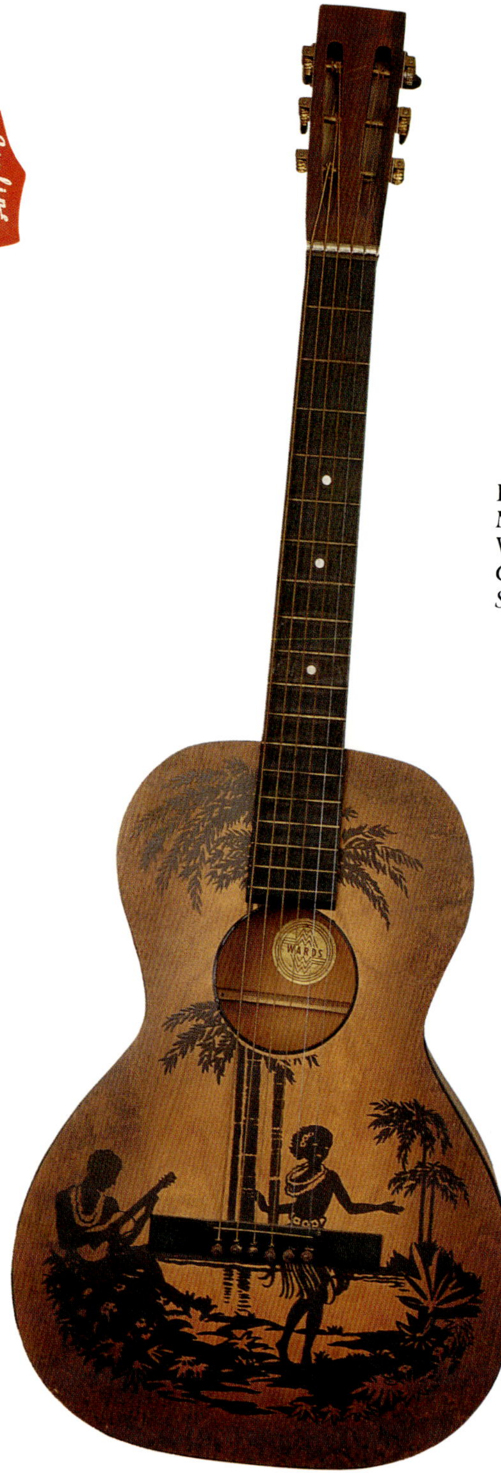

Hawaiian guitar, Montgomery Ward, c. 1940s. *Courtesy: Don Stewart.*

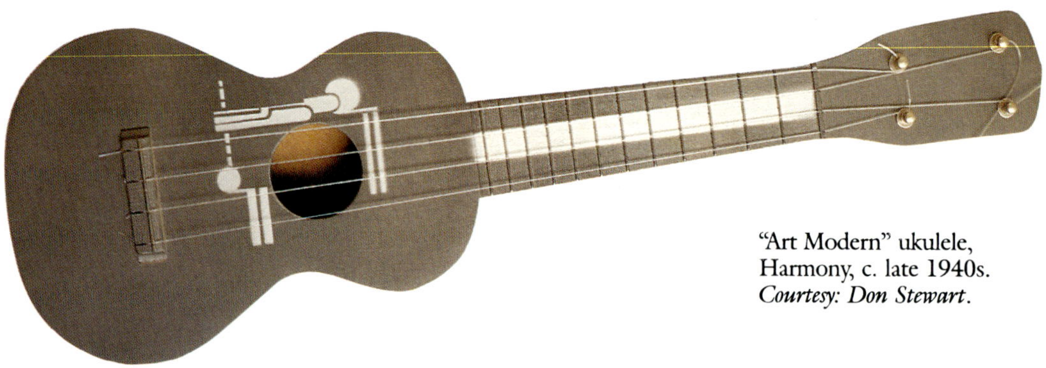

"Art Modern" ukulele, Harmony, c. late 1940s. *Courtesy: Don Stewart.*

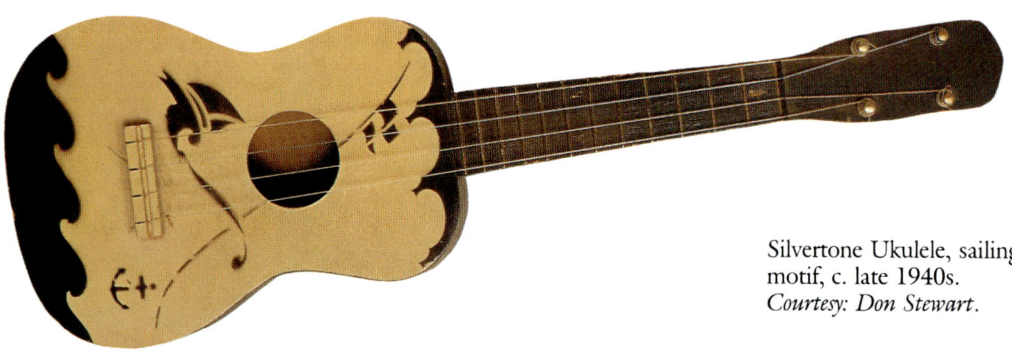

Silvertone Ukulele, sailing motif, c. late 1940s. *Courtesy: Don Stewart.*

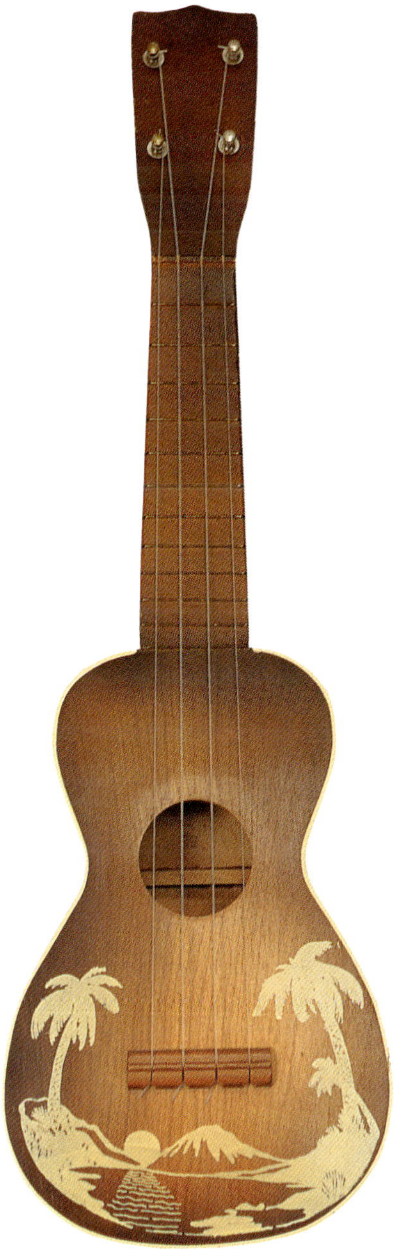

Harmony ukulele, palm tree motif, c. 1950s.
Courtesy: Don Stewart.

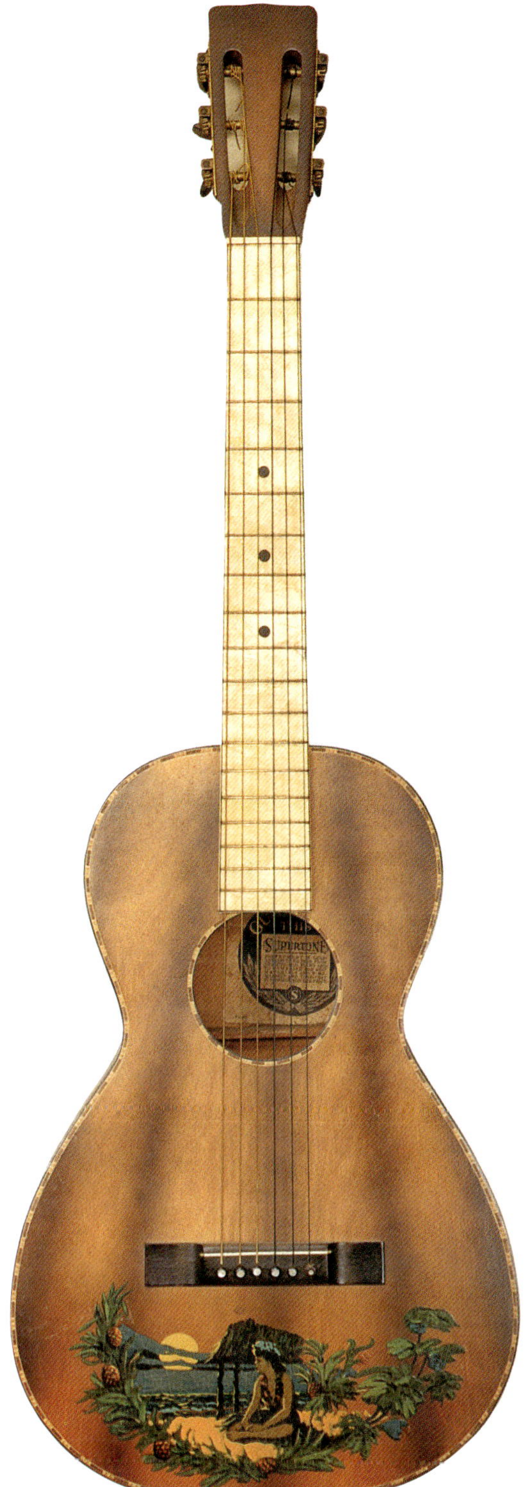

Silvertone Hawaiian Guitar, with plastic finger board, c. 1940s.
Courtesy: Don Stewart.

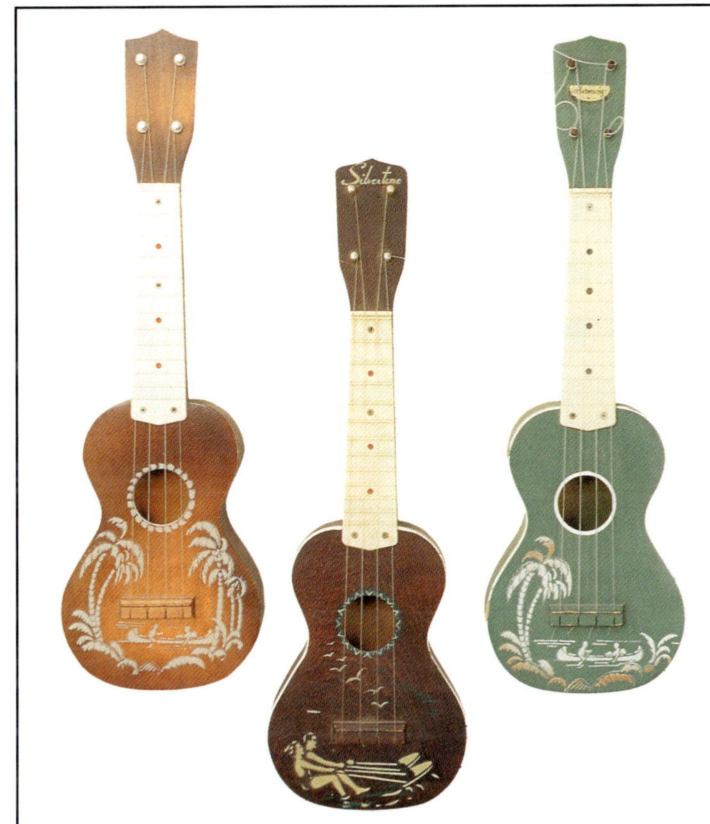

Three ukuleles, c. 1950s. Left to right: Harmony with palm tree motif; Silvertone with aquaplane motif; Harmony with canoe motif.
Courtesy: Don Stewart.

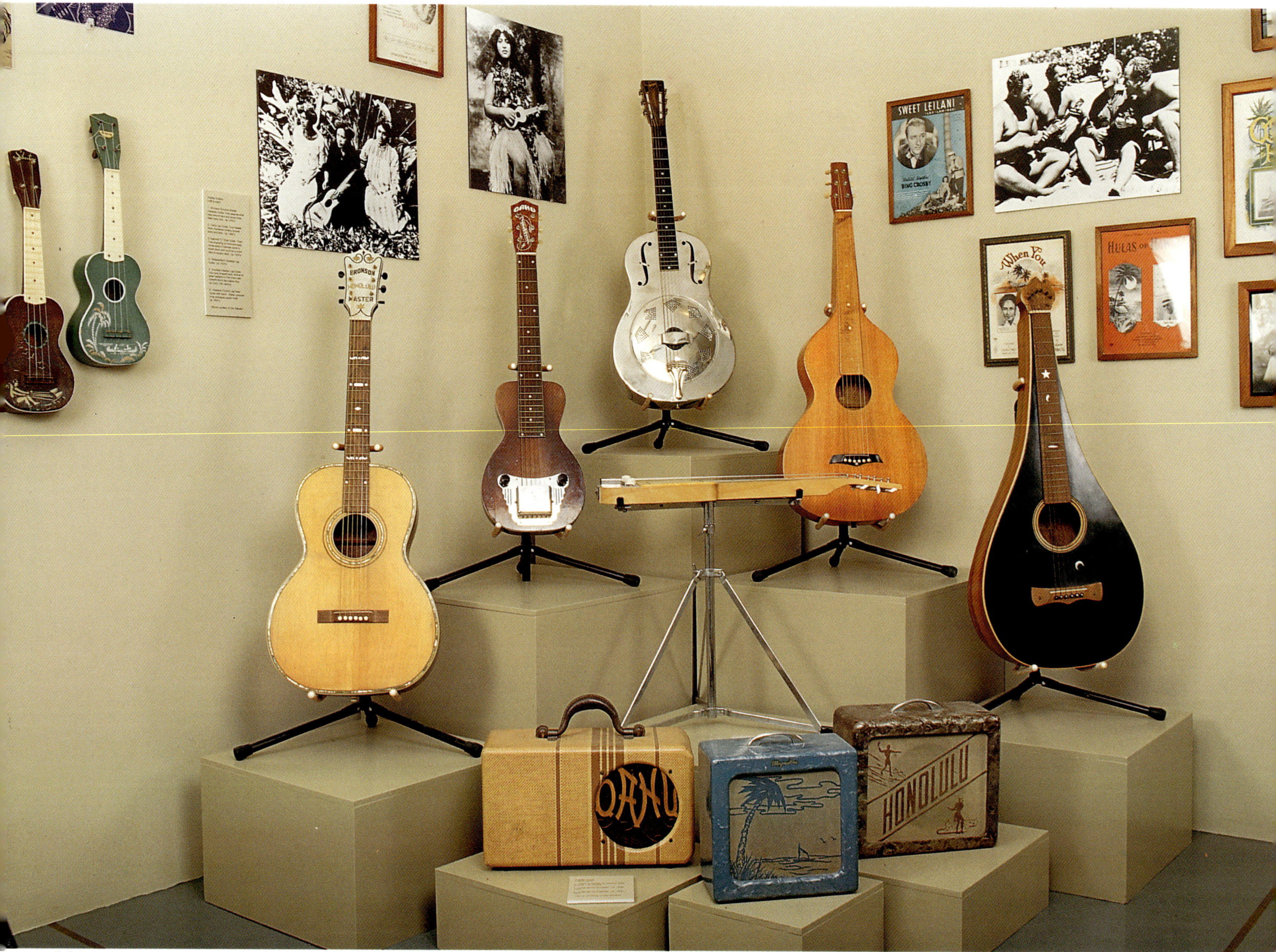
BRONSON
HONOLULU
MASTER
OAHU
SWEET LEILANI
BING CROSBY
When You
HULAS OF
OAHU
HONOLULU

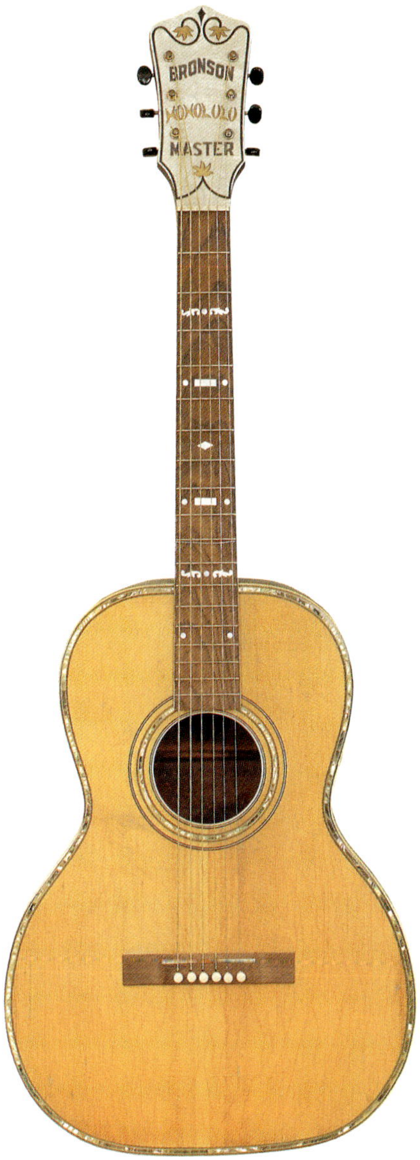

Bronson Honolulu Master Hawaiian Guitar, with deep body size and abalone shell inlay around the face and sound hole, c. 1930s. *Courtesy: Don Stewart.*

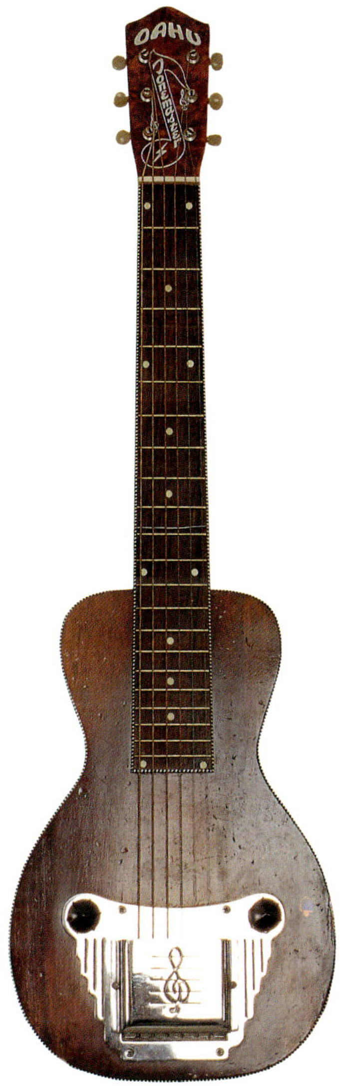

Oahu Tonemaster lap guitar with checkered binding around the neck and body, c. 1940s. *Courtesy: Don Stewart.*

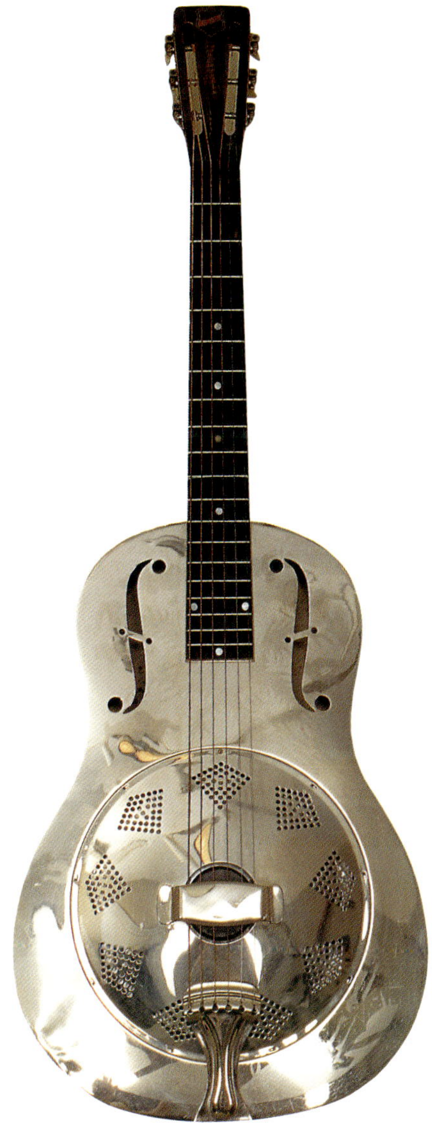

National "O" style guitar, constructed of German silver or nickel silver with palm tree engraving on front and back, it came with either a square or round neck, c. 1930s. *Courtesy: Don Stewart.*

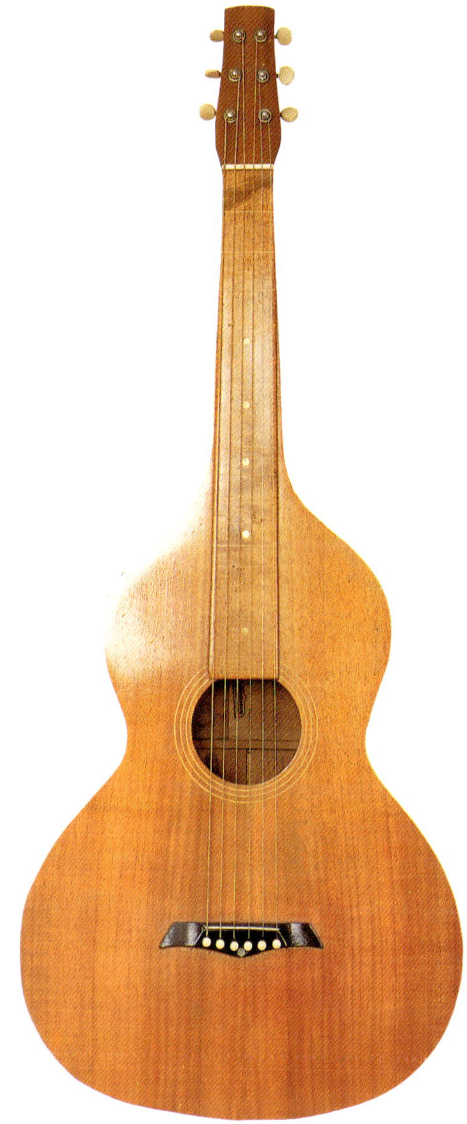

Weissenborn Hawaiian lap guitar, c. 1920s. *Courtesy: Don Stewart.*

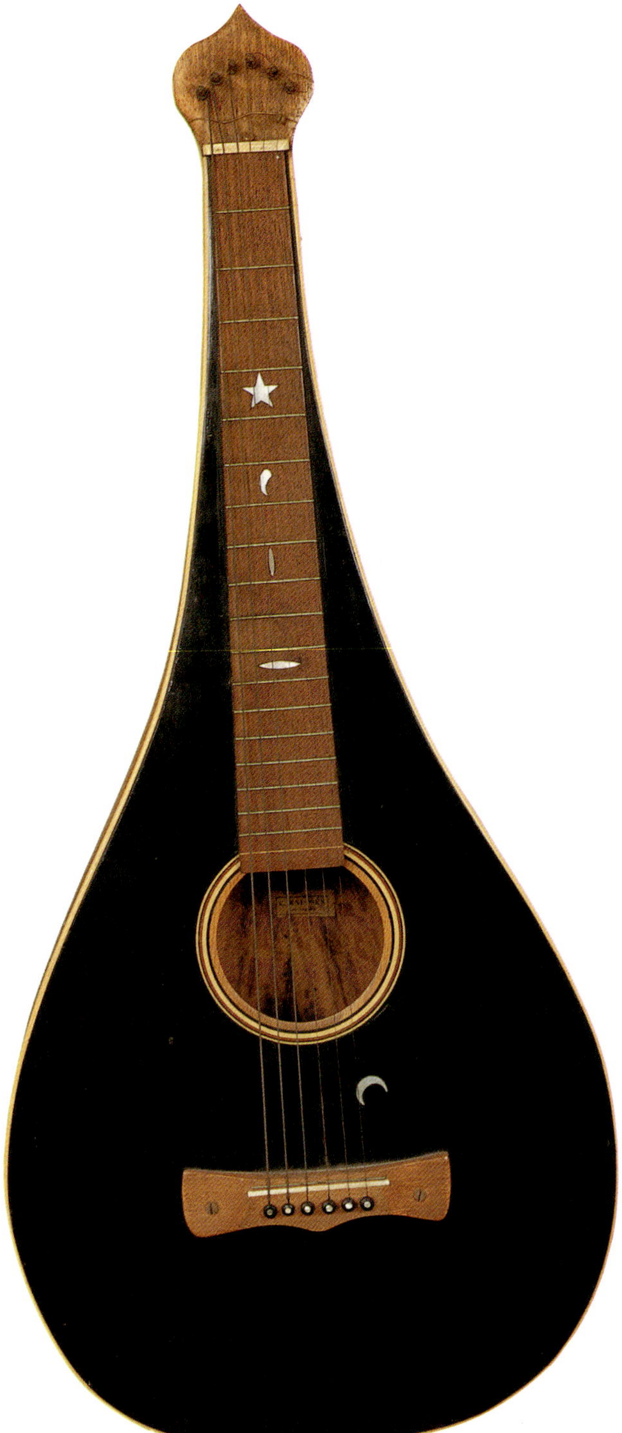

Knudsen Hawaiian lap guitar with pear-shaped body and mother of pearl inlay work, c. early twentieth century. *Courtesy: Michael Trotter*.

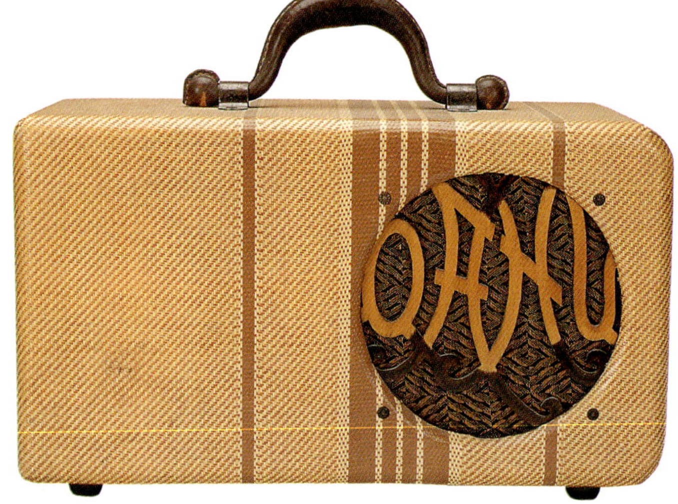

Oahu electric slide guitar amplifier. Fiber coated with leather handle. 1940s. *Courtesy: Don Stewart*.

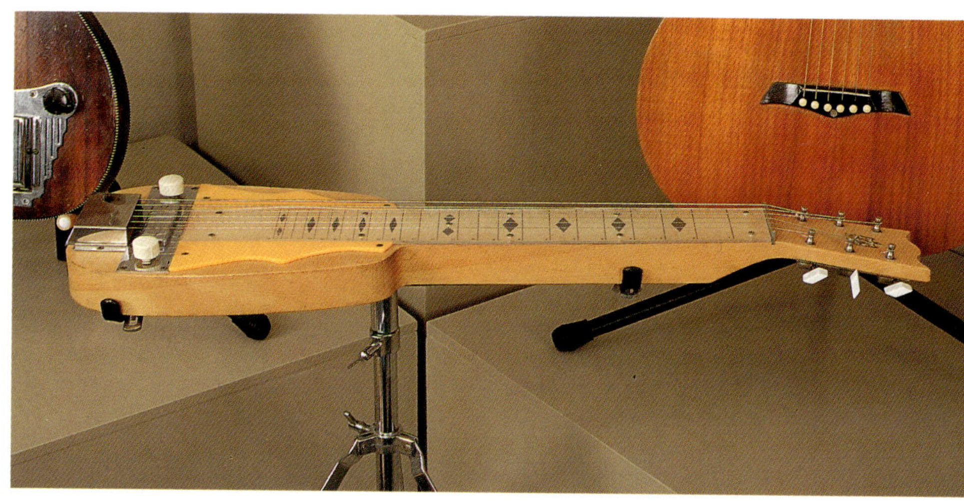

Hawaiian electric lap guitar with stand, maker unknown, c. 1950s. *Courtesy: Don Stewart*.

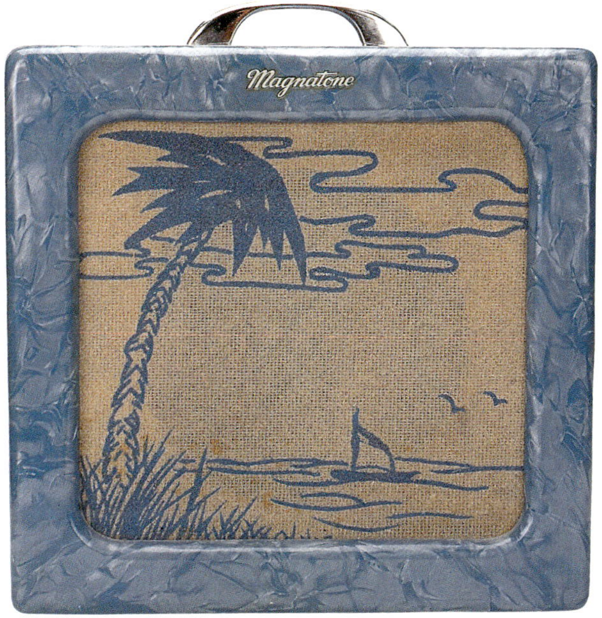

Magnatone guitar amplifier with tropical scene on the speaker screen. Plastic. c. 1940-1950. *Courtesy: Don Stewart*.

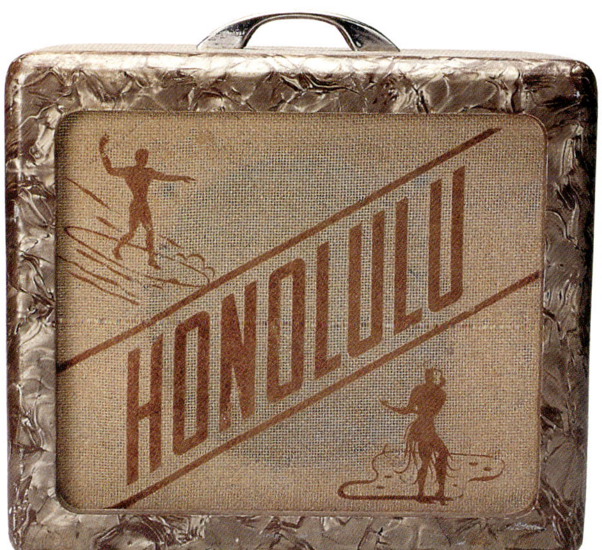

Magnatone Honolulu amplifier. Plastic. c. 1940-1950. *Courtesy: Don Stewart*.

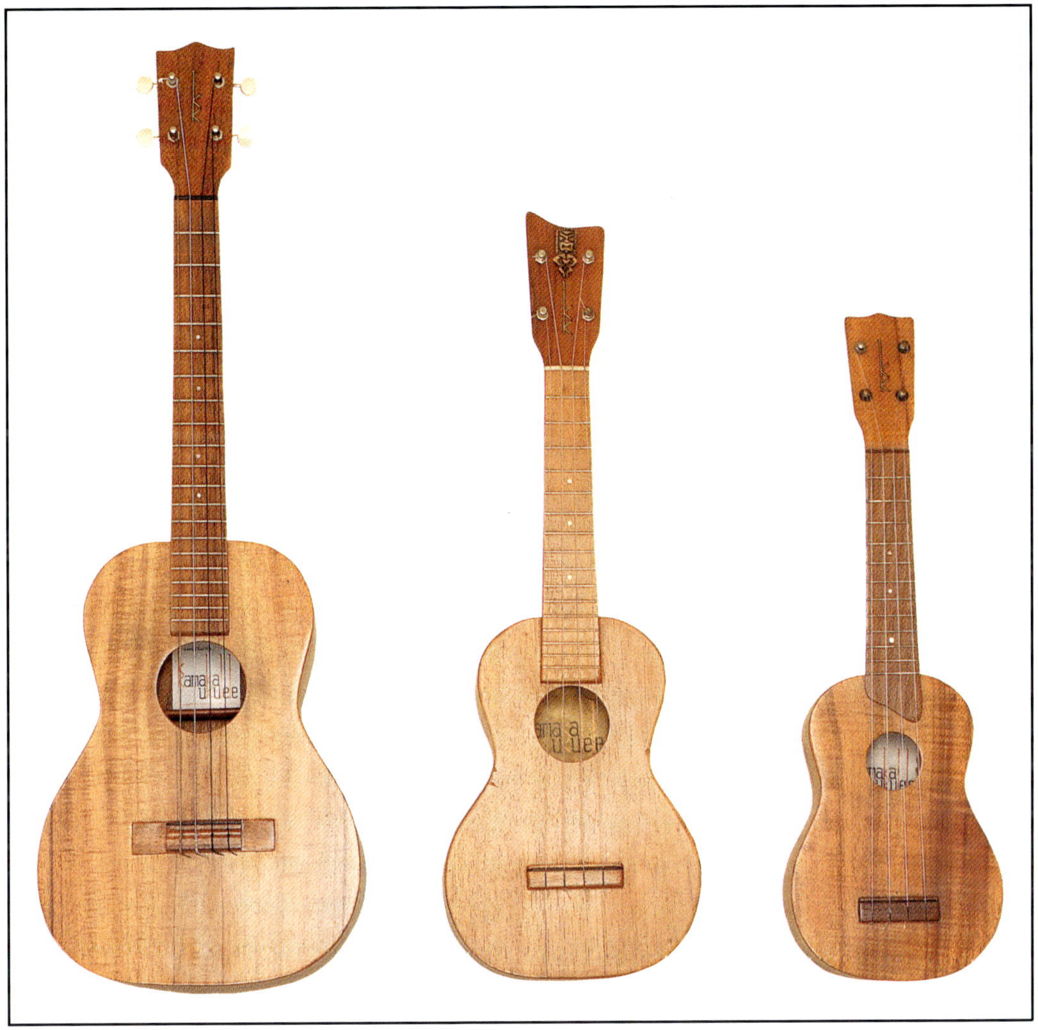

Kamaka ukuleles, koa wood, c. 1960s-1980. Left to right: Kamaka tenor ukulele; Kamaka concert ukulele; Kamaka soprano ukulele. *Courtesy: Don Stewart*.

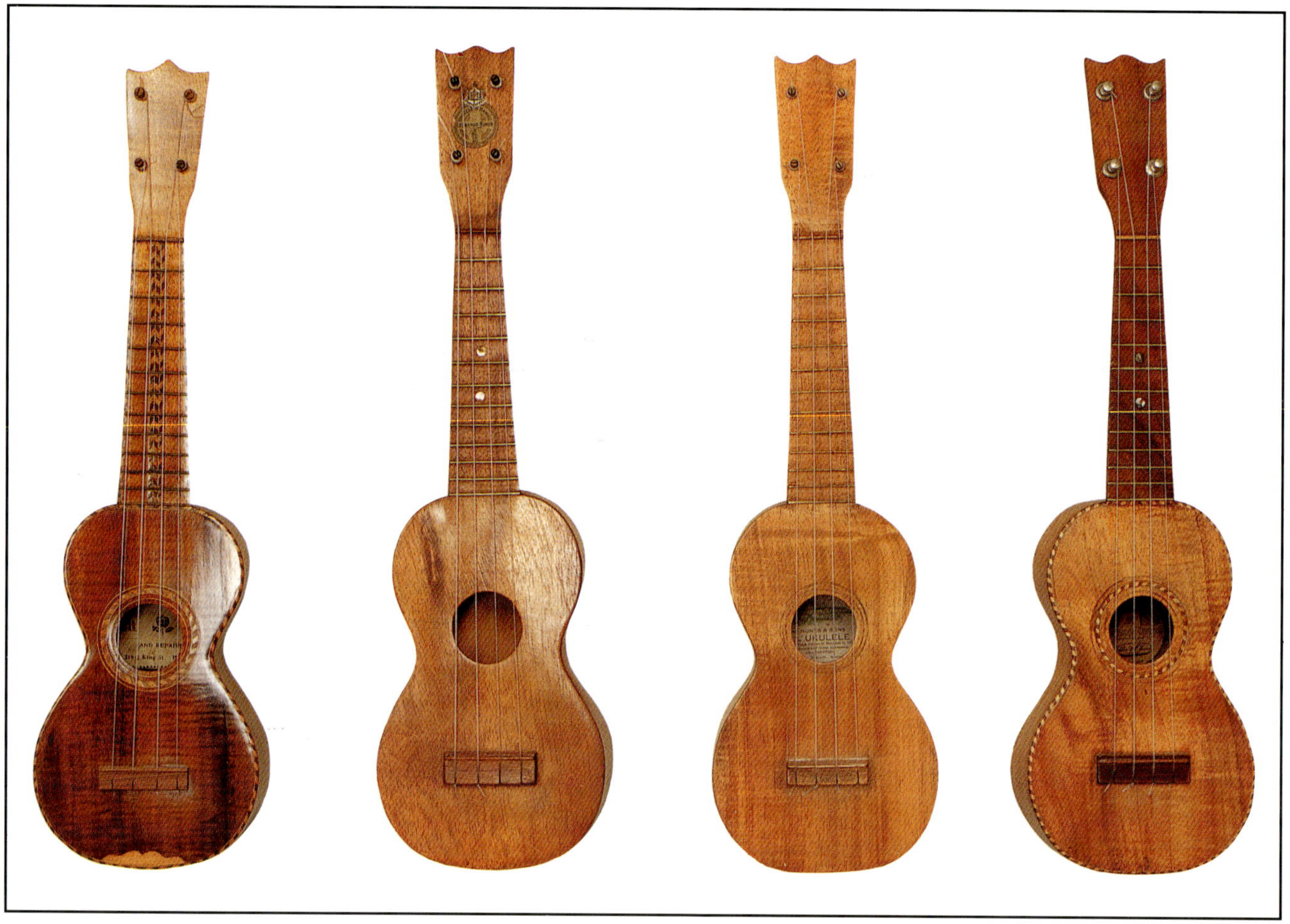

Left to right: Manuel Nunes ukulele, koa wood with friction tuners, rope binding around the neck and body, and inlay around the sound hole, mid-neck and at the base, c. 1910s-20s; Leonardo Nunes ukulele, koa wood friction tuners, c. 1910s-20s; Manuel Nunes and Sons ukulele, koa wood friction tuners, c. 1920s-30s; Leonardo Nunes ukulele with rope binding on face and sound hole, c. 1930s-40s. *Courtesy: Don Stewart and James O'Mahoney, S.B.S.M.*

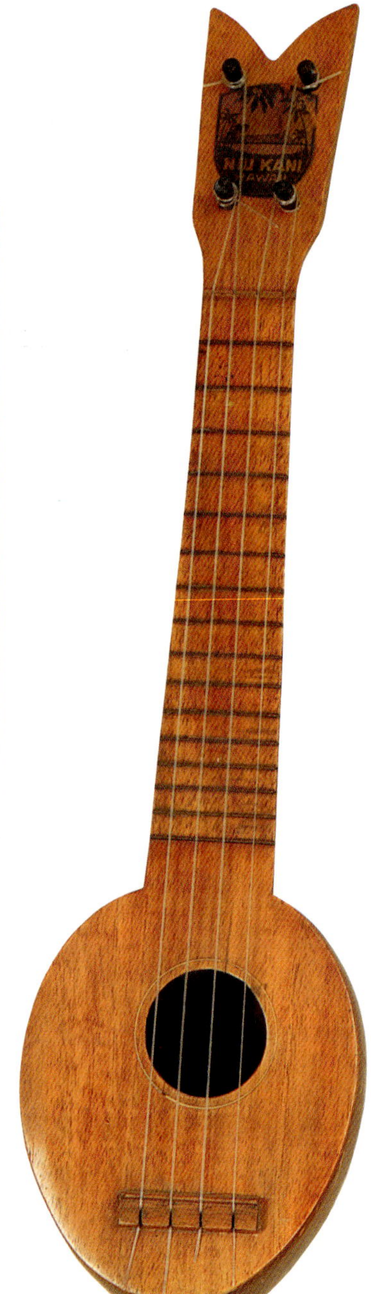

Niu-Kani Coconut koa wood ukulele, ebony friction tuners, c. 1920s.
Courtesy: James O'Mahoney, S.B.S.M.

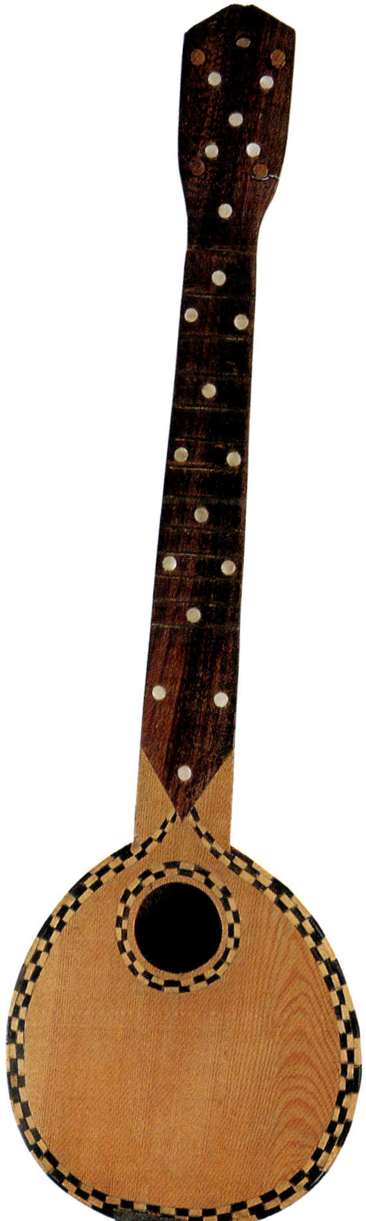

Coconut ukulele, with friction tuners and mother-of-pearl decoration on the neck. Maker and date unknown. *Courtesy: Don Stewart.*

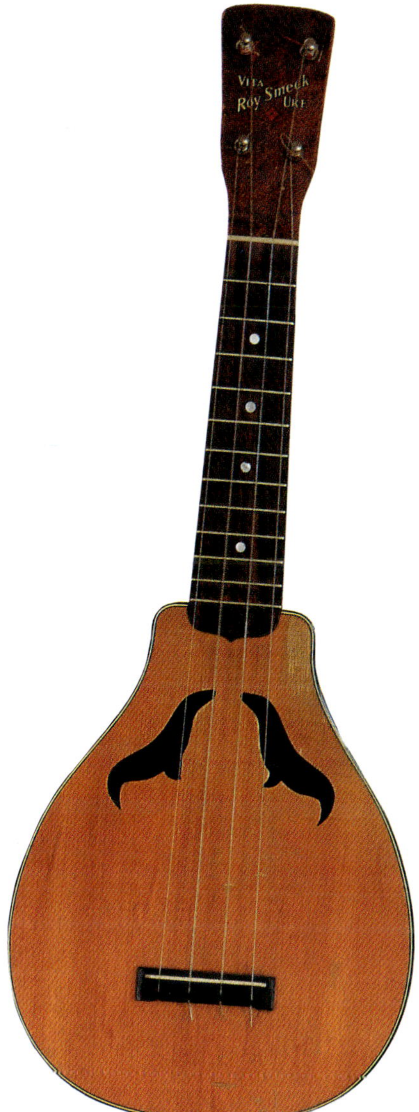

Roy Smeck Vita Uku, mahogany back and sides. It has an unusual shape and "seal " sound holes on the top. c. 1940s. *Courtesy: Don Stewart.*

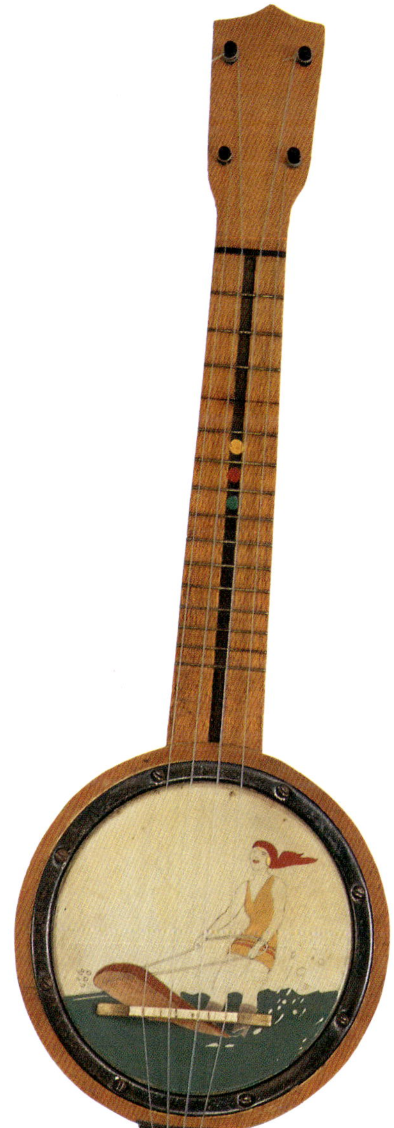

Banjo ukulele with a hand-painted aqua planer on the face and friction tuners. Maker unknown, c. 1920s. *Courtesy: Don Stewart.*

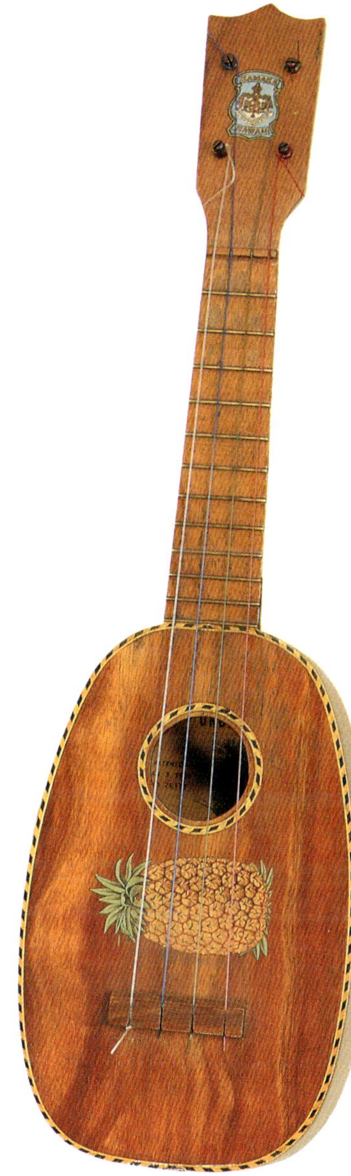

Kamaka Pineapple ukulele with friction tuners, c. late 1920s. *Courtesy: Don Stewart.*

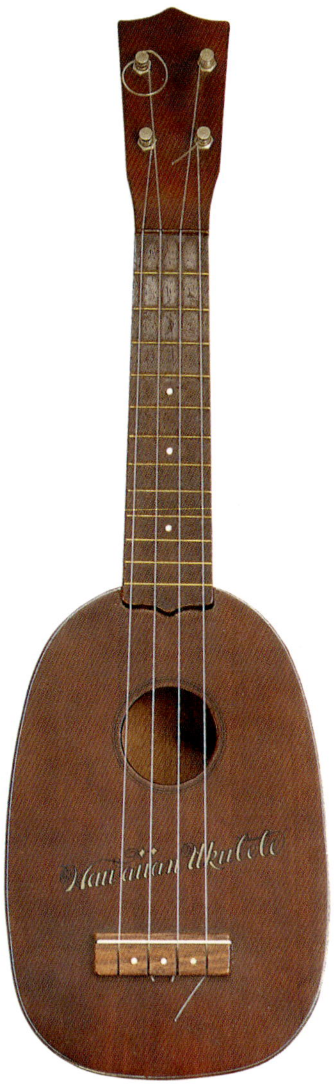

Pineapple ukulele with friction tuners, c. late 1920s. *Courtesy: Don Stewart.*

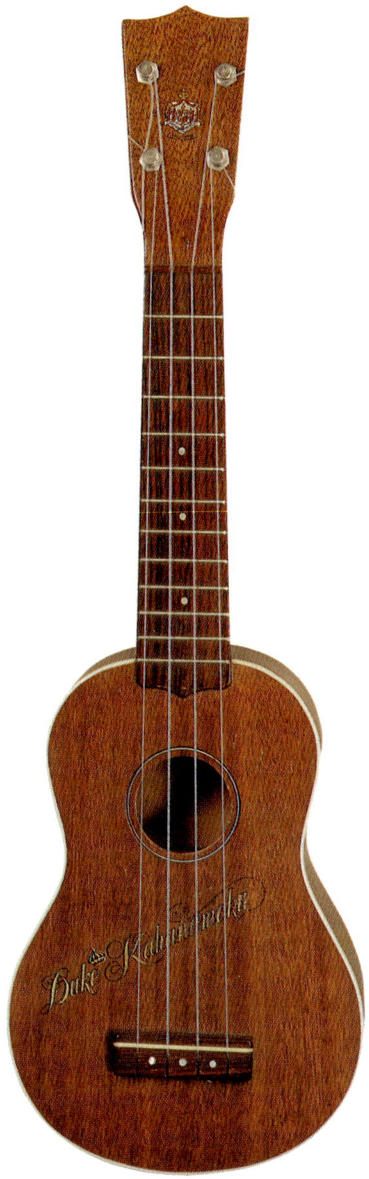

Duke Kahanamoku ukulele, mahogany, c. 1950-1960. *Courtesy: Don Stewart.*

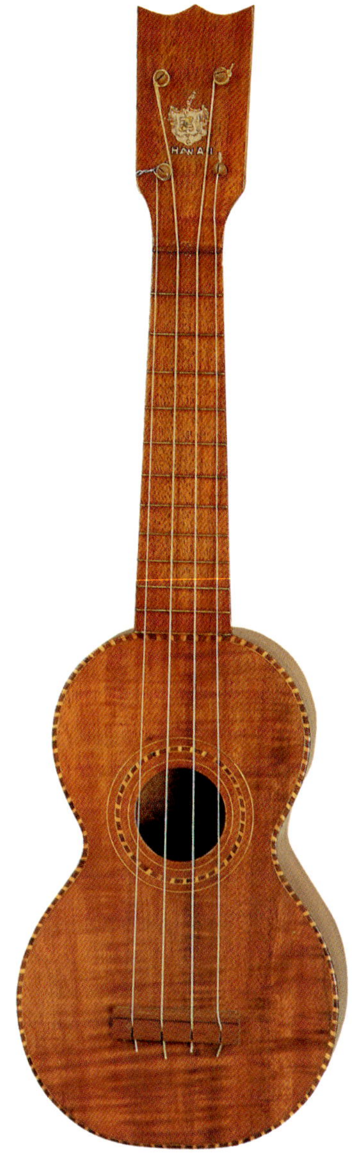

Kumulae ukulele, koa wood with friction tuners, c. 1920s. *Courtesy: Don Stewart.*

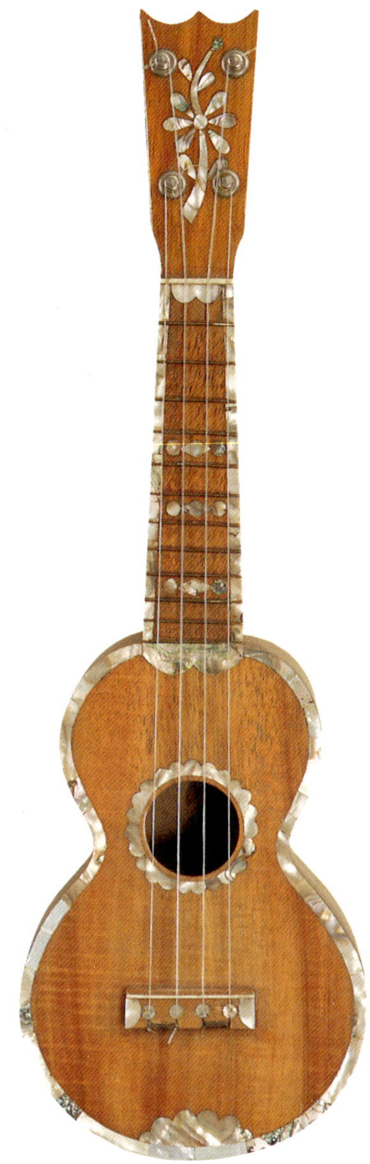

Koa wood ukulele with abalone trim around face and neck. Maker unknown, c. 1940s. *Courtesy: Don Stewart.*

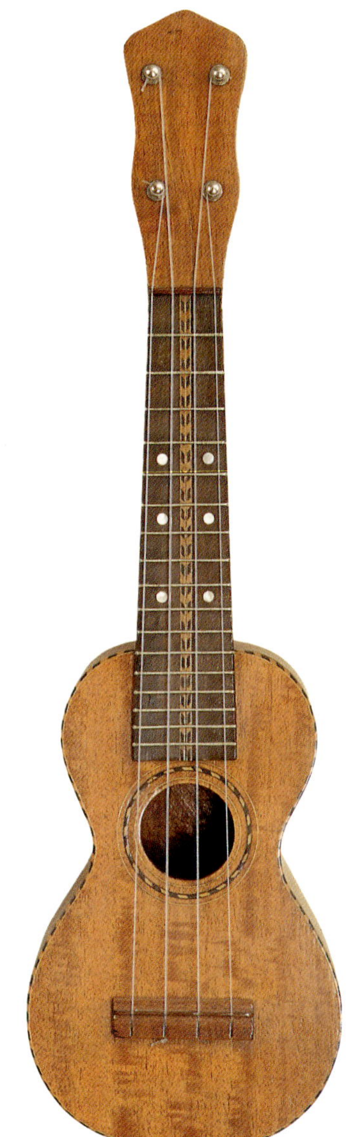

Koa wood ukulele, maker unknown, c. 1940s. *Courtesy: Don Stewart.*

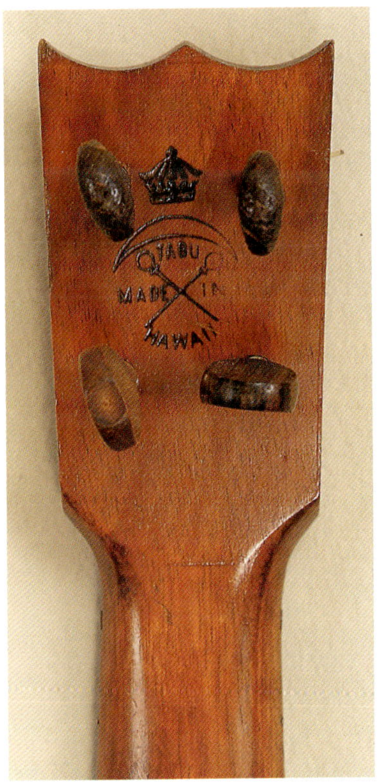

Koa wood ukulele, friction tuners, showing the "Tabu - Made in Hawaii" brand. c. 1920s. *Courtesy: Don Stewart.*

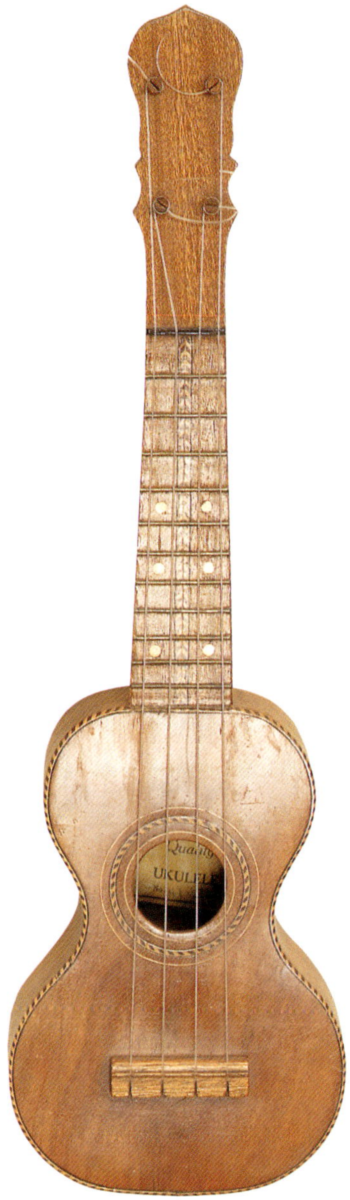

Conservatory of Music, koa wood ukulele with friction tuners. Note the body shape and the rope binding. c. 1920s. *Courtesy: Don Stewart.*

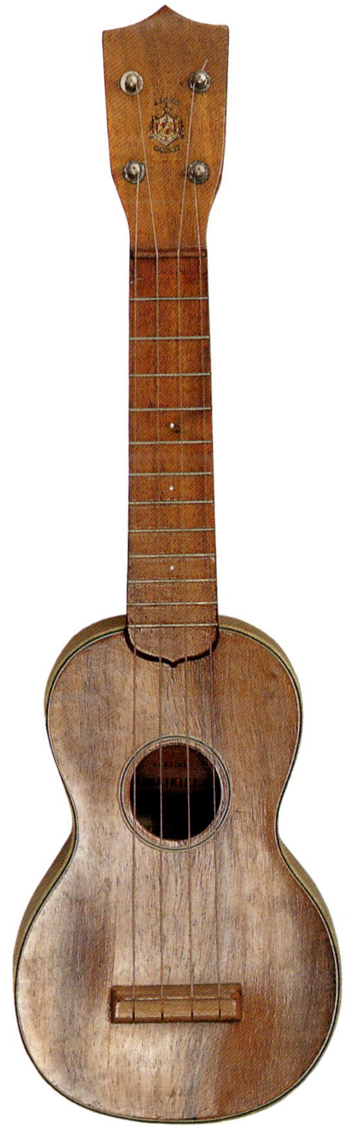

Harold L. Summers, koa wood ukulele, c. 1950. *Courtesy: Don Stewart.*

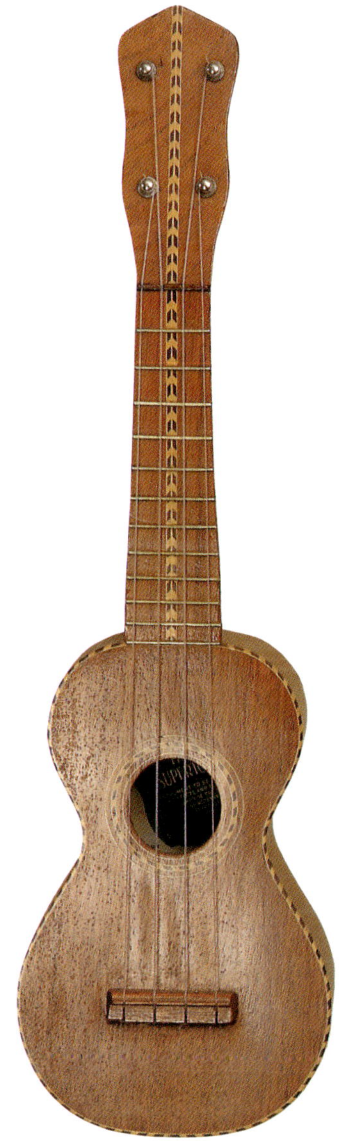

Supertone ukulele, mahogany, c. 1940. *Courtesy: Don Stewart.*

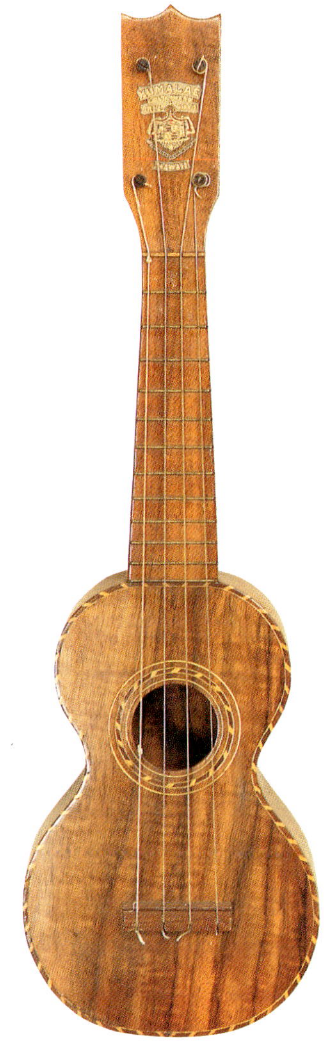

Kumalae ukulele, koa wood, with friction tuners and rope binding on the face, c. 1920s. *Courtesy: Don Stewart.*

Sheet Music and Records

The harmony of the Aloha Spirit was captured in the music of the Islands. Its popularization came with the publication of Queen Liliuokalani's "Aloha Oe." It became a hit around the world and so embodied the essence of Hawaii that even today it is nearly impossible to think about the Islands without the tune running through your consciousness.

But the queen was not alone. Many other Hawaiian songs made it into print as did songs about the Aloha experience. They were well received in this country, aided in part by the inclusion of Hawaiian singers on the vaudeville stages of the early twentieth century.

Where sheet music was the principle vehicle for a songs popularity in the early part of the century, as the years passed the phonograph record became much more important. Songs that were once heard while gathered around the parlor piano, with momma playing and dad singing, could now be heard over the Victrola, being performed by some of the most talented artists in the land. Hawaiian songs found their way onto many of these popular records and their fame spread.

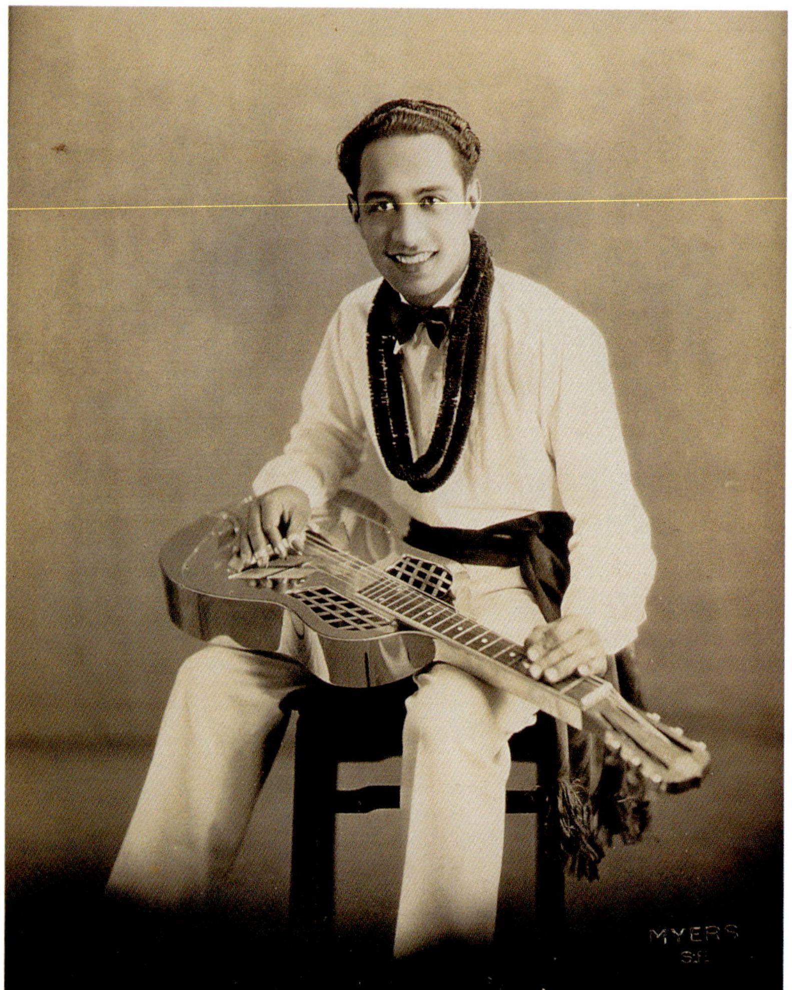

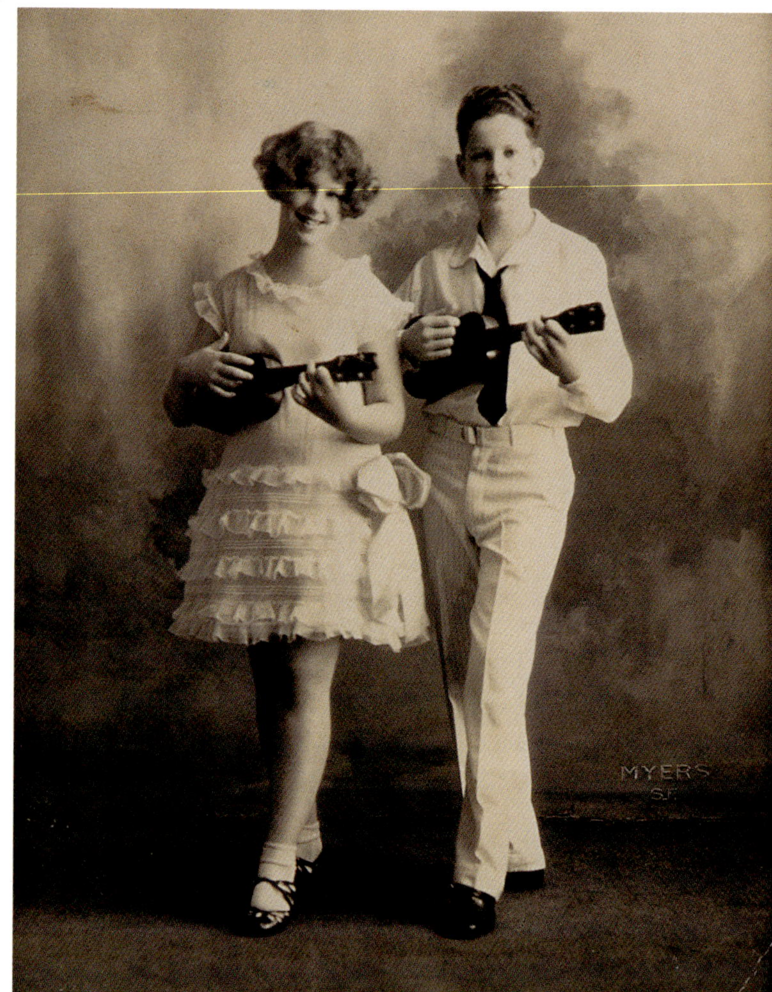

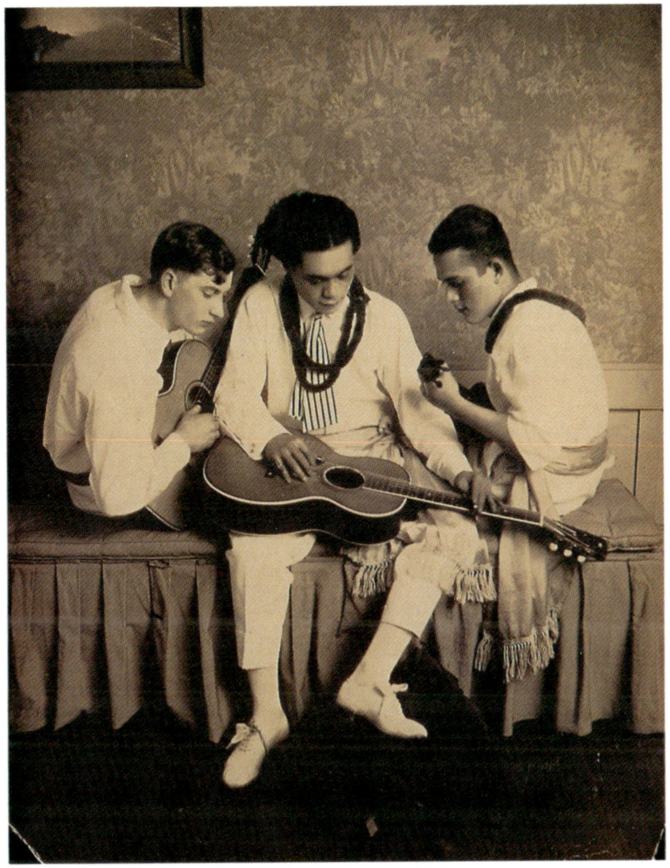

This trio seems to be preparing a new number. *Courtesy: Don Stewart.*

Promotional photo of Howard's Radio Hawaiian Dance Trio, making it clear that they are available for both radio and club work. Signed Phelps (?). *Courtesy: Don Stewart.*

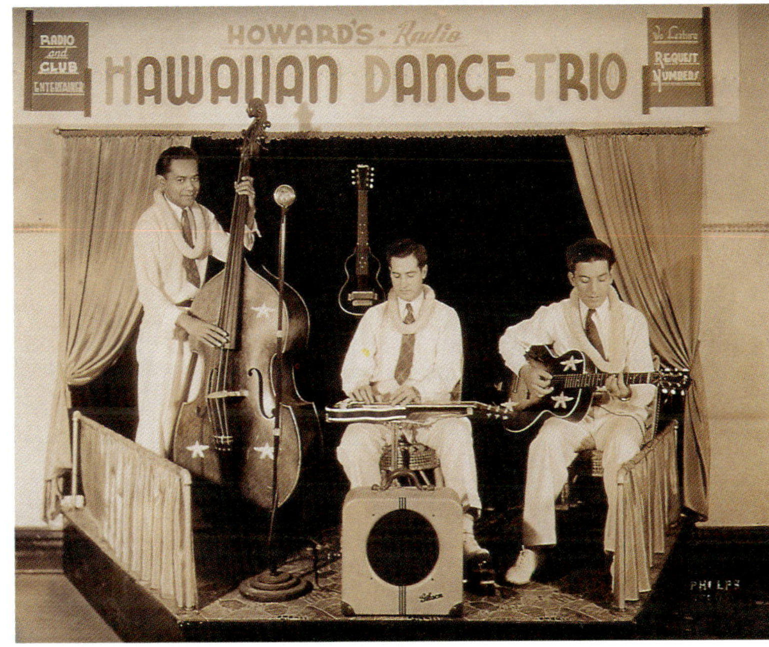

Opposite:
These two promotional photographs taken by Myers of San Francisco show two of a number of acts that toured the circuit performing Hawaiian tunes. As you can see, one need not be a native Hawaiian to appreciate or perform its music. *Courtesy: Don Stewart.*

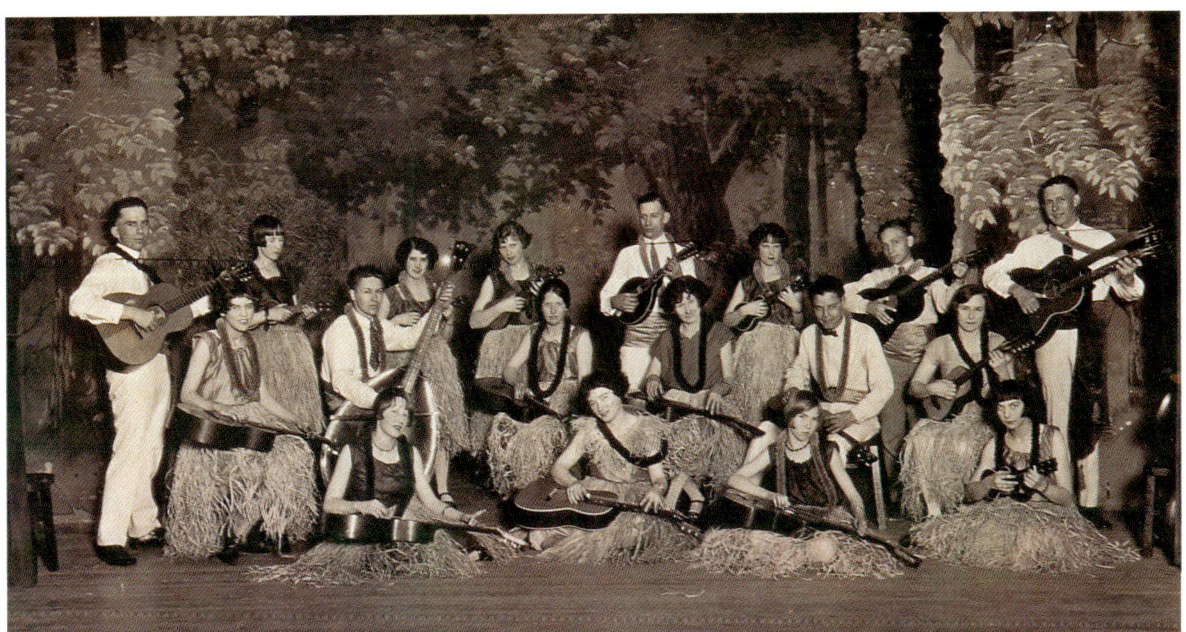

It is unclear whether these are professional performers or amateur. Whatever the case, they have clearly been swept up by the Aloha Spirit. *Courtesy: Don Stewart.*

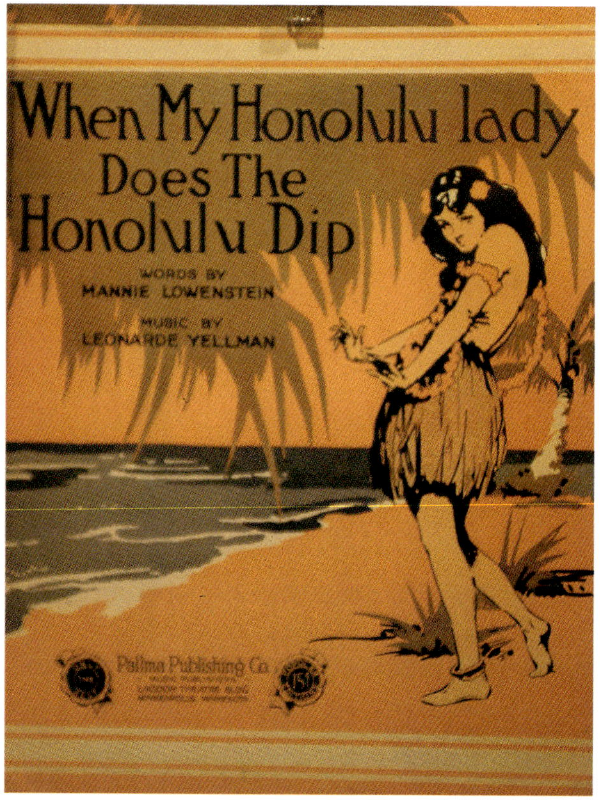

"When My Honolulu Lady Does the Honolulu Dip," words by Mannie Lowenstein, music by Leonarde Yellman. Published by Pallma Publishing, Minneapolis. *Courtesy: Susan Mast Enterprises.*

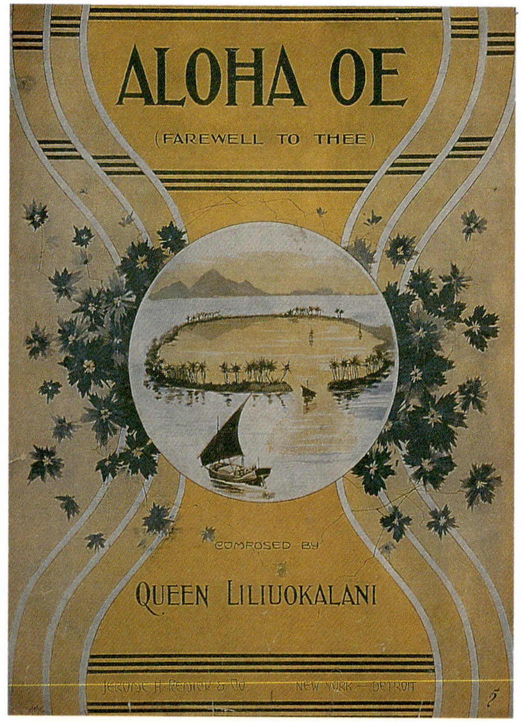

"Aloha Oe (Farewell to Thee)," by Queen Liliuokalani, published by Jerome H. Remick & Company, New York and Detroit. *Courtesy: Julie Cline.*

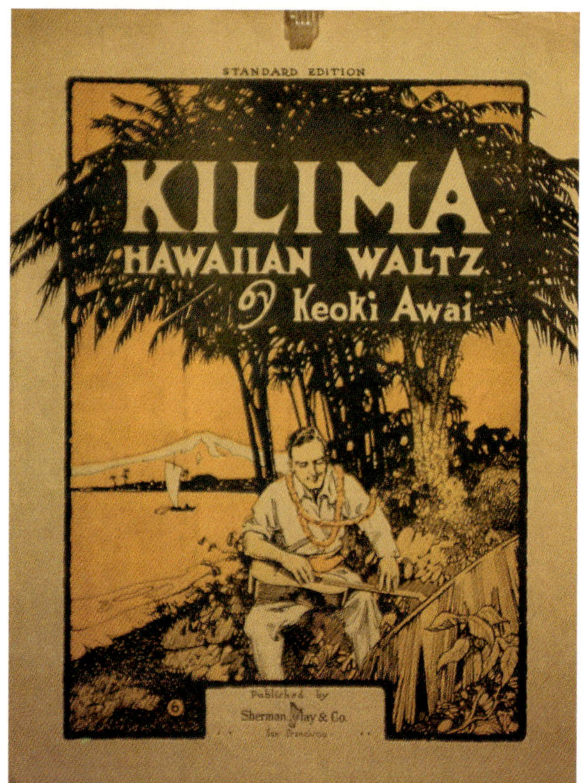

"Kalima Hawaiian Waltz," by Keoki Awai. Published by Sherman Clay & Co., San Francisco. *Courtesy: Don Stewart.*

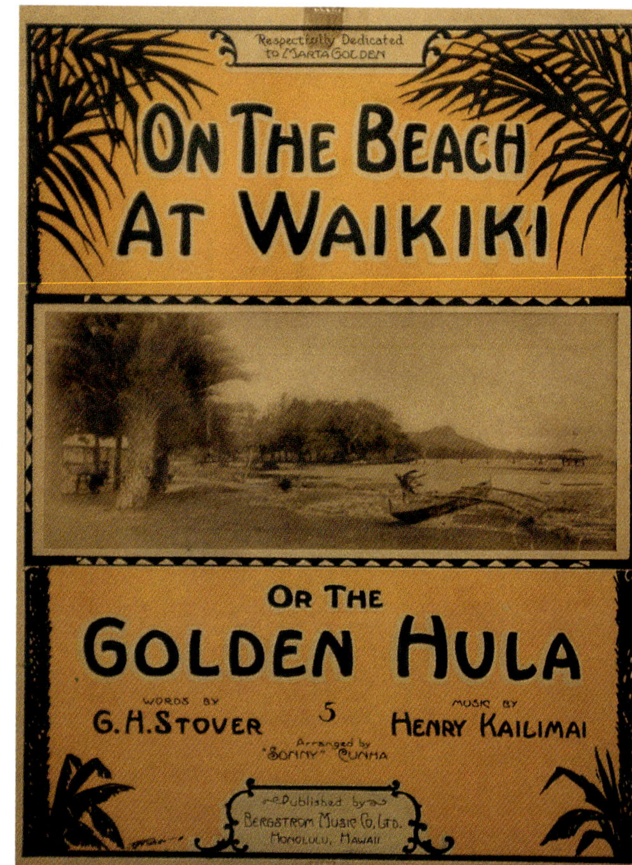

"On the Beach at Waikiki or The Golden Hula," words by G.H. Stover, music by Henry Kailimai. Published by Bergstrom Music Co., Honolulu. *Courtesy: Don Stewart.*

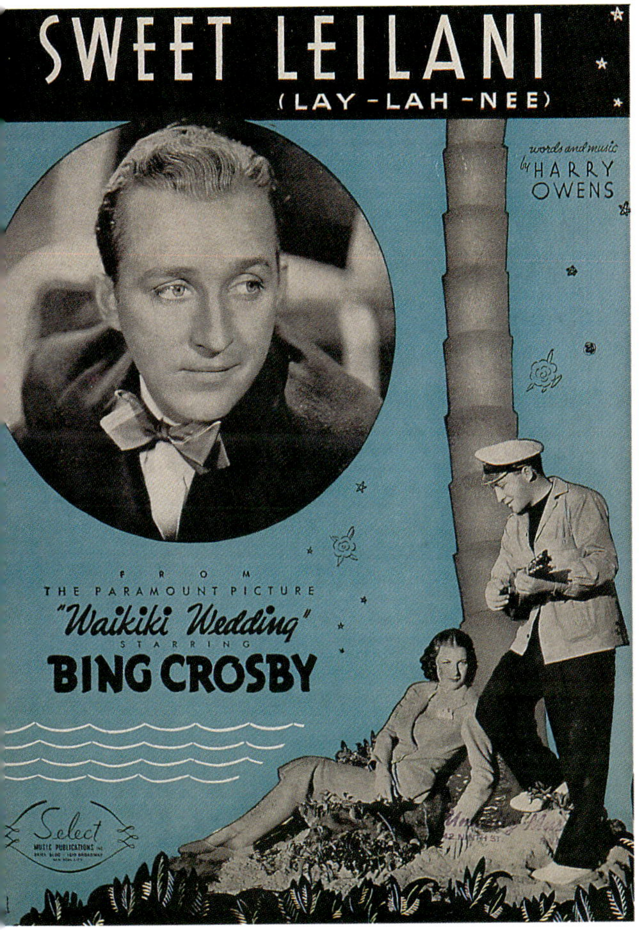

"Sweet Leilani," words and music by Harry Owens. Featured in Bing Crosby's film "Waikiki Wedding." Published by Select Music Co., New York. *Courtesy: the Collection of Brian Goddard & Gene Sweeney.*

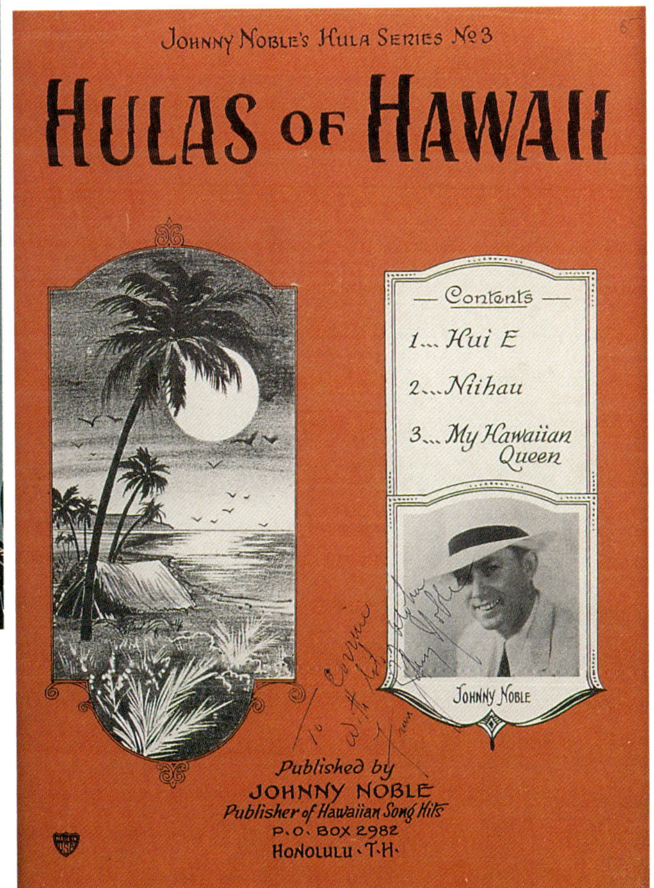

"Hulas of Hawaii," published by Johnny Noble, Hawaiian Song Hits, Honolulu. *Courtesy: Don Stewart.*

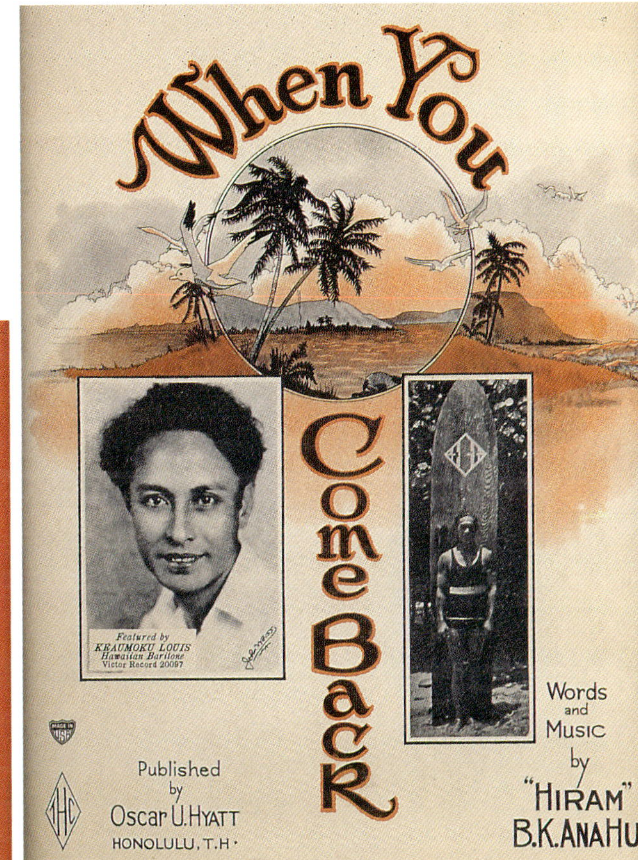

"When You Come Back," words and music by "Hiram" B.K. Anahu. Published by Oscar U. Hyatt, Honolulu. *Courtesy: Don Stewart.*

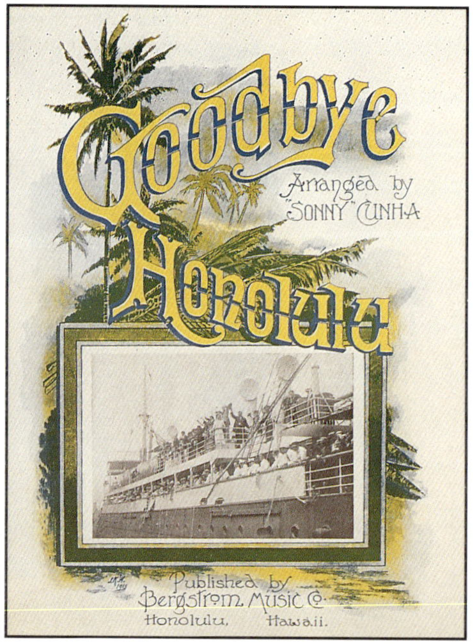

"Goodbye Honolulu," arranged by Sonny Cunha. Published by Bergstrom Music Co., Honolulu. *Courtesy: Don Stewart.*

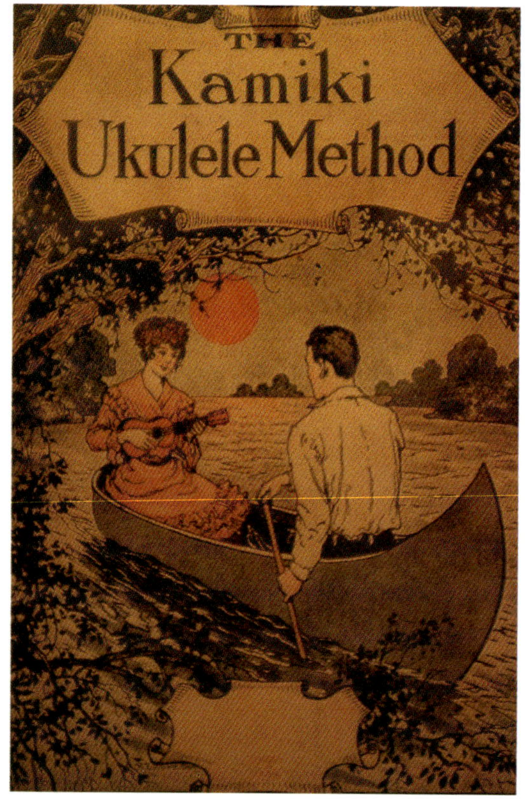

For tourists and others wishing to learn to play their new ukulele or Hawaiian guitar, several instructional books were available. This is an early "Kamiki Ukulele Method" featuring a woman serenading her rowing beau. *Courtesy: Don Stewart.*

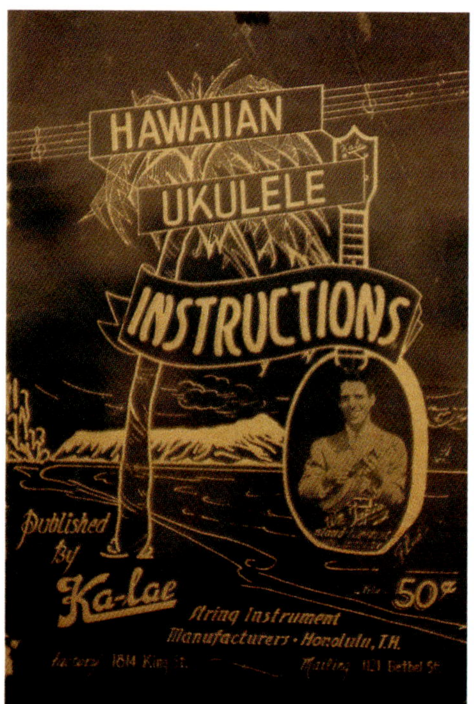

"Hawaiian Ukulele Instructions," published by Ka-Lae stringed instrument manufacturers, Honolulu. *Courtesy: Don Stewart.*

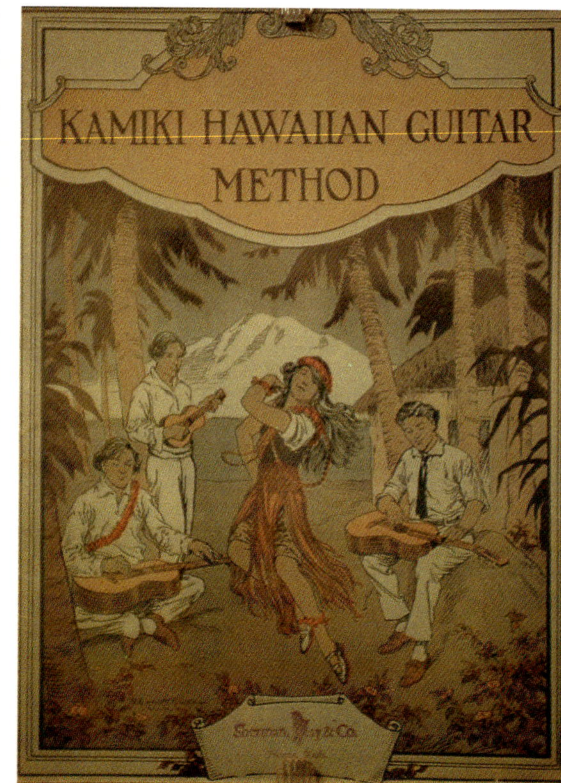

The "Kamiki Hawaiian Guitar Method" was published by Sherman Clay & Co., San Francisco. *Courtesy: Don Stewart.*

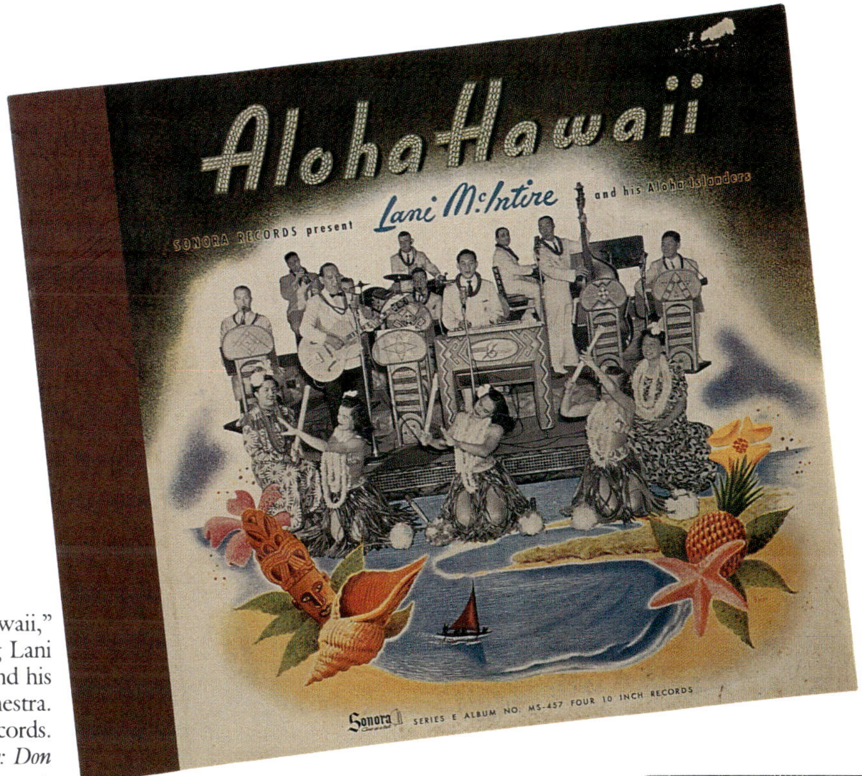

"Aloha Hawaii," featuring Lani McIntire and his Aloha Orchestra. Sonora Records. *Courtesy: Don Stewart.*

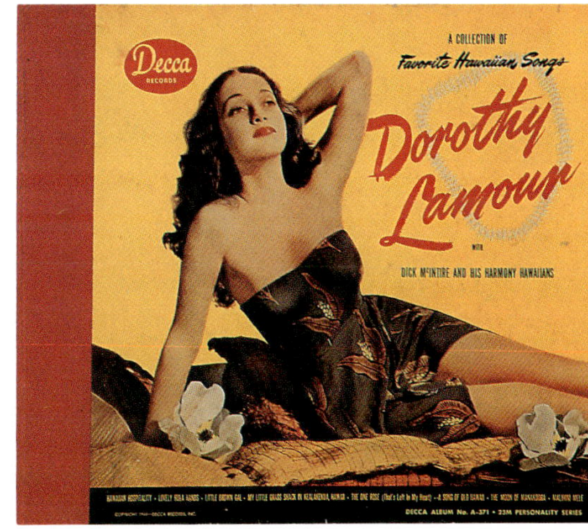

"A Collection of Favorite Hawaiian Songs," Dorothy Lamour with Dick McIntire and his Harmony Hawaiians. Decca Records, 1944. *Courtesy: Don Stewart.*

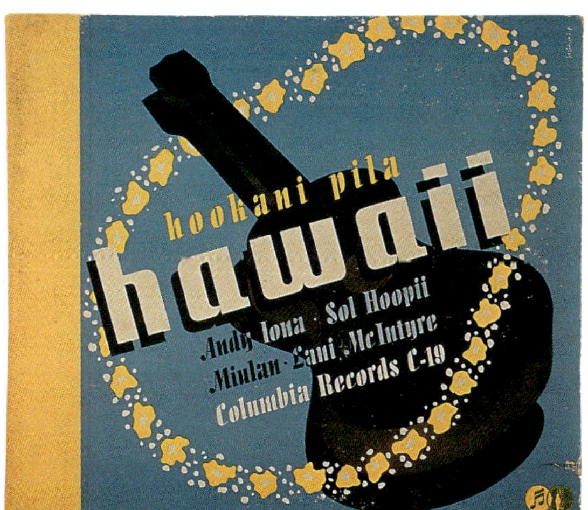

"Hookani Pila Hawaii," with Andy Iona, Sol Hoopii, Miulan, and Lani McIntire. Columbia Records. *Courtesy: Don Stewart.*

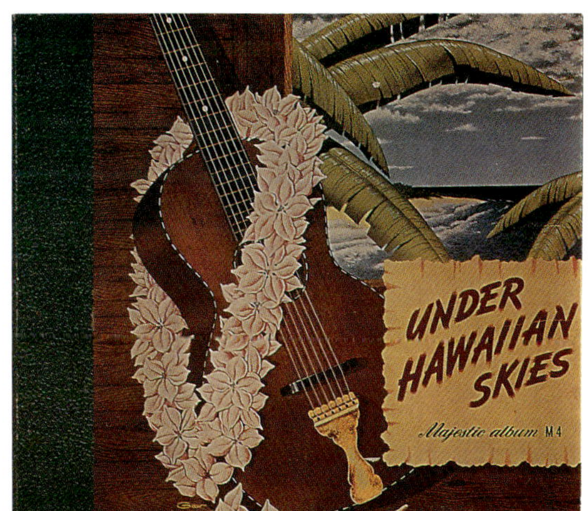

"Under Hawaiian Skies," Majestic Album M4, cover art by Gaw. *Courtesy: Don Stewart.*

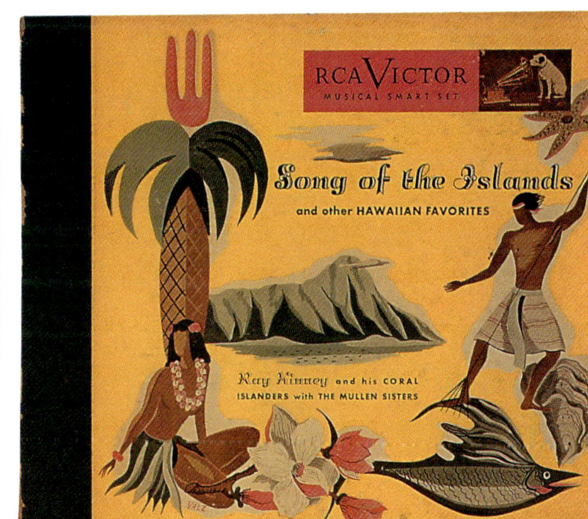

"Songs of the Islands and other Hawaiian Favorites," Ray Kinney and his Coral Islanders with The Mullen Sisters. RCA Victor. *Courtesy: Don Stewart.*

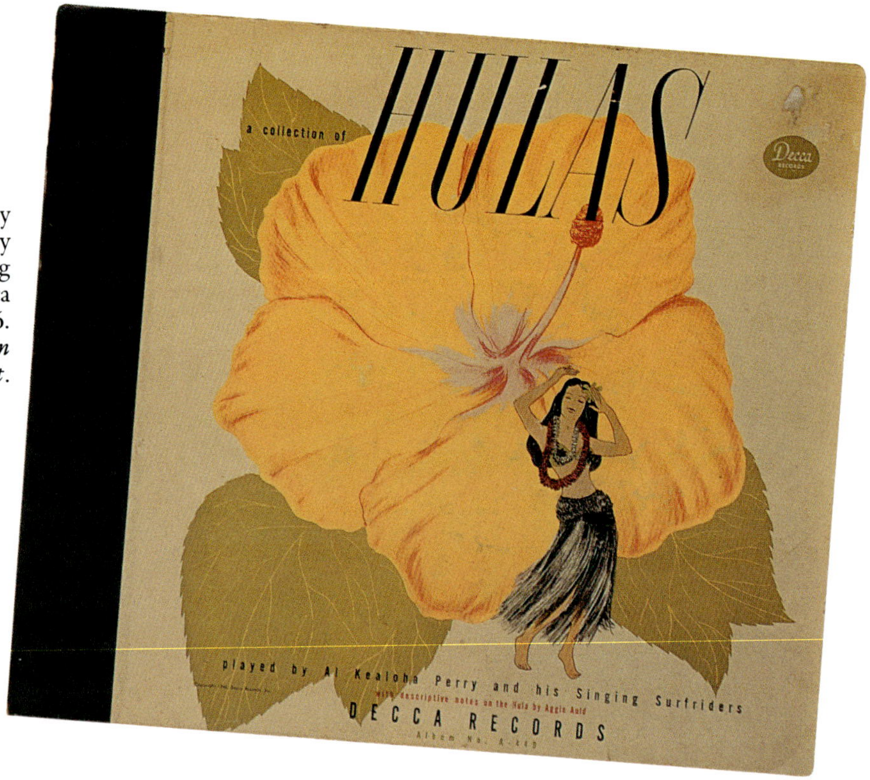

"Hulas," played by Al Kealoha Perry and his Singing Surfriders, Decca Records, c. 1946. *Courtesy: Don Stewart.*

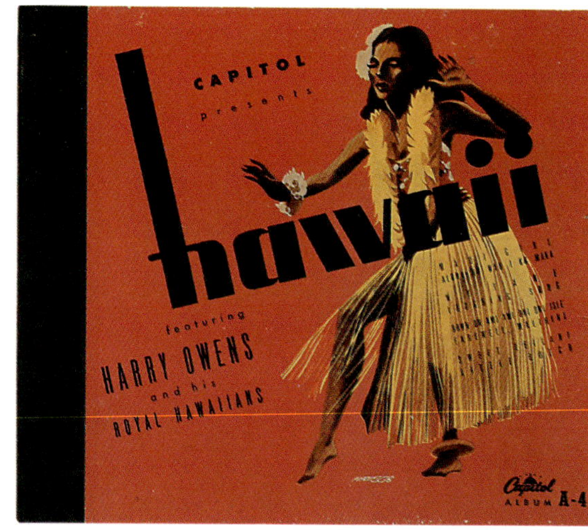

"Hawaii," featuring Harry Owens and his Royal Hawaiians. Capitol Records. *Courtesy: Don Stewart.*

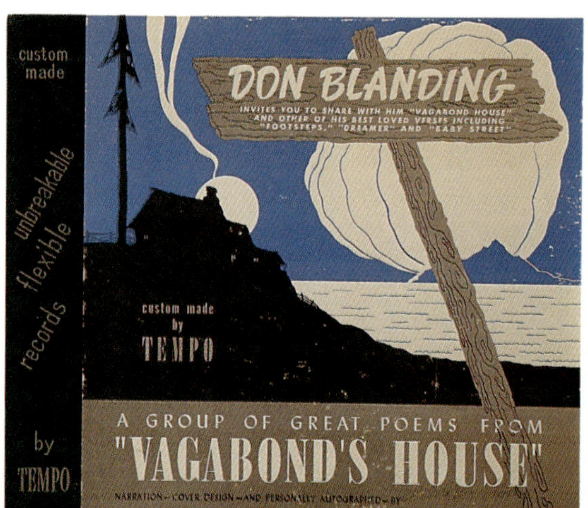

"A Group of Great Poems from 'Vagabond's House,'" narrated, cover design, and personally autographed by Don Blanding. Tempo Records. *Courtesy: Don Stewart.*

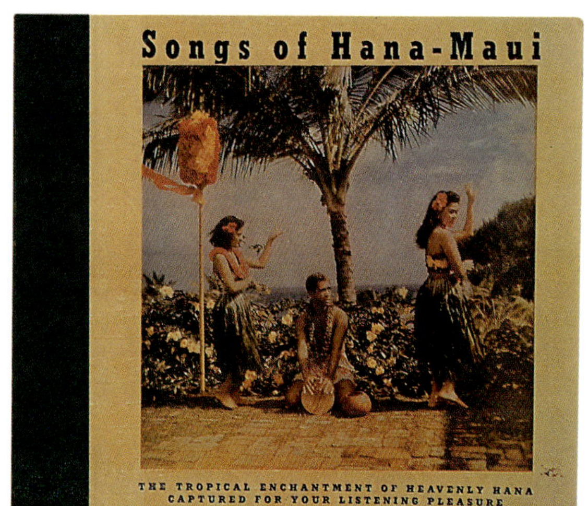

"Songs of Hana-Maui-The Tropical Enchantment of Heavenly Hana Captured for Your Listening Pleasure." *Courtesy: Don Stewart.*

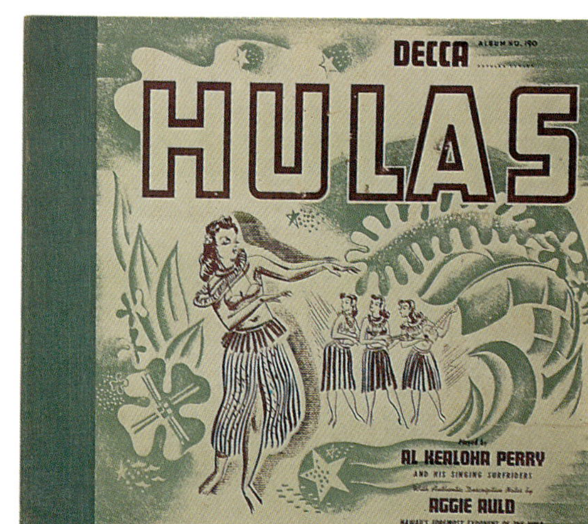

"Hulas," played by Al Kealoha Perry and his Singing Surfriders, Decca Records, date unknown. *Courtesy: Don Stewart.*

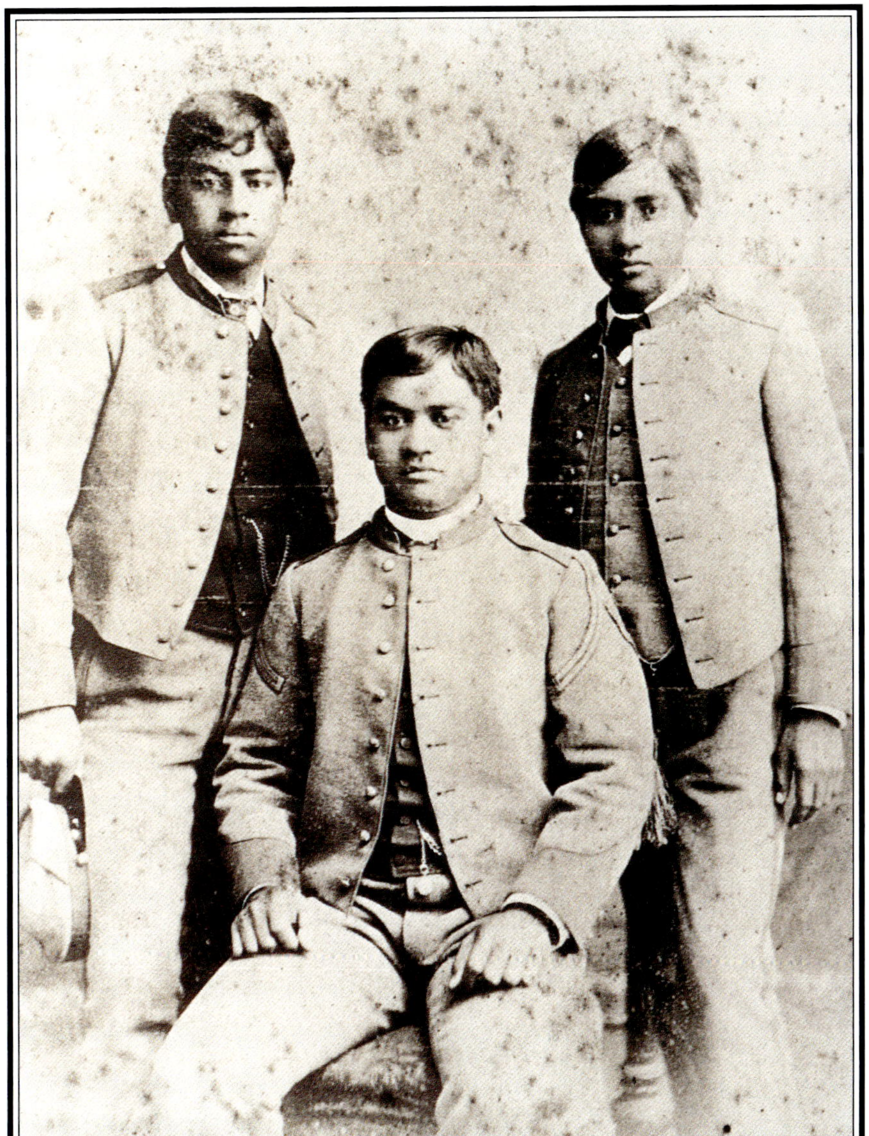

The three Hawaiian princes, c. 1885. They were nephews of Queen Kapi'olani, wife of Hawaii's last king, Jonah Kuhlio Keli'iahonui. They fashioned their California surfboards from Santa Cruz redwood. *Photograph courtesy of the Bishop Museum.*

Chapter 6

Surfing

Among Hawaii's cultural exports, none is as exciting as surfing. Originating in Oceania, probably Tahiti, it was brought to the Islands by early immigrants, probably between 800 and 1100 A.D. When Captain Cook came to Hawaii in 1778, surfing was a well-developed activity. It was an integral part of Hawaiian culture, intertwined with religious rites and the caste system.

Discouraged by missionaries in the 19th century, surfing suffered something of a slump. Only with the rise of tourism and the tourist's fascination with this local activity did it begin to make a comeback. In 1885 three Hawaiian princes studying at a military academy in Santa Cruz, California, may have been the first surfers on the mainland. The rest is history!

In 1907, George Freeth, an ace Hawaiian surfer, brought the "Sport of Kings" to southern California. Freeth's visit was a promotion sponsored by the Redondo/Los Angeles Railroad Company to introduce water sports to the public, in the hope of increasing the tourist business. Freeth gave wave riding demonstrations and offered surfing, swimming, and diving classes to youngsters. His life saving feats and advances are legendary. In Hawaii he taught Jack London to surf. When London's book *A Royal Sport* was published, it gave the new California sport a boost.

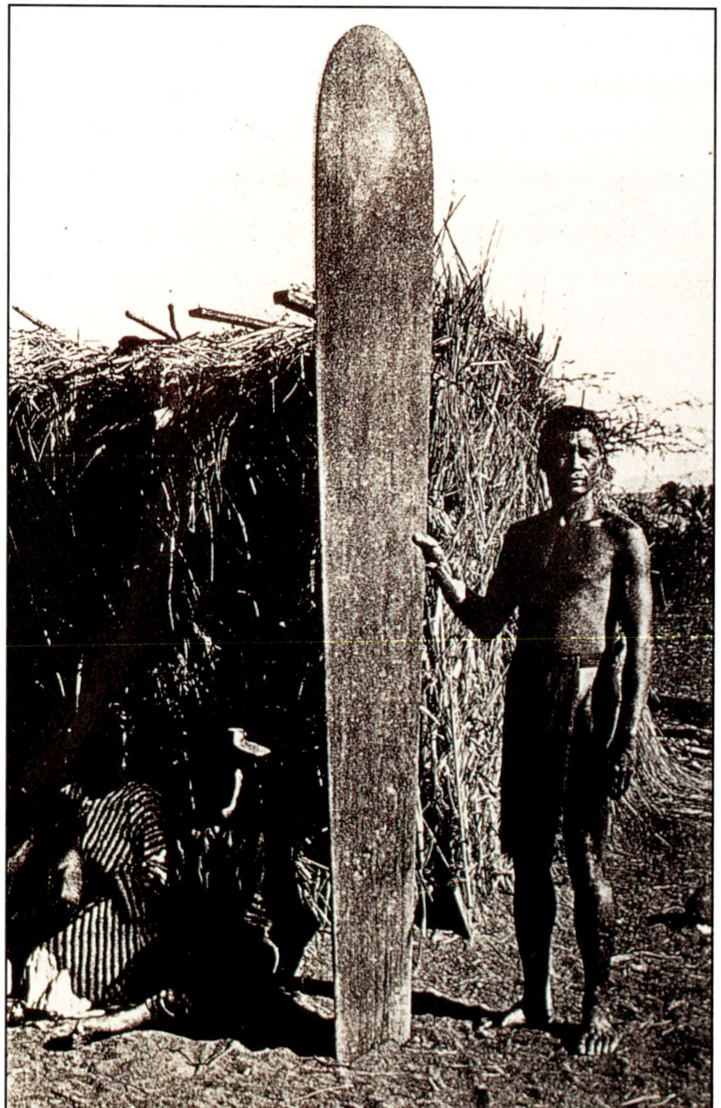

Ancient Hawaiian Surfer with Olo board. c. 1880s. *Courtesy: The Bishop Museum.*

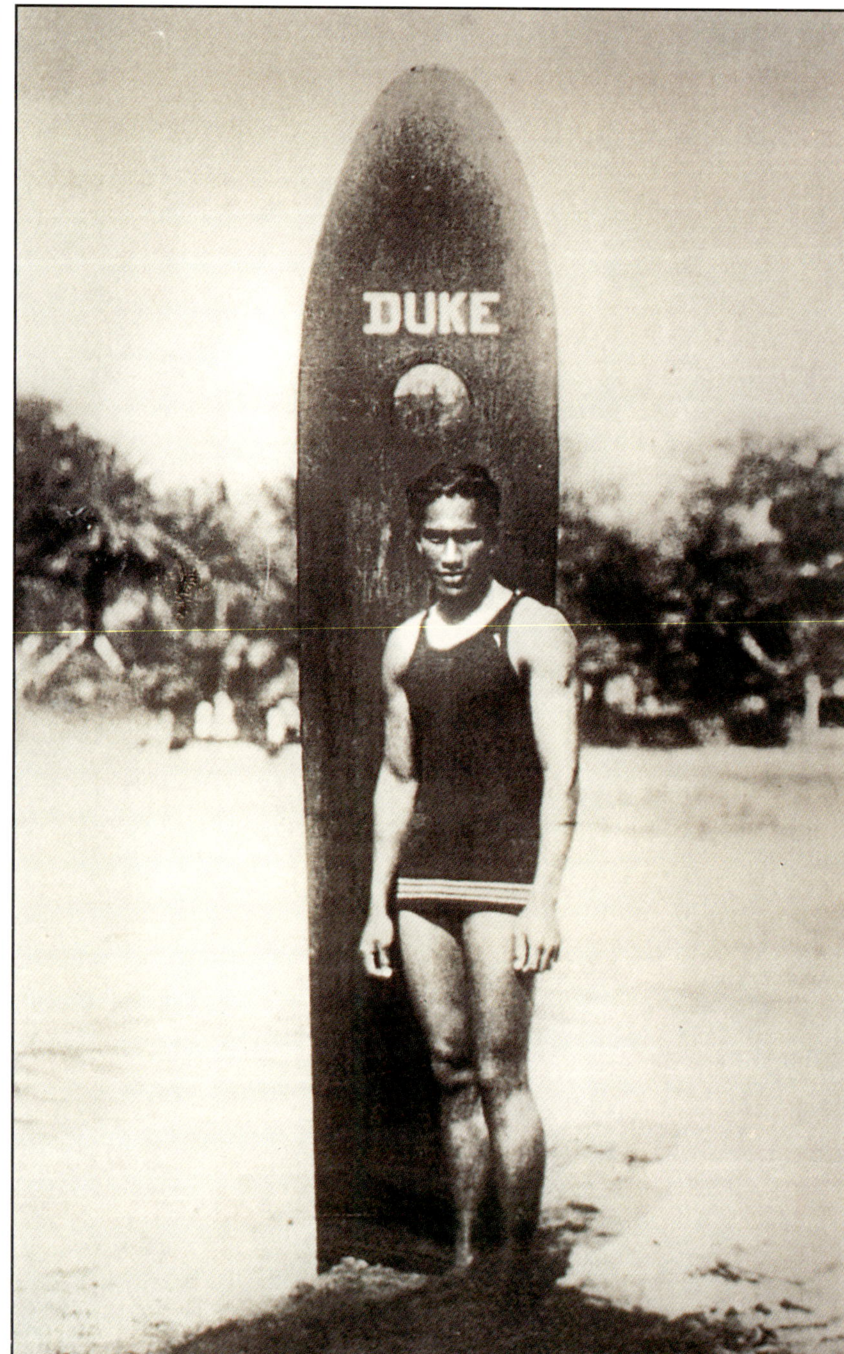

Duke Paoa Kahanamoku came to southern California on his way to the 1912 Olympics where he won a gold medal in 100 meter freestyle swimming. Duke astounded beach crowds at Santa Monica and Corona del Mar on his redwood surfboard. He is known as the grandfather of modern Hawaiian surfing. *Photograph: The Bishop Museum, Honolulu, Hawaii. Courtesy: the Bishop Museum.*

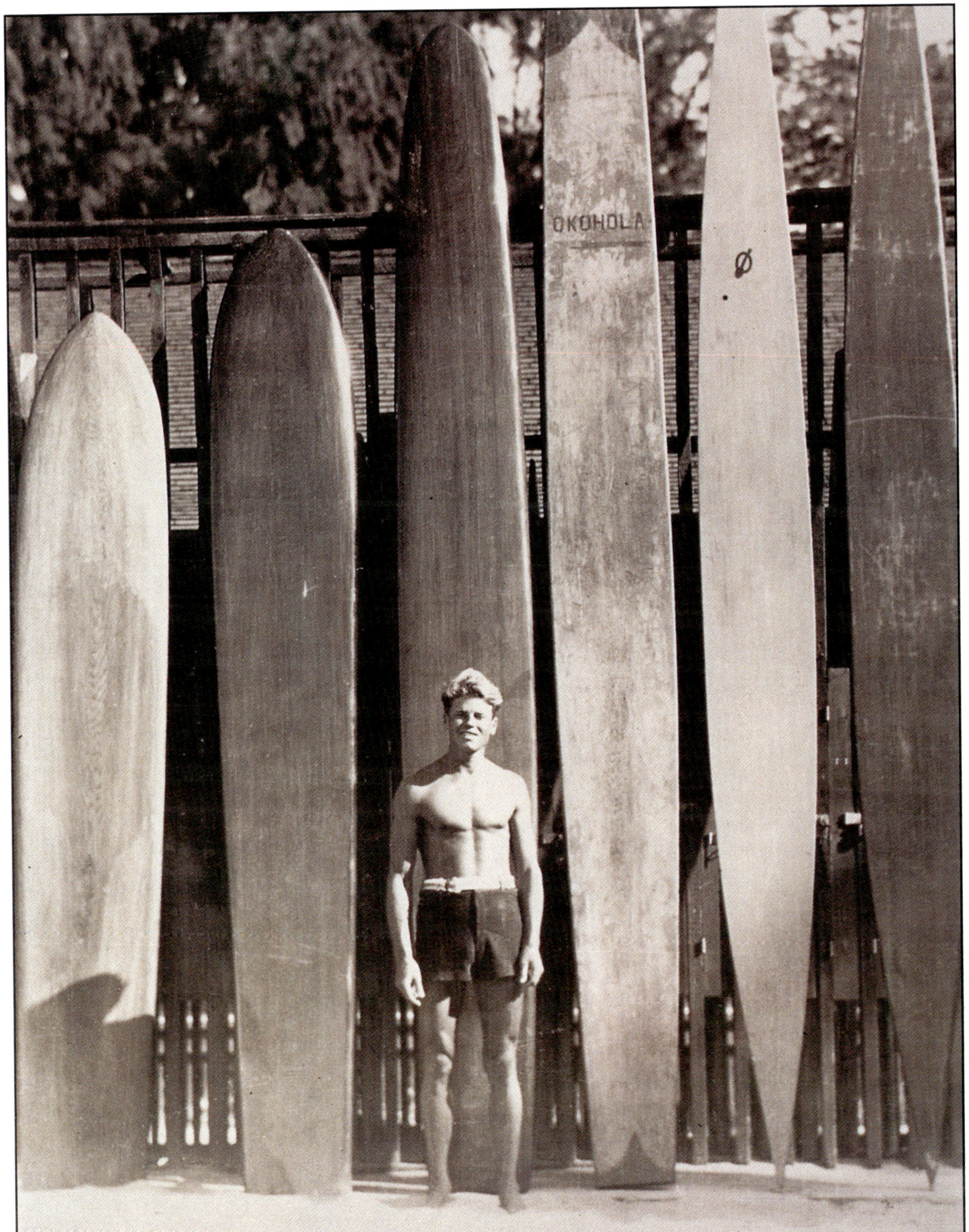

Tom Blake's contributions to surfing are landmarks in the sport. By applying common sense and an enthusiastic desire to make surfboard paddling and surfing more fun, Blake revolutionized the sport. After visiting the Bishop Museum in Honolulu and studying the large, heavy boards of old style Hawaiian surfing, Blake wondered if a lighter board would fare better.

"I wondered so much that in 1926 I built a duplicate of them as an experiment, my object being to find not a better board, but to find a faster board to use in the annual and popular surfboard paddling races held in southern California each summer." Blake "drilled [the duplicate board] full of holes to lighten and dry it out," then plugged the holes. Having invented the hollow board, Blake won every paddle board race he entered for several years.

In this self-portrait, Blake poses with six of his favorite boards, all but one of which he carved himself. From left to right: his favorite solid redwood board, 11' x 23" x 3.25" thick; a 12' red cedar board; for big waves, a hollow 14'6" x 20" board weighing 120 pounds; his reproduction of the ancient Hawaiian Olo; a light, hollow 16' board that broke all paddle race records at Waikiki; and a solid, heavy training board. *Photograph: Tom Blake. Courtesy: the California Heritage Museum Archives.*

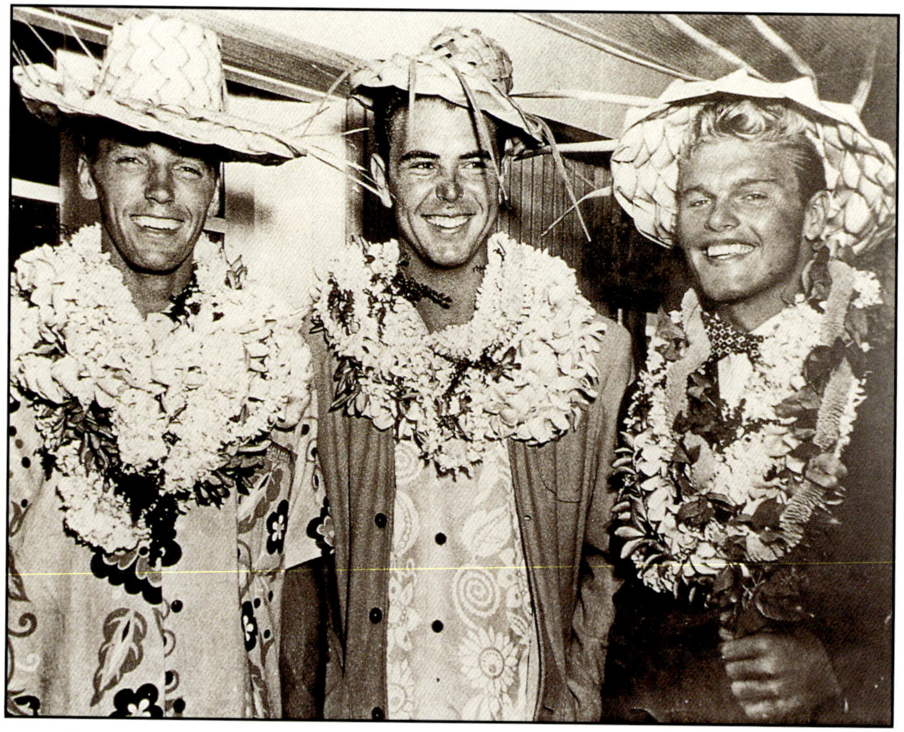

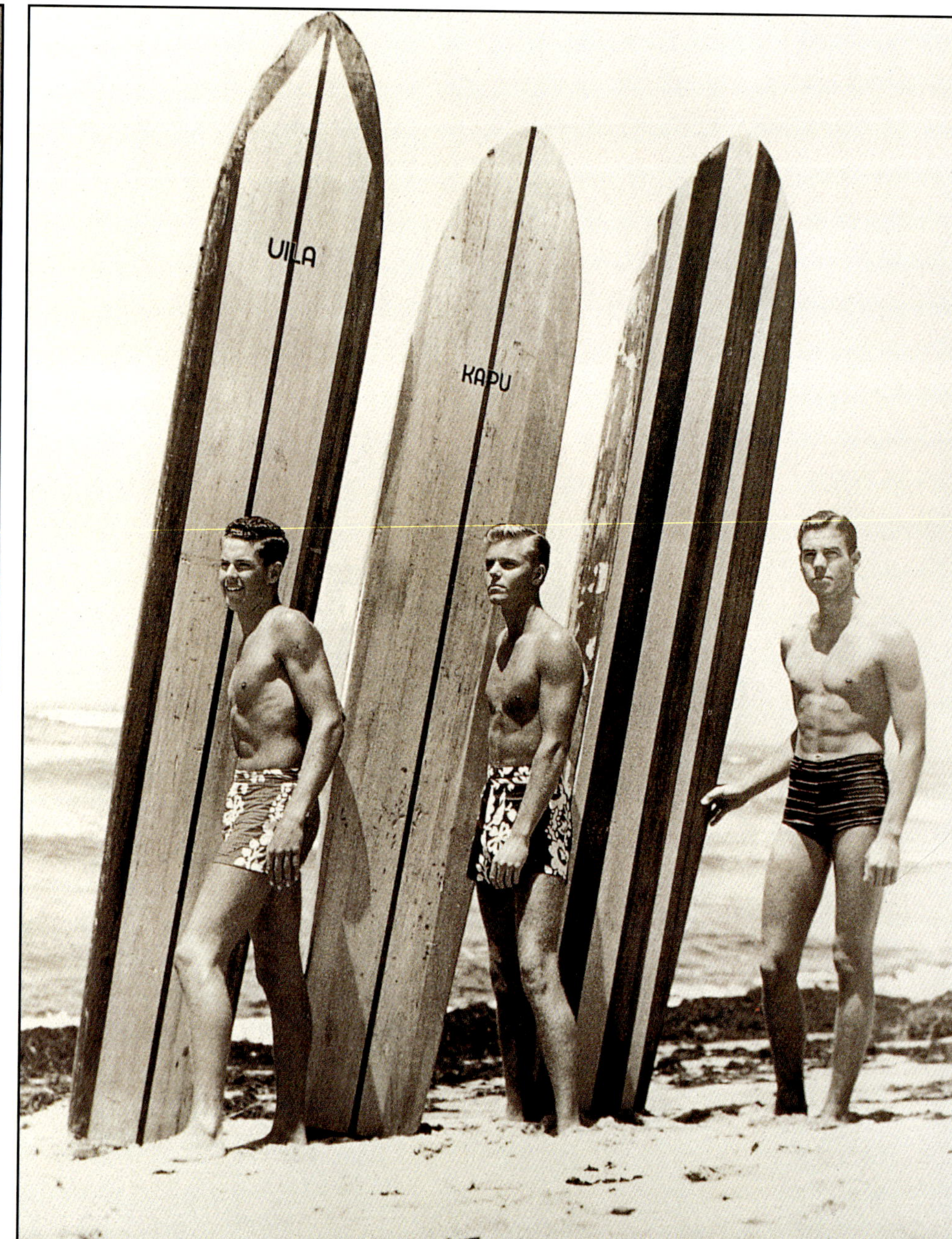

Above:
Malibu surfers Joe Quigg, Matt Kivlin, and Tommy Zahn bid Hawaii aloha and board the "S.S. Lurline" for Long Beach in 1952. Quigg and Kivlin were pioneers of the modern style of surfing and contributed many of the shape ideas presently found in the modern surfboard. In Hawaii, they offered their own balsa Malibu "Chip" boards for perusal, and brought back new knowledge of "hot curls" and "gun" shapes, to say nothing of the tropical fashion elements of coconut hats and aloha shirts. *Photo: Joe Quigg*.

Right:
Don James, Ed Fearon, and Bud Rice at San Onofre, 1939. "We dreamt of Hawaii; when we heard someone was going, we'd ask them to bring us flowered trunks from Lynn's in Waikiki," remembers Don. Note the Hawaiian names for the California-made surfboards. *Don James Photo. Courtesy: the California Heritage Museum Archives*.

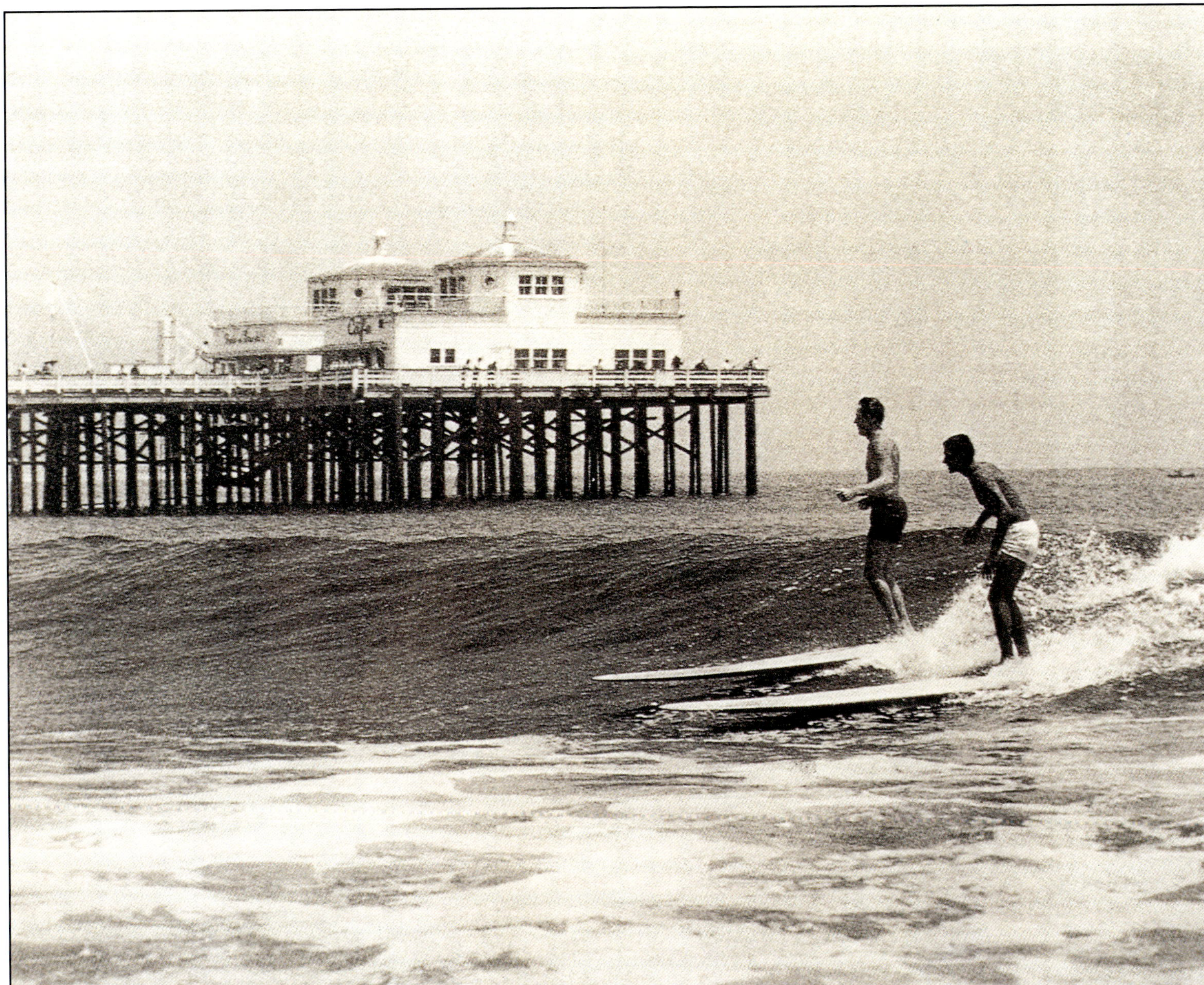

Peter Cole and a friend slide right at Malibu on their Simmons "Balsa Spoons." *Photo: Joe Quigg*.

In the corner is a solid California rockerless redwood plank, c. 1900, thought to have been shaped and owned by the Kahanamoku family and ridden by Sam and Dave Kahanamoku. The olo, ranging up to sixteen feet in length, was the surfboard of alii or royalty. It was used in places like Waikiki, where the breaking waves feathered and rolled in for great distances. 11'6" x 17".

The shorter Alaia board dates between 1890 and 1900, and is a varnished solid redwood rockerless plank. The Hawaiian Alaia surfboard ranged from six to nine feet in length and was generally the surfboard of choice for non-royalty, and therefore, usually ridden at surfing spots designated for non-royals. It is ironic that by today's standards, both the board shape (being smaller and more maneuverable) and the wave character (a better riding wave and location) would be considered far superior. A small victory for the working class! This board was found by Stuart Gimber in the 1980s in Hawaii when his dog stood on the beach barking at an object floating in the surf. 8' x 23". *Courtesy: California Surfing Museum.*

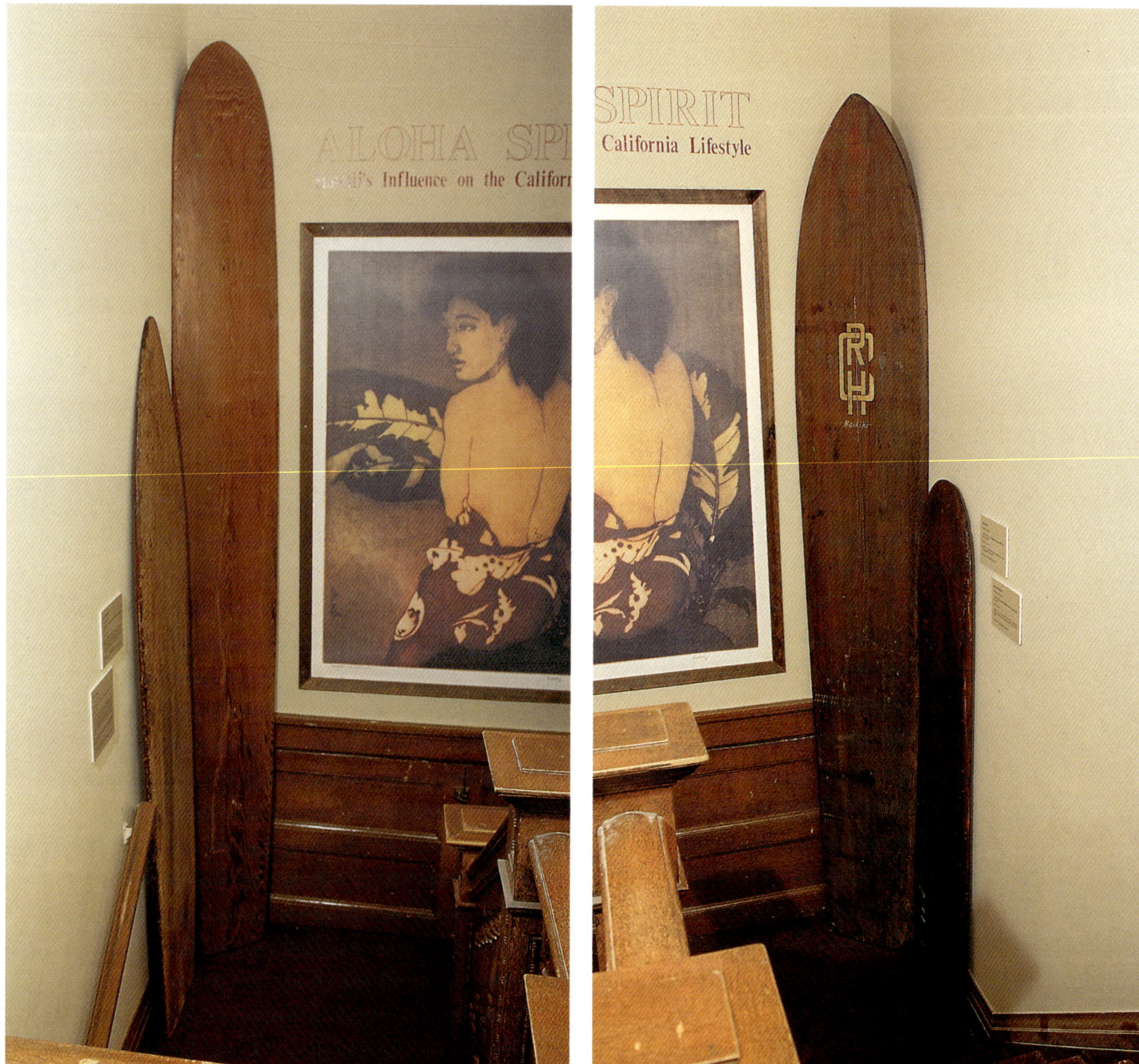

The board in the corner is solid redwood with marine varnish, c. 1920s. It has no rocker and is very heavy. It has the initials RHC framed with outrigger paddles, though the origin of the letters is unknown *(see detail)*. 10'1" x 21.5".

Beside it is a shorter solid redwood board dating to 1900-1910. It has no rocker and a slight "V" in the nose. Prior to the reintroduction of standing up on surfboards in the early 1900s, the surfer rode a smaller board on his belly or knees. 6' x 19". *Courtesy: Dan Pincetich.*

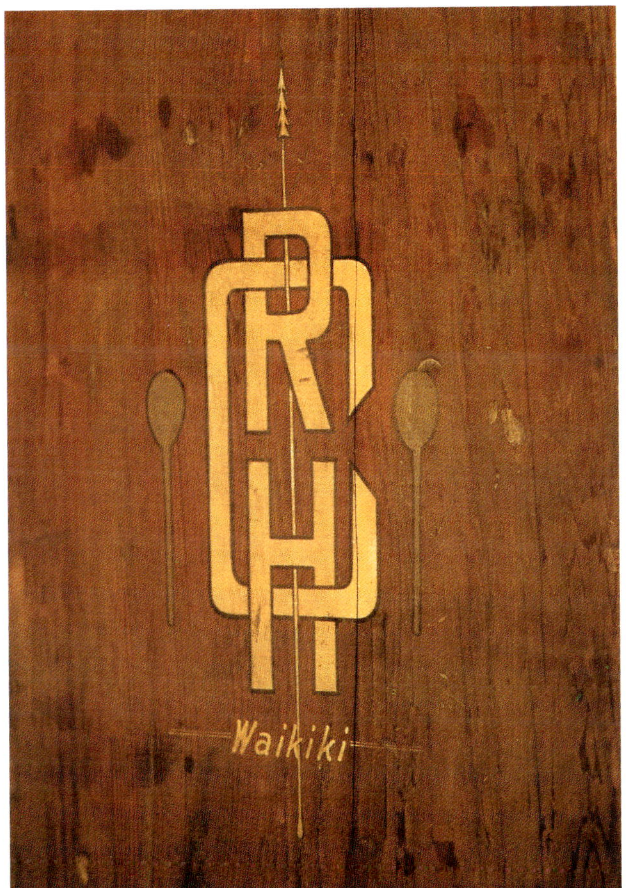

Detail of the 1920s redwood board. *Courtesy: Dan Pincetich*.

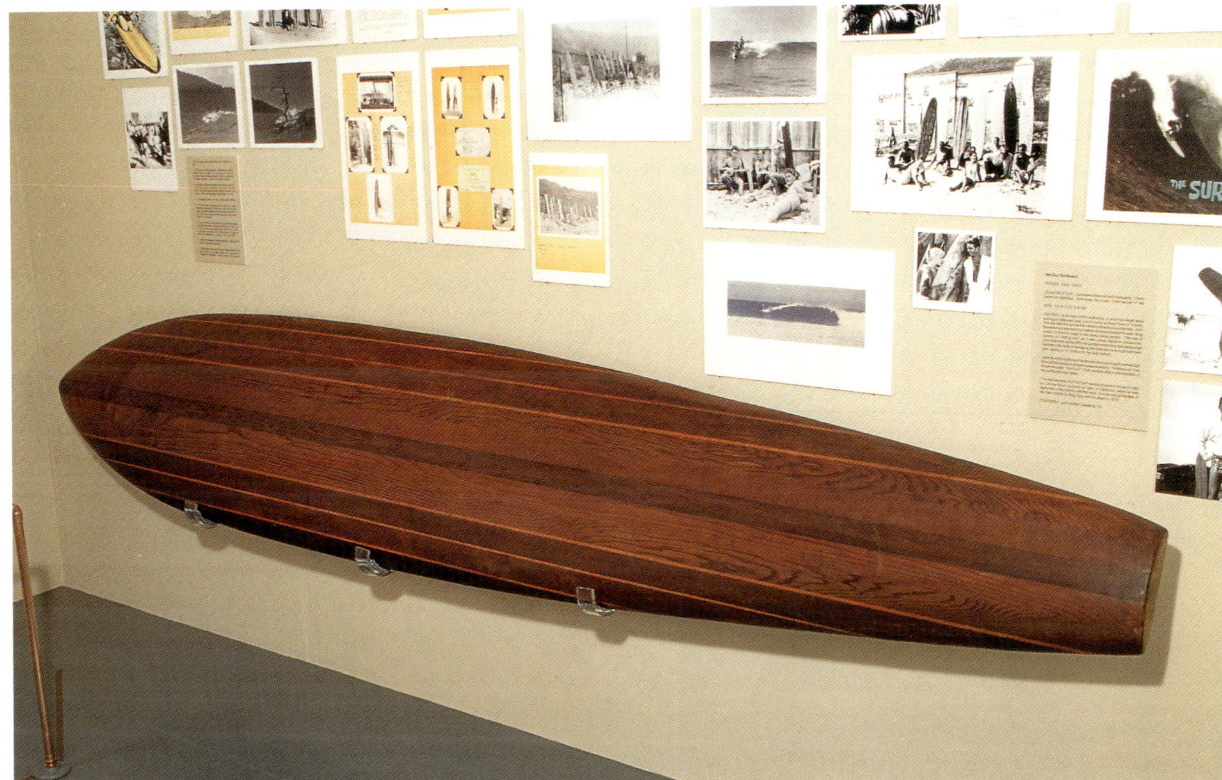

This hot curl surfboard dates to the early 1940s. It is laminated redwood and mahogany, chambered for lightness. It has a boat nose, no rocker, and a narrow "V" tail. In the late 1930s John Kelly, Jr. and Fran Heath were surfing breakwater near John's home at Black Point in Hawaii. The tide was low and as the waves hollowed out on the reef, John became frustrated that the traditional redwood plank he was riding could not hold an edge in the steep inside section. The loss of control, or "sliding ass" as it was called, became unbearable. John marched up the cliff to his garage where he used a small hatchet to reshape the wide tail into a much narrower one, adding a "V" contour to the tail's bottom.

Returning to the surf he stroked into a wave and trimmed high through the previous dangerous wave section. Paddling out, Fran Heath shouted "Hot curl!" and another step in the evolution of the surfboard was taken.

This fine example of a "hot curl" was purchased in Hawaii in 1945 by Connie Moss of California, while he was stationed there in the navy. Connie was a member of the San Onofre Surfing Club until his death in 1973. 10'4" x 21" (8" at the tail). *Courtesy: John Schell*.

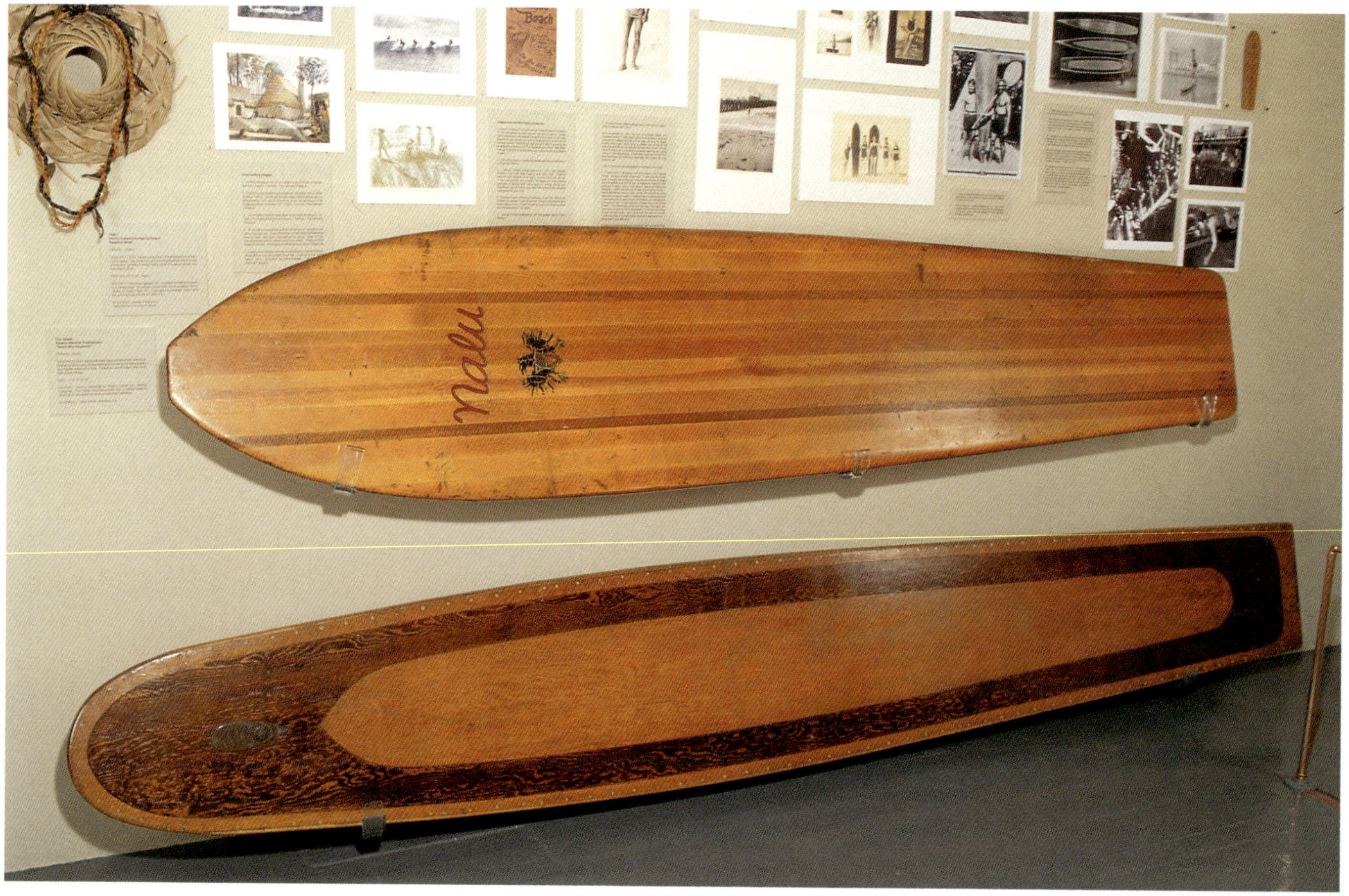

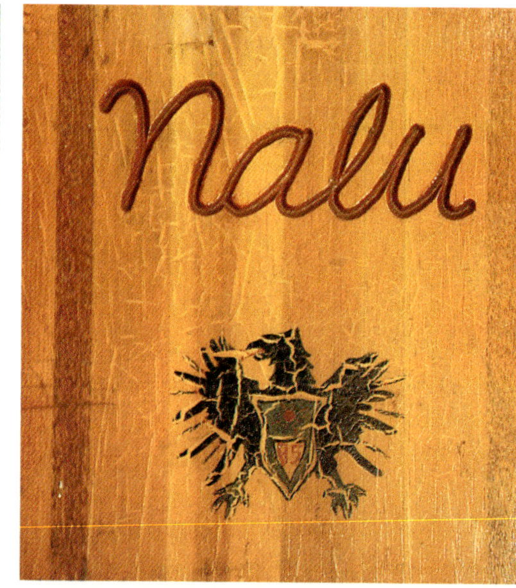

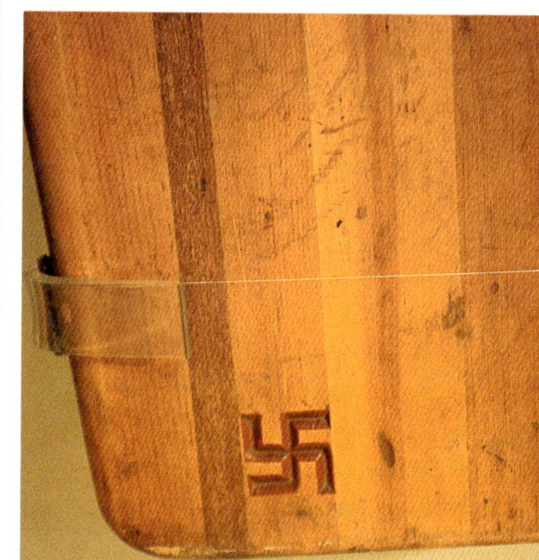

The "Nalu" board, at the top, is a production model manufactured by Pacific Systems Homes, Los Angeles, in the 1930s. One of the first production surfboards, this is a rare chambered model (partially hollow), made of sugar pine with two mahogany strips. This board, labeled "A5," traveled to Waikiki to serve as a rental board. As ultimate proof of her derring-do, Mrs. R.J. Huntington purchased the "Nalu" after learning to surf on it, and brought it home to California. Incidentally, the swastika is pre-Hitlerian and was a common good-luck symbol before the Nazis co-opted it for their own purposes. 9'8.5" x 23", heavy.

Below the Nalu is the Tom Blake/Rogers Hawaiian Paddle board known as the "Beach Boy Squaretail," from the 1930s. It has a varnished plywood skin, with solid rails on a wood frame, and is assembled with countersunk brass screws and marine waterproof glue. It features a brass drain plug with a screw-off cap. This was a production board made at the Rogers Ladder Co., Venice, California. The "Beach Boy Squaretail" was a hollow board or "kook box" designed for surfing more than paddling. 11'9" x 20.5". *Courtesy: John Schell, and James O'Mahoney, S.B.S.M.*

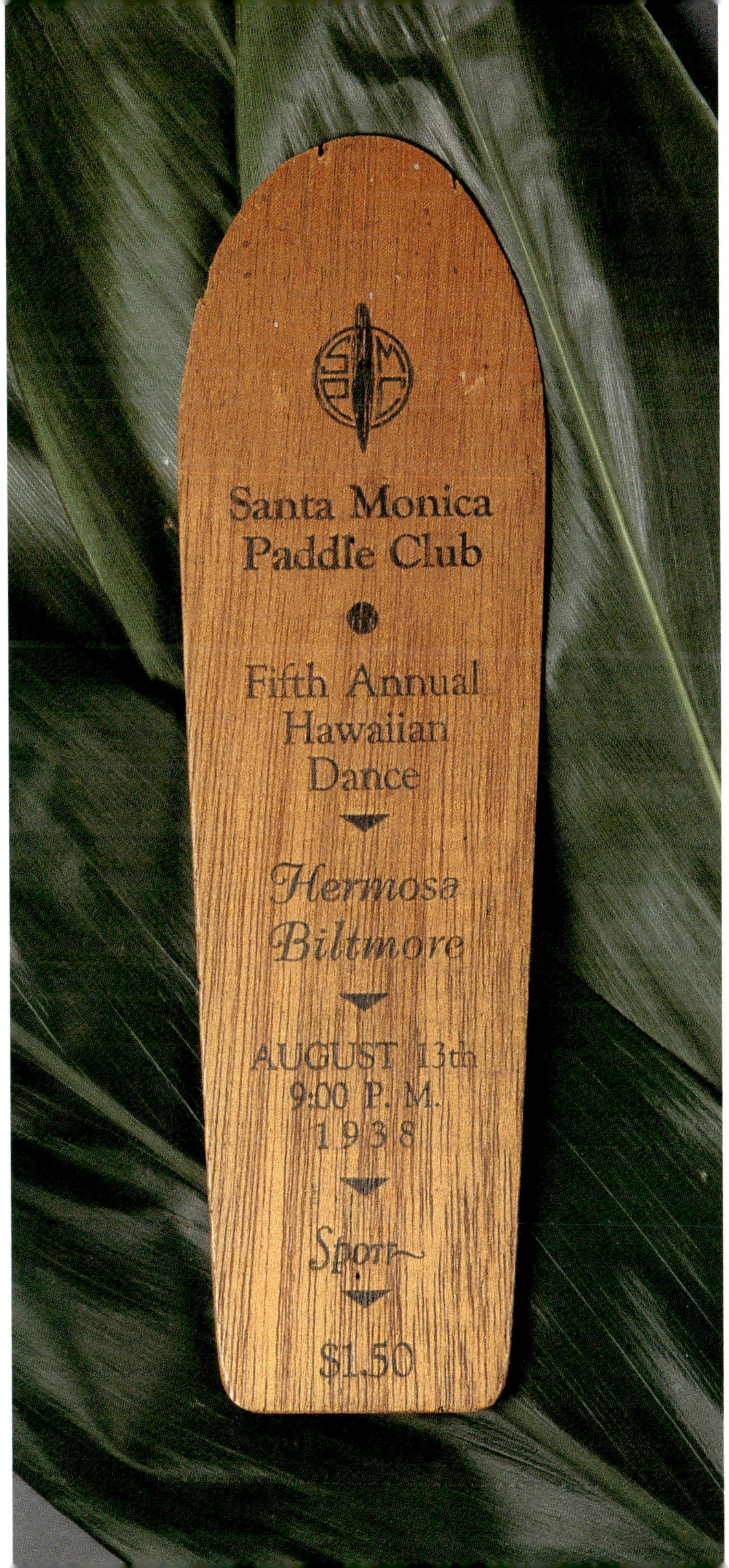

The smallest board in the exhibit is this favor for the Santa Monica Paddle Club's Fifth Annual Hawaiian Dance, August 13, 1938. It is about 6" long. *Courtesy: Michael Trotter*.

Bibliography

Blackburn, Mark. *Hawaiiana: The Best of Hawaiian Design*. Atglen, PA: Schiffer Publishing Ltd., 1996.

Brown, DeSoto. *Hawaii Recalls: Selling Romance to America*. Honolulu: Editions Limited, 1991.

Doi, Teruhito. *Master Book of Hawaiian Shirt*. Japan: Kesaharu Imai.

Feher, Joseph, ed. *Hawaii: A Pictorial History*. Honolulu: Bishop Museum Press, 1969.

Forbes, David W. *Encounters with Paradise: Views of Hawaii and its People, 1778-1941*. Honolulu: Honolulu Academy of Arts.

Fujii, Jocelyn. *Under the Hula Moon*. New York: Crown Publishers.

Hausman, Ruth L. *Hawaii: Music in its History*. Rutland Vermont: Charles E. Tuttle Company, 1968.

Nordyke, Eleanor C. *The Peopling of Hawaii*. Honolulu: University Press of Hawaii, 1977.

Piercy, Larue W. *Hawaii This & That*. Honolulu: Mutual Publishing, 1981.

Schiffer, Nancy. *Hawaiian Shirt Designs*. Atglen, PA: Schiffer Publishing Ltd., 1997.

Steele, H. Thomas. *The Hawaiian Shirt: Its Art and History*. New York: Abbeville Press Publishers, 1984.

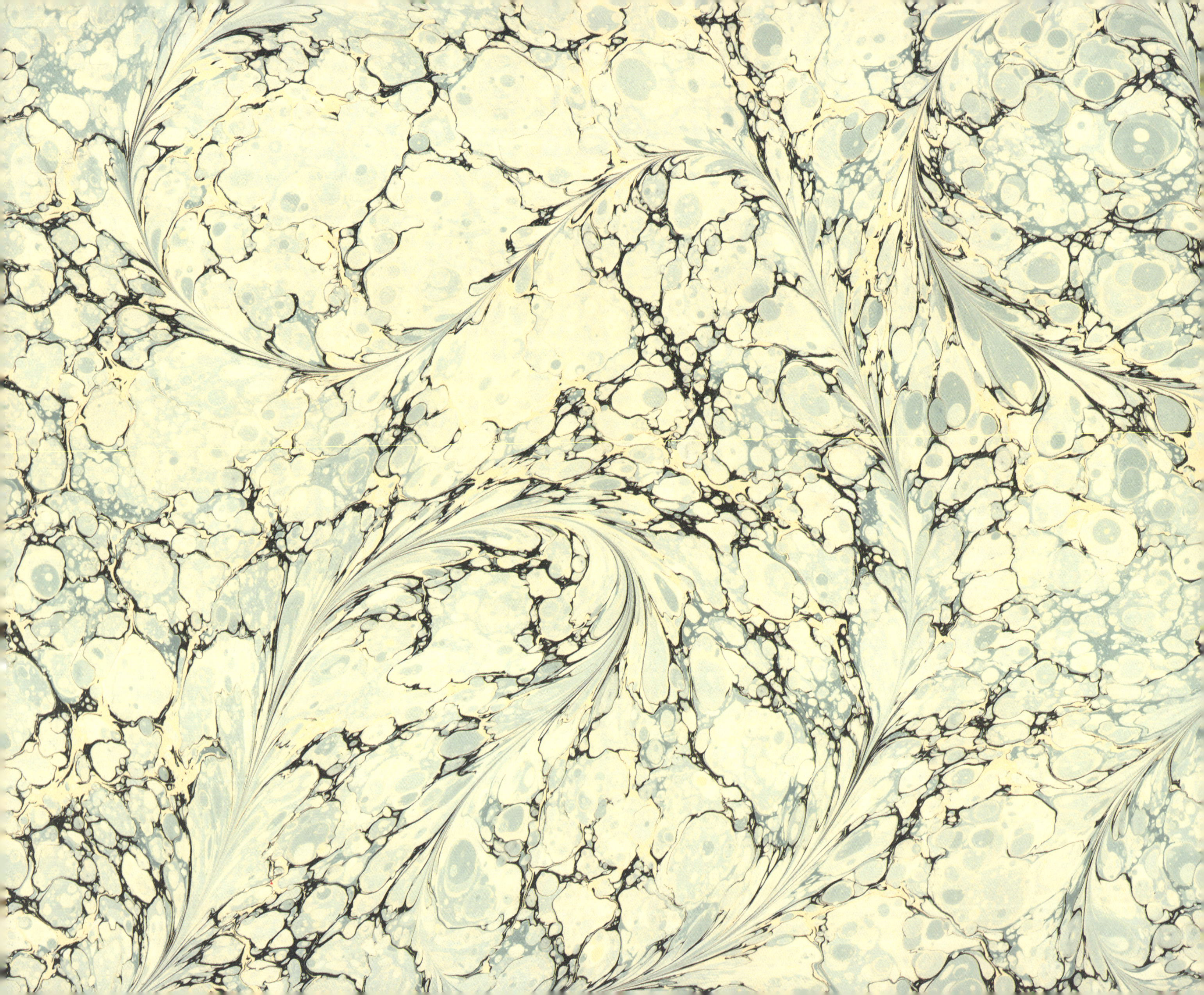